Global Dynamics in Travel, Tourism, and Hospitality

Nikolaos Pappas
The University of West London, UK

Ilenia Bregoli
University of Lincoln, UK

A volume in the Advances in Hospitality, Tourism, and the Services Industry (AHTSI) Book Series

Published in the United States of America by
    Business Science Reference (an imprint of IGI Global)
    701 E. Chocolate Avenue
    Hershey PA, USA 17033
    Tel: 717-533-8845
    Fax: 717-533-8661
    E-mail: cust@igi-global.com
    Web site: http://www.igi-global.com

Library of Congress Cataloging-in-Publication Data

Names: Pappas, Nikolaos, 1974- editor. | Bregoli, Ilenia, 1980- editor.
Title: Global dynamics in travel, tourism, and hospitality / Nikolaos Pappas
   and Ilenia Bregoli, editors.
Description: Hershey, PA : Business Science Reference, [2016] | Includes
   bibliographical references and index.
Identifiers: LCCN 2016003418| ISBN 9781522502012 (hardcover) | ISBN
   9781522502029 (ebook)
Subjects: LCSH: Tourism. | Tourism--Social aspects. | Hospitality
   industry--Management.
Classification: LCC G155.A1 G4876 2016 | DDC 338.4/791--dc23 LC record available at https://lccn.loc.gov/2016003418

This book is published in the IGI Global book series Advances in Hospitality, Tourism, and the Services Industry (AHTSI) (ISSN: Pending; eISSN: Pending)

British Cataloguing in Publication Data
A Cataloguing in Publication record for this book is available from the British Library.

All work contributed to this book is new, previously-unpublished material. The views expressed in this book are those of the authors, but not necessarily of the publisher.

For electronic access to this publication, please contact: eresources@igi-global.com.

Advances in Hospitality, Tourism, and the Services Industry (AHTSI) Book Series

ISSN: Pending
EISSN: Pending

MISSION

Globally, the hospitality, travel, tourism, and services industries generate a significant percentage of revenue and represent a large portion of the business world. Even in tough economic times, these industries thrive as individuals continue to spend on leisure and recreation activities as well as services.

The Advances in Hospitality, Tourism, and the Services Industry (AHTSI) book series offers diverse publications relating to the management, promotion, and profitability of the leisure, recreation, and services industries. Highlighting current research pertaining to various topics within the realm of hospitality, travel, tourism, and services management, the titles found within the AHTSI book series are pertinent to the research and professional needs of managers, business practitioners, researchers, and upper-level students studying in the field.

COVERAGE

- Service Training
- Service Management
- Tourism and the Environment
- Destination Marketing and Management
- Health and Wellness Tourism
- Leisure & Business Travel
- Travel Agency Management
- Service Design
- Casino Management
- International Tourism

IGI Global is currently accepting manuscripts for publication within this series. To submit a proposal for a volume in this series, please contact our Acquisition Editors at Acquisitions@igi-global.com or visit: http://www.igi-global.com/publish/.

Titles in this Series

For a list of additional titles in this series, please visit: www.igi-global.com

Corporate Social Responsibility in the Hospitality and Tourism Industry
Lipika Kaur Guliani (Panjab University, India) and Syed Ahmad Rizwan (Tourism Recreation Research, CTRD, India)
Business Science Reference • copyright 2016 • 356pp • H/C (ISBN: 9781466699021) • US $190.00 (our price)

Strategic Tools and Methods for Promoting Hospitality and Tourism Services
Alexandru-Mircea Nedelea (Stefan cel Mare University of Suceava, Romania) Maximiliano Korstanje (University of Palermo, Argentina) and Babu George (Fort Hays State University, USA)
Business Science Reference • copyright 2016 • 326pp • H/C (ISBN: 9781466697614) • US $195.00 (our price)

Handbook of Research on Global Hospitality and Tourism Management
Angelo A. Camillo (Woodbury University, USA)
Business Science Reference • copyright 2015 • 621pp • H/C (ISBN: 9781466686069) • US $345.00 (our price)

Emerging Innovative Marketing Strategies in the Tourism Industry
Nilanjan Ray (Royal Thimphu College, Bhutan)
Business Science Reference • copyright 2015 • 425pp • H/C (ISBN: 9781466686991) • US $215.00 (our price)

Current Issues and Emerging Trends in Medical Tourism
Malcolm Cooper (Ritsumeikan Asia Pacific University, Japan) Kazem Vafadari (Ritsumeikan Asia Pacific University, Japan) and Mayumi Hieda (St. Luke Clinic, Oita, Japan)
Medical Information Science Reference • copyright 2015 • 430pp • H/C (ISBN: 9781466685741) • US $235.00 (our price)

New Business Opportunities in the Growing E-Tourism Industry
Hajime Eto (University of Tsukuba, Japan)
Business Science Reference • copyright 2015 • 395pp • H/C (ISBN: 9781466685772) • US $205.00 (our price)

International Tourism and Hospitality in the Digital Age
Suresh Kumar (University Shimla, India) Mohinder Chand Dhiman (Kurukshetra University, India) and Ashish Dahiya (Central University of Haryana, India)
Business Science Reference • copyright 2015 • 326pp • H/C (ISBN: 9781466682689) • US $205.00 (our price)

Educational Strategies for the Next Generation Leaders in Hotel Management
Jiuguang Feng (Les Roches Jin Jiang International Hotel Management College, China) Sacha Stocklin (Les Roches Jin Jiang International Hotel Management College, China) and Wei Wang (Foreign Languages College, Shanghai Normal University, China)
Business Science Reference • copyright 2015 • 399pp • H/C (ISBN: 9781466685659) • US $200.00 (our price)

www.igi-global.com

701 E. Chocolate Ave., Hershey, PA 17033
Order online at www.igi-global.com or call 717-533-8845 x100
To place a standing order for titles released in this series, contact: cust@igi-global.com
Mon-Fri 8:00 am - 5:00 pm (est) or fax 24 hours a day 717-533-8661

Table of Contents

Section 2
Global Dynamics in Tourism

Detailed Table of Contents

Section 1
Global Dynamics in Travel

The first section of the edited book consists of five chapters and focuses on the travel contemporary issues and dynamics. It starts focusing on aspects relevant to information technology, proceeds to aviation and tourist agencies and concludes with an analysis of social effects stemming from travel.

This chapter looks into the concept of culture and its impacts on travellers' online information search behaviour. The study is focused on two culturally diametric countries: United Kingdom and China and they have been selected as case studies, representing values from the Western and the Asian cultures. In order to examine the effects of culture on online search behaviours, the research adopted a qualitative approach, and data was collected through interviews in order to enhance and elaborate the understanding on the subject studied. The results of this study show that culture influences the travellers' behaviour in the online environment, up to a certain extent, and as a result of this influences, different behavioural patterns between the British and the Chinese travellers emerged. Moreover, these findings bring implications for the marketers aiming at the British and the Chinese tourists, and they highlight the need to adopt different strategies in designing and marketing their tourism products for these two particular markets.

The visit of the favela or slum into a tourist destination is seen as a part of the so-called reality tours phenomenon and of the global circulation of the favela as a trademark. Tourist behaviour involves a search for leisure experiences from interactions with features or characteristics of places they choose to visit. Examples are the favelas in Brazil, the township of South Africa, the slum in India that have led to different definitions of "slum tourism", "poor-poor tourism", "reality tourism". Web heavily affect today most of the online activities and their effect on tourism is obviously rather important. The aim of the chapter is to discuss about slum tourism definitions. At the same time, taking Reality Tours and Travel

- a wholesaler slum websites - as a case, this study attempts to explore issues of the quality of strategic choices on the web. Considering that the content of web site includes a wide variety of technologies, is important that website offer also interactivity with e-tourists. Through the results of the study, it is possible to gain knowledge of the slum e-tourism.

    Marina Efthymiou, University of West London, UK
    Pavlos Arvanitis, Southampton Solent University, UK
    Andreas Papatheodorou, University of West London, UK

This chapter covers three areas of institutional changes in the European aviation sector that may significantly affect the dynamics of the tourism industry. Further to the introduction, airlines are discussed in section two; airports are analysed in section three; and air navigation service provision are presented in section four. The dynamics of these three pillars and the interrelationship with the tourism industry is explored in section five. Among others, the chapter argues that when a proper systemic approach is followed any smart relaxation of regulatory and infrastructural constraints will have positive repercussions on tourism growth and development not only of central places but also of more peripheral regions. Finally, section six concludes and discusses the way forward.

    Ilenia Bregoli, University of Lincoln, UK

Tourism is acknowledged to be highly experiential in nature, but despite these characteristics, in the tourism literature there are few articles that adopt the Service-Dominant logic (S-D logic) for studying tourism experiences. The aim of this paper is to apply the S-D logic to the case of Addiopizzo Travel, a Mafia-free project of responsible tourism set up in Sicily, Italy. Results show the role of Addiopizzo Travel as a central node of the network of firms involved in the project and the role that interactions among Addiopizzo Travel, stakeholders, and visitors have in the co-creation of tourists' experience.

    Maximiliano Emanuel Korstanje, University of Palermo, Argentina

Divorcing is a common-place practices that characterized our modern daily life. What is more than interesting to explore is why one of third takes after holidays. Are holidays accelerating the social decomposition the founding parents of sociology denounced in earlier century? or simply, as Maccannell puts it, tourism serves as a valve (mechanism) of cohesion similarly to the role played by religion/totems in primitive societies? To answer these questions, we present statistical information given by the Dirección General de Estadística y Censos (Ministerio de Hacienda GCBA). Although this information had its own limitations, which suggests more investigation is needed, we strongly beliefs the outcomes shed light to embrace the theory of vital cycles, as it has been formulated by Turner.

Section 2
Global Dynamics in Tourism

The second section of the edited book consists of seven chapters and focuses on tourism related aspects. The chapters discuss contemporary issues concerning tourism related post-conflict perspectives; women's role in innovation and internationalisation; digital marketing; rural wellbeing; risk and crisis management; and methodological insights on tourism research.

Chapter 6

The objective of this chapter is to organize, analyze and discuss information on tourism development in the Democratic Republic of East Timor, based on efforts from "development partners" countries between 2007 and 2011, principles of 2011 Development Strategic Plan (PED) and government programs from 2007 on. The analytical framework emerges from discussions on tourism in post-conflict countries and dependence and autonomy issues within post-colonial contexts. From a methodological perspective, reflections on East Timor are result of reading and government programs analysis since 2007, PED (2011-2030) and international cooperation reports from May 2012. In short, one observes in parallel to the slow growth of tourism in the island and the increase of the relevance of this issue in national documents that objective actions on behalf of tourism development in East Timor have been virtually absent in terms of international cooperation– even though they have been indirectly identifiable.

A significant challenge faced by the tourism and hospitality industries in a rapidly changing world, is the ability to sustain organisational growth. Some of the main strategies for achieving organisational growth are those related to innovation, internationalisation and networking. Addressing tourism studies' contemporary shift to a focus on social influences, this study investigates the relations between gender and organisational growth. Qualitative analysis of focus groups with managers from the seven administrative regions in Portugal provides an in-depth account of tourism and gender issues based on empirical evidence. Viewing the ways in which tourism managers contribute to organisational growth through the angle of gender, this chapter provides a compelling account of the delicate and often invisible interactions between economic and social transactions. Results illustrate how women as a labour source are paradoxically viewed as both an asset and an impediment to organisational growth strategies.

    Azizul Hassan, The Cardiff Metropolitan University, UK
    Roya Rahimi, University of Wolverhampton, UK

Upon understanding definition, features, application analysis of innovation and relevant theory of the Diffusion of Innovations, this study suggests Augmented Reality (AR) as a technological innovation. AR is an advanced stage of virtual reality that merges reality with computer simulated imageries in the real environment. This chapter synthesizes AR as an emerging and potential technology of digital tourism marketing and management. The aim of this analytical approach based chapter is to understand innovation from tourism product or services consumption perspective. Relevant evidences are also included on lenses of marketing, digitalization and innovation consumption. Results outline that, technology consumption is gradually reshaping and getting supported by the availability and accessibility of electronic formats as AR as a technological innovation. This symbolizes that the consumption of technological innovation as AR offers freedom to select, purchase and recommend in relation to the theory of Diffusion of Innovations.

    Anne-Mette Hjalager, University of Southern Denmark, Denmark
    Kaarina Tervo-Kankare, University of Oulu, Finland
    Anja Tuohino, University of Eastern Finland, Finland
    Henna Konu, University of Eastern Finland, Finland

Innovation in tourism does not take place in a vacuum. Innovators find inspiration from many sources. This article identifies ten innovation anchors, e.g. critical trends that can guide the long-term innovation activity and lead to fundamentally new products, services, delivery mechanisms, organizational models, means of collaboration etc. Innovation anchors are robust as they are found persistently in the recent scholarly literature and appear on a consistent base in business related evidence. Rural wellbeing tourism is area of inquiry. The study reveals that innovation, in the future, can take further advantage of the following: 1) Towards a holistic wellbeing, 2) Connecting with nature and its resources, 3) Altruism included, 4) The rural as a medical prescription, 5) Work-life balance, 6) Wellbeing diversification the rural way, 7) Taking advantage of the climate squeeze, 8) Opening the digital channels, 9) A new puritanism rural style, and 10) The gear dimension.

    Faye Taylor, Nottingham Trent University, UK

Numerous researchers have highlighted a relative lack of academic attention directly addressing the influence of political economy on achieving sustainability in post-disaster reconstruction. This chapter therefore extends existing academic debates and studies in a number of areas, drawing upon the context of Thailand in the post-Asian tsunami era. In existing academic debates concerning the political economy of post-disaster reconstruction there is a trend towards disaster capitalism. However, this did not occur on Phi Phi. Despite claims of a 'clean slate' being offered by the tsunami in developmental terms, this chapter provides explanation of why this did not and would never exist on Phi Phi, a finding that may be applied to other destinations in a post-disaster context.

Chapter 11

Nikolaos Pappas, University of West London, UK
Alexandros Apostolakis, Technological Educational Institute (TEI) of Crete & Greek Open University, Greece

The current recession has hit hard the European countries, and also affected tourism activity throughout the continent. Considering that several European countries (especially the Mediterranean ones) are heavily dependent upon tourism activity, the recent financial crisis has considerably affected their economy. This effect is strengthened with the parallel adoption of austerity measures aiming at economic recovery and exit from the recession. Despite the substantial magnitude and severity of this crisis, little is known about tourists' reactions in coping in with the recessionary effects. Contrary to the established practice of adopting a macroeconomic perspective in the examination of the impact of financial crises on tourism activity, this book chapter follows recent recommendations in the literature to examine the particular adverse effects of the current financial/economic crisis on individual behaviour and demand patterns. Thus, the research utilises a survey questionnaire to British tourists examining the effect of the current recession on travel and consumption patterns. Socio-demographically, the results reveal that the current recession appears to have a significant effect on gender, since male tourism expenditure is affected more than female one. Moreover, the uncertainty associated with income and employment levels during recession has a particularly strong effect on tourism expenditure. More specifically, uncertainty associated with both income and employment levels during the financial crisis has a negative and statistically significant effect on tourism expenditure. On the other hand, younger and middle aged tourists seem to be fairly unaffected by the financial crisis, as compared to more mature and senior tourists. In addition, the findings indicate that future expectations regarding income levels have no influence on current tourism expenditure patterns. Overall, those respondents that were unsure about the effect of the financial crisis on their current tourism expenditure patterns were also more likely to exhibit ambivalence about the future. The findings provide an interesting insight to tourism decision makers since they illustrate evidence regarding the turning points of demand, especially during periods of economic downturn.

Chapter 12

Maximiliano E. Korstanje, University of Palermo, Argentina & University of Leeds UK
Lourdes Cisneros Mustelier, University of La Habana, Cuba
Sylvia Herrera, University of Especialidades Turisticas, Ecuador

Over last years, the current growth of tourism flourished in a wealth of courses, Ph.Ds., Masters and academic offerings that positioned tourism as a good perspective for students. Jafar Jafari signaled to the term "scientifization of tourism" to explain the ever-increasing attention given to this new field. At a first stage, the great volume of bibliographic production offered an encouraging prospect in the pathways towards the maturation of this discipline. However, some epistemologists have recently alerted that not only tourism-research failed to develop a unified consensus of what tourism is, but also lack of a coherent epistemology that helps organizing the produced material. In this respect, tourism is subject now to an atmosphere of "indiscipline" where the produced knowledge leads to scattered (limited) conclusions.

Section 3
Global Dynamics in Hospitality

The last section of the edited book consists of four chapters and focuses on current trends in the hospitality industry. The chapters focus on hospitality aspects related to productivity; job satisfaction and turnover intention; physical attractiveness and self-confidence; social responsibility; and hospitality management facilitation.

Chapter 13

    Sigbjørn L. Tveteraas, University of Stavanger, Norway
    Martin Falk, Austrian Institute of Economic Research, Austria

This chapter introduces the global productivity challenge facing the hospitality industry. Global competition in the hospitality industry has led to increasing pressure on profit levels. To leverage profits hotels increasingly are forced to evaluate their operational performance. Specifically, the global productivity challenge entails that hotel managers to a greater extent must encompass a cost minimization perspective. With the integration of productivity-enhancing software systems in hospitality organizations hotels are becoming increasingly knowledge intensive. This chapter discuss measurement issues, productivity analysis and relevant research findings from empirical research. The empirical research on hotel productivity shows that there are many factors to keep in mind for managers that wish to improve productivity in their organizations. Hopefully this chapter will contribute to clear up the meaning of concepts and broadened the perspective of how productivity are related to all parts of the hospitality enterprise.

Chapter 14

    Chien-Wen Tsai, Chinese Culture University, Taiwan

The international tourist hotel industry that focuses on quality of the "tangible" service is a typical high-contact service. To survive in the recent competitive work environment, many enterprises enhance their competitiveness in the process of service employee selection and emphasize the importance of physical attractiveness. This study uses self-confidence as a moderator which is rare relevant empirical evidence to confirm the relationships between physical attractiveness, professional competence and service attitude. The results show that confidence of the service personnel, physical attractiveness and professional competence have positive significant correlation relationships with service attitude. Service personnel's "self-confidence" is the most important variable towards service attitude. The study borrows selection and training functions of human resource management to integrate the knowledge of psychology, marketing management to expand the theory.

The aim of this work is to study social responsible behavior in three, four and five star hotels found in Galicia and the Northern region of Portugal. To be able to carry out this investigation two types of analysis are carried out. First of all there is a descriptive statistical analysis about the group of variables contained in the used scale. Secondly a factor analysis is applied in which the factors that make up social responsibility in line with the triple dimension identified by Elkington (1997) are identified. The development of this methodology has made it possible to compare practices of social responsibility carried out by the hotels under study in two different countries, Spain and Portugal. From this investigation it can be concluded that the initial hypothesis is confirmed, corporations behave differently when it comes to social responsibility depending on the country they are in.

Chapter 16

This chapter explains the overview of hospitality management; the overview of tourism management; product quality, service quality, price, customer satisfaction, and consumer trust in hospitality and tourism management; the significance of hospitality management in global business; the significance of tourism management in global business; and the managerial implications of hospitality and tourism management. Tourism and hospitality industry is one of the most important industries in the modern business world. It is essential to acquire a driving enthusiasm for customer service and a strong sense of professionalism to develop and maintain customer satisfaction in the hospitality and tourism industry. Effective hospitality and tourism management positively affects customer satisfaction, firm growth, and productivity in global business. The chapter argues that facilitating hospitality and tourism management in global business has the potential to enhance organizational performance and reach strategic goals in the digital age.

Preface

In recent years, the growth of travel, tourism and hospitality has been faster than the growth of the wider economy and other significant sectors such as financial services, health care, and automotive (WTTC, 2015). Worldwide, tourism is the third largest economic activity in direct earnings (i.e. tour operators, hotels, travel agencies etc.) after petroleum and automotive industries, and, by far, it is the largest economic activity considering its indirect earnings (i.e. restaurants, events, indirect tourism consumption in local stores and shops etc.). In several countries, tourism acts as a developmental engine through the creation of direct and indirect employment (there are 235 million jobs in the tourism industry worldwide, accounting for one in every twelve jobs all over the world, approximately), and foreign exchange earnings. For instance, it is the only industry that several countries (i.e. Barbados, Dubai, Mauritius, Monte Carlo, San Marino, Seychelles, etc.) almost solely rely on for economic development (UNWTO, 2016). In addition, it contributes to approximately 5% of the world's GDP; and 6% of the world's exports in services, whilst it is the fourth largest export sector after fuels, chemicals and automotive products (UNWTO, 2016).

This rapid growth coupled with the dynamism within the industry due, for example, to the development of information technology, the sharing economy, as well as the spread of terrorism, just to mention a few, makes it fundamental to the tourism industry to be able to quickly adapt to this changing environment. Not only this rapid development within tourism and hospitality is linked to macro and micro-environmental factors, but it is also influenced by the multidisciplinary nature of the industry which can be studied from different perspectives such as economics, sociology, anthropology, marketing, management and geography. Hence, gaining a full understanding of the changes happening in tourism and hospitality is complicated but, at the same time, it is required in order to educate the tourism and hospitality operators of the future.

The dynamic character of the industry and the coexistence of a wide spectrum of different fields and disciplines, create the necessity of a holistic approach to tourism and hospitality operations, education, and research. For instance, the considerable influence of new trends and issues in tourism creates the necessity of a more flexible approach to education and training that, on the one hand is able to sufficiently assess the potential challenges of the new era and, on the other hand, help businesses to adapt in order to survive in the modern market place. Indeed, it is only through innovation and new ways of thinking that businesses can survive and develop (Sok & O'Cass, 2011). Thus, perspectives and research from different scientific fields and disciplines are considerably important for the understanding of the evolutionary travel, tourism and hospitality process.

In the light of the changing environment in which tourism and hospitality businesses are operating, this book aims at: 1) highlighting some of the challenges faced by the travel, tourism and hospitality industries; 2) bridging the gap between academic research and industry practice; 3) providing a core inter-disciplinary body of knowledge that can support the continuation of academic and applied research, and the understanding of current tourism and hospitality industry operations.

The "Global Dynamics in Travel, Tourism, and Hospitality" edited book provides quality research in contemporary aspects with a substantial business focus. It serves as a basis for academics to develop their research; as a guide for business managers to engage in innovative techniques and evaluate the current challenges and applications; and as a useful handbook for students seeking to enhance their understanding on specific aspects in travel, tourism and hospitality field.

This edited book is divided in three sections. The first section focuses on travel dynamics because the travel and transport industry is, by definition, one of the tourism key components. According to Reilly et al. (2010) tourists should eventually travel to and from the destinations they select, whilst this reality creates the need for extensive energy / fuel consumption, let alone when long-haul automobile or air travel transportation is involved.

The second part deals with global dynamics in the wider tourism field. During the last decades, the tourism industry has continued to rapidly expand and has become one of the highest-growth industries worldwide (Liu & Chou, 2016). This is because from a financial point of view the development of tourism can shape and transform not only localities and regions but even define national economies; and, at the same time, tourism impacts socially, culturally, and environmentally all destinations (Pappas, 2014).

The final section of the edited book concerns the dynamics within the hospitality industry. The hotel and accommodation industry is the largest sub-sector of tourism economy, and is also a significant ingredient of the tourism experience (Davidson et al., 2010). As Chen (2016) suggests, the development and evolution of the inbound tourism market is most likely to have a considerable effect on the hotel industry in terms of increase of the hotel occupancy rate and sales revenue. Thus, the developments and trends within the hospitality industry need to be further highlighted and analysed.

OVERVIEW OF THE BOOK

Chapter 1 presents the results of a study aimed at understanding the impact of culture on travellers' online information search behavior. The research focused on Chinese and British travellers since these two groups are culturally different according to the Hofstede's categorization. Results show that the behavior of these two groups presents some differences that can be attributable to cultural differences.

Chapter 2 focuses on slum tourism – i.e. the organized visits to places of poverty – and the businesses offering this type of service. In particular, the chapter analyses how new technologies and the Internet in particular are used by businesses offering slum tourism tours. By applying the eMICA model the author analysed the website of *Reality Tours and Travel*, an Indian tour operator offering slum tours.

Chapter 3 analyses the European aviation sector by focusing on the three pillars making it up, namely the airlines, the airports and the providers of air navigation services. In particular, the chapter illustrates the institutional changes affecting the three aforementioned areas and shows how all the three pillars are essential elements in the tourism development of destinations.

Chapter 4 investigates the case of a Sicilian tour operator that offers responsible travel to tourists who wish to visit Sicily without giving money to the Sicilian mafia. By adopting the lenses of Service-Dominant Logic the author analysed how experiences are co-created in a multi-stakeholder environment. In so doing the interactions between the tour operator, its service providers and visitors had been studied.

Chapter 5 investigates for the first time whether holidays have negative effects on marriages and consequently increase the number of divorces. Through official statistics on the number of marriages and divorces in Argentina and through qualitative data the author sheds light on a new perspective: i.e. holidays could not only bring about positive effects to individuals, but they could also be the cause of break-ups.

Chapter 6 focuses on east Timor tourism. More specifically, the chapter attempts to discuss the prospects of tourism development in post-conflict contexts. After an analysis of the historical process of tourism development in East Timor, and of the role of tourism in the political and economic agenda of the country; the author highlights and analyzes the impact of international cooperation on tourism development in East Timor.

Chapter 7 focuses on innovation, internationalisation and networking within tourism with the aim of understanding the role that women play in those areas. A qualitative research based on focus groups was carried out. The research involved tourism leaders working is the seven administrative regions of Portugal. Results shows that gender roles attributed to women limit their contribution to growth strategies of tourism businesses.

Chapter 8 synthesizes Augmented Reality as an emerging and potential technology of digital tourism marketing and management. The aim of this chapter is to understand innovation from both, tourism product and services consumption perspective. Results outline that technology consumption is gradually reshaping and getting supported by the availability and accessibility of electronic formats such as Augmented Reality.

Chapter 9 identifies specific innovation anchors and reveals that innovation, in the future, can take further advantage. More specifically, this article identifies ten innovation anchors, e.g. critical trends that can guide the long-term innovation activity and lead to fundamentally new products, services, delivery mechanisms, organizational models, means of collaboration etc.

Chapter 10 draws upon empirical research carried out in the wake of the Asian tsunami, with the aim of examining the role of a mega natural disaster upon tourism development and planning. More specifically, it examines the influence of a natural disaster upon destination redevelopment, and draws upon examples of other natural disasters that have affected the tourism industry in recent times.

Chapter 11 provides empirical evidence on the impact of the recent financial crisis on the British travellers. This research provides, on the one hand, a better understanding of tourist behaviour and demand patterns during periods of economic recession; and on the other hand, it offers evidence based insights to public policy makers and managers regarding the actions and initiatives they could initiate to fend off the negative effects of the crisis.

Chapter 12 critically discusses the main opportunities and limitations that epistemology faces today in tourism field, as well as the problems quantitative-oriented paradigms show. More specifically, (1) it debates on the needs of achieving a scientific definition of tourism, and (2) it departs towards a theory that triggers a review of John Tribe´s contributions to the epistemology of tourism.

Chapter 13 analyses the global productivity challenge faced by hotels and provides a conceptual discussion on the productivity measurement used in the hospitality industry. By adopting a microeconomic perspective, the chapter provides a standard theoretical framework that identifies the sources of productivity improvement.

Chapter 14 analyses the point of view of executives in five stars international hotels in order to investigate the role of hotel personnel during the service provision. Through a quantitative method the author investigated the impact of physical attractiveness, self-confidence, and professional competence on service attitude. This chapter shows that service attitude is affected by the other three variables, which represents areas on which hotel managers should pay attention.

Chapter 15 explores how three, four and five star hotels located in Galicia (Northwest region of Spain) and in the Northern Region of Portugal apply social responsibility. The study focused on three different areas of social responsibility, namely environmental, economic and social dimensions. Results show that, although the two regions are similar from a cultural point of view, hoteliers' behavior shows differences with regards to economic and social dimensions.

Chapter 16 aims to bridge the gap toward the practical and theoretical issues in tourism and hospitality management. More specifically it examines the relevant literature in an effort to describe the implementation of major theoretical applications in practice, since this aspect significantly impacts on the understanding of appropriate knowledge to both, practitioners and researchers.

Nikolaos Pappas
University of West London, UK

Ilenia Bregoli
University of Lincoln, UK

REFERENCES

Chen, M. H. (2016). A quantile regression analysis of tourism market growth effect on the hotel industry. *International Journal of Hospitality Management, 52*, 117–120. doi:10.1016/j.ijhm.2015.10.001

Davidson, M. C. G., Timo, N., & Ying, W. (2010). How much does labour turnover cost? *International Journal of Contemporary Hospitality Management, 22*(4), 451–466. doi:10.1108/09596111011042686

Liu, C. H. S., & Chou, S. F. (2016). Tourism strategy development and facilitation of integrative processes among brand equity, marketing and motivation. *Tourism Management, 54*, 298–308. doi:10.1016/j.tourman.2015.11.014

Pappas, N. (2014). The effect of distance, expenditure and culture on the expression of social status through tourism. *Tourism Planning & Development, 11*(4), 387–404. doi:10.1080/21568316.2014.883425

Reilly, J., Williams, P., & Haider, W. (2010). Moving towards more eco-efficient tourist transportation to a resort destination: The case of Whistler, British Columbia. *Research in Transportation Economics, 26*(1), 66–73. doi:10.1016/j.retrec.2009.10.009

Sok, P., & O'Cass, A. (2011). Achieving superior innovation-based performance outcomes in SMEs through innovation resource-capability complementary. *Industrial Marketing Management, 40*(8), 1285–1293. doi:10.1016/j.indmarman.2011.10.007

UNWTO. (2016). *Tourism and poverty alleviation*. Madrid: United Nations World Tourism Organisation.

Wang, J., & Ritchie, B. W. (2012). Understanding accommodation managers' crisis planning intention: An application of the theory of planned behaviour. *Tourism Management, 33*(5), 1057–1067. doi:10.1016/j. tourman.2011.12.006

WTTC. (2015). *Travel and tourism world economic impact 2015*. London: World Travel & Tourism Council.

Section 1
Global Dynamics in Travel

The first section of the edited book consists of five chapters and focuses on the travel contemporary issues and dynamics. It starts focusing on aspects relevant to information technology, proceeds to aviation and tourist agencies and concludes with an analysis of social effects stemming from travel.

Chapter 1

'The Impact of Culture on Tourists' Online Information Search Behaviour:
Evidence from the UK and China

Eleni Michopoulou
University of Derby, UK

Delia Gabriela Moisa
University of Derby, UK

ABSTRACT

This chapter looks into the concept of culture and its impacts on travellers' online information search behaviour. The study is focused on two culturally diametric countries: United Kingdom and China (Hofstede, 2001) and they have been selected as case studies, representing values from the Western and the Asian cultures. In order to examine the effects of culture on online search behaviours, the research adopted a qualitative approach, and data was collected through interviews in order to enhance and elaborate the understanding on the subject studied. The results of this study show that culture influences the travellers' behaviour in the online environment, up to a certain extent, and as a result of this influences, different behavioural patterns between the British and the Chinese travellers emerged. Moreover, these findings bring implications for the marketers aiming at the British and the Chinese tourists, and they highlight the need to adopt different strategies in designing and marketing their tourism products for these two particular markets.

INTRODUCTION

More than a decade has passed since the Internet was considered as this revolutionary 'big thing' that was changing everything, for the way we do business to the way we live (Buhalis & Law, 2008). However, today the impacts of the wide use of Internet are more apparent than ever. Considering the proliferation of the medium across the globe, it has become apparent that societies have been evolving and people's

DOI: 10.4018/978-1-5225-0201-2.ch001

lifestyles are changing. With a vast amount of information readily available, the Internet provides an opportunity for individuals in most parts of the world to connect, communicate and interact in an instant. During the year 2014, over 7 billion people had access to the Internet, an increase of 741.0% since the year 2000 (Internet World Stats, 2015), suggesting high rates of growth registered also in the travel sector. Developments in speed of networks, carrying capacities and search engines highly influence the numbers of travellers around the world using technology to plan and experience their travels (Buhalis & Law, 2008). Moreover, it has been recognized that the use of the Internet to search for travel information is highly more popular in contrast to traditional media, and this phenomenon continues to increase (Fesenmaier, Cook, Sheatsley & Patkose, 2009; Bai, Law & Wen, 2008; Tews & Merritt, 2007).

Recent statistics show that approximately 87% of the adult population in Great Britain uses the Internet (ONS, 2014). At the same time, the Asian market holds the highest numbers of Internet users in the world, with China accounting 632 million Internet users by the end of June 2014 (CNNIC, 2014). Considering this large population of Internet users, and the fact that China continues to be the largest outbound tourism market in the world for 3 consecutive years since 2012 (CIW, 2015), (together with the continuous increase in consumer spending), obtaining a better understanding upon the Chinese's preferences and the role Internet plays in their decisions becomes particularly relevant. Due to the vast amount of information available, searching and purchasing tourism products might be a daunting task. While the online market continues to grow at a relentless pace, the Western companies are facing a tough challenge and they find themselves in direct competition with Chinese providers like Renren, Baidu, or Sina Weibo (ISN, 2012). By understanding how individuals from cultures with very different index numbers (Hofstede, 2001) search for travel information on the Internet, marketers can develop and improve their strategies and tailor their services so that potential travellers become able to successfully navigate through the impressive amount of information available online, benefiting both the consumers and the providers.

Various authors acknowledged the different motives depriving the Chinese tourists from traveling overseas and using the Internet as a helping tool for planning and/or booking and these include: limitations and considerations concerning the visa application, income, preparation process for travelling, language concerns on booking tools, and safety concerns when using online systems (Wong, 2012; Zhang, 2009; Li & Buhalis, 2006). Moreover, it is widely well-known that the Chinese government developed sophisticated methods to monitor and repress social-media activities, through 'The Great Firewall'. The International Relations and Security Network (ISN) (2012) confirms that ''Beijing now sees the internet as a kind of safety valve for potential social unrest''. In case of any public interest event such as a strike, an environmental disaster, or a corruption scandal, the Chinese government pays a group of bloggers such as the Fifty Cent Party to 'shape' public debate online (ISN, 2012). Moreover, the Chinese Internet landscape is very different from anywhere else in the world. The limitations China is facing in terms of accessibility to some of the world's most famous search engines such as Google, social media platforms including Facebook, Twitter, means that multinational Internet companies are facing difficulties in penetrating the Chinese market, and therefore tourism suppliers need to adapt to their culture and tailor their services. The main players are all Chinese, but they all have equivalents from the western part of the world.

While Western companies remain focused on having a foothold in the world's largest online marketplace, it is important to recognize that once the population moves online, the consumer behaviour shifts. ICTs have not only changed the way in which tourism businesses are conducted in the marketplace, but also the how consumers interact with these organisations (Buhalis, 2003). Moreover, the flexibility of the Internet allows tourism organisations to address different target markets and to develop marketing propositions tailored to the needs of each market (Buhalis & Law, 2008). For this reason, it is vital for companies in the tourism industry to understand the why, when and how of the Internet and the way travellers utilize it. Therefore, this chapter will provide a better understanding upon the online tourists' behaviour and the impact of cultural variation and utilization of travel information search. By comparing the way users with different nationality utilize the Internet as a travel-related information tool, the differences towards consumer behaviour can be identified and allow tourism markets to develop effective strategies, by using appropriate communication and marketing channels, and to support and facilitate the exchange of worldwide information.

Hence, the objectives of this chapter are to:

1. Identify the key cultural differences between the Chinese travellers and British tourists, and how their cultural backgrounds influence their online information search behavior.
2. Identify major cultural themes that should be included in promotional strategies aiming at the Chinese and the British tourist market.

Keegan and Schlegelmilch (2001) state that culture only influences consumer behaviour on the environmental sensitive products such as food, where international companies are forced to respond to the nation's different tastes. However, it is more than just a language barrier which could easily be overcome by changing the settings on the Internet. While marketers mostly focus on increasing their visibility in the online environments through search engine optimizations, content creations, or paid advertisements, a high ranking in the search results might not result in higher traffic on the page, neither higher conversion rates. As a result, this chapter provides new insights into the cultural differences between the East and the West, affecting the users' way of accessing the Internet for travel-related purposes, and therefore contributing to the supplier side in developing and marketing their tourism products across the cultural context.

BACKGROUND

Tourist Behaviours in Information Search

The process of information search represents one of the very first steps of the travel decision making, and it includes the travellers' awareness of choice and selection regarding the destination visited, as well as on-site activities, accommodations, or tours (Chen & Gursoy, 2000; Fodness & Murray, 1998). Moreover, Engel, Backwell and Miniard (1995) defined the information search as a ''motivated activation of knowledge stored in memory or acquisition of information from the environment''. As the definition implies, the information can be either internal, such as previous experiences and knowledge, or external, involving a broad of other sources such as family, friends, media, and travel consultants (Gursoy, 2001).

There is a substantial number of previous studies attempting to understand the information search behaviour exhibited by travellers during their various stages of the travel planning process, with various authors confirming that tourists are motivated by functional, hedonic, innovation, and aesthetic needs (Peng, Xu & Chen, 2013; Vogt & Fesenmaier, 1998). This body of literature covers a range of subjects from information search and experience (Snepenger, Meged, Snelling & Worrall, 1990), information search and welcome centers (Howard & Gitelson, 1989; Gitelson & Perdue, 1987; Gitelson & Crompton, 1983), as well as information searcher typology (Fodness & Murray, 1998). In order to understand the why, what, where, when and how travellers search for information, most authors based their studies on the most influential theoretical frameworks: the strategic model, proposed by Snepenger et al. (1990) who focuses on the combination of information sources used by travellers, and the contingency model, where the information search behaviour depends on individual and product characteristics, situational influences, effort, number of sources used, and search outcomes (Gursoy, 2001; 2003; Fodness & Murray, 1999; Schul & Crompton, 1983). Furthermore, Gursoy and McCleary (2004) and Gursoy (2001) proposed the integrated model, a new approach focused on the pre-purchase information search behaviour of travellers, where the two previously discussed frameworks become complementary to each other, and it considers the psychological, motivational, economics and information processing factors (Gursoy & Chi, 2008).

While all these studies were based on the information search using the traditional forms of communication, including newspapers, brochures, radio, the development of the external information search tool, the Internet, changed radically the classic communication distribution model. The Internet, or the World Wide Web, became a dominant and ubiquitous means of delivering messages to hundreds of millions of travellers worldwide, allowing them to find any information about travel destinations and travel products (Gursoy & Chi, 2008). Based on the previous theoretical considerations in consumer behaviour, decision making in tourism, and e-shopping acceptance, the ''e-Tourism Usage Model'' (eTUM) in the figure below was derived, and it shows the various constructs that influence consumer's choice to use the Internet as travel planning channel including: the evaluation of the website, travel motivation, trip features, experience with e-commerce and/or e-tourism, Internet affinity, self-efficacy, involvement and trust. The traveller's attitude towards using the Internet for travel planning is therefore the main factor affecting the travellers' decisions of using the Internet as information and/or booking channel (Steinbauer & Werthner, 2007) (see Figure 1).

Hybrid Era

Thakran and Verma (2013) confirmed that we entered into a hybrid Era, where the customers are increasingly depending on online search, and they do this by using multiple screens at different times of the day. However, the new hybrid Era represents a renewed way of thinking, not only through the use of gadgets such as the iPhone or the Web, and its various applications including Twitter and Facebook, but rather to all technological inventions.

On one hand, advancements in the digital space have opened new ways of effectively marketing to the consumers, but on the other hand, these advancements have made travel and tourism management a complex task. The proliferation of the Information and Communication Technologies (ICT's) fundamentally revolutionized the way experiences are created and they support tourism consumers throughout all the stages, starting from the process of information search, to the process of information search, to the decision making process, planning, communication, retrieval of information, and sharing the experiences (Crouch & Desforges, 2003; Michopoulou & Buhalis, 2013; Stamboulis & Skayannis, 2003). The technologies are therefore implemented to support and facilitate travel activities and enhance the tourist experience, through the use of websites, blogs, recommendation systems, social networking, virtual communities, and mobile devices (Gretzel, Fesenmaier & O'Leary, 2006). A previous study on 15 participating countries in the Cisco Connected World Technology Report (2014) demonstrated that the Generation X (aged between 31 and 50) and Generation Y, also known as the Millennials (aged between

Figure 1. The e-tourism usage model (eTUM)
(Source: Steinbauer & Werthner, 2007, p. 68)

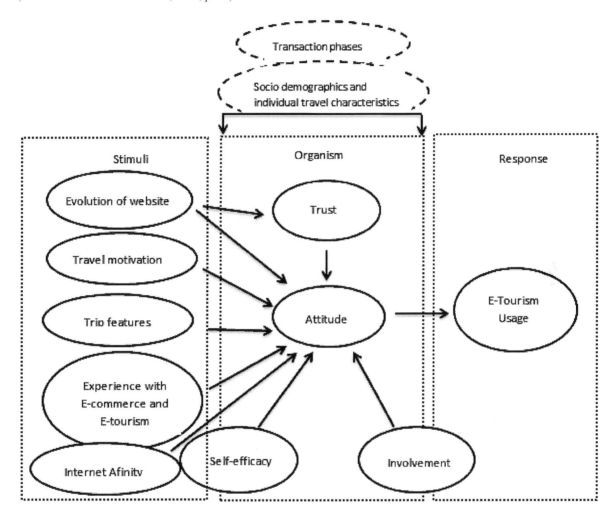

18 and 30) use two to three work and personal devices in their daily lives, with mobile internet becoming a more popular medium in travel information search rather than PC and traditional media (Okazaki & Hirose, 2009). They are technologically savvy, heavy Internet users (Nielsen, 2014), and the perceived social impact caused by sharing travel experiences is a considerable criterion for these generations. Social media stimulates tourists to ''dream'' about travelling experiences through the pictures, videos, and updates shared by their friends. Therefore, they engage with travel products and various brands without being in the stage of purchase or active travel information seeking (SE1 Media, 2015).

Literature on travellers' information search behaviour reveals that the way in which tourists look for information has often been used as a segmentation criterion in tourism studies (Bieger & Laesser, 2004; Buhalis & Michopoulou, 2011). Segmenting travellers becomes highly important when understanding individual behaviour (Wickens, 2002) and it brings high implications in terms of marketing purposes, and designing appropriate tourism products in order to establish appropriate communication channels to meet the needs and expectations of travellers from various segments (Alvarez & Asugman, 2006).

Gursoy and Chi (2008) stipulate that an important factor likely to influence the way travellers use the Internet or other sources of information, and influence their decision making process, is represented by the individual's culture. Considering the fact that human behaviour is culture-bound rather than culture free, the suppliers involved in distributing travel related services through the use of the Internet, must be able to cater for the needs of tourists from various backgrounds, and learn how to use appropriate communication and marketing channels.

Impact of Culture on Information Search Behaviour

Hofstede (2001) identified culture as an identity which helps to distinguish one group of people from another, and Keegan and Schlegelmilch (2001) suggest that the culture is formed within the community and over the years, being passed on from one generation to another. According to Doole and Lowe (2008), the essential components of the culture are the beliefs, values, and the customs. In other words, the culture offers a guideline for its members to decide how, what and why to do certain things; it shapes human behaviour by transmitting certain values, beliefs and norms. Culture dictates an individual's way of living, and thinking, an element that becomes highly important in this particular case, as it also brings implications for the usage of the Internet.

Hall's (1990, 1976) two dimensions of culture for context and time, argue that meaning is formed based on how information is perceived, and the form and function of information varies between cultures (Topi & Tucker, 2014). Therefore, the high context cultures mostly rely on implicit information, fast and efficient communication, embedded in a context of social cues such as body language, eye movement, and silence. In contrast, low-context cultures rely on explicit forms of communication coming directly through verbal channels.

For more than 30 years Hofstede's work (2010; 2005; 2001; 1991) has been the base on which various researchers relied in order to make comparisons based on country affiliation (Topi & Tucker, 2014), with his dimensions of power distance, individualism-collectivism, masculinity-femininity, uncertainty avoidance and long-term/ short-term orientation being frequently used in Information Systems research, and especially in e-commerce (Vyncke & Brengman, 2010). In 2010, a complementary dimension of Long versus Short-term orientation was added by an additional study labeled as Indulgence versus Restraint, which stands for societies which wither allow gratification of basic and natural human desires related to enjoying life and having fun, or societies which regulate these needs by means of social norms (Hofstede, 2011). While the validity of using Hofstede's (2001, 1991) finding has been widely questioned, the numerous quantitative and qualitative studies from various disciplines support his findings (Sondergaard, 1990; Straub, 1994) and Hofstede's classifications are often used in social psychological phenomena (Gefen & Heart, 2006), computer self-efficacy (Srite, Tatcher & Galy, 2008), and especially in studies of cross-cultural differences in an e-business context (Cyr, Head, Larios & Pan, 2009; Simon, 2001). Researchers agreed that culture determines the acceptable forms of communication, the nature and the degree of external search consumers utilize it (Gursoy & Umbreit, 2004; Chen & Gursoy, 2001; Engel et al., 1995). There is also a growing body of research examining the role of cultural differences in individual's use of computers and the Internet, online search behaviour and the perceived risk of using the Internet as a purchasing tool (Li & Kirkup, 2007; Park & Jun, 2003; Jarvenpaa, Tractinsky, & Saarinen, 1999). Nevertheless, only a small number of studies have researched the impact of culture on tourists' external information search behaviour in cross-cultural settings (Marcos, Garcia-Gavilanes, Bataineh, & Pasarin, 2013; Vuylsteke, Wen, Baesens & Poelmans, 2009; Gursoy & Umbreit, 2004).

Hofstede and Hofstede (2005) determined that cultural background contributes to the individual's tolerance levels of uncertainty and ambiguity, known as the uncertainty avoidance index. Such a cultural dimension shows that cultures with low uncertainty avoidance feel more comfortable in uncertain situations, while the opposite end, the cultures with a high uncertainty avoidance level, may feel anxious or threatened by such situations. Considering the fact the tourism activities can create situations with high levels of uncertainty for travellers, ranging from experiencing various cultures, languages, to reserving accommodations, travel activities without any prior experience, Kralisch, Eisend and Berendt (2005) showed that when searching on the Internet, travellers from cultural backgrounds with high levels of uncertainty avoidance preferred to collect more information, and used search engines to a greater extent rather than the cultures with low uncertainty avoidance, which are more comfortable gathering less information during their online information search.

The report from Iresearch (2012) shows that Chinese travellers generally search for travel information on search engines which eventually directs them to social media sites (Xiang & Gretzel, 2010), vertical search engines, portal travel channels, OTAs. Before making the decision of travel, the potential tourists incline towards the search of the online travel reviews (Doong, Law & Wang, 2009; Litvin, Goldsmith & Pan, 2008), mostly for accommodation decisions (Gretzel & Yoo, 2008). Chen, Johnson and Gherissi-Labben (2013) showed that American tourists are inclined to use the Internet for querying travel information, as well as the reservation channel, while the German and French tourists illustrate a much higher conversion rate regarding Internet usage and online reservation. Moreover, Jordan, Norman & Vogt's exploratory study (2012) revealed that Belgians like to explore many options before deciding upon purchase, adopting a 'browsing' web style, while the Americans tend to use the 'one shop stop' search style, make multiple booking products on a single website. Kim, Letho and Morrison's study (2007) demonstrated that there are substantial gender differences in terms of information channels preferred, as well as travel websites' functionality, and Zhou's study (2014) on Chinese students highlighted the actual gender differences when using the web for online information seeking, males being more engaged in search activities rather than females.

This chapter is designed to contribute to the growing body of literature, by examining a new aspect which has not been previously discussed: the online travel information search behaviour of individuals from China and the United Kingdom, while analyzing the connections between the travellers' use of online information sources in differentiating cultures. China and the United Kingdom were selected as representations for the Asian and the Western cultures for comparison for two reasons. First, the vast difference between the scores on Hofstede's (2001) depicted cultural maps provides a clear view of contrasting countries. According to these maps, while the United Kingdom rates relatively low in power distance, uncertainty avoidance dimensions, and long-term orientation, it rates high in masculinity and individualism dimensions. On the other hand, China rates high in power distance and long term orientation, and relatively low in individualism. Therefore, the study will analyze the manifestation of the specific cultural characteristics of English and Chinese culture in relation to their online information search behaviour. Secondly, Chinese students are required to learn English in primary schools, ensuring that both interviewed groups were proficient in the English language. Bolton and Graddol (2012) quoted a China Daily article and stated that approximately a third of the mainland Chinese population is currently learning English, excluding Hong Kong and Macau, where English is an official language. Wei and Su (2012) completes with more precise figures, claiming that 390.16 million Chinese people studied English in school as a foreign language.

METHODS

With a focus of understanding tourists behaviour and identifying possible explanations in terms of national likeliness and unlikeliness regarding the online information search, this subjective study lays emphasis on the holistic 'what, why, and how' of human behaviour and therefore it adopts a qualitative methodology. The qualitative research helps in understanding the phenomenon more deeply by analysing the reasons behind it (Creswell, 2003), it is pragmatic, interpretive and grounded in the lived experiences of people (Marshall & Rossman, 2006). The inductive approach of the study gives the researches a chance to explain the phenomenon studied, opening up new lines of enquiry without having any previous theories on the subject of interest (Saunders, Lewis, & Thornhill, 2007; Marshall, 1997). Furthermore, in order to understand the meaning people give to their use of the Internet in the process of travel information search, within their social setting, the qualitative research method adopted is the interview due to its effectiveness to help the researcher gain deep insights about people's experiences, feelings and interpretation of the social world (Mack, Woodsong, MacQueen, Guest, & Namey, 2005).

All the participating interviewees were asked for approval to be involved in the study, and certain rights including their anonymity was guaranteed. Considering the fact that the Generation Y, also known as the Millennials (ages between 18 and 30), are the technologically savvy, heavy Internet users (Nielsen, 2014), the two cultural representative groups were purposefully stratified according to their age, in order to obtain qualitative and meaningful answers from proficient Internet users. 10 native British travellers located in the United Kingdom, and 10 native Chinese travellers located in their home country took part in the interviews collected over a period of 3 weeks, starting from the 1st to the 22nd of March. Due to the geographical area covered by the research, the interviews were conducted face to face, or over the medium of the mobile phone and computer, by using social media means, such as WeChat, and Skype.

FINDINGS AND DISCUSSION

The results of the study indicate that there are differences between the British and Chinese online information behaviours, and that travellers are influenced to a certain extent by their cultural background. However, we, as humans, are simultaneously unique, and it becomes clear that culture only exists by comparison (Itim International, 2015).

The Table 1 illustrates the main themes and differences identified between the British and the Chinese travellers in terms of their online information search behaviour. These include information sources used by travellers, their attitude towards the Internet and confidence when booking online, as well as their usage patterns, regarding the frequency of use and types of websites accessed to look for tourism information. Furthermore, particulars regarding the booking of holiday packages, and social media engagement for travel related purposes, as well as the contribution to users' online opinions are going to be further discussed.

Information Sources

The main concept affecting the travellers' decision of using the Internet as an information tool or as a booking channel involves the user's attitude towards the Internet (Steinbauer & Werthner, 2007). As the

Table 1. Key similarities and differences between the British and the Chinese travellers

Themes	British Travellers	Chinese Travellers
Information sources	Internet (Google); Friends and family	Internet (Baidu, Google); Friends and family
Attitude: booker versus looker	Safety, technological concerns, less confident to complete the booking process	Feel safe and book online
Determinants of buying tourism products online	Speed of completing the task; convenience	Convenience; online sources perceived as cheaper rather than other sources
Usage patterns	Price-driven	Driven by brand recognition
Frequency of traveling/ buying tourism products online	Up to 5 times per year	Generally 2 times per year: National Day holidays, and Spring Festival holidays
Diversity of interests	Balance: price- product characteristics	Value for money, product characteristics and high value content about the destination
Holiday packages	Book holiday packages due to comfort, feeling of being more organized	Book separately, they like to DIY their trip
Planning required	Several months before –> cheaper	Between one week and one month
Social media engagement	Facebook, Instagram, Twitter, Google+, Youtube, LinkedIn	WeChat, Tencent QQ, Weibo, MaFengWo (social travel service)
Use of social media for travel related purposes	Travellers do not use social media for travel related purposes	Travellers read social media content, they have subscriptions to various travel related accounts
Importance of reviews	Important Main source: TripAdvisor	Very important Check review on the same websites where they book (Qunar, Ctrip, Agoda)
Contribution of users' opinions	Mainly read the reviews	Read and write reviews

study indicates, both the British and Chinese travellers feel confident at utilizing the Internet hence they use it as an information tool, and as a booking channel for travel products such as transportation and accommodation services. While previous studies showed that travellers first gather information from family and friends when choosing accommodation (Verma, Stock & McCarthy, 2012), this particular study indicates that consumer behaviours have changed over time, and the Internet became a highly reliable and a primary source of information. Both the British and the Chinese travellers confirmed that the Internet is the primary source accessed in order to look for travel information, and they often start the process of information search from the search engine. While the British travellers highly rely on the internationally used search engine Google where they type the key words of the destinations of their interest, and then scroll the search results, the study confirms that this also a common practice among the Chinese travellers as well. While the respondents confirmed to use the most popular Chinese search engine, Baidu, as a primary source of information, they also access the world's most popular search engine, Google (Krawczyk, 2014), although it is blocked in the country. From this point of view it is suggested that the generation of Millennials is highly influenced by the western culture, and they aspire to the freedom of information which they believe Google holds.

Attitude: Booker vs. Looker

Although the Internet is the most important tool for information search for both cultural groups studied, British and Chinese, travellers may still use different channels in order to make a decision, and end up making the purchase of travel products offline. As a country with higher levels of uncertainty avoidance, scoring 35 in Hofstede's dimensions (2001), compared to China which scores 30, travellers from the UK appear to feel more threatened by uncertain situations and therefore they try to avoid them. Buhalis and Law (2008) confirmed that in spite of the variety of choices available online, there are psychological barriers which may prevent travellers from completing transactions online. As this study suggests, while the Chinese travellers are very open at using the online booking systems, British travellers raise concerns related to potential technological issues, and they display less confidence, as well as safety concerns when providing personal information online. This justifies their inclination towards purchasing products off-line and asking help from third parties such as travel agencies. Comparatively, all the Chinese respondents confirmed to make travel bookings online directly through the Internet due to convenience. Moreover, Chinese travellers perceive online sources as being cheaper compared to other sources such as travel agencies, hence the reason for using the Internet as a booking channel.

Usage Patterns

When purchasing tourism products online, British travellers tend to focus their search around various websites, generally starting from the search engine Google, and accessing various websites from the results pages in order to find the best deal available online. This suggests that that the British travellers' search process is generally price-driven. On the contrary, the Chinese travellers generally access the same travel websites, mainly due to popularity within the country, with Ctrip, Elong and Qunar being mostly mentioned as websites with good reputation, and offering value for money. It is suggested that the Chinese travellers are driven by brand recognition and they base their decisions on Confucian ideology, and long-term orientation, as implied by Hofstede's (2001) dimensions. As a society which likes to maintain traditions and norms, it is reflected in the Chinese travellers' behaviours, where they all follow the same patterns of the general population within the country.

The frequency of searching for travel information and making travel purchases online is related directly to the travellers' frequency of traveling, which highly differs between the two cultures. The most recent dimensions added to the other six in Hofstede's (2011) theory is the indulgence versus restraint, and it is used to describe societies from the level of allowance to human desires related to enjoying life and having fun. According to Hofstede, Hofstede and Minkov (2010), with a high score of 69, the British culture is classified as indulgent, while China's low score of 24 suggests that it is a restraint society, regulated by social norms. The findings of this research confirmed that in terms of the frequency of travelling and frequency of buying tourism products, the British respondents travel for leisure up to 5 times per year, while the Chinese travellers take two holidays per year, during the most important Chinese holidays, which are the National Day and the Spring Festival. As an indulgent culture, the British travellers' responses confirmed that they generally possess a positive attitude, and they exhibit their desires and impulses concerning life enjoyment, as they place a much higher degree of importance on leisure time. Hence, the much higher frequency of traveling for leisure, compared to the Chinese travellers. On the contrary, as the study suggests, the Chinese restraint society is also reflected in their frequency of leisure travel, and the control on gratification of their desires. According to Hofstede's Centre, China is a country where people believe that indulging themselves is somewhat wrong (Itim International, 2015), and therefore they do not put an emphasis on leisure time.

Diversity of Interests

Chinese travellers do not plan their holiday around the hotel, as opposed to the British ones. They plan their travel around the destination, and therefore their goals when searching for information on the Internet differ. While the British travellers look for a balance between price, location and comfort, the Chinese are mostly interested in getting value for money, and other aspects involving high value content about the destination. The Chinese travellers do not go on holidays to relax, and they generally want to experience, visiting places completely different from their home environments, and therefore the information which interest them is related to visa requirements, traffic in the area, less crowds, season, and local tourism services. The study confirms that the group travelling habits of the Chinese old generation shifted, and the 'new' Chinese tourist is more independent. They do not look for package holidays, and the price is not the main reason for this. As the respondents of the study confirmed, they do not like to have a pre-established route, and they want to 'DIY' their trip. In accordance with Hofstede's dimensions (2001), China's relative low score in uncertainty avoidance is also reflected in the way they respond to travel information search behaviour. As this study suggests, Chinese travellers' planning is not detail oriented, and they are happy to change plans as they go along and new information is coming to light. This reason might also explain why the planning required for the Chinese travellers is considerably much shorter than for the British ones, and while the former cultural group takes up to several months in order to plan their travel, the Chinese generally finish the process between one week to one month. On the contrary, the British travellers might book earlier in order to get better prices, and they also prefer holiday packages mostly due to convenience, comfort, and feeling of being more organized.

Social Media Engagement

British respondents are all active on at least one social media platform such as Facebook, Twitter, Instagram, Youtube, LinkedIn, Google+, and they mostly use them for entertainment and communication purposes, without considering them for travel related purposes. However, one British respondent confirmed that ''on Facebook you always see in your news feed photos from your friends who go on holidays and how happy they look and it kind of makes you want to travel and you start thinking about it as a possible option to go there.'' This confirms the findings of the literature and through social media is proven to stimulate and engage users with tourism products without being in the active travel information seeking (SE1 Media, 2015). As far as the Chinese travellers are concerned, the majority confirmed to read social media information, and follow various travel accounts which provide updates regarding interesting destinations, and travelling journals. Another reason for having subscriptions to travel accounts is due to the offers they can get online, and they are active on social media platforms such as Facebook and Instagram, although these are blocked in China. Interestingly, they confirmed to use them as the people in their group use them as well, and also due to businesses in a foreign environment. These findings suggest that the content, comments and the reviews on these popular social networks are decisive elements for both cultural groups, and it influence especially the Chinese travellers' choices, hence presence on social media is a powerful tool in attracting tourists.

Importance of Reviews

The online reviews play an important part in the information search and decision making process for both cultural groups. British travellers, as well as Chinese travellers, confirmed to read reviews regarding travel products before making a decision. As the literature suggested, convenience, quality, social reassurance and risk reduction are the main factors which motivate customers to look for online travel reviews (Kim, Mattila & Baloglu, 2011). While the majority of the British travellers mentioned TripAdvisor as a main source to find customer reviews, the preeminent answer of the Chinese travellers relates to using the same source as the website where they make the booking, with very few respondents mentioning MaFengWo, the most popular travel website in China, where people share their experiences. Furthermore, the literature agrees with the theme related to the contribution of users' opinions, where according to Hofstede's (2001) findings, the UK scores high in individualism (89), while China scores low (20), being seen as a highly collectivist society, in which people's self-image is defined in terms of ''we''. The Hofstede Centre confirms that in individualist societies such as the UK, people tend to look after themselves and their direct family only (Itim International, 2015), while in collectivist societies, people belong to 'in groups'. This is reflected in the high contribution and engagement on social media, and as demonstrated in this study, in China, more than in the UK, social media is much more integrated into people's lives and peer reviews are highly trusted. Chinese travellers are much more likely to engage in cooperative behaviour and information sharing, and they use them as a reference before traveling. While anonymity does not impede to building trust, the Chinese respondents explained that ''the reviews are true'' and ''they are the reflection of the sincere feelings from the visitors from the past''. On the contrary, the British travellers trust the reviews to a certain extent only, they are usually useful and provide '' a slight idea of the place'', and ''every review has to be taken with a pinch of salt not every one of them will be true'', as the respondents stated.

Promotional Strategies

The findings identified between the British and the Chinese travellers in this study add credence to the call for managers to consider the importance of cultural differences and to respond promptly according to the customers' country of residence, and adopt adequate marketing strategies in correspondence with the needs and wants of the travellers. The study indicates that both the British and the Chinese travellers are connected 24 hours a day, they access the Internet every day, and they use at least two devices in order to access information. Moreover, the Chinese, more than the British use their mobile phones much frequently rather than a PC/laptop. It implies that digital and mobile marketing are critical when reaching these travellers, and developing dedicated mobile/iPad versions of the companies' websites and apps are mandatory. Most of the Chinese respondents confirmed that they do not check English travel websites, although they are proficient in English, as they confirmed that they can find all the information necessary in Chinese. While they might consider reading English information when planning to an overseas trip, they feel much more comfortable to access information in their native language. Therefore creating a website in Mandarin language is the key in order for a company to develop its presence in the Chinese market. Moreover, the Chinese travellers expect to find a lot more information related not only to the product characteristics, such as the hotel's facilities, but they need high value content about de destination as well. The inclusion of this kind of information on the company's websites aiming at attracting the Chinese market can therefore increase the companies' business.

There is a major difference between the British and the Chinese travellers when they search for information on search engines. The study revealed that the Chinese travellers are aware of the sponsored websites, and they generally avoid accessing them. Because sponsored links are generally not the most relevant ones, Baidu users are more likely to scroll down a little, and skip the results at the top of the page. This brings implications for the travel companies aiming at the Chinese market, which might believe that paying in order to be positioned at the top of the list in the search results might bring them more business, and the study suggests that it is not the case. On the contrary, British travellers confirmed that they generally access the results at the top of the page, without considering whether it is a sponsored link or not. Therefore, when aiming at the British market, travel companies may find marketing systems such as Google AdWords or alternatives such as Clicksor, Buy SellAdds or Yahoo! Bing Network as useful tools (Erin, 2014). Moreover, considering the fact that China holds the most active social media users in the world, with an approximately 95% of the total 600 million Internet users in the country having at least one account on social media (Tourism Marketing Agency, 2014) they are more willing to decide the destination, hotels and activities of their holidays that are mentioned and recommended on social media networks. As this study suggests, the Chinese travellers, are more likely rather than the British travellers to use social media in order to find information related to travel products. However, by reaching the Chinese market, companies must engage with the most popular social media sites in China including Wechat, Weibo, Tencent QQ, as the respondents confirmed to be highly active on these platforms.

However, it is important that companies understand that having a social network account does not ensure engagement, and as the literature confirmed, involvement on social media can be vital in generating interesting content, increasing awareness, and developing loyalty (Hays, Page & Buhalis, 2013; Parise, Guinan & Weinberg, 2008). Considering the fact the China is such a collectivist country, scoring 20 on Hofstede's (2001) dimensions, compared to the individualist UK with a 89 score, the users highly value interaction with online communities, where they usually contribute to users' opinions. This brings implications in terms of marketing strategies, and the message the ''we'' culture might be much more effective rather than ''me'' culture when aiming at the Chinese market. It is suggested that web designers should consider employing a group style by using pronouns such as ''us'', ''we'', and ''our'' in the websites' home pages, in order to reflect a sense of family within the country. Additionally, tourism companies must develop an approach to tailor to the Chinese travellers' expectations, and engaging with customers through social-media channels, connecting with individuals to solve problems, as well as being of assistance on a personal level are mandatory, and offering online discounts and promotions, and introducing loyalty schemes is crucial.

Literature has also confirmed that the higher the number of reviews, the more likely the company is to obtain conversions. As Ye, Law, Gu & Chen's (2011) study showed, 10 per cent higher traveller review ratings raised online bookings by more than 5 per cent. However, the findings of this study suggest that the travellers, the British ones more than the Chinese, are not engaged and although they value and read online reviews, they do not contribute to users' opinions online. One of the Chinese respondents mentioned that he writes reviews if there is a reward involved, which can therefore constitute a good strategy for companies trying to increase the numbers of reviews. Considering the findings of this study which suggest that British travellers do not incline towards contributions to users' opinions online, travel companies can develop reward schemes, or provide incentives or loyalty points as a way of motivating the travellers to write reviews, which would eventually increase the numbers of conversions. Additionally, providing special offers for travellers subscribed to a social media account would increase the level of engagement, and conversion rates. Although it has been previously mentioned the fact that the Internet is China is censored, none of the Chinese respondents mentioned that they would feel restricted to access to information. Moreover, the respondents confirmed that apart from the Chinese search engine Baidu, they also use Google as a primary source of information before traveling. However, companies must be aware of the fact that many sites commonly used around the world are blocked in China, and by using a website monitoring service, such as Website Pulse (Williams, 2015), companies can conduct article-blocking tests in order to find out whether the site can pass through the Great Firewall of China.

CONCLUSION

This chapter provided an understanding of the online information search behaviour of the two different cultural groups, Western and Asian travellers, and the way their cultural background influences behaviour patterns online. Moreover, by identifying key similarities and differences between the Western and Asian tourists' ways of searching for travel information online, the study provides key cultural themes and trends which companies aiming at these markets should take into account. The two culturally diametric countries: United Kingdom and China were selected as representatives for the Western, respectively Asian cultures, in correlation with Hofstede's (2001) dimensions which provide a clear view of contrasting countries. Moreover, considering the fact that China's large population holds the highest numbers of Internet users in the word, together with the Chinese' travellers increasing consumer spending, a better understanding into the Chinese travellers' preferences becomes highly relevant.

Various models have been proposed in order to understand why, what, where, when and how travellers search for information, with most authors basing their studies on the most influential theoretical frameworks: the strategic model, the contingency model, and the integrated model (Snepenger et al., 1990; Gursoy, 2001; Gursoy & Chi, 2008; Gursoy & McCleary, 2004). Based on these theoretical considerations, decision making in tourism, and e-shopping acceptance, the ''e-Tourism Usage Model'' (eTUM) was derived, and it shows the various constructs that influence consumer's choice to use the Internet as travel planning channel. Therefore, tourists make an evaluation of the website, and they consider travel motivation, trip features, experience with e-commerce and/or e-tourism, Internet affinity, self-efficacy, involvement and trust (Steinbauer & Werthner, 2007). The literature identified that the use of Internet to search for travel information highly more popular rather than the traditional media (Fesenmaier et. al., 2009; Tews & Merritt, 2007). While the phenomenon continues to increase, it has been agreed an important factor likely to influence the way travellers use the Internet or other sources of information, and influence their decision making process, is represented by the individual's culture (Gursoy & Chi, 2008). The most frequently used frameworks to describe various dimensions of culture belong to Hall (1960) and Hofstede (1991), and previous studies established the culture's link with the choice of one and the individual's use of the Internet (Li & Kirkup, 2007; Park & Jun, 2003). However, adapting tourism products to and marketing strategies to the specific market target represents a critical aspect which may decide on the company's success. For this reason, the main objectives of this research were to identify major cultural differences between the Chinese and the British travellers when searching for information online, and to identify cultural themes that should be included in promotional strategies aiming at these specific markets.

The study has found that there are distinct differences between the Chinese and the British travellers with regard to their search for travel information online. While both groups generally start their search from a search engine (Baidu, Google), the Chinese travellers feel safe in the online environment, and proceed with the booking, while the British travellers raised safety concerns when providing personal information online. Moreover, the two cultural groups display different usage patterns in terms of the websites accessed. The British respondents confirmed to access various websites to find the best deal, while the Chinese travellers generally access the same websites such as Ctrip, Qunar and Elong due to popularity within the country. Both cultural groups set as a priority the price and the products characteristics, however, for the Chinese more than for British, it is more important to obtain high value content about the destination. It implies that the Chinese travellers do not plan their holiday around the hotel, but around the destination. Hence, their preference of looking for separate transportation and accommodation facilities, instead of opting for holiday packages, they want to 'DIY' their trip and they like to make changes when travelling. Furthermore, both groups consider reviews are highly important, and they read reviews as part of their information search process; however, the ratio of posting on the consumer websites is much higher for the Chinese than for the British travellers.

The study confirmed that there have been changes manifested in the Chinese culture, and these are due to a mix of endogenous and exogenous factors. The new generation of Chinese travellers, the Millennials, adopt internationally used search engines such as Google, as a primary source of information, social media platforms such as Facebook, despite the fact that the Chinese government actively blocked such sources of information. Moreover, when making travel related purchases, they access internationally used online travel agencies, including Booking.com, Hotel.com, and Priceline. The western culture is accepted as a modern culture in the world (Odinye & Odinye, 2012) and it will always have influences on the Chinese culture. From this point of view, it is suggested that the 'global tourist' is emerging, and the Chinese travellers aspire to the freedom that the Western culture offers. With the popular media suggesting that communication technologies including the Internet will bring the people together in ''a global village where differences cease to matter'' (Hofstede et al., 2010), this study suggests that consumers select the information according to their own values. Based on the findings of this study, it is safe to confirm that markets and especially customers are differentiated, each person being unique. However, the culture does influence consumer behaviour up to a certain extent, and the travel companies aiming at different markets need to take cultural differences into consideration. The key is to think globally, and act locally.

Implications for the Industry

Taking into consideration the nature of the travel and tourism industry, and its worldwide coverage, together with the fast development of the Internet, it becomes important for businesses involved in the industry to tailor their strategies according to the market segment they are aiming at. Furthermore, the findings of this study have important implications for tourism professionals aiming at the British or Chinese market, and it reveals key aspects that need to be taken into account when developing their online presence. International marketers need to take in consideration the cultural dynamics of the tourism and hospitality industry, and adapt their strategies to the destination market, as follows:

- Digital and mobile marketing are critical when reaching British and/or Chinese travellers and developing dedicated mobile/iPad versions of the companies' websites and apps are mandatory;
- Although proficient in English, the Chinese travellers do not check English websites, and companies must create websites in Mandarin to attract the Chinese travellers;
- Adopt the ''we'' culture as marketing strategies aiming at the collectivist Chinese society, in order to reflect a sense of family;

- Ensure social media presence on the Chinese platforms including WeChat, Tencent QQ, Sina Weibo when aiming at the Chinese market;
- Online reviews are highly valued both in China and the UK, and companies can increase the users' contribution by offering rewards such as loyalty points, discounts;
- With TripAdvisor being the most popular source of customer reviews in the British travellers' culture, companies must ensure that they feature positive reviews on this platform, but also on their own website and other OTAs;
- Western companies aiming at the Chinese market must conduct article-blocking tests in order to find out if their website passes through the Great Wall of China.

Furthermore, the study suggested that the Internet is highly used for commercial information and therefore companies cannot neglect this marketing channel. Search engines play a much more important role in the British culture, rather than in the Chinese culture, where tourists generally access the most popular travel websites within the country. However, a well-targeted advertisement on consumer websites might be a good strategy, considering their popularity among the Chinese. Furthermore, paying the Chinese search engine, Baidu, in order to be listed on top of the search results might not be a good strategy, as this study suggests that Chinese travellers generally avoid sponsored links.

REFERENCES

Alvarez, M., & Asugman, G. (2006). Explorers versus planners: A study of Turkish tourists. *Annals of Tourism Research*, *33*(2), 319–338. doi:10.1016/j.annals.2005.12.001

Bai, B., Law, R., & Wen, I. (2008). The impact of website quality on customer satisfaction and purchase intentiond: Evidence from Chinese online visitors. *International Journal of Hospitality Management*, *27*(3), 391–402. doi:10.1016/j.ijhm.2007.10.008

Bieger, T., & Laesser, C. (2004). Information Sources for Travel Decisions: Toward a Source Process Model. *Journal of Travel Research*, *42*(4), 357–371. doi:10.1177/0047287504263030

Bolton, K., & Graddol, D. (2012). English in China today. *English Today*, *28*(3), 3–9. doi:10.1017/S0266078412000223

Buhalis, D. (2003). *eTourism: Information technology for strategic tourism management*. London: Pearson.

Buhalis, D., & Law, R. (2008). Progress in information technology and tourism management: 20 years on and 10 years after the Internet—The state of eTourism research. *Tourism Management*, *29*(4), 609–623. doi:10.1016/j.tourman.2008.01.005

Buhalis, D., & Michopoulou, E. (2011). Information Enabled Tourism Destination Marketing: Addressing the Accessibility Market. *Current Issues in Tourism*, *14*(2), 145–168. doi:10.1080/13683501003653361

Chen, J., Johnson, C., & Gherissi-Labben, T. (2013). Cross-cultural examination of decision elements: Youth tourism in Switzerland. *Anatolia*, *24*(2), 162–172. doi:10.1080/13032917.2012.741529

Chen, J. S., & Gursoy, D. (2001). An investigation of tourists' destination loyalty and preferences. *The International Journal of Contemporary Hospitality Management*, *13*(2), 79–85. doi:10.1108/09596110110381870

China Internet Network Information Center (CNNIC). (2014). *Statistical Report on Internet Development in China.* Retrieved March 5, 2015, from http://www1.cnnic.cn/IDR/ReportDownloads/201411/P020141102574314897888.pdf

China Internet Watch (CIW). (2015). *China, the Largest Outbound Tourism Market in 3 Consecutive years.* Retrieved May 25, 2015, from http://www.chinainternetwatch.com/13152/the-largest-outbound-tourism-market-3-consecutive-years

Cisco (2014). *Cisco Connected World Technology Report.* Retrieved February 15, 2015, from http://www.cisco.com/c/en/us/solutions/enterprise/connected-world-technology-report/index.html

Creswell, J. W. (2003). *Research Design Qualitative, Quantitative and Mixed Methods Approaches* (2nd ed.). Thousand Oaks, CA: Sage.

Crouch, D., & Desforges, L. (2003). The sensuous in the tourist encounter. *Tourist Studies, 3*(1), 5–22. doi:10.1177/1468797603040528

Cyr, D., Head, M., Larios, H., & Pan, B. (2009). Exploring human images in website design: A multi-method approach. *Management Information Systems Quarterly, 33*(3), 539–566.

Doong, H., Law, R., & Wang, H. (2009). An initial investigation of integrating innovation diffusion models for drawing first-time visitors. *Journal of Travel & Tourism Marketing, 26*(1), 19–29. doi:10.1080/10548400802656702

Engel, J., Blackwell, R., & Miniard, P. (1995). *Consumer Behaviour* (8th ed.). Fort Worth, TX: Dryden.

Erin, A. (2014). *7 Alternatives to Google AdWords for Small Businesses.* Retrieved April 26, 2015, from http://www.sitepronews.com/2014/10/08/7-alternatives-google-adwords-small-businesses

Fesenmaier, D. R., Cook, S., Sheatsley, D., & Patkose, M. (2009). *Travellers' Use of the Internet: 2009 Edition.* Washington, DC: Travel Industry Association.

Fesenmaier, D. R., & O'Leary, J. T. (2006). The transformation of consumer behavior. In D. Buhalis & C. Costa (Eds.), *Tourism business frontiers: Consumers, products and industry* (pp. 9–18). Oxford, UK: Elsevier.

Fodness, D., & Murray, B. (1998). A typology of tourist information search strategies. *Journal of Travel Research, 37*(2), 108–119. doi:10.1177/004728759803700202

Gefen, D., & Heart, T. (2006). On the need to include national culture as a central issue in e-commerce trust beliefs. *Journal of Global Information Management, 14*(4), 1–30. doi:10.4018/jgim.2006100101

Gitelson, R. J., & Crompton, J. (1983). The planning horizons and sources of information used by pleasure vacationers. *Journal of Travel Research, 21*(3), 2–7. doi:10.1177/004728758302100301

Gitelson, R. J., & Perdue, R. R. (1987). Evaluating the role of state welcome centers in disseminating travel related information in North Carolina. *Journal of Travel Research, 25*(1), 15–19. doi:10.1177/004728758702500403

Gretzel, U., Fesenmaier, D. R., & O'Leary, J. T. (2006). The transformation of consumer behavior. In D. Buhalis & C. Costa (Eds.), *Tourism business frontiers: Consumers, products and industry* (pp. 9–18). Oxford, UK: Elsevier. doi:10.1016/B978-0-7506-6377-9.50009-2

Gretzel, U., & Yoo, K. (2008). Use and impact of online travel reviews. In P. O'Connor, W. Hopken, & U. Gretzel (Eds.), *Information and Communication Technologies in Tourism 2008* (pp. 35–46). Vienna, Austria: Springer-Verlag Wien. doi:10.1007/978-3-211-77280-5_4

Gursoy, D. (2001). *Development of travellers' information search behaviour model.* (Unpublished doctoral dissertation). Polytechnic Institute and State University, Blacksburg, VA.

Gursoy, D. (2003). Prior product knowledge and its influence on the traveller's information search behaviour. *Journal of Hospitality & Leisure Marketing, 10*(3/4), 113–131. doi:10.1300/J150v10n03_07

Gursoy, D., & Chi, C. G. (2008). Travellers' information search behavior. In H. Oh (Ed.), *Handbook of Hospitality Marketing Management* (pp. 266–295). Oxford, UK: Elsevier.

Gursoy, D., & McCleary, K. W. (2004). An integrative model of tourist's information search behaviour. *Annals of Tourism Research, 31*(2), 353–373. doi:10.1016/j.annals.2003.12.004

Gursoy, D., & Umbreit, W. T. (2004). Tourist information search behaviour: Cross-cultural comparison of European Union Member States. *International Journal of Hospitality Management, 23*(1), 55–70. doi:10.1016/j.ijhm.2003.07.004

Hall, R. M. (1976). *Beyond Culture.* New York, NY: Doubleday.

Hall, R. M. (1990). *Understanding Cultural Difference.* Boston, MA: Intercultural Press Inc.

Hays, S., Page, S. J., & Buhalis, D. (2013). Social media as a destination marketing tool: Its use by national tourism organisations. *Current Issues in Tourism, 16*(3), 211–239. doi:10.1080/13683500.2012.662215

Hofstede, G. (1991). *Cultures and Organizations.* New York: McGraw Hill.

Hofstede, G. (2001). *Culture's Consequences: Comparing Values, Behaviours, Institutions, and Organizations Across Nations.* Sage Publications.

Hofstede, G. (2011). Dimensionalizing cultures: The Hofstede model in context. *Online Readings in Psychology and Culture, 2*(1). doi:10.9707/2307-0919.1014

Hofstede, G., & Hofstede, G. J. (2005). *Cultures and Organizations: Software of the Mind* (2nd ed.). McGraw-Hill.

Hofstede, G., Hofstede, G. J., & Minkov, M. (2010). *Cultures and organizations: software of the mind: intercultural cooperation and its importance for survival* (3rd ed.). New York: McGraw Hil.

Howard, D. R., & Gitelson, R. J. (1989). An analysis of the differences between state welcome center users and nonusers: A profile of Oregon vacationers. *Journal of Travel Research, 27*(1), 38–40. doi:10.1177/004728758902700406

International Relations and Security Network (ISN). (2012). *China, Corporations and Internet Censorship*. Retrieved March 11, 2015, from http://www.isn.ethz.ch/Digital-Library/Articles/Special-Feature/Detail/?lng=en&id=138039&contextid774=138039&contextid775=138031&tabid=138031

Internet World Stats. (2015). *Internet users in the world*. Retrieved March 3, 2015, from http://www.internetworldstats.com/stats.htm

Iresearch. (2012). *A research report on the Chinese online travellers' behaviours in 2012*. Retrieved January 17, 2015, from http:// www.iresearch.com.cn

Itim International. (2015). *National Culture*. Retrieved March 15, 2015, from http://geert-hofstede.com/national-culture.html

Itim International. (2015). *What about China?* Retrieved April 20, 2015, from http://geert-hofstede.com/china.html

Itim International. (2015). *What about the UK?* Retrieved April 20, 2015, from http://geert-hofstede.com/united-kingdom.html

Jarvenpaa, S. L., Tractinsky, N., & Saarinen, L. (1999). Consumer trust in an Internet store: A cross-cultural validation. *Journal of Computer-Mediated Communication*, 5(2), 1–37.

Jordan, E. J., Norman, W. C., & Vogt, C. A. (2012). A cross-cultural comparison for online travel information search behaviours. *Tourism Management Perspectives*, 6(1), 15–22.

Keegan, W., & Schlegelmilch, B. (2001). *Global marketing management* (6th ed.). Harlow, UK: Pearson Education Limited.

Kim, D. Y., Lehto, X. Y., & Morrison, A. M. (2007). Gender differences in online travel information search: Implications for marketing communications on the internet. *Tourism Management*, 28(2), 423–433. doi:10.1016/j.tourman.2006.04.001

Kim, E., Mattila, A. S., & Baloglu, S. (2011). Effects of gender and expertise on consumers' motivation to read online hotel reviews. *Cornell Hospitality Quarterly*, 52(4), 399–406. doi:10.1177/1938965510394357

Kralisch, A., Eisend, M., & Berendt, B. (2005). Impact of culture of Website navigation behaviour. In *Proceedings of the 11th International Conference on Human-Computer Interaction*.

Krawczyk, K. (2015). *Google is easily the most popular search engine, but have you heard who's in second?* Retrieved April 22, 2015, from http://www.digitaltrends.com/web/google-baidu-are-the-worlds-most-popular-search-engines

Li, L., & Buhalis, D. (2006). eCommerce in China: The case of travel. *International Journal of Information Management*, 26(2), 153–166. doi:10.1016/j.ijinfomgt.2005.11.007

Li, N., & Kirkup, G. (2007). Gender and cultural differences in Internet use: A study of China and the UK. *Computers & Education*, 48(2), 301–317. doi:10.1016/j.compedu.2005.01.007

Litvin, S. W., Goldsmith, R. E., & Pan, B. (2008). Electronic word-of-mouth in hospitality and tourism management. *Tourism Management*, 29(2), 458–468. doi:10.1016/j.tourman.2007.05.011

Mack, N., Woodsong, C., MacQueen, K. M., Guest, G., & Namey, E. (2005). *Qualitative research methods: A data collector's field guide*. Family Health International.

Marcos, M. C., Garcia-Gavilanes, R., Bataineh, E., & Pasarin, L. (2013). *Cultural Differences on Seeking Information: An Eye Tracking Study*. Retrieved April 28, 2015, from http://repositori.upf.edu/bitstream/handle/10230/20943/CHI_mcmarcos.pdf?sequence=1

Marshall, C., & Rossman, G. (2006). *Designing Qualitative Research (4th ed.)*. Thousand Oaks, CA: Sage Publications.

Marshall, P. (1997). *Research Methods: How to Design and Conduct a Successful Project*. Oxford, UK: How To Books, Ltd.

Michopoulou, E., & Buhalis, D. (2013). Information Provision for Challenging Markets: The Case of the Accessibility Requiring Market in the Context of Tourism. *Information & Management, 50*(5), 229–239. doi:10.1016/j.im.2013.04.001

Nielsen, J. (2014). *Millennials: much deeper than their facebook pages*. Retrieved February 15, 2015, from http://www.nielsen.com/us/en/insights/news/2014/millennials-much-deeper-than-their-facebook-pages.html

Office for National Statistics (ONS). (2014). *Internet Access – Households and Individuals 2014*. Retrieved March 5, 2015, from http://www.ons.gov.uk/ons/dcp171778_373584.pdf

Okazaki, S., & Hirose, M. (2009). Does gender affect media choice in travel information search? On the use of mobile Internet. *Tourism Management, 30*(6), 794–804. doi:10.1016/j.tourman.2008.12.012

Parise, S., Guinan, P., & Weinberg, B. (2008). *The secrets of marketing in a web 2.0 world*. Retrieved April 4, 2015, from http://online.wsj.com/article/SB122884677205091919.html

Park, C., & Jun, J.-K. (2003). A cross-cultural comparison of Internet buying behaviour: Effects of Internet usage, perceived risks, and innovativeness. *International Marketing Review, 20*(5), 534–553. doi:10.1108/02651330310498771

Peng, H., Xu, X., & Chen, W. (2013). Tourist Behaviours in Online Booking: A New Research Agenda. *Communications in Information Science and Management Engineering, 3*(6), 280–285.

SE1 Media Ltd. (2015). *Key trends in online customer behaviour: Experience driven content strategies*. Retrieved January 25, 2015, from http://thinkdigital.travel/opinion/key-trends-in-online-customer-behaviour-experience-driven-content-strategies

Saunders, M., Lewis, P., & Thornhill, A. (2007). *Research Methods for Business Students* (4th ed.). Harlow, UK: Pearson Education Limited.

Schul, P., & Crompton, J. L. (1983). Search behaviour of international vacationers: Travel-specific lifestyle and sociodemographic variables. *Journal of Travel Research, 22*(3), 25–31. doi:10.1177/004728758302200206

Simon, S. J. (2001). The impact of culture and gender on web sites: An empirical study. *The Data Base for Advances in Information Systems, 32*(1), 18–37. doi:10.1145/506740.506744

Snepenger, D., Meged, K., Snelling, M., & Worrall, K. (1990). Information search strategies by destination-naive tourists. *Journal of Travel Research, 29*(1), 13–16. doi:10.1177/004728759002900104

Sondergaard, M. (1990). Hofstede's consequences: A study of reviews, citations and replications. *Organization Studies, 15*(3), 447–456. doi:10.1177/017084069401500307

Srite, M., Thatcher, J. B., & Galy, E. (2008). Does within-culture variation matter? An empirical study of computer usage. *Journal of Global Information Management, 16*(1), 1–25. doi:10.4018/jgim.2008010101

Stamboulis, Y., & Skayannis, P. (2003). Innovation strategies and technology for experience-based tourism. *Tourism Management, 24*(1), 35–43. doi:10.1016/S0261-5177(02)00047-X

Steinbauer, A., & Werthner, H. (2007). Consumer Behaviour in e-Tourism. In M. Sigala, L. Mich, & J. Murphy (Eds.), *Information and Communication Technologies in Tourism 2007* (pp. 65–76). Vienna: Springer Vienna. doi:10.1007/978-3-211-69566-1_7

Straub, D. W. (1994). The effect of culture on IT diffusion: E-mail and fax in Japan and the US. *Information Systems Research, 5*(1), 23–47. doi:10.1287/isre.5.1.23

Tews, J., & Merritt, S. (2007). *Independent travel website satisfaction study.* Retrieved March 15, 2015, from http://businesscenter.jdpower.com/news/pressrelease.aspx?ID=2007277

Thakran, K., & Verma, R. (2013). The Emergence of Hybrid Online Distribution Channels in Travel, Tourism and Hospitality. *Cornell Hospitality Quarterly, 54*(3), 240–247. doi:10.1177/1938965513492107

Topi, H., & Tucker, A. (Eds.). (2014). *Computing Handbook: Information Systems and Information Technology* (3rd ed.). Boca Raton, FL: Taylor & Francis Group.

Verma, R., Stock, D., & McCarthy, L. (2012). Customer preferences for online, social media, and mobile innovations in the hospitality Industry. *Cornell Hospitality Quarterly, 53*(2), 183–186. doi:10.1177/1938965512445161

Vogt, C. A., & Fesenmaier, D. R. (1998). Expanding the functional information search model. *Annals of Tourism Research, 25*(3), 551–578. doi:10.1016/S0160-7383(98)00010-3

Vuylsteke, A., Wen, Z., Baesens, B., & Poelmans, J. (2009). *Consumers' Online Information Search: A Cross-Cultural Study between China and Western Europe.* Retrieved April 28, 2015, from http://www.aabri.com/OC09manuscripts/OC09043.pdf

Vyncke, F., & Brengman, M. (2010). Are culturally congruent websites more effective? An overview of a decade of empirical evidence. *Journal of Electronic Commerce Research, 11*, 14–29.

Wei, R., & Su, J. (2012). The statistics of English in China: An analysis of the best available data from government sources. *English Today, 28*(3), 10–14. doi:10.1017/S0266078412000235

Wickens, E. (2002). The sacred and profane: A tourist typology. *Annals of Tourism Research, 29*(4), 834–851. doi:10.1016/S0160-7383(01)00088-3

Williams, S. (2015). *China Inbound: how to prepare for Chinese guests.* Retrieved April 16, 2015, from http://www.hoteliermiddleeast.com/23481-china-inbound-how-to-prepare-for-chinese-guests/1/print

Wong, Y. (2012). Influences on Chinese online buying behaviour and decision making: The case of online booking for tourism products. *The International Hospitality and Tourism Student Journal, 4*(2), 135–145.

Xiang, Z., & Gretzel, U. (2010). Role of social media in online travel information search. *Tourism Management, 31*(2), 179–188. doi:10.1016/j.tourman.2009.02.016

Ye, Q., Law, R., Gu, B., & Chen, W. (2011). The influence of user-generated content on traveller behaviour: An empirical investigation on the effects of e-word-of-mouth to hotel online bookings. *Computers in Human Behavior, 27*(2), 634–639. doi:10.1016/j.chb.2010.04.014

Zhang, W. (2009). *The Motivations, Constraints and Decision Making of Beijing Outbound Tourism.* Hamilton, New Zealand: University of Waikato.

Zhou, M. (2014). Gender difference in web search perceptions and behaviour: Does it vary by task performance? *Computers & Education, 78*(1), 174–185. doi:10.1016/j.compedu.2014.06.005

Chapter 2
Poverty as a Tourism Attraction:
Travelling on the Web

Donatella Privitera
University of Catania, Italy

ABSTRACT

The visit of the favela or slum into a tourist destination is seen as a part of the so-called reality tours phenomenon and of the global circulation of the favela as a trademark. Tourist behaviour involves a search for leisure experiences from interactions with features or characteristics of places they choose to visit. Examples are the favelas in Brazil, the township of South Africa, the slum in India that have led to different definitions of "slum tourism", "poor-poor tourism", "reality tourism". Web heavily affect today most of the online activities and their effect on tourism is obviously rather important. The aim of the chapter is to discuss about slum tourism definitions. At the same time, taking Reality Tours and Travel - a wholesaler slum websites - as a case, this study attempts to explore issues of the quality of strategic choices on the web. Considering that the content of web site includes a wide variety of technologies, is important that website offer also interactivity with e-tourists. Through the results of the study, it is possible to gain knowledge of the slum e-tourism.

INTRODUCTION

Cities contain extremes of wealth and poverty, each concentrated in one or more sections. The wealthy areas are generally well insulated from the city around them; in contrast, areas inhabited by the poor are marginalised, i.e. generally unconnected to the social and economic life of the city flourishing around them. This leads to a number of questions: are poor people actually poor or are the contexts in which they live poor? Who are the poor? Although 'poor' may be a stable descriptive identity for people in some groups, for most, poverty is a situation, not an identity (Narayan, Pritchett, & Kapoor, 2009). Poverty is not defined in terms of low incomes, but uses broader concepts of deprivation and insecurity (Hossain, 2005).

Poverty is everywhere and anywhere to a different degree but often does not arouse interest. Conversely, poverty actually creates curiosity because of difference in ways of life. It is a common phenomenon

DOI: 10.4018/978-1-5225-0201-2.ch002

and is one of the top forms of tourism in some parts of the world (Delic, 2011). Examples are common throughout South and Central America as well as in Asian countries which have the same characteristics as the favela in Brazil, the townships in South Africa, or the slums in India, which have led to different definitions of favela, township and reality tourism: places where poverty is more concentrated in neighbourhoods.

Slums are particular, unstable areas representing otherness in terms of vandalism and deprivation with an emotive power denoting opposition to order and security (Durr, 2012a). The term slum usually has derogatory connotations. A slum is defined in several ways by different organizations. Slums are usually characterized by urban decay, high rates of poverty, illiteracy, and unemployment. According to the latest UN-Habitat publication regarding Urban Development and Management (2013), the absolute number of slum dwellers continues to grow, due to the fast time of urbanization. UN-Habitat states that the number of people living in slum conditions is now estimated at 863 million, in contrast to 760 million in 2000 and 650 million in 1990.

In recent times, due to changing social conditions and the development of international tourism, so-called *poverty* or *slum tourism* has increasingly come into focus: organised tours of destinations in degradation and poverty, and in some cases also illegal places fully run by gangs. In the past there have been a lot of violent confrontations between these gangs and states (e.g. favela in Brazil, barrio in Colombia). Tourism today is characterised by diversification and enrichment of the tourist product offered, where the tourist is satisfied not only by the contemplation of a landscape (authentic or romantic), but intends to turn it into an experience to feel a real part of (Schmitt, 1999).

Research of authentic and unexplored regions, places with forms of social tension and ethical issues, contrasts with the particularities that distinguish purely hedonistic and recreational, traditional tourism. The 'regular' tourist travels to sites for the purpose of learning and gaining knowledge and information. A slum tourist, in contrast, is seeking some sort of emotional pleasure and is interested in seeing 'reality', or gaining authenticity, insight into power relations or a window onto other lives when there are ethical sentiments.

At the same time, with consumers playing a participatory role in the production and consumption process (Buhalis & Law, 2008), it has become dominant for businesses to use technology to engage consumers in a more individual way. The internet is rapidly becoming the number one information source for travel. In fact, the choices of the consumer are aided by the information picked up through the Internet, which is an ideal place to communicate, promote, and 'sell' destinations and where potential clients can undertake comparisons and choices more responsibly. The more consumers submit their online interests, the more companies seek to offer solutions that meet their potential costumers. Porter (2001) demonstrated how the internet has changed industry forces. Previous research has shown that innovation, organisation and external factors can influence a firm's decision to adopt e-commerce as a marketing and selling strategy (Wan, 2002). The use of the Internet has become a key competitive tool and essential also for tourist destinations (Murphy et al., 2007) and offers great potential to influence consumers' perceived images. In addition internet promotes the mass customization of tourism products as it supports the tourist operators to target niche markets in different geographical locations (Buhalis et al., 2005; 2011).

As tourists have gained more experience in tourism travel, they have also grown more critical of tour wholesalers and their products. Online channels have played a crucial role in changing the attitude of them towards their customers. They have built a direct relationship with potential tourists. Following this trend, tour operators have also been adapting their strategies for online travel retail (Dwyer et al.,

2009). By using the web and the Internet as marketing tools, tourism organizations have gained some distinct advantages in cost reduction, revenue growth, marketing research and database development, and customer retention (Morrison et al., 1999). Wang and Fesenmaier (2006) argued that a successful web marketing strategy requires the integration and coordination of web-site features, promotion techniques and customer relationship management programmes. Thus integrating technologies with relationship marketing could help tourism organizations and destinations to maintain competitiveness and improve the management of business relationships with customers (Álvarez et al., 2007).

Therefore it is important to study tour salers sites as sources of tourist information (i.e. the ways in which these are seen online). Web-site performance can be measured in various ways (Buhalis et al., 2011).

This chapter first assesses the current literature on slum tourism and importance of the web sites to influence the perceived image of destination as a virtual experience for the tourist. It then goes on precedent research that evaluates tour operators websites to analyse strategic choices enacted, the attractiveness of the websites, tourist information given on slum tours and marketing effectiveness. The goal of the current study is to find out how organisations can improve their websites and gain competitive advantage in the marketing of slum tourism. A recent research (Privitera, 2015) show that slum tour organisations on the web are at a relatively sophisticated stage of development, it presents as a viable tool for promotion of slum tourism and complementary information channels. In fact an overview of websites of slum tourism operators were evaluated using the extended Model of Internet Commerce Adoption (eMICA), methodological approach which draws on the evolutionary development of electronic commerce. Now we are focusing on a case study *Reality Tours and Travel*, a well know and large tourism operator in Mumbai (India). This website has been selected due to its reputation and easy access to information for the purpose of a research study. The following study is of an exploratory nature. Finally, it highlights several critical managerial implications and discusses limitations and suggestions for further research. The results of the study allow a gainful contribution to the promotion of slum tourism on the web.

BACKGROUND TO THE DEBATE SURROUNDING POVERTY AS A TOURISM ATTRACTION

One of the major challenges facing urban planners globally is the proliferation of slums predominant in the urban economies of developing countries. The extent and spread of slums not only helps us to recognise that they are not anomalous and pathological phenomena in the urban landscape but also a manifestation of urban poverty (Goswani, 2013). The term slum, in vogue since the beginning of the 18th century, is used to describe squalid housing in densely populated areas of industrial cities. A slum is a compact area of an overcrowding population and poorly built congested dwelling conditions, an unhygienic environment usually with inadequate infrastructure lacking in proper sanitary and drinking water facilities (Goswami, 2013). The concept of slum varies widely from country to country and depends on a variety of defining parameters. In some countries slums are largely forgotten parts of a city; in others the poorest areas (Diekmann & Hannan, 2012).

From Rio de Janeiro to Mumbai, short, organised tours of poor areas have grown in popularity. And so too have ethical discussions on whether slum tourism or poverty tourism is educational and philanthropic, or voyeuristic and exploitative. Poverty tourism intersects with places of urban misery and their representation: slums representing the negative sides of cities, marginalised districts or ghettos and, in less developed countries, places of danger, crime and violence (Durr, 2012b). Slum tourism involves the commodification of urban deprivation (Durr & Jaffe, 2012). Slum tourism has expanded in popularity, probably due to the spread of communication routes (Delic, 2011) and media events; similarly, tourists who write about their experiences in virtual spaces create an increase in the demand for similar tours. Slum tourism is thus a mass tourism phenomenon occurring only in few destinations and a niche form of tourism in a growing number of other destinations (Frenzel et al., 2015). It's as viral marketing: from the Global South across destinations in Northern Europe. Recent estimates by Frenzel et. al. (2015) confirm an annual number of over one million slum tourists. Most of these tourists (80%) will do guided tours in just two destinations: the townships of South Africa and the favelas of Brazil.

The development of guided tours in destinations and places of poverty and degradation is controversial, probably because the combination of pleasure and poverty affects the sensitivity and moral values of public opinion (Freire-Medeiros, 2009). Researchers believe there are positive aspects of slum tourism (Steinbrink, 2012; Obrien, 2012) when proposed according to ethical and sustainable principles (Caldieron, 2013).

Exchanges can be positive but must improve the transformations of the neighbourhoods. In some cases, these tours offer travellers a glimpse of life in an area they might not visit otherwise, often because of logistic or safety concerns. But is slum tourism profiting from the poor? Slum tours can be unfair if communities aren't involved. In fact, it could be suggested that inhabitants have positive attitudes towards slum tourists (Mekawy, 2012), so that the appropriate form is collaborative and responsible participation in small-scale cooperatives (e.g. the government of Egypt uses cooperatives to reduce poverty). Another example is the social urbanism policy in Medellin, Colombia, a holistic approach to the development of the poorest areas, building a more authentic and inclusive image of the city (Hernandez-Garcia, 2013).

Slum tourism can be fabulously well-managed; an exchange of culture with local people ; very representative of a society; a confrontation with certain stereotypes; and at the same time an escape from monotony (MacCannel, 1976) or a search for absolutely real, objective authenticity, an experience which genuinely samples the culture of the society and the host people (Frenzel & Koens, 2012).

However, it appears that slum tourism is the organisation of tours in poor areas and thus different to 'dark' tourism, i.e. visiting sites, attractions, or events that have death, suffering or the macabre as a main theme (Stone & Sharpley, 2008) and different from pro-poor tourism. Specially pro-poor tourism (PPT) is aim to increase the net benefits for the poor from tourism, and ensure that tourism growth contributes to poverty reduction. PPT is not a specific product or sector of tourism as slum tourism but an approach (Ashley et al., 2001).

It is note that holidays are perfect opportunities for so-called experiential tourists, driven by their emotions, to see what is imagined and be immersed in a culture and lifestyle of a destination; or an affirmation of the so-called 'epidemic' of the imaginary (Zizek, 2004), in which images and desires tend to progressively replace reality. In fact, tourist experience seems less and less like a discovery and is characterised as more of a 'check'. The sociologist Urry (2002) has shown that in the era of hypermobility the tourist experience is mere observation of spectacular places. Tourists are quick and fleeting but must prove that they have also 'consumed' the holiday (Cohen, 1972). The tourism of poverty may therefore be defined as tourism diversion (Cohen, 2007; Ma, 2010) or experiencing a difference from the boredom of daily routine (Ryan, 2002), which are justified by curiosity but where a voyeuristic aspect is definitely a component (Williams, 2008). There are other important but not major reasons for travel, such as the provision of benefits to the environment and local communities, typical of social tourism (Butcher, 2003). In fact many tour operators say they give back to the communities they visit and create jobs (www.favelatour.com.br).

It appears that poverty tourism could include educational aspects typical of township tourism as defined by Ramchander (2004), such as the observation of expressions of culture and ways of life typical of South Africa, or the Brazilian *favela* as examined by Freire-Medeiros (2007; 2009), which became a trademark and at the same time was marketed as a tourist destination. Destinations may include any landscape, an ecological site, a tourist experience, extremes or places offering consumer goods (Duarte, 2010; Rolfes, 2010; Meschkank, 2011). Roogerson (2004; 2008) also includes poverty in this form of tourism, e.g. bringing visitors to the sites of significance to the anti-apartheid movement as well as improving tourists' understanding of poverty issues of historically oppressed communities.

Whyte et al. (2011) contend that the driving purpose is for tourists to observe poverty personally. They believe that the activities will provide an authentic experience of poverty and the decision to go on a tour does not involve meaningful collaboration and consent between residents and tourists. Also, Robertson (2007, p. 546), in downtown eastside Vancouver, for example, notes a form of "misery tourism" in which people visit the area solely to see its infamous poverty. The voyeuristic gaze of outsiders to the community has been remarked and decried, although this gaze is more regularly mediated through media rather than direct visits to the neighborhood.

Examples of organisations who organise such tours are numerous, but sometimes it is necessary to specify that there are operators with social or ethical purposes which benefit local residents and improve local economies. In this sense, the aim is to involve residents in decision-making processes, where they may receive benefits from this particular type of tourism. The studies demonstrate that isolated efforts from individual tourism companies have little tangible impact on the majority of people living in highly populated rural communities but impacts are substantial for the few people who directly benefit (Goodwin, 2009). Yet we need to ask which roles and functions illegal powers have developed in these areas. Much study on township tourism in South Africa has dealt with pro-poor aspects. Policy in South Africa is positive to promote township tourism as a tool of economic development so far business tourism is also likely to be a factor for tourism revenue for township (Frenzel, 2014; Rogerson, 2013). Other operators which offer regular sightseeing tours in cities have added the slum experience as an integral part of urban representation (Durr, 2012b) though slum tourism remains significant for creating economic opportunities in developing countries and contribute to shared growth in urban tourism (George & Booyens, 2014).

IMPORTANCE OF WEB: THE GEOGRAPHY OF INTERNET USERS

Internet and the new technologies have become an integrated part of our lives making is easier to communicate, research information and purchase any kind of products and services. The online transactions are becoming simpler and faster and have definitely made our lives easier since only one click can bring in a few days whatever we want. The web has an important role either to consumers than business operators. Previous research has shown that innovation, organization and external factors can influence a firm's decision to adopt e-commerce as a marketing and selling strategy (Guimaraes, 2012; Wan, 2002). There are 3.4 billions internet users in the world (see Table 1) with significant penetration ratios in countries like Asia (45.7%), Europe (19.2%) and North America (10.2%) (Internet World Stats, www.internetworldstats.com, 2014). Internet users in Europe as UK, Russia and Germany have a high amount: in 2014 the percentage of users exceeds 12-15%. Internet penetration in Europe is growing and travel e-commerce represents the largest item, surpassing more traditional uses such as internet banking or research information for health. Between top 20 Countries with the highest number of internet users there are Japan and Germany (86.2%), China (45.8%), Brazil (54.2%). However, the web also has the additional benefits of higher user involvement and user capture at opportune moments. Traditional mass media has been characterized by information push. In contrast, communication processes on the web are driven by information pull (Turban et al., 2008). Consumers control what information they access, which parts they explore, what routes they navigate, and when they view. The hyperlink function also allows users to move from one source of information to another. This further enhances user control in the communication process, and therefore allows users to pursue their specific interests. Therefore becomes important to study websites as places of business, the ways in which these can be seen online (Hax, 2010).

Globally, 4 billion people remain unconnected from the Web, 90% of whom are in the developing world. At the same time, we are currently undergoing a rapid shift from feature phones to smartphones, even in the world's less economically developed regions. Nowadays almost everyone, from children in playgrounds to seniors, have mobile phones or/and tablets connected to the internet and the number grows every year. At the end of 2014, half of the world's population had at least one mobile subscription, totalling over 3.6 billion unique mobile subscribers. The global mobile subscriber base increased by just over 5% in 2014 (GSMA, 2015). Millions are also converting to smartphones. In practice, the growing number of smartphones and tablets means significant changes in the behaviour of users (Kumar et al., 2006). This will affect the ways in which they spend their leisure time, the frequency of browsing the web, and increase their appetite for mobile apps (Rayport & Bernard, 2004). Mobile is confirmed as a strong youth medium with 48% of users between 18-34 years old, compared to 40% for the fixed Internet and 29% for the TV audience. Mobile is also more tilted towards men, who represent 63% of total users (GSMA, 2015).

STUDYING SLUM TOUR ORGANISATIONS WEBSITES

Methodology

As indicated in the research aims, the goal was to assess the attractiveness and other aspects of the websites as contributors to slum tourism. Some sites offering opportunities for consumers to interact had

Table 1. Global internet usage and demography in June, 2014 (in millions)

World Regions	Population (2014 Est.)	Internet Users -2000	Internet Users 2014 (Millions)	Penetration (% Population)	Growth 2000/'14%	Users %
Africa	1,125,7	4,5	297,9	26.5	6,498.6	9.8
Asia	3,996,4	114,3	1,386,2	34.7	1,112.7	45.7
Europe	825,9	105,0	582,4	70.5	454.2	19.2
Middle East	231,6	3,3	111,9	48.3	3,303.8	3.7
North America	353,8	108,1	310,3	87.7	187.1	10.2
Latin America -Caribbean	612,2	18,1	320,4	52.3	1,672.7	10.5
Oceania-Australia	36,8	7,6	26,8	72.9	251.6	0.9
World Total	7,182,5	360,9	3,035,7	42.3	741.0	100.0

Source: Elaborated data from Internet World Stats, www.internetworldstats.com, 2014

a higher number of unique features than other sites. Good quality website design is not only based on the developer's perceptions, but also customer acceptance and perception (Day, 1997). On the web, the competitive advantage of a "place" does not depend only of localizing factors, but also on the diffusion of information and on the image that it manages to create through the virtual experience.

The study of the tourism operators websites, in a precedent research (Privitera, 2015), was developed through fact-finding data collection using the eMICA model. In current literature of the quality of web sites it is possible to identify three groups of models (Mich et al., 2003). Some were created with the aim of developing instruments for automatically assessing quality, above all in the cases where it is necessary to assess a large number of web sites. The indicators used in this type of model are, for example, the average time needed to download the home page, the number of errors found in the code or in the script, the number of broken links which exist on the pages. Other models were created to respond to aim related to the evolution of the web site or to compare web sites, for example, in order to improve some particular aspects (usability, surfability, etc.). Finally, a third category is tied to the increasing importance that e-commerce has assumed. According to the original MICA model (Burgess & Cooper, 2000), an e-commerce model, a number of stages and layers of maturity are proposed (Figure 1), from infancy to maturity: promotion, provision, and processing. During the promotion stage, companies start simply by establishing a presence on the web. In doing so, they provide basic information covering business scope and post news relevant to their operations; some use animation and multimedia to draw visitors' attention toward an important promotion offered. Users, however, cannot send anything to the site and can only receive information from promotion websites.

Figure 1. The model of internet commerce adoption (MICA)
Source: Burgess, Cooper, 2000

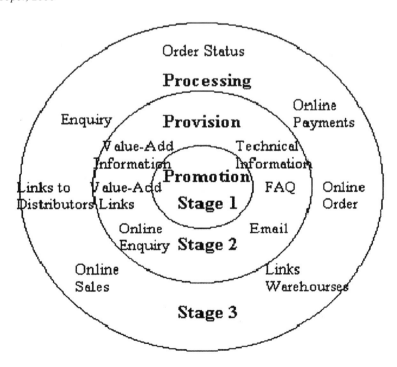

The second stage of website development (provision) is dynamic and offers users the functionality of sending and receiving information. This involves value-added links, access to search engines, and even choices of languages. More complex applications are also embedded as integral components of interactive websites. Customers or visitors can search for information regarding products and prices. They can also register online and take part in message boards. Interactive websites encourage and entice visitors to inquire, request, complain, challenge, or make recommendations.

In the processing stage, customers play the most influential role. One of the main utilities here is customer relationship management, from initiation to maintenance. Other electronic services such as online orders or inquiries are all completed through websites. In this layer the company creates an integrated function.

The reworking of the MICA model, or extended version, provides an increased number of layers within the three main stages with the aim of deepening the study of processes in terms of functionality and sophistication of the applications of e-commerce (Doolin et. al., 2002; Hashim et al., 2009; Karake & Shalhoub, 2007).

In the research, each website was evaluated and assessed. In total, 49 variables were defined; their composition differed from the MICA model. In fact the variables used in the study resulted from the adaptation of ideas from several authors who had previously published on the tourism sector (Pesonen & Palo-oja, 2010; Ting et al., 2013). This study covered a sample of websites in a group of developing economies for the first time: Africa nations (specifically Kenya), Brazil and India. The 19 websites (15.8% Brazilian operators, 31.6% Indian and 52.6% African) were evaluated in December 2013. The sample was drawn from various sources, including search engines (e.g. Google) utilising keyword searches using the names of countries in which slum tourism is prevalent[1].

Comparing the sites, we built a positioning map of the tour operators (Figure 2) in terms of market orientation. The questions about the sites were: the structure and navigation of the site adequate. The site reaches its communication objectives. The functions of the site are correct. The information content is appropriate to the purpose of the site. The operation of the site is well managed. Is it easily accessible to all. Although the technology of the web can allow users with little computer experts to realize in short time sites elementary, the design of professional sites, such as sites of companies or institutions, can be a very complex process. The research showed that all of the websites under examination were in the promotion and provision stages and only two were in the processing stage. One of this two was *Reality Tours And Travel*. A case study has become frequently used in the business context to describe leading industry cases as role models to increase success. Given the uncommon practical, and in turn theoretical, knowledge about businesses implementing technology for experience creation to date, the adoption of a case study was significant to gather the necessary practice insights, explain and clarify current practices. The adopted case study method, in particular was explanatory due to the nature of the research topic. Explanatory case studies offer the opportunity for explaining a case in a more understandable and meaningful way (Yin, 2012). The case study method is often criticised for the lack of objectivity. However, in comparison with other types of social science research methods, the case study method has wider validity for producing research based on issues relating to human behaviour (Merriam, 2014). The case study *Reality Tours And Travel* was selected based on three main defined criteria. First, the company had to be embedded in the tourism and hospitality context and second, it had to represent a best practice example by providing evidence for the current successful realization of slum experiences as demonstrate from travel reviews via Tripadvisor. The third, *Reality tours and Travel* is one with the major results after the application of eMica model.

Figure 2. Map of slum tour organisations (A= African sites; I= Indian sites; B= Brazilian sites)
Source: Privitera, 2015

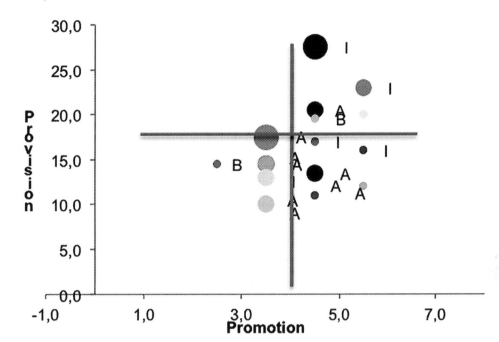

A Map of Slum Operators Websites

The map is based on two main dimensions: promotion and provision (variables detected in the two stages of the eMica model). These were also given a score for a third stage (processing), measuring the size of the point identified by the two previous measures.

Firstly, the concentration of sites near mid to high values for both stages is evident (x=4.2; y=15.7). The finding was: few tour operators that fully exploit the potential of the web to match demand and supply and to contribute to slum tourism promotion.

It was possible to hypothesise three sets of strategic behaviour. A first group is formed by a set of organisations that does not seem to attribute any importance to Web strategy. In this group, the levels of provision and promotion do not reach high scores. The sites appear as a presence on the Web with no particular goals (as basic information is not provided). There is a second group of sites among which the home page is dedicated to slum tourism and which are fairly complete from the point of view of information; the levels of interactivity reach discrete scores. The presence on the Web seems based on information content of a good quality, sometimes aimed at different users with respect to technological innovation. Finally, there is a third group of organisations which is very small (two sites), where in addition to levels of promotion and provision reaching satisfactory results, business transactions were also practised which gave international promotion to slum tourism. These operators have voluntarily designed a strategy behind the site and the use of the Web as a tool for image promotion and communication, as well as a vehicle of information for the market.

Some Empirical Evidence from a Case Study

The focus is to study the *Reality Tours and Travel* website (Figure 3). The goal of the *Reality Tours and Travel* is to provide authentic and thought-provoking local experiences through slum tours and to use the profits to create change in local communities, to promote cross-cultural understanding and local development. Their most famous tour takes people around the industrial and residential areas of Dharavi in order to breakdown negative stereotypes about slums and raise funds for community projects. 80% of the profits from the tours are used to fund local education projects through their sister-NGO Reality Gives.Reality Tours & Travel was founded in 2005 by Chris Way and Krishna Pujari. Chris Way, originally from England, moved to Mumbai in 2004 in order to bring slum tourism to Mumbai. Inspired by favela tours in Brazil, Chris wanted to use slum tours in India as a way to raise awareness about life in slums and to raise funds for community projects. Despite only having 367 visitors in 2006. The big break came when Lonely Planet included them in their 2007 guidebook. By 2011, Reality Tours was welcoming nearly 10,000 annual visitors into Dharavi. Reality currently runs six programs and supports eight others in the fields of education, health and livelihood. In 2011, Reality Tours started offering tours in South Mumbai with the creation of the Public Transport, Market Tours and Night Tour. They also made a first move outside of Mumbai with our 1 and 2 day village tours to Chinchoti. In 2013, they added an early morning Bicycle Tour and a Street Food Tour. In the summer of 2014, Reality Tours expanded to New Delhi and began working with the New Delhi slum, Sanjay Colony, which is located in the Okhla Industrial Area, India's largest industrial area.

The web site of *Reality* resulted with high scores located within the provision stage, particularly has numerous links to further information such as prices, awards and certification, photos. This result is supported by data of Rolfes (2010), where reports that the majority of operators intend to present an

Figure 3. The web site of Reality Tours & Travel
Source: www.realitytoursandtravel.com (accessed May 2015)

authentic image of slum, favelas to show the everyday and real life also to correct the public insight of these places, which is dominated by crime, violence. Also ethical information were ranked at the high position. The tour company have to work to economic aims but some of them remarked using a share of their profit to support particular projects in the local communities. Reality Tours and Travel started its operations in Dharavi in January 2006. Since then, most of the work of the Reality Group has been for the benefit of the Dharavi community. After, as Reality Tours and Travel expands its tours (Delhi and multi-day tours of Kerala and Rajasthan) they are also expanding projects to local communities in these areas.

Applying the eMica model at layers three and four of stage provision, the value-added site became increasingly interactive and included integration of social media (e.g. Facebook, Twitter) and to give virtual trips with many photos. Although the degree to which site were linked to other sites was satisfactory, the website did not include sitemaps or the date on which information had been updated. The site highlights travel reviews. Word of mouth marketing is very powerful this is the most frequently used source of information by consumers when booking or buying travel. Howewer, visitors tell about the best services they received, in the section "feedback".

An example:

From International Visitors

An essential part of a visit to India. The most thought provoking thing I have ever seen. Compassionately done with 80% of profits going to the slum. A real eye opener! (wwww.realitoursandtravel.com, May 2014 via TripAdvisor).

However, the incorporation of higher levels of functionality such as blogs was not evidenced in the site evaluated.

A significant finding is tourists to make bookings online and also buy the slum tours; generally on the websites of slum operators the potential client could fill in an inquiry form determining availability of tours. In the site is not present offered discussion forums; it had not a currency converter or others languages than English or meteo. These findings are surprising, especially since these organisation is geared towards promoting internationally orientated businesses like slum tourism. A point of weakness is the description of the team guides. An example from the site:

Krishna, co-founder of Reality Tours, is the tour guide for all of our multi-day tours. Born and raised in India, Krishna makes friends wherever he goes – he's your connection to the locals and will help you experience the "real" India all throughout your journey.

DISCUSSION AND PROSPECTS

There no doubt an important information channel is internet and the website's attractiveness of the operators. There are more and more studies about web site marketing effectiveness in tourism but it seems clear that slum tourism operators, like all operators, could benefit from good marketing of their products. There were no mistakes made regarding the identification of features that could attract tourists if a web strategy is developed. The entrepreneurial behaviour dynamics makes the analysis of websites and complex marketing tool. The transferability of finding highlighted is influenced by the specificity of studied context in relation to the product as slum tourism.

As the design and maintenance of an electronic marketplace on the web about slum tourism is still in relative infancy, there is limited knowledge for businesses. The results of the map can be interpreted as showing that the slum operators analysed are in order to learn and understand. Slum tourism represents a very actual concept not only in promoting the poverty communities values, but also in developing a new dimension of the tourism in a larger context of global change. A few of these organizations had strategies to rapidly develop and incorporate poverty tourism features into existing mainstream tourism plans. Slum tourism is not and has never been a political priority so the consequences is hard for the private small operators also for a web strategy. *Reality tours* is a good example but tourists products cannot be delivered without a strong distribution network with others operators as hotels, transports, institution, etc.. Since tour operators have the know-how in organising holiday travel, they are heading towards demonstrating their ability in adapting to new market trends. It is evident that the future of eTourism, which supported by Buhalis et al. (2011) will be focused on consumer-centric technologies that will support organizations in interacting with their customers dynamically. Howewer, the case study demonstrates the importance to be attractive according to the criteria used. Multimedia is also one of key area of technological development, in fact photo and short video to provide a tangible sense of place. It is here that *Reality tour*s operator have the opportunity to improve his offering distinct. It need to be borne in mind in this regard that tourists seek extensive travel information on a destination's website. The internet allows people to interact with the virtual tours so the experience on the web could communicate a sense of what the tour is like.

The results of the present study provide some guidelines for improving the possibilities of a website of slum operators. Yet they need of continual monitoring of development, functionality and more sophisticate. The eMica model displays the requirements and processes of technologies necessary for personalized experiences to be facilitated. In contrast to traditional static information collection from the consumer to the company and the one-way experience delivery from the company to the consumer, smart technologies have opened more dynamic service encounters, in which experiences are co-created in an agile manner. The integration of technologies for the creation of personalized experiences is critical for businesses to remain competitive in today's dynamic market place. This is of particular interest to the tourism and hospitality industry, in which commoditization, competition and high customer expectations drive the need for differentiation (Peterson 2011). Innovative technologies will support interoperability, personalization and competitiveness respect others tourist operators. It's important to slum wholesalers more education and training to optimize adoption on the Internet. Internet marketing and website design is important for all travel companies. In reality, it might not be the case as different companies have different marketing strategies. Some companies can emphasise on traditional brochures to reach their target markets whereas some use book guide or other media as a marketing channel.

The results of the study allow a gainful contribution to the promotion of slum tourism. It's true the potential opportunities for local development by enhancing tourism in slum, it is important to realise that the poor generally benefit little from slum tourism. This analysis is refers to provide managerial implications and the point of view is the perception of websites and specially of a case study. Existing market competition becomes ever more intense with the involvement of increased numbers of technology or product service providers. Existing literature and evidences demonstrate slum tourism can be a great opportunity to grow business plus online. This chapter points to is that built environment professionals with the interest and passion for advancing slum tourism plans must explore the approaches that successfully identifies, programmes and implements relevant and functional strategies. A limit of this analysis is that the results cannot be generalised because the case study is limited and exist between organisational dimensions and investments, especially in using the web to compete. Also is that tourist's opinions on their satisfaction of what was presented on the website were not included. Future research may therefore conduct tourist surveys since destination sites could be as competitive if it can attract potential slum tourists.

REFERENCES

Álvarez, L. S., Martín, A. M. D., & Casielles, R. V. (2007). Relationship marketing and information and communication technologies: Analysis of retail travel agencies. *Journal of Travel Research*, *45*(4), 453–463. doi:10.1177/0047287507299593

Ashley, C., Roe, D., & Goodwin, H. (2001). *Pro-Poor Tourism Strategies: Making Tourism Work For The Poor. A review of experience.* Available at: http://www.propoortourism.info/documents/Ashleyet-alPPTStrats.pdf

Buhalis, D., & Law, R. (2008). Progress in information technology and tourism management: 20 years on and 10 years after the Internet. The state of e-tourism research. *Tourism Management*, *29*(4), 609–623. doi:10.1016/j.tourman.2008.01.005

Buhalis, D., Leung, D., & Law, R. (2011). E-Tourism: Critical Information and Communication Technologies for Tourism Destinations. In Destination Marketing and Management. CAB International.

Buhalis, D., & O'Connor, P. (2005). Information communication technology – revolutionising tourism. *Tourism Recreation Research*, *30*(3), 7–16. doi:10.1080/02508281.2005.11081482

Burgess, L., & Cooper, J. (2000). A model of internet Commerce Adoption (MICA). In S. M. Rahman & M. S. Raisinghani (Eds.), *Electronic Commerce: Opportunity and Challenges* (pp. 189–201). IGI Global.

Butcher, J. (2003). *The Moralisation of Tourism*. London: Routledge.

Caldieron, J. M. (2013). Safety Perception and Tourism Potential in the Informal Neighborhood of "La Perla", San Juan, Puerto Rico. *International Journal of Safety and Security in Tourism*, *4*, 1–23.

Cohen, E. (1972). Towards a Sociology of International Tourism. *Social Research*, *39*, 64–82.

Cohen, E. (2007). Authenticity and Commoditisation in Tourism. *Annals of Tourism Research*, *1*(15), 371–386.

Day, A. (1997). A Model for Monitoring Web Site Effectiveness. *Internet Research*, *7*(2), 109–115. doi:10.1108/10662249710165244

Delic, J. M. (2011). *Trends in Slum Tourism*. Available at: https://dspace.lib.uoguelph.ca/xmlui/handle/10214/2473

Diekmann, A., & Hannan, K. (2012). Touristic mobilities in India's slum spaces. *Annals of Tourism Research*, *39*(3), 1315–1336. doi:10.1016/j.annals.2012.02.005

Doolin, B., Burgess, L., & Cooper, J. (2002). Evaluating the use of the web for tourism marketing: A case study from New Zeland. *Tourism Management*, *23*(5), 557–561. doi:10.1016/S0261-5177(02)00014-6

Duarte, R. (2010). *Exploring the Social Impacts of Favela Tourism*. Wageningen University. Retrieved from www.slumtourism.net/download/Duarte2010.pdf

Dürr, E. (2012a). Encounters Over Garbage: Tourists And Lifestyle Migrants In Mexico. *Tourism Geographies*, *3*(2), 339–355. doi:10.1080/14616688.2012.633217

Dürr, E. (2012b). Urban Poverty, Spatial Representation and Mobility: Touring a Slum in Mexico. *International Journal of Urban and Regional Research*, *36*(4), 706–724. doi:10.1111/j.1468-2427.2012.01123.x

Dürr, E., & Jaffe, R. (2012). Theorising Slum Tourism in Latin America and the Caribbean: Performing, Negotiating and Transforming Inequality. *European Review of Latin American and Caribbean Studies*, *93*, 113–123.

Dwyer, L., Edwards, D., Mistilis, N., Roman, C., & Scott, N. (2009). Destination and enterprise management for a tourism future. *Tourism Management*, *30*(1), 63–74. doi:10.1016/j.tourman.2008.04.002

Freire-Medeiros, B. (2007). Selling the favela: Thoughts and polemics about a tourist destination. *Revista Brasileira de Ciencias Sociais*, *22*(65), 61–72.

Freire-Medeiros, B. (2009). The favela and its touristic transits. *Geoforum*, *40*(2), 580–588. doi:10.1016/j.geoforum.2008.10.007

Freire-Medeiros, B. (2012). *Touring Poverty*. Oxon, UK: Routledge.

Frenzel, F. (2014). Slum Tourism and Urban Generation: Touring Inner Johannesburg. *Urban Forum*, *25*, 431-447. doi:10.1007/s12132-014-9236-2

Frenzel, F., & Koens, K. (2012). Slum Tourism: Developments in a Young Field of Interdisciplinary Tourism Research. *Tourism Geographies*, *14*(2), 195–212. doi:10.1080/14616688.2012.633222

Frenzel, F., Koens, K., & Steinbrink, M. (Eds.). (2012). *Slum-Tourism: Power Poverty Ethics*. Oxon, UK: Routledge.

Frenzel, F., Koens, K., Steinbrink, M., & Rogerson, C. M. (2015). Slum Tourism: State of the art. *Tourism Review International*, *18*(4), 237–252. doi:10.3727/154427215X14230549904017

George, R., & Booyens, I. (2014). Township tourism demand: tourists' perceptions of safety and security. *Urban Forum*, *25*, 449-467. doi:10.1007/s12132-014-9228-2

Goodwin, H. (2009). Reflections on 10 years of Pro-Poor Tourism. *Journal of Policy Research in Tourism. Leisure and Events*, *1*(1), 90–94. doi:10.1080/19407960802703565

Goswami S. (2013). The Slums: A Note On Facts And Solution. *Indian Streams Research Journal*, (3), 1-10.

Gretzel, U., & Yoo, K. H. (2008). Use and impact of online travel reviews. In P. O'Connor, W. Höpken, & U. Gretzel (Eds.), *Information and communication technologies in tourism*. New York: Springer. doi:10.1007/978-3-211-77280-5_4

GSMA. (2015). *The mobile economy 2015.* Retrieved June 2, 2015 from: http://gsmamobileeconomy. covaibalem

Guimaraes, T. (2012). Industry clockspeed's impact on business innovation success factors. *European Journal of Innovation Management, 14*(3), 322–344. doi:10.1108/14601061111148825

Hashim, N., Murphy, J., & Law, R. (2007). A review of hospitality website design frame-works. In M. Sigala, L. Mich, & J. Murphy (Eds.), *Information and communication technologies in tourism.* Wien: Springer.

Hax, A. C. (2010). *Reinventing your business strategy.* New York: Springer.

Hernandez-Garcia, J. (2013). Slum tourism, city branding and social urbanism: The case of Medellin, Colombia. *Journal of Place Management and Development, 6*(1), 43–51. doi:10.1108/17538331311306122

Hossain, S. (2005). Poverty, Household Strategies and Coping with Urban Life: Examining 'Livelihood Framework' in Dhaka City, Bangladesh. *Bangladesh e-. Journal of Sociology (Melbourne, Vic.), 2*(1), 1–12.

Karake Shalhoub, Z. (2007). Internet Commerce Adoption in the GCC Countries. *IRMA International Conference, Managing Worldwide Operations & Communications with Information Technology.*

Kumar, V., Venkatesan, R., & Reinartz, W. J. (2006). Knowing what to sell when to whom. *Harvard Business Review,* (May), 131–145. PMID:16515161

Ma, B. (2010). *A Trip into the Controversy: A Study of Slum Tourism Travel Motivations.* 2009-2010 Penn Humanities Forum on Connections. Available at: http://repository.upenn.edu/uhf_2010/12

MacCannell, D. (1976). *The Tourist: A New Theory of the Leisure Class.* New York: Schocken Books Inc.

Mekawy, M. A. (2012). Responsible slum tourism: Egyptian experience. *Annals of Tourism Research, 39*(4), 2092–2113. doi:10.1016/j.annals.2012.07.006

Merriam, S. B. (2014). *Qualitative Research: A Guide to Design and Implementation.* San Francisco: John Wiley & Sons.

Meschkank, J. (2011). Investigations into slum tourism in Mumbai: Poverty tourism and the tension between different constructions of reality. *GeoJournal, 76*(1), 47–62. doi:10.1007/s10708-010-9401-7

Mich, L., Franch, M., & Gaio, L. (2003). Evaluating and Designing the Quality of Web Sites. *IEEE MultiMedia, 10*(1), 34–43. doi:10.1109/MMUL.2003.1167920

Murphy, P., Pritchard, M. P., & Smith, B. (2007). The destination product and its impact on traveller perceptions. *Tourism Management, 21*(1), 43–52. doi:10.1016/S0261-5177(99)00080-1

Narayan, M., Pritchett, T., & Kapoor, M. (2009). *Moving Out of Poverty. Success from the Bottom Up.* The World Bank and Palgrave Macmillan. doi:10.1596/978-0-8213-7215-9

OBrien, P. W. (2011). Business, Management and Poverty Reduction: A Role for Slum Tourism? *Journal of Business Diversity, 11*(1), 33–46.

Pesonen, J., & Palooja, O. M. (2010). Comparing Internet Commerce Adoption Between the Finnish and the European Independent Accommodation Companies. In *Information and Communication Technologies in Tourism 2010,Proceedings of the International Conference*. doi:10.1007/978-3-211-99407-8_5

Porter, M. (2001). Strategy and the Internet. *Harvard Business Review*, *79*(3), 63–78. PMID:11246925

Privitera, D. (2015). Tourist Valorisation of Urban Poverty: An Empirical Study on the Web. *Urban Forum*, *6*(4), 373-390. doi:10.1007/s12132-015-9259-3

Ramchander, P. (2004). *Towards the responsible management of the socio-cultural impact of township tourism*. University of Pretoria, Department of Tourism Management. Available at: http://upetd.up.ac.za/thesis/available/etd-08262004-130507/

Rayport, J. F., & Bernard, J. J. (2004). Best face forward. *Harvard Business Review*, *82*(12), 47–52. PMID:15605565

Robertson, L. (2007). Taming space: Drug use, HIV, and homemaking in downtown eastside Vancouver. *Gender, Place and Culture*, *14*(5), 527–549. doi:10.1080/09663690701562198

Rogerson, C. M. (2004). Urban tourism and small tourism enterprise development in Johannesburg: The case of township tourism. *GeoJournal*, *60*(3), 249–257. doi:10.1023/B:GEJO.0000034732.58327.b6

Rogerson, C. M. (2008). Shared Growth in Urban Tourism: Evidence from Soweto, South Africa. *Urban Forum*, *19*(4), 395–411.

Rogerson, C. M. (2013). Urban tourism, economic regeneration and inclusion: Evidence from South Africa. *Local Economy*, *28*(2), 188–202. doi:10.1177/0269094212463789

Rolfes, M. (2010). Poverty tourism: Theoretical reflections and empirical findings regarding an extraordinary form of tourism. *GeoJournal*, *75*(5), 421–442.

Ryan, C. (2002). *The Tourist Experience*. New York: Continuum Books.

Schmitt, B. H. (1999). *Experential Marketing*. New York: The Free Press.

Steinbrink, M. (2012). We did the Slum! – Urban Poverty Tourism in Historical Perspective. *Tourism Geographies*, *14*(2), 1–22. doi:10.1080/14616688.2012.633216

Stone, P., & Sharpley, R. (2008). Consuming dark tourism: A thanatological perspective. *Annals of Tourism Research*, *35*(2), 574–595. doi:10.1016/j.annals.2008.02.003

Ting, P., Wang, S., Bau, D., & Chiang, M. (2013). Website Evaluation of the Top 100 Hotels Using Advanced Content Analysis and eMICA Model. *Cornell Hospitality Quarterly*, *54*(3), 284–293. doi:10.1177/1938965512471892

Turban, E., McLean, E. R., & Wetherbe, J. C. (2008). *Information technology for management*. John Wiley and sons, Inc.

Un-Habitat. (2013). *Streets as Public Spaces and Drivers of Urban Prosperity*. Available at: http://mirror.unhabitat.org

Urry, J. (2002). *The Tourist Gaze*. London: Sage Publications.

Wan, C. S. (2002). The web sites of international tourist hotels and tour wholesalers in Taiwan. *Tourism Management*, *23*(2), 155–160. doi:10.1016/S0261-5177(01)00048-6

Wang, Y. C., & Fesenmaier, D. R. (2006). Identifying the success factors of Web-based marketing strategy: An investigation of convention and visitors bureaus in the United States. *Journal of Travel Research*, *44*(3), 239–249. doi:10.1177/0047287505279007

Whyte, K. P., Selinger, E., & Outterson, K. (2011). Poverty tourism and the problem of consent. *Journal of Global Ethics*, *7*(3), 337–348. doi:10.1080/17449626.2011.635689

Williams, C. (2008). Ghettourism and Voyeurism, or challenging stereotypes and raising consciousness? Literary and non-literary forays into the favelas of Rio de Janeiro. *Bulletin of Latin American Research*, *27*(4), 483–500. doi:10.1111/j.1470-9856.2008.00280.x

Yin, R. K. (2012). *Applications of Case Study Research*. Thousand Oaks, CA: SAGE Publication.

Zizek, S. (2004). *L'epidemia dell'immaginario*. Roma: Meltemi.

KEY TERMS AND DEFINITIONS

Case Study: Documented, in-depth study about a specific situation or methodology used as a training tool.

Competitive Advantage: A superior performance relative to other competitors in the same market based on factors, like: skillful scientific and technical support of specialized knowledge, research, specific competence, innovative products, processes or new business models apply, high productivity.

E-Tourism: The use of Information and Communication Technologies (ICT) in the tourism industry. It involves the buying and selling of tourism products and services principally via internet but includes all intranet, extranet and internet applications as well as all the strategic management and marketing issues related to the use of technology.

Slum Tourism: Touristic tours to informal settlements in India metropolis. They are designed as reality tours. They focus on showing the tourists as realistic a view of real life in the slum.

ENDNOTE

[1]   Examples of keywords used were "poverty tourism", "favela tour", "slum tourism", "township tourism", and "poverty tour". An other source to construct the sample was Tripadvisor.it. It is important to mention the results about the reviews on tripadvisor.it with keywords used as "favela-tour", "slum tourism India", "township tour South Africa", "slum tour Kenya". The shortresearch (accessed on the web 02/09/2015) showed 31 tourists reviews about township tour South Africa (CapeTown), 47 about favela tour (Rio de Janeiro), 162 on slum walk tour India (New Delhi) and only 1 on Kenya (*Tour durch Kangemi Slum*). According to Gretzel and Yoo (2008), tourists have considered online consumer reviews as an information source when planning their trips. While it

is likely that other companies offering tours do exist the author contend that any others have very low online visibility (to deepen looks Privitera, 2015). It seems that so a few operators are actually selling the tours online in the studied Countries. Probably given that slum tourists often get booked into tours through hotels or traditional travel agencies, considered that the tourists' image of slum is not positive because is demonstrated that major percentage of tourists associate township with poverty and also crime before the booking of the tour (Rolfes, 2010).

Chapter 3

Institutional Changes and Dynamics in the European Aviation Sector:
Implications for Tourism

Marina Efthymiou
University of West London, UK

Pavlos Arvanitis
Southampton Solent University, UK

Andreas Papatheodorou
University of West London, UK

ABSTRACT

This chapter covers three areas of institutional changes in the European aviation sector that may significantly affect the dynamics of the tourism industry. Further to the introduction, airlines are discussed in section two; airports are analysed in section three; and air navigation service provision are presented in section four. The dynamics of these three pillars and the interrelationship with the tourism industry is explored in section five. Among others, the chapter argues that when a proper systemic approach is followed any smart relaxation of regulatory and infrastructural constraints will have positive repercussions on tourism growth and development not only of central places but also of more peripheral regions. Finally, section six concludes and discusses the way forward.

1. INTRODUCTION

According to the United Nations World Tourism Organization (UNWTO, 2015) international tourism accounts for 9% of world's GDP, 1 in 11 jobs is tourism related, generating over $1.5 trillion in exports. These figures refer to direct, indirect and induced impacts of tourism. International tourists have reached 1.13 billion with forecasts to reach 1.8 billion by 2030. In 2014 Europe received 582 million

DOI: 10.4018/978-1-5225-0201-2.ch003

international tourists (51% of the world market) who generated $509 billion tourism receipts (42% of the world). Globally, 54% of international tourists travelled to their destination by air; that is over 550 million tourists. The remainder (46%) travelled by surface transport, mostly by road (cars, coaches, buses). The trend over time indicates that air transport as a means of transport for tourists grows faster compared to other means of transport.

In fact, aviation is a major contributor into supporting tourism and has a strategic importance for the development of tourism, which results in economic growth and provision of economic and social benefits. The Air Transport Action Group (ATAG, 2014) estimates the aviation's global economic impact (direct, indirect, induced, and tourism catalytic) at US$2.2 trillion, equivalent to 3.5 percent of world gross domestic product (GDP). It also suggests that the air transport industry generates a total of 56.6 million jobs globally (8.4 million direct jobs in the airlines, airports, Air Navigation Service Providers and the civil aerospace sectors; 9.3 million indirect jobs through purchases of goods and services from companies in its supply chain; 4.4 million induced jobs through spending; and 34.5 million jobs globally through tourism). According to the International Air Transport Association (IATA, 2013) air transportation enables foreign direct investment (FDI), business cluster development, specialisation, and other spill-over effects. Air transportation is by far the most effective means of transportation for many destinations to be reached, offering speed, convenience and affordability at the same time (UNWTO, 2012). Aviation has contributed significantly to international tourism development by the smooth transport of passengers, who arrive at their selected destinations based on the enhanced connectivity through air (ICAO, 2006; World Economic Forum, 2013; ATAG, 2014).

The prevailing institutional framework and the emerging dynamics in terms of market regulation, deregulation and liberalization (the last two terms will be used interchangeably in the text in spite of some differences) may be regarded as the catalyst for the effectiveness of the air transportation system (Papatheodorou, 2002). The system per se comprises many components but its most important pillars are related to the airlines (with the aircraft, crew and services); the airports (with the infrastructure and ancillary services), the providers of air navigation services, i.e. ANSPs (with the en route and terminal Air Traffic Control in terms of both infrastructure and services); and the regulatory bodies oversighting the system. As expected these system components are structurally interrelated. Due to the fact that airlines often overfly more than one state, these are related to a number of service providers where regulation in several cases is less intrusive. ANSPs are associated with the area they cover and in the majority of cases they operate at a national level. Similarly, airlines are associated with the airports from which they take-off and land.

This chapter discusses the interrelations among the three main subsystems of the air transport sector and also their implications for the tourism industry. It is noteworthy that several air transport subsystems have been already liberalised, whereas others are in the process or even not yet subject to market liberalisation. This potential conundrum poses important challenges. On these grounds, this chapter covers three areas of institutional changes in the European aviation sector that may significantly affect the tourism industry. Airlines are discussed in section two of this chapter; airports are analysed in section three; and air navigation service provision are presented in section four. Building on Bieger and Witmer (2006) the dynamics of these three pillars and the interrelationship with the tourism industry is explored in section five, while section six concludes and discusses the way forward.

2. INSTITUTIONAL CHALLENGES IN THE EUROPEAN AIRLINE SECTOR

Interestingly, perhaps, the airline sector was the first to be regulated by the state and the first that was deregulated a century after (Dempsey and Goetz, 1992). The regulation of air transport services was deemed necessary to avoid destructive competition and market volatility (Graham, et al., 2008). The market failure led to the need for regulation and subsequently the failure of regulation brought deregulation. According to Graham et al. (2008) deregulation, liberalization and the power of competition resulted in a business environment where four business models currently co-exist in the market with differences among them occasionally blurred. These models are related to traditional carriers; charter airlines; low cost carriers (LCC); and all business-class carriers. Airlines are linked to tourism in quite a direct way e.g. charter airlines have been clearly contributing to the tourist flows from North to South Europe since their appearance in the market. Airline liberalization in Europe was pursued via three packages from 1988 to 1997 and led to the creation of the European Common Aviation Area (ECAA) (Graham, et al., 2008). Based on Council Regulations (EEC) 2407/92, 2408/92 and 2409/92, since the completion of the Third Liberalization Package in 1997 carriers belonging to any ECAA country can move freely in the European airspace (Dobruszkes, 2009a). Moreover, ten years later, i.e. in 2007 an Open Aviation Area between the EU and the U.S.A. was established (Graham, et al., 2008). In general, the degree of liberalization seems to be associated with the average income level of countries participating in a related agreement. A high degree of liberalization can be achieved only among countries with high incomes, while aviation agreements among countries with low income are generally restrictive (Piermartini & Rousova, 2008). Nationality restrictions on commercial operations like cabotage, ownership and wet-leasing often prove important obstacles in the liberalization process (Hindley, 2004).

According to Dobruszkes (2009b) there are two types of competition relating to the deregulation of the airline sector, i.e. competition associated with geography and competition associated with supply. Luring tourists and influencing destination choice through fare and level of service provision is of central importance. In fact, the airline liberalisation in Europe has resulted in an increased number of city-pair routes, higher frequencies and lower fares for the passengers/tourists. Several destinations in Europe have experienced a prolonged tourism season and a boom in the second home market as the cost of travelling to these destinations has been reduced. Moreover, the entry of low cost carriers into the market has significantly changed the role of charter carriers and the national/legacy carriers in terms of operation, route frequency, airport selection and aircraft utilisation. The dynamics of the airline industry resulted in the formation of international strategic alliances (i.e. Star Alliance, oneworld and SkyTeam); in the creation of greater airline networks; but also in the emergence of mergers and acquisitions (such as the merger between Air France – KLM and British Airways – Iberia) or even bankruptcies amongst European legacy airlines (e.g. Sabena in Belgium; Swissair in Switzerland, Malév in Hungary and more recently Cyprus Airways in Cyprus).

In any case, the number of passengers travelling by air for leisure and business purposes is constantly increasing in spite of the recent financial downturn that affected Europe and the rest of the world. The main driver for that growth has been the development of LCC which managed not only to steal market share from the existing legacy carriers but also to explore and develop new markets. Low fares led to an increase of both traffic flows and travel frequency. One important element of LCC is that they prefer regional airports because of their low charges and other privileges, thus new destinations have been developed where the LCC have a dominant position in terms of market share. LCCs expand their services by establishing bases at various geographical locations without investing resources to the extent a full service carrier would. It has been noticed that low cost carriers find it easier to start or cease operations between a given city-pair compared to a full service carrier, as it has fewer implications for their network. Countries like the United Kingdom, Germany, Italy, France and Spain have experienced the benefits of the LCC phenomenon since the late 1990s whereas countries that joined the European Union at a later stage like Poland, are currently in the process of experiencing similar benefits. Open skies agreements between the European Union and third counties such as Morocco have also resulted in a major boost of LCC traffic predominantly for leisure but also for visiting-friends-and-relatives (VFR) traffic.

As expected, the emergence of LCC led to a market disruption with important effects on traditional carriers. Since the early 2000s, the latter began to plan new strategies seeking ways to reduce their costs. There have been efforts to introduce wage cuts, more flexible labour laws and a simplification in fleet structures. Moreover, the traditional carriers had to continue reducing their fares to keep customers (Smeth et al., 2007). Another problem faced by traditional carriers is the problem of excess capacity. As with every sector where capacity exceeds demand, there tends to be a shakeout where some companies close down, others merge or create synergies. In the airline industry, mergers between airlines may prove complicated because of anti-competitive concerns expressed by government authorities. Instead of mergers, major airlines follow a practice called code sharing. Code-sharing enables airlines to sell seats on each other's planes, which allows them to offer more services and flight hours with little or even no extra charge (Smeth, et al., 2007). Moreover, full service carriers need to maintain their extensive feeder network as a lifeline for their long haul operations, supporting their hub-and-spoke structure.

Between 2010 and 2015 European airlines have predominantly focused on growing yields. Their commercial interests shifted away from adding new capacity and achieving network growth and moved towards serving core routes and larger airport markets. Moreover, the average number of passengers per aircraft movement has increased by approximately 20% - better utilization has also led to enhanced profitability. Since 2014 many European carriers have been in discussions with policymakers and institutions in order to re-establish the "grounds" of European air transport. Their actions are set in the context of a consultation process launched by the European Commission with the aim to propose an EU Aviation Package within 2015 (European Commission, 2015a). The new aviation policy is expected to have four distinct core strategic drivers, i.e. green efficiency and innovation, digitalization, internationalisation and humanisation. The new aviation policy will also underline the importance of regional and social cohesion. The European Commission suggests that there is no single solution, therefore collective thinking and collaborative work needs to be in place.

In essence, the European airline industry today is now far more competitive than it was 20 years ago. Airline carriers make brave moves to secure their future. These moves have and will present even more new challenges to the airline sector. Since competition has transformed the airline market, it will transform airports as well. Airports can no longer consider themselves simply as transport infrastructure, but they need to become sophisticated businesses if they hope to navigate successfully in the new landscape as now explored in the following section of this chapter.

3. INSTITUTIONAL CHANGES IN AIRPORTS

The changes in network characteristics, airline route planning and the changing business models of airlines are elements that need to be considered by airports (De Neufville & Odoni, 2013). As stated previously, air transport liberalisation has led to a massive growth in passenger traffic. On the other hand, air transport infrastructure developments have not kept apace thus raising concerns about the ability of the existing capacity (in terms of runway, parking and terminal facilities) to meet increased levels of demand. Moreover, seasonal traffic peaks to airports located in popular destinations create similar constraints which are not necessarily linked to airport capacity on the ground but airspace capacity and air navigation. According to a 2015 ACI Europe report there are 14 European airports serving more than 25m passengers a year; 23 airports serving 10-25m passengers; 34 airports serving 5-10m passengers; and 390 airports serving less than 5 million passengers. In 2015 total airport connectivity grew at 8.9% compared to 2014: this trend is reflected in direct connectivity, which has grown by +4.6%. Indeed, year-on-year direct connectivity growth in Europe between 2009 and 2014 was only +1.4%, with an actual decrease even occurring between 2011 and 2014 (ACI Europe, 2015). It seems though that large airports provide the highest connectivity levels, but small airports the greatest connectivity growth. In fact, traffic from large airports is not directed solely to similarly large airports but also heads to smaller ones. Similarly, smaller airports seek growth and connectivity in order to increase their customer base and passenger numbers resulting in a greater connectivity expansion.

The most worrying trend identified by a 2013 EUROCONTROL study is the sharp reduction in airport expansion plans noted since the previous forecasting exercise in 2008. That forecast saw a planned capacity expansion of 38% over the subsequent 22 years; the corresponding figure for 2013-35 is just 17% (EUROCONTROL, 2013). The EUROCONTROL study made various proposals to deal with the problem including a switch of flights to less-congested secondary/satellite airports; a shift of demand away from air and towards high speed rail; and/or a greater use of bigger aircraft or alternatively of off-peak traffic periods. Nonetheless, these measures may prove inadequate to deal with the binding airport infrastructure constraints especially in big hub airports where incumbent network carriers are in need of multiple scheduling options (Association of European Airlines, 2014). Changes in the existing airport slot allocation rules (as described in Regulation (EC) 793/2004, which amended Regulation 95/93) may provide some temporary comfort but are not expected to resolve the problem of infrastructure which largely relies on the undertaking of new investment. European airports with a large number of tourist arrivals during the peak summer season also face chronic capacity problems, thus delays in arrivals. For example, traffic to the Greek islands grew at a 17% rate in 2014 and many of the related airports currently operate at the limit of their current declared capacity. Problems relate to airport layout, terminal buildings capacity, poor airport slots scheduling, insufficient staff employed and lack of radar facilities.

Airport ownership is also another challenging issue. According to Graham (2008) and Ashford, Mumayiz and Wright (2011) the great majority of airports were publically owned until recently as part of a world-widely accepted industry norm of meeting utility-related state objectives. There are still many examples in Europe and other parts of the world where airports are owned partly or fully by the local authorities or governments. Nonetheless, several airports across Europe have gone private including some of the major ones like London Heathrow. In fact, the transition from public services to business entities has led to significant changes in the form of airport operation and ownership (De Neufville & Odoni, 2013) with emphasis on the introduction of commercial and financial management practices (Graham, 2014). Not surprisingly, the shift towards privatisation has led airports to operate in a more complex environment leading among others to different pricing strategies and the provision of incentives to carriers to operate to these airports. This development has resulted in a more dynamic and competitive environment amongst the airports seeking more connectivity and passenger numbers. Table 1 below shows the ownership status of airports in Europe.

Table 1. Ownership status of airports in Europe

Country/ Type of Ownership	Public	Mixed	Private
Albania			100%
Armenia			100%
Austria	80%	20%	
Belarus	100%		
Belgium	60%	40%	
Bosnia and Herzegovina	100%		
Bulgaria	50%		50%
Croatia	100%		
Cyprus			100%
Czech Republic	100%		
Denmark	33%	67%	
Estonia	100%		
Finland	100%		
France	72%	14%	14%
FYROM			100%
Georgia			100%
Germany	69%	26%	5%
Greece	98%	2%	
Hungary		100%	
Iceland	100%		
Ireland	60%	20%	20%
Israel	100%		
Italy	39%	61%	
Kosovo	100%		
Latvia	100%		
Lithuania	100%		
Luxembourg	100%		
Malta		100%	
Moldova	100%		
Montenegro	100%		
Netherlands		75%	25%
Norway	100%		
Poland	80%	20%	
Portugal	100%		
Romania	87%	13%	
Russia	62.5%	12.5%	25%
Serbia	100%		

continued on following page

Table 1. Continued

Country/ Type of Ownership	Public	Mixed	Private
Slovakia	100%		
Slovenia	50%		50%
Spain	100%		
Sweden	100%		
Switzerland	60%	40%	
Turkey		86%	14%
Ukraine	100%		
United Kingdom	32%	16%	52%

Source: ACI (2010)

The changing form of ownership has led to a series of transformations in the way airports operate. There has been a notable shift from the airline to the passenger, focusing more on the latter than the previous. Moreover, several airport operations have been subcontracted or provided by third parties such as handling (both air and landside). Although there is a dispute in both the academic and practitioner circles over the benefits of subcontracting such services, it is widely accepted that this practice has increased competition and level of service quality provided by each airport. In many cases, changing airport ownership has also become associated with increased commercialization as airports are interested in increasing non-aeronautical revenue from the provision of non-regulated services, related among others to airport terminal concessions, car parking and real estate developments outside the airport perimeter. According to Graham (2014) the fact that airports rely more on non-aeronautical or commercial revenues proves that airports have been commercialised and behave more like private corporations thus emphasising marketing (Halpern & Graham, 2013) even in cases where they are state-controlled. From a regulatory perspective, airlines usually argue in favour of a single-till approach. This usually imposes an overall price cap on airport activities; thus, if airports make substantial profits from their non-aeronautical activities, they would have to lower the fees related to their aeronautical services – this cross-subsidization would eventually prove to the benefit of airlines. On the other hand, airports are strong proponents of a dual-till approach arguing that only aeronautical services should be regulated since concessions and real estate developments do not possess natural monopoly characteristics (Frontier Economics, 2014).

In any case, the subsidization issue is of great important in airport operations and also largely associated with the issue of state aid. In February 2014, the European Commission adopted new guidelines regarding the circumstances under which a state aid to an airport may prove compatible with the European *acquis communautaire*. These rules are essential to safeguard institutional transparency of monetary transactions in a sector where hidden or even overt subsidies have often caused significant market distortion (European Commission, 2014). Being cautious about the very investment issue in capital intensive sectors is of crucial importance not only for airports but also for air navigation service provision as now analysed in the following section of this chapter.

4. INSTITUTIONAL CHANGES IN AIR NAVIGATION SERVICES (ANS) PROVISION

According to the European Commission (2015b) there are more than 150 scheduled airlines, a network of over 400 airports, and 37 air navigation service providers in the European economy. Airlines and airports alone contribute more than €140 billion to the European GDP. Air Navigation Services (ANS) provision is considered a vital element for air transportation. ANS includes five broad categories of services provided to air traffic during all phases of operation (area control, approach control and aerodrome control). These services are: Air Traffic Management (ATM), Communication services, Navigation services and Surveillance services (CNS), Meteorological services for air navigation (MET), Aeronautical Information Services (AIS) and Search and Rescue (SAR) (ICAO, 2012). In many countries, these air navigation services are not provided by a single entity; instead, several entities may be involved. Figure 1 provides a graphical breakdown of the organizational chart of air navigation services according to the guidelines set by the International Civil Aviation Organization (ICAO, 2012).

One very important aspect of the aviation industry is cost. As far as the cost of infrastructure is concerned according to IATA (2013:1) "Airlines and passengers are estimated to have paid at least US$92.3 billion for the use of airport and air navigation infrastructure globally in 2011, equivalent to 14.4% of the cost of transport". Cost efficiency is quite critical for an airline to compete and survive in such a competitive market. Cockpit and cabin crew, aircraft ownership, fuel, maintenance, handling and catering infrastructure, passenger services and distribution and other costs are the main costs for all airlines. ANS costs are the only ones that are the same for every carrier and the way the carriers operate does not impact the ANS cost significantly. All carriers are charged the same unit rate when they fly above a country.

Figure 1. The structure of air navigation services
Source: ICAO, 2012

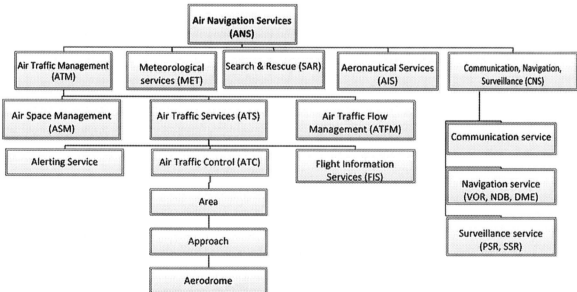

According to ICAO Doc 9980 (2012) the characteristics of ANS provision are much different from those of the airports. ANS rely on facilities and services provided by other states, since they extend over all the territory of the State concerned and sometimes beyond. ANS provision has an international dimension based on necessary multistate cooperation especially for route facilities and services. Air Navigation Service Providers (ANSPs) operate as natural monopolists. The transition of ANSPs to the market environment began in the 1980s and was rather slower in comparison to the airports and airlines; this is because ANSPs have been traditionally operated directly by governments. Over time, however, different organisational forms emerged, i.e.: a) government agencies (e.g. FAA-Federal Aviation Administration in USA); b) state owned or government business enterprise (e.g. DFS Deutsche Flugsicherung GmbH in Germany); c) private-public-partnerships (PPP[1]) (e.g. NATS in UK); and d) private entities (e.g. Nav Canada). All the different ownership and organisational forms exist and all have the potential to deliver excellent service under the condition of an appropriate governance structure (ICAO, 2013). Table 2 below shows the organisational and corporate arrangements for ANS providers in the European Common Aviation Area (ECAA).

The Cyprus ANSP was a government department until 2015, when new reforms were introduced. DFS in Germany is a Limited Liability Company. LVNL (The Netherlands) in 2002 was State enterprise and Slovenia Control was a government department. State enterprise is a government-owned corporate entity operating under a special statute, not normal commercial law (Performance Review Unit, 2004). Commercialization in ANSPs is deemed as a possible answer to financing and budgets constraints, as ANSPs were generally dependent on government budget for their capital and operational expenses. One important factor is reinvesting in the operational systems and enhancing performance and efficiency.

For instance, Nav Canada was the first fully private ANSP at a world level. It was created in 1996 and is the world's second largest ANSP by traffic volume. Nav Canada follows self-regulation, which means that it has an unlimited ability to set fees to airlines at a level sufficient to cover all of its costs, including reasonable reserves. Nav Canada is monitored by airline customers through membership on the board of directors (ICAO, 2012). On the other hand AEROTHAI, Aeronautical Radio of Thailand Limited, is a State enterprise in which 89 airlines had minority equity stakes in 2008, but the government controls the charges (ICAO, 2008). Charges for ANS is an important cost for airlines and thus for passengers' fares. Regarding Europe, UK is by far the most liberalised market in Europe. NATS was proposed as a PPP in 1998 and was finally formed as PPP in 2001. In 2001 Airline Group acquired 46% of NATS, the NATS staff took 5% and the remaining 49% was held by government. In 2009 NATS joined the A6 alliance of European ANSPs. In 2011 NATS created a partnership with Ferrovial Servicios, called FerroNATS. FerroNATS provides air traffic control services in the airports of Alicante, Valencia, Ibiza, Sevilla, Jerez, Sabadell, Cuatro Vientos, Vigo, La Coruña and Melilla (NATS 2015).

Under the rate of return regulatory regime (also called cost of service or cost plus regulation) ANSPs are required to obtain approval for the level of charges and investment. This regulation aims to limit the provider's rate of return on capital at the level prevailing in a competitive market. According to ICAO (2013) cost pass-through for both operating and capital expenditures is allowed, but this may provide an ANSP with a strong incentive for over-investment in order to increase the volume of its profit. The solution to this could be price cap regulation, under which the regulator sets a maximum chargeable rate. For example, prices of NATS are regulated in accordance with the price-capping formula (RPI-X) to create incentives for efficiency and are revised every five years taking into account, inter alia, major investment projects. Under performance regulation, ANSPs can charge up to a specific amount following a traffic risk sharing mechanism.

Table 2. Organisation and corporate ANSP arrangements in ECAA states

ANSP	Country	Organisational and Corporate Arrangements
Aena	Spain	State enterprise
ANS CR	Czech Republic	State enterprise
ARMATS	Armenia	Joint-stock company (State-owned)
Austro Control	Austria	Joint-stock company (State-owned)
Avinor	Norway	Joint-stock company (State-owned)
Belgocontrol	Belgium	State enterprise
BULATSA	Bulgaria	State enterprise
Croatia Control	Croatia	Joint-stock company (State-owned)
DCAC Cyprus	Cyprus	State body
DFS	Germany	Limited liability company (State-owned)
DSNA	France	State body (autonomous budget)
EANS	Estonia	Joint-stock company (State-owned)
ENAV	Italy	Joint-stock company (State-owned)
Finavia	Finland	State enterprise
HCAA	Greece	State body
HungaroControl	Hungary	State enterprise
IAA	Ireland	Joint-stock company (State-owned)
LFV	Sweden	State enterprise
LGS	Latvia	Joint-stock company (State-owned)
LPS	Slovak Republic	State enterprise
LVNL	Netherlands	Independent administrative body
MATS	Malta	Joint-stock company (State-owned)
M-NAV	F.Y.R.O.M.	Joint-stock company (State-owned)
MUAC	-	International organisation
NATA Albania	Albania	Joint-stock company (State-owned)
NATS	United Kingdom	Joint-stock company (part-private)
NAV Portugal	Portugal	State enterprise
NAVIAIR	Denmark	State enterprise
Oro Navigacija	Lithuania	State enterprise
PANSA	Poland	State body (acting as a legal entity with an autonomous budget)
ROMATSA	Romania	State enterprise
Skyguide	Switzerland	Joint-stock company (part-private)
Slovenia Control	Slovenia	State Enterprise
SMATSA	Serbia	Limited liability company
	Montenegro	

Source: Performance Review Unit (2012)

The liberalization of the air navigation service provision was preceded by the liberalization of airline activities. ANS in Europe started being liberalised through Single European Sky (SES) and Functional Airspace Blocks (FABs). SES intents to reduce delays, improve safety standards and flight efficiency, and encourage cost-savings related to service provisions. Regardless of the organizational format, according to Article 28 of the Chicago Convention, it is the State that is ultimately responsible for the provision and operation of air navigation facilities and services. The system before SES was deemed insufficient and costly. For instance the estimated costs of fragmentation of airspace amounts to 4 billion EUR a year and the 5 biggest ANSPs (AENA-Spain, DSNA-France, NATS-UK, DFS-Germany and ENAV-Italy) bear 60.3% of total European gate-to-gate air navigation service provision costs and they operate 54% of European traffic according to EC (2015). SES separated the National Supervisory Authorities and Civil Aviation Authorities (i.e. the regulators) from the ANSPs (i.e. the regulated service providers) to ensure safety and efficient supervision on the targets achievement. Under SES regulation aircraft should arrive within one minute of the planned arrival time regardless of weather conditions. On average, travel time will be reduced by 10 minutes compared to the pre-SES period and each of the 20 million flights per year will be handled with even greater levels of safety (European Commission, 2015b). Traffic risk sharing mechanism aiming to mitigate unexpected increases in costs or declines in traffic, and financial penalties or bonus for productivity and efficiency changes are now allowed provided that any profits are redistributed back to the airspace users. In any case, the value to passengers should be explicitly demonstrated in terms of shorter trips, enhanced safety and lower fares.

As for FABs, these were first proposed in 2004, then established in 2009 and eventually implemented in December 2012. Although on the air carrier side the private participation, privatization and commercialization process was faster than for airports and air navigation service providers (ICAO, 2003), the liberalisation and possibly consolidation of the air navigation service provision is deemed necessary for the efficiency of the system and for the generation of money and time benefits to the passenger. In fact, small ANSPs face difficulties in fully taking advantage of economies of scale and dealing with the high cost of investments. ATC services like meteorology and data communication services can be unbundled and outsourced, thus leading to reduced costs and overall efficiency gains (Finger, 2015).

Over the last few years the examples of changes in the ownership forms, pricing and investment regulation of air navigation service provision have been noteworthy. EC Performance Regulation 550/2004 brought a relative liberalisation by stating that the issue of certificates shall confer on ANSPs the possibility to offer their services to other ANSPs, airspace users and airports within the Community. In this way, there is no obligation on choice and the management of performance of the service provider is undertaken through an arm's length commercial contract. For instance, NATS has no monopoly on terminal ATM service provision and operates in 15 of the 90 or so UK airports where terminal ATC services are required. Furthermore, EC Regulation 2015/340 lays down technical requirements and administrative procedures related to air traffic controllers' licences and certificates aiming at a mutual recognition of the certificates issued by ATCO training organisations across the European Union and a harmonisation of the medical requirements for pilots and controllers facilitating the mobility of Air Traffic Controllers in Europe. (European Commission, 2015c)

In essence, sections 2-4 of this chapter identified and discussed important issues related to airlines, airports and ANSPs. As expected the relationship among these industry stakeholders has always been dynamic and controversial. Airlines have the advantage of investing on assets that can be utilised in such a way that maximises their return without necessarily operating on a certain geographical area (i.e. country, region airport). On the other hand, airports and ANSPs invest heavily on assets that cannot be transferred to another geographical area, i.e. they are spatially fixed. The common denominator is that airlines need airports to carry passengers and airports also need passengers to travel through them. Finally, ANSPs need both airlines to fly the designed routes and airports to host some of their activities and equipment. This interdependence will now be explored in the context of tourism.

5. TOURISM IMPLICATIONS OF AIRLINES, AIRPORTS AND AIR NAVIGATION SERVICES PROVISION

Air transportation cannot exist without the close cooperation of ANSPs, Airports and Airlines. ANS as a system is largely associated with the cost of services, en route and terminal charges, environmental issues and safety of flights given among others the infrastructural constraints at airports. The latter, on the other hand, need to consider the characteristics of operating airlines, the runway length, the available terminal capacity and the existing ground handling and ANS services. Likewise, airlines should take into account the type of aircraft, their flight frequencies and network structure, fare and cost issues and certainly the operational capacity and infrastructural constraints of airports and ANSPs. All these aspects are linked either directly or indirectly with each other; not surprisingly tourism destinations are largely affected by this interdependence in terms of securing enhanced connectivity and accessibility and a seamless (i.e. not bound by infrastructural over other constraints) travel experience of leisure, business and VFR passengers. Figure 2 expands on Bieger and Wittmer (2006) and depicts the relationship of the different entities as well as the emerging dynamics among their various characteristics.

Figure 2. The interdependence between air transport stakeholders and tourism
Source: Inspired by Bieger and Wittmer (2006)

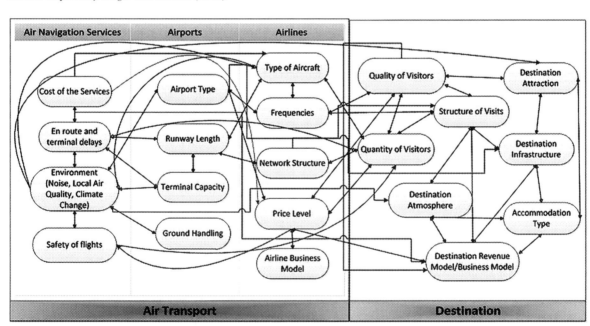

More specifically, the attractiveness of tourist destinations is linked to their natural and manmade resources as well as to the available hospitality and transport infrastructure. The latter usually blends with the natural resources determining in many cases the attractiveness of the tourist destination, since issues related to airport size and capacity affect the overall accessibility of the destination. Bieger and Wittmer (2006) put their emphasis on airports and airlines: the current approach adds ANS as another key pillar in the supply side. A new aspect which has lately become critical is related to environmental protection and regulation. Environmental constraints in the form of regulations on noise or Local Air Quality (LAQ) can affect the terminal capacity of an airport despite the implementation of Continuous Descent Operations (CDO). For example in order to reduce the noise exposure at night, night time operating restrictions were applied to Frankfurt, Heathrow, Gatwick and Stansted airport. The flights that can be accommodated in London are limited, thus the quantity of visitors arriving by airplane remains capped. If the tourism demand for London was not so high there would not be any restrictions in the capacity of the airport, the airline operations and the regulation of ANS. Following a chain reaction and a holistic approach the system of air transportation is closely connected with the tourism system. As part of the environmental protection at destination level, noise and air quality have been and are being discussed and regulated at several destinations and airports.

Airports, airlines and ANS differ on the aspects of asset specificity, their relative negotiating and bargaining power, the prevailing market conditions, as well as the level of regulation/deregulation they face. The ownership and control of airports, ANSPs and airlines, in conjunction with the specificity of various assets has led to a fierce battle between all parties where each one is trying to achieve most out of the other. The lights usually shine on the heavily congested airports with limited slot capacity and crowded passenger terminals. On the other hand, the majority of European airports underperform both in passenger numbers and financial results (ACI, 2015). In any case, air transport services depend on adequate infrastructure that can handle capacity in a cost-effective and safe manner. Airlines need airport infrastructure that can meet traffic demand in terms of capacity and quality, while complying with relevant safety and security standards. Air traffic management has to ensure safety and efficiently deal with traffic at peak hours especially at tourist airports with strongly seasonal traffic and binding infrastructural constraints.

The institutional changes in airlines, airports and air navigation service provision have enriched the city-pairs routes and their frequency; they have brought down the cost for the passenger and made many destinations reachable. The liberalisation in the airlines increased the passenger traffic, thus tourism. The deregulation on airports increased the city pairs and the connectivity. Increased passenger traffic and congested airports brought in the surface the need to improve the performance in terms of safety, environment, capacity and cost-efficiency of the air navigation service provision, thus institutional changes in ANS proved fundamental. Air transportation is serving the tourism industry by accommodating the tourists' need to reach their destination and at the same time by making traveling seamless, generates considerable demand for travelling, thus tourism.

A joint position on Open Skies by ACI EUROPE and the European Travel Commission (ETC - which represents National Tourism Organisations) was published in June 2015 stressing the need to expand Open Skies beyond Europe. Since tourism is a sector that will expand dramatically over the next decades, as a result of the emerging middle class in Asia, the demand for air travel is going to increase dramatically. Both aircraft manufacturers and tourism institutions predict that the demand for air travel will experience a positive growth. Therefore, airports but also possibly ANSPs in Europe should work closely with the travel distribution system (and primarily with tour operators and travel agents) to deliver an optimized tourist experience that will benefit all those involved as now also analysed in the concluding section of this chapter.

6. CONCLUSION AND THE WAY FORWARD

This chapter discussed institutional changes and emerging dynamics in the airline, airport and air navigation services sector and their implications for tourism. Among others, issues of regulation, deregulation and liberalization were extensively analysed given their important role in policymaking. It should be noted, however, that liberalisation of air services has not been a one-off event, but is rather an ongoing policy that has to be monitored and adjusted. In many cases no effective monitoring or compliance body exists that could intervene and correct violations against market liberalisation. Institutions should initiate policy discussions at high levels not only of air transport stakeholders but also of tourism communities concerned and involved in order to support adherence to agreed liberalisation. Finally, the private sector, represented by trade organizations such as IATA or major industries, such as aircraft manufacturing, must influence decision-makers at every opportunity to move toward and maintain a liberal policy when it comes to international air service agreements.

The international and European aviation sector seeks a fair regulation at an institutional level. The fact that there are different layers of regulation at national and/or regional level, in addition to the international ones, creates inconsistencies which the aviation industry needs to constantly address. The biggest challenge nevertheless remains the air space capacity and control as there is a direct conflict of interest amongst each member country. Apart from this, there is a long debate related to airport capacity (both in terms of runway and terminal size) as well as aircraft orders and delivery, in conjunction with emissions reduction, fuel consumption reduction, noise level reduction, and efficient aircraft utilisation and airline business models. Several airport operators stress the need for a more efficient air space utilisation and modernisation of the ANS, let alone the unification which will result in fewer costs and shorter flying times which will inevitably result in less fuel consumption and emissions. The amount saved by that reduction can actually fund the developments needed in the field of ANS. Provided that a proper systemic approach is followed any smart relaxation of infrastructural constraints will have positive repercussions on tourism growth and development not only of central places but also of more peripheral regions.

REFERENCES

Air Transport Action Group. (2014). *Aviation Benefits beyond Borders*. Geneva: ATAG.

Airports Council International. (2015). *Airport Connectivity Report*. Montreal: ACI.

Airports Council International Europe. (2015). *Economics Report 2014*. Brussels: ACI Europe.

Ashford, N., Mumayiz, S., & Wright, P. (2011). *Airport Engineering: Planning, Design and Development of 21st Century Airports* (4th ed.). New York, NY: John Wiley and Sons. doi:10.1002/9780470950074

Association of European Airlines. (2014). *Flightpath 2019: A Blueprint for the Future*. Brussels: AEA.

Bel, G., & Fageda, X. (2005). Is a Mixed Funding Model for the Highway Network Sustainable Over Time? The Spanish Case. *Research in Transportation Economics*, *15*, 187–203. doi:10.1016/S0739-8859(05)15015-X

Bieger, T., & Wittmer, A. (2006). Air transport and tourism: Perspectives and challenges for destinations, airlines and governments. *Journal of Air Transport Management*, *12*(1), 40–46. doi:10.1016/j.jairtraman.2005.09.007

Button, K., & Taylor, S. (2000). International air transportation and economic development. *Journal of Air Transport Management*, *6*(4), 209–222. doi:10.1016/S0969-6997(00)00015-6

Council Regulation (EC) No 550/2004 of the European Parliament and of the Council of 10 March 2004 on the provision of air navigation services in the single European sky (the service provision Regulation) OJ96/10

Council Regulation (EEC) No 2407/92. The introduction of harmonised requirements for an operating licence for EU airlines

De Neufville, R., & Odoni, A. (2013). *Airport Systems: Planning, Design and Management*. New York, NY: McGraw-Hill.

Dobruszkes, F. (2009a). Does liberalisation of air transport imply increasing competition? Lessons from the European case. *Transport Policy*, *16*(1), 29–39. doi:10.1016/j.tranpol.2009.02.007

Dobruszkes, F. (2009b). New Europe, new low-cost air services. *Journal of Transport Geography*, *17*(6), 423–432. doi:10.1016/j.jtrangeo.2009.05.005

EUROCONTROL. (2015). *NM Annual Network Operations Report 2014*. Brussels: EUROCONTROL.

EUROCONTROL-FAA. (2013). *Comparison of ATM-related performance: USA – Europe*. Brussels: EUROCONTROL.

European Commission. (2014). *State aid: Commission adopts new guidelines for state aid to airports and airlines*. Brussels: European Commission.

European Commission. (2015a). *Public consultation on the EU Aviation Package: Background information*. Available at: http://ec.europa.eu/transport/modes/air/consultations/doc/2015-aviation-package/background.pdf

European Commission. (2015b). *Air: Single European Sky*. Available at: http://ec.europa.eu/transport/modes/air/single_european_sky/index_en.htm

European Commission. (2015c). *Commission Regulation (EU) 2015/340 of 20 February 2015 laying down technical requirements and administrative procedures relating to air traffic controllers' licences and certificates pursuant to Regulation (EC) No 216/2008 of the European Parliament and of the Council, amending Commission Implementing Regulation (EU) No 923/2012 and repealing Commission Regulation (EU) No 805/2011*. Brussels: European Commission.

Finger, M. (2015, Spring). Liberalisation of air traffic management services: what role for EUROCONTROL? *Skyway*, 40-41.

Frontier Economics. (2014). *Setting airport regulated charges: the choice between single till and dual till*. London: Frontier Economics.

Graham, A. (2014). *Managing Airports: An International Perspective* (4th ed.). Oxford: Routledge.

Graham, A., Forsyth, P., & Papatheodorou, A. (2008). *Aviation and Tourism*. Aldershot: Ashgate.

Halpern, N., & Graham, A. (2013). *Airport Marketing*. Oxford: Routledgc.

Hindley, B. (2004). *Trade Liberalization in Aviation Services: Can the Doha round free flight?* Washington, DC: American Enterprise Institute Press.

International Air Transport Association. (2013). *IATA Economic Briefing – Infrastructure Costs*. Geneva: IATA.

International Civil Aviation Organization. (2003). *Commercialization and Liberalization* (working paper). Available at: www.icao.int/meetings/atconf6/.../workingpapers/atconf6-wp006_en.pdf

International Civil Aviation Organization. (2006). *Economic Contribution of Civil Aviation. International Civil Aviation Organization, 2006 Edition CD-ROM*. Aviatech Publications.

International Civil Aviation Organization. (2008). Ownership, Organisation and Regulatory Practices of Airports and Air Navigation Services Providers (report). Montreal: ICAO.

International Civil Aviation Organization. (2012a). Doc 9082 ICAO's Policies on Charges for Airports and Air Navigation Services. Montreal: ICAO.

International Civil Aviation Organization. (2012b). Doc 9980: Manual on Privatization in the Provision of Airports and Air Navigation Services. Montreal: ICAO.

International Civil Aviation Organization. (2013a). *Air Navigation Services Providers (ANSPs) Governance and Performance*. working paper. Available at: http://www.icao.int/Meetings/atconf6/Documents/WorkingPapers/ATConf.6.WP.073.2.en.pdf

International Civil Aviation Organization. (2013b). Doc 9161: Manual on Air Navigation Services Economics. Montreal: ICAO.

NATS. (2015). *Seamless Exceeding expectations on the ground and in the air*. Available at: http://www.nats.aero/wp-content/uploads/2013/01/NATS-Corporate-Brochure.pdf

Papatheodorou, A. (2002). Civil Aviation Regimes and Leisure Tourism in Europe. *Journal of Air Transport Management*, 8(6), 381–388. doi:10.1016/S0969-6997(02)00019-4

Performance Review Unit. (2004). *ATM Cost-Effectiveness (ACE) 2002 Benchmarking Report*. Brussels: EUROCONTROL.

Performance Review Unit. (2014). *ATM Cost-Effectiveness (ACE) 2012 Benchmarking Report with 2013-2017 Outlook*.Brussels: EUROCONTROL.

Piermartini, R., & Rousova, L. (2008). *Liberalization of Air Transport Services and Passenger Traffic*. Available at: http://www.wto.org/english/res_e/reser_e/ersd200806_e.pdf

Regulation (EEC) No 2408/92. The access for Community air carriers to intra-Community air routes.

Regulation (EEC) No 2409/92. The full freedom with regard to fares and rates.

Schlumberger, C., & Weisskopf, N. (2014). *Ready for Takeoff? The Potential for Low-Cost Carriers in Developing Countries*. Washington, DC: World Bank Group. doi:10.1596/978-1-4648-0282-9

Smeth, J. N., Allvine, F. C., Uslay, C., & Dixit, A. (2007). *Deregulation and Competition, Lessons from the Airline Industry*. Singapore: Sage Publications.

United Nations World Tourism Organization. (2012). *Global Report on Aviation: Responding to the needs of new tourism markets and destinations*. Madrid: UNWTO.

United Nations World Tourism Organization. (2015). *UNWTO Tourism Highlights 2015 Edition*. Madrid: UNWTO.

World Economic Forum. (2013). *The Travel and Tourism Competitiveness Report 2013*. Geneva: World Economic Forum.

KEY TERMS AND DEFINITIONS

ACI: Airports Council International.
ANS: Air Navigation Services.
ANSP: Air Navigation Service Provider.
CDO: Continuous Descent Operations.
EC: European Commission.
EEC: European Economic Community.
EU: European Union.
FAB: Functional Airspace Block.
LAQ: Local Air Quality.
LCC: Low Cost Carrier.
SES: Single European Sky.
VFR: Visiting Friends and Relatives.

ENDNOTE

[1]   Public-private partnership (PPP) provides private financing for infrastructure investment without immediately adding to government borrowing and debt, and can be a source of government revenue (ICAO, 2012b).

Chapter 4

Experience Marketing and Tourism:
An Application of Service–Dominant Logic to Addiopizzo Travel

Ilenia Bregoli
University of Lincoln, UK

ABSTRACT

Tourism is acknowledged to be highly experiential in nature, but despite these characteristics, in the tourism literature there are few articles that adopt the Service-Dominant logic (S-D logic) for studying tourism experiences. The aim of this paper is to apply the S-D logic to the case of Addiopizzo Travel, a Mafia-free project of responsible tourism set up in Sicily, Italy. Results show the role of Addiopizzo Travel as a central node of the network of firms involved in the project and the role that interactions among Addiopizzo Travel, stakeholders, and visitors have in the co-creation of tourists' experience.

INTRODUCTION

Consumer experiences are a topic that has attracted the attention of scholars in the tourism and marketing field for a long time. Indeed, scholars in the tourism field have been studying experiences since the 1970s (Uriely, 2005; Hosany & Witham, 2010), while in the marketing field experiences and experience marketing have been studied since the 1980s (Tynan & McKechnie, 2009), when the concept was first developed in the pioneering work of Holbrook and Hirschmann (1982). Experiences have been studied in B2B and B2C (Lemke et al., 2011) and in different services such as banking (Klaus & Maklan, 2012), hospitality (Jüttner et al., 2013), tourism (Kim, et al., 2012; Klaus & Maklan, 2011) and retail (Chang & Horng, 2010). Moreover, studies have focused on different aspects such as measurement of the experience quality (Lemke et al., 2011; Chang & Horng, 2010), the antecedents of the perceived value of experiences (Prebensen et al., 2013) and the impact that other customers have on the experience (Brocato et al., 2012). Moreover, different approaches to the development of experiences have been put forward.

DOI: 10.4018/978-1-5225-0201-2.ch004

For example, Pine II and Gilmore (1999) view experiences staged similarly to a theatrical play, while Schmitt (1999) stresses the need to stimulate the five senses.

Although several scholars have studied experiences, it must be acknowledged that little attention has been paid to the study of experiences in multi – stakeholder environments. On this topic, for example, Klaus and Maklan (2012) have highlighted that in literature the link between co – creation and the consumer experience is quite vague, as is the impact of social context on the consumer experience.

While looking at the literature on experiences taken from the tourism and marketing studies, it is possible to see that, while in marketing the Service-Dominant logic (S-D logic) has been applied to the study of experiences, in the tourism literature it has received little attention and just recently some attempts have been made to apply it. For instance, Shaw, Bailey, and Williams (2011) have adopted the S-D logic to the hotel industry and have focused their attention on the processes of co-creation of value with regard to innovation. However, even if the interest towards the S-D logic is increasing, it has been acknowledged that further research is needed (Li & Petrick, 2008).

Despite the lack of studies adopting the S-D logic to tourism, in literature there are some articles that stress some of the main points highlighted in the S-D logic, such as: (1) the concept of value of co-creation through which service providers and tourists are both engaged in the creation of value and they become, in this way, co-creators of value (Li & Petrick, 2008; Shaw, Bailey, & Williams, 2011); and (2) the relational nature of the exchange between, on the one hand, service providers and tourists and, on the other hand, tourists (Li & Petrick, 2008; Prebensen & Foss, 2011).

Due to the lack of studies that apply S-D logic to the field of tourism, this paper tries to fill in this gap by studying the case of *Addiopizzo Travel*, a project of responsible tourism that has been set up in Sicily, Italy. In so doing three different stages – the pre-trip, the travel, and the post-trip – have been analysed in order to assess how experiences are co-created. Special attention has been devoted to the analysis of relationships among *Addiopizzo Travel*, its network partners, and visitors.

LITERATURE REVIEW

Tourism Experiences and the S-D Logic

Tourist experiences have been usually studied by adopting two different perspectives that refer to the social sciences and the marketing, respectively. In the latter case the tourist experience has been associated to the consumer experience since tourists are consumers, thus the tourist experiences have been analysed by adopting a consumer behaviour approach (Quan & Wang, 2004). Although different approaches have been used in the study of tourism experiences, it is acknowledged that they share some common characteristics. They are subjective because they are lived by people who can give them different meanings according to the their own personal and cultural background. Moreover, tourist experiences are multi-phased because they start developing before the trip and continue evolving until the post-trip phase in which tourists recall the travel in their minds, this also means that experiences are variable over time. Finally, it is recognised that in order to develop a tourist experience it is necessary to involve both the suppliers of services and the demand (i.e. the tourists). Hence, tourist experiences cannot be shaped only by the tourism service providers, but also tourists play an active role and they can be considered, to all intents and purposes, to be co-producers of experiences (Quinlan Cutler & Carmichael, 2010; Ritchie & Hudson, 2009; Uriely, 2005). As a consequence, in this context the role of interactions between consumers and network partners is essential in the co-creation of the experience. For instance Quinlan Cutler and Carmichael (2010: 10) argue that "many experiences are in the presence of other people, who can influence levels of satisfaction and perceptions of quality. For example, a group of exciting and stimulating tourists will most likely enhance individual experiences". Similarly, Prebensen and Foss (2011) stressed the importance that the relationships between guests and stakeholders, on the one hand, and between guests, on the other hand, have in the development of tourist experiences in the context of organised tours. However, although the role played by interactions between stakeholders and tourists in the development of tourism experiences has been acnowledged in literature, there is still a lack of studies aimed at analysing how tourists' experiences can be co-created through interactions and the Service-Dominant logic (S-D logic) has been seldom applied in the tourism context.

The S-D logic was established as a new logic of marketing in which the service – "the process of providing benefit" (Lusch, Vargo, & O'Brien, 2007: 6) – was seen as the core of marketing. This new view of marketing was developed by Vargo and Lusch (2004) in their article published in the *Journal of Marketing*. In that first article, the new logic and the eight foundational premises on which it was based were described for the first time. Subsequently, those foundational premises were amended, one new premise was added, and nine derivative propositions were added (Lusch, Vargo, & O'Brien, 2007; Vargo & Lusch, 2008).

At the basis of S-D logic there are two main points: first, resources can be distinguished in operand and operant, the latter being a source of competitive advantage; second, the concept of co-creation of value and the need for collaboration between diverse actors is explicitly acknowledged (Lusch, Vargo, & O'Brien, 2007).

With regard to the resources, Vargo and Lusch (2004) have distinguished between operand and operant resources. The former are "resources on which an operation or act is performed to produce an effect" (Vargo & Lusch, 2004: 2), while the latter are "dynamic resources such as competences (skills and knowledge) that are capable of acting and producing effects in other resources" (Lusch, Vargo, & O'Brien, 2007: 8). Operant resources are usually deployed on operand resources in order to increase the value of other resources such as natural ones and, for this reason, operant resources represent one of the sources of competitive advantage. Indeed, operant resources are intangible, dynamic, and are able to produce effects on other resources. Among the operant resorces there are core competencies, organisational processes, customers, and firm's partners (Vargo & Lusch, 2004; Lusch, Vargo, & O'Brien, 2007).

The second fundamental aspect of S-D logic refers to the fact that value must be co-created rather than being embedded in products (Vargo & Lusch, 2004). This implies that value is not only created by the producers but that producers and customers collaborate in order to create value. As a result, it is essential that interactions and relationships develop between producers and customers at different stages, from the design of products to the consumption processes (Tynan & McKechnie, 2009; Vargo & Lusch, 2008). It must be pointed out, however, that relationships are not only limited to producers and consumers; indeed in the literature on S-D logic it is stressed the need to establish relationships between customers and members of a broader network consisting of diverse stakeholders that are linked to the company and to the customer, respectively such as "fellow customers, shareholders, external experts and opinion leaders, partners within the supply chain and other stakeholders such as the media, customers and members of brand communities" (Tynan & McKechnie, 2009: 507). As a consequence, for companies it is not sufficient to set up a one-way communication, but rather they must develop a dialogue with consumers that must "begin in the pre-experience stage to listen, get the consumer involved, to suggest an offer and to support imagining, searching, and planning activities. It must continue through to the post-experience stage to reinforce the positive outcomes" (Tynan & McKechnie, 2009: 510).

Similarly to the co-creation of value, experiences also require an active involvement of the consumers and other stakeholders that made up the company's and consumers' networks. Indeed, according to Gentile, Spiller and Noci (2007) and to Payne, Storbacka and Frow (2008), customer experiences originate from a set of interactions and relationships between the customer and the company's offer. However, what is important for a company is the ability to set up "good" relationships that create value for all parties involved and leave them "wanting to continue the relationship in some form" (Lusch & Webster Jr., 2011: 132). In this way, the idea of staged experiences developed by Pine II and Gilmore (1999), in which the company develops and offers to customers a staged experience, is overcome by a new idea in which consumers are actively involved in the co-creation of their own experiences and the role of the company is that of setting up the right infrastructure that allows consumers to co-create their own personal experiences (Gentile, Spiller, & Noci, 2007; Prahalad & Ramaswamy, 2004).

Since it is pivotal for a company to set up the right infrastructure for co-creating experiences with customers, the first step that is required for a business is to identify all possible network partners that might provide their competences and, in this way, facilitate the co-creation of experiences. Since the company does not own all the resources that are needed for the experience, it must play the role of "nodal" firm that coordinates all network partners (Prahalad & Ramaswamy, 2004). As a result, the role of the "nodal" firm is to set up an experience environment that will allow a personalised experience to be co-created according to the way each customer decides to interact with that experience environment (Prahalad & Ramaswamy, 2004).

Experience Quality and Value-In-Use

When studying customer's experiences it is important to take into account two dimensions: experience quality and value-in-use.

Experience quality is a construct that takes into account both tourists' perceptions about the quality of services consumed and interactions between various stakeholders involved in a trip (Lemke et al. 2011). More specifically, in a tourism context the interactions between consumers and service providers on the one hand, and between consumers and other stakeholders on the other, need to be considered. Apart from the explicit interactions, another element that must be taken into account is the degree of similarity between tourists. Indeed, it is recognised that the likelihood of consumers interacting with each other, consumers' intentions and behaviours and the consumer's perception of service quality are all influenced by similarities between consumers (Brocato et al., 2012). Indeed, the more similarly tourists perceive themselves to other stakeholders, the more likely they will be to start a relationship with them. Finally, it is necessary to consider the extent to which tourists co – create their own experiences both in the pre – travel phase, during travel and after travel. By so doing it is possible to take into account the multi – phased nature of tourism experiences.

Value – in – use refers to the value created for the consumers while they are using a service (Grönroos, 2011, 2008). This concept is linked to the idea that value for consumers emerges when the service is used and not when it is bought, because consumers are not interested in what they buy but in what they can do with the services they buy (Grönroos, 2008). Value – in – use can be utilitarian if it refers to the functional benefits obtained through the consumption of the offer, or hedonic if it refers to the achievement of experiential or enjoyment – related objectives (Chitturi et al., 2008). From their review of the literature, Lemke et al. (2011) have also included in their model other kinds of value – in – use, such as the relational benefits obtained when using the service and the cost/sacrifice. In addition a social value has been added in order to take into account the social benefits arising from the travel (Prebensen et al., 2013).

Apart from all these elements, it must be pointed out that the overall perception of the experience lived by tourists is also influenced by the tourists' personal values, involvement and motivations (Prebensen et al., 2013; Li and Cai, 2012).

METHODOLOGY

Case studies are suitable for gaining a deep understanding of the cases analysed (Creswell, 2007) and when the research is exploratory in nature (Yin, 2009). Since in tourism there is a lack of studies that analyse experiences by adopting the S-D logic, it was decided to use a case study in order to investigate the topic of this paper. Carrying out a case study usually entails the analysis of one or more cases through detailed data collection of multiple sources of information such as documentation, archival records, interviews, direct observations, participant observation, and physical artefacts (Creswell, 2007; Yin, 2009). In this research the analysis was based on secondary data (newspapers and magazine articles published in Italian, English, and French) and on primary data (interviews with the three founders of *Addiopizzo Travel*). All interviews were tape recorded and transcribed, and analysis was carried out on the transcripts.

Addiopizzo Travel is an association that was set up in 2009 as part of the main association *Addiopizzo* established in 2004 when a group of young people from Palermo pasted on the walls of the city a sticker in which it was written *"a whole people who pays the pizzo is a people without dignity"*. The aim of that action was to raise the awareness to the problem of *pizzo*, that is, protection money that businesses must pay in order to receive "protection" by Mafia. Following the reactions that arose from that action, those young people set up *Addiopizzo*, an association that promotes critical consumption in favour of those businesses that do not pay *pizzo* (http://www.addiopizzo.org/english.asp). As it was previously mentioned, *Addiopizzo Travel* is a member association of *Addiopizzo*. Indeed it was set up by three young people who are volunteering in the main association *Addiopizzo*. The idea of setting up this new association came from the recognition that in the market there was an unsatisfied need expressed by potential visitors who were asking *Addiopizzo* volunteers for suggestions on how to travel to Sicily and be sure that they were not financing Mafia.

Addiopizzo Travel offers to visitors "Mafia-free" tours in which visitors can learn about the problem of Mafia and about the anti-Mafia movement. In so doing, *Addiopizzo Travel* creates its tours by involving two kinds of stakeholders (Figure 1): on the one hand there are suppliers of services that are listed in the *Addiopizzo* list of businesses that do not pay *pizzo* – in this list there are almost 700 businesses working in different industries, not only in tourism. In this way, visitors are reassured that their money does not finance Mafia. On the other hand there are "witnesses", that is, stakeholders involved in anti-Mafia activities like prosecutors or anti-Mafia associations that are using goods confiscated to Mafia for social purposes like, for instance, *Libera Terra*. The organised tours aim at showing visitors not only the arts, history, and culture of some Sicilian destinations like Palermo, Monreale, and Cefalù, but also at showing them different ways of fighting Mafia. For instance, one of the interviewees explained:

Figure 1. The network of stakeholders of Addiopizzo Travel

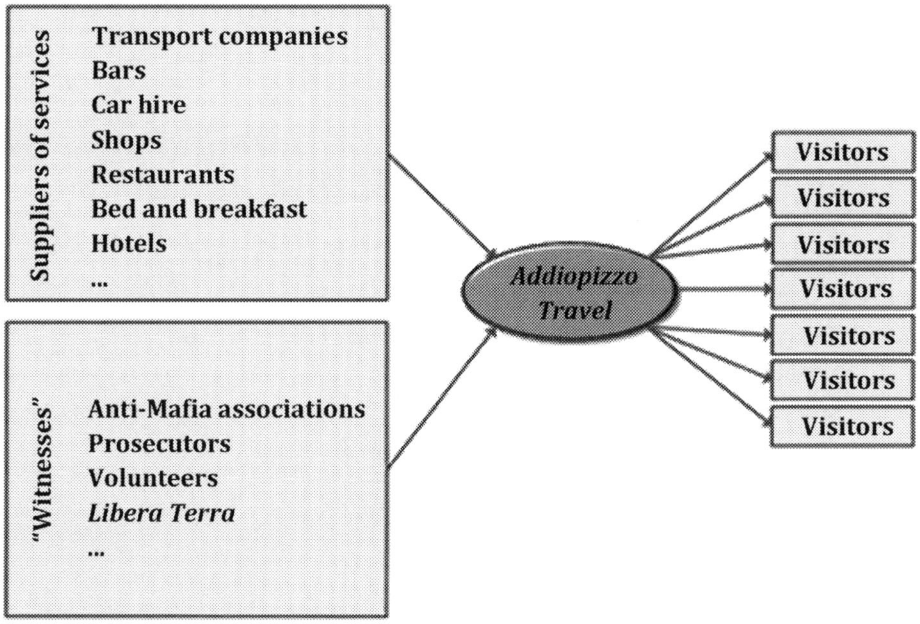

What we are trying to do through our tours is to make people appreciate the beauty of landscapes and the beauty of monuments but we also aim at making people appreciate those stories of resistance to Mafia and of those people that said "no", that didn't submit to Mafia violence, thus we are trying to offer both.

RESULTS

In this paper the experiences have been analysed by taking into account the relationship between *Addiopizzo Travel*, the nodal firm, and visitors in three different stages: the pre-visit, the travel, and the post-visit. Furthermore, interactions between *Addiopizzo Travel* and the actors involved in the network have also been considered.

Pre-Visit Stage

With regard to the pre-visit stage, people who want to travel with *Addiopizzo Travel* have the chance to join one of two standardised tours that are held in July and August of each year. These standardised tours are the starting point for the personalisation of tours that depends on individuals' preferences. In general the tour varies according to the specific target that wants to travel with *Addiopizzo Travel*, for instance, there are some visitors who want to travel independently and to discover Sicily on their own and, for this reason, they do not want to join any organised group, instead they ask *Addiopizzo Travel* to book services that are necessary during the trip (accommodation, transport, etc.) in order to be sure that they do not finance the Mafia. Moreover, a specific itinerary is set up and a guide book is given to these visitors who can travel independently and manage their holiday. On the contrary, when the tour is organised for schools, apart from showing the art and history of Sicily, a particular stress is given to the education to legality.

As one of the founders said, the final tour is the result of mediation between *Addiopizzo Travel* and the potential visitors:

We find an agreement in the sense that there are some days that are unavoidable given our idea of travel, while other days can be wishes, the need of analysis of some areas or of some perspectives that visitors wish to deepen. Thus, we try to find an agreement.

It is evident that reaching an agreement between *Addiopizzo Travel* and potential visitors is essential and, in order to do so, communication between the two parties is pivotal. This communication is mainly based on e-mail exchanges that develop over time. However, tours and the resulting experience cannot be fully personalised because *Addiopizzo Travel* can just involve those businesses that are not paying *pizzo* and that are included in the Addiopizzo list, thus it cannot involve all Sicilian businesses.

The Travel

In general, excluding trips for schools, the tour is done by small groups of people (between six and eight people). In this way visitors can easily make friends with other visitors and can have direct interaction with guides of *Addiopizzo Travel* and with other people they meet during the trip.

During the tour, visitors meet the "witnesses", that is, people who are actively involved in the anti-Mafia movement, for example, prosecutors, entrepreneurs who have denounced those who wanted to be paid the *pizzo,* friends and relatives of people who were killed by Mafia because they were fighting Mafia or denounced what Mafia was doing. For instance, during the tour visitors can meet Giovanni Impastato, brother of Peppino, who was killed by Mafia in 1978 because he was denouncing the local Mafia boss through the radio. Meeting these people is for visitors a highly emotional moment of the trip because visitors do not simply listen to the stories they are told, they also interact with the "witnesses". For instance, as one of the founders argued:

These meetings are seldom passive moments where visitors listen to […], the most beautiful thing is the interaction: from students of schools that chat with a prosecutor to adults […] that want to ask the question that eats you up in that moment and asking "how have you found the courage to do what you have done?".

During the travel visitors can do different activities. For instance, they can attend a cooking course to learn Sicilian recipes or visit the small TV station Telejato that is located in an area with a high presence of organised crime where visitors can meet the owner, Pino Maniaci. In the news of this small television Pino Maniaci denounces Mafia, and as a result he has been threatened several times and he was severely beaten by the son of a local Mafia boss. During this visit all visitors have the chance to host the news together with Pino Maniaci and read the news with him. In this way visitors can participate in the campaign "we are all Pino Maniaci" that was created to support him and its activity and show local people that he is not alone.

In these tours, due to the limited size of the groups of tourists, friendships develop. This is also facilitated by the fact that people on the tours usually share the same kind of values, as another founder stated:

This relationship is facilitated by the fact that visitors share the same kind of values [...]. Visitors recognize in other people the same motivations, the same spirit, and the same enthusiasm that brought them to do that travel.

Post-Visit Stage

In the post-visit stage the experience of visitors during the tour is reinforced through the *Addiopizzo Community*, the photos that are taken by visitors in a specific place visited during the tour, and the relationships that develop with people met on the tour.

Addiopizzo Community is the name given to the community that every person wishing to travel with *Addiopizzo Travel* joins by paying a fee that is comprised in the price of the tour. Thanks to this membership all visitors receive updates on the activities of the main association *Addiopizzo* and of *Addiopizzo Travel*. Moreover, the membership fee is used to support the associations and people involved in *Addiopizzo,* leaving, in this way, the feeling that visitors have contributed to the improvement of the areas visited and to give businesses involved in the project the feeling that they are not alone, as one founder stated:

[The membership fee] makes the tourist feeling to be part of the context visited because he feels that he has left something for improving the context that he has visited, while from the perspective of those people that are visited there is the feeling of not being alone.

Also, photos are used to enhance the visitors' experience, but in this case tourists are asked to send their photos to *Addiopizzo Travel* so that they can be uploaded on the website. These photos are taken on a hill in Capaci, nearby Palermo. Visitors are brought there because from there they can see the motorway where in 1992 the prosecutor Giovanni Falcone, his wife, and three police escorts were killed by a bomb placed there by Mafia. On that hill there is a building on which people from Capaci wrote "No Mafia" a couple of months after those killings. All visitors are asked to take photos with the building at their backs and are asked to send those photos to *Addiopizzo Travel*. As one of the interviewees stated, that photo represents a synthesis of the overall trip:

Taking a photo of all visitors in front of that building is a symbol of the overall travel, of all contents that there are in the travel, it is a synthesis.

Finally, the experience is strengthened through the relationships that develop with *Addiopizzo Travel* staff over time and involve a continued exchange of e-mails, as well as relationships with operators that visitors meet during the tour. For instance, there are visitors who spend their holidays in Sicily every year and stay in hotels run by people who they met on the *Addiopizzo Travel* tour. While in another case, not only the visitor kept in touch with one of the actors met during the tour, but when she found out that he was having economic problems she helped him by paying his electricity bills.

Relationship between *Addiopizzo Travel* and the Stakeholders

Addiopizzo Travel is the central node of the network of firms that offers services to tourists. Given this role, the relationship of *Addiopizzo Travel* with service providers is essential. In this case, the relationship is based on reciprocal trust and collaboration. For instance, actors help founders of *Addiopizzo Travel* sort out the technical aspects associated with the organisation of tours. Moreover, they give suggestions for developing new products or for adding new elements to the tour. This was the case, for instance, of a small producer of the traditional cap from Sicily, the *coppola*, that is now associated to Mafia. He suggested adding to the tour a visit to his workroom so that visitors could see how *coppola* are produced and, in this way, reaffirm the Sicilian origin of the cap. The relationship with actors is usually based on reciprocal trust. Indeed, as one of the interviewees stated:

With our suppliers, who are considered to be fellow-travellers rather than people with whom we have a commercial relation, there is reciprocal trust so that suggestions are made, discussed and in some cases can be realized and included into the itineraries.

Overall, this relationship is eased by the fact that actors perceive the benefit of being a member of the network of *Addiopizzo Travel*. Indeed, all tourists can only travel with providers who are members of *Addiopizzo* network and, as a result, they have received a positive economic impact from their choice.

CONCLUSION

The case presented in this paper has showed how experiences are created by a small Sicilian association, *Addiopizzo Travel,* that offers visitors "Mafia-free" tours. This case has helped highlight the role that relationships among *Addiopizzo Travel*, stakeholders, and visitors have in the co-creation of experiences at different stages of travel. In particular, it was shown that visitors are involved in the co-creation of the tour in order to satisfy their own specific needs and, in order to achieve this objective, interactions between visitors and *Addiopizzo Travel* are developed. During the trip interactions develop among diverse subjects, namely visitors, *Addiopizzo Travel* staff, and stakeholders belonging to *Addiopizzo Travel* network (i.e., service providers and "witnesses"). Finally, since these relationships continue in the post-visit phase through the membership to *Addiopizzo Community* and the visitors' photos shared with *Addiopizzo Travel*, the overall experience is enhanced. Furthermore, experiences are also created thanks to the relationships that *Addiopizzo Travel* has with its network members.

Consistent with the reviewed literature that stresses the role of relationships among the firm, customers, and other stakeholders involved in the firm's broader network in the co-creation of value and experiences (Prebensen & Foss, 2011; Tynan & McKechnie, 2009; Vargo & Lusch, 2008), the presented case shows how these relationships can be valuable in the development of a unique experience. Moreover, this case study has supported the view that not only is it important to establish relationships, but also that these relationships must be valuable for all parties involved and must lead them to continue that relationship over time (Lusch & Webster Jr., 2011). In this specific case, visitors who travel with *Addiopizzo Travel* have the chance to contribute to the fight against Mafia, while businesses involved in the network receive a positive economic impact and feel that they are not left alone in their fight. Finally, in light of the kind of relationships that develop among all parties involved, the relationships can develop over time even when the tour has concluded.

Even if this paper has highlighted the role that relationships have in the co-creation of experience, it is necessary to point out that this study is not free from limitations. First, in order to generalise results it is necessary to collect more data from visitors and from stakeholders who are involved in *Addiopizzo*

Travel network. In this way it would be possible to understand how relationships are considered by all parties involved. Second, it would be necessary to carry out a study on visitors to understand in depth how they perceive the experience lived during the travel and, in this way, to study the diverse components of customers' experience (Gentile, Spiller, & Noci, 2007). Finally, it would be interesting to carry out these studies on similar projects like those managed by *Libera Terra*, another association that provides Mafia-free holidays in accommodations that have been confiscated to Mafia.

To sum up, this study has shown how the development of relationships among people involved in travel is essential if a business wants its visitors to have a unique experience. This means that tourism businesses (tour operators in particular) should be aware of the contribution that all parties can give in the co-creation of experience. This means that, not only is it essential to pay attention to the relationships with visitors, but also to the relationships with stakeholders that make up the business network and provide services to tourists.

REFERENCES

Baron, S., & Harris, K. (2008). Consumers as resource integrators. *Journal of Marketing Management*, *24*(1-2), 113–130. doi:10.1362/026725708X273948

Brocato, E. D., Voorhees, C. M., & Baker, J. (2012). Understanding the Influence of Cues from Other Customers in the Service Experience: A Scale Development and Validation. *Journal of Retailing*, *88*(3), 384–398. doi:10.1016/j.jretai.2012.01.006

Chang, T.-Y., & Horng, S.-C. (2010). Conceptualizing and Measuring Experience Quality: The Customer's Perspective. *Service Industries Journal*, *30*(14), 2401–2419. doi:10.1080/02642060802629919

Chitturi, R., Raghunathan, R., & Mahajan, V. (2008). Delight by Design: The Role of Hedonic Versus Utilitarian Benefits. *Journal of Marketing*, *72*(3), 48–63. doi:10.1509/jmkg.72.3.48

Creswell, J. W. (2007). *Qualitative inquiry & research design. Choosing among five approaches*. Thousand Oaks, CA: SAGE.

Gentile, C., Spiller, N., & Noci, G. (2007). How to sustain the customer experience: An overview of experience components that co-create value with the customer. *European Management Journal*, *25*(5), 395–410. doi:10.1016/j.emj.2007.08.005

Grönroos, C. (2008). Service Logic Revisited: Who Creates Value? And who Co-creates? *European Business Review*, *20*(4), 298–314. doi:10.1108/09555340810886585

Grönroos, C. (2011). Value Co-creation in Service Logic: A Critical Analysis. *Marketing Theory*, *11*(3), 279–301. doi:10.1177/1470593111408177

Holbrook, M. B., & Hirschmann, E. C. (1982). The Experiential Aspects of Consumption: Consumer Fantasies, Feelings, and Fun. *The Journal of Consumer Research*, *9*(2), 132–140. doi:10.1086/208906

Hosany, S., & Witham, M. (2010). Dimensions of cruisers' experiences, satisfaction, and intention to recommend. *Journal of Travel Research*, *49*(3), 351–364. doi:10.1177/0047287509346859

Jüttner, U., Schaffner, D., Windler, K., & Maklan, S. (2013). Customer Service Experiences: Developing and Applying a Sequential Incident Laddering Technique. *European Journal of Marketing, 47*(5/6), 738–769. doi:10.1108/03090561311306769

Kim, J.-H., Ritchie, J. R. B., & McCormick, B. (2012). Development of a Scale to Measure Memorable Tourism Experiences. *Journal of Travel Research, 51*(1), 12–25. doi:10.1177/0047287510385467

Klaus, P., & Maklan, S. (2011). Bridging the Gap for Destination Extreme Sports: A Model of Sports Tourism Customer Experience. *Journal of Marketing Management, 27*(13/14), 1341–1365. doi:10.108 0/0267257X.2011.624534

Klaus, P., & Maklan, S. (2012). EXQ: A Multiple-item Scale for Assessing Service Experience. *Journal of Service Management, 23*(1), 5–33. doi:10.1108/09564231211208952

Lemke, F., Clark, M., & Wilson, H. (2011). Customer Experience Quality: An Exploration in Business and Consumer Contexts Using Repertory Grid Technique. *Journal of the Academy of Marketing Science, 39*(6), 846–869. doi:10.1007/s11747-010-0219-0

Li, X., & Petrick, J. F. (2008). Tourism marketing in an era of paradigm shift. *Journal of Travel Research, 46*(3), 235–244. doi:10.1177/0047287507303976

Lusch, R. F., Vargo, S. L., & O'Brien, M. (2007). Competing through service: Insights from service-dominant logic. *Journal of Retailing, 83*(1), 5–18. doi:10.1016/j.jretai.2006.10.002

Lusch, R. F., & Webster, F. E. Jr. (2011). A stakeholder-unifying, cocreation philophy for marketing. *Journal of Macromarketing, 31*(2), 129–134. doi:10.1177/0276146710397369

Payne, A. F., Storbacka, K., & Frow, P. (2008). Managing the co-creation of value. *Journal of the Academy of Marketing Science, 36*(1), 83–96. doi:10.1007/s11747-007-0070-0

Pine, J. B. II, & Gilmore, J. H. (1999). *The experience Economy: work is theatre and every business a stage*. Boston: Harvard Business School Press.

Prahalad, C. K., & Ramaswamy, V. (2004). *The future of competition. Co-creating unique value with customers*. Delhi: Harvard Business School Press.

Prebensen, N. K., & Foss, L. (2011). Coping and co-creating in tourist experiences. *International Journal of Tourism Research, 13*(1), 54–67. doi:10.1002/jtr.799

Quan, S., & Wang, N. (2004). Towards a structural model of the tourist experience: An illustration from food experiences in tourism. *Tourism Management, 25*(3), 297–305. doi:10.1016/S0261-5177(03)00130-4

Quinlan Cutler, S., & Carmichael, B. A. (2010). The dimensions of the tourist experience. In M. Morgan, P. Lugosi, & J. R. Ritchie (Eds.), *The tourism and leisure experience. Consumer and managerial perspectives* (pp. 3–26). Bristol, UK: Channel View Publications.

Ritchie, J. R., & Hudson, S. (2009). Understanding and meeting the challenges of consumer/tourist experience research. *International Journal of Tourism Research, 11*(2), 111–126. doi:10.1002/jtr.721

Shaw, G., Bailey, A., & Williams, A. (2011). Aspects of service-dominant logic and its implications for tourism management: Examples from the hotel industry. *Tourism Management*, *32*(2), 207–214. doi:10.1016/j.tourman.2010.05.020

Tynan, C., & McKechnie, S. (2009). Experience marketing: A review and reassessment. *Journal of Marketing Management*, *25*(5-6), 501–517. doi:10.1362/026725709X461821

Uriely, N. (2005). The tourist experience. Conceptual developments. *Annals of Tourism Research*, *32*(1), 199–216. doi:10.1016/j.annals.2004.07.008

Vargo, S. L., & Lusch, R. F. (2004). Evolving to a new dominant logic for marketing. *Journal of Marketing*, *68*(1), 1–17. doi:10.1509/jmkg.68.1.1.24036

Vargo, S. L., & Lusch, R. F. (2008). Service-dominant logic: Continuing the evolution. *Journal of the Academy of Marketing Science*, *36*(1), 1–10. doi:10.1007/s11747-007-0069-6

Yin, R. K. (2009). *Case study research. Design and methods*. Thousand Oaks, CA: SAGE.

KEY TERMS AND DEFINITIONS

Addiopizzo-Travel: Tour operator offering Mafia-free tours of Sicily.

Anti-Mafia Movement: People and associations that are fighting against mafia, e.g. prosecutors, businesses that are not paying pizzo, associations created by people whose friends and / or relatives were killed by mafia, etc.

Co-Creation of Experiences: Cases in which tourists are directly involved in the development of their travel experiences thanks to the involvement in the organisation of the travel, activities, etc.

Pizzo: Protection money.

Service-Dominant Logic: New logic of marketing in which the service is seen as the core of marketing.

Sicily: Biggest island in the Mediterranean Sea.

Value-in-Use: Value that customers receive when they use a product or service.

Chapter 5

Divorcing after Holidays:
From Sacredness to Post-Vacation Blues Syndrome

Maximiliano Emanuel Korstanje
University of Palermo, Argentina

ABSTRACT

Divorcing is a common-place practices that characterized our modern daily life. What is more than interesting to explore is why one of third takes after holidays. Are holidays accelerating the social decomposition the founding parents of sociology denounced in earlier century? or simply, as Maccannell puts it, tourism serves as a valve (mechanism) of cohesion similarly to the role played by religion/totems in primitive societies? To answer these questions, we present statistical information given by the Dirección General de Estadística y Censos (Ministerio de Hacienda GCBA). Although this information had its own limitations, which suggests more investigation is needed, we strongly beliefs the outcomes shed light to embrace the theory of vital cycles, as it has been formulated by Turner.

INTRODUCTION

Tourism has expanded worldwide due to two main factors, which are associated to its economic growth and the working condition improvements accelerated by the end of WWII. Today, for many family's holidays represent an acquired right not only because it liberates peoples from working rules, but consigning memorable moments. As a social mechanism of escapement, tourism revitalizes the psychological frustrations of daily life. Although some interesting studies focused on the daily habits or behavior during consuming leisure, less attention was given to tourism as a sacred-space (Krippendorf 1982; 2010; Deem, 1996; Urry, 1988; Korstanje & Busby, 2011). The metaphor of tourism as lost-paradise still remains unchecked (Korstanje & Busby 2011; Korstanje 2009; Cantallops & Cardona 2015). If tourism is characterized by a temporal stage where pleasure is maximized, what happens whenever the subject should be returned to working life, is one of the aspects now are being discussed by specialists and therapists. The concept of post-vocational syndrome, a pathology which ranges from depression towards divorce, is being explored by psychology. Some original hypotheses infer that holiday-makers

DOI: 10.4018/978-1-5225-0201-2.ch005

suffer some cognitive adjustments, at time they are rechanneled to the routine, from where they departed. The conceptualization of holidays as a lost Eden bespeaks of an eternal state of prosperity where all needs are fulfilled. As an ideal stage, holidays generate higher expectances sometimes are conjoined to violent reactions, when ideals do not match with reality. Even if the symptomatology of Post vacation-syndrome is very hard to grasp, some voices speculates there is some unstudied connection between the rate of divorces and holidays. Here two questions are raised, are people divorcing after returning from their holidays? to what extent tourism plays a crucial role in this process of disruption?

The goal of this chapter aims at discussing the negative effects of post vacation syndrome in order for policy makers to conduct efficient instrument of advertising. The fact is that efforts and sophistications of advertising sometimes produce idealized image of destinations that produce serious reactions when are suspended. We are daily bombarded by suggestive advertising whose primary aim is the conditioning of consumption, however, under some context, between the idealized image of the product and our possibilities there is a gap. The growing number of divorces may be very well a key factor that is accelerated by the divergence of cognitive dissonances caused by marketing and tourism-management.

The number of divorces is undoubtedly exceeding marriage worldwide. Not only, families are placed in context of change by the rise of informal civil unions but 50% of American families have a second marriage. Following this, the average impact of marriage/union interruption is almost 3/7 years. This social fragmentation produces negative consequences for children who spend less time with their parents or even inside the couple by the increase of intra-marital violence. Some ciphers show that in Argentina one of three divorces is encouraged by women. From 2001 to 2010, in Argentina were almost 564396 legal divorces. If in 80s decade almost 114 couples divorced in a daily basis, this decreased to 87. However, something changed from 2001 to 2010, where statistics reveal almost 172 divorces per day. One from 3 cases is divorces forced in post-holiday context (Himitian, 2012). The goals of these short notes of research are twofold. Originally, we explore on what specialists call as post vacation distress syndrome, which is explained as a state of depression formed by the divergence between the idealized image of holidays, the expectances posed to balance the daily frustrations ordinary people feel, and the return to work. It may range from bad mood, distress, lack of appetite, disorientation, insomnia, lack of motivation or even the rupture with the family. Although the material on this "post vacation blues syndrome" is slim (Hiltunen, et al 2004), it is important to determine to what an extent divorce results from the encounter between the dreamed and real world. Patients suffer at time they are re-entered to the normal routine, they originally wanted to escape. Secondly, we examine "how the metaphor of paradise" that exploits tourism marketing and destination policy makers is formed.

Preliminary Discussion

The act of traveling needs from trust and security. Though the etymological origin of tourism stems from Old Anglo Saxon, *torn*, which means going out of home to return later or roundabout travel (Korstanje 2007). Much has been written on the role of technological breakthrough in the configuration of modern travels. At some extent, tourism (in modernity) surfaced by a combination of different factors which range from betterments in working conditions to the acceleration in mobility systems (Towner & Wall, 1991; Towner, 1985; Kevan 1993; Seaton 1998). Put this in the terms of travel or not, George, Inbakaran & Poyyamoli (2010) focus on the needs to create an all-encompassing theory as to why people travel but return to home at a later day. Indeed, in what seems worthy discussing, tourism is an activity that denotes mobility and return. In perspective, not only people are subject to different consuming preferences during their stay, but destinations experience radical changes in their life-cycles. Traveling signals to an act of escapement or emancipation that revitalizes the daily frustrations. Though moving entails facing some risks which may very well jeopardize tourist´ ontological security, no less true is that the tourist motivation remains higher. Two type of motivations coexist in travellers, tourist and nativist. While the former appeals to the quest for "Other customs", cultures and exoticness, the latter one is a counter-act that leads to the known and certainness.

We also wanted to better understand how the two forces of touristic and nativistic motivators would interact to determine the 'destiny of a tourist'. Towards this end, first we developed a valid and reliable scale to measure nativistic motivation and later used this scale to see how, across the tourist life cycle, touristic and nativistic motivations negotiate with each other. It is to be acknowledged that, for a long time, motivation theory in tourism has not made a radical shift in its scope. This 'staticness' is shocking especially since tourism is a multidisciplinary area of research on the frontiers of disciplines, making it more likely to get a variety of theoretical perspectives. (George, Inbakaran & Poyyamoli, 2010, p. 405)

Tourism should be defined as something else than a commercial activity, or a mere industry. Furthermore, the current cultural values of postmodern societies confer to their citizens the autonomy to travel elsewhere, any geographical point of the globe. In Urry`s insight, tourism and consumption surged only in modern times. The meaning of tourism depends not only of the features enabled by geographical displacements, but (in this Urry coincides with MacCannell) in the intersections of leisure, consumption and labor. The tourist experience is based on an ongoing negotiation that changed the ways and how people gaze. Open to the logic of escapement, leisure allows the liberalization of all social constraints, which are fulfilled by the economy of desire (sign) and consumption. Unlike other sociologists, Urry acknowledges that tourism is a modern phenomenon associated to consumer services (Urry, 2002). However, some recent voices alert on the negative effects of tourism consumption in daily life. There is a type of new *Tourist consciousness* which merits being critically scrutinized (Tzanelli 2007; Virilio 2006; Meethan 2003; 2004; 2006; 2014; MacCannell 1973; 1984; 1988; 1992; 2001; 2011; 2012). As MacCannell (1976) puts it, the creation of Disneyland produced an uncanny situation, since technology helped modern societies to expand their hegemony over the so-called "primitive World" at the time, reserved in its core spaces of leisure and consumption. The paradox lies in the fact, this state of material stability resulted in the rise of diverse psychological frustrations, and pathologies that pressed thousands of citizens to consult therapists. To put this in bluntly we enjoy from modern tourism visiting exotic landscapes and culture while our trust in the neighbors declines.

Technology and Trust

From its inception, social sciences were concerned by the advance of industrialism. One of its founding parents, Emile Durkheim, who was widely influenced by Fustel de Coulange, emphasized on the importance of religion as a platform to enhance social cohesion. Modernity and the industrial mind, not only were based on a process of secularization that erodes the influence of religion, but also produces some social pathologies, associated to anomie (Durkheim 1987). Decomposition of social world has been accelerated by the introduction of "reflexivility and risk". Money serves as a symbolic mediator between human beings. The classic sources of power, based on the old aristocracy, ceded to a new type of "horizontality" that places in egalitarian conditions to all citizens. The gap left by capitalism is fulfilled by trade and globalization (Giddens, 1971; 1992; Batzell, 1991; Nisbet, 1993; Putnam, 1995; Buell, 1994). This begs a more than interesting point, is modernity corroding the marriages?

As the previous argument given, Denis Merklen (2013) argues convincingly that late-capitalism is not producing new institutions, as the specialized literature suggests, but is framing new citizens and their subjectivies. Appealing to neo-discourse associated to "social Darwinism", this global order encourages the competence of workers for reaching the success. Besides this allegory, anyway lies the vulnerability of workforce in favor of capital owners. One of the aspects that defines today how people is educates relates to risk-management. Unlike other times, ordinary people have been enabled to the power to shape their own destiny. This creates a sentiment of uncertainness that leads people to decline the trust in the other.

In this respect, Roland Inglehart (1997) explains that social systems are determined by the interaction with environment. At the time, society passed from feudality to modernity, rules and institutions suffered radical changes. In this token, the appearance of services and leisure industries not only tended to efface social relationships, but also accelerated the process of secularization. Whether traditional societies develop a high respect by authority, and attachment to God, the secular ones signal to a much profound sentiment of self-motivation that triggers divorce, abort and others practices. Other authorative voices as Bauman, Rosenberg & Arrambide (2005) observed that there was an abrupt epistemological rupture in the productive means, where the advent of virtual proximity, in the liquid times, made human connectivity more regular but weaker, or superficial than other decades.

In a seminal book, Jennifer Germann Molz (2014) observes that the first-world citizens have changed their habits to travel, their ways of figuring the "Other", as well as to forming their own identities. The adoption of digital technology empowered the creation of globalized networks where experiences are shared with others at the same time, travelers are abroad. The idea of "interactive travel" alludes to more fluid, rapid and intensive but weaker bondages. If decades ago, tourist plays a proactive role by gazing others, native or residents, today "tourists" are gazed by the blogs or the material uploaded in the global network. This happens simply because in our mobile society the possibility of escapement has diluted. The emergence of the internet, and social platforms promised a more cohesive society, however the ties are weaker than at other times. Are mobile technologies making a more sociable world, or rather, are they conducive to an irreversible social bond declination?

For Molz, we live in a new further mobile society, where the media organizes a set of paradoxes, into coherent performances. Travelling is now based on two contrasting forces, anxiety and aspiration. The emergence of internet, and social platforms promised a more cohesive society, however the ties are weaker than other times. One of the aspect this brilliant book addresses is the paradox of human sociability; at the time we use more technology to being close of our family, relatives, friends, we are farer than others, aliens, strangers, and so forth. The founding parents of sociology envisaged an apocalyptic world, where social ties disappeared by the advance of industrialization. To what extent this has occurred seems to be a question very hard to grasp (Germann-Molz 2014). At a closer look, the problem is not whether the media technology undermines the social bond; rather it is important to understand what types of relations it creates. Following this argument, a good point in the discussion arises. Is the metaphor of paradise fabricated by tourism what wakes up the needs to divorce?

Tourism as a Metaphor of Paradise

The recent prominence of tourism and its positive impacts on local economies led to over-valorize its economic nature. However, beyond the profits it generates, it still exhibits a social dynamic, enrooted in what anthropologists known as "rite of passages". Korstanje & Busby (2010) clarify that tourism may be equaled to a rite of passage that marks workers as leisure consumers, no less true is that we need to take distance from rules in a temporarily way. Holidays are inscribed to give society a space of revitalization, which is enrooted in the Hebraic belief of purification. As Campbell put it, the concept of paradise consists in remind the problems behind human´s greed. In this respect, etymologically the term derives from Persian Pairi (outskirts) and Daeza (prohibited or damned space). Because of the original sin, Bible says, humankind has fired from paradise. This evokes not only the idea of a lost-state of harmony between humans and Gods, but also a new sense of sins which needs to be expiated (Campbell 1968). In this respect, holidays can be seen as sacred-space of ritualization, where fire (sun) and water (sea) sublimates our souls. Whatever the case may be, Cohen adds, it is interesting not to lose the sight industrial societies have fabricated sacred paradises, emulating the lost-heaven which means a state of prosperity ended by the adoption of economy. Heaven as tourist destination are desired by two premier reasons, first it is related to the logic of consumption and grandiosity, but secondly it closes a privilege hermeneutic circle where only few are saved while the rest damned (Cohen 1982). The logic expressed as in-out from paradise was abundantly discussed in the ethnological anthropology (Maccannell, 1976; Korstanje, 2009, 2015; Salazar 2010). Any travel opens a temporal line of action, which are merged into a new subjective logic. The vital cycle theories, as it has been formulated by Victor Turner, evinces how symbolism is manufactured and altered following economic cycles, which are part of passages people face when they pass to superior statuses. The idea of rites of passage alludes to mark a person to change its status. This takes part of the theory of socialization, which formally may be articulated to three transitional phases, separation, liminality and incorporation. The first stage encourages people (candidates) to conduct a "detachment" from their original group. Once this is done, candidates are subject to liminal space (in-between states) which explains that one are not formally incorporated to the new group, but does not belong to the former one. This transition is accommodated to a last phase, anthropologists known as re-aggregation, where candidates are formally included in their new status and groups. Far from being harmonious, the vital cycles stimulate profound states of crisis, or ruptures between two worlds, the older and the newer ones which lead the candidate into a new status. The rites of passages exhibit a re-socialization of candidates to be replaced in new reference groups (Turner, 1999). Tourism, in respect to this, may be defined as a type of rites of passage since it contains all its elements (Cohen 1985; Korstanje & Busby, 2010; Noy & Cohen, 2012; Thirkettle & Korstanje, 2013).

Some specialists as Graburn (1983), Krippendorf (1982), Dos Santos (2005), Hiernaux (2000) & Lacanau (2003) confirmed not only that displacement produces anxieties and a rule change, but it wakes up an existential crisis which is regulated by a much profound archetype, posed by the society. Tourists are subject to rites of passage to validate their adscription to society, their rules and cultural values. Once they return to home, the most vital values of societies have been accepted and embraced. However, what is still unclear is why these idealized travels, whether most important for societal order as specialist discussed, are being the main reason of divorce. Marc Augé considers that tourism is an "impossible travel", which is based on the allegory of what is unreal. This fantasy is feed by "stereotyped forms of contact", where the "other is commoditized to fulfill the tourist´s needs. As a dream, the tourist travel appeals to create an impossible but desirable world where the discovery is closed to the visual hegemony of mass-media (Auge 1998).

Last but not least, Dean Maccannell made a diagnosis where tourism allows the formation of a "meth-pragmatic discourse" to legitimate the current economic production. In this stance, Maccannell´s viewpoint does not differ from Krippendorf. However, the American sociologist introduces the concept of "alienation" to explain why workers use tourism as a valve of "escapement". Breaking the rules of work at least temporarily entails not only a psychological revitalization for the Work-force, but also the acceptance of those cultural values (as consumption, hedonism or money) that are enrooted in the capitalist ethos. Nonetheless, here is in the way Maccannell sees tourism, first-world tourists are not ethical agents since they are not interested in coping with more peripheral others, nor in considering the world the "Others" have. What "the Other" gives me is only important according to my western stereotypes. In respect to this, "the other" serves as a commodity to meet my own desires. To put this in bluntly, tourism is to modern society what "totems" is for primitive mind. Both coadjuvates so that the society keeps united (Maccannell, 1976; 1992; 2001).

This archetype of lost-paradise is of paramount importance in marketing and managerial appliances because of two main assumptions. On one hand, the sociology of consumption has explored the dichotomy produced by expectances and its effects on consuming behavior. Whenever, ideals are higher than the affordable means that people followed, violence surfaces. At some extent, emphasis on the dream-destination may derive in pathological reactions whether the goals are not achieved. In some cases, this violence is channeled towards the couple aggravating a conflict-ridden situation that later is crystalized in a divorce. On another, to the already existent negative effects of tourism in communities, divorce still is unchecked. Though this matter has received little attention, it represents a fertile ground to understand post vacation syndrome. In this vein, the present chapter is aimed at responding to what an extent holidays and divorce would be inextricably linked.

Methodological Discussion

The information was provided by official institution Department of Statistics of Buenos Aires. It is based on the number of recorded divorces from 1990 to 2012. Though the information gathered here has not dispersions, it is limited only to Buenos Aires city, ignoring other provinces of Argentina. Quite from that, the outcomes obtained here are statistically representative of inhabitants of Buenos Aires and cannot be extrapolated to other contexts. The information was centered on separation legal proceedings initiated by one of the parts. Once the sentences are firm, the civil courts make publish all cases in the official website of Gobierno de la ciudad de Buenos Aires (Buenos Aires city Government). Since it does not imply any real fieldwork, the information is validated by means of three story lives tape-recorded from 2007-2010. Story of life is a method enrooted into ethnography, and as a qualitative instrument allows expand the understanding of complex issues otherwise would remain unchecked.

Divorce and Holidays

The present section contains statistical information obtained from the official department of Statistics of Buenos Aires, Government and Information managed by Dirección General de Estadística y Censos (Ministerio de Hacienda GCBA). Estadísticas Vitales (General Direction of statistics and Census, Ministry of Economy, GCBA. It is important to remind that outcomes of this research are not based on samples which are statistically representative Argentina all; for that reason, extrapolations beyond the present unit of analysis are not recommendable. The information discussed in this section applies only for Buenos Aires City, Buenos Aires Distrito Capital.

Table 1 evinces how the rate of divorce is not rising spectacularly. The rate of divorce, estimated in 1.000 inhabitants) reveals that in 1990 were 2.78 while this decreased to 1.9 for 2012.

Table 1. Rate of divorces (per 1.000 inhabitants)

	Rate Div.
1990	2,78
1995	2
2000	2
2005	2,3
2010	2,2
2012	1,9

Source: Office of statistics, Buenos Aires Government

However, if further attention is posed on the relation concerning marriage, the ciphers must be revisited.

In 1990 the divorce´s index, calculated from dividing the number of divorce over marriage, pulled out 36.4, in 1995, 35.4 which remained to 2000 in 35.8. Nonetheless, a radical shift is observed in 2005 and 2010. The index rose from 47.9 in 2005 to 49.2 in 2010. As experts agree, the rate of divorce, expressed in its index is being increasing in the time. Although the gross rate of divorces remained, even showing a subtle decrease, not only marriages have been slumped but also their weights in the divorces have been marginal in many senses (see Table 3).

Another interpretation may shed light on this whether we pay attention to Table 2, shown above, which indicates that in 2012 the 5.866 divorces, where 1206 are registered within 9 years of marriage, 1924 between 10-19 years and surprisingly, 2160 more than 20 years. The major numbers of divorces are related to couples of 20 years of marriage, which evinces the tendency of social decline or decomposition. In these terms, those couples ranged from 35-39 years of marriage have further divorces (1139 cases) than other cohorts. In consonant with the literature, this means that the experience in life-related marriage is not a valid variable to explain why people divorce. However, we have no further information whether the divorces are produced by holidays (see Table 4).

In 2012, January was the month with fewest cases of divorces, 206 followed by February with 359. Apparently, ciphers reveals that holidays are not a direct variable that explains the divorces, lest by this cipher escalates to 609 divorces by March. The index calculated by the percentage of divorces respecting to the total amount documented in 2012 indicates that in February we pass from an index of 6.12 to 10.38. Not surprisingly, months as October with 604, November 543 and December 524 register its

Table 2. Relation divorces/marriages

	Divorces	**Marriages**	**Index**
1990	7993	21966	36,4
1995	6005	16966	35,4
2000	6007	16766	35,8
2005	7045	14713	47,9
2010	6594	13390	49,2
2012	5866	12667	46,3

Source: Office of statistics, Buenos Aires Government

Table 3. Divorces per age, 2012 (marriage average length)

	Total	1-4 Years	5-9 Years	10-19 Years	20 or More
Total	5866	572	1206	1924	2161
20-24	30	17	13	-	-
25-29	262	123	121	18	-
30-34	816	227	384	205	-
35-39	1139	118	398	605	18
40-44	1003	31	162	607	203
45-49	910	21	63	276	550
50-54	729	12	21	113	583
55-59	445	10	18	52	365
60 +	495	9	15	36	435
Others	37	4	11	12	7

Table 4. Divorces per month or season, 2012

	Month	Index
January	216	3,68
February	359	6,12
March	609	10,38
April	477	8,13
May	552	9,41
June	572	9,75
July	402	6,85
August	527	8,98
September	488	8,32
October	604	10,30
November	536	9,14
December	524	8,93
Total	**5866**	

zenith, which lead us to say that holidays pave the ways for couples to present the proceeding for a legal separation to the corresponding to the competent authority. Gathering months in the trimester (jan-feb and March) we find alternative interesting observations.

The first trimester sums 1184 divorces, while the last one (Oct-Nov and Dec) appreciates a substantial more important cipher, 1664 proceedings. In view of this information, holidays are not the real cause of divorce but the key dates that alter the social bondage of family in some way. Starting from the premise that the major divorces are found in earlier month than charismas and New Year, than summer seasons, we understand that the emotional rupture are accelerated by the entrance of a new year, because it represents a "rite of passage" where the vital cycles of social life are revitalized, regenerated or broken. At some extent, this liminal process would engender some long-simmering conflicts which led the couple to the fragmentation. Although these statistics are not providing conclusive evidence, some hints are triggered to be continued in next approaches. Most likely, the post vocational stress would be not self-explanatory about why couples divorce more today.

Rodrigo, Maria and Juan

Because of time and space, it is difficult to synthetize the information of almost 3 years in few words. Following the ethical guidelines of anthropology and ethnology, real names are tergiversated an in any case individual behavior or information about interviewees is revealed. Rodrigo is male, Argentinian of 45 years old. He was married in three occasions in all cases they ended in failures. The last one took 10 years and gave a boy. Rodrigo is a middle-class clerk employed in the services of tourism. He is not only an experienced leading tour-guide, but also one of the well-recognized professional of travels in Buenos Aires. Professionally, he took part of many project invested by private sector as well as state. Per his testimony, one of the aspects that resonated in the decision to ask divorce to his wife, was the asymmetry of wages of the couple. While Rodrigo earned a salary of 10.000 per month, his wife doubled him to 20.000 in a monthly basis. When we asked what the reason behind divorce was, he replied,

Undoubtedly the lack of confidence on my wife was the key factor I opted for the legal separation. I decided to break the relation after 10 long years, particularly, we quarreled all time but the conflict reaches its peak whenever we are proxy to an important date, as birthday, baptism, holidays, or Christmas. This is ironically what I dealt with my therapist, these dates are pure celebrations one should be happy, not sad or drank because of the claims of my wife.

Rodrigo, nowadays, acknowledges he is happier and has the time for himself. In which case may be, he never had an affair beyond marriage with other woman until he was divorced. This, for him, was very important to keep things in a straight. "I opted to divorce from my wife, because love has gone forever, I feel sometimes people are not free to make this decision. If you ask me, guilt, which is experienced by infidelity, plays a crucial role to keep the marriage though both sides are not happy". Last but not least, he ensures this situation was better for him, his wife and the son the couple has in common.

Rather, Maria, who is 30 years old, was a businesswoman of tourism with high reputation in the market. Instead of Rodrigo, she kept an affair with other person almost 8 years. This infidelity made her thinking the idea of having children was not a good one. Instead of getting nervous at time of holidays or traveling, Maria was invited by Juan (her husbands) to exotic landscapes or fist class cruises but without any result. Beyond the privilege status this couple had, she never quarreled to him nor was hostile to be alone at home while he travelled. Not only the trust in the couple plummeted, but the lack of conflict was conducive to a sentiment of culprit that resulted in an ambiguous situation. This impeded for couple to separate, but induced them into a sentiment of secrecy that that paved the ways for the surge of infidelity. During his travels, Juan kept multiple romantic affairs which were kept under secrecy as well. United by an attachment to their economic position, both recurred to infidelity to save the couple. They, rarely, experienced situation of panic or anxiety while traveling together, but both re-directed their sentiments towards their respective mates of affairs. Evidence discussed here evinces two important assumptions. On one hand, holidays are not key factors towards divorce unless the couple is experiencing a situation of conflict; in which case, the hostility may rise. Since holidays are considered as a rite of passage, which means that rules are temporarily altered, an unresolved state of discrepancy may lead unknown channels. On another, in modern times tourism evolved under a paradoxical condition. At the time leisure industries play a vital role revitalizing the psychological deprivations suffered during the year, but it triggers some unexpected results which need further attention. The post-vacational syndrome offers an interesting conceptual framework to discuss to what extent, the inflation of hedonism and pleasure may connect with undesired consequences.

Managerial Implications

Why incorporating anthropological discussion to management studies? It is interesting to see how anthropology is a discipline that describes scientifically human organizations, no matter than their nature. Though from its inception, it associates to the role of native (as "other") in an ever changing world, fascinating approaches were given to the fields of management and marketing. In this vein, policy makers have devoted considerable time and efforts in designing the allegory of lost-paradise in tourism destinations. As a rite of passage, tourism enables the engagement of people with others, to see in their inner-world. Not only as a mechanism of escapement but inscribed in the core of production, tourism revitalize the social ties necessary for the society not to collapse. As social parents of sociology showed, touring is a good instrument to enhance the trust in the community. At time, the rise of divorce is an unquestionable reality, in some conditions irreversible, to what extent it is accelerated by tourism and holidays is one of the contributions this chapter offers. Psychologically speaking, travels may be considered as channels towards mental health, but in some conditions the worse come to worst. Travel may work dysfunctional accelerating serious problems or misbehaviors as drug-abuse, conflict and riots, and alcohol intoxications.

CONCLUSION

First and foremost, this exploratory study is framed on sources which are statistically representative, so findings should be limited to the present unit of analysis. Further, the collated evidence gives a new insight on the post-vacation distress syndrome, timidly explored by experimental psychology. Neither leisure-travels nor holidays produce the crisis that led couples towards legal separations alone but what Turner baptized as "crisis of vital cycles". Not only understanding tourism, but Christmas and New Year's celebrations as well as vital cycles, Turner argues that cultures elaborate rites of passage in order for the Gods to be thanked or claimed for the prosperity achieved or the material deprivation suffered. In this stage, everything can happen. Whenever social ties are not strong enough, as the case for modern social life, the involving group faces discrepancies and conflicts, which if not dully regulated may lead to decomposition. The global tendency to divorce not only seems to be unquestionable, but also advocates for the concern of founding parents of sociology, that indicates ties are being weakened. Limitations of this research should be detailed in view of the fact the sample has been drawn on the divorces of 2012 in Buenos Aires city (Registro Civil de la Ciudad de Buenos Aires). Since, the employed methods of sampling are changing by local government in annually basis it almost impossible to compare information year by year. This was the reason why qualitative ethnography complemented the already-produced outcomes. The qualitative research reveals that when the couple keeps its fidelity, rites of passage may lead to divorce if conflict is not reduced. Rather, in case one of the sides is committing adultery, the conflict is undermined and holidays do not represent a threat for marriage. This does not mean the couple will not break into pieces later. Anthropologically, tourism, even holidays are framed as a rite of passage, in which case laws, rules and loyalties are temporarily suspended or upended. If the couple is experiencing serious problems, no less true is that the likelihoods of further hostile atmosphere may arise. Though evidence is not conclusive, it opens the doors for further research that expands the current horizons of investigation in tourism fields. Divorced or sole travellers very well still are a segment which has been ignored from the specialized literature in marketing as to date. This represents a fertile ground for next approaches.

REFERENCES

Augé, M. (1998). *El viaje imposible: el turismo y sus imágenes*. Barcelona: Editorial Gedisa.

Baltzell, D. E. (1991). *The Protestant Establishment revisited*. New Brunswick, NJ: Transaction Publishers.

Buell, F. (1994). *National culture and the new global system*. Baltimore, MD: JHU Press.

Cantallops, A. S., & Cardona, J. R. (2015). Holiday destinations: The myth of the lost paradise? *Annals of Tourism Research*, *55*(4), 171–173. doi:10.1016/j.annals.2015.10.002

Chalmers, W. D. (2013). *America's Vacation Deficit Disorder: Who Stole Your Vacation?* Bloomington, IL: Universe.

Cohen, E. (1982). "The Pacific Islands, from utopian myth to consumer Product". *The Disenchantment Paradise. Cathiers du Turisme, Serie B.*, *27*, 1–17.

Cohen, E. (1985). Tourism as play. *Religion*, *15*(3), 291–304. doi:10.1016/0048-721X(85)90016-8

Deem, R. (1996). No time for a rest? An exploration of women's work, engendered leisure and holidays. *Time & Society*, 5.1, 5-25.

Dos Santos, J. R. (2005). Antropología, comunicación y turismo: la mediación cultural en la construcción del espacio turístico de una comunidad de pescadores en Laguna, Sc. Brasil. *Estudios y Perspectivas en Turismo*, *14*(4), 293-313.

Durkheim, E. (1997). *The division of labor in society*. New York, NY: Simon and Schuster.

George, B. P., Inbakaran, R., & Poyyamoli, G. (2010). To Travel or Not to travel: towards understanding the theory of nativistic motivation. *Turizam: znanstveno-stručni časopis*, *58*(4), 395-407.

Germann Molz, J. (2014). *Travel Connection: Tourism, technology and togetherness in a mobile world*. Abingdon, UK: Routledge.

Giddens, A. (1971). *Capitalism and modern social theory: An analysis of the writings of Marx, Durkheim and Max Weber*. Cambridge, UK: Cambridge University Press. doi:10.1017/CBO9780511803109

Giddens, A. (1992). *The transformations of intimacy*. Cambridge, MA: Polity.

Graburn, N. H. (1983). the Anthropology of Tourism. *Annals of Tourism Research*, *10*(1), 1–9. doi:10.1016/0160-7383(83)90110-X

Hiernaux, N. (2000). La fuerza de lo efímero. In *En Alicia Lindon Villoria (comp). La vida cotidiana y su espacio-temporalidad*. Editorial Anthropos.

Hiltunen, P., Jokelainen, J., Ebeling, H., Szajnberg, N., & Moilanen, I. (2004). Seasonal variation in postnatal depression. *Journal of Affective Disorders*, *78*(2), 111–118. doi:10.1016/S0165-0327(02)00239-2 PMID:14706721

Himitian, E. (2012). Hubo más de medio millón de divorcios en la última década. *La Nación*. Available http://www.lanacion.com.ar/1453694-hubo-mas-de-medio-millon-de-divorcios-en-la-ultima-decada

Inglehart, R. (1997). *Modernization and Postmodernization. Cultural, economic, and political change in 43 societies*. Princeton, NJ: Princeton University Press.

Kevan, S. M. (1993). Quests for cures: A history of tourism for climate and health. *International Journal of Biometeorology*, *37*(3), 113–124. doi:10.1007/BF01212620 PMID:7691761

Korstanje, M. (2007). The Origin and meaning of Tourism: An ethimologycal study. *E-Review of Tourism Resarch*, *5*(5), 100–108.

Korstanje, M. (2009). "Interpretando el Génesis del Descanso: Una aproximación a los mitos y rituales del turismo". *Pasos. Revista de Turismo y Patrimonio Cultural*, *7*(1), 99–113.

Korstanje, M. (2015). Entry: Paradise Tourism. In *Encyclopedia of tourism. Jafar Jafari & Xiao Honggen. Print to head*. Wien: Springer.

Korstanje, M., & Busby, G. (2010). Understanding the Bible as the roots of physical displacement: The origin of tourism. *E-Review of Tourism Research*, *8*(3), 95–111.

Krippendorf, J. (1982). Towards new tourism policies: The importance of environmental and sociocultural factors. *Tourism Management*, *3*(3), 135–148. doi:10.1016/0261-5177(82)90063-2

Krippendorf, J. (2010). *Holiday makers*. Oxford, UK: Taylor & Francis.

Lacanau, G. (2003). *El rito sagrado de las vacaciones: alimentos y género en la Argentina de 1930-1950. In Gastronomía y Turismo: cultura al plato* (pp. 203–216). Buenos Aires: CIET.

MacCannell, D. (1973). Staged authenticity: Arrangements of social space in tourist settings. *American Journal of Sociology*, *79*(3), 589–603. doi:10.1086/225585

MacCannell, D. (1976). *The tourist: A new theory of the leisure class*. Berkeley, CA: University of California Press.

MacCannell, D. (1984). Reconstructed ethnicity tourism and cultural identity in third world communities. *Annals of Tourism Research*, *11*(3), 375–391. doi:10.1016/0160-7383(84)90028-8

MacCannell, D. (1988). Turismo e Identidad [Tourism & identity]. Madrid: Juncar.

MacCannell, D. (1992). *Empty meeting grounds: The tourist papers*. London: Routledge. doi:10.4324/9780203412145

MacCannell, D. (1992). *Empty meeting grounds: The tourist papers*. London: Routledge. doi:10.4324/9780203412145

MacCannell, D. (2001). Tourist agency. *Tourist Studies*, *1*(1), 23–37. doi:10.1177/146879760100100102

MacCannell, D. (2011). *The ethics of sightseeing*. Berkeley, CA: University of California Press. doi:10.1525/california/9780520257825.001.0001

MacCannell, D. (2012). On the ethical stake in tourism research. *Tourism Geographies*, *14*(1), 183–194. doi:10.1080/14616688.2012.639387

Meethan, K. (2003). Mobile Cultures? hybridity, tourism and cultural change. *Journal of Tourism and Cultural Change*, *1*(1), 11–28. doi:10.1080/14766820308668157

Meethan, K. (2004). To stand in the shores of my ancestors. In T. Coles & D. Timothy (Eds.), *Tourism, Disaporas and Space* (pp. 139–150). London: Routledge.

Meethan, K. (2006). Introduction: narratives of place and self. In Tourism Consumption and Representation. CABI.

Meethan, K. (2014). Mobilities, Ethnicities and Tourism. In A. Lew, M. C. Hall, & A. Williams (Eds.), *Tourism*. New York, NY: Willey Blackwell. doi:10.1002/9781118474648.ch19

Merklen, D. (2013). Las Dinámicas contemporáneas de la individuación. In *Individuación, precariedad, inseguridad*. Buenos Aires: Paidos.

Nisbet, R. A. (1993). *The sociological tradition*. New Brunswick, NJ: Transaction publishers.

Noy, C., & Cohen, E. (Eds.). (2012). *Israeli backpackers: From tourism to rite of passage*. New York: SUNY Press.

Putnam, R. D. (1995). Bowling alone: America's declining social capital. *Journal of Democracy*, *6*(1), 65–78. doi:10.1353/jod.1995.0002

Salazar, N. B. (2010). Towards an anthropology of cultural mobilities. *Crossings: Journal of Migration & Culture*, *1*(1), 53–68.

Seaton, A. V. (1998). The history of tourism in Scotland: Approaches, sources and issues. *Tourism in Scotland*, *1*(2), 35–41.

Thirkettle, A., & Korstanje, M. E. (2013). Creating a new epistemiology for tourism and hospitality disciplines. *International Journal of Qualitative Research in Services*, *1*(1), 13–34. doi:10.1504/IJQRS.2013.054342

Towner, J. (1985). The Grand Tour: A key phase in the history of tourism. *Annals of Tourism Research*, *12*(3), 297–333. doi:10.1016/0160-7383(85)90002-7

Towner, J., & Wall, G. (1991). History and tourism. *Annals of Tourism Research*, *18*(1), 71–84. doi:10.1016/0160-7383(91)90040-I

Tzanelli, R. (2007). *The cinematic tourist: Explorations in globalization, culture and resistance*. Abingdon, UK: Routledge.

Urry, J. (1988). Cultural change and contemporary holiday-making. *Theory, Culture & Society*, *5*(1), 35–55. doi:10.1177/026327688005001003

Urry, J. (2002). *The Tourist Gaze*. London: Sage.

Virilio, P. (2006). Velocidad y política: Ensayo sobre dromología [Speed and politics: An essay on dromology]. Los Angeles, CA: Semiotext (e).

ADDITIONAL READING

Battuta, I. (2004). Travels in Asia and Africa: 1325-1354. Abingdon: Routledge.

Bishop, J. P. (1852). *Commentaries on the Law of Marriage and Divorce, and Evidence in Matrimonial Suits* (Vol. 2). New York, NY: Little, Brown.

Cohen, E. (1979). Rethinking the sociology of tourism. *Annals of Tourism Research*, 6(1), 18–35. doi:10.1016/0160-7383(79)90092-6

Cohen, E. (1984). The sociology of tourism: Approaches, issues, and findings. *Annual Review of Sociology*, 10(1), 373–392. doi:10.1146/annurev.so.10.080184.002105

Corsaro, W. A. (1997). *The sociology of childhood* (pp. 4–5). Thousand Oaks, CA: Pine Forge Press.

Eco, U. (1986). *Travels in hyper reality: essays*. New York, NY: Houghton Mifflin Harcourt.

Giddens, A., Duneier, M., & Appelbaum, R. P. (2003). *Introduction to sociology*. New York, NY: Norton.

Grabher, G. (2006). Trading routes, bypasses, and risky intersections: Mapping the travels of networks' between economic sociology and economic geography. *Progress in Human Geography*, 30(2), 163–189. doi:10.1191/0309132506ph600oa

Kitson, G. C., Babri, K. B., & Roach, M. J. (1985). Who divorces and why A review. *Journal of Family Issues*, 6(3), 255–293. doi:10.1177/019251385006003002 PMID:12313803

Korstanje, M. (2007). "Aportes de los viajes a las Ciencias Sociales: un relevamiento bibliográfico para un análisis teórico". Gest. tur.(Valdivia), 8, 25-46.

Korstanje, M. (2015). Constructing the Other by Means of Hospitality: The Case of Argentina. *Cultura (Asociación de Docentes de la Universidad de San Martín de Porres)*, 12(1), 145–157.

Mayo, E. J., & Jarvis, L. P. (1981). *The psychology of leisure travel. Effective marketing and selling of travel services. Wellingford*. CABI Publishing Company, Inc.

Rojek, C. (1993). *Ways of escape: Modern transformations in leisure and travel*. New York, NY: Macmillan Press Ltd. doi:10.1057/9780230373402

Smart, C., Neale, B., & Wade, A. (2001). *The changing experience of childhood: Families and divorce*. Cambridge: Polity Press.

Thornes, B., & Collard, J. (1979). *Who divorces?* Abingdon: Routledge.

Tzanelli, R. (2004). Constructing the 'cinematic tourist' The 'sign industry' of The Lord of the Rings. *Tourist Studies*, 4(1), 21–42. doi:10.1177/1468797604053077

Tzanelli, R. (2011). The Sociology of Tourism: European Origins and Development. *Tourism Analysis, 15*(6), 755–759.

Tzanelli, R. (2013). "On Avatar: digital commerce as activist pedagogy?".*Connexions: international professional communication journal\ revista de comunicação profissional internacional, 1.*1, 1-4.

Urry, J. (2003). Social networks, travel and talk1. *The British Journal of Sociology, 54*(2), 155–175. doi:10.1080/0007131032000080186 PMID:12945865

Urry, J. (2012). *Sociology beyond societies: Mobilities for the twenty-first century.* Abingdon: Routledge.

KEY TERMS AND DEFINITIONS

Divorce: Legal separation conferred to a couple to terminate a marriage.

Holidays: Leave given legally to after performing a job during a specific lapse of time.

Social Ties: In sociology the term is used to denote the reciprocity between two or more sides.

Vital Cycles: Term coined by Victor Turner to evince some organization changes that mould the life and identity of community.

Section 2
Global Dynamics in Tourism

The second section of the edited book consists of seven chapters and focuses on tourism related aspects. The chapters discuss contemporary issues concerning tourism related post-conflict perspectives; women's role in innovation and internationalisation; digital marketing; rural wellbeing; risk and crisis management; and methodological insights on tourism research.

Chapter 6
Tourism in East Timor:
Post-Conflict Perspectives

Thiago Allis
University of São Paulo (USP), Brazil

Maria Helena Mattos Barbosa dos Santos
Universidade Federal de São Carlos (UFSCar), Brazil

ABSTRACT

The objective of this chapter is to organize, analyze and discuss information on tourism development in the Democratic Republic of East Timor, based on efforts from "development partners" countries between 2007 and 2011, principles of 2011 Development Strategic Plan (PED) and government programs from 2007 on. The analytical framework emerges from discussions on tourism in post-conflict countries and dependence and autonomy issues within post-colonial contexts. From a methodological perspective, reflections on East Timor are result of reading and government programs analysis since 2007, PED (2011-2030) and international cooperation reports from May 2012. In short, one observes in parallel to the slow growth of tourism in the island and the increase of the relevance of this issue in national documents that objective actions on behalf of tourism development in East Timor have been virtually absent in terms of international cooperation– even though they have been indirectly identifiable.

INTRODUCTION

East Timor is a small insular country in Southeast Asia, located between northern Australia and eastern Indonesia (Sunda Islands), occupying 15,000km^2, consisting of two parts of Timor Island: half east and the Oe-Cusse enclave on the west, besides Ataúro Island on the north and Jaco Islet the east. Nowadays, the country has approximately 1.1 million people, speaking over twenty languages, among which the most expressive ones are Tétum, Mambae and Makasai. In 2002, the Constitution of the Democratic Republic of East Timor established Portuguese and Tétum as official languages, but Bahasa Indonesia, English and – to a far lesser extent – Mandarin are still used.

With over 70% of population living in the countryside, the country is divided in thirteen districts and 62 sub-districts, and has only two expressive urban agglomerations: Díli, the capital with approximately 230,000 inhabitants, and Baucau, 80km East of Díli, with approximately 60,000 inhabitants. The northern

DOI: 10.4018/978-1-5225-0201-2.ch006

Figure 1. Timorese-Indonesian border at Butugadé
(Source: Thiago Allis, 2012)

coast of the island is connected by road, linking the Indonesian border, in the city of Batugadé (Figure 1), with far East inTutuala, from where one accesses Jaco Islet (Figure 2).

The South Coast has fewer infrastructures however, but with the perspective of the oil sector developmenton-shore, it is expected that new cities such as Nova Suai, Nova Betano and Nova Viqueque will be built (Lao Hamutuk, 2013). Nowadays, off-shore oil production in Mar do Sul is the country's economic mainstay, accounting for almost 100% of revenues, virtually the main export product (plus, in small amount, coffee in the regionsof Ermera, Maubisse, Aileu and Liquiçá). With mechanisms

Figure 2. Partial view of Jaco Islet
(Source: Thiago Allis, 2012)

prescribed by the 2005 Petroleum Fund Law, the country can invest resources from oil production in financial assets abroad, making annual withdrawals for the composition of State budget. In March 2015, the Petroleum Fund had reached US$ 16.8 billion, and the investment return in the first quarter this year reached US$ 226.2 million (or 1.38% on the total). This year, 70% of the country's general budget (US$ 915 million) will be covered with the revenues from the Petroleum Fund (Ministry of Finance of East Timor [MFTL], 2015).

Tourism today is an important issue in the political agenda of East Timor, though with limited economic contribution when compared to oil exploration and agriculture. In spite of extensive limitation of basic and tourism infrastructure, tourist arrivals show significant growth in recent years: 144,565 for the period 2006-2010 and, only in 2013, it increased to 77,868, given civil and political stabilization (Breda & Ferreira, 2013, Thomaz, 2008; Tolkach et al, 2007). More recently a slight decay has been observed (around 60,000 in 2014), probably related to the progressive withdraw of personnel of United Nations (UN) and aid agencies after 2012, when the last peace mission was concluded. It has to be assumed that many travelers recorded as "tourists" by immigration authorities are, in fact, temporary workers or voluntary in charge of cooperation duties.

In 2014, Timorese government has scheduled investments of US$ 2.57 million for tourism projects – though only 41.7% of that amount was disbursed. When considered the item "Travel and Tourism" on the Balance of Payments for the years 2009 and 2011, there has been a clear imbalance: US$ 58 million and US$ 48 million in imports, respectively, and US$ 16 million and US$ 21 million of exports (Banco Central Timorense[BCTL], 2014).

In that panorama, it seems reasonable to understand, with more detail, the role of tourism in the political and economic agenda of this country, considering similar contexts in another nations emerged from separatist and racial conflicts, or even natural disasters of great proportions – where similarly international organizations also had key importance, such as in East Timor since the first intervention in 1999.

Aiming at organizing, analyzing and reflecting on initiatives of tourism development, considering specially the period after Independence restitution (2002) as well as the outcomes of international cooperation in Democratic Republic of East Timor, the authors have intended a historical reading of tourism development and the preliminary comprehension of the role attributed to this activity. For that purpose, three kinds of documents are analyzed: a) the Strategic Plan of Development (2011-2030), b) the reports developed by partner countries delivered in ceremony and made available to the public during the Meeting of East Timor Development Partners (TLDPM), written according a template developed by the National Board of Aid Effectiveness (NDAE) and the c) Programs of 4th, 5th and 6th Constitutional Government (2007-2012, 2012-2017 and 2015-2017, respectively). UN and UNDP reports were also considered – at first hand or from other studies, such as the one elaborated by Neves (2007) –, as well as reports elaborated by the Commission for Reception, Truth and Reconciliation of East Timor (CAVR).

In order to establish a theoretical framework, a literature review on post-conflict tourism has been undertaken, focused on in different places that emerged as tourist destinations or recovered its importance in the aftermath of local, regional or even global conflicts (Causevic & Lynch, 2011; Jallat & Schultz, 2010; Miles, 2010; Yasarata et al, 2010; Kim et al, 2007; Ioannides & Apostopoulos, 1999; Richter, 1999). The impacts of international cooperation on tourism development, the role attributed to this activity in the national political and economic agenda, as well as the issues that arise for the tourism development in countries in post-conflict context, in turn, was made considering perspectives of regional governance (Inácio et al, 2013), governance of international cooperation (Carrion & Santos, 2011), community-based tourism (Groot & Simons, 2015; Sanchez-Cañizares & Castilho-Canalejo, 2014), and tourism as tool for peace promoting (D'Alessandro-Scarpari, 2011).

In a short, the objectives of this chapter are:

- To discuss the prospects of tourism development in post-conflict contexts.
- To understand the historical process of development of tourism in East Timor, by investigating the role of tourism on the political and economic agenda of the country.
- To highlight and analyze the impact of international cooperation in tourism development in East Timor.

EAST TIMOR: SELF-DETERMINATION AND AUTONOMOUS DEVELOPMENT

East Timor was a Portuguese colony since the beginning of the sixteenth century until 1975, when the events of Revolução dos Cravos [Carnation Revolution] (1974), in Portugal, made room for an independence movement that led to a civil war, particularly because of Portugal omission about a decolonization plan (responsibility already previewed in UN Resolution 1514 of 1960, with the Declaration on Independence Concession to Countries and Colonial Peoples) and a colonialist-focused military regime in Indonesia, that had become independent from the Netherlands in 1949. Within this scenario, East Timor (then known as "Portuguese Timor"), a half-island in the Indonesian archipelago with over 18 thousand islands, was invaded by Indonesia in December 1975, that conducted a truculent military campaign supported by integrationalist forces of East Timor and some collusion of the USA – which, having recently suffered setbacks in Vietnam feared a diffusion of socialist movements in Asia.

For 25 years Indonesia imposed vile and inhuman measures upon Timorese people that resulted in the death of about ⅓ of the population, so that the region, considered the 27th province of Indonesia, started to draw more attention from the international community only in the 90's, particularly after the massacre of Santa Cruz, in 1991, carried out by the Indonesian army (TNI) on civilians during a demonstration in memory of student Sebastião Gomes – whose gravesite still attracts attention of Timorese and international visitors as well (Figure 3).

Figure 3. Gravesite of Sebastião Gomes, at Santa Cruz Cemetery
(Source: Thiago Allis, 2012)

The event was recorded and broadcasted by journalist Max Stahl. It was also a moment in which the *status quo* of Indonesian dictatorship was already breaking up, due to the resignation of dictator Haji Mohammed Soeharto in 1998 and constant public pressure – in favor of East Timor, even within Indonesia – and an economic crisis unfolding in the most populous country in Southeast Asia. Through UN (with direct participation of General Secretary Kofi Anan) and Portuguese diplomacy, besides several fronts of Timorese resistance (domestically and internationally), the Resolution 1279 of UN Security Council in May 1999 that became known as "New York Agreement", established an understanding with Indonesia for a consultation on the autonomy of the country, which would be ratified by 78.5% of voters on August 30th 1999.

Indonesia's departure was traumatic and left a scenario of material and human destruction, resulting in UN intervention through a peace mission (INTERFET), followed by other three missions, until 2002, under the leadership of Brazilian Sérgio Vieira de Mello (Transitorial Administration in East Timor [UNTAET]). This was unprecedented "unlike any previous peacekeeping operation", compared to UN "interim administration" in Kosovo. In East Timor, "for the first time, UN had sovereign control over a territory that it aimed to prepare for Independence. In other words, it was a case of agreement between UN government and the strategic objective of establishing an independent State". (Faria, 2011, p. 2). Since then, there have been five missions approved by the Security Council, with the latest of them (Integrate Mission for East Timor [UNMIT]) concluded in December 2012, after many renewals over the last decade.

After over 10 years of the first East Timor Constitution promulgation, there is a perspective of "peace-building", with consolidation of "peacekeeping" operations during the first years after the 1999 referendum. As an independent country, a local political, economic and social situation presents a series of changes, such as consolidation of electoral procedures, administrative institutions (still under way), implementation and recovery of infrastructures (such as electric power, mainly in the Capital), a system of justice, censuses and data analysis, among others. However, there are still important and persistent fragilities (the country holds the 120th position in the HDI ranking) that impose very unfavorable life conditions on Timorese people.

Within this context, support from the international community has focused on areas of immanent need, whose actions are distributed among UN official missions (with essential focus on security) several of its agencies (UNDP, ILO, WHO, WFP, UN Women, UNESCO, World Bank, Red Cross, among others) and specific projects of "development partners", countries with which the Democratic Republic of East Timor has established bilateral agreements. The countries as "partners" – through their cooperation agencies – have developed specific actions, including projects on selected issues (education, agriculture, security, justice, etc.).

The efforts for recognizing the basic right to self-determination that qualified the decolonization process have been marked by the assertion of collective and national identities, the defense of State-nation sovereignty and its territory, as well as the right to national destiny determination in administrative, economic, social and cultural terms, through democratic, fair and free processes that avoid external constraints (CAVR, 2005, 2010). However, contemporary issues related to the building of collective identities, the notion of State as fixed entity and subordination of its identity to territory and political frontiers present new elements for reflection on courses of action by States-nations and peoples in designing proposals of autonomous development, conformation of networks and social systems, participation in international political and economic systems, particularly considering globalization singularities (Barata, 2010).

The rapid transformations after 2002, mainly the construction of national identities and institutions, drive the Timorese society to new and multicolored cultural references and values both on the level of the daily lives and the institutional systems. The transformations due to these circumstances, enhanced by interpretations of rooted references and the appropriation of external ones (Agier, 2011;Canclini, 2013), gradually give a further boost to new landscapes and social meanings: the influence of Díli stretches over the country, by the mobility of Timorense currently living in the capital (students, public staff, etc originally from the "distritos"), as well as international personnel of cooperation agencies throughout the country – not rarely, as tourists!

POST-CONFLICT TOURISM: A REPORTING ANALYSIS

Causevic and Lynch (2011) coined the term "Phoenix Tourism" referring to Bosnia-Herzegovina after the ethnic conflicts between 1992 and 1995, from a re-analysis of the practice of "double burial", as reports in Anthropology theory. In the case of tourism, instead of treating reminiscences of the conflict in a "dark" manner, they understand that beyond the solemnity required, it is necessary to offer a positive perspective in which tourism can be the economic and social leverage factor. The relation between these situations – conflict, war, terrorism and tourism – may take many forms and perspectives, both by the nature of the region (and the roots of the conflicts), and by the approach given to the theme in a tourist development project.

Rwanda, an African country plagued by genocide and civil war during the 90's nowadays has had in its process of national reconstruction (or even construction) tourism as economic mainstay: if between 1995 and 1998, the tourism sector represented 20% of its revenues, between 2005 and 2008 this figure reaches 36%; in contrast, coffee exports fell from 37% of revenues to 11% within the same periods. In amounts, tourism incomes of the country rose from US$ 6 million 1995 (height of conflicts) to over US$ 200 million in 2008, the year when the volume of foreign tourists climbed over 980,000 (Ansoms, 2005; Nielsen & Spenceley, 2010).

One could assume that gorillas are one of the main forces for tourism. They gained worldwide expression with the work of Diane Fossey (subsequently represented in a movie starred by Sigourney Weaver). Nowadays, the contact with animals – particularly at Volcanoes National Park – is extremely controlled, requiring investments contrasting with the profile of traditional international tourists. Whether because "gorillas tourism", or other national tourist resources (mainly natural ones), it is possible to analyze, after internal conflicts, invasions, wars or natural disasters, a recovery of tourist activity – or at least its strengthening and expansion in subsequent periods. This has also been the case of Cambodia, which after long years of civil war foresees its most prominent icon – Angkor Wat – as an exclusive tourist asset. A similar scenario can be found in Sri Lanka, which from a "model of success" went through bloody conflicts between Tamil ethnicity and the established government – and that recently, within an insular context, has been recovering the weight of sun and beach tourism (Richter, 1999).

In Lebanon, quite close to European outbound tourism markets, tourism is also included on the list of national strategies, even after years of conflicts and main cities' infrastructure destruction (Jallat & Schultz, 2010). Even Iraq and Kuwait, former stage of the Gulf War, seek to build an image of secure and progressive countries, like other small oil nations around (Qatar, Bahrein, United Arab Emirates). Ionannides and Apostopoulos (1999), in turn, draw the attention to gaps in the studies on tourism development in microstates or insular countries, criticizing overly managerial and economic approaches, without attention to ethnic conflict issues like those in Cyprus, Sri Lanka and New Caledonia. In the case of Cyprus, despite its territorial exiguity, the country is divided in two portions, with Turkish Republic of Northern Cyprus recognized only by Turkey. Thus, the discussion about tourism development involves incorporation of insular resources advantages, plus geo-political aspects regarding to balance or tension between both parties. The authors wonder if there would be political-institutional maturity for both parties so they could promote themselves jointly as an only destination in the face of certain mature products' wear and loss of competitiveness (for instance, beaches, available through all Mediterranean basin), something that Egypt and Israel, despite their historical differences have been able to manage (Ioannides & Apostopoulos, 1999, p. 55).

When the subject are borders and instable States, the Middle East, particularly Palestine, depicts an important reference. In the case of Jerusalem, where conflicts are current and go through alternate waves or retraction and upsurge, Miles (2010) seeks to understand the practices and narratives of religious tourism phenomena, border tourism and "alternative tours". Particularly in the case of borders, one of the border checkpoints between Israel and Jordan, despite its aesthetic expression, ends up being the focus of curiosity for the mere appeal of its meaning. One will predict the future for tourism in the countries of Middle East, depending on the course of the ISIS's actions and the reactions of neighbor and western nations.

Still on borders, tourism developed between the two Koreas – technically still at war – has been appointed as a path to facilitate their reconciliation. It is a fact that visits to the border end up being a practice filled with fetishism, although exposing the issue of fragmentation of two parties ethnically united, but physically separated. Kim et al (2007) remind that tourism between the two Koreas may stimulate understanding in two ways: government-government and people-people, in which both parties have to find their way to establish a joint program for Mount Gumang Resort (in the northern part), allowing people to travel during their leisure moments (therefore, tending to leave their grudges behind) between both sides of the border.

Through the study of tourist development theories in post-conflict countries, it is possible to understand manifold features among the many international cases, aiming at general axis regarding the concept of "post-conflict tourism". In fact, one of the repeated characteristics is the presence of international organizations (mainly UN and its agencies) as conductors of actions in which tourism is appointed as:

- An activity to be recovered, because of a past that used to have some importance in earlier times. Cambodia and Sri Lanka are examples, where there used to be some tourism activity. Most recently, countries that lived the "Arab Spring", where tourism was significant due to the articulation with European source markets, are under observation with regards to recovering of tourism in line with political changes, such as in Tunisia and Egypt (where tourism accounted for 10% of the countries' GDP);
- A sector to be built, for the cases whose previous context did not have tourism as a highlighted factor, but which in the process of reconstruction, certain elements are considered as potentials for tourism and therefore, where able to contribute to economic and social recovery. From the cases studied, one can mention Rwanda and Pakistan, although social, political and cultural complexities still impose challenges to its advancement. Nowadays, some initiatives for tourism development in Haiti and even in Iraq have been noticed, not without critics (Hsu & Aristil, 2014; Kim, 2013).

Intermediary situations could also be considered, once as small as they may be, almost all these countries used to have some expression of tourism (for instance, Haiti). However, the categorization here serves as a methodological strategy in order to provide an analytical framework that in future studies may be object of specification, detail and critic.

East Timor lies within the second case, once in periods preceding independence (2002), little or no tourism activity was observed: up to the end of Portuguese colonialism in the country (1974), the colony was just a pass-by port, so global connections (and tourism itself) were not broadcasted on sufficient global scale to incorporate the poor and isolated settlement. With Indonesian occupation that lasted until 1999, the concern was to keep the country closed, particularly because of critiques that might emerge as result of the way Indonesia tried to incorporate East Timor as one of its provinces (*Timor Timur*).

Therefore, one can say that tourism was an alternative to future perspectives of development, asleep during Indonesia's occupation, that appear as a national development strategy only recently structured and implemented during the years after the referendum (1999). Tourism, then, is incorporated as an alternative of economic development in the political agenda established for East Timor, not only in the initiatives destined to alter the country's trade balance, but also as argument in the speeches on perspectives of future economic development, on the basis of which different projects have been developed by public and private institutions, in isolated actions or through partnerships.

TOURISM IN EAST TIMOR: A BRIEF REVIEW

Studies on tourism in East Timor are practically unheard of – which for more or less obvious reasons can be explained by the low dynamism of the sector itself, given the turbulent social and political context over the last three decades (a time when international tourism underwent important expansion and it has not included East Timor).

Even with data restriction, two more or less explicit periods can be observed in which tourism was treated and developed in different ways with several levels of priority in government agendas. Generally speaking, until the end of the colonial period, East Timor was a territory out of global tourism mainstream – despite the proximity with Bali, a "paradise" converted into worldwide tourist destination after the Dutch were in complete control of the possession in the 1930's. (Vickers, 2012, p. 114).

Within Indonesian occupation period (1975-1999), East Timor suffered the hardships of subjugation, mainly during the first years (marked by armed resistance of Timorese groups) and in the last years, with Santa Cruz Massacre (1991). In this period there little effort was made by Indonesia in order to promote tourism in East Timor, particularly by the nature of Suharto's dictatorship that came to suffer international pressure.

Thus, in spite of some mentions or attempts to promote an image of tourist paradise, the effective efforts – and even the business organization of sectors associated with tourism – did not result in expressive flows. With the process of independence (1999-2002), tourism reached the status of strategic element notwithstanding the capacity of generating revenues and contributing to the country's social and economic reconstruction under the auspices of international missions that succeeded each other between 1999 and 2012.

During this period, the role of international cooperation – both under the UN's umbrella and successive bilateral agreements with the independent nation – undertakes, in a subtle manner (despite the strength of the theme in national political speeches), tourism as an issue for support actions. Finally, with the closure of UN's mission, the withdrawal of peace forces and other groups in the mark of the agreement, the country seeks to tread autonomous footsteps in order to consolidate itself as a competitive tourist destination regionally – something that back in 2012 had been predicted, with the participation of East Timor in South Korea Universal Exposition, representing an effort of international insertion, speaking in terms of tourism (Figure 4).

Another recent milestone of these efforts, with almost triumphant importance, is the ship *Jewel* stopover in Díli, in mid-2015, with more than two thousand passengers, reinforcing expectations that the country may be included in international tourism networks, with diversification of activities in the field of agriculture and tourism (Lusa, 2015).

Nowadays, 85,000 entries have been registered with a little more than 36,000 for tourism purposes (that is, other than work or study) by immigration authorities (MTCI, 2012; Thomaz, 2008, p. 105). However, most of those who report "tourism" or "visit" purposes may in fact be for working purposes (although at the time of entry, without their working status adjusted, they report "tourism" as their trip purpose) (Tolkach et al, 2012, p. 302).

Figure 4. East Timor stand at Yeosu South Korea Universal Exposition
(Source: Thiago Allis, 2012)

From Colony to Indonesian Period (until 1999): Incidental Tourism

Luís Felipe Thomaz, an East Timor observer during the period corresponding to the last years of the Portuguese government, dedicated himself to information record, personal impressions and reflections on "local problems". He informed that in 1971 there were 4,468 entries of tourists in East Timor (focus of visitation in Tutuala and Baucau) and, while recognizing the increase in flow over the years, he wondered that "however much one dreams of oil, tourism and other pataca trees [*Dillenica indica*], the future of Timor still [will be], for many years, dependent on agriculture and cattle farming". (Thomaz, 2008, p. 70).

Moving through the territory during the 70's was quite limited, possible only overland, both for internal mobility, and for international access, of Timorese or tourists, a group rather unexpressive in qualitative terms and characterized as "hippie". For the Portuguese observer, "for those who live in Lisbon, Díli will appear perhaps the end of the world; but for those who live in Díli, the end of the world is a little farther; approximately in Bobonaro", stretch of "135 km that does not take less than seven hours, in leaps and bounds on stones or skating in zigzag on the dirt; but, after all, one goes". (Thomaz, 2008, p. 71).

Then, limitations for tourism development were related to absence of specific infrastructure (accommodation, restaurants), appropriate means of transport, valuing of existing attractions (beaches, mountains, landscapes, local customs, folklore and handicraft), and inexistence of oriented advertisement, a situation that represented a hindrance for more tourists attraction and a flow with higher purchasing power.

Baucau, today the second largest city in East Timor, would be presented as a "beautiful village", beneficiated by a direct air route and some infrastructure of support to tourism (hotel, bed & breakfast, cafes). Tutuala, in the island far east, is presented as a "paradisiacal place", from where one can spot some islands in the archipelago of "Maluco" – in fact, Jaco islet, nowadays one of the most important natural attractions in East Timor. In this period, the existence of archeological heritage in caves was already mentioned, "but there is not a guide that shows them, not even a reasonable path to get there". In short, it was understood that "therefore tourism can be an important factor for Timor's development – but it is not, surely, a magic potion to solve all its problems" (Thomaz, 2008, pp. 108-109). Indeed a very pertinent idea to the present context.

Tourism in the period is mentioned in direct association with the issue of development and establishment of a situation of East Timor greater economic independence towards the Metropolis (Portugal), constituting an issue discursively relevant of local political and economic agenda, but timidly treated under the aspect of initiatives. There was an expectation that an international company be installed simultaneously with the Timor Oil and Broken Hillin 1973, tourist development oriented (installation of five hotels in different locations), as well as the attraction of Australian investors interested in small-sized hotel development, could propitiate an encouraging scenario to the development of this activity. Although timid, during the late 60's and early 70's, the number of tourists in East Timor presented a growth trend, as well the input of resources from visits (Table 1).

With Indonesia occupation, the instability climate and the insecurity as result of violent actions by military contingents (against Timorese, Portuguese and Australian civilians and religious representatives, including the so called five Australian journalists), provoked significant alteration of tourist development trends presented in the early 70's. Between 1975 and 1999 there was the record of few visitors in East Timor, basically in official activities (civil and military authorities), small groups of professionals linked to communication sector and, at the end of the occupation period, a slight increase of domestic tourism with flow of Indonesians (CAVR, 2010; Thomaz, 2008).

Table 1. East Timor tourism data: 1969/1972

Year	Number of Tourists	Currency Entries (in "contos")	Hotels	
			Beds	Occupancy Rate
1969	2.425	2.640	-	-
1970	3.752	2.900	-	-
1971	4.468	3.120	13/221	20,5%
1972	4.854	4.000	15/239	26,7%

(Thomaz, 2008)

Tourism in the Independent Period (Post-1999): Reconstruction Strategy

The intervention of the UN in the country and the arrival of different cooperation agencies since 1999 stimulated the flow of foreigners, whose travel motivations categorized them as temporary workers (mainly related to international aid) and "volunteering tourism" (involving volunteers linked to religious and third sector organizations), so that experiences of cultural, ecologic and adventure tourism are timidly developed. According to data released by the General Direction of Statistics of Timorese Financial Ministry (2015), entered through Nicolau Lobato International Airport, 59,811 foreigners in 2014, compared to 77,868 in 2013. Between 2006 and 2010, 98,913 tourist visas and another 45,652 work visa were issued (Breda & Ferreira, 2013). However, a great proportion of visitors that mention "tourism" or "visiting" as a motivation to be in East Timor may, actually, be travelling for work.

In the years after the installation of INTERFET, along with efforts of peacekeeping and recovery of the country's basic infrastructure, there was the installation of infrastructure specifically focused on meeting elementary demands of professionals working in the country, which resulted in the construction of hotels (very simple or even pre-hotel structures), installation of food and beverage ventures, tour agencies and transport services. Nevertheless, external accessibility is still an important limitation for tourism in East Timor: air-connections are available mainly from Bali, and few direct flights from Singapore and Darwin (Australia) – with tickets relatively expensive, making the destination less competitive, especially because its insular location.

On the supply side, beaches are the main attractions (although very comparable to Southeast Asian competitors), mainly those at Northern coast, in the Islet of Jaco and Ataúro Island, whose demand is basically comprised of expatriates living in East Timor – so, technically speaking, domestic travel. Coral reefs that allow free or professional diving (including the surroundings of the capital, Díli) are seen as a great East Timor asset, and are among the best diving spots in the world (Lonely Planet, 2011). Calahan (2011), when analyzing "Lonely Planet East Timor", highlights, as background for the edition of the guide (2004), regional "political contexts", particularly in recent East-Timor-Australia relationships. Thus, "the role of the Australian traveler concerning East Timor includes connecting, somehow, with its national construction project" having as reference a complicated and contradictory past that in a sense "reveals how a moment of post-colonial culture can be extremely different from another" (Calahan, 2011, p. 97).

In the field of international cooperation, reports by country[1] - or "development partners" – bring data in line with the large areas stated by the Development Strategic Plan (2011-2030), for the period 2007-2011, as follows: a) Share Capital, b) Infrastructures Development, c) Economic Development and e) Institutional Framework. Figure for those years appoint an overall amount surpassing US$ 1 billion in international aid, but forecasts for the following period (2012-2016) indicate toward a slight decrease, a situation expected in face of East Timor's social, political and economic consolidation – particularly in relation to the expressive increase of revenues because of Petroleum Fund.

The analysis of disbursements does not reveal detailed information on projects regarding tourism, although indirectly expenses with certain items could indicate some warning to the sector. Only Portugal reports specific disbursement on Tourism (€60,365 in 2007 and €500 in 2011 – from a total of over €60 million for the period). Regarding total amounts, Australia is top ranked, having contributed with approximately 33% of the total for the period, followed by Portugal (ca. US$ 175 million or 17% of the total), USA (US$ 141 million or 14%) and France (US$ 115 million or 11%) (Table 2).

In the area of "Share Capital", measures in "Education & Formation", "Environment" and "Culture & Heritage" stand out and could somehow comprise support to tourism development. In the case of "Education & Formation", the resources come from all cooperative countries (Brazil, South Korea, USA, France, Ireland, Japan, New Zealand and Portugal), whose projects, in general, meet both primary education (mainly Brazil and Portugal due to the language), and higher education. In this last regard, support measures to East Timor National University are highlighted (Japan, in Engineering and Portugal, without specification) and granting of scholarships and supports for Timorese students formation (undergraduate and post-graduation) abroad (Portugal, USA, New Zealand and South Korea) – so that in these cases, only some superficial information on the areas of formation are presented (for instance, aviation in New Zealand, natural resources in South Korea). In "Environment", actions from three countries are identified: Brazil (without specification), USA (marine conservation and support in caring for Millennium Development Goals) and Japan (natural resources sustainable management, mainly water and forest). Finally, in the field of "Culture & Heritage", although cooperation initiatives are few they still exist, particularly those from France (archeological researches in Maubara and Suai, conservation

Table 2. Disbursements per international cooperation: 2007/2011

Country	Disbursement (US$)	% Total
Australia	342	33%
Portugal	174.39	17%
USA	141.88	14%
France	115	11%
Japan	79.07	8%
Germany	43.17	4%
China	33.32	3%
Brazil	31.38	3%
New Zealand	28.90	3%
Ireland	28.50	3%
Spain	17.50	2%
Norway	15.74	1%
TOTAL	1,050.85	100%

(Source: countries' aid agencies)

of Max Stahl audiovisual records and publication of the history book "Istória Timor Leste nian: husi pré-história to'o actualidade"); Portugal and Brazil reports register supports in this aspect, but do not explain their actions.

In the area of "Development of Infra-Structures", Japan, Australia and Ireland are the main highlights. In case of Japan, the support is provided basically for roads, bridges and ports' construction (including rehabilitation of Port of Díli) and cleanup improvement measures. Japan and Germany stand out in the issue of ports – Germany, for instance, donated and reformed *Berlin Nakroma*, a ship from World War II, today servicing regular routes between Díli-Oe-cusse (Pantemakassar) and Díli-Ataúro[2] (Figure 5).

In the "Economic Development" area, the main efforts are focused on rural and agriculture development, with all countries acting in this front. It is important to remember, for instance, the case of Spain, that develops important works through AECID in the District of Liquiçá, targeting the rural area, but that has in tourism one of the references for economic development (routes through the interior and display of products along their roads, with touristic signage). Still in this category, Portugal investments through project *Mós Bele* in Maubara (District of Liquiçá) stands out above all and see tourism as an activity of means for both implantation and expansion of a community development cluster (Figures 6 and 7). And finally, the participation of Norway stands out in the oil sector.

In the Institutional Framework" area, the actions are focused on security (Australia, Portugal, USA, France, New Zealand and Ireland) and in government and good governance, with measures of "training" or "institutional strengthening". Efforts of USA, France, Portugal, Japan, Brazil and New Zealand deserve attention, particularly in the support to the judiciary – Brazil, for instance, plays an important role in the establishment of public defender service.

By the general reading of cooperation reports, one could suggest some indirect measures in favor of tourism – for instance, in the area of Culture & Heritage and Environment (as basic concerns for valuing resources that may be used for tourism development), as well as Education & Formation (if measures of professional qualification are taken into account, it could allow professional engagement with tourism

Figure 5. "Berlin Nakroma" at Díli Harbour
(Source: Thiago Allis, 2012)

Figure 6. Beach Bar at Maubara, District of Liquiçá
(Source: Thiago Allis, 2012)

Figure 7. Handcraft on sale at Maubara, District of Liquiçá
(Source: Thiago Allis, 2012)

in the future), Rural Development (in cases of structuring tourist products on the basis of rural tourism, particularly considering the huge amount of population that still lives in the countryside) or even Institutional Framework (if efforts were focused on structuring tourism, as one of the issues, according to PDE, within the country's administrative scope).

Considering local national government initiatives since the independence (2002), tourism has been proposed as one of the mechanisms of economic reconstruction (along with other important sectors such as oil and coffee industry). In the "Program of 4th Constitutional Government of Democratic Republic of East Timor (RDTL 2007-2012)", tourism is cited explicitly as a factor of economic development, perceived through generation of revenues, work, installation of basic and tourist infra-structure and incentive of transport services development. Tourism is present in the document, but only illustrates the first attempts for the development of the sector without detailing priority operational actions, for example "to stimulate the creation of specific legislation for advancing tourism activity, ensuring occupation of national workforce and transference of knowledge to Timorese people" or "promoting the development of national tourism products development for the international market". (República Democrática de Timor-Leste, 2014).

In turn, the "Program of 5th RDTL Constitutional Government (2012-2017)" aggregates to tourism development a new role, that is, of affirmation – valuing – of East Timor peoples' history regaining the importance of the activity for the country's economical and social development. By recognizing its initial development stage, it takes a bold stand by figuring as regional leader in the markets of ecological, maritime, historical and adventure tourism on the following year, presents projects focused on tourism development and territory division in three distinct tourism areas: Central Tourism Zone (Díli, Ataúro and Maubisse), Western Tourism Zone (Northern coast road that goes from Balibó, Maliana, Bobonaro to Ermera) and Eastern Tourism Zone (Tutuala, Com beach, Baucau and the coastal road up to Hera). In this document, one observes an upgrading of proposals, with greater detail of actions in specific market segments ("Promotion of Sports Tourism, Religious Tourism and Archeological Tourism" and "Stimulation to enterprises development of Bed & Breakfast") and proposition of interventions in certain regions of the country, aiming to improve tourist attractions, qualify human resources and enhance processes of tourism communication ("Center of Formation in Tourism and Hotel Management in Díli", "Centers of Tourism Information in Díli, Los Palos, Balibo and Baucau", "Tourist Project for the Portuguese Fort in Balibó" or "Tourism Project for Aipelo Prison, with installation of a Museum" – this late, already a tourist site with some interpretation facilities (Figure 8) (República Democrática de Timor-Leste, 2014).

Finally, the "Program of the 6[th]RDTL Constitutional Government (2015-2017)" presents guidelines for tourism development in two different points in the document: the item on "Culture and Heritage", with emphasis on cultural tourism development and in the specific item on "Tourism", recovering a

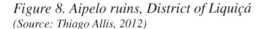

Figure 8. Aipelo ruins, District of Liquiçá
(Source: Thiago Allis, 2012)

major part of the text already published on the Program of the 6ᵗʰ Constitutional Government. The notion of cultural tourism presented focuses on valuing local cultural peculiarities (customs, rural communities ways of life, history, handicraft production, musical references and local dancing), associated to installation of tourism infrastructure. It aims to increase tourist flows to regions with cultural tourist attractions and information offer on these attractions within the world wide web environment. In comparison to the previous document, one notices a continuity of actions, which is partially explained by the fact that previous government has been interrupted and replaced by the program under discussion. The proposal of a "Tourism Master Plan", present in this program, suggests concern from central government to organize and plan thematic and regional specific actions (República Democrática de Timor-Leste, 2014).

Proposals for tourism development included in the Government Programs suggests an association with cultural and ecological peculiarities from different regions in the country and are recent references on the involvement of federal public institutions with the project of national economic development through tourism. However, following Carrion and Santos (2011), it depicts a clear emphasis on economic sector though the discourse embedded in those documents endeavors to shed some light on local peculiarities, as a priority in the tourism development.

TOURISM IN EAST TIMOR: PERSPECTIVES IN A GLOBALIZED WORLD

When aspects of East Timor recent history are analyzed – specially after 1999 – two views emerge: on one side, the argument that the country is a "young nation" and therefore is in the early phase of its political, social and economic organization – which to some extent would explain steps (forward and backward) in measures after Indonesia's evasion; and, on the other hand, the perception that the country has been through relevant changes, so that year by year landscapes, data, people and institutions among other aspects of daily life have been quickly and intensely modified. Therefore, for the observer, it means recognizing that the tension between permanence and transformation should be inescapable, particularly considering political and social frictions focused on coexistence and interrelations between the Timorese and foreigners, between local and external social systems in the capital, Díli.

Tourism appears, as perspective, in several documents and reports since the first moments of Timorese State Constitution. At the same time, through literature review on post-conflict tourism and local-based tourism, this issue comes up in association with reconstruction perspectives from the situation of political and racial conflicts, through several biases: memory value (Northern Ireland), economic development (Rwanda, Egypt, Peru, New Zealand, Cape Verde, Brazil, Kenya), opportunity of foreign investments (Lebanon), reconciliation (South Korea), coexistence between religions (Israel, Jordan), heritage conservation and enhancement (Libya).

As general inference, one could say that this orientation comes from views that provide to tourism a quick path for economic recovery and also an expectation that tourist potentialities – particularly concentrated on natural resources – may be developed in an obvious manner. However, one should not lose sight of the context vicissitudes (social and economic reconstruction of a country recently independent and virtually destroyed), including a history of colonialist plundering and low human development.

Furthermore, East Timor natural resources are quite similar to those of neighbor countries (especially Indonesia – particularly in the islands of Bali and surroundings), whose history of development and tourism structuring are well established, which includes an intense market share in of powerful international marketplaces, mainly from Europe. In addition, the location factor – between Oceania and South East

Asia – may at the same time represent a market advantage (for instance, proximity to regional market-places of Australia and Singapore) as an obstacle within the international context (distance of mature and far marketplaces such as Europe and North-America).

Through all the country, only 50 accommodations were registered, clearly concentrated in Díli, and most of them operate as temporary residences for contingents of international cooperation. In general, the Timorese tourism offer is clearly concentrated in the capital, Díli, and in Baucau, the main urban settlements in the country since the colonial era. The district of Lautém has also developed over the last years, particularly because of demands bounding to Jaco Islet or to Com Beach. As for tourist attractions, they can be mainly framed in the category of cultural heritage (approximately 150 citations) – like the world famous "uma lulik" or sacred houses of Los Palos District (Figure 9), having natural attractions as secondary, despite their diversity and conservation state (approximately 80 citations) (Figure 10).

In recent years, there has have particular efforts in Cristo Rei beach in order to arrange a leisure and tourist spot in the outskirts of Díli, where the statue of Christ The Redeemer stands since the 1990's, after the visit paid the Pope John II (Figures 11 and 12).

Figure 9. "Uma lulik", District of Los Palos
(Source: Thiago Allis, 2012)

Figure 10. Tourist supply in East Timor, by district: 2008-2015[3]

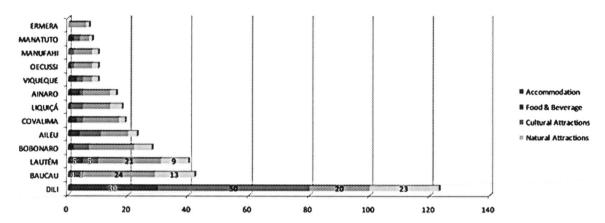

Figure 11. Cristo Rei beach from above, Díli
(Source: Thiago Allis, 2012)

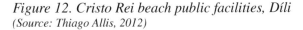

Figure 12. Cristo Rei beach public facilities, Díli
(Source: Thiago Allis, 2012)

Thus, considering local agents as active subjects in the process of tourism development, it will be indispensable that future papers take into account international contributions under an autonomous perspective, considering the valuation of national staff – that have been formed mainly at Timor Lorosa'e National University (UNTL) and that in turn is also inserted in higher education international cooperation plans.

Without disregard the country's cultural and landscape richness, the starting point for East Timor tourism development is not obvious, as official documents may suggest – whether PED (2011-2030), or the several reports from international agencies that have been operating in East Timor since the referendum of 1999 and mainly after the Independence in 2002 (like UNDP). Thus, through the process of international cooperation, not surprisingly, by meeting perspectives and desires of national projects, countries and partner entities would be concerned with the issue, specially because PED highlights at some extent tourism as development strategy.

Actions favoring tourism development from 2007 to 2011 are practically inexistent (in financial and content terms) in reports of countries and their cooperation agencies. However, since the country finds itself into a course of social, economic, structural and institutional development (although far ahead of what used to be observed in the early past decade), it is understandable that the issue tourism has a secondary role because of other more poignant demands in key-sectors (health, education, security, justice, sanitation, etc).

It would be important to discuss if cooperation should be focused on certain areas to be appointed by local government – among them, one could (or could not) include tourism. Anyway, for the moment, once this discussion is open, one can point out little attention from partner countries towards the issue tourism (directly or indirectly) – which does not mean a negligent attitude towards its participation as cooperative party.

There is no direct attention to tourism from partner countries: their reports do not recognize literal links with tourism, showing inattention to that issue in their cooperation programs – something that, as one notices, is recurrent in documents that deal with measures for East Timor social and economic reconstruction. However, indirect supports are pointed out (considering they simply exist!), then, this could subsidize tourism development through alternative ways (for instance, in the fields of Education & Formation, Heritage & Culture, Environmental, Airports, etc.).

The discussions undertaken in this chapter allow us to state outstanding international cooperation and aid initiatives to support national development in East Timor. In the case of tourism, however, these can be qualified as by its characteristics of early stage of development, given the basic infrastructure and, especially, tourist infrastructure – mainly provided by entrepreneurs and foreign private investors formally delinked from the official project of international cooperation and aid.

Though Sánches-Cañizares and Castillo-Canalejo (2011) noted that in community-based tourism the resident community assumes a key role not only in the development of projects, but also as beneficiary of tourism income, the literature points out that, in many cases, the situation of the localities has worsened in comparison to the previous situation. A significant array of impacts unforeseen and therefore distinct from expected highlights the great potential of negative impacts in community development. With regard to the empowerment of local communities, Groot and Simons (2015) reports that, in most cases, this occurs partially, because of the complexity and difficulty involved in the process. This is due to the complex nature of power relations, marked by inequalities and nonlinear behaviors, which impairs learning processes of the communities about the transformation of living conditions in the communities.

For the sake of communities' interests and needs, these issues, obviously, have to be considered when local development initiatives – whether in tourism sector or not – are undertaken in East Timor, including the role and the limits of international cooperation.

CONCLUSION

By looking at international experiences on post-conflict tourism, one notices that they are distributed throughout the globe, despite of religions, social-economical development level, territory size, races, etc. that is, the relation between tourism and conflict – and mainly what can be expected of post-conflict – should serve as reference for the philosophical construction of certain interventions and actions of international cooperation. Before thinking on the subject as something unusual, one could create a baseline for effective incorporation – even indirectly – of tourism as a vector for national reconstruction processes.

UN's work in the case of East Timor is a chapter to be studied in the field of international affairs for, if on one side, it represents the attention of international community paid to humanitarian causes (as many other cases in the world), on the other side, it calls into question the validity, concerns and effectiveness (and in to what extent) of international interventions on local causes. Anyway, the challenge has been to reject the scenario of "war territory" to a developing country, avoiding the idea of "underdeveloped country". In this sense, from a political point of view, the prestige of its leaders (mainly the Nobel Peace Prize winner, José Ramos-Horta, and Kay-Rala Xanana Gusmão) seems to have been decisive to insert East Timor in the main forums and communities of countries – for instance, the full membership campaign of East Timor at ASEAN, the country's articulation among Portuguese Official Language countries within the scope of CPLP, and more recently, the involvement in discussions with "G7+", focusing the needs of "fragile states" through a "New Agreement for the Involvement in Fragile States" of 2011.

Even recognizing limitation of sources, the systematization of available information has allowed a closer reading both of current and recent past tourism reality in East Timor. As it has already been observed, to report and discuss the history of tourism in East Timor with amplitude and from the expression of multiple voices is still a mission to be accomplished. Little attention has been given to artistic, gastronomic, territory use and management, architectural and intangible heritage references that express the cultural diversity both of different peoples and history of country's independence.

East Timor is result of the colonizer impetus of great navigations and, over the last decades, it was tossed in the whirlwind of globalization in ways that mix pain and hope. The intense flow of foreigners in the country – particularly in Dili – and the links between aid agencies, private institutions and institutions of Timorese government, stimulate the transformation of practices, processes and characteristic values of socio-political and cultural dynamics, both in the local and national scale. Within this melting pot, undoubtedly, tourism and all its practices, projects and representations will be ingredients increasingly present.

Only in public policy documents of the last two Constitutional Governments, proposals of tourism development have explicit alignment with an autonomous proposed national of development. This proposal is distinctly marked out by principles that have enhances self-determination arguments of the Timorese Nation in the independence process, strengthening political, social and cultural references, that are historically constituted and will be able to particularize the country in the international context.

At last, the authors understand that observing mediations carried out by Timorese amidst sociocultural systems, influenced by internal and external elements, resulted in a rich theoretical labor, once it helps out to explain self-determination, autonomy, development and social participation in this specific context. Down this road, in practical terms, further reflections can feed projects of tourism development in countries that strive, in the present, to manage the scars of local tragedies, hard to be erased from personal and national memories.

REFERENCES

Agier, M. (2011). *Antropologia da cidade: Lugares, situações e movimentos*. São Paulo: Editora Terceiro Nome.

Ansoms, A. (2005). Resurrection after civil war and genocide: Growth, poverty and inequality in post-conflict Rwanda. *European Journal of Development Research*, *17*(3), 495–508. doi:10.1080/09578810500209577

Anson, C. (1999). Planning for peace: The role of tourism in the aftermath of violence. *Journal of Travel Research*, *38*(1), 1–5. doi:10.1177/004728759903800112

Australian Agency for International Development (AusAID). (2012). *Australia Development Partner Handover Report 2012* (Unpublished). Díli, East Timor.

Barata, M. J. (2010). O Que e Quem é um Povo? O conceito de autodeterminação e o debate sobre a ontologia do actor internacional. In *Proceedings of Congress da APCP* (pp. 1-10). Retrieved July 4, 2015, from http://repositorio.ismt.pt/handle/123456789/254

BCTL. (2011). *Evolução Economia Nacional. In: Annual Report –Financial Year 2010-2011*. Retrieved November, 13, 2015, from https://www.bancocentral.tl/Download/Publications/Annual_Rep/Full_Report.pdf

BCTL. (2012). *Um ano de evolução da economia nacional 2011-12*. Retrieved November, 13, 2015, from https://www.bancocentral.tl/Download/Publications/Eco_Outlook_2012.pdf

BCTL. (2014). *Evolução Recente da Economia Nacional. In: Annual Report–Financial Year 2014*. Retrieved November, 13, 2015, from https://www.bancocentral.tl/Download/Publications/Annual_Rep/2014/Pt/BCTL_AR_2014_portuguese_Total.pdf

BCTL. (2015). Petroleum Fund of East Timor. *Quarterly Report, 11*(28). Retrieved July 4, 2015, from: http://www.bancocentral.tl/Download/Publications/Quarter-Report39_en.pdf

BrazilianCooperationAgency (ABC). (2012). *Cooperação Brasileira – Parceiros para o Desenvolvimento: Relatório para a Transição 2012* (Unpublished). Díli, East Timor.

Breda, Z., & Ferreira, A. (2013, July). *Turismo em Timor-Leste: passaporte para o desenvolvimento?* Paper presented at Timor Conference 2013, Díli, East Timor.

Calahan, D. (2011). Consuming and erasing Portugal in the Lonely Planet guide to East Timor. *Postcolonial Studies, 14*(1), 95–109. doi:10.1080/13688790.2011.542117

Canclini, N. G. (2013). *Culturas híbridas*. São Paulo: EDUSP.

Carrion, R. S. M., & Santos, C. G. (2011). Sobre a governança da cooperação internacional para o desenvolvimento: Atores, propósitos e perspectivas. *Revista de Administração Pública, 45*(6), 1847–1868.

Castillo-Canalejo, A. M., & Sánchez Cañizares, S. M. (2014). Community-basedislandtourism: The case of Boa Vista in Cape Verde. *International Journal of Culture. Tourism and Hospitality Research, 8*(2), 219–233.

Causevic, S., & Lynch, P. (2011). Phoenix tourism: Post-conflict tourism role. *Annals of Tourism Research, 38*(3), 780–800. doi:10.1016/j.annals.2010.12.004

CAVR. (2005). Chega! Relatório da CAVR. Díli, East Timor: CAVR.

CAVR. (2010). Timor-Oriental, Autodeterminação e a Comunidade Internacional – Audiência pública Nacional, 15-17 março 2004. Díli, East Timor: CAVR.

China Council for International Cooperation (CECID). (2012). *China Development Partner Handover Report 2012* (Unpublished). Díli, East Timor.

Cuban Embassy in Díli. (2012). *Republic of Cuba Development Partner Handover Report 2012* (Unpublished). Díli, East Timor.

D'Alessandro-Scarpari, C. (2011). Local territories, their power and their actions: Development as a weapon for peace. World Journal of Science, *Technology and Sustainable Development, 8*(2-3), 263–275.

Faria, V. S. (2011). *O desempenho da administração transitória das Nações Unidas em Timor-Leste: um estudo e análise do mandato do Conselho de Segurança das Nações Unidas segundo resolução n. 1272, de 1999.* LembahManah.

French Development Agency (AFD). (2012). *France Development Partner Handover Report 2012* (Unpublished). Díli, East Timor.

German International Cooperation Agency (GIZ). (2012). *Germany Development Partner Handover Report 2012* (Unpublished). Díli, East Timor.

Groot, E., & Simons, I. (2015). Power and empowerment in community-based tourism: Opening Pandora's box? *Tourism Review, 70*(1), 72–94. doi:10.1108/TR-06-2014-0035

Hall, D. (2002). Brand development, tourism and national identity: The re-imaging of former Yugoslavia. *Brand Management, 9*(4-5), 323–334. doi:10.1057/palgrave.bm.2540081

Hsu, J., & Aristil, J. C. (2014). *Haiti: Tourism Development on Île-à-Vache Island – Reconstruction or Another Disaster?* Retrieved 4 July, 2015, from http://www.globalresearch.ca/haiti-tourism-development-on-ile-a-vache-island-reconstruction-or-another-disaster/5393046

Inácio, R. O., Kern, J., Xavier, T. R., & Wittmann, M. L. (2013). Desenvolvimento regional: uma análise sobre a estrutura de um consórcio intermunicipal. *Revista de Administração Pública, 47*(4), 1041-1065.

Ionnides, D., & Apostolopoulos, Y. (1999). Political instability, war, and tourism in Cyprus: Effects, management, and prospects for recovery. *Journal of Travel Research, 38*(1), 51–56. doi:10.1177/004728759903800111

Irish Aid. (2012). *Irish Aid Development Partner Handover Report 2012* (Unpublished). Díli, East Timor.

Jallat, F., & Schultz, C. J. (2011). Lebanon: from cataclysm to opportunity: crisis management lessons for MNCs in the tourism sector of the Middle East. *Journal of World Business, 46*(4), 476–486. doi:10.1016/j.jwb.2010.10.008

Japan International Cooperation Agency (JICA). (2012). *Embassy of Japan & JICA Development Partner Handover Report 2012* (Unpublished). Díli, East Timor.

Jornal Diário Nacional. (2015, August 28). *Dragon Star Shipping Fasilita Barco Rapido – Dili-Oecusse Oras Tolu Deit.* Retrieved from: http://www.jndiario.com/2015/08/31/dragon-star-shipping-fasilita-barco-rapido-dili-oecusse-oras-tolu-deit/

Kim, S. (2013, July). *Iraq seeks threefold tourism rise despite unrest.* Retrieved 20 December, 2014, from http://www.telegraph.co.uk/travel/travelnews/10214243/Iraq-seeks-threefold-tourism-rise-despite-unrest.html

Kim, S. S., Prideaux, B., & Prideaux, J. (2007). Using tourism to promote peace on the Korean Peninsula. *Annals of Tourism Research, 34*(2), 291–309. doi:10.1016/j.annals.2006.09.002

Korea International Cooperation Agency (KOICA). (2012). *Korea International Cooperation Agency (KOICA) Development Partner Handover Report 2012* (Unpublished). Díli, East Timor.

Lao Hamutuk. (2013). *South Coast petroleum infrastructure project.* Retrieved July 4, 2015, from http://www.laohamutuk.org/Oil/TasiMane/11TasiMane.htm

Lusa. (2015a, June 25). *Construtora sul-coreana ganha contrato de 720MD para projeto em Timor-Leste.* Retrieved from: http://noticias.sapo.tl/portugues/info/artigo/1445592.html

Lusa. (2015b, Jun 13). *Timor-Leste recebe com êxito enchente de turistas de cruzeiro australiano.* Retrieved June, 23, 2015, from http://www.sapo.pt/noticias/timor-leste-recebe-com-exito-enchente-de_557bfaea60753b3619188ed6

MFTL (Ministry of Finance of East Timor). (2015). *Aprovação unânime do Orçamento Geral do Estado para 2015*. Retrieved July 4, 2015, from https://www.mof.gov.tl/wp-content/uploads/2015/01/MoF_Press_Release_Budget_2015-_pt.pdf

Miles, W. S. (2010). Dueling border tours: Jerusalem. *Annals of Tourism Research, 37*(2), 555–559. doi:10.1016/j.annals.2009.11.003

Neves, G. N. S. (2007). O paradoxo da cooperação em Timor-Leste. In K. Silva & D. S. Simião (Eds.), *Timor-Leste por trás do palco: cooperação internacional e a dialética da formação do Estado* (pp. 97–121). Belo Horizonte: UFMG.

Nielsen, H., & Spenceley, A. (2010). *The success of tourism in Rwanda: gorillas and more*. Retrieved September, 20, 2012, from http://anna.spenceley.co.uk/files/publications/nature%20based%20tourism/Tourism_Rwanda%20gorillas.pdf

Norwegian Agency for Development Cooperation (NORAD). (2012). *Norway Development Partner Handover Report 2012* (Unpublished). Díli, East Timor.

Portuguese Development Agency (IPAD). (2012). *Portugal Development Partner Handover Report 2012* (Unpublished). Díli, East Timor. Retrieved 20 June, 2014, from http://timor-leste.gov.tl/?cat=39&lang=pt&bl=16

República Democrática de Timor-Leste. (n.d.a). *Programa do V Governo Constitucional*. Retrieved 20 June, 2014, from http://timor-leste.gov.tl/?cat=39&lang=pt&bl=7569

República Democrática de Timor-Leste. (n.d.b). *Programa do VI Governo Constitucional*. Retrieved 20 June, 2014, fromhttp://timor-leste.gov.tl/?cat=39&lang=pt&bl=11688

Richter, L. K. (1999). After political turmoil: The lessons of rebuilding tourism in three Asian countries. *Journal of Travel Research, 38*(1), 41–45. doi:10.1177/004728759903800109

Spanish Agency of International Cooperation for Development (AECID). (2012). *AECID (Spanish Agency of International Cooperation for Development) Development Partner Handover Report 2012* (Unpublished). Díli, East Timor.

The New Zealand Aid Programme. (2012). *New Zealand Aid Programme Development Partner Handover Report 2012* (Unpublished). Díli, East Timor.

Thomaz, L. F. (2008). *Achegas para a compreensão de Timor-Leste*. Instituto Português do Oriente, Fundação Oriente.

Tolkach, D., King, B., & Pearlman, M. (2007). Prospects for the establishment of a community-based tourism network in Timor-Leste. In M. Lech, N. C. Mendes, A. B. Silva, B. Bougthon, & A. C. Ximenes (Eds.), *Peskiza foun konaba Timor-Leste* (pp. 302–307). Hawthorn: Swinburne Press.

United Nations World Food Programme (WFP). (2012). *United Nations World Food Program Development Partner Handover Report 2012* (Unpublished). Díli, East Timor.

United States Agency for International Development (USAID). (2012). *The US Mission Development Partner Handover Report 2012* (Unpublished). Díli, East Timor.

Vickers, A. (2012). *Bali: a paradise created*. Singapore: Tuttle.

Yasarata, M., Altinay, L., Burns, P., & Okumus, F. (2010). Politics and sustainable tourism development: Can they co-exist? Voices from North Cyprus. *Tourism Management*, *31*(3), 345–356. doi:10.1016/j.tourman.2009.03.016

KEY TERMS AND DEFINITIONS

Colonialism: Expanding influence of European modern nations (Portugal, Spain, France, England, the Netherlands among others) through economic, political and cultural subjugation of traditional territories and its populations.

Decolonization: Independence wave emerged mainly in Asia and Africa after mid-20th century, resulting in politically independent nations, formerly colonies of European countries.

Malay Archipelago: Geological complex of more than 18.000 islands, in the confluence of Pacific and Indic Oceans, housing over 250 million inhabitants, including Indonesia, Malaysia and East Timor.

Multiculturalism: The existence and recognition of multiple cultures, including the expressions of behaviors, values, beliefs and traditions shared by particular groups.

Portuguese Colonialism: Formation of a world mosaic of exploitation colonies under Portuguese dominance in America, Africa and Asia, through the great navigations initiated in the 16th century.

Post-Conflict Tourism: Tourist activities undertaken in nations or regions recently emerged from ethnical/political conflicts, as a strategy to boost social and economic development

Self-Determination: The right of particular territories to reclaim political autonomy, with respect the sense of nationality expressed by historical and cultural issues.

ENDNOTES

[1] For this study, first-hand reports of cooperation agencies of 13 countries have been analyzed, as follows: Australia (AusAid), Brazil (ABC), China (CECID), Cuba (Cuban Embassy in Dili), France (AFD), Germany (GIZ), Ireland (Irish Aid), Japan (JICA), Korea (KOICA), Norway (NORAD), Portugal (IPAD), Spain (AECID), New Zeland (NZAid) and United States of America (USAid). These reports were available for the participants of the "Meeting of East Timor Development Partners (TLDPM)", sponsored by East Timor government in May, 2012.

[2] In August, 2015 a new boat service has been started, providing a safer, faster (3h, instead of 12h of Berlin Nakroma) and more confortable link between Díli and Oe-Cusse. This service was assigned to a private business man, as part of improvements to develop the recent stablished Oe-Cusse Special Economic Zone (Jornal Diário Nacional, 2015).

[3] From 62 sub-districts in the country, it was possible to collect information and data about tourist potentiality or presence of tourist infrastructure for 40 sub-districts. This information was identified through field research along the year of 2012 and documents collected by the authors who were visiting professors at Timor Lorosa'e National University. Data updating was carried out through research in documents and institutions on the *worldwide web*, among them: *East Timor Lonely Planet Tourist Guide, TripAdvisor, Booking.com, Portal de Turismo do Mundo Lusófono* (http://webviagens.net.), *Memorial de Dare* (http://darememorialmuseum.com) and other East Timor public sources (http://timor-leste.gov.tl).

Chapter 7
"Female Charm":
Women's Role in Tourism Internationalization, Innovation, and Networking Strategies

Carlos Costa
University of Aveiro, Portugal

Fiona Eva Bakas
University of Aveiro, Portugal

Zélia Breda
University of Aveiro, Portugal

Marília Durão
University of Aveiro, Portugal

Isabel Pinho
University of Aveiro, Portugal

ABSTRACT

A significant challenge faced by the tourism and hospitality industries in a rapidly changing world, is the ability to sustain organisational growth. Some of the main strategies for achieving organisational growth are those related to innovation, internationalisation and networking. Addressing tourism studies' contemporary shift to a focus on social influences, this study investigates the relations between gender and organisational growth. Qualitative analysis of focus groups with managers from the seven administrative regions in Portugal provides an in-depth account of tourism and gender issues based on empirical evidence. Viewing the ways in which tourism managers contribute to organisational growth through the angle of gender, this chapter provides a compelling account of the delicate and often invisible interactions between economic and social transactions. Results illustrate how women as a labour source are paradoxically viewed as both an asset and an impediment to organisational growth strategies.

INTRODUCTION

Creating gender analyses of tourism processes is essential for a more holistic representation of today's reality (Ferguson & Alarcón, 2015). This is because gender roles and relations silently order social dynamics, thus invisibly influencing economic structures, such as organizational growth strategies. There is a need to investigate the ways in which gender influences the discourses surrounding gendered eco-

DOI: 10.4018/978-1-5225-0201-2.ch007

nomic structures, in order to open space for alternative conceptualizations of the economy that are more realistic and representative of people's experiences. Since the underlying processes of the economy are constituted through economic discourse (Barker, 2005), where discourse is created through language, social institutions and practices, the ways in which economic discourse is gendered, is investigated in this study through qualitative analysis.

Drawing on feminist economics theorizing, such as Gibson and Graham's (2006) feminist analysis of the capitalist economic system, this paper aims to expose the ways in which the organizational growth strategies of internationalization, innovation and networking are gendered.

The subject area of tourism is currently characterised by a critical turn as scholars are increasingly questioning the social constructions that act to maintain unequal power relations and the structures upholding socio-economic processes that restrict human potential (Bramwell & Lane, 2014). Critical theory is used to critique neoclassical economic interpretations of these growth strategies as being predominantly embedded within a masculinised discourse. Critical theory seeks to interrogate taken-for-granted assumptions about theories and hence is useful in uncovering the ways in which gender roles are embedded within economic structures.

By challenging mainstream economic theorizing and questioning the relationship between power and knowledge, this study opposes the coercion of a unified scientific discourse, drawing attention to the ways in which hegemonic masculinity is present within organizational growth strategy discourse. Whilst there are many things that influence managerial style, such as age, class, ethnicity, sexual orientation and the social distribution of power and influence, in this study we focus upon the variable of gender. As is true for all gender research, it is important to bear in mind that findings are relative and context specific.

Since many organisations privilege masculine norms of managerial communication, women and feminised men often face systematic discriminations (Ashcraft, 2009). Indeed, past literature echoes the overarching discourse of "think manager-think male", which continues to be a barrier to women's progress in management and consequently their involvement in organisational growth strategy creation (Gherardi & Murgia, 2014, p. 691). Indicative of this limitation is the low number of women in managerial positions, especially in executive positions. For example, in 2013, only 14.6% of Fortune 500 companies where headed by women (Soares, Barkiewicz, Mulligan-Ferry, Fendler, & Wai Chun Jun, 2013). In Portugal, only 7.3% of stock indexed companies were led by women in 2014, which is one of the lowest percentages in Europe - a masculine dominance in top-level management that illustrates how gender roles influence economic discourse (Catalyst, 2015).

The performance of stereotypical gender roles are particularly evident within tourism, that is a highly gendered area with strong horizontal segregation (Baum, 2013) of occupations (e.g. women are chambermaids, men are bus drivers), a prevalence of men in top-level management positions and the use of sexualised images of young, attractive women to advertise holiday destinations (Jordan, 1997). Not surprisingly, tourism is one of the sectors with the largest pay-gap, with women earning on average 26.3% less than men in Portugal in 2011 (Carvalho, Costa, Lykke, & Torres, 2014). Like many of the countries in Southern Europe, Portugal has a dominant patriarchal identity (Costa, Carvalho, & Breda, 2011) with stereotypical masculine and feminine gender roles being common practice.

Past research finds that gender acts as a background identity that influences the performance of managers in the name of organizational roles (Ridgeway, 2009). Being a cultural frame that coordinates behavior, gender influences tourism processes and this study offers insight into the ways in which things could be different, if an alternative conceptualization of economic discourse was adopted. Responding to a recent call to investigate the role of gender within tourism processes (Figueroa-Domecq, Pritchard,

Segovia-Pérez, Morgan, & Villacé-Molinero, 2015), this chapter aims to fill a gap in literature on the role of gender in tourism organizational growth strategies. Despite the significance of organizational growth strategies such as innovation, internationalization and networking within tourism development, little has been written about the influence of gender in organizational growth strategies that tourism companies employ in order to increase productivity and efficiency.

In this study we question the ontological position that there exists a shared social reality regarding how gender equality at work is perceived by leaders in the Portuguese tourism industry and suggest instead that there are multiple, context-specific truths. Using the method of focus groups to gather the empirical evidence relied upon to construct versions of what constitutes the 'truth' in this study, we draw out the complexity, nuance and contradiction through participants' conflicting opinions. In this way, knowledge is co-constructed amongst participants and researcher. Focus groups allow for the more 'natural' behaviour of participants, than would be exhibited for example in a one-to-one interview (Leavy, 2014). Hence, drawing on recent research conducted in Portugal in 2013 on a nation-wide scale, this paper uses qualitative analysis to investigate gender's role in tourism organizational growth strategies.

BACKGROUND

Critical theory is used to deconstruct masculinised neoclassical economic discourses surrounding the company growth strategies of internationalization, innovation and networking. Literature on these areas is explored in order to provide a nuanced angle of investigation on this critical feminist economic analysis of tourism labour dynamics. However, initially, an understanding of the ways in which gender roles operate is fundamental in order to better comprehend the ways in which gender permeates the tourism company growth strategies investigated in this chapter.

Gender roles, represent beliefs about behaviours that are appropriate for members of each sex (Wood & Eagly, 2010), influencing behaviours ranging from sexual behaviour to leadership style and entrepreneurial behaviour. As such, participants in this study represent gendered economic subjectivities. Gender encapsulates all the cultural markers a society uses to account for biological difference. Gender is not exactly something that someone *is* or something that a person *has*, it is the *mechanism* by which notions of what constitutes masculine and feminine are produced and normalised. Enacting or "doing" gender is the act of performing complex "socially guided...micropolitical activities" (Bruni, Poggio, & Gherardi, 2005, p. 37) that are taken as expressions of what is seen as gender-related natural behaviours. Gender can indeed be considered society's "most pervasive organising principle" (H. Ahl & Nelson, 2010, p. 7) as it is a form of social power. An understanding of current gender roles is important in creating policy and promoting development that has a positive effect on people.

Having explained how gender roles influence economic processes, some background is provided on the economic processes focused on in the chapter, drawing attention to the ways in which gender permeates these processes.

Whilst, historically, tourism is a phenomenon characterised by immense innovativeness, it is only in the last decade that research on innovation in tourism is increasingly focused upon. Despite this surge in interest, there are limited empirical studies on the level and nature of innovative activities and even less research on the gendered nature of innovation, as a tourism business growth strategy. The reasons why tourism businesses do not innovate are largely shrouded in mystery, perhaps because of the lack of a common definition of what constitutes an innovative practice. The dictionary definition of innovation is "to renew", "to create something new". Within the EU, innovation is defined as new or improved products, services, processes and models (European Commission, 2010). Innovation in this study is defined as the process of bringing any new problem-solving idea that reaches the stage of implementation and commercialisation, into use (Hjalager, 2010). Within tourism, innovation is often linked to government policies. An example is the proliferation of low-budget airlines after air-traffic regulations were modified. Tourist needs also stimulate innovation to take place, such as the merging of cosmetic manufacturers with wellness centres (Mair, 2005).

Innovation has become an increasingly strategic topic in politics, research and the public debate all over the world. In politics, innovation topped the European Union agenda, in 2009 which was declared as "the year of creativity and innovation as a prerequisite for sustainable growth". Since the ultimate resource in contemporary society is novelty, this explains why innovation has been turned into the utmost competitive means of winning the game. However, research into innovation and gender highlights how innovation discourse is built on stereotypical notions of gender; promoting men and certain forms of masculinity as the norm (Blake & Hanson, 2005; Lindberg, 2012; Nyberg, 2009; Pettersson, 2007). Feminist studies are full of stories of women made invisible, but whose actions have been crucial to innovative practices. An example of an innovative invisible women is Grace Hopper, the founder of programming language (Beyer, 2009).

The gender composition of team members within the enterprise is also an important factor for understanding innovation, since a diverse workforce contributes to diversity in the knowledge base. Enterprises with a balanced workforce (50-60% of same gender) are almost twice as likely to innovate compared to those with a segregated workforce (Danilda & Thorslund, 2011).

Internationalisation is another way in which tourism organisations gain competitive advantage, and is defined in this study as "the process of becoming aware of the importance of international transactions for the future development of the firm, as well as the process of investing in and undertaking business transactions in other countries" (Calof & Beamish, 1995, p. 119). Portuguese tourism companies have long been involved in international operations in the domestic market, but only started investing abroad in the late 1990s (Bernardino & Jones, 2008). While, depending on definitions, the internationalization of tourism can be traced back centuries, tourism internationalization has intensified in recent decades, largely because of improved connectivities (Shaw & Williams, 2004). References to internationalization litter the tourism literature, and it is variously referred to as a driver, a shaper, or an outcome of change. Indeed, internationalization within tourism is distinctive because of tourism's nature of being by definition mobile beyond the immediate locality. Some of the advantages of internationalizing for larger tourism companies such as hotel chains, are the high growth rates that companies who invest outside the host company get, and the international branding which applies to domestic and international clients. One of the ways in which internationalization occurs is through trade fairs which exhibit the tourism company's products to an international audience.

The tourism industry, which is made up primarily of SMEs, has specific considerations regarding internationalization as a business strategy. SMEs typically rely extensively on network relationships as they pursue international expansion (Coviello, 2006) and experience difficulties in involving competent managers in highly time-consuming activities (Mutinelli & Piscitello, 1998). Since the extent to which female managers can engage in 'highly time-consuming' activities is limited by gender roles that connect femininity to caring, this creates gendered assumptions about women's ability to be effective within internationalization strategies.

Whilst the internationalisation of a firm can be defined as a dynamic process of incremental learning from foreign markets that develops over time, more recently, this concept has evolved by including network relationship and so internationalisation is seen as an evolutionary process of developing networks that form bridges to foreign markets (Brida, Driha, Ramón-Rodríguez, & Scuderi, 2015).

Networks are of significance both within internationalization and innovation processes in tourism. As knowledge becomes the most important strategic asset for organisations in the 21st century, "networks and networking are fundamental to the knowledge development and sharing processes" (Durbin, 2011, p. 101). However, women's entry and participation in formal and informal types of networks is often constrained by gendered barriers. For example, whereas informal networks boost men's professional lives, they work as an obstacle to women's career development (Kotiranta, Kovalainen, & Rouvinen, 2007a; Zhong & Couch, 2007). The informal nature of networks makes it difficult to fight discrimination since organisations are not legally responsible for these informal work ties.

Formal networking, for example that carried out at trade fairs, also presents similar constraints to women who may have limited availability to travel. Whilst the internet plays an increasingly important role in the maintenance of networks through social networking websites, physical presence is still essential for networking to occur (Sigala, Christou, & Gretzel, 2012). Indeed, Linehan and Scullion (2008, p. 36) find that the two main obstacles for female managers regarding networking are: "(i) access to male networks, and (ii) having less time available for networking due to domestic commitments". Hence networking discourse is influenced by gender roles connecting femininity to caring, and consequently the expectation that women are more likely than men to have caring responsibilities that limit their availability to network.

METHODS AND METHODOLOGY

The research presented in this book chapter is part of a larger research project covering all seven administrative regions in Portugal, aiming to answer the umbrella research question: 'Does gender equality have a say in the boost of innovative forms of economic growth? Reviving the economy through networks and internationalisation in the tourism sector'. From this main research question, other research questions emerged. The one examined in this chapter is: 'How do gender roles influence the organizational tourism growth strategy discourses of innovation, internationalization and networking?

The method of focus groups was chosen as a valid method of collecting qualitative data for this particular project as it is in-line with the methodology that posits knowledge is co-constructed between researcher and researched (Fine, 1994). Whilst the meanings created in human interactions can be perceived as a "shifting carnival of ambiguous complexity" (Scheurich, 1995, p. 243), thus effectively limiting the possibility of any joint construction taking place, every attempt has been made to represent participants opinions as best possible. Focus groups can provide rich interpretative data as participants try to make sense of the fluid concept of gender by engaging in discussion with other participants and building upon their findings as a group, which also potentially contains an element of awareness-raising for participants themselves (Silverman, 2010). Focus groups are hence recognized as having overlapping pedagogical, political and traditionally empirical purposes (Leavy, 2014).

Focus groups took place in each of the seven Portuguese administrative regions (Nomenclature of Territorial Units for Statistics - NUTS) – Continental Portugal: Norte (North), Centro (Centre), Alentejo,

Algarve, and (Lisboa) Lisbon, and also, Madeira and Açores (Azores) –, with the objective of collecting information concerning the regional specificities of the tourism industry and tourism employment from the perspective of the key stakeholders in each region. The focus groups took place within five months, between November 2013 and March 2014. Each focus group had an average number of 11 participants, lasted for about 3 hours and was conducted in the style of a brainstorming session.

The participants were selected according to their representativeness, job creation capacity, level of connectivity with other agents (within the regional tourism network) and their role in the definition and implementation of regional and local policies for the tourism sector. A total of 79 tourism leaders from the private and public sector participated in the focus group discussions. The focus groups were relatively evenly balanced in terms of male and female participants with 36 female participants and 43 male participants, which amounted to 46% female participants and 54% male participants in the focus groups overall.

Content analysis methods were used for a systematic examination of the collected data, using an inductive approach. Whilst no approach can be completely classified as inductive due to the influence of theories and prior experiences of the researcher which are such that the researcher does not arrive at the analysis scene as a blank receptacle, this research does endeavour to be inductive (Denzin & Lincoln, 2011). An inductive approach is adopted by creating the categories which focus group data is coded into, using themes emerging from the transcripts, rather than solely from the initial questions. Doing so, we deny that it is possible to create laws that explain social processes and hence accept that reality is context bound.

GENDERED ORGANISATIONAL GROWTH STRATEGIES

This section's main aim is to make sense of all the rich information that emerged during the focus groups, by situating it within current discourse, literature and theories. The concept of world-making (Hollinshead, 2009) which is the actions individuals perform to privilege dominant representation of their 'world', is important to take into consideration when investigating deeply embedded social norms such as gender roles which often make the operation of these social structures, invisible. Hence, viewing participants as the embodiment of gendered economic subjectivities, this analysis focuses on the ways in which participants' narratives reveal how hierarchies that determine social life, shape tourism organisational growth strategies.

Innovation

Innovation is about facilitating market access, which requires the unbiased interaction of business members, and can be achieved by amending business structure. One of the problems is that innovative ideas don't just need to be synthesised, they also need to find their way to the ears of decision-makers. This gendered bias was echoed by participants who felt that a lack of innovation from women was partly because women do not occupy higher hierarchical levels and hence do not have the opportunity to get their ideas heard. As one participant says: *'The barrier that women face is often the hierarchy itself, which is composed of men and does not allow women to show their ideas to head managers.'* Indeed, recent research shows that employing more women in hierarchical positions would reduce gendered segregation and thus the symbolic associations between innovation, men and masculinities (Andersson,

Berglund, Gunnarsson, & Sundin, 2012). This gender bias within management structures, operates to men's favour, constituting men as more innovative, as illustrated in the words of a participant, who says: *'Men benefit without a doubt from more opportunities to innovate because they are, as a general rule, in higher hierarchical levels'*. This shows how gender silently operates to create perceptions of men as innovative, based on the economic structures that place them in higher management positions in the first place, which also relates to networking.

This section discusses the ways in which the various characteristics that participants associate with innovation discourse are gendered, focusing on creativity, credibility and risk-taking. Finally, some of the strategies employed by companies to involve women more in the innovation process are presented.

Creativity, Credibility and Innovation

Focus group participants concentrate on the ways in which innovativeness is a masculine or feminine trait, attempting to describe the 'natural' roles women play in innovative business practices. Most participants believe that women are more innovative and creative than men as *'they [women] effectively have a spirit of innovation, creativity'*, whereas men *'are very basic'*. One participant illustrates this by saying that 70% of new ideas in the company he represents were generated by women. However, despite this, the majority of participants feel that women were not very well represented or recognised within the innovative process because of various barriers.

Whilst creativity is the result of various factors such as type of parenting (Miller, Lambert, & Speirs Neumeister, 2012), it is often perceived as a feminine characteristic, as seen in social behaviour research on androgynous female and feminine male students (Stoltzfus, Nibbelink, Vredenburg, & Hyrum, 2011). However, despite the obvious connection between creativity and innovation and even though women are perceived as more creative than men, gendered limitations on the hierarchical positions that women can achieve, mould the roles within business that women can take, effectively limiting the role women play in providing innovative business solutions.

Whilst women are thought of as being creative, there are gendered perceptions of women lacking credibility. In the present research, gender influences women's hierarchical ascension and their role within decision-making positions. We find that even when women reach the top, they *'face the barrier of credibility'* as one participant quoted. Credibility is related to gendered perceptions of leadership effectiveness. Recent research finds that although men and women are perceived as equally effective as leaders, hence potentially having similar credibility, whilst women are more competent, men are more confident giving the illusion that masculinity is connected to credibility (Paustian-Underdahl, Walker, & Woehr, 2014). Credibility is a complex concept, but is based on two main pillars, trustworthiness and expertise (Henderson, 2005). In general, men are perceived as having more expertise, perhaps because they are more confident than women, hence appearing to be more credible.

Risk-Taking and Innovation

Indeed, confidence is closely related to another characteristic which is perceived as masculine, that of risk-taking (Charness & Gneezy, 2012). A link between the perceived masculine characteristics of innovation and risk-taking is pointed out by participants who say that the lack of innovation on women's side is *'related to the risk aversion that women have'* and progress to reinforce the idea that a propensity to take risks is correlated with innovativeness by saying that: *'The power of initiative and innovation are strongly correlated with a low level of [risk] aversion'*. However this explanation may be greatly influenced by gender roles that constitute masculinity to be connected with risk-taking. As gendered characteristics often operate at the exclusion of the other (i.e. a masculine characteristic cannot be a feminine one and vice versa) this means that femininity is not associated with risk-taking. The connection between femininity and an aversion for risk-taking is seen in research on female CEOs who were found to exhibit less corporate risk-taking behaviour (Elsaid & Ursel, 2011) and female leaders who were less likely to take the risk to invest than male leaders (Charness & Gneezy, 2012). However these type of studies also have received criticism for not representing reality as they lack methodological and analytical vigour by basing their methods and analysis on superficial understandings of gender roles (Nelson, 2014). Since the connection between risk-taking and femininity is ambiguous, so is the assumption that women do not excel in innovative growth strategies because they are risk adverse.

Strategies to Involve Women in the Innovative Process

As well as illustrating the reasons why women are less involved in organisational growth through innovation, some participants suggest ways in which companies can involve women more in the innovative process. This change in strategy comes from tourism managers realising that *'women can have an extremely important role in terms of potential in increasing the final quality of the tourism product'*. Indeed, incorporating women (and sectors which employ a lot of women) into the symbolic understanding of innovation can help deconstruct the link between innovation, men and masculinities and reconstruct a link between innovation, women and areas associated with women (Lindberg, 2012). This is because it is the very way that different industries are characterized, which creates and maintains segregating and hierarchical gender constructions.

Some participants say that their companies promote gender equality in the innovative process by creating systems *'that allow women to give suggestions for improvement of product and processes'*. As noted earlier, one of the main problems is that although women have suggestions, they cannot reach the positions where their suggestions will be heard. Although the details of how suggestions are being submitted and if the submitter is rewarded are not elaborated on further, this company policy indicates a positive change as the lack of women's contributions to the innovative process is actually recognised and acted upon. Another participant also mentions a similar program, called *'market/fair ideas'* which aims to *'give everyone in the company the opportunity to come up with innovative ideas'*. This was put into place just three years ago, showing how the realisation that women's contribution is important to company performance is a relatively new concept. The need to put such as system into place also shows that gendered constraints have often prohibited women's contribution, who apparently have a *'sprit of innovation'*.

Moving on to internationalisation, it is interesting to note the direct relationship that innovation and internationalisation have. Past research highlights how in fact internationalisation, is a form of innovation, essential to achieve higher company growth rates. Indeed, the topic of how an innovation perspective can contribute to the challenge of deepening theoretical understanding in the area of internationalisation has recently been addressed (Williams & Shaw, 2011).

Internationalization

While, depending on definitions, the internationalisation of tourism can be traced back not just centuries, but even millennia, tourism internationalisation has intensified in recent decades, because of the intensification of connectivities (Shaw & Williams, 2004). However, developing an understanding of the constitutive economic relations in this field remains a largely unfulfilled adventure for tourism researchers. Hence, this section analyses how tourism managers in Portugal define internationalisation and how they perceive it to be gendered, revealing the intimate connection between internationalisation and networking.

Defining Internationalization

In the current study, some confusion regarding the definition of the concept of internationalisation was present, as one participant says: *'with regards to internationalisation strategies, I had some difficulties in understanding what you meant... our strategy of internationalisation is to conquer customers of all nationalities without the chimera of making our accommodation international through franchising'.* This statement reveals the ambivalence felt by some participants in translating the concept of internationalisation as attracting international clientele or becoming internationalised as a company. However, drawing on internationalisation literature, both interpretations of internationalisation are equally valid. Firms grow either by launching a new venture on international soil or by attracting new customers or by using a mixed strategy (Kyläheiko, Jantunen, Puumalainen, Saarenketo, & Tuppura, 2011).

The majority of participants when asked to comment on gender roles within internationalisation concentrated on the aspect of internationalisation related to knowledge transfer. Accordingly, most participants chose to discuss if, why and how women are involved in attending international trade fairs. Attending international trade fairs, talks to the importance of developing networks of business relationships in other countries in order to internationalise (Breda, 2010). A focus on internationalisation as being largely dependent on trade fair attendance, highlights the importance of effective knowledge transfer conduits to firms wishing to internationalise.

Importance of Networks to Internationalization

Participants' focus on women participating in trade fairs does brings up an important aspect of internationalisation, that of the significance of networks to successful internationalisation. International literature identifies the significance of networks to internationalisation and highlights the ways in which different types of networks are needed at different stages of internationalizsation. For example, it is suggested that strong ties are better at the beginning of the process where as weaker ties are preferable as the venture develops (Musteen, Francis, & Datta, 2010). Other authors question whether business networks are more important that social networks, revealing a complex relationship between having cognitive capital (which is common amongst groups of people from the same country) and internationalisation success, as more cognitive capital means better sharing of information among team members of foreign market opportunities (Rosenbaum, 2013).

Drawing on the network approach to internationalisation, the majority of participants in the current study express how women are underrepresented in networks that facilitate internationalisation of tourism, largely because of gender roles that associate femininity with primary care-giver positions. Femininity is culturally related to motherhood and especially in Western cultures, these ideals involve *intensive* mothering, which competes for time with paid employment such as tourism work (Fox, 2006). The caring roles that women take on, are because gender is a "result of upbringing and social interaction" (Ahl, 2006, p. 597). Women are socialised from a young age to assume these caring positions based on expectations that they are primarily responsible for family care (Bakas, 2014). This gendered responsibility influences their perceived 'availability' to contribute to internationalisation processes.

Women are thus excluded from internationalisation through gendered ideals of a 'good' woman staying at home, which consequently limits their ability to travel to trade fair shows. Feminine ideals of remaining within the private sphere are common in patriarchal countries of Southern Europe, such as Greece (Dubisch, 1993) and prominent in Muslim countries such as Turkey (Tucker, 2007). These gendered ideals mean that husbands or other male members of the family may prohibit women from travelling or staying away from the house for too long as this is not considered 'proper' female behavior. All these, often conflicting 'ideals', are in a constantly alternating relationship with current politico-economic conditions that influence familial and individual priorities. The changing conditions mean that negotiations start occurring among family members, as social relations are re-ordered to fit with current demands on time and economic needs (Fenstermaker & West, 2013).

This is illustrated by how one participant says that women can go on work trips because *'the husband understands'* and how the *'husband keeps quiet'* about his wife's travelling, because it is for work. However, the shocking thing is that the same participant brings to light the rigidity of gender roles connecting women's confinement to the private sphere with 'good woman' ideals, by saying how *'in some families this [women's travelling] would end up with violence'*. A major review of academic literature on household abuse shows that gender traditionalism plays an important role in heterosexual intimate terrorism (Sugarman & Frankel, 1996) and that patriarchal societies are particularly at risk of such behaviour. This is a further illustration of how gender roles constrain women's involvement in tourism internationalisation.

'Availability' and Future Trends in Internationalization Discourse

Many participants say that a gendered limitation to women's involvement in tourism internationalisation strategies, is that women have limited 'availability to travel'. As one participant says: *'the woman is at a disadvantage in internationalisation, to have to travel abroad'*. Another participant points out how a woman has to sacrifice her personal life in order to play an active role in internationalisation, by saying: *'...for the woman to have the availability to do so [travel to trade fairs], she largely abdicates of her personal life; then she can accomplish internationalisation'*. Indeed, one participant comments how women's availability to take part in internationalisation is *'defined by family responsibilities'*.

Trade exhibitions which are perceived by most participants as almost a synonym to internationalisation, are considered, as one participant puts it as *'male territory'*. However, this is changing as one participant remarks: *'when a woman went to the trade fairs, at the beginning it was almost all men, but today the situation has reversed'*. This changing trend in women's involvement in tourism companies' internationalisation strategies, through their participation in trade fairs and exhibitions is echoed by the majority of participants who cite examples of women participating in international trade fairs. One participant says: *'if we look at who travels to attend trade shows and promotional actions, we see that there are a lot of women, and many have children'*. The participant's comment that these women 'have children' is interesting as it hides the gendered assumption that women who have children are primarily responsible for them. This double standard is visible in how no participant comments if a man who travels for work has children or not, as children are not automatically assumed to be a man's direct responsibility. Indeed, literature shows that having young children reduces the travel activity of women, whereas there is no similar effect among men (Gustafson, 2006). Mobility is often related to career development and being able to play a significant role in internationalisation. Internationalisation through mobility is increasingly equated to excellence in career prospects, as seen in research on female academics whose propensity for mobility means better career opportunities (Ackers, 2013).

Participants also indicate that more women are in charge of international market expansion, citing examples such as *'the woman in charge of the European market is also our official representative in international trade fairs'* or how their company has *'a female oenologist promoting our wines in national and international markets'*. Hence, participants note an increased participation of women in the internationalisation of tourism, which reflects international trends of more women participating in the workforce (Costa, Caçador, Carvalho, Breda, & Costa, 2014), but which has not been investigated before specifically in relation to tourism internationalisation.

Networks

As knowledge becomes the most important strategic asset for organisations in the 21st century, "networks and networking are fundamental to the knowledge development and sharing processes" (Durbin, 2011, p.101). Networking is significant within tourism organization growth strategies, because as one participant conceptualises it: *'Networking is a facilitator for new experiences and promotes excellence'*. Gender plays a role in the benefits accrued by professionals engaging in networking. According to Forret & Dougherty (2004, p. 430), certain networking behaviours enhance career outcomes, with gender differences in the returns of the networking behaviour as a career-enhancing strategy. In this section, the ways in which gender permeates discourses of networking according to participants is analysed, focusing on how informal networking is particularly gendered.

Significance of Networking to Tourism Organisations

The majority of participants, both male and female, felt that women were missing from many networking opportunities for various reasons. There are two main types of networking, formal and informal, both of which are equally important for business and individual progress. As one participant points out: *'both formal and informal networks are valuable'*. Indeed Wolff and Moser (2009, p. 202) find that "networking behaviours can contribute to differential salary growth over time" and also that "individuals who engage in networking behaviours are more satisfied with their careers". Indeed, a participant also notes that *'networks have influence on important decisions made with the company'*. Another participant comments on the significance of networking to his business saying that: *'One of the things that helped my company at the beginnings were precisely these networks.'*

How Informal Networks Exclude Women

Men's informal networks are much more established than women's informal networks. As one participant says, *'informal networks of men are natural in Portugal'*. 'Old boys' networks are occupied by "high status white men" (McDonald, 2011, p. 328), facilitating access to privileged information within the organisation, enhancing the formation of alliances and increasing the professional opportunities of their members. These networks operate on an informal basis at senior management level, and their exclusionary tactics to women have been well documented in various industries, including tourism (Forret & Dougherty, 2004; Liff & Ward, 2001). Particular network features influence differential access to social capital, namely "gender and race composition of networks are associated with access to job information and high status network alters" with homophily being "positively associated with vouching assistance from job contacts" (McDonald, 2011, p. 327).

Indeed, within the current study, tourism managers express how the exclusion of women from informal networks used to be on a formal basis, with men's clubs, like Feitoria Inglesa in Porto, having, up until very recently, regulations prohibiting the acceptance of female members. As one participant says: *'only recently have women been able to enter Feitoria Inglesa'*. Informal networks hence boost men's professional lives, but work as an obstacle to women's career development (Kotiranta, Kovalainen, & Rouvinen, 2007b; Zhong & Couch, 2007). As Durbin (2011) states: "If excluded from informal male networks, women may miss out on important opportunities for promotion as they are viewed as being poor in social capital." (p. 99). In addition, the informal nature of these networks makes it difficult to fight discrimination since organisations are not legally responsible for these informal work ties.

One participant very succinctly describes how informal networking is gendered, by saying: *'If the boy who has the ball only talks to that group of boys, for sure he will pass the ball to one of them, right? If there are no girls in the group, the girl would never get the ball'*. Here the participant is referring to the often strict segregation between men and women's informal networks. Indeed, the very fact that male informal networks have a long established history of research on them and even a special name for them – 'old boys' networks – highlights how research itself privileges masculine dominance within business literature, as women's informal networks are given less attention.

Women's Informal Networks as 'Gossip Groups'

Although women's informal networks do exist and are very influential, they are often devalued as 'gossip groups' as one participant calls them, rather than being given the value they deserve. Indeed, participants have the opinion that women's and men's informal networking groups are inherently different, which justifies the differential success of each. As one participant says: *'the men protect each other and have a very different group spirit from the spirit of women's groups. While women attack each other when they are in groups, men protect each other when they are in a group. They [men's group] show a united front, whereas women's groups do not.'* However, drawing on evidence of very successful women's groups, such as women's agrotourism cooperatives where poor, underprivileged women work excellently together, these 'excuses' seem weak (Aggelopoulos, Kamenidou, & Pavloudi, 2008; Malo, Beundia-Martinez, & Vezina, 2012). Whilst the sexist perception that women fight each other when in groups is prevalent in patriarchal societies, the plethora of women's groups ranging from handicraft societies, to cooking groups, to new mothers groups, it is obvious that women are efficient at operating within groups. Indeed, even taking a gendered view that the very 'nature' of women is to be the cohesive material within families, highlights how women are particularly skilled at diplomatically handling group relationships.

The main difference between formal networking and informal networking is that the former occurs during work hours and the later occurs outside work hours, often after a formal meeting. This networking issue is highly associated with time availability, which is gendered as women are often held responsible for caring and household work. As one participant says: *'women are not represented [in networks] because they make the natural choice of choosing motherhood'*. The concept of femininity being linked to primary responsibility for childcare is a gender role prominent in Portuguese society, reinforced by the Catholic Church's teachings. Gender-traditional religions such as Catholicism, tend to emphasize ontological differences between men and women, noting that men are predisposed to leadership and a strong work ethic, while women are naturally nurturing, passive, and receptive (Burke, 2012).

Should an 'Ideal Woman' Network?

Networking requirements can come at odds with perceptions of what the 'ideal' woman should be like, causing working women's partners to restrict women's time spent networking. One participant expresses this by saying: *'the husband at home does not accept very well that the woman goes out at 3am to have a drink with 2 male directors/colleagues'*. Indeed, female managers who are able to network, count themselves 'lucky' to have a husband who does not restrict their movements. One female participant recounts this as follows: *'Sometimes my husband says: 'what kind of job is yours?'. If he weren't a civilized person, maybe I couldn't have this job.'*

Gendered restrictions to female participation in networking extend even to the actual action of networking, rather than just the time availability. So when women do find the time for networking, they face additional problems, as one participant illustrates: *'I know some cases when a woman has tried to be part of these groups and go out with them to have dinner or some drinks; and if that woman shows to be independent or very confident of herself, men tend to wrongly interpret this attitude, which can raise problems of sexual harassment...'*. This raises the issue of how gendered beliefs can lead to sexual harassment, illustrating an extreme form of barrier to female managers' ability to partake in networking events. Sexual harassment is largely the result of men's skewed adherence to masculine gender roles that carry the perception of superiority and control (Johnson, 2011).

CONCLUSION

Drawing on the qualitative analysis of fresh empirical evidence, this chapter furthers knowledge on the ways in which gender operates within Portuguese tourism companies' organisational growth strategies. Looking at historical discourses associated with organizational growth strategies (Andersson et al., 2012), we note that these are largely masculinised, following neoclassical economic discourse where the productive rational self is perceived as male. Using a feminist economics viewpoint to deconstruct and critique neoclassical economic theory, this chapter reveals how gender strongly influences economic subjects' decisions and roles in tourism companies' growth strategies. Focusing on innovation, internationalisation and networking, it is found that gender permeates what are perceived as gender-neutral economic processes.

These often invisible permeations of gender are highlighted by the contradictory accounts of tourism managers regarding women's suitability for what are often perceived as 'male' domains. Whilst female tourism employees are presented as more creative, innovative and persistent than men, all of which are desirable characteristics of successful innovators, they are not well represented within then implementation of innovation practices. According to participant accounts, innovation is associated with masculine characteristics such as risk-taking and credibility, and less so by feminine characteristics of creativity which is a reason why women are not involved in innovation. However, since aversion to risk-taking is not an inherently male characteristic, we find that one of the main reasons for the exclusion of female tourism employees is that they do not occupy hierarchical positions that would involve them in innovation strategies. Furthermore, women's involvement in internationalisation *'is defined by familial responsibility'* as one participant says. Indeed, literature on gender and vertical segregation indicates that the reasons behind women's low representation at hierarchical positions relates to the connections between femininity and a primary care-giving role (Kulik & Olekalns, 2012).

However, there are more barriers than just women's prioritisation of familial responsibilities. Tourism managers point out that men's networks actively operate to exclude women from internationalisation and networking in an attempt to eliminate competition. The criticism of female tourism employees who partake in informal networking at night and the undermining of female tourism employees' networking groups as 'gossip groups', are examples of how women in this study are excluded from organizational growth strategies by drawing on gendered stereotypes of what constitutes 'correct' feminine behavior.

One way of increasing the number of women within tourism organizational growth strategies would be through the introduction of 'gender quotas', which refers to the legal requirement of the number of women on company boards. However, this measure should be approached cautiously as recent research within Spanish political parties (Verge & de la Fuente, 2014) finds that gender quotas on their own do not result in greater gender equality as the masculine behavior is valued (such as fist thumping and barking orders). The authors argue that since many business decisions are actually taken during informal networking, from which women are often excluded and for which 'gender quotas' do not exist, other measures should be taken to ensure more gender equality within workplaces. Since changing the way informal network operate, increases women's agency and limits men's power over women, it is a very significant goal in improving tourism organizational growth strategies' effectiveness.

The study finds that gender roles continue to limit women's contribution to tourism companies' organisational growth strategies, however, it also indicates that changes are occurring. Tourism managers mention how they are actively encouraging further contributions by women, illustrating how contemporary capitalist pressures to accumulate are progressively displacing socio-culturally imposed gender roles. In fact, the emergence of a new group of male tourism managers who are divorced and have childcare responsibilities, is giving rise to the novel concept of 'working father' as a new ideal of masculinity (Ranson, 2012). As new masculinities emerge, space for acceptance of feminized behavior is made possible.

Finally, we find that increasingly, gender equality goals are equated to economic gain for companies, making their adoption more frequent. Whilst this leaves the question of who is responsible for social reproduction unanswered, this study illustrates the need for tourism organizational growth strategies to be informed by in-depth analysis that takes gendered economic discourses into consideration, in order to improve tourism companies' development.

ACKNOWLEDGMENT

This article results from a research project on gender issues in the tourism sector, which is entitled 'Does gender equality have a say in the boost of innovative forms of economic growth? Reviving the economy through networks and internationalisation in the tourism sector' (PTDC/CS-SOC/119524/2010). The authors would like to thank the support provided by the Portuguese Foundation for Science and Technology, as well as the co-financing of the European Union through the National Strategic Reference Framework, European Regional Development Fund, and the Operational Program for Competitiveness Factors.

REFERENCES

Ackers, L. (2013). Internet mobility, co-presence and purpose: contextualising internationalisation in research careers. *Sociología Y tecnociencia/Sociology & Technoscience/Sociologia E Tecnociência, 3*(3), 117–141.

Aggelopoulos, S., Kamenidou, I., & Pavloudi, A. (2008). Women's business activities in Greece: The case of agro-tourism. *Tourism, 56,* 371–384.

Ahl, H. (2006). Why Research on Women Entrepreneurs Needs New Directions. *Entrepreneurship: Theory & Practice, 30*(5), 595–621. doi:10.1111/j.1540-6520.2006.00138.x

Ahl, H., & Nelson, T. (2010). Moving forward: Institutional perspectives on gender and entrepreneurship. *International Journal of Gender and Entrepreneurship, 2*(1), 5–9. doi:10.1108/17566261011044259

Andersson, S., Berglund, K., Gunnarsson, E., & Sundin, E. (2012). *Promoting Innovation - Policies, practices and procedures* (Vinnova Re). VINNO VA –Verket för Innovationssystem /Swedish Governmental Agency for Innovation System.

Ashcraft, K. L. (2009). Gender and diversity: other ways of making a difference. In M. Alvesson, T. Bridgman, & H. Willmott (Eds.), *The Oxford Handbook of Critical Management Studies* (pp. 304–327). Oxford, UK: Oxford University Press. doi:10.1093/oxfordhb/9780199237715.003.0015

Bakas, F. E. (2014). *Tourism, female entrepreneurs and gender: Crafting economic realities in rural Greece.* (PhD Thesis). University of Otago, Dunedin, New Zealand.

Barker, D. K. (2005). Beyond Women and Economics: Rereading "Women's Work.". *Signs (Chicago, Ill.), 30*(4), 2189–2209. doi:10.1086/429261

Baum, T. (2013). *International Perspectives on Women and Work in Hotels.* Geneva: Catering and Tourism.

Bernardino, L., & Jones, M. (2008). *Internalization and performance: an empirical study of high-tech SMEs in Portugal.* Bookonomics Lda.

Beyer, K. W. (2009). *Grace Hopper and the invention of the information age.* Cambridge, MA.: MIT Press.

Blake, M. K., & Hanson, S. (2005). Rethinking innovation: Context and gender. *Environment & Planning, 37*(4), 681–701. doi:10.1068/a3710

Bramwell, B., & Lane, B. (2014). The "critical turn" and its implications for sustainable tourism research. *Journal of Sustainable Tourism, 22*(1), 1–8. doi:10.1080/09669582.2013.855223

Breda, Z. (2010). *Redes relacionais e a internacionalização da economia do turismo. Departamento de Economia, Gestão e Engenharia Industrial.* Aveiro: University of Aveiro.

Brida, J. G., Driha, O. M., Ramón-Rodríguez, A. B., & Scuderi, R. (2015). Dynamics of internationalisation of the hotel industry: The case of Spainnull. *International Journal of Contemporary Hospitality Management, 27*(5), 1024–1047. doi:10.1108/IJCHM-11-2013-0527

Bruni, A., Poggio, B., & Gherardi, S. (2005). *Gender and entrepreneurship: an ethnographic approach.* New York: Routledge. doi:10.4324/9780203698891

Burke, K. C. (2012). Women's Agency in Gender-Traditional Religions: A Review of Four Approaches. *Social Compass*, 6(2), 122–133. doi:10.1111/j.1751-9020.2011.00439.x

Calof, J. L., & Beamish, P. W. (1995). Adapting to foreign markets: Explaining internationalization. *International Business Review*, 4(2), 115–131. doi:10.1016/0969-5931(95)00001-G

Carvalho, I., Costa, C., Lykke, N., & Torres, A. (2014). An Analysis of Gendered Employment in the Portuguese Tourism Sector. *Journal of Human Resources in Hospitality & Tourism*, 13(4), 405–429. doi:10.1080/15332845.2014.888509

Catalyst. (2015). *2014 Catalyst Census: Women Board Directors*. New York: Author.

Charness, G., & Gneezy, U. (2012). Strong Evidence for Gender Differences in Risk Taking. *Journal of Economic Behavior & Organization*, 83(1), 50–58. doi:10.1016/j.jebo.2011.06.007

Costa, C., Caçador, S., Carvalho, I., Breda, Z., & Costa, R. (2014). The Influence of Gender and Education-related Variables on Career Development: The Case of Portuguese and Brazilian Tourism Graduates. In The Tourism Education Futures Initiative: Activating Change in Tourism Education. Routledge.

Costa, C., Carvalho, I., & Breda, Z. (2011). Gender inequalities in tourism employment: The Portuguese case. *Revista Turismo & Desenvolvimento*, 15, 37–52.

Coviello, N. E. (2006). The network dynamics of international new ventures. *Journal of International Business Studies*, 37(5), 713–731.

Danilda, I., & Thorslund, J. G. (2011). *Innovation & Gender*. Västerås: Edita Västra Aros AB.

Denzin, N. K., & Lincoln, Y. (2011). *The SAGE Handbook of Qualitative Research*. SAGE Publications.

Dubisch, J. (1993). "foreign chickens" and other outsiders: Gender and community in Greece. *American Ethnologist*, 20(2), 272–287. doi:10.1525/ae.1993.20.2.02a00040

Durbin, S. (2011). Creating Knowledge through Networks: A Gender Perspective. *Gender, Work and Organization*, 18(1), 90–112. doi:10.1111/j.1468-0432.2010.00536.x

Elsaid, E., & Ursel, N. D. (2011). CEO succession, gender and risk taking. *Gender in Management: An International Journal*, 26(7), 499–512. doi:10.1108/17542411111175478

European Commission. (2010). Europe 2020 – A European strategy for smart, sustainable and inclusive growth. Brussels: Author.

Fenstermaker, S., & West, C. (2013). *Doing gender doing difference*. Hoboken, NJ: Francis Taylor.

Ferguson, L., & Alarcón, D. M. (2014). Gender and sustainable tourism: Reflections on theory and practice. *Journal of Sustainable Tourism*, 1–16. doi:10.1080/09669582.2014.957208

Figueroa-Domecq, C., Pritchard, A., Segovia-Pérez, M., Morgan, N., & Villacé-Molinero, T. (2015). Tourism gender research: A critical accounting. *Annals of Tourism Research*, 52(0), 87–103. doi:10.1016/j.annals.2015.02.001

Forret, M. L., & Dougherty, T. W. (2004). Networking behaviors and career outcomes: Differences for men and women? *Journal of Organizational Behavior*, 25(3), 419–437. doi:10.1002/job.253

Fox, B. (2006). Motherhood as a class act: the many ways in which "Intensive mothering" is entangled with social class. In K. Bezanson & M. Luxton (Eds.), *Social reproduction: feminist political economy challenges neo-liberalism*. Montreal: McGill-Queen's University Press.

Gherardi, S., & Murgia, A. (2014). What makes a "good manager"? Positioning gender and management in students' narratives. *Equality, Diversity and Inclusion:International Journal (Toronto, Ont.)*, *33*(8), 690–707. doi:10.1108/EDI-05-2013-0040

Gibson-Graham, J. K. (2006). *The end of capitalism (as we knew it): a feminist critique of political economy*. Minneapolis, MN: University of Minnesota Press.

Gustafson, P. (2006). Work-related travel, gender and family obligations. *Work, Employment and Society*, *20*(3), 513–530. doi:10.1177/0950017006066999

Henderson, J. (2005). Influence: The Impact of language, credibility and gender. *The Conservator*, *29*(1), 63–72. doi:10.1080/01410096.2005.9995213

Hjalager, A.-M. (2010). A review of innovation research in tourism. *Tourism Management*, *31*(1), 1–12. doi:10.1016/j.tourman.2009.08.012

Hollinshead, K. (2009). Review - tradition and the declarative reach of tourism: Recognizing transnationality - the articulation of dynamic aboriginal being. *Tourism Analysis*, *14*, 537–555. doi:10.3727/108354209X12596287114417

Johnson, M. P. (2011). Gender and types of intimate partner violence: A response to an anti-feminist literature review. *Aggression and Violent Behavior*, *16*(4), 289–296. doi:10.1016/j.avb.2011.04.006

Jordan, F. (1997). An occupational hazard? Sex segregation in tourism employment. *Tourism Management*, *18*(8), 525–534. doi:10.1016/S0261-5177(97)00074-5

Kotiranta, A., Kovalainen, A., & Rouvinen, P. (2007a). *Female Leadership and Firm Profitability*. Finnish Business and Policy Forum.

Kotiranta, A., Kovalainen, A., & Rouvinen, P. (2007b). *Female Leadership and Firm Profitability*. EVA. Retrieved from http://www.europeanpwn.net/files/eva_analysis_english.pdf

Kulik, C. T., & Olekalns, M. (2012). Negotiating the Gender Divide: Lessons From the Negotiation and Organizational Behavior Literatures. *Journal of Management*, *38*(4), 1387–1415. doi:10.1177/0149206311431307

Kyläheiko, K., Jantunen, A., Puumalainen, K., Saarenketo, S., & Tuppura, A. (2011). Innovation and internationalization as growth strategies: The role of technological capabilities and appropriability. *International Business Review*, *20*(5), 508–520. doi:10.1016/j.ibusrev.2010.09.004

Leavy, P. (2014). *The Oxford Handbook of Qualitative Research*. Oxford, UK: Oxford University Press. doi:10.1093/oxfordhb/9780199811755.001.0001

Liff, S., & Ward, K. (2001). Distorted Views Through the Glass Ceiling: The Construction of Women's Understandings of Promotion and Senior Management Positions. *Gender, Work and Organization*, *8*(1), 19–36. doi:10.1111/1468-0432.00120

Lindberg, M. (2012). A Striking Pattern. Co-construction of Innovation, Men and Masculinity in Sweden's Innovation policy. In S. Andersson, K. Berglund, E. Gunnarsson, & E. Sundin (Eds.), *Promoting Innovation. Policies, Practices and Procedures.* Stockholm: VINNOVA.

Mair, H. (2005). Tourism, health and the pharmacy: Towards a critical understanding of health and welness tourism. *Tourism, 53*(4), 335–346.

Malo, M. C., Beundia-Martinez, I., & Vezina, M. (2012). A conceptualization of women's collective entrepreneurship: From strategic perspectives to public policies. In M. A. Galindo & D. Ribeiro (Eds.), *Women's entrepreneurship and economics.* New York: Springer. doi:10.1007/978-1-4614-1293-9_14

McDonald, S. (2011). What's in the "old boys" network? Accessing social capital in gendered and racialized networks. *Social Networks, 33*(4), 317–330. doi:10.1016/j.socnet.2011.10.002

Miller, A. L., Lambert, A. D., & Speirs Neumeister, K. L. (2012). Parenting Style, Perfectionism, and Creativity in High-Ability and High-Achieving Young Adults. *Journal for the Education of the Gifted, 35*(4), 344–365. doi:10.1177/0162353212459257

Musteen, M., Francis, J., & Datta, D. K. (2010). The influence of international networks on internationalization speed and performance: A study of Czech SMEs. *Journal of World Business, 45*(3), 197–205. doi:10.1016/j.jwb.2009.12.003

Mutinelli, M., & Piscitello, L. (1998). The entry mode choice of MNEs: An evolutionary approach. *Research Policy, 27*(5), 491–506. doi:10.1016/S0048-7333(98)00063-8

Nelson, J. A. (2014). Are women really more risk-averse than men? A re-analysis of the literature using expanded methods. *Journal of Economic Surveys*, 1–20. doi:10.1111/joes.12069

Nyberg, A.-C. (2009). *Making Ideas Matter: Gender, Technology and Women's Invention.* Luleå University.

Paustian-Underdahl, S. C., Walker, L. S., & Woehr, D. J. (2014). Gender and perceptions of leadership effectiveness: A meta-analysis of contextual moderators. *The Journal of Applied Psychology, 99*(6), 1129–1145. doi:10.1037/a0036751 PMID:24773399

Pettersson, K. (2007). *Men as male as the norm? A gender perspective on innovation policies in Denmark, Finland and Sverige.* Stockholm: Nordregio.

Ranson, G. (2012). Men, Paid Employment and Family Responsibilities: Conceptualizing the "Working Father.". *Gender, Work and Organization, 19*(6), 741–761. doi:10.1111/j.1468-0432.2011.00549.x

Ridgeway, C. L. (2009). Framed before we know it how gender shapes social relations. *Gender & Society, 23*(2), 145–160. doi:10.1177/0891243208330313

Rosenbaum, G. (2013). Toward an understanding of how entrepreneurs access and use networks/social capital to internationalize: A gender perspective. In H. Etemad, T. K. Madsen, E. S. Rasmussen, & P. Servais (Eds.), *Current Issues in International Entrepreneurship* (pp. 296–316). Cheltenham, UK: Edward Elgar Publishing. doi:10.4337/9781781953426.00018

Shaw, G., & Williams, A. M. (2004). *Tourism and tourism spaces.* London, UK: SAGE.

Sigala, M., Christou, E., & Gretzel, U. (2012). *Social media in travel, tourism and hospitality: Theory, practice and cases*. Ashgate Publishing, Ltd.

Soares, R., Barkiewicz, M. J., Mulligan-Ferry, L., Fendler, E., & Wai Chun Jun, E. (2013). *2013 Catalyst Census: Fortune 2013 Women Executive Officers and Top Earners*. Retrieved September 18, 2015, from http://www.catalyst.org/knowledge/statistical-overview-women-workplace

Stoltzfus, G., Nibbelink, B. L., Vredenburg, D., & Hyrum, E. (2011). Gender, Gender Role, and Creativity. *Social Behavior and Personality: An International Journal, 39*(3), 425–432. doi:10.2224/sbp.2011.39.3.425

Sugarman, D. B., & Frankel, S. L. (1996). Patriarchal ideology and wife-assault: A meta-analytic review. *Journal of Family Violence, 11*(1), 13–40. doi:10.1007/BF02333338

Tucker, H. (2007). Undoing Shame: Tourism and Women's Work in Turkey. *Journal of Tourism and Cultural Change, 5*(2), 87–105. doi:10.2167/jtcc089.0

Verge, T., & de la Fuente, M. (2014). Playing with different cards: Party politics, gender quotas and women's empowerment. *International Political Science Review, 35*(1), 67–79. doi:10.1177/0192512113508295

Williams, A. M., & Shaw, G. (2011). Internationalization and innovation in tourism. *Annals of Tourism Research, 38*(1), 27–51. doi:10.1016/j.annals.2010.09.006

Wood, W., & Eagly, A. H. (2010). Gender. In *Handbook of Social Psychology* (5th ed.; pp. 629–667). New York, NY: Oxford University Press. doi:10.1002/9780470561119.socpsy001017

Zhong, Y. G., & Couch, S. (2007). Hospitality Students' Perceptions of Facilitators and Constraints Affecting Women's Career Advancement in the Hospitality Industry. *Family and Consumer Sciences Research Journal, 35*(4), 357–373. doi:10.1177/1077727X07299993

KEY TERMS AND DEFINITIONS

Economics: The study of production, transfer and consumption of wealth and labour power.

Feminism: The philosophy and movement promoting the radical idea that women should have equal opportunities as men.

Gender: Behaviors that produce what is perceived as 'masculine' or 'feminine'. Not necessarily related to biological sex.

Innovation: The action of producing something with novelty value that is commercially successful.

Internationalisation: Completing transactions with international partners and/or investing internationally.

Networks: The ways in which knowledge is transferred in a business sense.

Organisational Growth Strategies: The actions an organisation needs to take in order to achieve long-term goals that increase revenue.

Chapter 8

Consuming "Innovation" in Tourism:
Augmented Reality as an Innovation Tool in Digital Tourism Marketing

Azizul Hassan
The Cardiff Metropolitan University, UK

Roya Rahimi
University of Wolverhampton, UK

ABSTRACT

Upon understanding definition, features, application analysis of innovation and relevant theory of the Diffusion of Innovations, this study suggests Augmented Reality (AR) as a technological innovation. AR is an advanced stage of virtual reality that merges reality with computer simulated imageries in the real environment. This chapter synthesizes AR as an emerging and potential technology of digital tourism marketing and management. The aim of this analytical approach based chapter is to understand innovation from tourism product or services consumption perspective. Relevant evidences are also included on lenses of marketing, digitalization and innovation consumption. Results outline that, technology consumption is gradually reshaping and getting supported by the availability and accessibility of electronic formats as AR as a technological innovation. This symbolizes that the consumption of technological innovation as AR offers freedom to select, purchase and recommend in relation to the theory of Diffusion of Innovations by Rogers (1962).

INTRODUCTION

Tourism is the world's largest industry that continuously contributing global economy. The economic and market structures of countries across the world are diverse that necessitates technology application to cater growing demands of both consumers and businesses. Technology application in tourism is said as linked with Information and Communication Technology (ICT). ICT has been continuously contrib-

DOI: 10.4018/978-1-5225-0201-2.ch008

uting business activities including tourism. The extended roles and capacities of ICT are also diverging traditional means of technology adoption in tourism. ICT has witnessed a sharp rise of up gradation over the last few decades where, innovations in ICT have contributed largely. This is thus significant that, ICTs in present days are more innovative than ever before that simultaneously affecting the tourism enterprises. The attachment of innovative natured technologies is adopted by both traditional and electronic tourism enterprises. On the other side, the gradual excellence of technology has given rise to innovative technologies as Augmented Reality (AR). AR is seen as blending computer simulations of digital imageries in a real environment (Dadwal & Hassan, 2015; Jung et al., 2015). The growing demand is one of the key reasons to introduce and adopt technological innovation as AR in the particular area of digital marketing.

Innovation is expressed through creativity or excellence and thus the process is simultaneously well balanced with product or service development. Through all of these, innovation is responsible for both of application and maintenance the use and application of technological standards. The outcome of technological innovations can appear in diverse forms and in numerous forms. The term invention as followed by innovation is more focused on the society and the human being. These can also generate both positive and negative effects those can have immense effects on both of the humans and the society, itself. Innovations normally widens in more areas through their adoption and application. However, in tourism this is well manageable with destination management, service or product development. Technological innovation relates interests and general understanding of the general academia. Still, studies related to innovation show conceptual directions to develop general marketing approaches in tourism (Buhalis & Law, 2008; Hassan, 2012a, Hassan 2013b; Hassan & Rahman, in press; Hassan & Rahman, 2015; Hassan & Iankova, 2014). Thus, the development of innovation researches in tourism is critical and challenging from many perspectives. This becomes more evident with the involvement of internet supported technologies those are adopted in diverse forms by numerous agents having active presence in tourism marketing.

Upon understanding this theory, definition, features and application analysis of innovation suggests AR as a technological innovation. This study considers AR as an innovation and relies on the Diffusion of Innovations Theory of Rogers (1962). Thus the aim of this chapter is to critically explain the consumption of technological innovation. AR is the example of such innovation relying on digital format as Internet. Rapid digitalization helps expanding tourism product or service markets as well as increasing consumption capacities. Relevant evidences and examples are also been presented to support arguments.

INNOVATION IN TOURISM

A number of researches outlines that, technologies of innovative nature surely are affecting tourism trade (Hassan & Dadwal, in press; Hassan & Donatella, in press; Hassan, 2015; Azim & Hassan, 2013a; Azim & Hassan, 2013b). Innovation is a relatively an uncommon concept that mostly relates to technological excellences. According to Sarker (2007), the word 'Innovation' is derived from the Latin word 'in+novare' that means to make new, to renew or to alter. Sarker (2007) also suggests that, theoretically innovation is intertwined with entrepreneurship that supports unlocking opportunities of a new market leading to enhanced efficiency and economic growth. Finally, Sarker (2007) defines innovation as about to have or apply a new idea or even applying other people's idea in novel and new ways. From a general understanding, innovation refers to the process of advancement as concerned with application of updated technologies (Dodgson & Gan, 2010). Such technological innovations have expanded to more areas of human lives through their adoption and application. The adoption and consumption of a specific technology that can be termed as an innovation is not attached to a single factor rather, an accumulation of diverse factors generated from different perspectives. A consumer's capacities can vary in terms of spending, knowledge and interests to use technologies. From this perspective, innovation refers to a process that is attached more with application and use than planning or manufacturing (Fahrer, 2012).

In general, innovation is not attached with a single factor rather, an accumulation of diverse factors and artefacts of different perspectives. Innovation in a more applied understanding resembles its relatedness with science or arts and the application of theoretical understanding into practice for the well-being of the entire human being. Also, this is more related with the process of offering diverse social benefits. Innovations can appear in many types where, technological gadgets can replace the position of existing applications or machines, or even the entire systems (Penn State, 2013).

Innovation as the core of technological advancements can have applications in several business areas where, tourism sector can become a valid example for this. The online and web based technologies are demanding more priorities, in terms of their access and nature of uses in travel and tourism sector (Morrison, 2013). However, tourism service sector visibly renders better prospects to serve the entire innovation adoption process and thus to ensure better business profitability. In tourism, the offers and demands of services or products remain immense and are changing constantly. However, the application of technological innovation at least can support the innovation process to reach a certain stage of development that otherwise would remain difficult to reach. This is more understandable that, innovations can be beneficial for the entire tourism market development mainly through their non-conventional features. From consumer perspective, these situations in turn can emphasize more on developing services or products innovations for tourism. This creates more spaces for the application of technological innovation to support the tourists from harms across destinations in the world. Innovation can become a part of tourism strategy development towards embracing different market situations and abilities to adopt in diverse market conditions (Chang & Cheung, 2001). The relevance and requirement of tourism product or service innovations remains as a requisite for the comprehensive development of tourism industry in different countries across the world. These patterns and approaches always remain as challenging those need to be updated in accordance with both existing and potential demands. In a dynamic tourism market place where, the level and rhythm of competition are fierce and the involvement of competitors is strong, this is less likely that marketers can exist in competition without adopting valid sets of technological innovations. Enterprises ranging from medium to small scale has to adopt and apply technological innovations in accordance with their given capacities and limitations (Olsson & Väänänen-Vainio-Mattila, 2013). In case, when technological innovations are not adopted in an expected form and volume, the acceptability and validity of tourism market dynamics turn as less effective. This claim becomes evident not only for big scale in tourism enterprises but also, for small and medium scale enterprises, indeed.

Innovation Consumption

The general understanding of technological innovation consumption involves common practices and thus to attempt to apply the knowledge gathered so far (Yu & Tao, 2009). This is more aligned with product or service betterment through a way that concentrates on tourism market development through increased participation of parties or stakeholders. Innovation consumption is an important area while discussing innovation. Innovation consumption of a certain technology, product or service relies on users' habit, behaviour or consumption pattern (Shavininia, 2003). Innovation in a more applied understanding resembles its relatedness with science and technology and its theoretical motive to be placed into practice for well-being of the humans (McMeekin, 2002). Through all of the understandings, innovation is viewed to maintain and apply an updated technological standard.

Firm based innovation is playing crucial roles in technology application in tourism. One of the key examples of firm based innovation is the involvement of many firms to develop AR. The reshaping of AR is also hugely contributed by tourism firms aiming to bring further excellences in this sector. The outcome of a technological innovation can appear in diverse forms and in numerous areas. Technological innovation involves general practices and the attempt to apply such knowledge for human kind. Thus, from user acceptance and consumption perspective for a technology, the term invention as followed by innovation is more focused on the society and the human being (Swann, 2009). This is more related with the process of offering diverse benefits for users. Technological innovation relates to the understanding of general academic paradigms and shifting trends of knowledge to benefit both concepts and marketing approaches. The development of tourism marketing is critical and challenging from many perspectives. Marketing in tourism can appear in a type; where, technological gadgets can replace the existing applications or machines, or even the systems (Francesconi, 2012). Such trend of replacement becomes more evident with the involvement and support of internet that is adopted in diverse forms by numerous active agents of tourism marketing. Innovation is viewed as creativity or excellence and as a process that simultaneously balances well with product or service development and consumer use. However in tourism, the use of technology is seen as well managed in destinations across the world through effective management, service or product development (Hall & Allan, 2008). Innovation consumption in tourism is more aligned with product or service betterment that concentrates on tourism market development through increased participation of consumers, tourists, parties or stakeholders (Cox & Rigby, 2013).

Market based innovation is getting more attention and development over the last few decades. Tourism market is passing through so many changes and is getting familiar with so many technologies that, this is very often difficult to identify the nature and types of technologies those can be viewed as innovations (SAS Institute Inc., 2015). Tourism industry is also experiencing growing demands, modifications or developments and these are mostly technology supported. Such things in common can consequence to dramatic changes in the global tourism marketplace. For example, tourism industry has been passing through many unexpected situations and many of them can be viewed as fully undesired like war and attack on tourists (Conrady & Buck, 2011). Certain incidents as and accidents necessitate the demand and application of technological innovation for ensuring tourist safety. Lack of security and war issues can have negative effects on the growth of tourism business in certain countries of the world. Unexpected situations aggregate when life risks of tourists are also involved (Mihart, 2012). These create more crises in many areas of tourism industry and thus the improvement of existing situation becomes more critical and essential to get rid of ill effects of such incidents. Technological innovation adoption thus becomes necessary to minimize risks of such unexpected situations.

Augmented Reality (AR)

AR by name might appear as something that emerges from a different planet. However, the technology has been in use for quite a long time under different label of virtual reality. AR is thus seen as an advanced format of an earlier technology to concentrate on creating bridge between reality and augmentation. This technology is a visibly a blend of reality and computer generated simulation related to improve users' visual and motion capacities. Several types of AR technologies exist to cater demands of diverse consumer bases in visitor management, in museums, destination image formation or even in tourism related education (Hassan & Ramkissoon, in press; Hassan, 2013; Hassan, in press; Hassan & Sharma, in press; Hassan& Jung, in press; Shabani & Hassan, 2015; Hassan & Shabani, 2015). However, in general mobile AR is viewed as an advanced form to address increasing and multi-fold demands of tourists. The technology relies on using a mixed set of sensors for measuring 'data' from surroundings of a mobile device user for visualizing relevant information on mobile phone display as based on that specific perspective (Azim & Hassan, 2013). The data of such measurement can be anything but, depends on sensor capacities of the mobile phone or a particular electronic gadget. Thus, this is relevant to view AR as a medium to display a user's surroundings on either a mobile phone or any other electronic device. This is normal that the capacities and accessibilities of certain electronic gadgets can vary in accordance with the make and also considering market potentials. However, in general almost all Smartphones are more or less equipped with technologies those tend to support AR to meet increasing consumer demands. Still, this is a bit confusing to which degree or level a technological device can become able to support AR in both applications and device hardware.

AR brings changes in both the ways general users interact with a specific technology. Following advancements, this technology offers added benefits to general consumer bases and creates more opportunities to become popular within diverse consumer bases. AR is actually makes technology easier to reach and access with ensuring better outcomes. In many cases, future potentials of AR become visibly more reliable as developments of this technology have been made in recent times. In case more sensors are added in Smartphones, the capacities of AR are expected to reach a content level (Kounavis et al., 2012). For example, a user walks down a trendy shopping district and looks for an exclusive brand cloth. A particular brand stays in the user's mind and unexpectedly, the user cannot find that brand store. The user then starts using AR app using Smartphone's camera to get street image that stays ahead. AR overlays name of each store in streets that sells cloths of that particular brand. Then provides information of that particular and directs. Also, the user points Smartphone's camera on a specific store and gets information about products or brands those are carried in that store. The user then clicks the button and gets information about business hours of that particular store and plan shopping in accordance. AR technology tends to perform symmetrically both inside and outside the store to make shopping easier and comfortable for shoppers and users.

With the input of computer generated sound, information, graphics, video or GPs data, AR provides a live view in a real world or physical environment. The origin and development of AR is less questionable and clear. In particular, the existence of this technology cannot be less than decades. Boeing (2015) confirms that during the 1990s, this technology was used by the leading aircraft manufacturer Boeing. This time, AR was used with head mounted displays to support aircraft wiring assembly. This is one of the most complex jobs in aircraft manufacturing and the person who was in responsible for his job had a screen in front of them. The screen was overlaid with data showing the exact place to put the wires followed by identifying right colours and the functions of these wires and so on. However, the technology has been gradually changing over the years and these days this technology is no longer a complex technical task. AR has been turned as a relatively easier technology to be accessed by the general users and mass populations through using computer devices or mainly Smartphones. Several apps in Smartphones allow users to get familiar and access to AR technology. By using specific apps and phone's camera, AR technology allows users are entertained. For example, a user place the phone camera on a distant mountain and the app simultaneously overlays name of that mountain on the phone screen. The user then touches the button and gets detailed information about that particular mountain, its natural fauna, elevation and related information. This is not a miracle and technology brings information to users. AR apps in Smartphones use the phones in built digital compass, motion sensors and GPS to detect the positioning of that user. This particular technology is advancing rapidly on the basis of recent technological inventions. AR makes technology application livelier to the users through its diverse applications.

The Diffusion of Innovation Theory

Due to the unavailability of required number of literature, critical discussions about the Diffusion of Innovation Theory can hardly be elaborated and widened to understand academic stances related to this theory. As because there are shortage of relevant and sufficient number of literature, focuses are also need to be made on both core and peripheral research areas of technological innovation diffusion from tourism marketing contexts. The development of a critical understanding of technological innovation depends on sound academic knowledge. This requires critical understanding of discussed subject matters that entirely depends on both subjective and objective awareness of a researcher in tourism. For a relatively new researcher within the academic paradigm of tourism marketing, technological innovation can become an interest topic. Theoretically, technological innovation is attached with diffusion and can be assumed as a subject matter for further checks in terms of its application and acceptability.

The Diffusion of Innovation theory by Rogers (1962) is a widely popular concept for other knowledge areas including marketing, information technology and so on. But for tourism, its application is widely limited related to technology adoption. This is obvious that this theory of Rogers (1962) however, can make appeal to business entrepreneurs and tourism products or service consumers, symmetrically. This theory developed in 1962 but, there has been a long way to understand its application in recent tourism market structures. There are almost no scopes to ignore the importance and relevancy of technological innovation diffusion as an interesting subject area in tourism research. The application of technological innovation with their effective application have been left as understudied and unexplored for a long time. This is a key fact of tourism marketing that deserves proper attention both from the academic and practical senses. This is evident from the lack of available literatures those have concentrated on these study areas. A proper review of literature sometimes becomes impossible due to the unavailability of literatures in these identified areas. The adoption of technology through numerous innovations is brought to consumers through tourism enterprises. These enterprises cannot be identified as traditional rather they are more focused into technology and its purposeful application. Even almost every aspects of technology adoption become valid in the current tourism marketing context. Still, this is very unlikely that technological innovation diffusion gets sufficient focus from the concerned academics and researchers. Technological innovation diffusion can appear as a valid and promising research topic of tourism marketing. Also, in a world where, technology as an essential element deserves to be widely available and accessible in almost every spheres of human livelihood there are very low space to ignore the importance of technology in practical life. Thus, technological innovation diffusion as part of a research and study deserves due attention and particularly from academic tourism marketing perspective. Each aspects of the Diffusion of Innovation theory by Rogers (1962) require proper attention, discussion, description, critics and application from tourism research perspectives. This is particularly important to allow fellow researchers to advance further research in this defined knowledge area.

Following the Diffusion of Innovation theory by Rogers (1962), an innovation by the nature needs to be will matched and harmonized with the existing values or norms of a specific society. This should help to allow innovation to create specific type of impacts, in accordance. An innovation should create link between the innovators, practitioners and users, simultaneously. This should also benefit a society in terms of advancements and well performance. Also, the diffusion of a specific technological innovation has to be well accepted by the specific industry. Tourism industry in particular can be an example where, there are still lots of spaces left to improve and accelerate the patterns of both diffusion or adaption of innovations. Innovations need to be simple to use and their adaption should also be well documented, in terms of their applications and potentials. A simpler characteristic of innovation increases the chances for better affectivity and thus to create further opportunities for getting more popular. Relatively, newer types of innovations demand skills and knowledge transfer to turn them as more prepared for substantial use in practical grounds. The other feature of innovation is the triability that is, innovations demand experimentation in limited capacities. This is crucial because, previous trials offer innovations to generate better results and thus to turn them as more capable to match with demands of both of the existing and potential customer bases. The later feature is observation that is; innovations are required to be well adapted by individuals. Better outcomes of an innovation can produce the better acceptability of individuals, groups or customers. Possible results of innovations can encompass both visual and non-visual aspects. As the visual results of an innovation can have better capacities to attract certain number of individuals or customers. Visible results of an innovation can act as a way to spread the features of an innovation to allow them to create more interests among the friends, relatives or family members.

Features of the Diffusion of Innovation theory by Rogers (1962) can raise interests among a considerable number of customers, individuals or groups. These can also help to identify the weaknesses of an innovative product or service and thus to offer some sort of suggestions to improve them to reach a certain limit of betterment. The Diffusion of Innovation theory by Rogers (1962) is affecting tourism industry and has managed to create interests within certain individuals or customers. This theory has also become able to stimulate researchers to focus on identified individuals or customer base's demand fulfilment. This is thus very important to understand the limit or boundaries of the working capacities of this theory. The contexts or working spaces of this theory can vary and also can raise specific disputes among the target audiences. In the particular scene of tourism industry, outcomes of this theory thus lie within the entire tourism industry. This is evident that, innovations in tourism are taking place in terms of technologies and their applications. There are also elaborated credentials to outline the potentials of this theory that is; this theory may not have similar affectivity in every situation where, the variables vary over the years, places or circumstances. This is also essential to end any unexpected situations or circumstances those can have negative impacts on the entire tourism industry. Later discussion in this chapter is aimed to view augmented reality as an innovation in digital tourism marketing based on the above critical analysis of the Diffusion of Innovation theory by Rogers (1962).

Augmented Reality as an Innovation

On the basis of the Diffusion of Innovation theory by Rogers (1962), AR can be defined as an innovation. This questionable to identify the similarities between AR with mobile phone or other electronic devices followed by the contexts of its usage. Although AR is seen as an innovation but, its application has been present from the sixties, in terms of physical interaction of a certain technology with the humans. AR blends with virtual reality and offers multiple features including sound, visuals and physical sensations. The technology interacts in real time on the grounds of these three diverse aspects. These three different aspects can be viewed as stimuli. Different industries have utilized AR technology in different times but, the aeronautical industry becomes the pioneer to advance this specific type technology. Boeing is the leading player of this technology's global popularization followed by the unprecedented development of research initiatives in this specific technology. During the 90s, Boeing developed a special type AR goggle for engineers in wire harness assembly process. However, recent time's developments have witnessed AR to accumulate both visual data visualization as well as the local environment. Later on, several other industries have initialized the technology to certain limits covering entertainment and others.

Recent researches in tourism have explored different approaches of tourism by using AR for enhancing tourist experiences as a technological innovation. This technology has been viewed as more beneficial for the development of tourism and related research. Even followed by recent popularity of AR, there has been very low number of researches to identify AR as an innovation in tourism. The recent penetration of mobile, portable and wearable smart devices has in fact brought revolution in defining technological innovation in tourism. This has resulted the rise of demands of personalised items as smartphone devices to meet increasing demands of customers. The technology has offered various types functions to users those are mostly concerned with technological innovation development. Also, AR as a non-traditional technology has been placed in diverse technological gadgets ranging from mobile phone devices, recently developed Smartphones and wearable devices as Smart watches and many other devices those are expected to appear in the near future.

Countries across the world have applied or started applying AR in tourism. The European countries are way too forward in such endeavours. The Natural History Museum, the British Museum or even the Manchester museum in the United Kingdom has applied AR technology. France has applied the technology in many areas of tourism operation including Museum. The Louvre Museum is the basic example. Germany has applied AR in city based tourism where, the most prominent example in Berlin. Visitors in the Acropolis Museum in Greece have experienced AR. Numerous examples of AR application have been witnessed in countries many countries.

This technology has been expanded to mobile devices thus giving rise to mobile AR technology. AR has offered users with benefits of applying situational information that are based on their movements. Recently developed applications are mostly attached with identifying and offering information of user movements like sensor or positioning information to help users materializing desired outcomes. The increasing number of mobile phone users has actually expanded the entire market of AR application leaving more spaces for involving more users. Friendly attitudes of users towards a specific technological device have widened the boundaries of a specific technology use as AR. User friendly feature of this technology has been experiencing fierce competition in terms of experience sharing and advertising in mobile phone and wearable devices. AR has been appearing as a promising element of advertisement to create more interests among diverse consumer bases. Also, traditional mobile AR applications are getting attached with advertisements to offer the augmenting Point of Interest (POI) service (Juniper Research, 2015). However, this service relies on the positioning system of both user and their surroundings.

AR has prospects to offer in situ and essential information. Still, mainly due to the satellites' margin error, this technology has a sort of limitation to offer concrete and prompt information to the users. Also, the gross rate of failure to provide straightforward and accurate information in relation to real and visible information can be judged as crucial to get more concentration. This is evident that AR applications are interesting and capable to generate fun or entertainment. Still, the proper development of this eserves more attention from the authorities concerned to make it profitable and benefit . The both way communication between AR application and users need proper attention to e error margin those are caused by satellites. Thus, the satellite positioning denotes importance ase functionalities of AR technology. The technology offers both promises and prospects but, the accessibility and complex nature of usability restricts its mass use leaving it more sophisticated and less demanding in every parts of the world.

Not only in tourism but also in different other areas of marketing AR technology have been applied. One of the popular examples of such application that has been influenced by digital marketing strategies is IKEA. According to IKEA (2015), the world's leading furniture brand IKEA determines to address this issue in their 2014 catalogue. Following this catalogue application, users can be able to superimpose a specific product straightaway from the catalogue to a specific area of their home or office to check its match or position in the given room or office space. Thus a customer can be able to see and feel a desired furniture item without even going to an IKEA store or spending time. However, innovation is a relatively uncommon concept in the tourism academia and particularly related to technology application. The features of innovation are diverse and depend on certain backgrounds to adopt. In order to be termed as 'innovation' in tourism, a technology application followed by the use of gadgets as Smartphones or computers needs to be workable in a complex market system. Also, such technological innovation needs to be unique, technically excellent and risk minimized features with its user friendliness (Abernathy & Clark, 2007). The presentation of a novel technological innovation in tourism needs to be apparently prospective for marketing. Thus, an innovation in tourism typically has to be new and focused towards serving diverse consumer demands.

Digital Marketing in Tourism

Digital tourism denotes the marketing of services or products by using digital channels (Holloway, 2004). Internet stands as the key platform of such type marketing to reach consumers. In principal, the basic objective of digital marketing remains as to introduce, promote or marketing of brands on different forms of Internet supported media (Middleton et al., 2009). In tourism, digital marketing in most cases can hardly expand over the use of Internet to reach target consumers for marketing purposes (McCabe, 2013). Digital marketing in tourism remains as the most reliable and measurable Integrated Marketing Communication (IMC) component in tourism (Morrison, 2013).

The conventional types of marketing strategies can in many cases show less affectivity and this is why, the adoption of innovation becomes more powerful. The management of tourism destination can become less effective without using technological innovations on the base of their along innovative applications (Mariaani et al., 2014). This becomes specifically important when, destinations mostly rely on conventional technological processes (Turban et al., 2008). Typically, the management of tourism destinations is based on theoretical aspects and less likely to involve any form of dynamism of products or services development. In certain cases, existing strategies attached with destination marketing can become less effective followed by relatively poor capabilities to produce better outcomes and avoiding complexities. In a complex and more advanced market structure, the relevancy and adaptation level of technology can vary in relation to their capacities and the demand of situations.

Information technology is becoming amalgamated with manufacturing turning as more capable to offer product or service betterment for a specific industry, as a whole.

Product or service innovation has relatively more importance in tourism to fully exploit the capacities of technology adoption to represent technological advancements of improvements.

Increasing number of tourists is facilitating the process of innovation adoption through their wider forms of roles and abilities. Also, there are many cases those appear as aggravated and irrelevant when an increasing demand to meet diverse types of consumers is related. The trends and features of tourist bases across the world are constantly changing followed by the increasing number of ageing tourists (Yang, 2004).

The capacities to offer a memorable tourism experience are crucial and are influenced by the application of technological innovation into practice. Innovations need to be market demand driven than only focusing on using advanced technologies (Candela & Figini, 2012). The adoption and application of innovations mainly can then lead to fulfil the requirements of customers with the space for creating more opportunities. Technological innovation in tourism can improve the common market place.

Global marketing approaches in tourism are potential and the level of such potentials become less valid when, innovations cannot be applied at their expected pattern. This is very common that over the years almost every developed country in the world have passed through economic advancements based on technological innovations (Michopoulou & Buhalis, 2013). Such developments are mostly viewed as more effective towards creating opportunities for socio-economic development. Innovation creates roadmap for creating a specific industry to be featured as more wealthy. Such industry in a country therefore can become beneficial for serving demands of huge consumer bases. The existing market patterns in tourism in developed countries do not always support niche markets. Still, these markets are relevant for benefitting entire tourism market structures across the world to reach the optimum level. To ensure this, effective participation and involvement of both existing and potential customers is essential. These examples are viewed as replicable for other nations those are termed as developing nations (Wynne et al., 2001). The emergence of new markets can have huge impacts on the existing tourism market structure by both generating and supporting increased number of tourists. Brazil, India or China are example and expected to be major players of global tourism in coming years.

Augmented Reality Consumption in Digital Tourism Marketing

AR is actually a game changer for a business enterprise that relies on digital platforms as Internet. Business enterprises related to sports or entertainment has closer interaction with AR as well as with social media. The increasing popularity of AR can be actually viewed as the start of a potential technology application aimed to dominate the future technology world. This is expected that over the next few years AR is not only leaving huge effects on the existing technology led lifestyle but also; create scopes to interact with the whole world mainly by wearable technological gadgets (Breeze, 2014; Buchholz, 2014).

The involvement of social elements to AR is an interesting fact to be considered for the general development of this particular technology. For example in a busy crowd or meeting, a general pedestrian needs to reach home quickly (Mitropoulos & Tatum, 2008). In reality he is lost in the crowd and fails to identify the shortest route to escape from such crowd. AR application is brought in use and the app shows the direction of crowd with exits to reach home within the shortest possible time. This example has been brought in reality by a San Francisco based start-up company named CrowdOptic. Invention of this company allows users to identify the exact direction to which peoples' crowd pointing their phones. By using the app developed by CrowdOptic, users can then become able to invite others to see the displays of those phones. Again, in busy and big racing track at a NASCAR race many visitors could not see the track. These spectators then point their phones towards a distant track, get relevant photos with videos those closer viewers were watching and gathered (AR blog, 2015).

According to inc (2015), a recent research shows that by the end of 2015, approximately 2.5 billion AR applications should be downloaded per year and expects to generate a minimum of US $ 1.5 billion as revenue. Several agencies and entrepreneurs become involved with developing and using AR to serve specific purposes. AR can be viewed as passed its infancy stage and becoming more mature. 3Pillar Global is a company that builds applications mostly AR for reputed companies as PBS and CARFAX. 3Pillar builds an attractive app for the Ballston Business Improvement District that allows attendants at the Taste of Arlington event to pose for pictures with DC sports celebrities virtual version as the Washington Capitals' Alex Ovechkin, DC United's Chris Pontius and the Washington Wizards' John Wall. Such approach in a sense can be featured as great to promote a specific event on the way this is moves on and allows the experiences live longer even after the attendees go back home. David DeWolf, the Chief Executive Officer of 3Pillar Global identified three specific ways within which AR supports customer experiences to change expected interactions with the physical environment. These three ways as mentioned above are innovative.

The first innovative way is to support physical product purchase. If a company is aimed to sell physical products as decorative items or furniture the most difficult barrier appears before them is their ability to visualize how the product would look or fit in a desired space as the consumer's home or office. According to AR-Media (2015), AR as technology can work both inside and outside of store or place. For example, a customer tends to purchases a specific product from a warehouse that is massive in size. Out of hundreds of products, the customer's demand to buy a tiny item of a plant is visibly very difficult. The customer tend to find assistants but could not find one and then wanderer from aisles to aisles and still could not find the desired plant item. The customer then brings augmented reality technology in use on the basis of built app in Smartphone. The customer tells the Smartphone the actual plant name and details. The customer then pans around the Smartphone camera and have the AR app activated. As the customer moves inside the store a small arrow on the Smartphone screen starts directing from one aisle to the other and thus showing the exact place where the plant is displayed. Thus, both visibly and practically, AR makes life easier as well as customary shopping patterns of the users (Azuma, 1997).

The second innovative way is to get engaged with customers in novel ways. Turning a general customer as loyal for years cannot be simple job. This requires clear engagement both before and afterwards purchases. Customer relationship management is a more theoretical notion that has been placed as an interesting subject matter for years. J. Walter Thompson (2015) affirms that, Johnson & Johnson's is mainly a leading medical equipment and toiletries product manufacturer. This company has expanded operation across the world by both adopting dynamic marketing strategies and using technology applications. One of its products, Band-Aid Magic Vision becomes a good example for following customer relationship. AR application for this product is simply innovative in a way that engages an important target market with a consumer package goods company. The target market is defined as two to eight year old consumers. The time when a user points the camera of their device that is mostly a Smartphone a t a braded Band-Aid, they can see video messages from Muppets characters. These Muppets characters are commonly viewed as popular. This is one of the basic ways to maintain customer engagement even after making purchases.

The third innovative way is to enhance on-site customer experiences. According to Prote (2015), Bacon technology and AR is used in the Peter Paul Rubens Museum in Antwerp. These technologies widen user experiences by offering an interactive guide that is virtual and provides added information on their surroundings relying the location. Such application benefits visitors by providing extra information about the museum's art work, interactive games and guided tour services. A business that ensures the presence of a brick-and-mortar, similar applications can be used to capitalize possibilities of both in- store and direct marketing.

A changed purchase and consumption patterns exists to accept and gradually direct marketing initiatives for tourism. Gartner (2013) expects that, on the basis of continual technological advancements, general public will be highly accepting the AR technologies in 2014. However, AR applications as marketing instruments are still subject of further explanation where, technology for mass consumer base cannot be always readily available (Yovcheva et al., 2012). Recently developed technological gadgets are harnessing such technologies those the users have not experienced in their previous use. One of such examples is that AR tends to become a popular means of entertainment and have started to expand in other relevant areas as education (Shen et al., 2011).

CONCLUSION

This conceptual chapter mainly concentrates on aspects technology innovation consumption in tourism marketing with AR as an example. AR is seen as an innovative technology that is emerging in marketing. In tourism, innovation is a common word and mostly related to technological excellences and from a more general understanding, innovation refers to the process of advancement that is concerned with the improvement of technological applications. From a more tourism conceptual perspective, innovation refers to a process that is attached with both planning and manufacturing of an idea at the same time. This is involved with the development of ideas, placing ideas into action, examining, experimentation and the manufacturing of a specific product or service. Thus, these features can clearly outline AR as a technological innovation. AR is also outlined by something that is not existed or that is more in advanced form than present. This chapter confirms the introduction and presence of technological innovation as AR in different activities of consumption. The wider availability of technology through many types of innovations has made both commercialization and marketing easier than ever before. In particular, this chapter considers the case of AR as example to outline a shift from conventional to non-conventional. On the basis of Rogers (1962), the Diffusion of Innovations Theory, the chapter identifies AR as an innovation. In addition citing many examples of consumption, behaviour this study defines AR as a valid tool of technology supported marketing. The chapter proposes that a clear understanding of technological innovation consumption is required to learn gradual or potential changes. Technology application expands the capacities of consumers allowing them more freedom for marketing. The changing patterns of tourism product or service consumers' behaviour, attitude or perception about particular technological innovation consumption requires more attention from both academics and practitioners. This is obvious that the capacities of AR to appear as a marketing instrument are convincing as well as challenging. Innovation as a notion has been mostly popularised by Rogers (1962) through the 'Diffusion of Innovations' theory. Basic limitations of this chapter are the lack of available literature and absence of primary data. These two concerns can be seen as key drawbacks of this particular chapter. Future research areas can cover more technological innovations those can potentially be viewed as emerging to dominate future market settings.

REFERENCES

Abernathy, W., & Clark, K. B. (2007). Innovation: Mapping the winds of creative destruction. *Research Policy, 14*(1), 3–22. doi:10.1016/0048-7333(85)90021-6

AR-Media. (2015). *Augmented reality and the future of printing and publishing opportunities and perspectives*. Retrieved from: http://www.inglobetechnologies.com/docs/whitepapers/AR_printing_whitepaper_en.pdf

Augmented Reality Blog. (2015). *How augmented reality can revolutionize the hospitality industry*. Retrieved from: http://www.augmentedrealitytrends.com/augmented-reality/hospitality-industry.html

Azim, R., & Hassan, A. (2013). Impact analysis of wireless and mobile technology on business management strategies. *Journal of Information and Knowledge Management, 2*(2), 141–150.

Azim, R., & Hassan, A. (2013a). *Understanding Recent Wireless and Mobile Technological Changes for Business Management Practises*. The 6th International Conference on Business Market Management (BMM). The University of Bamberg. Available at: http://bit.ly/Ns5u1C

Azim, R., & Hassan, A. (2013b). *Analysing the impact of mobile and wireless technology on Business Management Strategies*. The 6th International Conference on Business Market Management (BMM). The University of Bamberg. Available at: http://bit.ly/Ns5u1C

Azuma, R. (1997). A survey of augmented reality. *Presence (Cambridge, Mass.), 6*(4), 355–385. doi:10.1162/pres.1997.6.4.355

Boeing. (2015). *Boeing's working on augmented reality, which could change space training, ops*. Retrieved from: http://bit.ly/1SquO89

Breeze, M. (2014). *How augmented reality will change the way we live*. Retrieved from: http://tnw.co/1nEDN6O

Buchholz, R. (2014). *Augmented reality: New opportunities for marketing and sales*. Retrieved from: http://bit.ly/1nMCLYO

Buhalis, D., & Law, R. (2008). Progress in information technology and tourism management: 20 years on and 10 years after the internet-The state of eTourism research. *Tourism Management, 29*(4), 609–623. doi:10.1016/j.tourman.2008.01.005

Candela, G., & Figini, P. (2012). *The economics of tourism destinations*. Berlin: Springer. doi:10.1007/978-3-642-20874-4

Chang, M. K., & Cheung, W. (2001). Determinants of the intention to use Internet/ WWW at work: A confirmatory study. *Information & Management, 39*(1), 1–14. doi:10.1016/S0378-7206(01)00075-1

Conrady, R., & Buck, M. (2011). *Trends and issues in global tourism 2011*. London: Springer. doi:10.1007/978-3-642-17767-5

Cox, D., & Rigby, J. (2013). *Innovation policy challenges for the 21st century*. New York: Routledge.

Dadwal, S., & Hassan, A. (2015). The Augmented Reality Marketing: A Merger of Marketing and Technology in Tourism. In N. Ray (Ed.), *Emerging Innovative Marketing Strategies in the Tourism Industry* (pp. 78–96). Hershey, PA: IGI Global. doi:10.4018/978-1-4666-8699-1.ch005

Dodgson, M., & Gan, D. (2010). *Innovation: a very short introduction*. Oxford, UK: Oxford University Press. doi:10.1093/actrade/9780199568901.001.0001

Fahrer, N. (2012). *Innovation and other useless things: a jump-start for discussions*. New York: Norman Fahrer.

Francescon, S. (2012). *Generic integrity and innovation in tourism texts in English*. Academic Press.

Gartner Incorporated. (2014). *Gartner technology research*. Retrieved from: http://gtnr.it/1nvU5Bb

Hall, M. C., & Allan, W. (2008). *Tourism and innovation*. Oxon, UK: Routledge.

Hassan, A. (2012a). Key Components for an Effective Marketing Planning: A Conceptual Analysis. *International Journal of Management & Development Studies*, *2*(1), 68–70.

Hassan, A. (2012b). Rationalization of Business Planning Through the Current Dynamics of Tourism. *International Journal of Management & Development Studies*, *2*(1), 61–63.

Hassan, A. (2013). Perspective Analysis and Implications of Visitor Management - Experiences from the Whitechapel Gallery, London. *Anatolia: An International Journal of Tourism and Hospitality Research*. DOI: 10.1080/13032917.2013.797916

Hassan, A. (2015). The Customization of Electronic Word of Mouth: An Industry Tailored Application for Tourism Promotion. In S. Rathore & A. Panwar (Eds.), *Capturing, Analyzing and Managing Word-of-Mouth in the Digital Marketplace* (pp. 61–75). Hershey, PA: IGI Global.

Hassan, A. (in press). Destination Image Formation: The Function Analysis of Augmented Reality Application. In M. Khosrow-Pour (Ed.), *The Encyclopaedia of Information Science and Technology* (4th ed.). Hershey, PA: IGI Global.

Hassan, A., & Dadwal, S. (in press). Search Engine Marketing – An Outlining of Conceptualization and Strategic Application. In W. Ozuem & G. Bowen (Eds.), *Competitive Social Media Marketing Strategies*. Hershey, PA: IGI Global.

Hassan, A., & Donatella, P. S. (in press). Google AdSense as a Mobile Technology in Education. In J. L. Holland (Ed.), *Handbook of Research on Wearable and Mobile Technologies in Education*. Hershey, PA: IGI Global. doi:10.4018/978-1-5225-0069-8.ch011

Hassan, A., & Iankova, K. (2012). Strategies and Challenges of Tourist Facilities Management in the World Heritage Site: Case of the Maritime Greenwich, London. *Tourism Analysis*, *17*(6), 791–803. doi:10.3727/108354212X13531051127348

Hassan, A., & Jung, T. (in press). Augmented Reality as an Emerging Application in Tourism Education. In D. H. Choi, A. Dailey-Hebert, & J. S. Estes (Eds.), *Emerging Tools and Applications of Virtual Reality in Education*. Hershey, PA: IGI Global.

Hassan, A., & Rahman, M. (2015). Macromarketing Perspective in Promoting Tourism: The Case of the Buddhist Vihara at Paharpur. *Tourism Spectrum*, *1*(2), 13–19.

Hassan, A., & Rahman, M. (in press). World Heritage Site as a Label in Branding a Place. *Journal of Cultural Heritage Management and Sustainable Development*.

Hassan, A., & Ramkissoon, H. (in press). Augmented Reality for Visitor Experiences. In J. N. Albrecht (Ed.), *Visitor Management*. Oxfordshire, UK: CABI.

Hassan, A., & Shabani, N. (2015). *eMarketing Adoption in Tourism and Hospitality Industry in London: Industry Analysis and Some Narratives*. The 4th International Interdisciplinary Business-Economics Advancement Conference (IIBA). Available at: http://bit.ly/1BQqGnI

Hassan, A., & Sharma, A. (in press). Wildlife Tourism: Technology Adoption for Marketing and Conservation. In M. A. Khan & J. K. Fatima (Eds.), *Wilderness of Wildlife Tourism*. Waretown: Apple Academic Press, Inc.

Holloway, J. C. (2004). *Marketing for tourism*. Essex, UK: Pearson Education Limited.

IKEA. (2015). *2014 IKEA Catalogue Comes To Life with Augmented Reality*. Retrieved from: http://bit.ly/1uQHR86

inc. (2015). *3 smart ways augmented reality is changing the customer experience*. Retrieved from: http://www.inc.com/eric-holtzclaw/using-augmented-reality-to-enhance-the-customer-experience.html

Jung, T., Chung, N., & Leue, M. (2015). The determinants of recommendations to use augmented reality technologies: The case of a Korean theme park. *Tourism Management*, *49*, 75–86. doi:10.1016/j.tourman.2015.02.013

Juniper Research. (2015). *Mobile augmented reality IFx1 2013-2018*. Retrieved from: http://www.juniperresearch.com/researchstore

Kounavis, C. D., Kasimati, A. E., & Zamani, E. D. (2012). Enhancing the tourism experience through mobile augmented reality: Challenges and prospects. *International Journal of Engineering Business Management*, *4*, 1–6.

Marcello, M., Baggio, M. R., Buhalis, D., & Longhi, C. (2014). Tourism management, marketing, and development: volume I: the importance of networks and ICTs. New York: Palgrave McMillan.

McCabe, M. (2013). *The Routledge handbook of tourism marketing*. New York: Routledge.

Mcmeekin, A., Tomlinson, M., Green, K., & Walsh, V. (2009). *Innovation by demand: an interdisciplinary approach to the study of demand and its role in innovation (new dynamics of innovation and competition MUP)*. Manchester, UK: Manchester University Press.

Michopoulou, E., & Buhalis, D. (2013). Information provision for challenging markets: The case of the accessibility requiring market in the context of tourism. *Information & Management*, *50*(5), 229–239. doi:10.1016/j.im.2013.04.001

Middleton, V. T. C., Fyall, A., Morgan, M., & Ranchhod, A. (2009). *Marketing in travel and tourism*. Oxford, UK: Butterworth Heinemann.

Mihart, C. (2012). Impact of Integrated Marketing Communication on Consumer Behaviour: Effects on Consumer Decision – Making Process. *International Journal of Marketing Studies*, *4*(2), 121–129. doi:10.5539/ijms.v4n2p121

Mitropoulos, P., & Tatum, C. B. (2008). Forces driving adoption of new information technologies. *Journal of Construction Engineering and Management*, (September-October), 340–348.

Morrison, A. M. (2013). *Marketing and managing tourism destinations*. Oxon, UK: Routledge.

Okazaki, S. (2005). Mobile advertising adoption by multinationals: Senior executives' initial responses. *Internet Research*, *15*(2), 160–180. doi:10.1108/10662240510590342

Olsson, T., & Väänänen-Vainio-Mattila, K. (2013). Expected User Experience of Mobile Augmented Reality Services. *Personal and Ubiquitous Computing*, *17*(2), 287–304. doi:10.1007/s00779-011-0494-x

Penn State. (2013). *Factors identified that influence willingness to use new information technology*. Retrieved from: http://news.psu.edu/story/267639/2013/03/07/science-and-technology/factors-identified-influence-willingness-use-new

Prote. (2015). *iBeacon*. Retrieved from: http://bit.ly/1embSQh

Rogers, M. E. (1962). *Diffusion of Innovations*. New York: Free Press.

Salvadori, N., & Balducci, R. (2005). *Innovation, unemployment, and policy in the theories of growth and distribution*. Cheltenham, UK: Edward Elgar Publishing. doi:10.4337/9781845428167

Sarker, S. (2007). *Innovation, market archetypes and outcome: An integrated framework*. New York: Physica-Verlag.

SAS Institute Inc. (2015). *Digital marketing-what is it and why it matters*. Retrieved from: http://bit.ly/1cRj6SG

Shabani, N., & Hassan, A. (2015). *Innovative Technology Diffusion in Hospitality: Concept and Industry Perspective*. The 5th International Interdisciplinary Business-Economics Advancement Conference (IIBA). Available at: http://bit.ly/1BQqGnI

Shavinina, L. V. (2003). *The international handbook on innovation*. Oxford, UK: Elsevier Science Limited.

Shen, Y., Ong, S. K., & Nee, A. Y. C. (2011). Vision-based hand interaction in augmented reality environment. *International Journal of Human-Computer Interaction*, *27*(6), 523–544. doi:10.1080/10447318.2011.555297

Swan, G. M. P. (2009). *The economics of innovation: an introduction*. Cheltenham, UK: Edward Elgar Publishing.

Turban, E., McLean, E. R., & Wetherbe, J. C. (2008). *Information technology for management*. John Wiley and sons, Inc.

Werthner, H., & Klein, S. (1999). *Information technology and tourism - a challenging relationship*. Vienna: Springer-Verlag. doi:10.1007/978-3-7091-6363-4

Wynne, C., Berthon, P., Pitt, L., Ewing, M., & Napoli, J. (2001). The impact of the Internet on the distribution value chain- the case of the South African tourism industry. *International Marketing Review*, *18*(4), 420–431. doi:10.1108/EUM0000000005934

Yang, C. C. (2004). Exploring factors affecting the adoption of mobile commerce in Singapore. *Telematics and Informatics*, *22*(3), 257–277. doi:10.1016/j.tele.2004.11.003

Yovcheva, Z., Buhalis, D., & Gatzidis, C. (2012). Smartphone augmented reality applications for tourism. *e-Review of Tourism Research*, *10*(2), 63-66.

Yu, C.-S., & Tao, Y. H. (2009). Understanding business-level innovation technology adoption. *Technovation*, *29*(2), 92–109. doi:10.1016/j.technovation.2008.07.007

ADDITIONAL READING

Gartner Incorporated. (2014). Gartner Technology Research. Retrieved from: http://Online.gartner.com/technology/home.jsp> (accessed: the 29th September, 2014).

Herbst, I., Braun, A.-K., Mccall, R., & Broll, W. (2008). TimeWarp: Interactive time travel with a mobile mixed reality game. Retrieved from: http://citeseerx.ist.psu.edu/viewdoc/download;jsessionid=7001C F82F69CEA5001A5B74F7C8CD1B9?doi=10.1.1.368.5238&rep=rep1&type=pdf (accessed: the 01st January, 2015).

Jung, T., & Han, D. (2014). Augmented reality (AR) in urban heritage tourism. e-Review of Tourism Research, p. 1.

Marketing Society. (2015). Pepsi pushes augmented reality to the MAX. Retrieved from: https://www.marketingsociety.com/the-library/pepsi-pushes-augmented-reality-max (accessed: the 01st January, 2015).

Preexamples (2015). Paddy Power augmented reality campaign brings the Queen's face on £10 note to life. Retrieved from: http://bit.ly/1CRur13 (accessed: the 09th January, 2015).

prweb (2011). Digital frontiers media uses augmented reality to market St. Pete/Clearwater tourism with miles media. Retrieved from: http://www.prweb.com/releases/2011/03/prweb5141134.htm (accessed: the 01st January, 2015).

Seo, B.-K., Kim, K., & Park, J. (2011). Augmented reality-based on-site tour guide: A study in Gyeongbokgung. *Lecture Notes in Computer Science*, *6469*, 276–285. doi:10.1007/978-3-642-22819-3_28

Social Media and Games Law Blog. (2015). Recently in augmented reality category. Retrieved from: http://www.socialgameslaw.com/augmented-reality/ (accessed: the 01st February, 2015).

Spencer, A. J., Buhalis, D., & Moital, M. (2011). A hierarchical model of technology adoption for small owner-managed travel firms: An organizational decision-making and leadership perspective. *Tourism Management*, *33*(5), 1195–1208. doi:10.1016/j.tourman.2011.11.011

Suh, Y., Shin, C., Woo, W., Dow, S., & MacIntyre, B. (2011). Enhancing and evaluating users' social experience with a mobile phone guide applied to cultural heritage. *Personal and Ubiquitous Computing, 15*(6), 649–665. doi:10.1007/s00779-010-0344-2

Sung, J., & Cho, K. (2012). User experiences with augmented reality advertising applications: Focusing on perceived values and telepresence based on experiential learning theory. *Lecture Notes in Electrical Engineering, 182*, 9–15. doi:10.1007/978-94-007-5086-9_2

Total Immersion. (2015). The Future of augmented reality. Retrieved from: http://www.t-immersion.com/augmented-reality/future-vision (accessed: the 01st January, 2015).

KEY TERMS AND DEFINITIONS

Augmented Reality: Augmented reality is an advanced stage of virtual reality that merges reality with computer simulated imageries in the real environment.

Digital Tourism Marketing: The non-conventional form of marketing that involves electronic platform mainly the Internet for operation.

Innovation: From a general understanding, innovation refers to the process of advancement as concerned with application of updated technologies.

Chapter 9
Robust Innovation Anchors in Rural Wellbeing Tourism

Anne-Mette Hjalager
University of Southern Denmark, Denmark

Anja Tuohino
University of Eastern Finland, Finland

Kaarina Tervo-Kankare
University of Oulu, Finland

Henna Konu
University of Eastern Finland, Finland

ABSTRACT

Innovation in tourism does not take place in a vacuum. Innovators find inspiration from many sources. This article identifies ten innovation anchors, e.g. critical trends that can guide the long-term innovation activity and lead to fundamentally new products, services, delivery mechanisms, organizational models, means of collaboration etc. Innovation anchors are robust as they are found persistently in the recent scholarly literature and appear on a consistent base in business related evidence. Rural wellbeing tourism is area of inquiry. The study reveals that innovation, in the future, can take further advantage of the following: 1) Towards a holistic wellbeing, 2) Connecting with nature and its resources, 3) Altruism included, 4) The rural as a medical prescription, 5) Work-life balance, 6) Wellbeing diversification the rural way, 7) Taking advantage of the climate squeeze, 8) Opening the digital channels, 9) A new puritanism rural style, and 10) The gear dimension.

INTRODUCTION

Tourism is a phenomenon under perpetual change and development. The geographical features constitute imperative attraction values (Hall & Page, 2014). Simultaneously, the material and immaterial features of the geography stimulate the innovation of new touristic products and services. In an era of increasing local as well as global completion, the careful and creative interpretation of what happens in the geographical space becomes more important.

The purpose of this chapter is to identify and discuss the foundations – innovation anchors - for the future of innovation in tourism. Innovation anchors are robust piles in the ground, they are developments and prospects that are likely to be of guiding value for innovating enterprises and destinations (Hjalager, 2002; Kozak, 2014; Mei et al, 2012). Accordingly, the study addresses trends in tourism, and there is a specific emphasis on wellbeing tourism.

DOI: 10.4018/978-1-5225-0201-2.ch009

The study also aims at contributing to the rural tourism research, hopefully with the future oriented view stimulating new directions in a research tradition which has had a focus on mainly authenticity and stability. There is a distinct need for further inquiries into innovations at the business level illuminating new business models in rural wellbeing. The study also attempts to move innovation studies further.

By definition, rural wellbeing tourism is a form of tourism that takes place in rural settings and that interconnects actively with local nature and community resources. Based on the rural tangible and intangible, openly accessible and commercial ingredients, wellbeing tourism is holistic mode of travel that integrates physical and mental wellness and health and contributes to wider positive social and individual life experiences.

Rural wellbeing tourism is related to wellness and health tourism, for example as defined by Sheldon and Bushell (2009), but it has a broader stance, and it might be seen as a further development of historical spa and wellness trends (Connell, 2006; Erfurt-Cooper & Cooper, 2009; Müller & Lanz Kaufmann, 2001; Smith & Puczkó, 2009, 2014). Over the past decades spa and wellness tourism has increased in popularity, and a mushrooming of concepts takes place, for example into facets of spiritual tourism, thalasso specialities, occupational wellness tourism, yoga and meditation, and many forms of sauna (Smith & Puzckó, 2009, 2014). The development of the traditional spa and wellness resorts towards a more holistic paradigm is prevalent. According to García-Altés (2005) diverse demographic, economic and lifestyle related factors have enhanced this. Many people are stressed by living in work-obsessed, time-pressured, materialistic and over-individualistic societies (Laing & Weiler, 2008; Sheldon & Bushell, 2009; Smith & Puzckó, 2009, 2014). In addition, the aging population, changes in lifestyle and alternatives in tourism, where experienced travellers seek new experiences (Konu & Laukkanen, 2010), add to the increased emphasis on more holistically oriented wellness products (Koh et al., 2010; Lehto et al., 2006; Mak et al., 2009).

Smith and Puzckó (2009) have listed both internal and external factors that affect the growth of and the increased demand for wellness tourism. External factors include governmental policy, nutrition, psychology, therapy, and healing and medicine. Internal factors are the search for a community, a desire to "downsize", new spirituality, time-poor and cash-rich elite manners, and curiosity. They also mention fashion and tradition, obsession with self and celebrity, and fitness and sport.

It can be concluded that the main motivating push factors in the wellbeing and wellness tourism sector seem to be relaxation, escape, pampering, physical activity, avoiding burn out and mental wellbeing. Relaxation is in many cases connected to "rest" and "physical relaxation". Escape is in many studies seen as one of the most important motivations. Pampering seems to be a motivation that is characteristic of wellness and spa tourism (Laesser, 2011; Mak et al., 2009). Pampering is also connected to the enjoyment of comfort (Laesser, 2011). Physical activity includes sports and multiple activities, and also physical health and appearance with wellbeing implications. Mental wellbeing is a motivation that can be seen to be specific to wellness tourism. It includes motivations such as "to seek mental peacefulness" (Mak et al., 2009) and "to help me gain a sense of balance" (Lehto et al., 2006).

Health tourism and medical tourism concepts are used in conjunction with wellness tourism. According to García-Altés (2005) health tourism is based on travelling outside the home to take care of one's health, and the purpose of the trip can be healing illness or preventing it and promoting general health related wellbeing (Finnish Tourist Board, 2005; Kandampully, 2013; Suontausta & Tyni, 2005). In addition to preventing illness and maintaining wellbeing, the goal of wellbeing tourism is to experience pleasure and luxury. As forms of tourism, wellbeing tourism and healthcare tourism are not very distant from each other. For instance, healthcare tourists may travel to the same destinations and use the

Figure 1. The rural wellbeing tourism arena

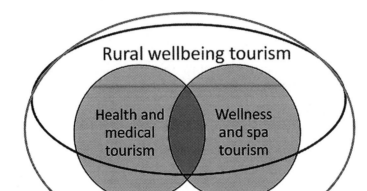

same recreational services as wellness tourists (Finnish Tourist Board, 2005; Müller & Lanz Kaufmann, 2001; Suontausta & Tyni, 2005) (see Figure 1).

The ambition in this chapter is to loosen the backward looking perspectives on traditions and cultural heritage, so often seen when addressing the prospects for rural tourism (Briedenhan & Wickens, 2004; Hoggart et al., 2014; Roberts & Hall, 2001). It is also the aim to widen the ideas of wellbeing and the traditional spa and wellness phenomenon. Hence, the plan is to investigate tendencies for the future that might positively or negatively affect what actors can make of wellbeing tourism in a rural setting.

Trend Studies as Guidance for Innovation Processes

Trend and future studies have been well-known for a large number of years, and they seem to remain of importance as the speed of change is amplifying and the complexities of societies tend to increase. This also accounts for tourism related issues and (rural) places that accommodate for tourism. Trend and future studies can be regarded as indispensable instruments in continual development processes. The future will, of course, always be open and unpredictable, and trend research does not have the full capacity to predict long-term (or even medium- and short-term) situations with any impressive accuracy (Slaughter, 1995). However, the worthy aim of the endeavour is to raise attention, at the earliest possible stage, to changes that might eventually affect the normal lives of people, enterprises or communities. Trend and future studies try to travel into the future in order to inform the present. This is about creating both individual and collective foresight and planning aptitude. Users of trend studies are business sectors, governmental bodies and NGOs. Early awareness can lead to a suitable reaction or pro-action to exploit opportunities or, for that case, to prevent disasters.

Trend and future studies are recognised as being informative contributions to innovation processes, mainly in the first phases where ideas are generated (Cuhls & Johnston, 2008), but also on a continual base when enterprises need to adjust and develop. Trend studies are elements in a long list of tools available for destinations, as the geographical aspects are crucial in tourism (Kozak, 2014; Moutinho et al, 2013).

Marketing research has applied trend studies to a significant extent (Aburdene, 2007; Naisbitt & Aburdene, 1990; Varey, 2013; von Groddeck & Schwarz, 2013). In fact, from a broader tourism perspective, such studies have been applied to a considerable extent in tourism fields, for example in attempting to predict the risks and implications of environmental developments (Edwards et al., 2008; Gössling et al., 2010) and as a means of identifying new customer segments and understanding their behaviour (Buhalis et al., 2006; Leigh et al., 2013). Wellbeing travel activity (and particularly wellness and spa tourism) has also received immense attention in academic and trade trend studies (Smith & Puczkó, 2013, 2014). Currently, broader wellbeing perspectives are included in tourism trends studies, but the field is still emerging (Hjalager et al., 2011; Konu, 2010).

In this chapter, a trend is understood as *the particular direction that something, over time, is developing into. The situation is not yet there in extended forms, but possibly there in embryonic forms.*

Trend analysis is the practice of collecting information and attempting to spot a pattern, or *trend*, in the available information. It includes for example forecasting based on historical data. Additionally, studies may detail the driving factors that enhance embryonic tendencies into mainstream futures. Analysis can also consist of the identification of upcoming phenomena among first-mover customers and enterprises. Methods are many and include extracting information from interviews or behavioural studies, where such first-movers expose their thoughts, tastes and preferences.

Leaning on the literature, in particular Aburdene (2007), Naisbitt and Aburdene (1990), Varey (2013) and von Groddeck and Schwarz (2013) it makes sense to distinguish between the trend formats at different levels. At higher levels, the impact may be comprehensive, and the possibility to affect limited, and strategies will mainly be adaptive in nature. At lower levels, actors e.g. enterprises, governments and organisation, will, to a higher extent, be able to become game changers.

- **Gigatrends:** Large evolutions, for example demographic shifts, refer to changes in various aspects of population statistics, such as size, racial and ethnic composition, birth and mortality rates, geographic distribution, age and income. Gigatrends may also comprise major science and technology inventions. Economic dynamics are changes in the production and exchange of goods and services globally, and gigatrends map principal changes in the policy approaches to prices, unemployment, banking, capital and wealth distribution etc. Environmental changes and challenges can be considered important gigatrends. Eventually, gigatrends define social and cultural shifts in core values, beliefs, ethics and moral standards.
- **Paradigms:** Ways of understanding how society operates, for example how political ideas and regulations can shape the prospects for enterprises and the lives of people. Paradigms are prevalent for example in the fields of health and welfare, where they govern the way that facilities are provided for citizens. Paradigms – for example, ideas about certification and data openness – emerge to be of relevance for tourism and wellbeing. In some cases the sophisticated interlinkage of paradigms takes place in order to create a higher level of political coherence and synergy.
- **Megatrends:** Patterns that last for some years or even decades and define how people choose to live their lives. Megatrends include for example holiday patterns that reflect the fact of an ageing population or the development towards one-person households. Megatrends include values related to leisure and spirituality, and attitudes to responsibility in health and wellbeing. Megatrends also embrace issues about the nature of human interaction including the role of technology in enhancing human connectivity. Megatrends may express comprehensive prospected changes in consumption patterns; for example as a response to environmental or economic constraints.
- **Fashions:** Short-term changing styles and consumption manners. This is about new food products, upcoming colour schemes and tastes and also must-experience hypes related to tourism. To a considerable extent, fashions are adopted by people in order to mark their social connectivity.

In practice the distinctions between these four categories are not entirely clear, but nevertheless the list provides an idea of levels. In this chapter the trends provided will mainly have a focus on megatrends but with references to paradigms as well as to examples from fashions.

APPROACHES AND METHODOLOGIES

This trend study is elaborated with the following interrelated steps:

A literature review of academic sources has been performed, with a particular emphasis on contributions that address not only wellness but also a wider range of wellbeing and health prospects. This study does not have a uniformly rural perspective as new trends and consumer needs may emerge in urban agglomerations yet be applied in rural settings and contexts to raise new and different market perspectives. The literature review also looks into sources that address ecosystems services, thus assuming that human wellbeing is in this context based on daring reinterpretations of how nature and rural space can serve the desires of tourists.

Further, the process includes a search through commercial and trade-based trend studies with an emphasis on tourism and wellness. These sources are plentiful and tend to draw attention to the commercially directed demands of "first movers". They offer particular insight into consumption patterns and fashions, which can provide supplements to the academic literature.

A "trend workshop" with 21 participants in the ProWell research project group was organized. The participants were business and DMO professionals mixed with a group of tourism researchers from five countries: Denmark, Finland, Latvia, Lithuania and Norway. The trend session took place in two phases. First, sub-groups of three were asked, in a moving and dynamic process, to respond to possible future scenarios, some of these less likely occur than others. Those proposed elements had emerged from the literature and trade search as described above, presented to the participants in preparatory session. During the second phase reshuffled groups were, in a similarly dynamic process, urged to suggest more specific innovative rural wellbeing products with a commercial twist and consumer appeal.

The material from the workshop, in the form of many post-its, was the first step in the elaboration of trend proposals for this text. The statements provided were organized according to topic, and then reorganized on a "disruption axis" (Hjalager, 2014). Disruptive innovations are such technological social, institutional or other changes than may lead to the replacement of otherwise well-established products, services with entirely new ones. In the process some enterprises may fail and die, while others will thrive. The post-its were then again re-grouped by the researchers so as to generate coherent trends. A quite large majority of the contributions from workshop participants suggested trends with fairly cautious attitudes to the future, and some participants struggled with escaping the links to past trajectories. They mainly came up with bids and ideas for sustaining and enhancing natural resources. Many of these were, at an early stage of the trend building, omitted from the process. Dimensions of radical disruption were seen but not often, but did occur, particularly in the fields of enterprise internal service improvements. This analysis of the workshop contributions led to critical reconsiderations of the potential speed and scope of future changes. Thus, the process of analysis has raised reflections that might be of importance for an assessment of actors' inclination not only to envisage changes but also to proactively work for their occurrence at an accelerated speed.

In the following, the ten identified innovation anchors will be presented.

Innovation Anchor 1: Towards Holistic Wellbeing

Tourism no longer just provides opportunities to relax and recover from arduous daily lives with stressful working conditions, overburdened and spatially confined family lives, long commutes and polluted city climates. For many holidaymakers in modern welfare societies daily life is actually challenging and beneficial, and people are used to high-class facilities at or near home, or even at the workplace. However, that does not lower the demand for interesting and rewarding holiday experiences but requirements in terms of quality and variety tend to increase.

Tourists may seek contrasts to their daily life but also the enhancement of preferred lifestyle elements and life endeavours. Holidays are intermingled with and are part of a whole-life progression where it is essential to keep a balance, remain capable to face changes and prevent lifestyle related negative symptoms (such as burn-out, tension, stress) with a sense of control.

Wellness centres and spas are responsive to this change, and many of them are changing names and practices towards "body and mind". The range of water-based treatments, balance exercises, massages, muscle therapies, acupuncture services, chiropractic care, reflexology services etc. are being continuously developed. But increasingly, such spas and wellness facilities also include, for example, yoga, stress coaching, training of communication skills etc. "Whole individual" concepts lead to the integration of nutritional counselling, psychotherapy, emotional guidance and other elements of functional body and mind care.

From a rural perspective this trend can be regarded as highly promising, as the use of outdoor facilities in the body and mind integration may become far more prevalent. Reconnection with nature is shown to improve mental and emotional wellbeing more than just indoors relaxation, exercising or receiving therapy and guidance. Traditional spas expand outside with gardens and trails into nature. Entrepreneurs in the field provide, for example, riding therapy or other facilities that allow a (re)connection with animals. Kayaking, trekking or other physical sports and activities are also reinterpreted into body and mind totality concepts. Spiritual training and stress therapy may rely on the interpretative interlinkages between nature and healing but also relate directly to narratives of healing "powers" and "flows" in specific natural environments.

Many people now in their fifties and sixties are captivated by the concepts of body and mind wellness. They are well aware of the potentially longer lifespans that they may face and the need for preventive health and fitness. They want to go on holiday, but they will not want to return home feeling sluggish and weighing three kilos more than when they left.

Innovation Anchor 2: Connecting with Nature and its Resources

Traditional wellness products tend to be international, and wellness concepts travel. It is possible to acquire Dead Sea treatments all over the world, and Wat Pho traditional Thai wellness massage may be more well-recognized in the US than in Thailand. Volcanic rocks are shipped to equip hot stone massages in many non-volcanic places. However there is a tendency to relate wellbeing tourism more with the specific local and natural resources, and base it on what is available in order to ensure the development of new wellbeing products and services.

For example, thalassotherapy is well-known but there can be an emphasis on exploring local algae, seaweed and alluvial mud in combination with climates and marine environments so as to not only create new touristic experiences but also to efficiently link up the local and regional spaces in a way that can assist recognition, image and branding.

Food is a major object for this endeavour, used to reconnect and to boost the wellbeing dimensions in rural tourism. Shying away from typical tourist behaviour, tourists express an interest in authentic experiences and community-based exploration, and food allows them to get to know locals in a meaningful way. A tendency consists of the inviting attitudes that intersect soundly with wellness travel, for example, the opportunity to attend cooking classes, learn about local agriculture and to participate in river and open sea fishing. It is a particular experience to follow food on its way from the farm/sea to the table that emphasizes the emotional, social, intellectual and sustainable aspects of wellbeing. Local food related traditions and events may also be opportunities in terms of wellbeing developments, such as "medical food plant festivals", an "apple and cider harvesting, preparation and tasting event" etc.

Working with ambience, for example how it is created by building style and building materials, underlines the connectivity between tourism facilities and rural resources. A rural setting can encourage the use of stone, wood, water, clay creating an ambience that can enhance the feeling of wellbeing and also create distinctive images of place and space while also emphasising multidimensional connectivity with nature.

Innovation Anchor 3: The Altruistic Fling

Very clearly, traditional spas and wellness centres have a focus on the individual's ego, his or her enjoyment and pleasure (Pesonen & Komppula, 2010). The products and services can be described as pampering, often also with the social element of being together with others with the same aspirations. Habitually, a prime matter of attention for customers in spas is the quality level that is likely to be synonymous with the standard of luxury.

However, new strata of holidaymakers tend to recognize that they do not necessarily leave a wider responsibility at home when they travel to their holiday destination. It is not only about having a good time but also about being responsible and taking care of the social and physical environment. There are enhanced psychological and economic links between altruism and wellbeing. Giving back is often found to be more joyous than receiving, and it is correlated positively with happiness and health. "Voluntourism" has become an increasingly popular travel option. Affluent and well-educated travellers looking for personal growth and discovery are turning to experiences that connect them to charitable causes and local communities while on vacation. The pleasure of contributing to a higher purpose is indeed a wellbeing issue.

This can be considered an opportunity for many rural areas. However, altruism is not a product that develops itself and it is demanding in terms of entrepreneurial creativity, initiative and local follow-up. Touristic products can consist of, for example, letting tourists assist in fields or help out in environmental and nature regeneration projects. Less strenuous versions can be the "adoption" of environmentally vulnerable trees, endangered species or historical buildings, where tourists both co-finance and commit themselves to operating as ambassadors for the protection of such resources.

Spiritual resources (religious sites, magical natural phenomena etc.) may be particularly powerful in terms of creating platforms for relationships between locals and guests in a way that may lead to a beneficial feeling of wellbeing. There is a plea for considerate rural wellbeing entrepreneurs with high ethical standards. Wellbeing products in this category require reciprocity.

Innovation Anchor 4: Rural as a Medical Prescription

Welfare economies in the EU are under financial pressure, and the constraints may increase with an ageing population, but also paradoxically as a consequence of better medical treatment opportunities. There is a trend that there will be an intensified focus on preventive medicine in order to stop expanded public expenditure, and populations will be required to take more self-preventive action.

It is not unusual for persons with health risks to take trips on their "doctor's orders", as physicians increasingly prescribe vacations as antidotes to stress. Doctors may recommend various kinds of physical activity to combat obesity and diabetes. In this development, rural areas can potentially become the location for a niche health business with services in care and treatments, and in the training of citizens so that they raise the level of their self-care competences.

Nature as a healer is widely discussed and quite well documented but still to some extent it lacks commodification. For example, silence may be a health remedy but enjoying silence properly prompts a demand for supplementary accommodation, catering, transport etc.

A restriction to such prospects may be the requirement for standardized and certified medical treatment provided by trained and professional staff. Such human resources might be lacking in areas far from urban agglomerations. Presently, preventive health provision in rural areas is often mainly found in unorthodox medical specialties. Overcoming the barriers and building bridges between alternative medical practices and mainstream health systems is a task for rural actors who will want to exploit the potential that emerges from this trend. This strategy alley also embraces inviting new health experts to start businesses in rural areas.

Innovation Anchor 5: Work–Life Balance

This trend represents a challenge to the standard understanding of citizenship. The assumption is that "dual" or even "triple" or "quadruple" citizenships will emerge, and people will not only live in one single place. Technology allows the emergence of virtual workspaces and simultaneously work will become less spatially restricted – the workplace can be moved between urban and rural localities. In the future, the inclination to combine work, leisure and tourism in outdoor environments will become more pronounced and integrated into comprehensive life strategies. We are talking about creating an optimal work–life balance for families with young children, semi-retired professionals and also for people in other phases of their lives.

The customers for rural wellbeing in this category will be private persons and possibly also enterprises. Occupational health issues related to work–life balance may become reshuffled, particularly in the case of indispensable employees with scarce qualifications and competences. If indispensable staff suffers from stress and also health threatening obesity, mental problems etc. it is a major concern for employers. Embracing employers as potential customers for wellbeing tourism may call for entirely new types of spatial organization and modes of collaboration. Partnerships with insurance companies and professional medical bodies may also become more prevalent.

Rural areas, particularly in attractive vicinities of urban agglomerations, may have to organize spaces and services in order to be more attractive for beta citizens. Beta citizens have homes in several places and they feel at home, for example, both in towns and in rural areas. Typically, they are mobile job-wise. In terms of adding to the wellbeing profile of a rural community, it is a core challenge and undertaking to make these inhabitants feel like citizens and not like just tourists or guests. The term "tourist" may become less concise, and there is a necessity to reconceptualize the idea of a rural community and what is a "homeland". In addition, there is a demand for reconsidering the locations and designs of beta homes for beta citizens, possibly also including mobile categories thereof.

Innovation Anchor 6: Wellbeing Diversification the Rural Way

Above, it was emphasized that rural areas possess many resources of relevance for human wellbeing, resources that are specific for areas outside urban agglomerations and related to the existence of geographical breadth and open spaces. The rural also comprises resources that are related to rural traditions and practices that can be integrated into the development of new products. Any ambition to develop and innovate wellbeing tourism products may include the material or immaterial assets of the place. Rural wellbeing tourism may become significantly more than accommodation and spa facilities in rural areas.

However it must also be envisaged that rural areas are in competition with urban areas and that resources, however firmly defined as rural, may not be sacred and strapped to the rural environment. Continuously urban areas are found to steal, copy, transfer, and reconstruct rural wellbeing resources. For example, London is planning a green bridge over the Thames, which is a natural area in the middle of the city. Copenhagen has a scheme to establish a large ski-mountain, integrated into the harbour leisure development. It makes it increasingly difficult for rural areas to genuinely distinguish themselves and to profit from their rural resources. These are not "real" rural facilities, but in the mindset of some city-dwellers these facilities can nonetheless be perfect substitutes, and "rubanization" is a very consistent and strong trend, such as illustrated by Gražulevičiūtė-Vileniškė & Zaleskienė, (2014).

Good odds may exist if rural areas can maintain an interlinked, multidimensional rural profile. Such composite styles and trends will be harder to mimic by urban wellbeing actors. It will require a significant collaborative organizational setup in rural areas, if the image of the rural should transgress the products of several providers in a larger area.

A consistent and constant reinvention of traditional rural tourism products may also be a crucial ingredient. In addition, this will require professional inputs as well as local commitment and foresight.

It is worth noticing that rural wellbeing products, as they are now, mainly rely on fairly "superficial" and easily understandable resources, for example forests, wind, water, food etc. Less intensively, attempts are seen to include "hidden" and "intricate" resources. An outsider's view is essential to "excavate" such resources. Future rural wellbeing may embrace the extraction of resources less "beautiful" and obvious, for example resources available in mining areas, on seabeds or in less accessible nature areas in general. This can, for example, inventively lead to "shock" therapies or "dirty" experiences. The excavation of nonconformist resources can include new types of raw materials for the portfolio of spa products or food ingredients and also experiences where the tourists interact with the resources as part of wellbeing consumption. This kind of diversification may be less replicable by actors in urban settings and thus be a way to maintain a competitive profile and distance.

Innovation Anchor 7: Taking Advantage of the Climate Squeeze

There are many predictions about the changed and changing climate, but quite consistently, scientists assume that the weather in Northern Europe is likely to become more unstable, with more severe, rough incidents with heavy rain, storms and flooding. Gradually, the average temperature will probably rise. For better or worse, these are very important signals for rural wellbeing tourism.

Basically, warmer temperatures will benefit the rural tourism product as much of the experience takes place in outdoor environments. Biodiversity may benefit or degrade in a changed climate. Seasons may be prolonged. However, unpredictable weather conditions will urge a need to develop products that will be attractive no matter what the weather conditions are. This may consist of an increased emphasis on indoor facilities, possibly with opportunities to gaze at nature, in case outdoor environments are not accessible all the time and in all seasons. In winter sports areas, climate changes are particularly complex and ambiguous.

Alternatively, the development of touristic wellbeing products may take advantage of the volatility and enhance products that can make sense of and take advantage of, for example, heavy rainfalls or extreme winds. New categories of outdoor equipment may be invented for this purpose, with narratives that support the experience to follow. Likewise, the development may include safety equipment, remedies and procedures so that the wellbeing element is not compromised.

Slowly, sustainability is moving into tourism as a managerial prerequisite. Some spa facilities are taking their environmental footprint very seriously. The dimensions such as savings of water and energy are readily delivered in awareness messages to customers.. However, the distinct rural particularities – in general and in the specific locality – still need emphasis and communication to a tourism audience.

Innovation Anchor 8: Opening the Digital Channels

Social media influences all aspects of tourism. However, the communication imperative can be so intense that people nearly become "digital addicts", and in this case rural wellbeing can be a chance to turn off the mobile phone and the computer, and become disconnected for a period of time – for example for the purpose of reducing stress or addressing other health issues. The rural may offer medically supported help for digital addition victims. Thus, the rural environment can be an escape, a hideaway from the monstrous "surveillance" of daily life, and the tourist can be provided with the freedom to do things that are socially not fully accepted.

However, digital connectivity may offer opportunities in the completely opposite direction for rural wellbeing tourism. Potentially, users of social media do not want to be disconnected. This can be considered essential, which intrinsically means moving away from the social variety and turmoil of agglomerated places, but staying in digital contact. People may seek rural silence and peacefulness but within limitations: social media provides the (self-controlled) possibility to stay connected. While on holiday they may even increase their inclination to tell others about their experiences and thus compensate for disadvantages of geographical distance. They will be the nodes in interrelatedness across geographies. For rural tourism destinations and facilities the high frequency of updates is a "viral word of mouth".

Social media is entering the rural and outdoor experiencescapes in other important ways. Tracking instruments can map personal performances on trails – for example distance, speed, endurance, moods and feelings. Systems can tag places of particular interest visited. The results are "personal" data, which may affect the individual's behaviour. The performance data and tagging can, however, also be shared with friends, and they can be the initiators of new relationships, for example with other people who incidentally happen to be in the same rural area at the same time. Indirectly and through social media, valuable marketing may take place outside the specific region. The e-rumour is, of course, difficult or impossible for rural destinations or wellbeing enterprises to control. Working in social media environments is a new discipline for rural wellbeing operators, and integrating them into rural storytelling and ever-evolving narratives is a challenge.

In this process of adapting to new ways of communication, rural actors will have to reinterpret their roles and the roles of the visitors. Visitors are not only customers; they may also be friends, associates, collaborators and information pushers. If the relationship goes wrong, the visitors may become communicators with negative implications; disseminating reproachful and, in the worst case, wrongful information.

Innovation Anchor 9: New Puritanism – The Rural Style

Immanently, the rural has connotations with being "pure", "clean" and "healthy". Taking a wider stance, the rural can be the environment for initiating a healthier lifestyle, and popular self-help literature offers many allegations for this endeavour, for example de-clotting, de-toxication, simplicity, recycling, slow living etc. The rural may be the perfect place to acquire the genuine competences and skills to shift from an over-complex and hectic modern lifestyle to a purer one.

This wellbeing trend manifests itself in many, although not exactly coherent, ways. Enterprises in the rural tourism wellbeing field may grab this opportunity, for example by providing "grow-your-own food" and "collect-your-own herbs" courses and events, offering simple health treatments using local plants and foods in detox etc. The built ambience can also illustrate a strategic pureness, for example in the use of building materials, the handling of waste etc.

However, an honest shift may include a wider community in order to give an air of solemnity and urgency. The emerging "Slow Cities movement" demonstrates an indication of how a concept can gain some momentum by a comprehensive and coordinated attention and branding. Slow Cities is also an illustration of the fact that models must become global in order to gain dynamism and the power of persuasion. This is a challenge for small and remote rural areas, which are not always well accommodated within these context relevant competences and high quality global connections.

Innovation Anchor 10: The Gear Dimension

Rural wellbeing tourism can appear to be extremely simple, for example it may just consist of taking a walk in pastures bordered with wild flowers, listening to birdsong. Equally unpretentious is gazing at natural phenomena or relaxing in the midst of rural features. However, rural wellbeing tourism may also require a whole range of range of equipment, technologies and gear for the visitor to get the full benefit of the experience. There is a drift towards experiences that are enhanced, expanded and enriched by the use of technological add-ons. Examples are prevalent in wilderness and outdoor adventure travel, where the variety of gear is expanding, for example in terms of tents, clothing, communication and navigation equipment, safety tools, food and drink gadgets, fashion accessories etc. Likewise, traditional spa facilities are also being filled up with many types of spa products, cosmeceuticals, sauna choices, fitness and massage tools etc. and spa enterprises strive to augment the variety of provided attractive sounds, tastes etc. for the totality of outdoor and indoor enjoyment.

The gear, equipment and tools for wellbeing tourism are often of international standards, produced (in China) without any particular local aesthetic or functional accent. The trend is, however, to add local flavours and specifications for the enjoyment of the guests. Spa products can be produced using local herb ingredients. Healthy food can be grown and prepared in the area. However, seemingly little is done to widen the range of local products co-innovated with the wellbeing tourism industry.

Achievement in this field might benefit the visitors by providing a wider variety and more interesting experiences. Technology can also be a remedy to lower the cost of wellbeing services, so that they can be available to the less affluent strata. Another impact is that gear, equipment and tools can be purchased in the rural destination and taken home; this can eventually create economic activity and employment in other business sectors than tourism. Finally, the image of a destination travels with the gear – for example a type of equipment that carries the name of a place or is related to, for example, a special type of locally specific treatment or activity. Accordingly, the gear dimension can constitute a multidimensional diversification tactic.

CONCLUSION AND PERSPECTIVES

This chapter sought to capture ten trends that may affect the future of rural wellbeing tourism:

- A movement towards holistic wellbeing.
- Connecting with nature and its resources.
- The altruistic fling.
- The rural as a medical prescription.
- Work–life balance.
- Wellbeing diversification the rural way.
- Taking advantage of the climate squeeze.
- Opening digital channels.
- New puritanism – the rural style.
- The gear dimension.

Noticeably, modern tourists will want the rural wellbeing product. However, demand changes due to complex demographic, environmental, economic and other shifts in society. In spite of the fact that spa tourism has demonstrated considerable growth rates over the past decades (Bushell & Sheldon, 2009; Voigt & Pforr, 2013), rural wellbeing is far more than just building additional spas. The process applied in the study suggests that destinations and providers would support and recommend a gradual and not too fast development of new products and services rather, and they are sceptical about changing the ideas about the products drastically. In rural practice, the pace of innovation in destination will have to reflect both market forces and entrepreneurial capacities.

Going in greater detail, the outline of the trends suggests that rural areas have development and market opportunities in the wellbeing fields, and there are distinctive nature-based resources available that can be the foundation of innovative progressions of products. It also becomes clear that rural areas are in multifaceted and rather severe competitive situations with urban areas, and they will have to take a closer look at trends and cultivate a suitable anticipation of their prospects. However, the trends illustrate that rural areas need to foster strategic relationships with actors in urban areas, as rural communities and actors seldom possess the full array of skills and investor potential for a massive expansion into wellbeing tourism in its wider varieties.

The trend analysis is far from definite, and there are considerable uncertainties about the when and how changes will affect rural practices. A micro-spatial approach is required to assess this. There is also a significant ambiguity about where in space new ideas will be created and how they will disseminate to other geographical areas. The study includes the participation of a number of countries in Northern Europe, and these countries represent quite different economic backgrounds, traditions, institutional structures and policy directions. Progress with rural wellbeing anchors and ideas will hardly be entirely uniform across this geographical area.

The literature about innovation processes in tourism at the enterprise and destination levels is still only modestly developed, and more diverse arrays of tools could be tested following the initial effort in this study. Preferably increased interest will be in studies that are experimental in nature and that takes place in collaboration between researchers, wellbeing tourism services and possibly also such groups of customers who can be regarded as "first-movers". In addition, future research is needed to uncover the capabilities of change in rural areas and the nature of competition between rural and urban wellbeing providers. Such endeavour based on empirical evidence may lead to grounded theoretical re-orientation of the innovation-in-tourism research. Each of the ten anchors raises a number of more specific prospects and problems and many of these lack solid academic inquiry. In particular the suggested trajectories in anchors 9 and 10 touch upon issues that have only recently emerged in the research literature, and where further inquiry is needed.

REFERENCES

Aburdene, P. (2007). *Megatrends 2010: The rise of conscious capitalism*. Hampton Roads Publishing.

Briedenhann, J., & Wickens, E. (2004). Tourism routes as a tool for the economic development of rural areas—vibrant hope or impossible dream? *Tourism Management*, *25*(1), 71–79. doi:10.1016/S0261-5177(03)00063-3

Buhalis, D., Costa, C., & Ford, F. (Eds.). (2006). *Tourism business frontiers*. London: Routledge.

Bushell, R., & Sheldon, P. J. (Eds.). (2009). *Wellness and tourism: Mind, body, spirit, place*. New York: Cognizant Communication.

Connell, J. (2006). Medical Tourism: Sea, Sun, Sand and Surgery. *Tourism Management*, *27*(6), 1093–1100. doi:10.1016/j.tourman.2005.11.005

Cuhls, K., & Johnston, R. (2008). Corporate foresight. In C. Cagnin, M. Keenan, R. Johnston, F. Scapolo, & R. Barré (Eds.), *Future-Oriented Technology Analysis* (pp. 102–114). Springer Berlin Heidelberg. doi:10.1007/978-3-540-68811-2_8

Edwards, D., Mistilis, N., Roman, C., Scott, N., & Cooper, C. (2008). *Megatrends underpinning tourism to 2020: Analysis of key drivers for change*. CRC for Sustainable Tourism.

Erfurt-Cooper, P., & Cooper, M. (2009). *Health and Wellness Tourism. Spas and Hot Springs*. Bristol: Channel View Publications.

Finnish Tourist Board. (2005). Hyvinvointi- ja wellness-matkailun peruskartoitus. Helsinki: Finnish Tourist Board A:144. Suunnittelukeskus Oy.

García-Altés, A. (2005). The development of health tourism services. *Annals of Tourism Research*, *32*(1), 262–266. doi:10.1016/j.annals.2004.05.007

Gössling, S., Hall, C. M., Peeters, P., & Scott, D. (2010). The future of tourism: Can tourism growth and climate policy be reconciled? A mitigation perspective. *Tourism Recreation Research, 35*(2), 119–130. doi:10.1080/02508281.2010.11081628

Gražulevičiūtė-Vileniškė, I., & Zaleskienė, E. (2014). Landscape Research Trends and Some Insights from Rurban Landscape. *Environmental Research. Engineering and Management, 67*(1), 43–53.

Hall, M. C., & Page, S. J. (2014). *The geography of tourism and recreation: Environment, space and place*. London: Routledge.

Hjalager, A. M. (2002). Repairing innovation defectiveness in tourism. *Tourism Management, 23*(5), 465–474. doi:10.1016/S0261-5177(02)00013-4

Hjalager, A.-M. (2014). Disruptive and sustaining innovations: the case of rural tourism. In Handbook of Research on Innovation in Tourism Industries (pp. 56-83). Edward Elgar. doi:10.4337/9781782548416.00009

Hjalager, A. M., Konu, H., Huijbens, E. H., Björk, P., Nordin, S., & Tuohino, A. (2011). Innovating and re-branding Nordic wellbeing tourism. Oslo: NICe.

Hoggart, K., Black, R., & Buller, H. (2014). *Rural Europe*. Routledge.

Kandampully, J. (2013). Service Management a New Paradigm in Health and Wellness Services. In J. Kandampully (Ed.), *Service Management in Health & Wellness Services* (pp. 1–6). Dubuque, IA: Kendall Hunt.

Koh, S., Yoo, J. J.-E., & Boeger, C. A. (2010). Importance performance analysis with benefit segmentation of spa goers. *International Journal of Contemporary Hospitality Management, 22*(5), 1–20.

Konu, H. (2010). Identifying potential wellbeing tourism segments in Finland. *Tourism Review, 65*(2), 41–51. doi:10.1108/16605371011061615

Konu, H., & Laukkanen, T. (2010). Predictors of tourists' wellbeing holiday intentions in Finland. *Journal of Hospitality and Tourism Management, 17*(1), 144–149. doi:10.1375/jhtm.17.1.144

Kozak, M. W. (2014). Innovation, Tourism and Destination Development: Dolnośląskie Case Study. *European Planning Studies, 22*(8), 1604–1624. doi:10.1080/09654313.2013.784597

Laesser, C. (2011). Health travel motivation and activities: Insights from a mature market – Switzerland. *Tourism Review, 66*(1/2), 83–89. doi:10.1108/16605371111127251

Laing, J., & Weiler, B. (2008). Mind, Body and Spirit: Health and Wellness Tourism in Asia. In J. Cochrane (Ed.), *Asian Tourism: Growth and Change* (pp. 379–389). Amsterdam: Elsevier. doi:10.1016/B978-0-08-045356-9.50037-0

Lehto, X. Y., Brown, S., Chen, Y., & Morrison, A. M. (2006). Yoga tourism as a niche within the wellness tourism market. *Tourism Recreation Research, 31*(1), 5–14. doi:10.1080/02508281.2006.11081244

Leigh, J., Webster, C., & Ivanov, S. (Eds.). (2013). *Future Tourism: Political, Social and Economic Challenges*. Abingdon, UK: Routledge.

Mak, A., Wong, K. K., & Chang, R. C. (2009). Health or self-indulgence? The motivations and characteristics of spa-goers. *International Journal of Tourism Research, 11*(2), 185–199. doi:10.1002/jtr.703

Mei, X. Y., Arcodia, C., & Ruhanen, L. (2012). Towards tourism innovation: A critical review of public polices at the national level. *Tourism Management Perspectives, 4*, 92–105. doi:10.1016/j.tmp.2012.05.002

Moutinho, L., Rate, S., & Ballantyne, R. (2013). Futurecast: an exploration of key emerging megatrends in the tourism arena. In C. Costa, E. Pnayik, & D. Buhalis (Eds.), *Trends in European Tourism Planning and Organisation* (pp. 313–325). Bristol, UK: Channel View Publications.

Müller, H., & Lanz Kauffman, E. (2001). Wellness Tourism: Market analysis of a special health tourism segment and implications for the hotel industry. *Journal of Vacation Marketing, 7*(1), 5–17. doi:10.1177/135676670100700101

Naisbitt, J., & Aburdene, P. (1990). *Megatrends 2000*. New York: William Morrow.

Pesonen, J., & Komppula, R. (2010). Rural Wellbeing Tourism: Motivations and Expectations. *Journal of Hospitality and Tourism Management, 17*(1), 150–157. doi:10.1375/jhtm.17.1.150

Roberts, L., & Hall, D. (2001). *Rural tourism and recreation: principles to practice*. Wallingford: Cabi Publishing. doi:10.1079/9780851995403.0000

Sheldon, P., & Bushell, R. (2009). Introduction to wellness and tourism. In R. Bushell & P. J. Sheldon (Eds.), *Wellness and Tourism. Mind, Body, Spirit, Place* (pp. 3–18). New York: Cognizant Communication.

Slaughter, R. (1995). *Future tools and techniques*. Melbourne: DDM.

Smith, M., & Puczkó, L. (2013). Regional trends and predictions for global health tourism. In Wellness Tourism: A Destination Perspective. Abingdon, UK: Routledge.

Smith, M., & Puczkó, L. (2014). *Health Tourism and Hospitality: Spas, Wellness and Medical Travel*. Routledge.

Smith, M., & Puzckó, L. (2009). *Health and Wellness Tourism*. Oxford, UK: Butterworth-Heinemann.

Suontausta, H., & Tyni, M. (2005). *Wellness-matkailu – hyvinvointi matkailun tuotekehityksessä*. Helsinki: Edita Prima Oy.

Varey, R. J. (2013). Marketing in the flourishing society megatrend. *Journal of Macromarketing, 33*(4), 354–368. doi:10.1177/0276146713489150

Voigt, C., & Pforr, C. (Eds.). (2013). *Wellness tourism. A destination perspective*. Abingdon, UK: Routledge.

von Groddeck, V., & Schwarz, J. O. (2013). Perceiving megatrends as empty signifiers: A discourse-theoretical interpretation of trend management. *Futures, 47*, 28–37. doi:10.1016/j.futures.2013.01.004

Chapter 10
Tourism and Crisis:
Clean Slates, Disaster Capitalism, and Vulnerability

Faye Taylor
Nottingham Trent University, UK

ABSTRACT

Numerous researchers have highlighted a relative lack of academic attention directly addressing the influence of political economy on achieving sustainability in post-disaster reconstruction (Klein, 2008; Hystad and Keller, 2008; Olsen, 2000; Faulkner, 2001; Glaesser, 2003; Ritchie, 2004). This chapter therefore extends existing academic debates and studies in a number of areas, drawing upon the context of Thailand in the post-Asian tsunami era. In existing academic debates concerning the political economy of post-disaster reconstruction there is a trend towards disaster capitalism (Klein, 2005; Harvey, 2007; Saltman, 2007a). However, this did not occur on Phi Phi. Despite claims of a 'clean slate' being offered by the tsunami in developmental terms (Pleumarom, 2004; UNDP, 2005; Dodds, 2011; Ko, 2005; Nwankwo and Richardson, 1994; Rice, 2005; Altman, 2005; Brix, 2007; Ghobarah et al., 2006; Dodds et al., 2010), this chapter provides explanation of why this did not and would never exist on Phi Phi, a finding that may be applied to other destinations in a post-disaster context.

INTRODUCTION

This chapter will draw upon empirical research carried out in the wake of the Asian tsunami, intended to examine the role of a mega natural disaster upon tourism development and planning. This tsunami, which took place on 26th December 2004, triggered by an underwater earthquake of 9.3 on the Richter scale off the coast of Banda Aceh, Northern Indonesia (Ghobarah et al. 2006) affected nineteen countries including Indonesia, Sri Lanka and Thailand, resulted in over 300,000 deaths and left 1.5 million people homeless (Ghobarah et al. 2006). A specific focus upon Thailand will be taken, more precisely the island of Koh Phi Phi in the Southern Andaman, a popular backpacker and day-tripper destination, the epitome of a paradise location (Fahn, 2003; Cummings 2005), which, when struck by the tsunami, suffered a tremendous loss of life and vast destruction of island infrastructure to support both tourism and local livelihoods (Bergman, 2005). The island's reconstruction is still ongoing today. This chapter intends to explore some of the following discussions and debates using the Asian tsunami as a primary

DOI: 10.4018/978-1-5225-0201-2.ch010

focus but will also draw upon examples of other natural disasters that have affected the tourism industry in recent times.

Regarded as one of the most catastrophic crises of our times (Wong, 2009), the Asian tsunami left a long-lasting global footprint (Rice, 2005). This event was locally devastating, but also lingered in the global consciousness on account of the intense media coverage, and the fact that many of the areas affected were those that we have personal familiarity with through tourism (Rice, 2005). Historically, the development of Phi Phi, including tourism, had been subject to widespread criticism (Fahn, 2003; Hart, 2005; Dodds, Graci & Holmes, 2010), due to the unsustainable nature of infrastructure development and lack of strict regulation and planning, particularly with regard to the alleged 'sell-out' of Phi Phi Le's Maya Bay (part of Hat Nopparat Thara National Marine Park) following the filming of Fox's motion picture *The Beach* (Noikorn, 1998; Ekachai, 1998; Fuengprichavai, 1998).

The chapter will address four key concerns. Firstly, the observation within literature on the political economy of post-disaster reconstruction, of a trend towards 'disaster capitalism' (Klein, 2008) or 'smash and grab capitalism' (Harvey, 2007, p. 32) and 'attempts to accumulate by dispossession' (Saltman, 2007a, p. 57). The author's research found that this did not occur on Phi Phi. Despite claims of a 'clean slate' being offered by the tsunami in developmental terms (Pleumarom, 2004; UNDP, 2005; Brix, 2007; Ghobarah et al., 2006), this chapter will provide evidence and explanation of why this did not and would not occur on Phi Phi, a finding that may be applied to other destinations in a post natural-disaster context.

Secondly, in response to Blaikie et al.'s (2004) concerns that vulnerability is often reconstructed following a disaster and may create the conditions for a future disaster, this chapter will extend discussions of disaster vulnerability through an adapted application of Turner et al.'s (2003) Vulnerability Framework. The chapter will refine their work to identify a detailed framework of vulnerability factors intertwined with factors of political economy, presenting a post-disaster situation in Phi Phi that remains highly vulnerable and non-conducive to sustainability. This is also in response to Hystad & Keller's (2008) recognition that there are a lack of long-term studies, which not only show how disaster has shifted the nature of the destination and tourism product, but also identify successful strategic processes and actions in disaster response.

Thirdly, the strategic response to the tsunami in Thailand will be analysed, through an adapted Strategic Disaster Management Framework (Ritchie, 2004). This will identify the shortcomings of the disaster response and help comprehend how such a disaster has influenced tourism development and planning in Thailand, showing that this was a mirror opposite to how a disaster should be handled according to existing research (Ritchie, 2004; Miller et al., 2006; Coppola, 2015; Faulkner, 2001; Baldini et al., 2012).

Finally, the chapter will discuss the notion of 'strategic drift' (Johnson, 2009, p. 179) and 'boiled frog syndrome' (Richardson, Nwankwo & Richardson, 1994, p. 10) to explain how host attitudes to tourism may increase disaster vulnerability. These discussions will provide theoretical and practical insights that may support the process of identifying destination vulnerability and limitations in disaster response and recovery.

The objectives of the chapter are as follows:

- To examine the influence of a natural disaster upon destination redevelopment.
- To critically assess the prospect of a clean slate in development terms post-disaster.
- To assess the evidence of disaster capitalism in the context of Thailand post-tsunami.
- To identify shortcomings in disaster response and recovery following the Asian Tsunami in Thailand and consider the bases of destination vulnerability in light of potential crisis.

LITERATURE REVIEW

Conceptualising Crises within Tourism

It is widely accepted that the tourism industry is extremely sensitive to external shocks (Sonmez et al., 1999; Bonn & Rundle-Thiele, 2007), whether natural or man-made, and that such shocks are increasing in frequency (Faulkner, 2001; Ritchie, 2004; Hall, 2010). This increasing frequency, particularly of natural shocks, are alleged by many to be a result of the 'current state of the world' (Brammer, 1990, p.18); the pressure of economic development upon the environment, a notion also supported by Richardson (1994); human activity; and the pressures of globalisation (Jessop, 1999).

There have been many attempts to categorise crises in order to better understand them, mostly according to severity as presented by Parsons (1996) and through Burnett's (1998) Crisis Classification Matrix. Ritchie (2004) explains that through classification, one can develop strategies to deal with such events based on an understanding of time pressure, extent of control and magnitude. In particular, Burnett's (1998) model acknowledges the difference between hazards and disasters and notes that not all hazards will become disasters, the determinants of which are vulnerability and risk (Coppola, 2015). The proposal here by Coppola (2015) is that several countries may be exposed to the same hazard, but some are more vulnerable than others based upon physical, social, economic and environmental factors. A disaster in this sense, therefore, as defined by Faulkner (2001, p. 136), refers to: 'situations where an enterprise (or collection of enterprises in the case of a tourist destination) is confronted with sudden unpredictable catastrophic changes over which it has little control.'

Many researchers note the profound effects of disaster upon tourism destinations, particularly supply side impacts and the perception of risk associated with the destination (Sonmez et al., 1999; Hall, 2010). Terrorism severely intimidates the travelling public (Hall, 2010); natural disasters are similarly off-putting (Sonmez et al. 1999) but arguably have a greater effect upon the fabric of the tourism destination (Lee and Harrald, 1999). Authors in this field (Ritchie, 2004; Fink, 2000; Faulkner, 2001; Coppola, 2015) have traditionally focused upon the development of prescriptive life cycle models of disaster, which share a common goal of aiding understanding of the crisis and future proactive and strategic management of crises. The assumption of these models is that disasters follow a series of sequential stages and that strategies can be developed at each stage to prohibit progression onto the next.

In more recent years, the 'pre-event' stage of disaster management in tourism locations has become more significant. In Miller et al.'s (2006) framework, equal weight is given to the stages pre-disaster and the stages of prevention or 'mitigation' and 'preparedness' Disaster managers recognise what should be done to prevent the disaster, reduce its impact and minimise its losses (Baldini et al., 2012; Miller et al., 2006). In preparedness, the inference here is that facilities and resources are ready to respond (Baldini et al., 2012). Classic mitigation measures include more stringent building codes for new construction and more readily enforced land use regulations (Olsen, 2000), whilst preparedness measures incorporate programmes such as public education and awareness, warning systems and evacuation plans (Olsen, 2000).

Whilst Ritchie (2004) suggests that humans have limited ability to prevent disasters (particularly natural ones) and whilst pre-warning is minimal (Tsai & Chen, 2010), the effects of a disaster can be managed and mitigation measures can be put in place (Coppola, 2015). In fact some accounts of social and ecological resilience to coastal disasters (Adger et al., 2005) recognise that disaster preparedness may be either heightened or eroded, which in turn affects vulnerability, through established practices of living with, and learning from, change and unexpected shocks. Such practices as the transmission of indigenous knowledge as in the fisher-people of Simeulue Island, west of Sumatra, enabled their survival through inherited local knowledge of tsunamis (Adger et al., 2005). Erosion of inherited knowledge in Thailand had the opposite effect, and weakened ecosystems such as mangrove swamps and coral reefs not only removes natural barriers, but reduces or slows economic recovery (Adger et al., 2005).

Other explanations of destination vulnerability to disasters may be drawn from the notion of a 'boiled frog syndrome', which is acknowledged within the literature surrounding strategic management of organisations and business failure, however to a much more limited extent within the literature on the strategic management of tourism destinations and disaster. However, the theory presents some clear parallels with the experiences on Phi Phi, which will be discussed later on in the chapter. Coined initially by Villiers in 1989 in respect of business, Richardson, Nwankwo, & Richardson (1994) explain that if you:

put a frog into a container of hot water, it will feel the heat and jump out. Put a frog into cool water and then gently heat the water to boiling point and the frog will happily sit there unaware of the incremental, dangerous change occurring in its environment. This well-observed, generic form of business failure has its roots in the tendency of organization managers to become trapped in their own "boiled frog syndromes (Richardson, Nwankwo & Richardson, 1994, p. 4)

This phenomenon is a key feature of complacent managers who remain 'blissfully unaware whilst the environment around them heats up' (Richardson et al., 1994, p. 4), something Johnson (1998) describes as strategic drift.

Importantly, their model shows that inertia in changing circumstances increases the likelihood of a crisis. In a tourism context, Sonmez et al. (1999) recommend that tourism destinations vulnerable to crises should incorporate strategic crisis management planning into their overall sustainable development and marketing strategies in order to protect and rebuild a positive destination image and re-establish the area's functionality. Certainly perception management is an important consideration when managing crises (Faulkner, 2001; Rittichainuwat, 2006; 2011). In fact, researchers suggest that the effectiveness and speed of a destination's recovery hinges on the efficiency of re-establishing tourism facilities and sending clear, consistent messages that the destination is once again ready for business (Rittichainuwat, 2011; Henderson, 1999). Misinformation is considered one of the greatest barriers to recovery (Bierman, 2006). In Bonn & Rundle-Thiele's (2007) research concerning strategic decision-making following shock events, they observe that the manner in which this is undertaken will differ significantly from institutional decision-making in a stable environment. Post-shock decision-making can be more intuitive; less analytical and less inclined to consult (Bonn & Rundle-Thiele, 2007.). In light of this, Ritchie (2004) has developed a strategic disaster management framework (Figure 1). This framework stresses the significance of a strategic and proactive approach to disaster management.

Again it can be seen that in the tourism models, greater emphasis is placed upon the response and recovery over the mitigation and preparedness. However, lack of preparedness appears in a vast amount of the literature (Morgan et al., 2006; Calgaro & Lloyd, 2008). These reports note deficiencies in both mitigation and preparedness, most significantly the complete absence of a disaster warning system in the Indian Ocean at the time of the 2004 tsunami. There is similar evidence that the Thai Meteorological Office were aware of the tsunami threat in advance, but decided not to issue a warning due to the potential damage that it might wreak upon the tourism industry should the tsunami not occur (The Nation, 28/12/04; Bangkok Post, 29/12/04).

Figure 1. Strategic disaster management framework
(Source: Ritchie, 2004)

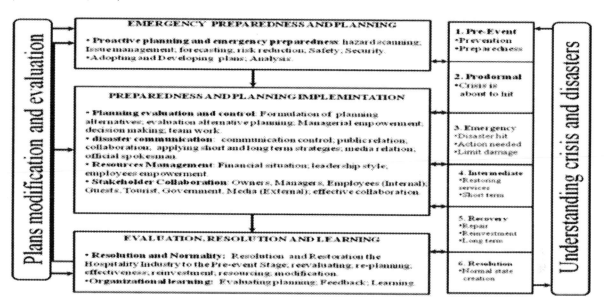

The Thai Government did, however, act swiftly following the tsunami, to restore confidence in the security and safety of Thailand as a tourism destination, attempting to alleviate the perception of risk that can create further damage to the tourism industry in a post-disaster situation (Ritchie, 2004; Faulkner, 2001). However, as Huan, Beaman & Shelby (2004) argue, crisis management plans are all too often reactive rather than proactive, as would appear to be the case here. A National Disaster Warning Centre has now been in operation since 31st May 2005 with the key actors and processes shown in Figure 2, with warning towers erected across the provinces of Ranong, Phuket, Krabi, Phang Nga, Satun and Trang. The tsunami evacuation plan has been in place since 2006 with annual drills held and a full evacuation held last on the 21st August 2009 across all provinces (Svetasreni, 2009). Sadly, it is often found that reactive policies and long lead in times responding to disaster may further heighten the vulnerability of populations (Ingram et al., 2006).

Ingram et al.'s (2006) work in Sri Lanka post-tsunami recognized the socio-economic disparities created by a hastily-designed coastal buffer zone policy of a 100-200m gap between buildings and the shoreline, which led to significant displacement of coastal populations, who were subject to the 'discriminating impact the wave had on poorly constructed buildings' (Ingram et al., 2006, p. 2; Khazai, 2006). At the same time, wealthier citizens and hoteliers benefited from rapid expansion of rebuilt structures (Rice, 2005). Ingram et al. (2006) applied Turner et al.'s (2003) Vulnerability Framework to show that 'adjustment and adaptation' plays a critical role in influencing vulnerability. Rather than removing coastal communities (quickly reducing exposure to risk in the short term), Ingram et al. (2006) recommend that attention needs to be given to underlying sensitivity issues such as socio-economic disparities, lack of economic diversification, and directing attention to sustainable mitigation measures, including conservation of natural protective resources such as mangroves and reefs (Figure 3).

Figure 2. Structure of disaster early warning system
(Source: Svetasreni 2009, Tourism Authority of Thailand)

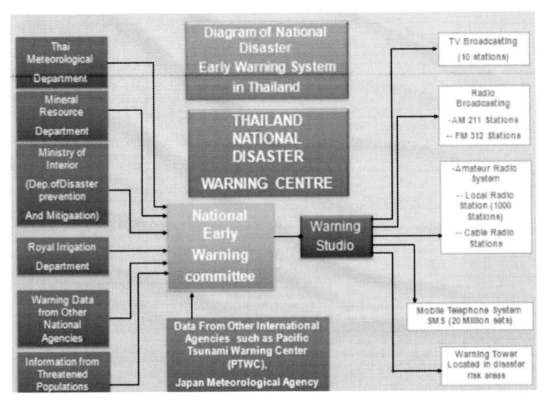

Figure 3. Turner et al.'s (2003) Vulnerability framework contextualised for the tsunami-affected areas
of Sri Lanka
Adapted by Ingram et al. (2006)

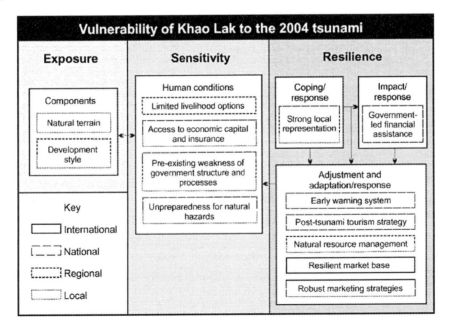

Within their model, solid lines represent the interactions between components of vulnerability (Turner et al. 2003). Dashed lines represent a deviation from these interactions in post-tsunami Sri Lanka as a result of the buffer zone policy. The framework demonstrates the manner in which resource entitlements and usage are influenced by socio-political and environmental processes, and additionally that vulnerability is affected by multiple stressors (Calgaro & Lloyd, 2008).

This framework has also been applied and developed by Calgaro & Lloyd (2008) in the context of Thailand post-tsunami, specifically Khao Lak, in order to expose the causal factors that contributed to the exposure, sensitivity and resilience of Khao Lak in the wake of the tsunami. Their findings presented thirteen factors that they felt influenced Khao Lak's vulnerability; to include the impact of natural terrain and local development style, a lack of preparedness for natural hazards, limited livelihood options and weaknesses in government structure and processes (Calgaro & Lloyd, 2008).

The findings of their research were significant as they offered important contextual information that may have be applicable to Phi Phi due to the similarity of context, but also a basis for comparison. Turner *et al* (2003) offered a framework that could be applied to Phi Phi to establish the root causes of Phi Phi's vulnerability, permitting recommendations for future sustainable development of the island and exposing socio-political factors that have exacerbated vulnerability, allowing the author to identify whether these same factors influenced the nature of the post-disaster redevelopment. Importantly, as Blaikie *et al* (1994) point out, the factors of vulnerability are often reconstructed following a disaster and as such may create frame conditions for a repeat disaster. Calgaro & Lloyd's (2008) work also recognised how a destination's unique socio-political conditions influence vulnerability, notably their recommendation that further longitudinal research in other tsunami-affected locations is required to refine their framework.

Rigg et al. (2005), in their research concerning the socio-economic impacts of the tsunami in Thailand, based their empirical study on three locations, including Phi Phi. They revealed a 'dysfunctional' response to crisis. Of specific relevance, Rigg et al. (2005) observed uneven geographies of recovery, stating that social capital plays an important part in mobilising towards recovery and that this is highly dependent on the cohesiveness of pre-existing community and social networks. To illustrate these differences, they noted that, in Koh Lanta, organisations such as UNICEF, the Thai Red Cross and UNDP played an active part in working with communities to aide recovery, whereas in Phi Phi, the community response was less unified and less local (Rigg et al., 2005). In Phi Phi, the reliance upon transnational social capital was notable. Rigg et al.'s (2005) research notes that after evacuation, community members were scattered across multiple sites and no clear strategy to re-establish the community was proposed.

Conversely, while the devastating effects of crisis are widely acknowledged, some commentators, as in Faulkner's (2001, p. 136) notion of a 'triggering event', recommend that events may be sufficiently significant to 'challenge the structure, operations and survival of an [organisation]' and this may lead to positive transformational connotations (Prideux et al., 2003).

While the body of literature concerning management of disasters in tourism areas is undoubtedly growing (Hystad & Keller, 2008; Beirman, 2003; Ritchie, 2004) and the need for disaster management plans is urged, there is recognition of a lack of longer-term studies, which not only would elaborate how disaster has shifted the nature of the destination and tourism product, but also identify successful strategic processes and actions in disaster response (Hystad & Keller, 2008.). Hedman (2005, p.5) recognises that the substantial shortcomings in the response to the tsunami draw attention to relations of power and politics within affected nations and that a range of protection concerns have been revealed, including 'access to assistance, enforced relocation, sexual and gender-based violence, safe and voluntary return, loss of documentation and restitution of property'.

Political Economy and (Re)Construction Post Disaster

There are a range of cases, which demonstrate the influence of political economy upon development and reconstruction at different levels of analysis. These cases may be useful as a basis for understanding the dynamics and experiences of Phi Phi's reconstruction and be the basis of comparative analysis, grounded in the fact that they represent examples of the influence of political economy upon reconstruction in a post-natural disaster context (Hurricane Mitch and Katrina; The Asian Tsunami on Sri Lanka). The analysis may not only provide a theoretical background through which to understand the experiences on Phi Phi but also assist theoretical building resulting from this research, on the basis that experiences on Phi Phi are reflected in other cases. The analysis spans down to more localised examples within Thailand and on Phi Phi itself.

Klein's work (2005 and 2008) specifically is significant because it elaborates, through cases dating back to the 1950s, how the principles of shock therapy allegedly applied at McGill University under Dr Ewen Cameron were mirrored through economic shock therapy preached by the Milton Friedman Chicago School movement, whereby starting with Pinochet's Coup in 1972 in Chile, large-scale shocks were exploited to impose extreme capitalist takeovers (Klein, 2008) under the guise of neoliberalism. Klein's work on shock therapy through disaster capitalism (2005; 2008) offers a critical discussion of the reconstruction effort of the Bush Administration following events such as the wars in Iraq and Afghanistan, and natural disasters in Haiti, Hurricane Mitch and the post-tsunami relief effort, hinting at the trend towards 'disaster capitalism'.

Klein (2008, p. 385) criticises reconstruction agents including consulting firms, NGOs, government and UN aid agencies and international financial institutions, suggesting that there is a 'rise of a predatory form of disaster capitalism that uses the desperation and fear created by catastrophe to engage in radical social and economic engineering.' 'Terra nullius' is diminishing, particularly in the case of tourism, whereby tourists increasingly seek out 'new, exotic places' (Poon, 1993) and therefore a 'clean slate' in developmental terms might be quite appealing. Should this 'clean slate' be used as an opportunity to redevelop a longstanding unsustainable tourism destination along more considerate lines, thus enhancing the quality of life of the host community, then perhaps some hope can be gleaned from such disaster. If, however, Klein's (2005, p.3) claim is true that 'disaster is the new terra nullius' whereby financial institutions such as the World Bank and IMF can provide reconstruction loans in the form of structural adjustment policies with crippling conditions, enabling the privatisation of industry and loss of control to foreign corporations, then disaster reconstruction may present an unsustainable future for those countries affected (Willis, 2011).

Her (Klein, 2008, p.386) subsequent publication 'The Shock Doctrine' explored these issues further through a variety of post-disaster cases including that of Sri Lanka. Her research uncovered many issues of significance to this research. Most notably, her discussions with coastal communities highlight widespread dissatisfaction with a mass evacuation plan in the name of 'building back better'. New rules imposed on coastal communities forbade rebuilding for safety reasons within two hundred metres of the shoreline, making the beach 'off limits' for small boat fisher-people. However, tourist resorts were exempted from the buffer zone rule, on the condition that they classified their reconstruction work as 'repair'. New homes would be found for the fishing communities several kilometres inland (Klein, 2008). It was proposed that the tsunami was the answer to the prayers of businessmen and politicians, 'since it literally wiped these coastal areas clean of the communities, which had previously stood in the way of their plans for resorts, hotels, casinos and shrimp farms' (Klein, 2005, p. 3; 2008). Klein (2008, p. 402) likens the post-tsunami situation to colonial times: 'if the land was declared empty or wasted, it could be seized and its people eliminated without remorse.'

Other global cases where the political economic influences of reconstruction are evident are plentiful. Hurricane Mitch is mentioned by Klein (2005), and supported by Bradshaw (2002, p.871) in her critique of the reconstruction processes in Nicaragua, highlighting that 'disasters tend to reveal existing national, regional and global power structures, as well as power relations within intimate relations' (as adapted from Enarson and Morrow, 1998, p. 2). In this case, it is clear that the reconstruction processes are the result of existing power struggles and structures and that rarely do disaster responses contribute towards long-term development: they can in fact undermine it (Bradshaw, 2002).

In a similar vein, Harvey (2006; 2007, p. 29) acknowledges a rise in attempts to 'accumulate by dispossession', a new form of imperialism seeking to preserve the hegemonic position of the US in global capitalism. In fact, neoliberal approaches to development are cited by Harvey as an hegemonic discourse in itself: 'with pervasive effects on ways of thought and political-economic practices to the point where it is now part of the common sense way we interpret, live in, and understand the world' (Harvey, 2007, p. 21). Other researchers have critiqued disaster capitalism as a form of neoliberal thought through study of its impact upon public services; specifically, education in New Orleans post-Hurricane Katrina (Owen, 2011), Democracy "Promotion" in Iraq, and Chicago's Renaissance 2010 project and the impact of No Child Left Behind (NCLB) (Saltman, 2007a; 2007b). Similar studies have been conducted on Healthcare provision by Berggren et al. (2006) post-Katrina and by Fletcher (2012) who notes that addressing the climate change crisis has become a boom industry in its own right. Saltman's (2007a; 2007b) work draws many parallels with Klein's (2008) when he considers how disasters both natural and manmade have been used by businesses and power brokers to profiteer from the educational sector. Saltman identifies 'smash and grab capitalism', which he claims threatens democracy in the US.

At a regional level, Klein's (2005; 2008) and Saltman's (2007a; 2007b) observations are further reinforced in the case of post-disaster reconstruction following the tsunami. Following widespread destruction across numerous developing countries, the challenges and conflicts faced by host communities are comparable. Important work had commenced surrounding the political economy of post-tsunami reconstruction in Thailand as part of a PhD study by Dararat Kaewkuntee, Government official in the Office of Natural Resources and Environmental Policy and Planning. Tragically, Khun Kaewkuntee passed away in February 2006, leaving her work unfinished. Her published work up unto that point discussed the complexity of land rights problems in Thailand, highlighting that the tsunami only served to 'unveil' the conflict that awaited community members, governments and private investors (Kaewkuntee 2006, p.15). She states that in Thailand land rights are a nationwide issue and that 'many communities have been making use of public land both before and after the public land and national forest law', thus creating a situation whereby ownership and land boundaries are hazy. The issue is heightened, however, owing to the fact that land in Thailand is one of the country's most precious commodities that may be exploited, particularly when significant sums of money are offered by private investors to get their hands on prime beachfront land. In the name of capitalism, therefore, minor landowners and traditional inhabitants are tempted to sell their sought-after land for brief economic gain and retreat to inland locations, or alternatively encroach on public land (Kaewkuntee, 2006).

There were many examples of conflict following the tsunami in the Andaman Region, including Ban Namken, Tungwa, Ban Laem-Pom and Tubtawan communities (Kaewkuntee, 2006; Krauss, 2005). The stories follow a familiar pattern: following the tsunami these communities have been forcibly relocated by the government under the claim that they have been encroaching on public land (Rigg et al., 2005).

Another common tale is that ownership rights have been claimed over the land, usually by a development company or someone with close Governmental links (Pleumarom, 2005). Inhabitants report returning to the place where their home used to be to find armed guards and barbed wire fence encircling the settlement (Rigg et al., 2005). Land rights therefore remain of pivotal concern in the post-tsunami reconstruction effort. Saltman (2007b) further claims that the tsunami permitted large corporations to seize coveted shoreline properties for resort development, a claim that is supported by Klein (2008) and research undertaken in the Andaman Region by Tourism Concern (Rice, 2005).

METHODOLOGY

The methodology adopted for the empirical research was interpretivist, in which primary data was gathered using an inductive, mixed methodology. Methods of data collection included online research, comprising the design and operation of a tailored website to overcome geographical and access limitations; and offline methods such as visual techniques to monitor change and confirm opinions offered by participants; in-depth face-to-face interviews with hand-picked stakeholders of Phi Phi's development; open-ended questionnaires with tourists; and extended answer Thai script questionnaires.

Establishing Contacts

This research mapped the form of touristic development on Phi Phi from an initial visit to the islands in 2005 to the present day. Methodologically, a fundamental requirement of this research was to establish contacts amongst stakeholders. This purpose was threefold: to identify key literature to form the basis of the literature review; to obtain opinions from stakeholders to provide the basis for future contacts and targeted interviews as the research evolved; and to keep abreast of new developments. Contacts were sought in a variety of areas. Firstly, during a visit to Phi Phi Don in June 2005, contact details of local businesses, accommodation providers and tour operators were obtained. Upon return, emails were sent to these businesses to introduce the research and ask permission to contact them again in the future. Other contact with stakeholders was established through a visit to the Hi Phi Phi shop and subsequent postings on the Hi Phi Phi website and discussion forum. Once the tailored research website was designed, the URL was also posted on the Hi Phi Phi website. This ensured that contact was established with islanders, volunteers, expatriates, tourists and local businesspeople.

Through contacting key tourism industry and government personnel in the region, a report on a workshop for the implementation of WTO sustainability indicators in Phuket (The Phuket Action Plan) was obtained. An annex of this document detailed potential contacts, which were followed up and proved fruitful. Contacts were then established with industry and government representatives, key authors and researchers, national media representatives and pressure groups. This provided the basis for future contacts and other key stakeholders were subsequently directed to the author using snowball-sampling techniques.

Data Collection Methods

In total, 26 in-depth interviews were conducted between April and November 2006, using a combination of purposive and snowball sampling techniques based upon stakeholder theory (Swarbrooke, 1999; Weaver & Lawton, 2014). Respondents were selected purposively and on the basis of their role and familiarity with Phi Phi.

Research in the literature and observations from initial field visits in 2006 suggested that one of the greatest influencing factors in shaping the island's future development was the tourist market. Therefore, in order to ascertain the typology of tourists visiting Phi Phi to comprehend the nature of demand and subsequent impacts of tourism (in line with proposals made by Plog (2001), Wickens (2002) and Cohen (1979)), a snapshot, convenience-sampled, short-answer questionnaire was developed. The questionnaire was designed provide a profile of the tourists visiting the island, and to learn more about the needs, motivations and desires of the tourist market at this time, as was similarly undertaken by Dodds et al. (2010) approximately six months later. The questions posed therefore had these goals in mind. The questionnaire was designed to be short for ease of completion, as respondents were approached in a variety of environments including the beach, ferries, restaurants, bars and in tourist accommodation. The majority of questions were open-ended to solicit unbiased responses.

The language barrier between the researcher and Thai respondents, in addition to the temptation to 'answer to please' (Van Esterik, 2000; Mulder, 2000), was further addressed during phase two of the field study (April 2008), whereby research questions translated into Thai script were developed and handed by the researcher to 38 inhabitants of Koh Phi. These questions were pre-tested with a Thai colleague to ensure comprehension. These questionnaires were left with the respondents for half a day or a whole day, to enable them to write a full, unbiased response in Thai. This went some way toward overcoming language barriers and biases introduced through the face-to-face interviews (which were predominantly in English), and also enabled respondents to express themselves clearly their own language.

Banks (2002; 2005) discusses the use of visual data, including photography as a 'visual notebook'. Most certainly, in a study seeking to document change, and project future change, this method would seem highly appropriate. Film and photography may be used to gain understanding of societies and cultural forms (Edwards, 1992) and the study of spatial behaviour (Hockings, 2003). Within this research therefore, this method was used in combination with other data collection techniques as detailed. The purpose of using visual data was to document change over time (2006-2011) and to validate observational field notes and interview data. Banks (2005) discusses how images may be used. The photography in this research was not intended as visual anthropology, but rather as a visual record and *aide memoire* (Knowles & Sweetman, 2005).

RESULTS AND DISCUSSION

Influence of the Tsunami upon Tourism Planning

The influence of the tsunami was not the strongest within the emergent themes from the data. This may be on account of being informed early on (Interview respondent 1) that it was inappropriate to dwell on the past and therefore the author's sensitivity was heightened to avoid questioning that may cause emotional distress to respondents, in line with ethical principles. Additionally, the author was informed that nothing has changed; the situation is not different after the tsunami; the tsunami only served to uncover problems that existed before and temporarily slow the pace of development down (Electronic Respondent 11, non-Thai resident), a finding that supports the initial empirical findings of Kaewkuntee (2006) in Khao Lak, Thailand, post-tsunami. In fact, sub-themes within the influence of the tsunami elaborate upon these problems, including incidence of abuse, a lack of preparedness and how vulnerable the island and its community was in the light of shock events. The nature of this vulnerability will be explored later on in the chapter through an adaptation of Turner et al.'s (2003) Vulnerability Framework.

Whilst the opportunity was presented to take stock and reconsider an alternative form of tourism to the island (as it appears the government wanted), this was not taken: 'The appeal of the island has not changed, it remains a beautiful place. The tsunami did not change the island's appeal, but rather continued poor environmental practices and poor building regulations continue to decrease the beauty of Phi Phi' (Electronic respondent 6, a Thai-based academic). This may be on account of concerns, as voiced by Rice (2005) in a post-tsunami assessment study by Tourism Concern, that the secondary impacts of the tsunami would be almost destructive as the tsunami itself i.e. loss of earnings and livelihoods from the tourism industry. It is no wonder, therefore, that to rebuild lives through the only way they know (tourism) is one of the key shaping influences post-tsunami.

Systems put in place to ensure the safety of the island inhabitants were being used ineffectively: 'there is a tsunami warning system in place to warn the local population of an impending problem. In reality the system is used to tell people of an event in the local school. The road posts informing people where to go in the event of an incoming tsunami have either been removed or are swamped by other advertising signs' (Electronic respondent 7, Thai resident). In fact, the research findings provide empirical evidence of the limitations in the strategic management of the tsunami disaster on Phi Phi and as such highlights that the actions taken towards the management of the crisis are in fact contrary to the recommendations made in the literature surrounding disaster management in tourism areas.

Whilst in the literature there was a profusion of viewpoints that recommended that the island use the tsunami as an opportunity for a 'clean slate – the opportunity to build anew in areas that had had been developed in environmentally and socially unjust ways' (Tangwisutijit & Warunpitikul, 2005; UNDP. 2005; Cummings, 2005), there is minimal evidence that this opportunity has been taken. Respondents argue that the tsunami has had no real impact in terms of reassessing the development philosophy and has only served to heighten (and in some way, permit) further destruction. Electronic respondent 8, an ecotourism operator, and Interview respondent 7, a Thai-based academic, had similar views: 'the tsunami was an excuse to build high rises on Phi Phi. I doubt that any credible land use planner anywhere would consider high rises appropriate on the formerly beautiful island' (Electronic respondent 8).

Interview respondent 7 explained how, through their own research, they have observed a trend in the development of Thai island destinations, which in government rhetoric is focused upon sustainability, but in practice results in a transfer from small-scale, local- owned enterprises to outside investment, highlighting a clear conflict in the interpretation of sustainability:

this was a major thing after the tsunami. They took the opportunity to grab more land and then they said it is as part of this sustainable tourism plan because when the big investors come in, they all do it in an orderly way, you know, and not ... backpacker[s], crazy people who pollute the sea, build shacks on the beach and so on. In Koh Samet also it was the same situation. In these small businesses they all produce the dirt, so they come in and they build the posh hotels. For that they set up the staged authenticity fishing communities, which look like a living museum. That is what their vision of sustainable tourism is.

The images below illustrate the impact that the tsunami had upon the central 'apple core' area. It can be seen how densely populated Tonsai village was pre-tsunami. Significantly, this land is only two metres above sea level at its highest point (see Figures 4 and 5).

The image below illustrates the extent of the devastation following the tsunami.

Figure 4. Map of construction in the central area of the island pre-tsunami (taken 29.3.2006)

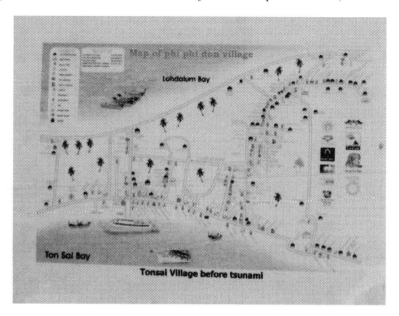

Figure 5. The so-called 'clean slate' (taken 11.12.2005)

One can see how the government might have viewed the opportunity to revert this 'apple core' area back to an area of no construction post-tsunami. However, within their original plan, this would involve moving all remaining construction up onto the hillside. It would also mean that the major landowners' land and high-rise accommodation would be affected. It is therefore no wonder that the plans did not proceed, due to the level of power retained by the landowners on account of their wealth, land ownership, knowledge and status. The results of the research, therefore, present empirical evidence that, although a shock event such as a tsunami may temporarily stall the pace of development, it does not create a clean slate situation, on account of the pre-existing ideology. The desire in the aftermath of the shock event is to recreate that which existed before, with haste.

Discussions of Disaster Capitalism

Despite Klein's (2005; 2008) claims of 'disaster capitalism', there was minimal evidence found of this at a local level. Claims of an increased takeover of global powers and a dangerous level of power held by multinationals are not apparent in this localised case study. There is a trend in Thailand for high-end tourism; however, this is not exclusively pursued through selling out to international hotel chains, and in fact this is restricted by policies favouring national interest (Noy, 2011; Konisranukul & Tuaycharoen, 2010; Krutwaysho & Bramwell, 2010) and a focus upon what can be regarded an inward facing 'sufficiency economy' (Noy, 2011; Krongkaew, 2004). Where there are international hotel chains on Phi Phi (e.g. Intercontinental Hotels Group and Holiday Inn), development took place in association with Thai landowners, further strengthening their control over the future development of the island, through the establishment of international bonds and support structures, an example of local elites perpetuating their own interests under dependency theory. There was a loss of local control on Phi Phi, but this occurred in the early 1990s when the traditional inhabitants sold their land to wealthy business people from the mainland. There is limited evidence of the 'radical social and economic engineering' that Klein (2005; 2008) speaks of.

Far more fitting for the case of Phi Phi would be the considerations of Pleumarom (1999), and Bradshaw (2002), who note the inequalities that exist within society and the influence that these have over developmental outcomes. Inequalities are certainly apparent on Phi Phi. Those who own land on the island, and specifically the four major landowners have the greatest influence over development. One may argue that there may have been a desire to 'capitalise' on the disaster, as the government has been accused of trying to do, but this was not borne out. Bradshaw's (2002) observations would be most apt for the situation on Phi Phi, that, 'reconstruction processes are not newly constructed in the light of the disaster but are the result of existing power struggles and structures'. Scheyvens (2002) adds strength to this argument, highlighting due to the complex interplay of class, values and power that exists at a destination level, it ultimately may result in a lack of equitable participation and consultation in planning for tourism. This would certainly appear to be the case on Phi Phi, whereby, on account of economic power and landownership, the key players in shaping the future of Phi Phi's development are the landowners.

In the literature surrounding the political economy of post-disaster reconstruction it became evident that there were two clear schools of thought concerning Koh Phi Phi's reconstruction: firstly, that the tsunami had created a 'clean slate' and hence opportunity should be taken to pursue a more sustainable future; and secondly that global neoliberal policies have incited a trend towards disaster capitalism, in which disaster capitalists would use desperation and fear created by catastrophe to engage in radical re-engineering of affected areas. Neither school of thought has been wholly correct in respect of Phi Phi.

These outcomes are strongly influenced by the political economy of the island and as such make the experiences on Phi Phi a contribution to the existing knowledge on post-disaster tourism redevelopment.

Although the research demonstrated a desire by the Thai government to capitalise on the disaster in terms of reclaiming encroached land and changing the face of the island to pursue a lower-density, high-end model, the tsunami did not, as Klein (2008), Bradshaw (2002), Saltman (2007) and Harvey (2007) predicted reflect a growing trend in disaster capitalism. It is worth exploring why that did not occur. The table below elaborates the evidence of 'disaster capitalism' in tourism destinations post-tsunami, the manner in which these experiences were or were not present on Phi Phi and a subsequent explanation of why this occurred. It can be seen that the tsunami did present the opportunity for disaster capitalism but the political economy surrounding Thai tourism development and development on Phi Phi did not permit this to happen (see Table 1).

The opportunity was presented to consider an alternative form of tourism (as it appears the government wanted), but this was not taken. The tsunami did not change the island's appeal, but rather continued

Table 1. A summary of why Phi Phi avoided 'disaster capitalism'

Characteristic of Disaster Capitalism	Presence Post-Tsunami	Presence and Influence on Phi Phi
Shock event	Earthquake off west coast of Sumatra measuring over 9 on the Richter scale Sea receded to 100 metres from the Andaman coast for about five minutes; three staggered waves hit the Andaman Coast, up to 10m in height; one hour inundation 5395 Killed 2817 missing 58,550 affected 120,000+ lost livelihoods in tourism	3m (10ft) wave hit from Tonsai Bay 5.5m (18ft) wave hit from Ao Lo Dalaam Devastated low-lying land 70% of buildings destroyed 850 bodies (approx.) recovered 1500 missing The tsunami had a profound effect on the central area of Phi Phi Don Island, destroying 70% of the infrastructure and presenting what was considered by some to be a blank canvas The disaster was characteristic of a low intensity, low threat, low control event with limited response options, shock event
Slate wiped clean	Mass evacuation plan in Sri Lanka, displaced fishing communities 1km inland Rules imposed on fishing communities in Sri Lanka and Khao Lak in Thailand forbade rebuilding for 'safety' reasons Communities in Ban Namken, Ban Laem-pon, and Tubtawan forcibly removed from coastal homes	70% of infrastructure in the 'apple core' destroyed Islanders evacuated for a month following the Tsunami, accommodated in disparate locations across the Krabi province and in refugee camps Rubble cleared 30m setback imposed New inland homes provided Resistance, delays and inaction resulted in islanders 'forging ahead' with rebuilding the island despite ban on construction As explained in Table 27, a clean slate can never exist in development terms unless 'terra nullius' as the landscapes of development that preceded the tsunami cannot and will not be erased. The tsunami has shown the challenges that face this community in 'high colour' Strong political-economic structures at a local level on Phi Phi Don resisted government plans Strong support from the international backpacker and volunteer community strengthened resistance
Increased takeover of global powers	Ambiguity in foreign ownership laws in Thailand Foreigners cannot own land in Thailand, but can own buildings separate from the land Thailand restricts and prohibits economical areas and business categories for foreigners primarily in the Foreign Business Act (A.D.1999). Sector specific legislation on foreign ownership of 49% stake Many 'loopholes'	Multinational hotel chain Intercontinental develops as the management company of the Holiday Inn through co-operation with local landowner High levels of control are maintained by dominant landowners through status, predominantly 'outsiders' (Thais who are not native of the area – Cohen, 1983) Islanders are rushing to rebuild homes to avoid any claim on the land by wealthy families Anti-liberalisation stance and emphasis on 'sufficiency economy' places power back in the nation of Thailand Strong socio-political structures created by major landowners prevented takeover

continued on following page

Table 1. Continued

Characteristic of Disaster Capitalism	Presence Post-Tsunami	Presence and Influence on Phi Phi
Increase in multinationals	Set back or 'buffer' zone policy of 100m imposed in Sri Lanka represents a state-sponsored dislocation of coastal populations 10m setback policy for hotels The Thai government has liquidated public land holdings in tsunami-affected areas. In Nai Lai the local government has sold 240 acres of public land to developers, and 1,800 acres has been bought from villagers. Rather than favouring Multinationals this favours big business in Thailand.	Presence of multinationals arises from co-operation between landowners and foreign operators and shows dependency theory. At present Intercontinental have two developments on the island using this means but these are in the Laem Tong area, not Tonsai Pursuit of high-end tourism across Thailand. On Phi Phi this is realised in the northern and eastern beaches although it does not involve solely multinational corporations. Phi Phi Island Village and Zeavola are considered 'high-end' however there is no involvement of international capital, moreso favouring national 'big business'
Extreme capitalist takeover	Tourist resorts in Sri Lanka and Khao Lak exempted from the buffer zone ruling as works classified as 'repair'; used as a means to acquire land	Phi Phi differs from Khao Lak in that the central part of the island (80% of which) is owned by a small collection of landowners who form a strong resistance against capitalist takeover in the same sense as other tsunami affected locations such as Sri Lanka, however these landowners can be seen as the capitalists themselves. Ownership has not shifted therefore following the tsunami, capitalist takeover occurred on Phi Phi in the 1980s
Reconstruction loans with crippling conditions for the privatisation of industry	The Thai government refused 'disaster relief' only accepting 'technical assistance' in light of a resistance to be bound to neoliberal measures imposed by the World Bank post-Asian Financial Crisis	Focus on 'sufficiency economy' pioneered by the King, focuses upon fostering national interests General populace against neoliberalism post-Asian Crisis experience Resultant inward facing development programmes favour national interest over external assistance Funds for the reconstruction of the island generated predominantly through private capital (landowners) and volunteer fundraising retained local ownership
Highlights existing power relationships and the inequalities that exist within society	Unveiled complexity of land rights problems in Thailand	Presented delays in reclaiming land by original owners and identifying who held the title deeds Landowners asserted power by reclaiming land from tenants for new developments as new terms of lease were established resulting in erosion of trust and strong community bonds
Used by power brokers to profiteer	Land seized, ownership rights to coastal land claimed by development companies with close governmental links	This took place on Phi Phi long before the tsunami. Wealthy investors made connections with indigenous landowners in the 1980s, who would be willing to make land claims on the investor's behalf. Title deeds claimed under the pretence that the land was being used for farming

(Sources: Author's empirical research; Klein, 2008; Bradshaw, 2002; Saltman, 2007; Kaewkuntee, 2006; Rigg et al., 2005; Scott, 1985; Rice, 2005; Department for Disaster Prevention and Mitigation, Ministry of Interior, Thailand, 2004)

poor environmental practices and poor building regulations, which continue to decrease the beauty of Phi Phi. This may be on account of concerns that the secondary impacts of the tsunami would be almost as destructive as the tsunami itself i.e. loss of earnings and livelihoods from the tourism industry. It is no wonder, therefore, that the islanders chose to rebuild their lives the only way they know how, and tourism is the key shaping influence post-tsunami. As academic commentators have observed, an event on this scale has the potential to radically transform structures and processes, representing a break in the trajectories of existence (Rigg et al., 2005), This thesis suggests that a 'clean slate' never existed in development terms and the reasons behind this are derived from both primary and secondary data and are elaborated in Table 2.

There is an assumption that Phi Phi will always be a success in terms of tourism and therefore inhabitants treat it as a cash cow. Respondents claimed that the general attitude is to grab as much money as they can from the island. The warning signs noted by Pleumarom (2004) and Thongpra (2005) that the desire to rebuild and accommodate tourism again would far supersede any consideration for sustainability have been borne out. The importance of marketing to boost tourism seems to be a philosophy

Table 2. Justification of the absence of a 'clean slate' on Phi Phi

Reasons Why 'Clean Slate' Opportunity Could Not Be Taken	Evidence
Prevailing development philosophy on the island pre-tsunami is economic	Theme [Development philosophies]; Theme [Future Desires]; Theme [Past reflection]
Lack of economic diversity, nurturing of tourism monoculture	Pleumarom, 2004; Theme [Development philosophies]; Dodds, 2011; Ko, 2005;
Preference for the 'tried and tested' model of tourism development	UNDP; Theme [Future Desires]; Theme [Development philosophies]
Complacency born of competitive success	Theme [Development philosophies]; Nwankwo and Richardson, 1994; Argenti, 1976
Failure to see the interconnectedness of environmental viability and economic sustainability	Theme [Conceptualisations of sustainability]; Theme [Development philosophies]
Island still does not have a robust system of basic infrastructure	Theme [Needs]; Theme [Community Challenges]; Brix, 2007; Ghobarah et al., 2006; Dodds et al., 2010
Fear, confusion and improper communication surrounding future plans for the island were met with suspicion and resistance	Theme [Communication]; Theme [Future Plans]; Theme [Fear]; Theme [Conflict]; Rice, 2005; Altman, 2005
Inaction and delays in the release of plans, caused islanders to forge ahead illegally with rebuilding as there was an immediate need to secure livelihoods	Rice, 2005; Theme [Barriers]; Theme [Future Plans]; Theme [Economic impacts of tourism]; Theme [Conflict]; Theme [Lawlessness]
Strong political-economic structures maintained by major Landowners who also have ties with local government deter ongoing government involvement	Theme [Power Relationships]; Theme [Lawlessness]; Theme [Conflict]
The Tsunami not only creates new challenges but uncovered existing ones	Theme [Influence of the Tsunami]; Theme [Community Challenges]; Theme [Conflict]; Theme [Lawlessness]
The psychological effect of tourism development cannot be erased	Theme [Economic impacts of tourism]; Theme [Social impacts of tourism]; Theme [Influence of the Tsunami]

(Sources: Pleumarom, 2004; UNDP, 2005; Dodds, 2011; Ko, 2005; Nwankwo & Richardson, 1994; Argenti, 1976; Rice, 2005; Altman, 2005; Brix, 2007; Ghobarah et al., 2006; Dodds et al., 2010 and Researcher's own empirical evidence)

that is common to Thai government representatives and within discussions of sustainability originating in Thailand, but it does not engage in discussions of sustainability within literature of Western origins.

Given that the results of the research, combined with evidence presented within existing literature, have exposed significant critique concerning the manner in which the tsunami was handled in respect of Phi Phi, it is appropriate at this juncture to apply Ritchie's (2004) strategic disaster management framework to identify the shortcomings of the disaster response and use this in line with the research objectives to comprehend how such a disaster has influenced tourism development and planning on the island. In essence, what can be seen here through the experiences on Phi Phi is a mirror opposite to the manner in which a disaster should be strategically handled; according to the academic debates on disaster management (Ritchie, 2004; Miller et al., 2006; Coppola, 2015; Faulkner, 2001; and Baldini et al., 2012, amongst others). An exploration of why this occurred is linked with discussions of vulnerability (see Figure 6).

The tsunami uncovered problems that already existed, and also brought them to the forefront due to the attention that was paid to the island post-tsunami. The main issue was land conflict. The tsunami revealed the extent of gradual encroachment onto National Park Land and the severe lack of adequate facilities for a community to survive and prosper.

Figure 6. Framework of shortcomings in the strategic management of the tsunami on Phi Phi
(Taylor, 2012, Author's own comprised through data collection)

Prevention (prevent, reduce impact, minimise losses pre-Tsunami)
- Building codes ignored
- Land use regulations not enforced
- Lack of zoning, environmental management plan and carrying capacity
- High density, poorly planned development of weak structural performance
- Loss of natural 'buffers' and undermined protective ecosystems

Preparedness (capabilities built for response pre-Tsunami)
- Absence of national disaster warning system and evacuation plans
- Absence of public awareness campaigns
- Erosion of indigenous knowledge concerning the threat of Tsunami
- No established practice of living with or learning from shock events
- Absence of post disaster marketing plan
- Warnings ignored by the Thai Meteorological Department of impending Tsunami
- Lack of cohesive community

Emergency
- Two waves enveloped the central low lying area of Phi Phi Don, devastating homes and businesses
- 850 bodies recovered, 1500 missing
- Loss of productive and business assets
- Salinisation of clean water supply
- Reservoir flooded
- Geographical isolation hampered rubble removal
- A break in the trajectories of existence

Response
- Island closed for 1 month, displacement of inhabitants
- Immediate repatriation of tourists
- Tourist flows redirected
- Media exacerbated risk perception through misinformation
- Encouragement of 'dark tourism'/ day trippers
- Thai government refused international assistance
- Co-ordinated through outsider volunteer effort, establishment of volunteer organisations
- 100 day mourning period, then inappropriate to dwell on the tragedy
- Desire to take advantage of an alleged 'clean slate' and threat of 'disaster capitalism'

Recovery
- Ongoing Land conflicts, loss of documentation
- Ongoing political problems delayed the release of plans for the island
- Neo-liberal development philosophy favouring tourism growth
- Completed projects such as the wetlands system function ineffectively
- Resistance of government plans
- Lack of reconstruction assistance
- A recreation of the pre-tsunami development trajectory
- Lack of social-psychological expertise in embassy staff
- Absence of socio-psychological support for survivors
- Lack of robust infrastructure and system of utilities

Perceptions of Vulnerability

It can be seen that vulnerability played a significant role in the immediate and long-term effects of the crisis, and through a more comprehensive analysis of Phi Phi's vulnerability, as Calgaro & Lloyd (2008) advised was required in order to refine their framework developed from empirical study in Khao Lak, other socio-political factors influencing the tourist development on the island may also be uncovered. The factors contributing to Phi Phi's disaster vulnerability are thus presented in the author's own context bound and refined adaptation of Calgaro & Lloyd's (2008) work.

The descriptions of a perfect beach resort with palm trees, hammocks, beach huts and white sand beaches with crystal-clear water suitably described Phi Phi twenty years ago and the image captured by Alex Garland in *The Beach* (1997) and the subsequent film that caused so much controversy. One of the greatest contradictions of Phi Phi is that it was selected as the location for the filming of stereotypical paradise location and yet paradise had to be cosmetically enhanced, which wrought environmental destruction on Maya Bay (Fahn, 1998; Shelby-Biggs, 2000) and contravened the 1992 Environmental Protection Act and the 1961 National Park Act (The Nation, 11.11.1998).

In respect of inhabitants, this phenomenon is also evidenced. Commentators on Phi Phi liken this to what is called 'boiled frog' syndrome. This is a phenomenon not newly applied in business but in the business of tourism it is, nevertheless clear parallels can be drawn. In relation to Phi Phi, this 'strategic gap' can be viewed in several ways. Firstly, a lack of action in implementing measures to manage tourism impacts, control the nature and volume of tourism development and developing sustainable tourism practices creates a crisis of tourism 'killing the golden goose' (Respondent 26), degrading the environment upon which the tourist product is based. Secondly, a lack of proactive action by the Thai government in terms of disaster preparation and complacency about the probability of such an event, a resistance to act for fear of harming the tourism industry exacerbated the strategic gap created by a rapidly-changing environmental situation. A further strategic gap developed on account of delays by the Thai government in agreeing and delivering redevelopment plans in the recovery phase. This represents a further 'crisis' due to the time elapsed between the Prodromal (pre-impact) phase (Ritchie, 2004) of 26th December 2004, and Resolution (normal or improved state resumed), which, arguably, has still not been reached due to rebuilding work taking place in many areas of the island including shoreline developments near the pier in Tonsai and shop houses adjacent to the Wastewater Treatment Plant and wetlands. This notion of 'strategic gap' is embedded in the authors' model of Vulnerability (see Figure 7) as a factor that has heightened the vulnerability of Phi Phi.

Whilst the age of previous academic research on the concept of the boiled frog is noted (Argenti, 1976; Richardson *et al*, 1994; Villiers, 1989), a subsequent search for more recent studies or application to the study of tourism development yields results applied only in the context of generic management. The closest application is Faulkner's (2000) observation that the impacts of a threatening situation (disaster) are often only realised following a triggering event, implying that a gradual onset of adverse changes affords less recognition of a crisis situation than that of a triggering event, such as a tsunami. More recently still, Johnson's (2009) work applies the boiled frog concept to encourage hospitality students to develop self-awareness in their attitudes to change, whilst Hardiman & Burgin (2010) in their research on 'canyoning' in the Blue Mountains National Park in Australia likens the lack of care for ecological damage to the boiled frog phenomenon. This research, however, demonstrates the relevance and applicability of Richardson, Nwankwo & Richardson's (1994) ideas, in order to comprehend how disaster

Figure 7. A framework of factors influencing Koh Phi Phi's vulnerability to disasters
(Taylor, 2012, Author's own comprised through data collection)

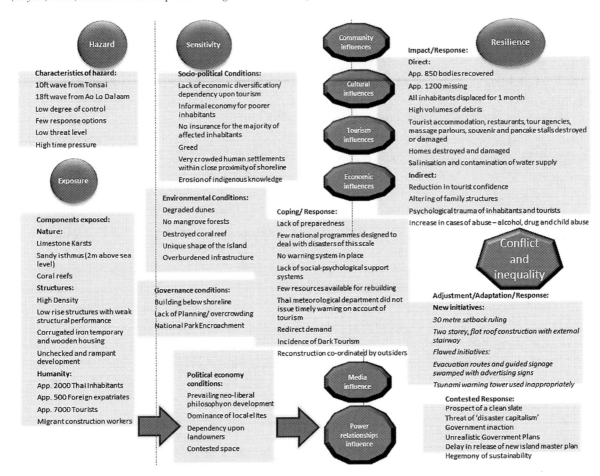

vulnerability can be heightened and how a gradual onset of detrimental changes without remedial action being taken represents a crisis situation.

CONCLUSION

This chapter has outlined the reasons why Phi Phi avoided the type of capitalism experienced by disaster affected tourism destinations elsewhere. Despite claims of a 'clean slate' being offered by the tsunami in developmental terms (UNDP, 2005), evidence and explanation of why a 'clean slate' did not and would never exist on Phi Phi has been provided, a finding which may offer practical relevance to other tourism destinations in a post disaster context.

The chapter has refined the work of Calgaro & Lloyd (2008) in order to identify a detailed framework of vulnerability factors intertwined with factors of political economy, presenting a post disaster situation, which remains highly vulnerable and non-conducive to sustainability. Through the experiences post-disaster on Phi Phi, the strategic response has been analysed through an adapted Strategic Disaster Management Framework (Ritchie, 2004) to identify the shortcomings of the disaster response and use this to comprehend how such a disaster has influenced tourism development and planning on the island. In essence, what can be seen here is a mirror opposite to the manner in which a disaster should be strategically handled according to the literature (Ritchie, 2004; Coppola, 2015; Baldini et al., 2012. amongst others). The author has drawn on the notion of 'strategic drift' (Johnson, 1998) and 'Boiled frog syndrome' (Richardson, Nwankwo & Richardson, 1994) which have been previously applied within strategic management but to a very limited extent within tourism studies in order to explain how host attitudes to tourism may increase vulnerability. Both of these practical and managerial contributions can be used assist in the identification of destination vulnerability and to highlight limitations in disaster response and recovery.

This has enabled one to observe that the island's development followed a linear path of destination development and provides a practical illustration of how shock events, stakeholder relationships and human agency can impact upon this predicted model of destination evolution. The tsunami illustrates limitations in models of destination evolution in that it acts as an intervention in the linear path of development. Destinations following this intervention can take many paths. Phi Phi had an opportunity to reassess the development model, but sought to regain the level of development they had pre-tsunami as quickly as possible. One may note that while the infrastructure was removed, the philosophy predetermining that level of development certainly wasn't. Klein's (2008) observations on disaster capitalism, which took root in the notion of shock therapy, designed to erase and remake the human mind and likened to Friedman's search for a 'laissez-faire laboratory' under which he could employ his capitalist 'shock treatment' (Klein 2008, p. 49), can be applied differently in this case. Certainly a shock did occur on Phi Phi, which presented the opportunity for disaster capitalism, which would be enabled through neoliberal policies, but the ideology and 'memory' of the island had not been wiped clean and therefore could not be remade. The power of the landowners and their development hegemony did not permit this and was more powerful an influence than the hegemony of Western sustainability discourse.

The tsunami has exposed pre-existing problems on Phi Phi, such as the extent of encroachment onto National Park Land and the lack of adequate utilities. Without the tsunami, the challenges faced by this community would undoubtedly not have received such attention and interest. Through context bound adaptations of Ritchie's (2004) Strategic Disaster Management model and Turner et al.'s (2003) Vulnerability Framework, the sources of vulnerability on Phi Phi have been analysed and limitations in the disaster response highlighted (both of which have their roots in the political economy of the island). The author suggests that under the existing political economic climate, pursuit of an alternative development paradigm will not be possible and the island will remain highly vulnerable in line with Blaikie *et al's* (1994) observations that the factors of vulnerability are often reconstructed following a disaster and as such may create frame conditions for a repeat disaster. The research has re-presented adapted versions of both Ritchie's (2004) and Turner et al.'s (2003) work in light of Phi Phi's experiences and hence progresses the debates on post-disaster tourism redevelopment, demonstrating the conditions of vulnerability on Phi Phi which may create a repeat disaster.

SUGGESTIONS FOR FURTHER RESEARCH

The following recommendations are made to researchers considering embarking on research within this field and to practitioners or agents responsible for policy formation/implementation and the rebuilding and sustainable development of tourism destinations post-disaster.

The agents responsible for the redevelopment of tourism destinations following a disaster need to have a full comprehension of the power structures and political economy prevalent in that destination, particularly in destinations that have a strong hierarchical society, as the overt and covert values of high-status individuals will strongly influence development.

Tourism planners need to understand that, no matter how sophisticated and effective the plans produced for the destination appear to be, political economic factors will determine the shape of the future development and this may undermine sustainability, unless strong governance measures are implemented without fear of corruption.

The research recommends that barriers to sustainability be fully understood by development stakeholders. It is essential to establish if present needs are being met within a community before consideration of future generations is made. If barriers to sustainability are understood, efforts to diminish them can be made. It is essential to ascertain if present community needs are being met and make provision for these needs in terms of a robust infrastructure and adequate utilities at a fair cost prior to consideration of future needs.

There is potential to investigate whether the claims of Klein (2008) in respect of 'disaster capitalism' were evident in any of the destinations affected by the tsunami. Evidence would suggest this occurred in Sri Lanka and Khao Lak. However, longitudinal research is required to ascertain the eventual shape of the tourism development of affected coastal areas and the manner in which this has affected destination sustainability and coastal communities. There is potential for further research surrounding the political economy of post-disaster tourism redevelopment to ascertain if other affected destinations avoided 'disaster capitalism' using similar means to Phi Phi.

In respect of disaster response, it is recommended that the World Tourism Organisation develop guidelines on how to deal with disasters in densely populated tourist areas. There is a need to build capacity to deal with emotional trauma. Embassy staff, responsible for liaising with and repatriating tourists post-shock event, are rarely trained as counsellors and therefore are arguably not the best people to fulfil such a role. Rather than rushing to repatriate tourists as quickly as possible post-shock event it is better for their psychological wellbeing to remain *in situ* and work through the post-trauma stage while rehabilitation is carried out. Tourists and non-tourists should remain together following such an event, in order to share their emotional recovery and answer the many questions they have.

There is potential to apply the author's adapted Strategic Disaster Management and Vulnerability Frameworks to other post-disaster tourism contexts to comprehend the effectiveness of the disaster response and recovery, and to establish the root causes of vulnerability.

REFERENCES

Adger, W. N., Hughes, T. P., Folke, C., Carpenter, S. R., & Rockstrom, J. (2005). Social-Ecological Resilience to Coastal Disasters. *Science*, *309*(5737), 1036–1039. doi:10.1126/science.1112122 PMID:16099974

Altman, M. (2005). *Treading Water*. Thai Day.

Aoyama, Y., Olds, K., Dicken, P., Kelly, P., Kong, L., & Yeung, H. (2001). Globalisation and the Asia-Pacific: Contested Territories. *Economic Geography*, *77*(2), 201. doi:10.2307/3594066

Baldini, G., Oliveri, F., Braun, M., Seuschek, H., & Hess, E. (2012). Securing disaster supply chains with cryptography enhanced RFID. *Disaster Prevention and Management, 21*(1), 51–70. doi:10.1108/09653561211202700

Banks, M. (2001). *Visual methods in social research*. London: Sage.

Berkeley.edu. (2005). *UC Berkeley team visits Thailand to open dialogue on impacts of tourism*. Author.

Boisjoly, R., & Argenti, J. (1978). Corporate Collapse: The Causes and Symptoms. *Southern Economic Journal, 45*(2), 638. doi:10.2307/1057698

Bonn, I., & Rundle-Thiele, S. (2007). Do or die—Strategic decision-making following a shock event. *Tourism Management, 28*(2), 615–620. doi:10.1016/j.tourman.2006.04.021

Bradshaw, S. (2002). Exploring the gender dimensions of reconstruction processes post-hurricane Mitch. *Journal of International Development, 14*(6), 871–879. doi:10.1002/jid.932

Brammer, H. (1990). Floods in Bangladesh: Geographical Background to the 1987 and 1988 Floods. *The Geographical Journal, 156*(1), 12. doi:10.2307/635431

Brix, H., Koottatep, T., & Laugesen, C. (2007). Wastewater treatment in tsunami affected areas of Thailand by constructed wetlands. *Water Science and Technology, 56*(3), 69. doi:10.2166/wst.2007.528 PMID:17802840

Burnett, J. (1998). A strategic approach to managing crises. *Public Relations Review, 24*(4), 475–488. doi:10.1016/S0363-8111(99)80112-X

Calgaro, E., & Lloyd, K. (2008). Sun, sea, sand and tsunami: Examining disaster vulnerability in the tourism community of Khao Lak, Thailand. *Singapore Journal of Tropical Geography, 29*(3), 288–306. doi:10.1111/j.1467-9493.2008.00335.x

Chester, D. (1995). Blaikie, Piers, Cannon, Terry, Davis, Ian and Wisner, Ben, "At Risk: Natural Hazards, People's Vulnerability and Disasters" (Book Review). *Third World Planning Review, 17*(3), 357.

Cohen, E. (1979). Rethinking the sociology of tourism. *Annals of Tourism Research, 6*(1), 18–35. doi:10.1016/0160-7383(79)90092-6

Cohen, E. (1983). Insiders and Outsiders: The Dynamics of Development of Bungalow Tourism on the Islands of Southern Thailand. *Human Organization, 42*(2), 158–162. doi:10.17730/humo.42.2.45767335470438t0

Coppola, D. (2015). *Introduction to international disaster management* (3rd ed.). Oxford, UK: Butterworth-Heinemann.

Cummings, J. (2005). *Andaman Coast Post-Tsunami Landscape: Island Recover*. TAT Governor Corner.

Denscombe, M. (2010). *The good research guide* (4th ed.). Maidenhead, UK: Open University Press.

Dodds, R. (2011). Koh Phi Phi: Moving Towards or Away from Sustainability? *Asia Pacific Journal of Tourism Research, 15*(3), 251–265. doi:10.1080/10941665.2010.503615

Dodds, R., Graci, S., & Holmes, M. (2010). Does the tourist care? A comparison of tourists in Koh Phi Phi, Thailand and Gili Trawangan, Indonesia. *Journal of Sustainable Tourism, 18*(2), 207–222. doi:10.1080/09669580903215162

Easterby-Smith, M., Thorpe, R., & Lowe, A. (2012). *Management Research* (4th ed.). London: Sage.

Edwards, E. (1992). Anthropology and photography, 1860-1920. New Haven, CT: Yale University Press in association with the Royal Anthropological Institute, London.

Ekachai, S. (1998). What it all boils down to is greed. *The Bangkok Post.*

Faulkner, B. (2001). Towards a framework for tourism disaster management. *Tourism Management, 22*(2), 135–147. doi:10.1016/S0261-5177(00)00048-0

Fink, S. (2000). *Crisis management.* New York, NY: American Management Association.

Fuengprichavai, R. (1998). At the movies or at the beach, where were you. *Nation (New York, N.Y.).*

Garland, A. (1997). *The beach.* New York: Riverhead Books.

Ghobarah, A., Saatcioglu, M., & Nistor, I. (2006). The impact of the 26 December 2004 earthquake and tsunami on structures and infrastructure. *Engineering Structures, 28*(2), 312–326. doi:10.1016/j.engstruct.2005.09.028

Hall, C. (1999). *Sustainable tourism: a geographical perspective.* Harlow: Pearson Education.

Hardiman, N., & Burgin, S. (2010). Adventure recreation in Australia: A case study that investigated the profile of recreational canyoners, their impact attitudes, and response to potential management options. *Journal Of Ecotourism, 9*(1), 36–44. doi:10.1080/14724040902863333

Harvey, D. (2006). *Spaces of global capitalism.* London: Verso.

Harvey, D. (2007). Neoliberalism as Creative Destruction. *The Annals of the American Academy of Political and Social Science, 610*(1), 21–44. doi:10.1177/0002716206296780

Hedman, E-L. (2005). The Politics of the Tsunami Response. *Forced Migration Review.*

Henderson, J. (1999). Managing the Asian Financial Crisis: Tourist Attractions in Singapore. *Journal of Travel Research, 38*(2), 177–181. doi:10.1177/004728759903800212

Hockings, P. (2003). *Principles of visual anthropology.* Berlin: Mouton de Gruyter.

Huan, T., Beaman, J., & Shelby, L. (2004). No-escape natural disaster. *Annals of Tourism Research, 31*(2), 255–273. doi:10.1016/j.annals.2003.10.003

Hystad, P., & Keller, P. (2008). Towards a destination tourism disaster management framework: Long-term lessons from a forest fire disaster. *Tourism Management, 29*(1), 151–162. doi:10.1016/j.tourman.2007.02.017

Ingram, J., Franco, G., Rio, C., & Khazai, B. (2006). Post-disaster recovery dilemmas: Challenges in balancing short-term and long-term needs for vulnerability reduction. *Environmental Science & Policy, 9*(7-8), 607–613. doi:10.1016/j.envsci.2006.07.006

Johnson, G. (1988). Rethinking incrementalism. *Strategic Management Journal, 9*(1), 75–91. doi:10.1002/smj.4250090107

Johnson, K. (2009). Corporate sperm count and boiled frogs. *Int J Contemp Hospitality Mngt, 21*(2), 179–190. doi:10.1108/09596110910935679

Kaewkuntee, D. (2006). Land Tenure, Land Conflicts and Post-Tsunami Relocation in Thailand. *Mekong Update and Dialogue, 9*(2).

Klein, N. (2007). *The shock doctrine*. New York: Metropolitan Books/Henry Holt.

Knowles, C., & Sweetman, P. (2004). *Picturing the social landscape*. New York, NY: Routledge.

Ko, T. (2005). Development of a tourism sustainability assessment procedure: A conceptual approach. *Tourism Management, 26*(3), 431–445. doi:10.1016/j.tourman.2003.12.003

Konisranukul, W., & Tuaycharoen, N. (2010). *Public Participation In Sustainable Island And Tourism Planning*. Faculty Of Science And Technology.

Krauss, E. (2005). *Wave of destruction*. London: Vision.

Krongkaew, M. (2004). The development of the Greater Mekong Subregion (GMS): Real promise or false hope? *Journal of Asian Economics, 15*(5), 977–998. doi:10.1016/j.asieco.2004.09.006

Krutwaysho, O., & Bramwell, B. (2010). Tourism policy implementation and society. *Annals of Tourism Research, 37*(3), 670–691. doi:10.1016/j.annals.2009.12.004

Lee, K. (2006). Fahn, James David. 2003. A Land on Fire. The Environmental Consequences of the Southeast Asian Boom. Boulder, CO: Westview Press. *Global Environmental Politics, 6*(4), 135–136. doi:10.1162/glep.2006.6.4.135

Lee, Y., & Harrald, J. (1999). Critical issue for business area impact analysis in business crisis management: Analytical capability. *Disaster Prevention and Management, 8*(3), 184–189. doi:10.1108/09653569910275382

Miller, H., Engemann, K., & Yager, R. (2006). Disaster planning and management. *Communications Of The International Information Management Association, 6*(2), 25–36.

Morgan, O., Sribanditmongkol, P., Perera, C., Sulasmi, Y., Van Alphen, D., & Sondorp, E. (2006). Mass Fatality Management following the South Asian Tsunami Disaster: Case Studies in Thailand, Indonesia, and Sri Lanka. *PLoS Medicine, 3*(6), e195. doi:10.1371/journal.pmed.0030195 PMID:16737348

Mulder, N. (2000). *Inside Thai society*. Chiang Mai, Thailand: Silkworm Books.

CNN News. (2005). Land Wars in Post-Tsunami World. *CNN News*.

Noikorn, U. (1998). Green protest at film slammed. *The Bangkok Post*.

Olsen, R. (2000). Toward a politics of disaster: Losses, Values, Agenda and Blame. *International Journal of Mass Emergencies and Disasters, 18*(2), 265–287.

Parsons, W. (1996). Crisis management. *Career Development International, 1*(5), 26–28. doi:10.1108/13620439610130614

Pleumarom, A. (2004). *Tourism and the Tsunami disaster with a focus upon Thailand.* Third World Network.

Plog, S. (2001). Why Destination Areas Rise and Fall in Popularity. *The Cornell Hotel and Restaurant Administration Quarterly, 32,* 14–24.

Poon, A. (1993). *Tourism, technology, and competitive strategies.* Wallingford: CAB International.

Rice, A., & Haynes, K. (2005). *Post-tsunami reconstruction and tourism: a second disaster?* London: Tourism Concern.

Richardson, B. (1994). Crisis Management and Management Strategy-Time to "Loop the Loop"? *Disaster Prevention and Management, 3*(3), 59–80. doi:10.1108/09653569410795632

Richardson, B., Nwankwo, S., & Richardson, S. (1994). Understanding the Causes of Business Failure Crises. *Management Decision, 32*(4), 9–22. doi:10.1108/00251749410058635

Rigg, J., Law, L., Tan-Mullins, M., & Grundy-Warr, C. (2005). The Indian Ocean tsunami: Socio-economic impacts in Thailand. *The Geographical Journal, 171*(4), 374–379. doi:10.1111/j.1475-4959.2005.00175_3.x

Ritchie, B. (2004). Chaos, crises and disasters: A strategic approach to crisis management in the tourism industry. *Tourism Management, 25*(6), 669–683. doi:10.1016/j.tourman.2003.09.004

Rittichainuwat, B. (2006). Tsunami recovery: A case study of Thailand's Tourism. *The Cornell Hotel and Restaurant Administration Quarterly, 47*(4), 390–404. doi:10.1177/0010880406289994

Rittichainuwat, B. (2011). Ghosts: A Travel Barrier to Tourism Recovery. *Annals of Tourism Research, 38*(2), 437–459. doi:10.1016/j.annals.2010.10.001

Saltman, K. (2007). *Schooling in Disaster Capitalism: How the Political Right is using Disaster to Privatise Public Schooling.* Teacher Education Quarterly Spring.

Saunders, M., Lewis, P., & Thornhill, A. (2003). *Research methods for business students.* Harlow, UK: Prentice Hall.

Scheyvens, R. (2002). *Tourism for Development: Empowering Communities.* Harlow: Pearson Education.

Shelby-Biggs, B. (2000). *The Two faces of Leo.* The Envirolink Network.

Sonmez, S., Apostolopoulos, Y., & Tarlow, P. (1999). Tourism in Crisis: Managing the Effects of Terrorism. *Journal of Travel Research, 38*(1), 13–18. doi:10.1177/004728759903800104

Svetasreni, S. (2009). *Tourism Management in a Critical Period.* JATA World Tourism Congress.

Swarbrooke, J. (1999). *Sustainable tourism management.* Wallingford, UK: CABI Pub.

Tangwisutijit, N., & Warunpitikul, Y. (2005). *Post-Tsunami Development – The lessons not learned.* Third World Network.

The Nation. (2004). Tsunami Warning rejected to protect Tourism. *The Nation.*

The Phuket Gazette. (2006). Big Phi Phi Meeting makes small progress. *The Phuket Gazette.*

Tsai, C., & Chen, C. (2010). An earthquake disaster management mechanism based on risk assessment information for the tourism industry-a case study from the island of Taiwan. *Tourism Management,* *31*(4), 470–481. doi:10.1016/j.tourman.2009.05.008

Turner, B. L., Kasperson, R. E., Matson, P. A., Mccarthy, J. J., Corell, R. W., Christensen, L., & Schiller, A. et al. (2003). A framework for vulnerability analysis in sustainability science. *Proceedings of the National Academy of Sciences of the United States of America,* *100*(14), 8074–8079. doi:10.1073/pnas.1231335100 PMID:12792023

UNDP, World Bank, & FAO. (2005). *Joint Tsunami Disaster Assessment Mission.* Ft. Belvoir: Livelihood Recovery and Environmental Rehabilitation.

Van Esterik, P. (2000). *Materialising. Thailand.* Oxford, UK: Berg.

Villarreal, E. (2009). Capitalizing on Disaster: Taking and Breaking Public Schools - By Kenneth J. Saltman. *Anthropology & Education Quarterly,* *40*(4), 438–439. doi:10.1111/j.1548-1492.2009.01059.x

Villiers, C. (1989). Boiled Frog Syndrome. *Management Today,* 121-124.

Weaver, D., & Lawton, L. (2014). *Tourism Management* (5th ed.). Queensland: Wiley.

Wickens, E. (2002). The sacred and the profane: A Tourist Typology. *Annals of Tourism Research,* *29*(3), 834–851. doi:10.1016/S0160-7383(01)00088-3

Willis, K., & Dawson, B. (2011). *Theories and practices of development.* London: Routledge.

KEY TERMS AND DEFINITIONS

Boiled Frog Syndrome: A phenomenon associated with inaction and business failure. The premise is that if one remains complacent in the face of changing circumstances, a strategic gap emerges, which increases the likelihood of a crisis.

Capitalism: A political-economic system in which a nation's trade and industry is privately, rather than state controlled.

Disaster: Is a serious and significant disruption to the functioning of a community or society which brings about damages, loss and/ or destruction of livelihoods and infrastructure.

Disaster Vulnerability: The characteristics and circumstances of a destination that make it susceptible to the damaging effects of a hazard.

Discourse: Verbal or written discussion and/or debate.

Hegemony: Leadership or dominance of one group or viewpoint over another.

Ideology: An accepted normative belief that guides and influences behaviour.

Strategic Gap: Associated with the boiled frog concept. A strategic gap can emerge when the behavior and actions of stakeholders is not in line with changes in the business environment.

Chapter 11
Financial Crisis and Tourism Activity:
Evidence from the UK

Nikolaos Pappas
University of West London, UK

Alexandros Apostolakis
Technological Educational Institute (TEI) of Crete & Greek Open University, Greece

ABSTRACT

The current recession has hit hard the European countries, and also affected tourism activity throughout the continent. Considering that several European countries (especially the Mediterranean ones) are heavily dependent upon tourism activity, the recent financial crisis has considerably affected their economy. This effect is strengthened with the parallel adoption of austerity measures aiming at economic recovery and exit from the recession. Despite the substantial magnitude and severity of this crisis, little is known about tourists' reactions in coping in with the recessionary effects. Contrary to the established practice of adopting a macroeconomic perspective in the examination of the impact of financial crises on tourism activity, this book chapter follows recent recommendations in the literature such as Brooner and de Hoog (2012) Kaytaz and Gul (2014) to examine the particular adverse effects of the current financial/economic crisis on individual behaviour and demand patterns. Thus, the research utilises a survey questionnaire to British tourists examining the effect of the current recession on travel and consumption patterns. Socio-demographically, the results reveal that the current recession appears to have a significant effect on gender, since male tourism expenditure is affected more than female one. Moreover, the uncertainty associated with income and employment levels during recession has a particularly strong effect on tourism expenditure. More specifically, uncertainty associated with both income and employment levels during the financial crisis has a negative and statistically significant effect on tourism expenditure. On the other hand, younger and middle aged tourists seem to be fairly unaffected by the financial crisis, as compared to more mature and senior tourists. In addition, the findings indicate that future expectations regarding income levels have no influence on current tourism expenditure patterns. Overall, those respondents that were unsure about the effect of the financial crisis on their current tourism expenditure patterns were also more likely to exhibit ambivalence about the future. The findings provide an interesting insight to tourism decision makers since they illustrate evidence regarding the turning points of demand, especially during periods of economic downturn.

DOI: 10.4018/978-1-5225-0201-2.ch011

INTRODUCTION

The recent financial crisis that plagued the majority of European countries recently has had a particularly negative effect on tourism activity across national economies. The direct effects of the recent financial crisis on tourism activity are evident in terms of tourism consumption (tourism demand) and expenditure patterns (Smeral, 2009). According to Sheldon and Dwyer (2010), tourism expenditure has experienced greater falls than any other form of discretionary consumer expenditure during the peak of the financial crisis. Indicative of the extent of the problem is the fact that in 2009 the international credit crunch and the financial crisis resulted into a slow down of international demand for foreign travel in the EU by 5% in real terms, whilst more that 10 million jobs are accounted to accommodation and food services sector, which is 4% of total EU employment (European Parliament, 2014).

It is common ground that tourism is not immune from crises (Bramwell & Lane, 2003; Wang & Ritchie, 2012). As IMF (2009) indicated international tourism has been considerably declined since 2008, whilst the tourist consumer patterns have been deeply affected with negative psychology in terms of the duration, depth and implications of the recession. As a consequence, the current recession has severely affected tourism and hospitality industry, producing sharp consumption declines throughout the economic sector (Novelli et al., 2012) that have substantially reduced tourism revenues (Sariisik et al., 2011). At this stage, several tourism and hospitality companies fear that that during this recession they may solely focus on the reduction of prices no matter the costs, a route which is likely to prove very dangerous to follow (Papatheodorou et al., 2010).

Despite the magnitude and severity of the financial crises on tourism activity, very little is being done in terms of understanding how the tourism sector is coping during times of economic recession (Henderson, 1999; Okumus and Karamustafa, 2005). Following the recommendations by Song et al. (2010), this investigation could provide interesting insights to public sector managers and policy makers since it provides evidence regarding the turning points of demand, especially during periods of economic downturn.

The particular aim of this book chapter is to provide empirical evidence on the impact of the recent financial crisis on the British travellers. Our research objectives are set twofold.

- First, to provide a better understanding of tourist behaviour and demand patterns during periods of economic recession.
- Second, to offer evidence based insight to public policy makers and managers regarding the particular actions and initiatives they could initiate to fend off the negative effects of the crisis.

Contrary to the established practice of adopting a macroeconomic perspective in the examination of the impact of financial crisis on tourism activity, this book chapter follows recent recommendations in the literature (Song *et al.,* 2010, Sheldon and Dwyer, 2010) to examine the particular adverse effects of the current financial/economic crisis on individual behaviour and demand patterns. For that purpose, we utilise evidence from a unique dataset put together through the distribution of a survey questionnaire on British tourists.

RESEARCH METHODOLOGY

Research Characteristics

The study was conducted from October till end of November 2010 at the International Airport of Manchester in United Kingdom. The most appropriate method considered in order to obtain the primary data, was through structured personal interviews. According to Sekaran (2000), this is the most versatile and productive communication method, enabling spontaneity, and also providing the skill of guiding the discussion back to the topic outlined when discussions are unfruitful.

In order to select a sample frame, the process adopted was the following: A random starting method was selected in order to reach the respondents. Every fifth passenger passing from flight's check in desk was selected to participate in the sampling frame. The selected passengers had to be permanent residents of the U.K. All the respondents had to be adults, travelling for leisure purposes. As previous researches such as Pappas (2010) reveal, in crisis aspects there is a high proportion of perspectives differentiation towards gender. Thus, the research sample is based on gender stratification in order to collect equal responses on this socio-demographic characteristic.

Sample Size Determination

The representativeness of the sampling size was a fundamental criterion in order to determinate the amount of the sample. Since the proportions of population were unknown, it has taken a conservative response format 50 / 50, meaning the assumption that 50% of the respondents have negative perceptions of tourism impacts, and 50% have not. At least 95% confidence and 5% sampling error was selected. The sample size is:

$$N = \frac{(t - table)^2 (hypothesis)}{S^2} \Rightarrow N = \frac{(1.96)^2 (0.5)(0.5)}{(0.5)^2} \Rightarrow N = 384.16$$

Rounded to
400

The calculation of the sampling size is independent of the total population size hence the sampling size determines the error (Aaker and Day, 1990). Based on the estimation above, the selected population sample was 400 individuals. Due to gender stratification, 200 men and 200 women were examined. The statistical error for the total sample and per gender is 4.9% and 6.9% respectively.

Data Collection and Analysis

The questionnaire consists of 26 questions. These questions were:

- 23 Likert Scale (1 – 5) questions assessing passengers' perspectives toward:
  ○ Influence of global economic recession (five questions).
  ○ Influence of economic recession in travel and tourism over the last year (13 questions).
  ○ Perspectives for future impacts of the economic recession (five questions).
- Four socio–demographic questions (age, gender, frequency of travel, and educational attainment).

For the analysis of the collected data, the Statistical Program for Social Sciences (SPSS, 16.0) was used. To identify the existence of statistical significances between the variables, the analysis used t-Test and ANOVA. In addition, logistic regression has been implemented in order to explore the importance of variables. The indication of statistical significance is at the 0.05 level of confidence. For the contradiction and presentation of the research findings, cross tabulations were also used.

Selection of Variables

The variance of the expressed opinions and the statistical significances that are formulated toward the expressed perceptions are directly connected with the individual characteristics of the sample population. A series of studies reveal that gender is the main factor affecting individual perceptions (Fairburn-Dunlop, 1994; Kinnaird and Hall, 1996; Mason and Cheyne, 2000). Others such as Trakolis (2001), Collins and Tisdell (2002), and Tretheway and Mak (2006) reveal that age considerably influences the formulation on expressed perspectives. Moreover, the frequency of travel is also considered as an important factor for perceptions' variances (Berendien and Liebe, 2010; Berendien et al., 2011). Finally, the sample's level of education is considered as a crucial factor for the creation of significant differences in the expressed perspectives (Baloglu and McCleary, 1999; Teye et al., 2002). This study takes under consideration all the above studies and researches, and examines the variation of perceptions toward gender, travel frequency, and level of education.

RESEARCH FINDINGS

The Profile of Respondents

The sample profile (Table 1) is – as mentioned – stratified toward gender. There are five age groups, structured by decade, with the largest one relating to respondents from 25 till 34 years old. Almost 2/3 of respondents travel up to six times for leisure purposes annually both domestically and overseas. The sample also seems to be somehow equally spread as far as the level of respondents' educational attainment, with somewhat more respondents to report compulsory level education qualifications.

Financial Crisis

Dealing with the influence of the financial crisis on respondents' behavioural patterns (Table 2), the higher agreeable trend seems to appear in employability, followed by the after tax income. Furthermore, these are also the actual statements that produce statistical significance.

Toward age, there is statistical significance in both statements. Concerning after tax income it seems that the older the respondents were, the more they perceived that recession influences them. In younger age groups (18 – 34) the overall agreements reached 70.7 per cent (123 respondents) while in people between 35 till 54 years old the proportion was 82 per cent (141 respondents). On the other hand the elder most age group had an agreeable rate in 55.6 per cent (30 respondents). A rational explanation is that the older people are, the higher the salaries are since they can gain senior occupational posts and their after tax income is more influenced by financial variances because of the economic recession. On the contrary retired people (elder most age group) have a stable pension, which is not really affected by the

Table 1. Profile of the sample

	N	%
GENDER		
Male	200 (Stratified)	50 (Stratified)
Female	200 (Stratified)	50 (Stratified)
AGE		
18 – 24	69	17.25
25 – 34	105	26.25
35 – 44	94	23.5
45 – 54	78	19.5
Over 54	54	13.5
TRAVEL FREQUENCY		
0 – 3	128	32
4 – 6	135	33.75
7 – 9	95	23.75
Over 9	42	10.5
EDUCATION		
Compulsory	214	53.5
Higher	186	46.5

overall economic environment. Focusing on employability, many previous researches such as Sakata & MacKenzie (2004) reveal that the younger a person is the more possible is to face unemployment issues at least in short-term periods, while there is an increase of these effects in times of recession.

In terms of travel frequency the employability factor plays an important role. People travelling annually up till six times for leisure purposes seem to be more affected by employability issues than those who travel more than six times. In the first two groups (up till six leisure trips) the overall agreements reached 77.2 per cent (203 respondents), while for respondents travelling more than six times the percentage was 77 (96 respondents). The high amount of annual leisure travels indicates a sufficient expenditure for this purpose, directly connected with high income and, in parallel, employment stability. Profoundly, leisure expenditure is one of the first victims where generated income is at stake (Fleischer et. al., 2011; Jang et. al., 2004). As a result, occupational uncertainties – and hence low employability – minimize leisure travel patterns.

Travel and Tourism

As the results indicate (Table 3), dealing with travel and tourism several statistical significances appear in most statements, in all socio-demographic characteristics. Towards gender, women seem to be more affected by the economic crisis under the perspective on selecting a tourist destination in both abroad and home. On the other hand, men are more influenced from recession in terms of expenditure patterns in both, abroad and home, something which is directly connected with the accommodation selection

Table 2. Influence of global economic recession

	After Tax Income	Employability	Consumption Patterns	Consumption (Tangibles)	Consumption (Services)
MEANS	2.23	2.19	2.63	2.63	2.73
Std. Deviation	.946	1.014	.905	.928	.972
GENDER					
Male	2.28	2.25	2.71	2.74	2.81
Female	2.18	2.14	2.56	2.51	2.65
T Ratio	1.004	1.135	1.716	2.384	1.650
Significance	.540	.675	.735	.629	.612
AGE					
18 – 24	2.55	1.80	2.74	2.81	2.84
25 – 34	2.10	1.82	2.74	2.72	2.82
35 – 44	2.03	2.12	2.49	2.43	2.63
45 – 54	2.04	2.40	2.67	2.64	2.74
Over 54	2.70	3.26	2.48	2.52	2.57
F Ratio	8.203	28.033	1.631	2.293	1.056
Significance	.000	.000	.166	.059	.378
TRAVEL FREQ.					
0 – 3	2.09	2.10	2.51	2.53	2.63
4 – 6	2.29	2.07	2.76	2.75	2.86
7 – 9	2.35	2.39	2.62	2.58	2.66
Over 9	2.21	2.40	2.64	2.62	2.76
F Ratio	1.555	2.803	1.656	1.309	1.392
Significance	.200	.040	.176	.271	.245
EDUCATION					
Compulsory	2.22	2.27	2.65	2.67	2.76
Higher	2.25	2.11	2.61	2.57	2.69
T Ratio	-.291	1.565	.514	1.107	.699
Significance	.217	.649	.565	.477	.983

* Statistical significance is at .05 level of confidence

(abroad) where the overall agreements from men reached 22 per cent (44 respondents) while the same proportion for women was 6 per cent (12 respondents).

Toward age, the statistical significances produced by travel mean reveal that the younger the population is the more influenced is from the economic recession. As Aksoy et al., (2003) state differences in consumer profiles as age, are important factors for transportation selection. In general terms, the age of population is also connected with income, since younger people usually have lower salaries due to limited experience, occupational background, time lack of opportunities to achieve senior posts etc.

The younger groups' income efficiency and higher unemployment rates also have a considerable influence to travel frequency in both home and abroad. In addition this influence is also revealed through

Table 3. Influence of the economic recession in travel and tourism over the last year

	Travel Means		Travel Frequency		Tourist Destinations	Length of Stay		Expenditure Patterns		Tourist Destinations		Tourist Accommodation	
	Abroad	Home	Abroad	Home		Abroad	Home	Abroad	Home	Abroad	Home	Abroad	Home
MEANS	2.50	2.46	2.38	2.47	2.15	2.47	2.64	2.02	2.14	2.06	2.27	3.20	3.33
Std. Deviation	.968	.975	.1.029	.996	.770	.855	.931	.518	.574	.815	.795	.750	.795
GENDER													
Male	2.50	2.46	2.37	2.46	2.25	2.35	2.57	1.97	2.09	2.14	2.40	2.98	3.11
Female	2.50	2.46	2.39	2.48	2.04	2.59	2.71	2.06	2.19	1.97	2.14	3.42	3.55
T Ratio	.000	.000	-.194	-.201	2.684	-2.892	-1.452	-1.841	-1.835	2.220	3.244	-6.051	-5.683
Significance	.634	.458	.736	.749	**.000**	.204	.154	**.043**	**.036**	**.001**	**.001**	**.012**	.185
AGE													
18 – 24	2.17	2.16	2.04	2.16	2.28	1.87	2.10	2.03	2.17	2.13	2.28	3.09	3.28
25 – 34	2.17	2.14	2.11	2.22	2.29	2.17	2.37	2.00	2.12	2.20	2.45	3.24	3.33
35 – 44	2.47	2.40	2.39	2.47	2.11	2.51	2.67	2.11	2.23	2.03	2.27	3.16	3.27
45 – 54	2.94	2.91	2.81	2.92	2.00	2.65	2.76	2.04	2.10	1.92	2.15	3.18	3.31
Over 54	2.98	2.91	2.69	2.70	2.00	3.50	3.65	1.85	2.00	1.91	2.07	3.39	3.52
F Ratio	13.886	12.859	8.798	8.758	2.645	47.185	31.481	2.172	1.606	1.972	2.585	1.402	1.008
Significance	**.000**	**.000**	**.000**	**.000**	**.033**	**.000**	**.000**	.071	.172	.098	**.037**	.232	.403
TRAVEL FREQ.													
0 – 3	2.41	2.36	2.27	2.34	2.14	2.38	2.55	2.03	2.13	2.04	2.22	3.24	3.38
4 – 6	2.50	2.46	2.37	2.49	2.16	2.25	2.41	2.5	2.17	2.06	2.28	3.23	3.37
7 – 9	2.56	2.53	2.47	2.52	2.21	2.79	2.94	1.95	2.06	2.15	2.18	3.14	3.24
Over 9	2.67	2.62	2.55	2.69	2.00	2.76	3.00	2.02	2.24	1.88	2.57	3.14	3.24
F Ratio	.928	.973	.1.167	1.460	.734	10.162	8.865	.811	1.130	1.064	2.644	.507	.825
Significance	.427	.405	.322	.225	.532	**.000**	**.000**	.488	.337	.364	**.049**	.677	.481
EDUCATION													
Compulsory	2.52	2.44	2.40	2.51	2.07	2.50	2.67	2.01	2.15	1.99	2.25	3.20	3.35
Higher	2.47	2.48	2.35	2.42	2.23	2.44	2.61	2.03	2.12	2.13	2.29	3.20	3.30
T Ratio	.517	-.353	.456	.948	-2.018	.807	.700	-.338	.449	-1.683	-.535	-.045	.619
Significance	.834	.651	.849	.502	**.008**	.139	.230	.483	.277	**.020**	.093	.606	.608

* Statistical significance is at .05 level of confidence

the production of statistical significances to the statements focusing on the length of stay. More specifically, the percentages on overall agreements of the age group of 18 till 24 were 92.7 (abroad) and 75.4 (home), from 25 till 34 were 78.1 (abroad) and 63.8 (home), from 35 till 44 were 57.4 (abroad) and 46.8 (home), from 45 till 54 were 43.6 (abroad) and 38.5 (home), and for people over 54 years old were 11.1 per cent in both, home and abroad. The profound decrease of income efficiency the younger people are has direct impact on the length of stay for leisure purposes. Moreover, the ability on having higher rate of leisure travels indicates a lower impact to the actual length of stay. Thus the respondents travelling up till six times seem to be more influenced concerning their leisure length of stay.

Dealing with the independent variable of education, statistical significances appear on the statement focusing on the selection of tourist destinations, especially those abroad. The strong agreements in destination selection on the compulsory and higher education graduates were 16.8 (36 respondents) and 13.4 per cent (25 respondents) respectively, while the agreements were 64 (137 respondents) and 59.1 per cent (110 respondents) respectively. On the statement examining the selection of tourist destinations abroad for the same groups, the overall agreements were 82.2 (176 respondents) and 75.3 (140 respondents) per cent respectively. The higher the education is the more possible the respondents to have a higher familiarity with internet (meaning more opportunities to seek out for destinations and select the most suited one), to succeed higher stability on their employability, and to occupy senior occupational posts (meaning higher salary). These three reasons, either separately or combined, can give the justification on why higher education graduates have a relatively lower impact on destination selection because of the economic crisis, in comparison with the compulsory education graduates.

Forthcoming Influence of Economic Recession

The influence of the nowadays economic crisis in future leisure and tourism was one more parameter that had to be examined. As the results indicate (Table 4), the most important influence is expected on the forthcoming holiday spending patters. Not only the general trends of the examined population appear to be more agreeable, but it is also the statement that produces most of the revealed statistical significances.

Toward age, the first statistical significance appears on the tax income the forthcoming year. The younger the respondents were the less they perceived that the economic recession will influence their income. More specifically, the overall agreements for people from 18 till 24 years old were 1.4 percent (only one respondent), from 25 till 34 were 8.6 per cent (9 respondents), from 35 till 44 were 24.5 percent (23 respondents) from 45 till 54 were 33.3 per cent (26 respondents), and for those over 54 years old were 64.8 per cent (35 respondents). The younger age groups were actually the first victims from the economic crisis. These people were the first who felt the consequences on their income, their employability opportunities, and the occupational liquidity. It seems that trough their responses they actually arise the question on how worse can it become. On the other hand, the older people are the more they are afraid for the forthcoming income impacts of the crisis. More and more companies and firms start to face financial liquidity problems, and start firing personnel even from senior posts, while the retired ones start to experience the economic crisis's impacts on their pensions through generated inflation and severe state budget cuts in health and insurance policies.

The produced statistical significances on holiday spending patterns seem to have a higher impact to younger people and to respondents that don't travel many times for leisure purposes. Between ages the overall agreements for people from 18 till 24 years old were 69.6 (abroad) and 59.4 per cent (home), from 25 till 34 were 66.7 (abroad) and 59 per cent (home), from 35 till 44 were 56.4 (abroad) and 52.1 per cent (home), from 45 till 54 were 64.1 (abroad) and 57.7 per cent (home), and for respondents over 54 years old were 20.4 (abroad) and 22.2 per cent (home). This can be explained that the income of younger age groups was already affected more the older ones, hence they already need to drastically minimize their expenses in microeconomic level. As a result they gained higher familiarity with the perspective that the forthcoming year their leisure expenses will be minimal, if not existed at all. Focusing on travel frequency and holiday expenditure patterns, in general terms, the higher the rate of leisure trips was the less the respondents were influenced. The exception for this trend comes from the group that has the highest frequency (over nine leisure trips annually). These respondents appear to understand the need

Table 4. Perspectives for future impacts of the economic recession

	After Tax Income	Travel Ability		Holiday Spending Patterns	
		Abroad	Home	Abroad	Home
MEANS	3.09	2.96	3.09	2.45	2.53
Std. Deviation	.835	.872	.881	.845	.858
GENDER					
Male	3.32	2.91	3.07	2.42	2.50
Female	2.86	3.02	3.12	2.48	2.56
T Ratio	5.794	-1.262	-.624	-.650	-.757
Significance	.258	.277	.752	.426	.644
AGE					
18 – 24	3.87	2.91	3.01	2.19	2.32
25 – 34	3.31	2.86	2.97	2.20	2.30
35 – 44	2.96	2.98	3.04	2.50	2.59
45 – 54	2.83	3.10	3.19	2.42	2.51
Over 54	2.24	3.02	3.37	3.20	3.17
F Ratio	49.618	1.004	2.331	17.194	11.678
Significance	**.000**	.405	.055	**.000**	**.000**
TRAVEL FREQUENCY					
0 – 3	3.20	2.93	3.08	2.27	2.38
4 – 6	3.11	3.03	3.13	2.44	2.47
7 – 9	3.01	2.96	3.5	2.69	2.77
Over 9	2.86	2.88	3.10	2.45	2.60
F Ratio	2.101	.447	.172	4.653	4.064
Significance	.100	.719	.915	**.003**	**.007**
EDUCATION					
Compulsory	3.01	2.96	3.08	2.50	2.52
Higher	3.17	2.97	3.11	2.39	2.53
T Ratio	-1.895	-.059	-.318	1.215	-.103
Significance	.810	.373	.297	.223	.401

* Statistical significance is at .05 level of confidence

to reduce their expenditure patterns if they still want to have the ability to frequently continue travelling for leisure purposes. Still, the greatest impact remains of the group that has the lowest frequency of leisure trips (up till tree times annually) having a proportion in overall agreements of 68.75 (abroad) and 62.5 per cent (home). It has to be noted that almost half (49.2 per cent) of this group consists from respondents coming from the two youngest age groups (18 till 24 and 25 till 34 years old). This can explain the high rate of overall agreements on holiday spending patterns in both, younger people and less frequent travelers.

Econometric Results

The direct effects of the recent financial crisis on tourism activity are evident in terms of tourism consumption (tourism demand) and expenditure patterns (Smeral, 2009). According to Sheldon and Dwyer (2010), tourism expenditure has experienced greater falls than any other form of discretionary consumer expenditure. The current recession is extensively discussed in the media but the evaluation of tourism attributes and behaviour is still limited (Smeral, 2009) due to the unavoidable delay caused by the crisis itself and the resulting research opportunities, and also considering the time needed for publication (Brooner & de Hoog, 2014). For the moment it is clear that recession leads to a fall in disposable income resulting in a decrease in consumption, and that luxury goods and services such as tourism are likely to be more sensitive during periods of economic turmoil (Eugenio-Martin & Campos-Soria, 2014). In order to evaluate the effect of the recent financial crisis on tourism activity in general and tourism expenditure more specifically, we distinguish between tourism expenditure patterns at home and away (travel abroad). Contrary to the established practice of adopting a macroeconomic perspective in the examination of the impact of financial crises on tourism activity, this study follows recent recommendations in the literature (Song *et al.,* 2010; Sheldon and Dwyer 2010) to examine the particular adverse effects of the current financial/economic crisis on individual behavior and demand patterns.

In terms of the analysis of the results, the study first deals with the evidence pertaining to tourism expenditure patterns taking place both abroad and at home (evidence summarized on Table 5 below), and then move on to examine log – odds ratios derived from the empirical analysis. According to Westergren *et al.* (2001: 268), "The odds ratio is one of a range of statistics used to assess the risk of a particular outcome (or disease) if a certain factor (or exposure) is present. In the current case study, odd ratios can be explained as the ratio of the odds of a subgroup with a given characteristic (i.e., males) being exposed to an event (i.e., economic recession) divided by the odds of the same subgroup of demand with the same characteristics not being affected or exposed to the said event (economic recession). Thus, the odds ratios is a relative measure of risk, that tells us how much more likely is for someone with a particular characteristic to behave or react to an event (in this case the event is tourism expenditure), as compared to someone who does not share the same characteristic with that individual.

The empirical evidence from Table 5 illustrates that the overwhelming majority of factors considered in the model would have a negative effect on tourism expenditure abroad. Thus, young (18 – 24 years of age) and middle aged (35 – 44 and 45 – 54 years of age categories) respondents' expenditure patterns abroad were more likely to be negatively affected by the financial crisis, when compared to mature/ senior tourists. On the other hand, tourism expenditure at home, during the period of the financial crisis does not seem to exert a statistically significant effect on consumption levels (measured in financial terms). Thus, it seems that out of the two events, tourism expenditure abroad seems to be more seriously affected by the financial crisis in the UK.

More particularly, the examination of the log odds for holidays abroad indicate that tourism expenditure abroad among young tourists (18 to 24 years of age) is 56% more likely to be adversely affected as compared to their senior counterparts. Rather unexpectedly, the older the tourist, the more severe the effect of the financial crisis on tourism expenditure abroad is. This is to be expected given the fact that the more senior segment of the population is always to suffer first the adverse effects of the economic downturn. Hence, tourists between 35 to 44 age group, are almost 60% (59%) more likely to be affected by the financial crisis as compared to senior tourists. Similarly for tourists 45 to 54 years of age, their

Table 5. Logistic regression coefficients

	Expenditure Abroad	Expenditure at Home
Socio-Demographic		
Gender (Male)...............................	.037 [1.037]	.308**[1.35]
Age 1 (18 – 24)...............................	-.575* [.562]	-.094 [.910]
Age 2 (25 – 34)...............................	.111 [1.121]	.071 [1.073]
Age 3 (35 – 44)...............................	-.526* [.590]	-.153 [.857]
Age 4 (45 – 54)...............................	-.461* [.630]	.150 [1.163]
Frequency 1 (Up to 3 times)................	-.604** [.546]	.763*** [2.144]
Frequency 2 (Up to 6 times)................	-.508** [.601]	.599** [1.820]
Frequency 3 (Up to 8 times)................	-.411* [.662]	.776*** [2.172]
Compulsory Education.....................	-.118 [.888]	-.015 [.098]
Economic Influences		
Effect on Income............................	-.022 [.978]	.087 [1.091]
Effect on Employment......................	-.558** [.572]	-.078 [.924]
Consumption Patterns		
Daily Consumption Patterns................	.218 [1.243]	-.278 [.758]
Consumption in Goods......................	-.265 [.762]	-.508** [1.661]
Consumption in Services...................	-.210 [.810]	-.033 [.967]
Obs.	400	400
LL	-133.655	-205.977
McFadden R	.499	.507

Odd Ratios in squared brackets, * significant in 10% level of confidence, ** significant in 5% level of confidence, *** significant in 1% level of confidence

tourism expenditure abroad is 63% more likely to be negatively affected during periods of economic uncertainty.

Overall, this piece of evidence is rather anticipated with younger and middle aged tourists to be more affected by the financial crisis as compared to overseas tourism expenditure, as compared to mature travelers. From a policy perspective this empirical finding seems to accord with the current theorising over the significance of 'generation Y' onto tourism consumption. The current literature in the field (Glover and Prideaux 2009, Grougiou and Pettigrew 2011)) argues that the mature segment of the population represents the most dynamic part of the tourism industry and the one that marketing managers and advertisers are desperately trying to relate to. During periods of financial uncertainty it seems that certain age groups (namely the young and those still on the labour force) tend to behave more constrained during their overseas holidays.

The above point seems to be replicated when the empirical analysis considers the effect of frequency of travel on tourism expenditure (both abroad and at home). Thus, individuals that travel up to eight times per year are more likely to report a negative effect on their tourism expenditure patterns abroad as compared to first time tourists. In other words, individuals who indicated that they were travelling for up to eight times per year, were also the ones more likely to suffer (in terms of their expenditure patterns) as compared to first time travellers. Actually, it appears that all other categories but first time visitors seems to be negatively affected by the financial crisis as far as their expenditure patterns are concerned.

In actual terms, and looking at the information provided by the odds ratios, the negative effect on expenditure patterns seems to follows in proportion to the frequency of travel. Thus, those travelling for up to 3 times are 54.6% more likely to be negatively affected by the financial crisis as compared to fist time tourists. The same applies with those travelling for up to 6 times (almost 60% more likely to be negatively affected) and those travelling for up to 8 times (66.2% more likely to be negatively affected, as compared to those travelling for first time travelers. Hence, the more frequently one travels abroad, the more likely is that his/her tourism expenditure will be negatively affected. This could be one argument against the current policy and managerial norm regarding the added emphasis put on the building a life-long relationship with a tourist/visitor.

In contrast to what is the case for tourism expenditure abroad, tourism expenditure at home is positively affected by occasional (up to 3 times), frequent (up to 6 times) and very frequent travelers (up to 8 times). Thus, during recessionary periods, and periods of financial uncertainty, home destinations (and to that extent tourism expenditure at home) tend to be preferred from occasional and frequent travelers as compared to first time travellers. In particular, occasional travelers (travelled for up to 3 times) are 2.14 times more likely to spend more as compared to first time visitors at home. The same applies for those travelling for up to 6 times (1.82 times more likely to spend more as compared to first time tourists) and those travelling for up to 8 times (2.17 times more likely to spend more as compared to first time tourists). The effect of frequency to travel on tourism expenditure at home is not as linear as in the case of overseas tourists, although it is of a much stronger/positive effect. From a policy and managerial perspective the abovementioned information provides a strong indication towards greater emphasis on the development of new tourism products and services, especially during periods of financial crisis. From this perspective, the concept of "staycation" becomes even more relevant and appealing. What is more, the empirical findings indicate that life-long tourist relations tend to be more rewarding and effective when initiated close to home.

The effect of frequency of travel on tourism expenditure patterns is an interesting one and we ought to examine this collectively for home and tourism destinations abroad. On the one hand, the more frequent traveller the individual is, the more destinations and attractions at home will benefit, whereas on the other hand, the more frequent traveller the individuals to more destinations and attractions abroad are going to suffer. For destinations in the UK, frequency of travel has a positive effect on tourism expenditure. In particular, respondents travelling up to three times per year were more than twice more likely to spend more on a home destination during the financial crisis as compared to other tourists travelling more frequently (nine or more times per year). The same applies to those travelling up to six times (1.8 times more likely as compared to very frequent tourists) and those travelling up to 8 times (twice more likely as compared to very frequent visitors). On the other hand, respondents travelling up to three times per year reported that their tourism expenditure abroad was almost 55% more likely to suffer as compared to very frequent travelers (9+ trips). Interestingly, the odds of an individual reporting an adverse effect on tourism expenditure during recession seem to increase along with frequency of travel per year. So, those travelling for up to 6 times per year are 60% more likely to report a negative turn on their tourism expenditure abroad during periods of financial crisis as compared to very frequent tourists. The corresponding figure for those travelling up to 8 times is 66% respectively.

Next, the analysis turns into the examination of gender influences on tourism consumption patterns during the financial crisis. Interestingly, males' tourism expenditure at home appears to be positively affected by the financial crisis, as compared to their female counterparts. In other words, males tend to spend more on tourism consumption at home as compared to females. In actual terms, males are 1.35 times more likely to outspend their female counterparts when travelling at home. This is rather unusual behavior and it could mean that male respondents tend to exhibit higher substitution patterns in favour of domestic destinations as compared to female tourists.

Finally, the empirical results indicate that those travelling abroad seem to be particularly affected by the general climate of financial and employment uncertainty. This is evident when considering the effect of the employment variable on tourism expenditure patterns abroad. Respondents with uncertain employment prospects were more likely to reflect this on their tourism expenditure abroad. These individuals were 57% more likely to cut back on their tourism expenditure abroad as compared to those that did not face any uncertainty in their professional lives. This point to the fact that higher levels of uncertainty in the economy would translate into individual tourists adjusting their tourism expenditure patterns abroad accordingly. In practical terms this piece of empirical evidence suggests that during periods of economic uncertainty, tourists would still choose to visit destinations abroad, and at the same time try to stretch their limit budget by cutting back on tourism expenditure at the destination. In simple terms, when considering the various categories of tourist costs, income elasticity of demand appears to be significantly more affected by the economic downturn as compared to transportation elasticity of demand.

For home destinations, tourists reported that the financial crisis would entice them to think more carefully about the tourism goods they consume during their holidays. In particular, those respondents that had switched towards cheaper goods during this period of economic uncertainty were 1.6 times more likely to report that their tourism expenditure at home has also been affected. Hence, this empirical evidence suggests that during periods of economic downturn, individuals would choose to divert their spending on cheaper tourist goods. Compared to the evidence presented earlier, this finding indicates that tourists holidaying at home follow similar strategies to those travelling abroad to make their budget go further (stretch holiday budget). Tourists travelling abroad choose to cut back on tourism expenditure, whereas tourists travelling at home destinations would choose to spend on cheaper goods (substitute dearer to cheaper goods).

CONCLUSION

The fragile global economic environment surely reflects on tourism flows and travelers' decision making. The first 'victims' are people with low income and younger are, while men seem to be more influenced than women. Issues of employability and potential income decrease also reflect on future holiday spending patterns. Furthermore, the selection of travel means, destinations, and length of stay face direct impacts from the economic recession. All the above create the necessity to formulate sufficient policies and strategies under the perspective of further leisure opportunities – especially to economically weaker market segments – higher customer satisfaction, and larger and wider 'value for money' input.

The contribution of the book chapter in the field can be considered from a number of different perspectives.

- First, this study represents a rare application of the examination of the financial crisis into tourism activity from a microeconomic perspective, as opposed to a macroeconomic one. Following Song *et al.* (2010), this approach is better suited to assist public policy and managerial decision making. Most of previous evidence regarding the effects of past economic crises on tourism has been accumulated as part of the examination of the 1997 financial crisis on Asian countries (Wang, 2009; Song et al., 2003). At the same time, there is another stream of research, growing in parallel, focusing on the effect of a number of other devastating events on the tourism industry (Kuo *et al.*, 2008; Bonham *et al.*, 2006). All of the aforementioned papers have adopted a macroeconomic perspective on the examination of the effects of the financial crisis on tourism activity.

- Second, this approach considers rather uniquely both domestic and international or long haul tourism activity. The survey questionnaire distributed to a sample of 400 individuals enquires about the effect of the financial crisis on their tourism behavioural patterns both at home and abroad. Thus, the study addresses a major gap in the research literature in the field, namely the importance of domestic tourism activity as a substitute to international and long haul tourism activity (Sheldon and Dwyer, 2010).

- Third, the book chapter considers a number of different categories of discretionary tourism expenditure (accommodation, transportation components) as well as a number of other variables (frequency of travel abroad, and at home) and their effect on individual tourism behaviour during periods of financial uncertainty.

Within the borders tourism is less affected by the economic crisis since respondents perceive that it is cheaper and is more applicable to their ability of tourism consumption. That gives a great opportunity to destination decision makers to develop further strategies for the enlargement of domestic tourism, something that can partially cover the financial losses from international tourists. In addition, marketing and communication techniques can help to fear reduction in terms of perceived high expenditure on destinations abroad. Moreover, for sensitive market segments (i.e.: young population, low paid people) the creation of specific premium tourist packages can help their increase of travel frequency.

The effects of global economic recession are expected to be significant at lest in the nearby future. In order to overpass these difficulties it is also vital to understand the consumers' consumption patterns in microeconomic level, and try to help them overpass their fears and worries, since these psychological factors directly affect tourists' decisions and hierarchy of needs and wants. Tourism and hospitality industry is significantly affected by travelers' leisure decisions and spending minimization. Thus, every formulated tourism policy needs to focus on the industry's long-term prosperity and viability.

Despite the contribution of this research, several limitations also arise. First, the research has been focused on permanent adult residents of U.K.. The same research in tourists having different backgrounds (financial, national, cultural, job vulnerability etc) may produce different results. Thus, any generalisation of the current study's results should be made with caution. Second the research reflects the perspectives of tourists in a specific time. The perspectives of respondents are likely to change throughout time, thus relevant research is suggested to be repeated in frequent time periods. Third, the current study does not examine the perspectives of tourism and hospitality stakeholders, but solely focuses on travellers' perceptions. The inclusion of more interest groups in research and the cross examination of the findings can illustrate more holistically the impacts of the current recession, and provide a further understanding of the factors affecting tourism decisions.

REFERENCES

Aaker, D., & Day, G. (1990). Marketing Research. (4th ed.). Wiley.

Aksoy, S., Atilgan, E., & Akinci, S. (2003). Airline Services Marketing by Domestic and Foreign Firms: Differences from the Customers' Viewpoint. *Journal of Air Transport Management*, *9*(6), 343–351. doi:10.1016/S0969-6997(03)00034-6

Baloglu, S., & McCleary, K. W. (1999). US International Pleasure Travellers' Images of Four Mediterranean Destinations: A Comparison of Visitors and Nonvisitors. *Journal of Travel Research*, *38*(2), 114–129. doi:10.1177/004728759903800207

Berendien, L., Douglas, A., & Zambellis, J. (2011). An Application of the Airport Service Quality Model in South Africa. *Journal of Air Transport Management*, *17*(4), 224–227. doi:10.1016/j.jairtraman.2010.08.001

Berendien, L., & Liebe, L. (2010). The Perceived Value of Devices to Passengers Across the Airline Activity Chain. *Journal of Air Transport Management*, *16*(1), 12–15. doi:10.1016/j.jairtraman.2009.02.002

Bonham, C., Edmonds, C., & Mak, J. (2006). The Impact of 9/11 and Other Terrible Global Events on Tourism in the United States and Hawaii. *Journal of Travel Research*, *45*(1), 99–110. doi:10.1177/0047287506288812

Bramwell, B., & Lane, B. (2003). Tourism and sustainable development in an economic downturn. *Journal of Sustainable Tourism*, *11*(1), 1–2. doi:10.1080/09669580308667188

Brooner, F., & de Hoog, R. (2012). Economizing strategies during an economic crisis. *Annals of Tourism Research*, *39*(2), 1048–1069. doi:10.1016/j.annals.2011.11.019

Claros, E., & Di Tella, A. (2014). *Tourism in the EU economy*. European Parliament.

Collins, D., & Tisdell, C. (2002). Age-Related Lifecycles: Purpose Variations. *Annals of Tourism Research*, *29*(3), 801–818. doi:10.1016/S0160-7383(01)00081-0

Eugenio-Martin, J. L., & Campos-Soria, J. A. (2014). Economic crisis and tourism expenditure cutback decision. *Annals of Tourism Research*, *44*, 53–73. doi:10.1016/j.annals.2013.08.013

Fairburn-Dunlop, P. (1994). Gender, Culture and Tourism Development in Western Samoa. In V. Kinnaird & D. Hall (Eds.), *Tourism: A Gender Analysis* (pp. 121–141). Chichester, New York: Wiley.

Fleischer, A., Peleg, G., & Rivlin, J. (2011). The Impact of Changes in Household Vacation Expenditures on the Travel and Hospitality Industries. *Tourism Management*, *32*(4), 815–821. doi:10.1016/j.tourman.2010.07.003

Glover, P., & Prideaux, B. (2009). Implications of Population Ageing for the Development of Tourism Products and Destinations. *Journal of Vacation Marketing*, *15*(1), 25–37. doi:10.1177/1356766708098169

Grougiou, V., & Pettigrew, S. (2011). Senior Customers' Service Encounter Preferences. *Journal of Service Research*, *14*(4), 475–488. doi:10.1177/1094670511423785

Henderson, J. (1999). Managing the Asian Financial Crisis: Tourist Attractions in Singapore. *Journal of Travel Research*, *38*(2), 177–181. doi:10.1177/004728759903800212

Jang, S., Bai, B., Hong, G., & O'Leary, J. T. (2004). Understanding Travel Expenditure Patterns: A Study of Japanese pleasure Travelers to the United States by Income Level. *Tourism Management*, *25*(3), 331–341. doi:10.1016/S0261-5177(03)00141-9

Kaytaz, M., & Gul, M. C. (2014). Consumer response to economic crisis and lessons for marketers: The Turkish experience. *Journal of Business Research*, *67*(1), 2701–2706. doi:10.1016/j.jbusres.2013.03.019

Kinnaird, V., & Hall, D. (1996). Understanding Tourism Processes: A Gender Aware Framework. *Tourism Management*, *17*(2), 95–102. doi:10.1016/0261-5177(95)00112-3

Kuo, H., Chen, C., Tseng, W., Ju, L.-F., & Huang, B.-W. (2008). Assessing Impacts of SARS and Avian Flu on International Tourism Demand to Asia. *Tourism Management*, *29*(5), 917–928. doi:10.1016/j.tourman.2007.10.006

Mason, P., & Cheyne, J. (2000). Residents' Attitudes to Proposed Tourism Development. *Annals of Tourism Research*, *27*(2), 391–411. doi:10.1016/S0160-7383(99)00084-5

Novelli, M., Morgan, N., & Nibigira, C. (2012). Tourism in a post-conflict situation of fragility. *Annals of Tourism Research*, *39*(3), 1446–1469. doi:10.1016/j.annals.2012.03.003

Okumus, F., & Karamustafa, K. (2005). Impact of an Economic Crisis; Evidence from Turkey. *Annals of Tourism Research*, *32*(4), 942–961. doi:10.1016/j.annals.2005.04.001

Papatheodorou, A., Rossello, J., & Xiao, H. (2010). Global economic crisis and tourism: Consequences and perspectives. *Journal of Travel Research*, *49*(1), 39–45. doi:10.1177/0047287509355327

Pappas, N. (2010). Terrorism and Tourism: The Way Travelers Select Airlines and Destinations. *Journal of Air Transport Studies*, *1*(2), 76–96.

Sakata, K., & MacKenzie, C. (2004). The Accumulation of Human Capital and the Sectoral Shifts Hypothesis for Different Age Groups. *Mathematics and Computers in Simulation*, *64*(3-4), 459–465. doi:10.1016/S0378-4754(03)00111-3

Sariisik, M., Sari, D., Sari, S., & Halis, M. (2011). Tourism sector in order to recovering from the recession: Comparison analyses from Turkey. *Procedia: Social and Behavioral Sciences*, *24*, 181–187. doi:10.1016/j.sbspro.2011.09.070

Sekaran, U. (2000). *Research Methods for Business: A Skill – Building Approach* (3rd ed.). New York: John Wiley & Sons Inc.

Sheldon, P., & Dwyer, L. (2010). The Global Financial Crisis and Tourism: Perspectives of the Academy. *Journal of Travel Research*, *49*(3), 3–4. doi:10.1177/0047287509353191

Smeral, E. (2009). The Impact of the Financial and Economic Crisis on European Tourism. *Journal of Travel Research*, *48*(1), 3–13. doi:10.1177/0047287509336332

Song, H., Lin, S., Witt, S., & Zhang, X. (2010). Impact of Financial/Economic Crisis on Demand for Hotel Rooms in Hong Kong. *Tourism Management*, *32*(1), 172–186. doi:10.1016/j.tourman.2010.05.006

Song, H., Wong, K., & Chon, K. (2003). Modeling and Forecasting the Demand for Hong Kong Tourism. *International Journal of Hospitality Management, 22*(4), 435–451. doi:10.1016/S0278-4319(03)00047-1

Teye, V., Sonmez, S., & Sirakaya, E. (2002). Residents' Attitudes toward Tourism Development. *Annals of Tourism Research, 29*(3), 668–688. doi:10.1016/S0160-7383(01)00074-3

Trakolis, D. (2001). Local Peoples' Perceptions of Planning and Management Issues in Prespes Lakes National Park, Greece. *Journal of Environmental Management, 61*(3), 227–241. doi:10.1006/jema.2000.0410 PMID:11381950

Tretheway, M., & Mak, D. (2006). Emerging Tourism Markets: Ageing and Developing Economies. *Journal of Air Transport Management, 12*(1), 21–27. doi:10.1016/j.jairtraman.2005.09.008

Wang, J., & Ritchie, B. W. (2012). Understanding accommodation managers' crisis planning intention: An application of the theory of planned behaviour. *Tourism Management, 33*(5), 1057–1067. doi:10.1016/j.tourman.2011.12.006

Wang, Y. (2009). The Impact of Crisis Events and Macroeconomic Activity on Taiwan's International Inbound Tourism Demand. *Tourism Management, 30*(1), 75–82. doi:10.1016/j.tourman.2008.04.010

ADDITIONAL READING

Antonakakis, N., Dragouni, M., & Filis, G. (2015). How strong is the linkage between tourism and economic growth in Europe? *Economic Modelling, 44*, 142–155. doi:10.1016/j.econmod.2014.10.018

Beirman, D. (2003). *Restoring tourism destinations in crisis: A strategic marketing approach*. Oxon: CABI.

Dahles, H., & Susilowati, T. P. (2015). Business resilience in times of growth and crisis. *Annals of Tourism Research, 51*, 34–50. doi:10.1016/j.annals.2015.01.002

Henderson, J. C. (2007). *Managing tourism crises*. Oxford: Butterworth – Heinemann.

Jucan, C. N., & Jucan, M. S. (2013). Travel and tourism as a driver of economic recovery. *Procedia Economics and Finance, 6*, 81–88. doi:10.1016/S2212-5671(13)00117-2

Martin, J. C., Rodríguez-Déniz, H., & Voltes-Dorta, A. (2013). Determinants of airport cost flexibility in a context of economic recession. *Transportation Research Part E, Logistics and Transportation Review, 57*, 70–84. doi:10.1016/j.tre.2013.01.007

Pappas, N. (in press). Marketing hospitality industry in an era of crisis. *Tourism Planning and Development*.

Pappas, N. (in press). Achieving competitiveness in Greek accommodation establishments during recession. *International Journal of Tourism Research*.

Pearce, B. (2012). The state of air transport markets and the airline industry after the great recession. *Journal of Air Transport Management, 21*, 3–9. doi:10.1016/j.jairtraman.2011.12.011

Poudyal, N. C., Paudel, B., & Tarrant, M. A. (2013). A time series analysis of the impact of recession on national park visitation in the United States. *Tourism Management, 35*, 181–189. doi:10.1016/j.tourman.2012.07.001

Ritchie, B. W. (2009). *Aspects of Tourism: Crisis and disaster management for tourism*. Buffalo: Channel View Publications.

Sariisik, M., Sari, D., Sari, S., & Halis, M. (2011). Tourism sector in order to recovering from the recession: Comparison analyses for Turkey. *Procedia Social and Behavioral Studies, 24*, 181–187. doi:10.1016/j.sbspro.2011.09.070

Visser, G., & Ferreira, S. (2013). *Tourism and crisis*. London: Routledge.

KEY TERMS AND DEFINITIONS

Consumer Behaviour: It is the purchasing behaviour of consumers in terms of personal or household shopping.

Crisis: It is originated from the Greek word "krisi" (κρίση), which means judgement, and refers to a condition of danger, destruction and/or instability that can lead to a decisive change.

Recession: A time period of economic downturn, usually limited in scope, and duration.

Risk: The potential exposure to a danger, destruction and/or instability that can result to losses, problems or even crises.

Tourism Activity: The tourism oriented process of planning and engaged in certain activities.

Tourism Consumption: It is the process of buying or using goods and/or services in the wider field of travel, tourism, and hospitality.

Tourism Demand: It is the overall number of people who use tourism facilities, products and services away from their place of residence. Its three basic components deal with: (i) actual or effective demand (ii) suppressed demand, and (iii) no demand.

Travel: The action of transporting people from one place/country to another.

Chapter 12
Understanding the Indiscipline of Tourism:
A Radical Critique to the Current State of Epistemology

Maximiliano E. Korstanje
University of Palermo, Argentina & University of Leeds UK

Lourdes Cisneros Mustelier
University of La Habana, Cuba

Sylvia Herrera
University of Especialidades Turisticas, Ecuador

ABSTRACT

Over last years, the current growth of tourism flourished in a wealth of courses, Ph.Ds., Masters and academic offerings that positioned tourism as a good perspective for students. Jafar Jafari signaled to the term "scientifization of tourism" to explain the ever-increasing attention given to this new field (Jafari & Aeser, 1988; Jafari, 1990, 2005). At a first stage, the great volume of bibliographic production offered an encouraging prospect in the pathways towards the maturation of this discipline. However, some epistemologists have recently alerted that not only tourism-research failed to develop a unified consensus of what tourism is, but also lack of a coherent epistemology that helps organizing the produced material. In this respect, tourism is subject now to an atmosphere of "indiscipline" where the produced knowledge leads to scattered (limited) conclusions.

INTRODUCTION

Over last years, the growth of tourism studies has been duplicated and crystalized in Ph. Doctorates, Master degrees, books, journals and academic courses (Leiper, 1981; Jafari, 1990; Sheldon 1991; Hall, Howey et al 1999; Williams & Lew 2004). As Jafar Jafari put it, the scientifization of tourism was based on the increasing attention given by scholars to tourism as their primary object of study (Jafari & Aeser, 1988;

DOI: 10.4018/978-1-5225-0201-2.ch012

Jafari, 1990; 2005). Though this volume of prolific production accelerated the disciplinary maturation of tourism, some epistemologists have alerted that applied research failed to reach a unified consensus (epistemology) about what tourism means, but the production evolved on a fragmentary platform which was dubbed by John Tribe as "the indiscipline of tourism". (Tribe 1997; 2005; 2010; Korstanje & Thirkettle, 2013; Korstanje & Skoll 2014; Escalona & Thirkettle, 2011). In this context, the present chapter is aimed at discussing critically the main opportunities and limitations that epistemology faces today in tourism fields, as well as the problems quantitative-oriented paradigms show. For some reasons, which remains obscure, researchers are prone to employ quantitative over qualitative instruments (Walle 1997; Decrop 1999). Though this chapter does not represent an attack to any scholar or position, no less true is that the current state of the art is experiencing an epistemological fragmentation which prevents a clear diagnosis of what tourism is. A fragmentation of this caliber leads to serious difficulties in order for the discipline to be seriously taken as a maturated academic option. The aims of this text are twofold; on one hand we debate on the needs of achieving a scientific definition of tourism. On another, we depart towards a theory that triggers a review of John Tribe´s contributions to the epistemology of tourism. The first section explores preliminary the problem of transdisciplinarity and the intervention of different social sciences to take tourism as the main object of their approaches but leaving behind a shared definition. As a second option, an in-depth insight is done over the prone of fieldworkers to opt for quantitative research, ignoring the benefits other types of instruments offer. In this vein, it is important to review the criticism posed by John Tribe respecting not only to the "indiscipline of tourism", but the pervasive role played by Academy in allowing a conceptual chaos in the produced bibliography. However, Tribe´s diagnosis does not present the reasons why the bibliographic production is scattered. To fulfill this gap, an alternative explanation on the indiscipline of tourism is given in fourth section.

Towards a Theory of Tourism

It is unfortunate that tourism-researchers not only have developed a sentiment of admiration for social sciences, but also borrowed their main epistemologies for their own field-works (Ryan 1991). It resulted in the proliferation of multi-disciplinary approaches which leaves further doubts than answers. Some voices have proposed to embrace a new post-disciplinary method combining the best of many disciplines towards the transdisciplinarity of tourism (Coles, Hall & Duval, 2006).

As an object of study, tourism has been examined by diverse social sciences, as anthropology (Graburn, 1983), Sociology (Maccannell 1976; Cohen 1984), Geographies (Mitchel & Murphy, 1991; Britton 1991; Williams & Lew, 2014), Psychology (Pearce 1982), Politics (Richter 1983; 1989), economy (Krippendorf, 1984), mobilities (Urry, 2007; Hannam, Sheller & Urry, 2006), history (Towner, 1985) and so forth. Beyond the great divergence of all these studies, two main waves emerged. Both will attempt to respond the following question, though from diverse angles: Is tourism an productive activity resulted from industrial revolution?, or is it a social institution inherited to sedentary tribes?.

Doubtless American and European perspectives discussed to what extent tourism is a modern phenomenon or an ancient practices other ancient civilizations. In this respect, Jost Krippendorf ignited a much deeper discussion to explain the logic of leisure not only traverses cultures and times, but also it is enrooted in the psychology of our mind. No matter than the time, tourism is not previously determined by the capital as American sociology precludes, but by the needs of "escapement" which is common to many human sedentary organizations. A great variety of cultures in the globe has historically performed similar practices of recreational leisure and travels which suggests that tourism is an all-encompassing social institution. One of the aspects of leisure, even tourism, depends on its efficacy to revitalize the psychological frustrations people suffered during their working time. The sense of novelty and discovery not only are enrooted in human nature, but serves to enhance social cohesion. Cultural values are socialized to new members of society from their childhood. These values conform what Krippendorff dubbes as "consciousness". Those behavior and acts committed during holidays are culturally determined by the "tourist consciousness" which is instilled in holiday-makers from their early home. Since without tourism, society would not prosper, Krippendorff adds, it is not surprisingly that a scientific-oriented platform should think this activity as a social institution which transcends the borders of geography and economy as the orthodoxy suggests (Krippendorf, 1975; 1982; 1984; 1986; 1987a; 1987b; 1989; 1995).

In sharp contrast with Krippendorf, Maccannell conceives that tourism consolidated just after the mid of XXth century, or the end of WWII. Not only the expansion of industrialism, which means a set of benefits for workers as less working hours and salaries increase but the technological breakthrough that triggered mobilities were responsible from the inception of tourism. There was nothing like an ancient form of tourism, Maccannell notes. Taking his cue from the sociology of Marx, Durkheim, and Goffman, Maccannell argues that tourism and staged-authenticity work in conjoint in order for the society not to collapse. If totem is a sacred-object that confers a political authority to chiefdom in aboriginal cultures, tourism fulfills the gap between citizens and their institutions which was enlarged by the alienation lay people face. The current industrial system of production is finely-ingrained to expropriate workers from part of their wages. A whole portion of earned salaries is spent to leisure activities, even in consuming tourism. As Krippendroff, Maccannell believes, industrialism forged a "tourist consciousness" that revitalizes the glitches and deprivations produced by economy. Tourism would be a type of totem for industrial societies that mediates among citizens, officials and their institutions. In this context, tourism, like a chamanized totem in primitive communities, revitalizes psychological frustrations and alienation proper of urban societies. Not surprisingly, Maccannell adds, Marx was in the correct side at denouncing the oppression suffered by the work-force. Nonetheless, leisure, far from being an ideological mechanism of control (as in whole Marxism), prevents the social disintegration (Maccannell, 1976; 1984). Over recent years, he was concerned by the lack of ethics in tourism consumption. Coalescing contributions of Giddens with Derrida, he points out that globalization entails to type of mobilities. Nomads who are defined as forged-migrants are pitted against tourists who are encouraged to consume landscapes and exotic cultures. Since tourists are conferred by a certain degree of freedom, this leads them to think they are part of a privilege class, sentiment that is reinforced by the quest of "the local other". Reluctant to contact others, tourists affirm their own self-esteem enjoying the precarious conditions where natives live. If this is not controlled tourism may produce a progressive process of dehumanization (Maccannell, 1973; 1976, 1984; 1988; 1992; 2001; 2009; 2011; 2012).

A more radical insight, initiated by Dean Maccannell, but continued by other sociologists as G. Debord, E. Chambers, K. Meethan, T. Edensor and others, (like J. Krippendorff) acknowledged that the advance of tourism and the consuming style of life is oppressive for citizens. However, they thought that the consolidation of industrial age was possible due to many factors such as working time reduction, wages and working conditions improvements as well as more efficient technologies that prompted to discover new markets for Europe and US. Based on the psychological need of mobilities, tourism drew a new geography which stimulated the consumption of signs, or symbols. This school envisaged exclusively tourism as a modern institution, observable only through the inception of modernity. Starting from the premise that there was nothing like holidays before the advance of industrial society, scholars who adopted this stance confirmed that tourism worked as an ideological instrument in order to control the newfound workforce resulted from the expansion of capitalism. At the time, workers earn further money it is transferred to capital owners in forms of consumption in leisure, tourism and mobility industries. Sooner or later, capital is centralized and rechanneled from consumers-workers to producers. In this vein, the sociology of tourism took from historians the belief that tourism was a trend surfaced during the start of modernity; because their familiarity with other ancient civilizations or their lack of knowledge in archeology, historians developed a western-centered orientation that focused on Middle Age as the starting point of their studies. In view of the internal wars and feuds that led to political atomization, Europe faced a dark period that left behind the travels and infrastructure of Roman Empire. Following this, historians of tourism did not pay the necessary attention to ancient civilizations as Assyrians, Romans, even Muslims where an earlier network facilitated the exchange of goods and persons paving the pathways for the performance of practices very similar to tourism. Let´s explain that term *feriae (in Latin)* was used to give a leave to Roman citizens to stimulate they visit their relative or friends in the periphery, beyond the Italian Peninsula. Those Romans who worked hard during 9 months had timeframe of 3 months to enjoy outside the main cities of Empire. Not only this was not pretty different to modern holidays, but some European as German or Portuguese languages keep its linguistic legacy in words as *Ferias or Ferien* which undoubtedly, deserves the attention on the fact that a much deeper discussion should be done in next years in regards to the roots of tourism. Though ancient history would play a fertile ground to study tourism, it was discarded from the onset. Instead, the economic-based paradigm was enthralled.

Methodological Discussions

In the forewords of their book, *Tourism Research Methods,* B. W Ritchie, P. Burns and C. Palmer (2005a) noted tourism research was caught between two fronts, business vs. social science-led methodologies. The programs at main European and American Universities are hosted in managerial business faculties or in social science division according to the discretion of the establishment. Even those textbooks written by sociologists or anthropologists, in tourism research, are not based on empirical cases or study cases. Far from asking for the unification of syllabuses authors highlighted on the needs of integrating theory with practice.

The tension, which is described above, pits industry-based researchers against social scientists. During decades, sociology was reluctance to accept tourism as a serious discipline. This happens because sociologists express their worry knowledge-production has increased to the extent to be bogged down. The attempts to expand the research volume resulted in a disordered expansion that today is very hard to grasp. Moreover, much of the influence of positivism as well as economic functionalism has undermined the objectivity of current business studies. Furthermore, the conceptual fragmentation given the lack of a coherent epistemology has led to take exorbitant attention to the role played by taxonomies in the fieldwork. In consequences, the current applied research, which is overtly published in top tier journals, focuses its studies on the tourist-experience alone (Ritchie, Burns & Palmer 2005b).

To what an extent the illustrating outcomes of empirical-research are derived from the optimization in the efficacy in selecting methodologies for expanding the fieldwork, is a point discussed by Chris Ryan. Based on the concept of experience in Plato, Ryan adheres to fieldwork sometimes is subject to a great variety of sources, where the experience of tourists is the primary criterion of validation (Ryan 2005). At some extent, experts feel that the only valid ways towards true, is the interview or the close-ended questionnaire at airports or train stations. It is important not to lose the sight we need new additional sources of investigation to escape from the established positivism. Over years, epistemologists have discussed the pro and cons of qualitative and quantitative methods within different disciplines. However, for some reason, this discussion is incipient in tourism fields. In a book edited by Dwyer, Gill & Seetaram the needs of combining qualitative and quantitative methods remind us that while the advance of business-related journals accepted the introduction of a quantitative viewpoint, sociology and anthropology launched to develop qualitative instruments (Dwyer, Gill & Seetaram 2012). As M Korstanje and Geoffrey Skoll evinced, the fact is that both techniques have their benefits and limitations. At a first glance, by measuring a sample one may obtain correlation between two or more variables, but nobody knows if this link explains the issue. To set an example, the findings of research may show that females are frightful to some risks as terrorism, natural disasters and food contamination, while males are not prone to risk perception. In view of this information, the report concludes that females are risk prone in comparison to males. Even, readers may validate these remarks according to the used methodologies and the steps in designating the sample. From a qualitative view, this rests in a great fallacy because of two main reasons. The first and most important, risks are social construes, which do not depend on the genre by the previous cognitive filter where each genre is educated. Women would perceive more risk because she is being socialized to express their concerns, and fears. Besides, she takes a proactive role in caring their families. Rather, men not only repress their emotions because it undermines their archetype of masculinity, but are educated to sublimate their fears in violence. Secondly, perception of risk may not provide any time of shock in the psychological mind. Even, some tourists are strongly interested to be in risky destinations while others are risk-avoiders (Korstanje & Skoll 2015). In the fieldwork, for example ethnographies, anthropologists find often how consulted natives lie or simply are unfamiliar with their behaviors. The same happens in tourism at time a tourist is interviewed. The obtained results are useful to establish trends in consumptions but not as conclusive evidences which explain the issue. Furthermore, even though qualitative-driven research offers a lot of alternatives in discovering new horizons, field-workers should never be students. It is widely acknowledged that professional researchers recruit students to collate dataset from the fieldwork. Why this is not a recommendable decision should be discussed in depth in the methodological section.

In perspective, the employment of student for professional investigations exhibits two main problems. Firstly, students are not familiar with the design of research as well as the conceptual discussion senior researchers had with its colleagues, which means that young fieldworkers administer questionnaires and interviews as automats. Not only they ignore those expressions which would be of importance to keep in mind, but also, a lot of details are missing between interviewee and interviewer. Secondly, students want to sympathize with their tutors; this leads not only by tergiversating the outcome of fieldwork (to get good marks) but are prone to make the much they can. Indeed, these amateur researchers think erroneously that the large of the sample gains veracity in the hypothesis they want to test. No matter what interviewees respond, they look for obtaining the largest number of cases.

Particularly, there are qualitative approaches as (self) ethnography, story life, participant observation, projective drawings which are not based in the number of case but in the deepness of content. Most of these techniques are successfully achieved after a long period of time to warm up with participants. Even, in the fieldwork anthropologists never interview the entire community they only take one key informant who is considered as a valid source to understand the habits and customs of the rest. During the fieldwork, the key informant would be of help not only in assisting the ethnographer, but also in weaving the network of politics, economics proper of the studied society. What these types of methodologies valorize seems to be the meaning instead of measuring. Then, the logic of multi-variable comparison, where rests many of quantitative techniques, has no sense in ethnography. An excellent ethnology may be achieved with only one case. As Clifford Geertz puts it, a person may wink the eye to others, but this act, may have two diverse interpretations. It can be a nervous habit or an insinuation of any type. Metaphorically speaking this is exactly what happens with qualitative methods (Geertz, 1994). Examples of good ethnographies or projective drawing application can be seen in the following investigations: The Tourist (Dean Maccannell, 1976), The Power of Projective Drawings (Maximiliano Korstanje, 2010), Envisioning Eden (Noel Salazar 2013), Traversing Paris (Charlie Mansfield, 2005) and others. An additional obstacle relates to the divergence between what peoples say and do. I do remember my ethnography in the "Sanctuary of Cromañón", a dark-tourism site where 194 teenagers died while attending a rock and rock festival. One day, a person came to me explaining me he was a privilege eye-witness of everything what happened that sad night. In respect to this, the interview lasted roughly 5 hours and was tape-recorded. The information I obtained from this young was very important for me at a preliminary stage. Nonetheless, with the passing of months I have advanced my ethnography comparing the collated information by what I can hear and see. Not only I realized that the original interview was completely false, because the involved key-informant wanted to attract attention and exaggerated his stories, but he felt the needs to tell something to me. The importance of this story was not determined by its credibility. He had not lost anyone in the disaster of Cromañon, though developed a strange attachment for the event, for the other´s suffering. This empathy led him to alter his sense of reality. Paradoxically, although this interview was a fake, it underpinned the main hypotheses in my research opening the doors to new cosmologies and opportunities to be empirically validated. This reflects two important lessons, sometimes people imagine events which are unreal but it speaks of their inner world. In addition sometimes interviewees lie or are unfamiliar with the reasons behind their behaviour. Whenever quantitative-techniques are applied in this slippery context, results are misleading.

Some epistemologists have exerted a radical critique on qualitative view because its inconsistency to be replicated in other environs than the original where the experiment was conducted. This lack of standardization, which was widely explored by historians of anthropology, suggests that two ethnographers who visited the same culture can see different things. This type of methodological relativism, far from unifying concepts, leads to some contradictions at time of interpreting evidence. However, to what extent, quantitative methods resolves this problem is a point of discussion open to date. At time one object is clarified, other remains obscure. For example, at time the design of investigation reminds us on the importance on sampling 1500 cases to conduct the fieldwork. The sample not only is statistically significant, but was carefully selected following complex algorithms and soft-wares. The main topic of this investigation is associated to risk perception. The results indicate that 70% of participants are risk-avoiders while 30% restant are risk-seekers. The correlations of variables operate over a little portion of the universe, which means the 70% of the sample who manifested aversion to the risk. Results will say nothing on the rest 30% of interviewees. The quantitative methods should be used to express trends, but they often fail to explain reasons. To solve this pitfall, some experts suggest "triangulation" as a valid source to combine the best of quantitative with qualitative methods. In tourism fields and additional methodological problem lies on the lack of a scientific definition of the object of study. This raises the question, Why are the key factors for tourism to be disorganized in islands or tribes of knowledge?.

A Review of the Indiscipline of Tourism in John Tribe

A wide range of research delved in the economic nature of tourism, but in so doing, it failed to produce a firm platform to avoid the divergence of schools and networks each of them dotted with a particular vision of the industry (Dale & Robinson, 2001; Botterill, 2001; Tribe 2007). "The indiscipline of tourism", following Tribe, was a result not only of the passive role played by Academy to fix issues, but the lack of identity to forge a shared epistemology (Tribe 1997a; 1997b; 2005; 2006; 2009; 2010). As Graham Dann observed, the Academy of Tourism built its legitimacy in an "up-hill city" following the business-based paradigm, where tourism was conceived as a mechanism to enhance profits. Certainly, studies promoted by The International Academy for the Study of Tourism frowned the intromission of social sciences, prioritizing an economic orientation, which was more interested in protecting the lucrative interests of entrepreneurs than in understanding the tourist behaviour (Dann 2009; 2011).

In this respect, other critical voice echoed Dann´s concerns, John Tribe. Today, Tribe is considered one of the most authorative voices in the fields of epistemology of tourism. He has developed a critical look respecting to the role played by Academy of Tourism and the produced knowledge. His most limitations and approaches will be placed under the lens of scrutiny in next section.

The philosophical concerns of tourism scholars led to question why tourism has not been consolidated as a serious discipline. In this discussion, John Tribe, who serves as Chief Editor of Annals of Tourism Research, starts from the needs of establishing the basis of a new epistemology of tourism beyond of what it has been already written. As noted in his preface, overtly acknowledges, tourism research has advanced considerably over last decades. Not only in the number of specialized journals but also books and other post-graduate programs. However, this was not accompanied with the solidification of a solid argumentative epistemology (Tribe 2005; 2006; 2010). What is more than important to discuss is the state of contemporary research in tourism today. Citing Giddens in his book *Philosophical Issues in tourism,* Tribe (2009) coins the term "run-away tourism" to signify the uncontrolled liberal forces that situates the industry out of control. Following this argument, tourism research has been monopolized by the advance of managerial disciplines, which it can be added, promote the profit of industry instead of laying the foundation of a durable episteme. Tribe main argument may be divided in four relevant points,

- Tourism has gained recognition to produce an important volume of knowledge but it is not enough to be seen as a science.
- The nature of tourism seems still to be not easily to define.
- There are unresolved delineations in the commonalities and differences between tourism and mobility.
- Since tourism, even, has been framed as a naïve activity, tourists normal-wise refuse to be labelled as "tourists", they preferably use to be called as "travellers".

It is clear that problems and concerns by researchers in defining an established academic discipline was subject to empirical problems of validations. Although Tribe's compilation attempts to contribute in the formation of solid definition of tourism and hospitality, it fails in the aspect that did not provide a clear explanation why tourism has not been a serious academic alternative up to date. Though we formally recognize the valuable efforts of Tribe to resolve the epistemological problems of tourism, much of reviews done after the release of the book not only were superficial, but also did not understand the point where the argument goes to.

To fulfil this gap, we do not offer a response to the question why tourism has not reach a point of maturation in the standardized guidelines of science, because it stems from the particular interests of some scholars to give formal recognition to their Marketing-related programs. Rather, we will explain further on the boundaries between classical and postmodern disciplines. This sheds light on the reason behind the "fragmentation of tourism", Tribe originally denounced.

The Postmodern Disciplines

The problem is not how knowledge is produced, but the context where the cosmology of the world evolves. In some perspective, the forms of production, science and the cosmology are inextricably intertwined. In times where society integrated centralized forms of production, creating imperial powers, a unified vision of the world is imposed. This means that academic disciplines are formed resulting from the societal order and its respective economy. Instead of interrogating on the failure of Enlightenment as an all encompassing project, Tribe takes much attention to the phenomenology of tourist experience.

Nonetheless, he fails to give credible explanation about the factors that coadyuvated in the "indiscipline of tourism". In this sense, we propose an alternative answer. At a closer look, one might realize the science has evolved into three differentiated stages. The scientific thought is determined by three basic pillars: The inference of laws; The replicability of the data; The explanation of phenomena.

The sources and processes should be duly documented and the results should be capable of being repeated by another researcher. Lastly, science should, by observation, permit the comprehension and explanation of the variation and connection of the variables of the problem. Thus, all scientific research begins with a question, which is answered by following a method.

For a long time, the positivists, not knowing about the contributions of the Viennese School, introduced relativity in the evaluation of results. Thus, science came to be determined not by the method but by the falsability of the results. This suggests an investment in the production of knowledge in which the result comes to be more important than the intervening steps. As a result of this epistemological confusion, many scientists fell into conceptual relativity which has led to great fragmentation. The form of research then gave way to methodological subjectivity, which, being linked to the situation and politics, facilitates the consolidation of modernity as a general way of life.

In this context, it is worth clarifying that all science rests on two forms of generating knowledge. The first is called '1st state' and is characterised by the isolation of those variables which are studied, generally in laboratories, and which seek to learn about the laws which govern the universe. Physics is one of the sciences which operate under the principle of direct observation. The environment, in this type of situation, is totally controlled. The scientist should always conduct experiments in the present in order to draw inferences about the future. However, '2nd state' science is totally different. Under certain conditions, the grade of repeatability cannot be isolated in a determined frame of time and space, and the researcher must 'reconstruct' the causes of the problem from the past. Within this classification are the so-called social sciences, which include psychology and sociology, among others. As capital expands its influence, breaking down the former notions of time and space with globalisation, knowledge is produced by a great variety of research centres with few links between them. Their results are so dispersed that there is little or no dialogue between the different schools of thought. The most established disciplines accuse newer bodies of knowledge of not being able to infer laws, and this becomes a motive for their rejection. Given the general laws of science, it is of interest to know that historical evolution of science has changed through the years. We may explain our model of *The three phases of science'* as follows:

From antiquity until the end of the middle ages, mankind was interested by questions concerning the connection between people and its cities. His economy was purely a subsistence economy linked to cattle farming and primary agriculture. There was an important link between a man and his territory and lineage, as there was no concept of salaried work as we know it today, or in other words the possibility of a person to choose where, for what wage, and for whom he would work. The disciplines which governed life were philosophy, astrology, medicine and astronomy among others. We term this phase 'the primary production of knowledge'. In the late middle age, we enter into a second phase, which we term 'the secondary production of knowledge' in which the Industrial and Cromwellian Revolutions have left their mark. Work and the relationship of a person with his lineage started to lose their strong linkage, due to the consensus that labour should be sold according to the conditions of the context. Little by little man ceased to be subject to God, his city, and his master in order to become part of the capitalist adventure based on speculation, control of the results, and calculation. During this process, from the 19th century until the middle of the 20th century, new disciplines wee born. These included psychology, anthropology and sociology. These new disciplines were totally orientated to the study of man, but rather than seeking the answers to abstract universal questions, they were specific with emphasis on industrial work, poverty, and development, for instance.

The 'social sciences' entered into conflict with the established disciplines, and so sociology confronted philosophy, and psychology confronted medicine (and psychiatry). Without doubt, we inevitably begin to see a fragmentation in the method of generating and interpreting knowledge. These forms of the production of science cannot be studied outside the context of the standardisation of the modern means of production in general. Systemic standardisation (that is, the possibility of the accumulation of comparative data, as defended by the positivists) was directly proportional to mass production. Society and human behaviour begin to be considered as a systemic whole, where there are inputs, processes and outputs which indefinitely feed back into other systems. Social interaction is the conceptual base which these new sciences claimed to study. Nevertheless, the situation changed radically towards the end of 20th century, or to be more exact in about 1970 when capitalist countries began to realise that they could not guarantee serial production for ever in a sustainable way. This was due to the energy crisis provoked by the Arab-Israeli War, in which industries had to introduce a new form of consumption so that capital, which had been born out of the Industrial Revolution, could become electronic. The production of capital for the purchase of goods did not now seem to be as important as the opposite situation, where goods become a pre-condition for the production and general accumulation of money. The classic relationship is replaced by symbolic mediators, such as money, generating a total solipsism, or the view that the self is the only thing that really exists. We may call this third state the 'fragmented stage of knowledge' in which the new disciplines (communication, journalism, tourism, gastronomy, management and publicity, for example) begin to gain ground in comparison with second stage disciplines such as sociology. As two of the main characteristics of post-modernity have been social fragmentation and subjectivity, theses new forms of knowledge have been oriented towards consumption and the aesthetic. These new values of society are rejected by the already established second stage sciences (Harvey, 1989)

It is tempting to say that sociology and anthropology claim that tourism is a science which does not have its foundations in serious reason. These are the same claims that sociology had confronted from its own predecessors. In order to summarise this model and enable the reader to achieve a greater understanding of the phenomenon, we might synthesise the main aspects which distinguish third stage sciences as follows:

They are disciplines which are linked to the creation of necessities, in order to explain them.

1. They consider social reality as a product.
2. They follow parameters which are similar to market engineering.
3. Their considerations and findings are isolated, and cannot be integrated into a coherent whole.
4. They show great fragmentation or lack an academic base to orientate research.
5. Information plays an important role in the construction of their discourse, but is not integrated.
6. They appeal to multi-disciplinarity but their results are mere second-order explanations.
7. They are purely descriptive.
8. They are strongly influenced by the aesthetic and appearance.
9. They focus on experience as their principal strength, but lack an integrated.

In other terms, as they define as an abstract form of thinking, these new disciplines can express principles, which do not have any real direction. These new post industrial sciences are incomplete projects, which are aimed at explaining what must be done, instead of focusing in the fact. They are centered on studding effects, not reasons. Tourism has consolidated as a discipline in a moment where the concept of Truth was broken into pieces. This is the reason why, it keeps serious difficulties to produce unified concepts.

CONCLUSION

In this chapter, we have addressed two major points, the indiscipline of tourism as it has formulated by John Tribe and the overemphasis for quantitative viewpoints which get misleading results. Neither the Academy nor, the reasons given by Tribe are responsible for the dispersion of tourism. Rather, as we have explained, it corresponds with a much deeper issue enrooted in the productive system. At the time, The Project of Enlightenment set the pace to "relativism", determined by the Oil Embargo in 70s decade, the concept of reality turned into subjective pieces. From that moment on, the concept of truth was inextricably linked to subject perception. The lemma, "everybody is an individual" synthetized a new allegory of the World, where all-encompassing models turned in atomized projects. In this context, tourism, communication, and marketing surfaced. Some established options as sociology and anthropology not only mocked on the fact tourism is considered valid discipline, but focused on the methodological limitations of its fieldworkers. The effort of some scholars to unify methods discussing quantitative and qualitative instruments was in vain since the discipline was gradually monopolized by profit-oriented interests. Today, instead of consolidating a scientific-paradigm that explains tourism, researchers are more interested in protecting the interests of stakeholders optimizing their profits.

The appetite for captivating more segments engenders two consequences which lead to the fragmentation of discipline. The first corresponds with the accumulation of definitions, all of them conducive but limited to businesses alone. The ever-growing number of definitions about tourism prevents to achieve a "unified epistemology" to work on. In parallel, epistemologists call to the importance of "multidisciplinary approach" to understand the complexity of tourism. That way, discursively, scholarship has adopted the belief that maturation of discipline depends on the richness of used methods and voices. This engenders a vicious circle which aggravates the state of dispersion of produced knowledge.

REFERENCES

Bertaux, D., & Kohli, M. (1984). The life story approach: A continental view. *Annual Review of Sociology, 10*(1), 215–237. doi:10.1146/annurev.so.10.080184.001243

Botterill, D. (2001). The epistemology of a set of tourism studies. *Leisure Studies, 20*(3), 199–214. doi:10.1080/02614360127084

Britton, S. (1991). Tourism, capital, and place: Towards a critical geography of tourism. *Environment and Planning. D, Society & Space, 9*(4), 451–478. doi:10.1068/d090451

Chambers, E. (2009). *Native tours: the anthropology of travel and tourism.* Waveland Press.

Cohen, E. (1984). The sociology of tourism: Approaches, issues, and findings. *Annual Review of Sociology, 10*(1), 373–392. doi:10.1146/annurev.so.10.080184.002105

Coles, T., Hall, C. M., & Duval, D. T. (2006). Tourism and post-disciplinary enquiry. *Current Issues in Tourism, 9*(4-5), 293–319. doi:10.2167/cit327.0

Dale, C., & Robinson, N. (2001). The theming of tourism education: A three-domain approach. *International Journal of Contemporary Hospitality Management, 13*(1), 30–35. doi:10.1108/09596110110365616

Dann, G. (2009). How international is the International Academy for the Study of Tourism? *Tourism Analysis, 14*(1), 3–13. doi:10.3727/108354209788970180

Dann, G. M. (2011). Anglophone hegemony in tourism studies today. *Enlightening Tourism: A Pathmaking Journal, 1*(1), 1-30.

Debord, G. (1998). *Comments on the Society of the Spectacle* (Vol. 18). London: Verso.

Decrop, A. (1999). Triangulation in qualitative tourism research. *Tourism Management, 20*(1), 157–161. doi:10.1016/S0261-5177(98)00102-2

Dwyer, L., Gill, A., & Seetaram, N. (2012). *Handbook of Research Methods in Tourism: quantitative and qualitative approaches.* Cheltenham, UK: Edward Elgar Publishing Ltd. doi:10.4337/9781781001295

Edensor, T. (2001). Performing tourism, staging tourism (Re) producing tourist space and practice. *Tourist Studies, 1*(1), 59–81. doi:10.1177/146879760100100104

Escalona, F. M. O. D., & Thirkettle, A. (2011). General theory of tourism? the case of war and terrorism. *International Journal of Tourism Anthropology, 1*(3), 208–225. doi:10.1504/IJTA.2011.043706

Geertz, C. (1973). *The interpretation of cultures: Selected essays* (Vol. 5019). New York: Basic books.

Geertz, C. (1994). Thick description: Toward an interpretive theory of culture. *Readings in the Philosophy of Social Science*, 213-231.

Goffman, E. (1959). *The presentation of self in everyday life.* Garden City, NY: Anchor.

Graburn, N. H. (1983). The anthropology of tourism. *Annals of Tourism Research, 10*(1), 9–33. doi:10.1016/0160-7383(83)90113-5

Hall, C. M., Williams, A. M., & Lew, A. A. (2004). Tourism: Conceptualizations, institutions, and issues. *A Companion to Tourism*, 3-21.

Hannam, K., Sheller, M., & Urry, J. (2006). Editorial: Mobilities, immobilities and moorings. *Mobilities*, *1*(1), 1–22. doi:10.1080/17450100500489189

Howey, R. M., Savage, K. S., Verbeeten, M. J., & Van Hoof, H. B. (1999). Tourism and hospitality research journals: Cross-citations among research communities. *Tourism Management*, *20*(1), 133–139. doi:10.1016/S0261-5177(98)00099-5

Jafari, J. (1990). Research and scholarship: the basis of tourism education. *Journal of Tourism Studies*, *1*(1), 33-41.

Jafari, J. (2001). The scientification of tourism. In V. L. Smith & M. Brent (Eds.), *Hosts and guests revisited: Tourism issues of the 21st century* (pp. 28–41). New York: Cognizant Communications.

Jafari, J. (2005). Bridging out, nesting afield: Powering a new platform. *Journal of Tourism Studies*, *16*(2), 1–5.

Jafari, J., & Aaser, D. (1988). Tourism as the subject of doctoral dissertations. *Annals of Tourism Research*, *15*(3), 407–429. doi:10.1016/0160-7383(88)90030-8

Korstanje, M., & Skoll, G. (2014). The inception of the rational platform. *Turismo y Desarrollo Local*, (17), 1-9.

Korstanje, M. E. (2010). The power of projective drawings: A new method for researching tourist experiences. *e-Review of Tourism Research, 8*(5), 85-101.

Korstanje, M. E., & Skoll, G. (2015). Exploring the Fear of Travel: study revealing into tourist´s mind. *Revista Turismo: estudos e práticas, 4*(1), 56-63.

Krippendorf, J. (1975). *Die Landschaftsfresser: Tourismus u. Erholungslandschaft*. Bern: Hallwag.

Krippendorf, J. (1982). Towards new tourism policies: The importance of environmental and sociocultural factors. *Tourism Management, 3*(3), 135–148. doi:10.1016/0261-5177(82)90063-2

Krippendorf, J. (1984). *Holiday makers*. Oxford, UK: Heinemann-Butterworth.

Krippendorf, J. (1986). The new tourist—turning point for leisure and travel. *Tourism Management, 7*(2), 131–135. doi:10.1016/0261-5177(86)90025-7

Krippendorf, J. (1987). Ecological approach to tourism marketing. *Tourism Management, 8*(2), 174–176. doi:10.1016/0261-5177(87)90029-X

Krippendorf, J. (1987). *The Holiday-makers: Understanding the Impact of Travel and Tourism*. Oxford, UK: Butterworth-Heinemann.

Krippendorf, J. (1989). *Fur einen Anderen Tourimus: Probleme-Perspektiven*. Frankfurt Am Main: Fischer-Taschenbuch Verl.

Krippendorf, J. (1995). *Freizeit & Tourismus: eine Einfuhrung in Theorie und Politiks*. Bern: FIF.

Leiper, N. (1981). Towards a cohesive curriculum tourism: The case for a distinct discipline. *Annals of Tourism Research, 8*(1), 69–84. doi:10.1016/0160-7383(81)90068-2

MacCannell, D. (1973). Staged authenticity: Arrangements of social space in tourist settings. *American Journal of Sociology, 79*(3), 589–603. doi:10.1086/225585

MacCannell, D. (1976). *The tourist: A new theory of the leisure class.* Berkeley, CA: University of California Press.

MacCannell, D. (1984). Reconstructed ethnicity tourism and cultural identity in third world communities. *Annals of Tourism Research, 11*(3), 375–391. doi:10.1016/0160-7383(84)90028-8

Maccannell, D. (1988). Turismo e Identidad [Tourism & Identity]. Madrid: Juncar Edition.

MacCannell, D. (1992). *Empty meeting grounds: The tourist papers.* London: Routledge. doi:10.4324/9780203412145

MacCannell, D. (2001). Tourist agency. *Tourist Studies, 1*(1), 23–37. doi:10.1177/146879760100100102

MacCannell, D. (2009). Dmitri Shalin Interview with Dean MacCannell about Erving Goffman entitled "Some of Goffman's Guardedness and Verbal Toughness Was Simply a Way of Giving Himself the Space and Time That He Needed to Do the Work That He Really Loved". *Bios Sociologicus: The Erving Goffman Archives,* 1-37.

MacCannell, D. (2011). *The ethics of sightseeing.* Berkeley, CA: University of California Press. doi:10.1525/california/9780520257825.001.0001

MacCannell, D. (2012). On the ethical stake in tourism research. *Tourism Geographies, 14*(1), 183–194. doi:10.1080/14616688.2012.639387

Mansfield, C. (2005). *Traversing Paris: French Travel Writing Practices in the Late Twentieth Century: An Analysis of the Work of Annie Ernaux, François Maspero and Jean Rolin.* VDM Verlag.

Meethan, K. (2005). Tourism in global society. Place, culture, consumption. *Relaciones Estudios de Historia Social (Madrid, Spain), 26*(103), 270–277.

Mitchell, L. S., & Murphy, P. E. (1991). Geography and tourism. *Annals of Tourism Research, 18*(1), 57–70. doi:10.1016/0160-7383(91)90039-E

Muñoz De Escalona, F. (2014). La Epistemología Y El Turismo (Epistemology and Tourism). *Anuario de Turismo y Sociedad, 15*(1), 187–203.

Pearce, P. L. (1982). *The social psychology of tourist behaviour.* New York: Pergamon Press.

Richter, L. K. (1983). Tourism politics and political science: A case of not so benign neglect. *Annals of Tourism Research, 10*(3), 313–335. doi:10.1016/0160-7383(83)90060-9

Richter, L. K. (1989). *The politics of tourism in Asia.* Honolulu, HI: University of Hawaii Press.

Ritchie, B. W., Burns, P., & Palmer, C. (2005a). Preface. In *Tourism Research Methods, integrating theory with Practice* (pp. ix–x). Wallingford: CABI Publishing. doi:10.1079/9780851999968.0000

Ritchie, B. W., Burns, P., & Palmer, C. (2005b). Introduction: reflection on the Practice Research. In *Tourism Research Methods, integrating theory with Practice* (pp. 1–8). Wallingford: CABI Publishing. doi:10.1079/9780851999968.0001

Ryan, C. (1991). *Recreational tourism: A social science perspective*. London: Routledge.

Ryan, C. (2005). Ethics in Tourism Research: objectivities and Personal Perspectives. In *Tourism Research Methods, integrating theory with Practice* (pp. 9–20). Wallingford: CABI Publishing. doi:10.1079/9780851999968.0009

Salazar, N. B. (2013). *Envisioning Eden: Mobilizing imaginaries in tourism and beyond* (Vol. 31). Oxford, UK: Berghahn Books.

Sheldon, P. J. (1991). An authorship analysis of tourism research. *Annals of Tourism Research, 18*(3), 473–484. doi:10.1016/0160-7383(91)90053-E

Thirkettle, A., & Korstanje, M. E. (2013). Creating a new epistemiology for tourism and hospitality disciplines. *International Journal of Qualitative Research in Services, 1*(1), 13–34. doi:10.1504/IJQRS.2013.054342

Towner, J. (1985). The Grand Tour: A key phase in the history of tourism. *Annals of Tourism Research, 12*(3), 297–333. doi:10.1016/0160-7383(85)90002-7

Tribe, J. (1997a). The indiscipline of tourism. *Annals of Tourism Research, 24*(3), 638–657. doi:10.1016/S0160-7383(97)00020-0

Tribe, J. (1997b). The indiscipline of tourism. *Annals of Tourism Research, 24*(3), 638–657. doi:10.1016/S0160-7383(97)00020-0

Tribe, J. (2005). New tourism research. *Tourism Recreation Research, 30*(2), 5–8. doi:10.1080/02508281.2005.11081468

Tribe, J. (2006). The truth about tourism. *Annals of Tourism Research, 33*(2), 360–381. doi:10.1016/j.annals.2005.11.001

Tribe, J. (2007). Critical tourism: Rules and resistance. In I. Altejevic, A. Pritchard, & N. Morgan (Eds.), *The critical turn in tourism studies: Innovative research methodologies* (pp. 29–40). Oxford, UK: Elsevier. doi:10.1016/B978-0-08-045098-8.50007-6

Tribe, J. (2009). *Philosophical Issues in tourism*. Bristol: Channelview.

Tribe, J. (2010). Tribes, territories and networks in the tourism academy. *Annals of Tourism Research, 37*(1), 7–33. doi:10.1016/j.annals.2009.05.001

Urry, J. (2002). *The Tourist Gaze*. London: Sage.

Urry, J. (2007). *Mobilities*. Cambridge, MA: Polity Press.

Walle, A. H. (1997). Quantitative versus qualitative tourism research. *Annals of Tourism Research, 24*(3), 524–536. doi:10.1016/S0160-7383(96)00055-2

Williams, S., & Lew, A. A. (2014). *Tourism Geography: Critical Understandings of Place, Space and Experience*. Abingdon, UK: Routledge.

Section 3
Global Dynamics in Hospitality

The last section of the edited book consists of four chapters and focuses on current trends in the hospitality industry. The chapters focus on hospitality aspects related to productivity; job satisfaction and turnover intention; physical attractiveness and self-confidence; social responsibility; and hospitality management facilitation.

Chapter 13
The Productivity Challenge Facing the Global Hospitality Industry

Sigbjørn L. Tveteraas
University of Stavanger, Norway

Martin Falk
Austrian Institute of Economic Research, Austria

ABSTRACT

This chapter introduces the global productivity challenge facing the hospitality industry. Global competition in the hospitality industry has led to increasing pressure on profit levels. To leverage profits hotels increasingly are forced to evaluate their operational performance. Specifically, the global productivity challenge entails that hotel managers to a greater extent must encompass a cost minimization perspective. With the integration of productivity-enhancing software systems in hospitality organizations hotels are becoming increasingly knowledge intensive. This chapter discuss measurement issues, productivity analysis and relevant research findings from empirical research. The empirical research on hotel productivity shows that there are many factors to keep in mind for managers that wish to improve productivity in their organizations. Hopefully this chapter will contribute to clear up the meaning of concepts and broadened the perspective of how productivity are related to all parts of the hospitality enterprise.

INTRODUCTION

Around a decade ago, a Scandinavian GM commented that "running hotels is no rocket science, basically it is a business of cleaning rooms." His self-effacing comment poorly reflects the complexity of running hotels in today's business environment. Globalization and tougher competition have forced hotels to become ever more streamlined and efficient in their operations. This has led to an increased attention to measurement and improvement of operational efficiency and productivity. An increasing share of hotels has adopted tools that previously were more associated with industrial processes in terms of optimizing the use of its resources. The objective of this chapter is to discuss the importance

DOI: 10.4018/978-1-5225-0201-2.ch013

of operational productivity in today's competitive environment, which is reflected in the increased usage of measurements like total revenue management (TRM) and gross operating profits per available room (GOPPAR) (Kimes, 2011). Specifically, the objectives of this chapter are threefold. First, to provide arguments that productivity improvements in the hospitality companies are increasingly important for overall performance. Second, to clarify the meaning and measurement of productivity using standard microeconomic theory. Third, to identify sources of productivity differences among hotels based on the findings from a growing literature on productivity in hospitality research. While studies that directly estimate productivity performance in hospitality firms obviously provide relevant evidence, there are also other studies on e.g. human resource (H.R.) issues that provide relevant perspectives on sources of productivity differences.

This chapter starts by putting the spotlight on the global productivity challenge facing hotels. Next, follows a conceptual discussion of productivity measurement used in the hospitality industry. The standard theoretical framework from microeconomics is presented, which provides a conceptual framework that allows us to identify sources of productivity improvements. The discussion of productivity measurements and theory is used as a departing point to look at sources of productivity differences among hotels. Here productivity issues that are relevant for the hospitality industry discussed, relevant productivity measures and methods to estimate hotel productivity are reviewed; empirical findings on productivity in the hospitality industry are presented; and, finally, some managerial implications on optimizing operational performance in hotels are discussed.

THE GLOBAL PRODUCTIVITY CHALLENGE

The main benchmarking performance measure in the hospitality industry is revenue per available room (REVPAR). The overall trend in inflation-adjusted REVPAR following the post financial-crisis period of 2008 have either been flat or negative depending on which region one looks at. For example, REVPAR in Europe and Asia has increased less than the general inflation level based on global hospitality data from Smith Travel Report (STR). This could imply that prices of inputs (e.g., labour, food and energy) have been increasing more than room revenue and, as a result, have put pressure on hotels' profit margins.

To understand why growth in earnings have been flat we need to look at the effects of globalizations. Importantly, the Internet has completely changed the marketing and distribution channels for hotel rooms during the last couple of decades (Buhalis & Law, 2008). On the one hand, the Internet has led to a far wider distribution making it easy for travelers to book rooms worldwide, but, on the other hand, the Internet has also changed the profit distribution in hospitality companies' disfavor. Specifically, the explosion of Internet distribution channels such as Expedia, Tripadvisor and Hotels.com have shifted market power from hotels to online distributors and customers (Lee, Denizci Guillet, & Law, 2013). For example, Expedia ask hotels commission of up 25% of sold room rates. This not only means that revenue growth has stagnated but the share of revenue going to hotel companies is also decreasing putting hotels' earnings under pressure. Thus, the market power issue in hospitality has widened from the typical worry about, say, tour operators negotiating power in relation to contracting hotel capacity (Tveteraas, Asche, & Lien, 2014), to a much wider impact of online distribution channels. Furthermore, the increased transparency of hotel pricing through the Internet has made room pricing more efficient due to consumers' exploitation of arbitrage opportunities.

An implication of these changes in the hotel marketplace is that fewer smart pricing decisions remain. Thus, while yesterday's challenge in the hotel industry to a larger degree was linked to revenue management (i.e., how to sell the right room to the right customer at the right price), the current challenge to a greater extent encompasses strategic questions like the marketing mix (i.e., how we sell), the product mix (i.e., what we sell) and the input mix (i.e., how we deliver our services) (Kimes, 2011). In other words, to leverage profits hotels increasingly are forced to evaluate their overall value proposition and their operational performance. This is also noted by Cullen and Helsel (2010) who observes that: "Over the last several years, the industry has recognized that revenue management can no longer be a tactical approach to room and pricing management only. With technological and management support, revenue management must be and is being integrated into all aspects of hotel marketing and operational strategies ... In addition to total revenue contributions, revenue management will examine *various costs and ensure the cost factors are taken into consideration allowing the focus to be on profit and not just revenue.*" [Our italics].

The view expressed by Cullen and Helsel (2010) contrasts the traditional strong focus on REVPAR in the hospitality industry. Singh and Schmidgall (2002) suggest that the use and reliance on revenue management programs could be an explanation of REVPAR's perceived importance. Other explanations for its popularity could be easy availability (it only requires data on total room revenue and number of available rooms), easy-to-interpret, and a presumed strong correlation with profits. While the latter is true, it is also important to understand that there are other factors that influence profitability (O'neill & Mattila, 2006). This is also implied by a US study that shows that REVPAR have little predictive power of stock values of hospitality companies (J. Chen, Koh, & Lee, 2011). The traditional marketing-perspective-bias suggests that the hospitality industry has paid more attention to sales at the expense of the operational side and costs (Baker & Riley, 1994; Kimes, 2011; Singh & Schmidgall, 2002). These skewed incentives have caused many hotels to operate on sub-efficient productivity levels.

To exemplify differences in operational performance across hotels, we can look Figure 1. Figure 1a) shows the relationship between REVPAR and number of sold rooms per work hour – a productivity measure – for 131 hotels in Scandinavia belonging to three different chains in 2013. The regression line shows a modest positive relationship between REVPAR and productivity. The positive association between the two variables could be that higher demand (i.e., more hotel guests) leads to more efficient use of labour force. However, optimization of labour scheduling is about minimizing the cost of labour and other inputs, while maintaining the desired service level. An important component to achieve this is by scheduling work hours according to the level of demand. If a hotel is unable to plan well its labour scheduling one will observe over- and understaffing more frequently. This is captured in figure 1b) where the horizontal axis now is the standard deviation of number of sold rooms per work hour. This measure is an indicator of mismatch between demand level and staffing level. As Figure 1b) shows there is a negative association between REVPAR and the standard deviation of the staffing level. The highest REVPAR is obtained by having relatively consisting level in the sales/staffing ratio, and conversely REVPAR tends to be lower when the sales/staffing ratio varies a lot. This gives one illustration of the importance of staff scheduling for hotel performance.

Many hotels now try to optimize all parts of its operations from housekeeping, food menus, procurement, employees and so forth. Accordingly, stronger competition has contributed to shift the focus from revenue per available room (REVPAR) to gross operation profits per available room (GOPPAR) as the most important performance indicator (Kimes, 2011). However, even among hotels that have adopted productivity enhancing software systems there sometimes appears to be confusion and disagreement over what productivity is and what these systems try to do. This is not surprising as there appears to be confusion of what are the appropriate productivity measurements in the hospitality industry (Sigala,

Figure 1. a) Boxplot of REVPAR and average number of sold rooms per work hour and b) REVPAR and st.dev. of number of sold rooms per work hour (d2o)

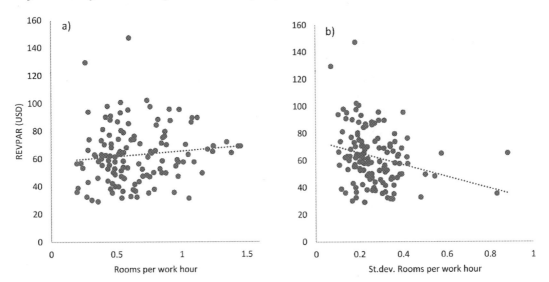

Jones, Lockwood, & Airey, 2005). Traditionally, the hospitality industry has paid more attention to systematic measurement of revenue than of productivity, as evident from benchmarking activity of hotels performance (Singh & Schmidgall, 2002). The inadequate attention given to productivity measurements makes it important to first clarify the productivity concept. This follows in the next section, which also provides an overview of some relevant productivity measures in the hospitality industry and how these can be used to evaluate hotel performance.

PRODUCTIVITY MEASUREMENT IN HOSPITALITY

Defining Productivity

It is challenging to define productivity in a hospitality context where output can be intangible and difficult to measure. Productivity is usually defined as the ratio of outputs over inputs (i.e., productivity = outputs/inputs). This definition has a clear meaning in the goods-producing-industries where the outputs are tangible. However, there are different perceptions of what productivity means in the context of the hospitality industry. One reason is the intangible nature of services where aspects like quality and guest satisfaction are important. No services deliveries are exactly alike because production and consumption occur in the same moment and, consequently, different people will experience the service exchange differently (Sigala et al., 2005). Moreover, the service level differ depending on the customer segments that a hotel targets, as reflected by the star rating system. The fact that service delivery is heterogonous complicates measurement of output, especially when comparing different hotels (Harnisch, 2008).

These complications is no reason why usual definitions of productivity are not applicable in the hospitality industry. A key aspect to take into consideration when measuring hotel productivity are quality differences. Productivity is therefore defined here as a ratio between input and output *at a given quality level*. Productivity grows when the ratio increases, since it entails that one obtain relatively more output per unit of input. This definition is logical and clean cut. In other words, we say that productivity should be measured at a same level of service quality. This does not pose any challenge when a hotel benchmarks its operational productivity with its own past performance. Comparison of operational productivity across different hotels requires some type of control for the quality differences among those hotels. This is an issue we will return to later.

Operating Ratios

When operationalizing the basic productivity definition above another complication that arise is choice of inputs and outputs (Andersson, 1996). In hospitality firms, the same inputs often serve to produce different outputs. For example, reception staff will attend the regular room guests in addition to daytime conference visitors. Overnight guests and daytime visitors for a conference can be viewed as two different markets served and, consequently, two different outputs. The hospitality industry's tradition for dealing with this challenge of definition and measurement is to use operating ratios that covers many different aspects of operations. For example, there is an operating ratio food cost percentage that is calculated as food cost divided by food sales. Another operating ratio is labour cost percentage, which is calculated as labour cost divided by total revenue. Furthermore, the operating ratios are broken down on department levels.

These operating ratios can be viewed as inverted productivity measures, since higher values are associated with slack in productivity. There are several more such operating ratios that hotels use to measure productivity. Normally each department in the hotel will have its own operating ratios. For example cost of F&B staff could be compared to food sales, while the front desk is compared to the number of check-ins and check-outs. One can also have ratio for food costs (excluding staff costs) in comparios to food sales. However, ratios involving the use of labour is usually the most important operating ratios because hotels are labour intensive and, consequently, account for a large share of operational costs.

The operating ratios are often measured in monetary in terms, while the traditional or textbook usage of productivity is the number of physical outputs over the physical inputs. For example, why not measure the number of guests hotels handle as output over the number of work hours as input? Such a productivity measurement can be used – and are also used - but one argument for using monetary-based productivity measures is the quality aspect of service deliveries. Hotel guests will usually pay more for a room in five star hotel compared to a three star hotel because they receive higher service level. Thus, by measuring output by revenue one also obtains a measure of the service level. Therefore even if number of sold rooms are used in productivity measurement, it also makes sense to treat as an output room revenue. Dollar sales per employee is also used as productivity measure for studies in other industries (Guthrie, 2001).

Although operating ratios have a long history in hospitality operations, this does not mean that hotels traditionally have applied sophisticated systems for optimizing the use of its staff and other resources. Adopting systems for optimizing productivity like those used in goods-producing-industries requires a systematic and integrated approach. Measurement of operating ratios is an important first step, but the next step is to obtain a proper understanding of how inputs and outputs are related to each. For example, Gary M. Thompson and Goodale (2006) show that the number of employee hours and a desired service-level of output can be nonlinear. Understanding these types of relationships will allow management to apply and interpret the performance measures for improving productivity. This chapter will discuss several aspects in relation hotel productivity and will refer to some relevant research findings. First, however, the main theoretical and methodological framework for analyzing productivity is introduced. This will give a better understanding of what is being measured when we study productivity.

ANALYSING SOURCES OF PRODUCTIVITY DIFFERENCES

Technical Efficiency

The goal of productivity measurements is ultimately to measure *efficiency*. According to the X-inefficiency theory, technical efficiency refers to "the ability to avoid waste, either by producing as much output as technology and input usage allow or by using as little input as required by technology and production function" ((Fried, Lovell, & Schmidt, 2008), p. 5).

Efficiency levels can be influenced by differences in production technology (e.g. more or less capital intensive hotels); differences in the scale of operations (e.g. hotel chain vs independent hotel or e.g. small hotel vs large hotel); differences in operating efficiency (e.g., how efficient is labour use compared to similar hotels); differences in the operating environment in which production occurs (e.g. urban vs. rural, seasonality etc.). For example, A. G. Assaf and Barros (2013) find that national and international hotel chains are more efficient than independent hotels, indicating that one determinant of efficiency in hospitality is scale of operations. This suggests that chains are able to centralize some functions that leads to efficiency gains.

Technical efficiency is a useful concept that refers to the ability to avoid waste either by producing as much output as technology and input usage allow or by using as little input as required by technology and output production. Figure 2 shows a frontier production function that shows the maximum amount of output for different levels of input. Hotels that operate with waste (i.e., on an inefficient level) will be located below the production frontier, for example, as illustrated with the point (y^A, x^A). With the x^A input level it is possible to produce more output than y^A, and the difference from (y^A, x^A) to the production frontier represents waste. This model framework is the theoretical "workhorse" of productivity estimations and has been widely used in applied production analysis (Daraio & Simar, 2007; Greene, 1997).

Figure 2. The production frontier model

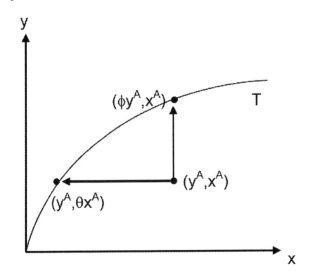

Methods for Productivity Estimation

Productivity research in hospitality received sparse attention before the turn of the millennium, but thereafter many studies on efficiency in hotels have appeared. As argued earlier in this chapter, a high level of efficiency and productivity is a key priority for growth and survival of hospitality enterprises in the current competitive climate. Now there are several studies that have investigated the level of efficiency and productivity of hotels (R. Anderson, Lewis, & Parker, 2000; R. I. Anderson, Fish, Xia, & Michello, 1999; A. Assaf, Barros, & Josiassen, 2010; A. G. Assaf & Josiassen, 2015; Barros, 2005; C.-F. Chen, 2007; Chiang, Tsai, & Wang, 2004; J.-L. Hu, Chiu, Shieh, & Huang, 2010; Hwang & Chang, 2003; Johns, Howcroft, & Drake, 1997; Manasakis, Apostolakis, & Datseris, 2013; Morey & Dittman, 1995; Sigala, 2003; Tveteraas, Roll, Jørgensen, & Tveterås, 2015). These models will typically have one or more outputs that are dependent on usually a number of different inputs. The quality aspect of hotels can be controlled for by using service level indicators such as number of hotel stars as an explanatory variable. Alternatively, the quality aspect can be capture by using output measurements that reflect the service level. For example, REVPAR will usually be higher in full-service hotels compared to limited-service hotels. However, there is no standard model formulation and specification for estimating hospitality, and each study will usually have some different variables or measurements compared to the others.

The type of estimation method also differs, mainly between parametric techniques represented by econometric stochastic frontier models or non-parametric techniques like data envelopment analysis (DEA). The empirical hospitality productivity literature leans more heavily towards using non-parametric methods such as data envelopment analysis (DEA) and the free disposal hull (FDH) method (A. Assaf et al., 2010; Hwang & Chang, 2003). The non-parametric methods have been criticized by econometricians for being extremely sensitive to outliers and measurement error. An advantage with stochastic front analysis model compared to DEA is that it allows stastistical tests of the functional form and about the importance of different factors (Barros, 2006). However, one of the main advantages of DEA is its ability to handle multiple outputs, when evaluating productivity. Recently, the so-called partial frontier approaches have been introduced that are less sensitive to few dominant observations (Cazals, Florens, & Simar, 2002). In particular, the partial frontier method is a generalization of the free disposal hull (FDH) method by allowing super efficient observations to be located outside the production frontier and thereby accounting for possible measurement error. As we can see, each approach has its advantages and disadvantages. Summarized by A. G. Assaf and Josiassen (2015): "The nonparametric approach is more flexible in the sense that it does not require a specification of a functional form for the relationship between inputs and outputs. Its main limitation, however, is that it does not allow for random error. Hence, it is highly sensitive to noise in the data. The parametric approach, on the other hand, includes a random error, but imposes so much structure on the functional form [of the production function]".

In their meta-analysis of frontier studies covering the hospitality industry A. G. Assaf and Josiassen (2015) noted that the approach to studying productivity in this sector appeared more divergent compared to that of other industrial sectors. They noted that the factors used to explain productivity varies substantially from study to study, which raises questions about what is the right model specification. This led them to advice productivity researcher to choose a more theory-driven approach to model formulation, taking into account the large body of research on hospitality and tourism productivity drivers.

Another issue they raised in relation to econometric stochastic frontier approach is that there seems to be little thought about the functional form used. Specifically, they noted that many times constant returns to scale where assumed, because of using the Cobb-Douglas production function. The constant-returns to scale assumption is very restrictive as it assumes that all hotels in the sample operate at an optimal scale. A final reservation of A. G. Assaf and Josiassen (2015) that is mentioned here is that there seems to be little thought about whether and input orientation (i.e., minimizing input usage for a given output level) or output orientation (i.e., maximizing output for a given input level) should be used. Instead, the choice of orientation appears to be very much data-driven, that is, given by the availability of data. These latter comments points to some challenges in productivity estimation for future researchers. This chapter will not discuss these methodological concerns further. Instead, the chapter now turns the attention to the findings in the empirical studies on productivity with the objective of putting the spotlight on sources of productivity differences in the hospitality sector.

SOURCES OF PRODUCTIVITY DIFFERENCES

Staff Management and Productivity

Hotels are labour intensive, which means that staff productivity is key when evaluating operational productivity. Several studies have pointed out that hotel management do not control all factors that affect staff productivity (Barros, 2005; Sigala, 2004). For example, much of the variation in demand is outside the control of a hotel GM. Nonetheless, hotels control the denominator of the productivity ratio, staff hours (or cost). By forecasting demand variability and planning staffing levels accordingly hotels can maintain productivity at a relatively steady level, even if the nominator – room sales - changes. In this way, hotel management hold an important key to staff productivity.

This does not mean that guests cannot be catered by different levels of staffing. Consequently, there need not be a high correlation between inputs and outputs if GMs are not actively managing this ratio. Poor planning of staffing schedule with respect to anticipated changes in demand will lower the correlation between sales and labour hours, everything else equal. On the one hand, when staffing levels are very low this will generate waiting times for serving guests and could lead to unsatisfied customers. On the other, a high staffing level relative to number of sold rooms will tend to decrease productivity. Moreover, a high staffing level might even affect the service level negatively if it influence employee effort (Tan & Netessine, 2014). Thus, planning of staffing levels to avoid under- or overstaffing should be a goal of hotel manager. In addition, it seems likely that a more predictable work schedule would be a plus for its employees. A study from Israel suggests that while hotels are willing to hire and fire according to seasonal adjustments, they are unwilling or unable to fully synchronize staffing to demand (Krakover, 2000). However, there are systematic differences with an urban area such a Tel Aviv having a larger degree of adjustment in staffing levels.

Lewis and McCann (2004) find that staff related issues are the most frequent cause of service failure in hotels. Service failures include issues such as inefficient staff, unfriendly or unhelpful receptionists, and that staff would not put themselves out to help. Several other service failures that were considered serious are also related to staffing issues such as slow check-in check-out, slow restaurant service, and room not clean. Some of these service failures are affected by staff level and, as such, shows the importance of planning for the right number of staff. However, it also shows that productivity depends on both the attitude and the aptitude of staff. This means that not only number of work hours are important but also staff training.

The topic of training is also relevant in the measure of productivity, because hotels will normally account for both productive and nonproductive hours. Nonproductive hours include those hours where staff receive training. A relevant question therefore is what to do with these hours in productivity measurement. Harnisch (2008) argues that it makes sense to include hours of training as labour cost when measuring productivity. Although this will drag down productivity in the short run, the long run yield of training could be great on revenue. This perspective also makes sense due to the importance of service quality and service failures on guest satisfaction (Lewis & McCann, 2004). For example, in a survey and interview of managers in 55 hotels in Northern Cyprus, the five most important factors for productivity were identified as staff recruitment, staff training, customer expectations, multi-skill training programmes and the role of management (Kilic & Okumus, 2005). This study is interesting in that unlike the more quantitative studies, it shows that managers perceive human factors to be at the heart of productivity performance.

Another key issue relating to staff productivity in the hospitality industry is employee turnover. The industry is known to have a high turnover rate of employees and one suspects this also affects labour productivity negatively (Tracey & Hinkin, 2008). To the degree that employee turnover negatively affects hotel performance it also means that human resource management (HRM) is important for maintaining productivity. Cho, Woods, Jang, and Erdem (2006) tested if several different HRM practices had any impact on labour productivity in hotels, but did not find any significant statistical relationships. Chand (2010), however, found that HRM practices can improve the service quality offered by hotels.

It has already been pointed out that training of hotel employees can be positive for productivity, but another question is how productivity is affected by the level of education of its employees. Marchante and Ortega (2012) offer some insight on this topic with evidence from the Spanish hotel industry. They find that that a mismatch between the employees' education levels and the education required for a job can explain differences in labour productivity. Employees with a suitable education are more efficient than those whose education is not matched to the job. Also, undereducated employees are less efficient than overeducated ones. Finally, Marchante and Ortega (2012) also found evidence that hotel employees with an average tenure of more than ten years have superior performance in terms of labor productivity. This latter result support the notion that high employee turnover is bad for productivity in hospitality.

Non-Staff Issues That Affect Labour Productivity

The previous section discussed the importance of planning staffing level and staff training in relation to productivity. Next this chapter turn to other relevant factors that influence labour productivity. In the short run, hotels will exert little influence over many of these factors. Based on earlier studies we can list some of the most important factors assumed to influence productivity (Barros, 2005; B. A. Hu & Cai, 2004; Sigala, 2004):

- Location – rural, city centre, suburban.
- Property size.
- Hotel design – old / new.
- Ownership – independent or chain.
- Business format – owned, franchised.
- Demand variability.
- Level of repeat custom.

- Average length of stay.
- Market segments served.
- Distribution channels.
- Proportion of part-time staff.
- Manager capabilities.

Location is key to performance in hospitality and with the increasing urbanization trend globally it is also clear that where hotels locate will not only influence revenue (Falk & Hagsten, 2015), but also staff productivity in terms of access to a larger pool of qualified personnel. Typically, hotels situated in urban districts and that are part of a chain will have access to a large pool of employees and a greater flexibility in adjusting staff level (Riley, 1990).

However, maybe the most important non-staff factor for productivity is overall demand variability. Hotels can influence demand through marketing strategies and revenue management, but there will be seasonal factors (Fernández-Morales & Mayorga-Toledano, 2008), business cycles (Guizzardi & Mazzocchi, 2010) and other events of economic significance (Crotts & Mazanec, 2013) of which the hotel exert little influence and that affect the occupancy rate and revenue. Demand is often seasonal, where there are certain months of the year where more guests arrives than others and this pattern will differ among markets (Fernández-Morales & Mayorga-Toledano, 2008). Also there can be certain weekdays where there are more business than others. Hotels geared towards business travelers will usually receive more guests on weekdays, while hotels that receives more leisure travelers will typically have higher occupancy in weekends. If staffing level during the seven weekdays is constant productivity will become higher during either weekdays or weekends depending on which of the two descriptions apply. In relation to the productivity challenge, this creates another distinction for the hospitality industry compared to that of traditional goods-producing industries; while productivity in the latter is usually about maximizing the output for a given level of input, the former is more about adjusting the input level to the output level (i.e., demand level). That is, hotels need to adjust the staffing level and food purchases according to the number and type of guests visiting.

In their study, Jones and Siag (2009) tests if housekeeping productivity is affected by size, age, location (urban vs. non-urban), service level (full size vs. limited size service level) and demand variability of 48 UK hotels. They do not find any difference in productivity levels among the hotels associated with differences in any these factors. This indicates that hotels exert more influence on the productivity level than what we sometimes are lead to believe. This is also in line with the comment we made earlier that hotels are in control of the denominator of the productivity ratio. The study of Jones and Siag (2009) uses rooms cleaned per housekeeping work hour as productivity measurement, implying that this study only gives a partial look at productivity. As such, the study suggests that cleaning rooms is a fixed proportions technology with little flexibility in adjusting effort.

ICT and Quality Management

The hospitality industry is increasingly adopting integrated systems to make operations more efficient. Many hotels use information and communications technology (ICT) tools that not only optimize pricing and booking but also contributes to optimize the use of inputs, such as labour and food. This can be observed as hotels introduce new software systems that contain tools for optimizing these parts of operations. For example, a dedicated distributor lists 243 software systems in the marketplace aimed at different parts of hotel management (Capterra, n.d.). The purpose of introducing these kinds of tools and systems is to increase productivity and minimize costs. This is also based on an important realization that profits are not solely reliant on the demand level, but that hotels in fact control many of the factors influencing the productivity of its employees and thereby can leverage profits (Jones & Siag, 2009). For example, Tan and Netessine (2014) found that when a restaurant chain introduced labour scheduling software the chain could reduce staffing level, significantly increase sales and lower labour costs.

This does not imply that the issue of labour productivity can be reduced to a question about introducing ICT management tools. Li (2014) finds that introduction of ICT systems does not generally improve hotel staff productivity. A drawback with his study is that it does not investigate ICT systems which particular objective is to optimize staffing, but instead look at general usage of ICT systems in hotels. However, a successful implementation of new productivity systems depend on that the entire organization understands what are the objectives and measurements of productivity (Harnisch, 2008). This again points to the importance of training.

Other studies have expanded the focus to look at the effect of hotel quality management programs on productivity (Benavides-Chicón & Ortega, 2014; Skalpe & Sandvik, 2002). Benavides-Chicón and Ortega (2014) found that increased investments in total quality management (TQM) systems improved productivity in Spanish hotels. This indicates that implementation of systems that require more organizational discipline and planning is good for productivity. Further findings from Spain suggests that only the standards and quality models specific to the hotel industry increase labour productivity and only when these are fully implemented (Sanchez-Ollero, García Pozo, Marchante-Lara, Okumus, & Okumus, 2015). This shows the importance of choosing relevant productivity measures and that the organization is fully immersed in those systems that are implemented.

MANAGERIAL IMPLICATIONS

The discussion of hotel productivity in this chapter shows that there are many factors to keep in mind, from measurement and analysis to the implementation of productivity systems. As a result, hotel management needs to have their strategic objectives clear before adopting productivity systems. It is also important that the employees understands productivity and what one tries to achieve when introducing such systems (Harnisch, 2008). In the end, the employees are the key to the level of service quality and productivity of a hotel property.

The basis of all productivity improvements is based on systematic measurement of productivity performance and requirements. A staff scheduling system needs to have imbedded how to interpret productivity measurements and how to act on that information. For example, the main contribution of specialized software systems that assist in optimizing work schedules and food purchases is to link room demand forecasts with resource requirements. These new systems for improved productivity performance imply that hospitality organizations are becoming increasingly knowledge intensive. In principle, this is not any different from, say, a budgeting system, which is rendered useless unless the resource constraints imposed by those budgets are actually upheld. Likewise, the introduction of labour scheduling system is only useful insofar that the organization adapts to its requirements and recommendations. This is no easy task but requires long-term planning and investment in relevant competencies and changes to operational routines.

As Ernst, Jiang, Krishnamoorthy, and Sier (2004) put it: "It is extremely difficult to find good solutions to these highly constrained and complex [labour scheduling] problems and even more difficult to determine optimal solutions that minimize costs, meet employee preferences, distribute shifts equitably among employees and satisfy all the workplace constraints." Although their study reviewed general labour scheduling problems across industries, these challenges are also present specifically in the hospitality industry. In a series of four papers Gary Thompson outline the challenges for hotelier managers that want to optimize labour scheduling (Gary M Thompson, 1998a, 1998b, 1999a, 1999b). These involve forecasting demand, knowing how many on-duty employees to schedule, and developing a labour schedule. Finally, after all the planning have been done, hotel managers need to deal with realtime problems in service delivery, because of mismatch between the demand that was planned for and the one that actually materialized itself. And important insight from Gary M Thompson (1999a) is that it need not be inconsistent to satisfy employee preferences for work schedule and delivering the service efficiently. This is an important motivator for managers to invest in capacitation of developing efficient labour scheduling schemes.

The non-staff related productivity is to a larger degree related to investments decisions – the how and where and for whom hotels are built. Modern hotels are normally designed to be more streamlined in terms of employing its staff and other resources in a more efficient way. More generally, this discussion implies that the productivity aspect is important to incorporate when planning new hotels.

CONCLUDING REMARKS

The hospitality industry has become increasingly aware of the productivity challenge it is facing. The introduction of *total revenue management* reflects this insight, as it encompass all factors that affect profits, including operational costs (Cullen & Helsel, 2010). Total revenue management reflects a partial shift in focus from tactical pricing to issues related to strategic pricing and operational efficiency. This requires that the industry becomes increasingly knowledgeable of productivity and all its relevant aspects.

Hopefully this chapter have contributed to clear up the meaning and concepts productivity and broadened the perspective of how productivity are related to all parts of the hospitality enterprise. An important recommendation for future research is to link human resources factors such as motivation, abilities, training and labour turnover with the factual productivity and effiency levels. This will give hotel managers a firmer grip on the types of investments in its employees and what types of management styles and labour scheduling systems are compatible with high productivity levels.

REFERENCES

Anderson, R., Lewis, D., & Parker, M. (2000). Hotel industry efficiency: An advanced linear programming examination. *American Business Review, 18*(1), 40–48.

Anderson, R. I., Fish, M., Xia, Y., & Michello, F. (1999). Measuring efficiency in the hotel industry: A stochastic frontier approach. *Hospital Management, 18*(1), 45–57. doi:10.1016/S0278-4319(98)00046-2

Andersson, T. (1996). *Traditional key ratio analysis versus data envelopment analysis: a comparison of various measurements of productivity and efficiency in restaurants.* London: Cassell.

Assaf, A., Barros, C. P., & Josiassen, A. (2010). Hotel efficiency: A bootstrapped metafrontier approach. *International Journal of Hospitality Management, 29*(3), 468–475. doi:10.1016/j.ijhm.2009.10.020

Assaf, A. G., & Barros, C. P. (2013). A global benchmarking of the hotel industry. *Tourism Economics, 19*(4), 811–821. doi:10.5367/te.2013.0230

Assaf, A. G., & Josiassen, A. (2015). Frontier Analysis: A State-of-the-Art Review and Meta-Analysis. *Journal of Travel Research*. doi:10.1177/0047287515569776

Baker, M., & Riley, M. (1994). New perspectives on productivity in hotels: Some advances and new directions. *International Journal of Hospitality Management, 13*(4), 297–311. doi:10.1016/0278-4319(94)90068-X

Barros, C. P. (2005). Measuring efficiency in the hotel sector. *Annals of Tourism Research, 32*(2), 456–477. doi:10.1016/j.annals.2004.07.011

Benavides-Chicón, C. G., & Ortega, B. (2014). The impact of quality management on productivity in the hospitality sector. *International Journal of Hospitality Management, 42*(0), 165–173. doi:10.1016/j.ijhm.2014.07.004

Buhalis, D., & Law, R. (2008). Progress in information technology and tourism management: 20 years on and 10 years after the Internet—The state of eTourism research. *Tourism Management, 29*(4), 609–623. doi:10.1016/j.tourman.2008.01.005

Capterra. (n.d.). *Best Hospitality Property Management*. Retrieved March 25, 2015, from http://www.capterra.com/hospitality-property-management-software/

Cazals, C., Florens, J.-P., & Simar, L. (2002). Nonparametric frontier estimation: A robust approach. *Journal of Econometrics, 106*(1), 1–25. doi:10.1016/S0304-4076(01)00080-X

Chand, M. (2010). The impact of HRM practices on service quality, customer satisfaction and performance in the Indian hotel industry. *International Journal of Human Resource Management, 21*(4), 551–566. doi:10.1080/09585191003612059

Chen, C.-F. (2007). Applying the stochastic frontier approach to measure hotel managerial efficiency in Taiwan. *Tourism Management, 28*(3), 696–702. doi:10.1016/j.tourman.2006.04.023

Chen, J., Koh, Y., & Lee, S. (2011). Does the Market Care About RevPAR? A Case Study of Five Large U.S. Lodging Chains. *Journal of Hospitality & Tourism Research (Washington, D.C.), 35*(2), 258–273. doi:10.1177/1096348010384875

Chiang, W., Tsai, H., & Wang, L. (2004). A DEA evaluation of Taipei hotels. *Annals of Tourism Research, 31*(3), 712–715. doi:10.1016/j.annals.2003.11.001

Cho, S., Woods, R. H., Jang, S., & Erdem, M. (2006). Measuring the impact of human resource management practices on hospitality firms' performances. *International Journal of Hospitality Management, 25*(2), 262–277. doi:10.1016/j.ijhm.2005.04.001

Crotts, J. C., & Mazanec, J. A. (2013). Diagnosing the impact of an event on hotel demand: The case of the BP oil spill. *Tourism Management Perspectives, 8*, 60–67. doi:10.1016/j.tmp.2013.07.002

Cullen, K., & Helsel, C. (2010). *The Evolving Dynamics of Revenue Management. In Advanced Robust and Nonparametric Methods in Efficiency Analysis: Methodology and Applications* (Vol. 4). Springer Science & Business Media.

Ernst, A. T., Jiang, H., Krishnamoorthy, M., & Sier, D. (2004). Staff scheduling and rostering: A review of applications, methods and models. *European Journal of Operational Research, 153*(1), 3–27. doi:10.1016/S0377-2217(03)00095-X

Falk, M., & Hagsten, E. (2015). Modelling growth and revenue for Swedish hotel establishments. *International Journal of Hospitality Management, 45*, 59–68. doi:10.1016/j.ijhm.2014.11.009

Fernández-Morales, A., & Mayorga-Toledano, M. C. (2008). Seasonal concentration of the hotel demand in Costa del Sol: A decomposition by nationalities. *Tourism Management, 29*(5), 940–949. doi:10.1016/j.tourman.2007.11.003

Fried, H. O., Lovell, C. K., & Schmidt, S. S. (2008). *The measurement of productive efficiency and productivity growth.* Oxford University Press. doi:10.1093/acprof:oso/9780195183528.001.0001

Greene, W. H. (1997). Frontier production functions. Handbook of applied econometrics, 2, 81-166.

Guizzardi, A., & Mazzocchi, M. (2010). Tourism demand for Italy and the business cycle. *Tourism Management, 31*(3), 367–377. doi:10.1016/j.tourman.2009.03.017

Guthrie, J. P. (2001). High-involvement work practices, turnover, and productivity: Evidence from New Zealand. *Academy of Management Journal, 44*(1), 180–190. doi:10.2307/3069345

Harnisch, O. (2008). Productivity Management in the Hospitality Industry. *Hospitalitynet.org.* Retrieved from http://www.hospitalitynet.org/news/4035884.html

Hu, B. A., & Cai, L. A. (2004). Hotel labor productivity assessment: A data envelopment analysis. *Journal of Travel & Tourism Marketing, 16*(2-3), 27–38. doi:10.1300/J073v16n02_03

Hu, J.-L., Chiu, C.-N., Shieh, H.-S., & Huang, C.-H. (2010). A stochastic cost efficiency analysis of international tourist hotels in Taiwan. *International Journal of Hospitality Management, 29*(1), 99–107. doi:10.1016/j.ijhm.2009.06.005

Hwang, S., & Chang, T. (2003). Using data envelopment analysis to measure hotel managerial efficiency change in Taiwan. *Tourism Management, 24*(4), 357–369. doi:10.1016/S0261-5177(02)00112-7

Johns, N., Howcroft, B., & Drake, L. (1997). The use of data envelopment analysis to monitor hotel productivity. *Progress in Tourism and Hospitality Research, 3*(2), 119–127. doi:10.1002/(SICI)1099-1603(199706)3:2<119::AID-PTH74>3.0.CO;2-2

Jones, P., & Siag, A. (2009). A re-examination of the factors that influence productivity in hotels: A study of the housekeeping function. *Tourism and Hospitality Research, 9*(3), 224–234. doi:10.1057/thr.2009.11

Kilic, H., & Okumus, F. (2005). Factors influencing productivity in small island hotels: Evidence from Northern Cyprus. *International Journal of Contemporary Hospitality Management, 17*(4), 315–331. doi:10.1108/09596110510597589

Kimes, S. E. (2011). The future of hotel revenue management. *Journal of Revenue and Pricing Management, 10*(1), 6272. doi:10.1057/rpm.2010.47

Krakover, S. (2000). Partitioning seasonal employment in the hospitality industry. *Tourism Management, 21*(5), 461–471. doi:10.1016/S0261-5177(99)00101-6

Lee, H. A., Denizci Guillet, B., & Law, R. (2013). An Examination of the Relationship between Online Travel Agents and Hotels: A Case Study of Choice Hotels International and Expedia.com. *Cornell Hospitality Quarterly, 54*(1), 95–107. doi:10.1177/1938965512454218

Lewis, B. R., & McCann, P. (2004). Service failure and recovery: Evidence from the hotel industry. *International Journal of Contemporary Hospitality Management, 16*(1), 6–17. doi:10.1108/09596110410516516

Li, X. (2014). An analysis of labour productivity growth in the Canadian tourism/hospitality industry. *Anatolia, 25*(3), 374–386. doi:10.1080/13032917.2014.882850

Manasakis, C., Apostolakis, A., & Datseris, G. (2013). Using data envelopment analysis to measure hotel efficiency in Crete. *International Journal of Contemporary Hospitality Management, 25*(4), 510–535. doi:10.1108/09596111311322907

Marchante, A. J., & Ortega, B. (2012). Human Capital and Labor Productivity: A Study for the Hotel Industry. *Cornell Hospitality Quarterly, 53*(1), 20–30. doi:10.1177/1938965511427698

Morey, D., & Dittman, D. (1995). Evaluating a hotel's GM performance: A case study in benchmarking. *The Cornell Hotel and Restaurant Administration Quarterly, 36*(5), 30–35.

O'neill, J. W., & Mattila, A. S. (2006). Strategic Hotel Development and Positioning The Effects of Revenue Drivers on Profitability. *The Cornell Hotel and Restaurant Administration Quarterly, 47*(2), 146–154. doi:10.1177/0010880405281519

Riley, M. (1990). The labour retention strategies of UK hotel managers. *Service Industries Journal, 10*(3), 614–618. doi:10.1080/02642069000000063

Sanchez-Ollero, J. L., García Pozo, A., Marchante-Lara, M., Okumus, F., & Okumus, F. (2015). Measuring the effects of quality certification on labour productivity: An analysis of the hospitality sector. *International Journal of Contemporary Hospitality Management, 27*(6), 1100–1116. doi:10.1108/IJCHM-02-2014-0057

Sigala, M. (2003). The information and communication technologies productivity impact on the UK hotel sector. *International Journal of Operations & Production Management, 23*(10), 1224–1245. doi:10.1108/01443570310496643

Sigala, M. (2004). Using data envelopment analysis for measuring and benchmarking productivity in the hotel sector. *Journal of Travel & Tourism Marketing, 16*(2-3), 39–60. doi:10.1300/J073v16n02_04

Sigala, M., Jones, P., Lockwood, A., & Airey, D. (2005). Productivity in hotels: A stepwise data envelopment analysis of hotels' rooms division processes. *Service Industries Journal, 25*(1), 61–81. doi:10.1080/0264206042000302414

Singh, A., & Schmidgall, R. S. (2002). Analysis of financial ratios commonly used by US lodging financial executives. *Journal of Retail & Leisure Property, 2*(3), 201–213. doi:10.1057/palgrave.rlp.5090210

Skalpe, O., & Sandvik, K. (2002). The economics of quality in the hotel business. *Tourism Economics, 8*(4), 361–376. doi:10.5367/000000002101298188

Tan, T. F., & Netessine, S. (2014). When Does the Devil Make Work? An Empirical Study of the Impact of Workload on Worker Productivity. *Management Science, 60*(6), 1574–1593. doi:10.1287/mnsc.2014.1950

Thompson, G. M. (1998a). Labor scheduling, part 1: Forecasting demand. *The Cornell Hotel and Restaurant Administration Quarterly, 39*(5), 22–31. doi:10.1177/001088049803900507

Thompson, G. M. (1998b). Labor scheduling, Part 2: Knowing how many on-duty employees to schedule. *The Cornell Hotel and Restaurant Administration Quarterly, 39*(6), 26–37. Retrieved from http://cqx.sagepub.com/content/39/6/26

Thompson, G. M. (1999a). Labor Scheduling, Part 3: Developing a workforce schedule. *The Cornell Hotel and Restaurant Administration Quarterly, 40*(1), 86–94. doi:10.1016/S0010-8804(99)80019-6

Thompson, G. M. (1999b). Labor Scheduling, Part 4: Controlling workforce schedules in real time. *The Cornell Hotel and Restaurant Administration Quarterly, 40*(3), 85–96.

Thompson, G. M., & Goodale, J. C. (2006). Variable employee productivity in workforce scheduling. *European Journal of Operational Research, 170*(2), 376–390. doi:10.1016/j.ejor.2004.03.048

Tracey, J. B., & Hinkin, T. R. (2008). Contextual factors and cost profiles associated with employee turnover. *Cornell Hospitality Quarterly, 49*(1), 12–27. doi:10.1177/0010880407310191

Tveteraas, S., Asche, F., & Lien, K. (2014). European tour operators' market power when renting hotel rooms in Northern Norway. *Tourism Economics, 20*(3), 579–594. doi:10.5367/te.2013.0291

Tveteraas, S., Roll, K. H., Jørgensen, H., & Tveterås, R. (2015). *Workload Management and Staff Performance in the Hospitality Sector.* Paper presented at the Nordic Symposium of Tourism and Hospitality, Reykjavik, Iceland.

Chapter 14
Is Physical Attractiveness More Important than Professional Competency?
The Moderator of Self-Confidence

Chien-Wen Tsai
Chinese Culture University, Taiwan

ABSTRACT

The international tourist hotel industry that focuses on quality of the "tangible" service is a typical high-contact service. To survive in the recent competitive work environment, many enterprises enhance their competitiveness in the process of service employee selection and emphasize the importance of physical attractiveness. This study uses self-confidence as a moderator which is rare relevant empirical evidence to confirm the relationships between physical attractiveness, professional competence and service attitude. The results show that confidence of the service personnel, physical attractiveness and professional competence have positive significant correlation relationships with service attitude. Service personnel's "self-confidence" is the most important variable towards service attitude. The study borrows selection and training functions of human resource management to integrate the knowledge of psychology, marketing management to expand the theory.

INTRODUCTION

Due to the rapid changes and developments in our current environment, we are looking for ways to find the best differentiated competitive advantages for enterprises in this competitive world. For the services industry, in addition to hardware facilities (appearance and equipment); the soft service (media); namely, the "front-line service personnel," has become the most representative means of enterprises and the organizations, creating first impressions of the enterprise for customers. The enterprise being the first-line of services delivered, must maintain the service provided by the service personnel of a high quality (Nickson et al., 2005); in order to gain competitive advantage (Rapert & Wren, 1998). The

DOI: 10.4018/978-1-5225-0201-2.ch014

importance of the front-line service staff to the enterprise (Luoh & Tsaur, 2009) is obvious, especially for the international tourist hotel industry, which has a lot of contact with the customers and emphasizes the "tangible" service quality. However, Parasuraman, Zeithaml and Berry (1985) believe it is difficult to make an accurate assessment of service quality, due to some of its features such as un-storability and being invisible; therefore, the service quality could be replaced by the service attitude (Parasuraman et al., 1988). During the 'moment of truth' in service contact, customers would pre-set their views and expectations of the service staff, as well as presume what situations may occur in the environment (Lockwood & Jones, 1989), thus, forming possible stereotypes and influence the evaluation of the services (Fischer, Gainer, & Bristor, 1997).

Therefore, many industry executives believe: during this 'moment of truth' regarding contact, customers would establish their first impressions of the service staff and judge whether the physical attractiveness of the service staff could affect the service provided (Berger, Fisek, Norman, & Zelditch, 1977). Previous studies also show that the good-looking service staff may influence the cognition of service personnel's service attitude (Luoh & Tsaur, 2009). And if the service personnel are neatly dressed, it would motivate customers to generate a positive perception (Sirgy et al, 2000) and make them feel appreciated and respected. Therefore, the international tourist hotel industry believes that to enhance the competitive advantages and increase service differentiation, it could be achieved by the physical attractiveness of the service personnel (Warhurst et al., 2000; Spiess & Waring, 2005).

This is the era of the "professional" certificate, according to the 104 Job Bank survey, there are more than 82.2% of enterprise executives in Taiwan who believe that owning international certificates is helpful to one's pay rise and promotion. According to AH&LA, a series of professional certificate training courses for hotel professionals, including Certified Hospitality Supervisor (CHS) supervisory staff training, operation and management of customer service, food and beverage management and human resource management courses, has been established to become compulsory certificates for tourist hotel personnel worldwide to enhance their service quality. It is obvious that the professional competence of international tourist hotel service personnel is important for the industry and to enhance the service quality is a vital element of meeting the customers' expectations. However, could physical attractiveness and professional competence enhance good service attitude of the service personnel? What causes service personnel to believe that if he/she is physically attractive or is professionally competent, he/she could provide a good service attitude? A person's psychological state and level of self-confidence could influence his/her interpersonal skill performance as well. Jane (2006) believes that if we increase the service personnel's self-confidence, it would improve the service quality of the service personnel as well as their work efficiency. Li Tien-hsu (1993) also indicated that, especially in the service-oriented industry, if the service staff lacks self-confidence, not only would this affect their work efficiency, but also generate a negative impact on their service objectives. Service staffs that have positive self-esteem tend to perform well at work (Benabou et al., 2003). It also shows that self-confidence plays an important role between the two variables, but few studies have shown how the self-confidence of the service personnel would affect the physical attractiveness, professional competence and service quality when providing services.

Therefore, the objectives of the chapter is to attempt to apply psychology, human resource management selection and training knowledge to cut into the expansion of the marketing management theory and to explore the way international tourist hotel industry's select their service personnel, which one would be more important, physical attractiveness or professional ability? From the executives' viewpoint, how would physical attractiveness and professional ability influence the service attitude of the service staff and what is the role of self-confidence amongst these factors? Because the previous literature seldom mentioned this aspect, this study was designed to compensate for the lack of empirical facts and to extend the original theory. In practice, the results of this study are provided from the international tourist hotel executives, we could thus further understand the operational direction of the industry and the study also provides business owners with suggestions on human resource planning, training and selection

BACKGROUND

1. The Relationship Between Physical Attractiveness and Service Attitude

Before 1985, the social sciences didn't provide a definition for physical attractiveness. After 1985, different research fields have given different meanings; researchers have investigated physical attractiveness. To provide reference standards for the subjects who took the test, Patzer (1985) defined physical attractiveness as: "the pleasing degree an individual possesses that affect other people". Hatfield& Sprecher (1986) also suggested in their research that physical attractiveness is: "an ideal image of an individual and in the meantime, this image also trigger the most pleasant feelings for the person in her mind". Staats (1981) made a more concrete definition of physical attractiveness; she believed that: "physical attractiveness should have three basic functions or characteristics: attitude, reinforce and directive. In other words, attractive appearance could not only trigger a human's positive emotions and generate positive reinforce effects, but could further prompt the intentions or behaviour of other people attempting to make an approach, such as: to invite, help, smile, chat, etc." (Burns,1987). While Strzalko & Kaszycka (1990) considered it in the same way; they suggested that: "physical attractiveness is certain features of the individual's shape or physical appearance, which could surely trigger positive emotions and prompt the direction of behaviour and approach to a stimulus"

According to environmental psychologist, Baker (1987), the service environment could be divided into three categories:

1. The potential factors that are difficult to be perceived by customers (air-quality, aroma and cleanliness) which are internal and external constructions;
2. Design factors that don't concern actual contact with the customers (aesthetically appealing, architectural colour, functional configuration, comfortableness); and
3. Social factors (people, appearance and behaviour).

While the "people" of the social factors here refers to the "people" in the environment (including the appearances of both the service personnel and the customer, their behaviour and the number of people could also affect the customer's behaviour when the service personnel provide services to the customer). It shows that the physical attractiveness of the service staff is part of the environment in terms of consumer psychology, and has a certain influence.

Garner (1997) suggests that our body is our personal billboard, providing others with 'first-and sometimes only-impressions'. Therefore, previous studies also stated: "What is beautiful is good," which explained the stereotyping of physical attractiveness (Dion et al., 1972) and suggested that when someone is physically attractive, it could prompt other people to feel agreeable (Hatfield & Sprecher, 1986). As a result, most people would assume beautiful people are more passionate, hardworking, and skilful and have more positive interactions, in addition to other stereotypes (Dion et al., 1972). In hotels, supervisors would prefer to recruit attractive labour service staff because supervisors believe that service staff who are 'a pleasure to behold' provide better labour and could increase sales quality (Chris & Dennis, 2005; John, 2007). Hence, if the industry people emphasize the charisma aspect of labour, they would pay more attention to the physical attractiveness of the service staff and they will also believe that service staff with an attractive appearance would increase service quality (Warhurst & Nickson, 2007).

Service quality is often regarded as a measure of whether the industry could provide superior service (Parasuraman, Zeithaml, & Berry, 1985, 1988). Because service quality has features which are unstorable and invisible, it is difficult to evaluate. Therefore, many empirical researches replace service quality with service attitude (Parasuraman et al., 1988). Kuo (2007) suggests that the service approach of international tourist hotel service staff should be measured by their friendliness, problem solving ability, sympathy and positive services. It is found in previous studies that physical attractive service staff may certainly affect the service attitude of the service personnel (Luoh & Tsaur, 2009) and the attitude of international tourist hotel's service personnel (Tsai & Lin, 2008). Therefore, during the 'moment of truth', the physical attractiveness of the frontline service personnel is very important (Megumi et al., 2003). For international tourist hotel executives, the appearance of service staff would influence his/her service attitude. Hereupon, the study proposed the first hypothesis.

H1: The physical attractiveness of the service staff has an obvious positive impact on the service attitude.

2. The Relationship between Professional Competency and Service Attitude

Jarvis' (1990) study explains that the profession often contains two characteristics:

1. Professional competence that is of a specific industrial field.
2. Ethics covering professional services.

Omae Kenichi (2006) mentioned in her book "The Professionalism" that a "professional" could control emotions and keep on being rational; have higher expertise, techniques and ethics; adhere to the faith that customers come first; an endless curiosity and entrepreneurial spirit, in addition to strict self-discipline, as well as having four required abilities: "the ability of foresight," "the ability of conceiving," "the ability of discussion" and "the ability of adapting to contradiction." People equipped with the aforementioned four abilities could thus be called "professional." Jarvis (1990) also explained in her research that professional competency covers professional expertise, skills and attitudes; she also suggests that the judgment of professional competency is based on the professional that achieved this in a particular period of time; that is, as the technology and time advance, the required skills and expertise of the professional competency would vary as well. Chisholm and Ely (1976) pointed out that professional competency includes three elements, which are knowledge, expertise and attitude; while those three elements also have reciprocal interactions with one another. Hill et al (1989) especially mentioned that when selecting professional service personnel, whether the service staff has professional expertise is the most influential element because it would doubtless affect the service attitude of the service personnel when providing services. Since international tourist hotels are an industry that are based on personal contact and the emphasis is on providing service, previous studies suggest that the service personnel of international tourist hotels should be equipped with professional expertise (understanding the job description, working environment, language aptitude, organizational system, regulations and so forth), attitudes (having occupational ethics, set an example for the others; the spirit of dedication, etc.) and expertise (the expertise of catering services, communication and problem solving, etc.) (Horng & Wang, 2003) would also influence consumers' impressions towards the business people (John & Richard, 2007). Therefore, by observing the interaction between the service staff and the customers, we could decide whether the service staff are equipped with professional expertise (Bitner, Booms, & Tetreault, 1990; Bitner, Boom, & Mohr, 1994), while professional expertise of the service personnel is one of the crucial factors influencing consumers to decide whether the attitude of the service staff is good or bad (Tsai & Lin, 2008; Sasser, Olsen & Wyckoff, 1987); hence, the deduction is that international tourist hotel supervisors believe that if the service personnel have good professional expertise regarding their specific capacities, it would have a positive effect on the service attitude. Hereupon, this research proposes the second hypothesis.

H2: The professional competency of service personnel has an obvious positive effect on his/her service attitude.

3. Moderator of Self-Confidence

Self-confidence is when one believes in herself/herself, having confidence in his/her knowledge and capacity, having no doubt about his/her decisions and judgments and can successfully implement a specific mission (Chang Chun-hsing, 1989;Modified from Luthans et al., 2004). Because one believes that he/she could deal with any project and accomplish it, regardless of how complicated the situations may be when handling the project, he/she would accomplish it with courage (Kohn & Schooler, 1973). Self-confidence sometimes is called "predominance" (e.g., Marshall, 1991). Many studies suggest that if one can effectively build self-assurance or self-assuredness, then it would also be helpful in enhancing one's efficacy (Kempen et al., 2000; Rejeski, Miller, Foy, Messier, & Rapp, 2001). Previous researches sometimes would refer to self-confidence as "self-efficacy." Self-efficacy means: "when someone is learning new things and carrying out missions, having the self-confidence required to implement each mission with one's expertise (Maurer, 2001). Bandura (1997) considers self-efficacy as having three levels:

1.   Having the self-efficacy of completing specific missions;
2.   Having the self-efficacy in a certain field;
3.   Having the self-efficacy that could handle ordinary situations.

4. The Relationship of Physical Attractiveness and Self-Confidence

In her research, Chun-Hsing Chang (1989) mentioned that self-confidence is one's trust in oneself, one's confidence in one's knowledge and capabilities, and the lack of doubt that one has for one's actions and decisions. Therefore, self-confidence represents one's confidence in one's ability to complete work tasks, missions, studies, etc. Mowday (1978) suggested that when a person makes a decision about a situation, the influencing factors are "major components of motive and ability" or, simply, "confidence". Chusmer, Koberg, and Stecher (1992) once mentioned that whether or not a person has confidence relates to the role one plays regarding a certain situation. When one is attempting to achieve a goal within the conditions of a particular activity, a person's confidence may be influenced by environmental factors (such as resources or friends), which ultimately affect the final result of the actions taken (Bandura, 1986, 1997; Schunk & Pajares, 2002; Richard & Ruiling, 2008). In recent years, for example, information spread by social media that touching everyone's lives has proven that physical image can positively affect people in the workplace (McCabe & Ricciardelli, 2003). In their research into physical attraction, Dipboye, Arvey, and Terpstra, (1977); Dipboye, Fromkin, and Wiback, (1975); Cash, Gillen, and Burns, (1977); and Watkins and Johnston (2000) all produced evidence that supports that a job candidate's physical attractiveness may affect her ultimate "station". Keith and Rennae (2000) applied the effects of overall appearance and hair styling to management, secretarial, sales, and service staff and found that overall appearance may affect work performance. Therefore, Megumi et al. (2003) suggested that attractiveness is important. Many people undergo cosmetic surgery to enhance their appearance in search of beauty (Chu-Ching Lin, 2007; Wen-Hua Chang, 2006) in order to get ahead in the workplace (Min-Ping Chen, 2015). One study investigating weight control found that people who lost a significant amount of weight had more confidence, indicating that enhancing one's confidence through dieting and weight loss can be effective for reaching one's goals (Richman, Loughnan, Droulers, Steinbeck, & Caterson, 2001). Therefore, one can enhance one's confidence in one's ability to lose weight by becoming thinner and, in turn, possibly improve one's weight loss results. This finding shows that physical appearance affects one's level of self-confidence. Wood and Stagner (1994) stated that those who are more confident about their judgements are "highly confident people" and less affected by the opinions of others. Through external environmental factors (resources, friends) and accumulation of experience, almost everyone has the ability to enhance their existing self-confidence. For example, if a service person is highly self-confident, she will easily believe her own subjective assessment of her actions and thus be less affected by external factors. Therefore, the following can be inferred when international hospitality industry service personnel come into contact with guests: Because guest contact is usually brief, service personnel must demonstrate the highest level of service within a short time frame, and because a service person is more confident when "she is confident in her physical appearance", possessing a confident smile can help her demonstrate a better, more positive attitude when providing customer service. Therefore, when a service person is self-confident, her awareness of her service attitude increases (Lisa, 2003), and the service quality experienced by the guest, as well as her supervisor, may also increase accordingly. Hence, this study proposes Hypothesis 3a of this research:

H3a: As far as a service person's supervisor is concerned, her self-confidence has a significant influence on the existing relationship between her physical attractiveness and service attitude.

5. The Relationship of Professional Competency and Self-Confidence

Many studies focused on the self-confidence of service staff in the field of human resource management (Vithessonthi, Chaiporn; Schwaninger, Markus, 2008); most enterprises compare the service staff learning abilities and self-development to their own work performances, having a positive effect on the company. Wood and Stagner (1994) suggest that people with high self-confidence tend to believe their own subjective viewpoints rather than being influenced by external factors, compared with people with low self-confidence. People with high self-confidence deliver better work performance (Benabou et al., 2003). Vithessonthi & Schwaninger (2008) also suggest that self-confidence is very important as it influences the work performance of service personnel and plays a vital role when providing services (Johnson, 2001); the self-confidence of the service staff also represents that one could make an effective service decision to protect herself/herself and to prevent customers to question his/her professional expertise when providing a service. According to the study of Lin Wen-chen (2001), the competency of successfully implementing a duty requires both explicit characteristics (knowledge, expertise and interpersonal skills) and implicit characteristics (attitude, motivation and concept). Thus, if the service personnel's self-confidence could be increased, it would also enhance the work performances of the service staff (Curry, Dobbins & Ladd, 1994).

According to Benabou et al. (2003), a person with a high level of self-confidence will perform well on the job. Vithessonthi and Schwaninger (2008) also indicated the importance of self-confidence. Johnson (2011) found it to affect service personnel work performance and to play an important role in the process of service delivery. According to research by Pick, Xocolotzin, and Ruesga (2007), if a service person possesses all the necessary knowledge and skills and can resolve guest problems and answer their questions, she will feel more self-confident. Furthermore, according to research by Yu-Chen Cho (2007) on technology university students who graduate on schedule, confidence is the most important factor when it comes to choosing a professional direction within the range of their respective professional abilities. Therefore, management in the international tourist hotel industry feel that if their service personnel can become familiar with their work and be highly confident, then they will provide the best performance in the course of providing services as well. When a service person is highly effective, she will have a progressive, positive attitude at work (Zhao, Seibert, & Hills, 2005). From the perspective of an international tourist hotel direct supervisor, a service person's self-confidence influences her work attitude when she provides services. Therefore, when such a person provides services to guests, her professional competency shall subsequently raise her confidence in her service ability. Therefore, a service person's self-confidence is an important factor influencing her service. A service person with enough self-confidence often reflects her confidence in herself and others through her facial expressions in her eyes and smile. Therefore, a service person's direct supervisor will believe that an employee's self-confidence will influence her service attitude. Based on this belief, the study hereby propose Hypothesis 3b of this research.

H3b: From the perspective of a service person's direct supervisor, the service person's self-confidence has a significant influence on the existing relationship between her professional competency and her service attitude.

Previous studies show that industry people could improve the service personnel's appearance and expertise by recruiting, selecting and training, (Tsai & Lin, 2008; Warhurst & Nickson, 2001; Wharhurst, Nickson, Witz & Cullen, 2000) in order to leave a good impression and service attitude when 'the moment of truth' in terms of customer service. In international tourist hotels, guest service personnel represent the hotel's corporate image, and the overall appearance and service quality of front-line Guest Service Representatives (GSRs) maintain the general images of their companies (Yi-Ting Chen, 2006). As such, direct supervisors at international tourist hotels believe in the importance of employing GSRs with attractive appearances and mannerisms. They also believe that being attractive with regard to appearance and mannerisms will increase GSRs' self-confidence when providing guest services, thus improving the overall service process and satisfying guests throughout their stay. Therefore, direct supervisors will greatly value appearances when hiring guest service personnel, believing that the related high self-confidence will positively affect the service they provide. Shu-Hua Chen (2002) expressed that food and beverage (F&B) students must enrich themselves with F&B related knowledge and skills before they can establish self-confidence. Likewise, if service personnel in international tourist hotels become highly capable regarding their applicable professional knowledge and skills, they will have increased self-confidence when providing service, which will correlate with their improved work performance. In this way, their professional knowledge and capabilities will subsequently improve guest satisfaction (Yu-Feng Tsai, 2001). Therefore, service personnel supervisors in international tourist hotels believe that possessing the professional competency necessary for the work will increase a service person's self-confidence, in turn positively influencing the person's service quality.

SOLUTIONS AND RECOMMENDATIONS

1. Method

This research surveyed the direct supervisors of service personnel working at five-star international tourist hotels, and based on the supervisor's cognition towards the service personnel when providing customer services. In addition, to make the questionnaire valid, this research has gained the permission of the HR of the international tourist hotel beforehand and 23 five-star international tourist hotels have granted us permission to do this questionnaire. The researcher sent out the questionnaires to 100 front-line mid-level managers and randomly assigned one service member as target, asking the specific service member's direct supervisor to make an assessment of the aforementioned staff member. The direct supervisor would make an evaluation on the spot in accordance with the service member's physical attractiveness, professional competency, self-confidence and service attitude; the questionnaire would be returned immediately. In order to prevent the possible influence of the gender of the service personnel, this research is limited to female service personnel. A total of 100 questionnaires have been given out, validity rate is 100%. According to Tabachnick & Fidell (2007) and Wu Min-lung (2007), although SEM analysis of a large number of samples is better, the latest statistic approach is estimated to allow the SEM model less than 60 observations. In this study, the sample size was 100, suitable for a SEM statistical analysis.

This study used the Cronbach α created by L. J. Cronbach, to analyse the interitem consistency to measure the reliability of the questionnaire and make some appropriate amendments. The study also adopted Analysis of Moment Structure (AMOS) 17.0 ver. for the path analysis between each relevant factor to clarify the factor relationship analysis of recognition factors on physical attractiveness, professional competency, and service attitude. The items are based on the features of the international tourist hotel industry; appropriate wording changes have been made and measured by Likert Scale: 1 indicating strong disagreement, and 5 indicating strong agreement.

A. Measurement of Employee's Physical Attractiveness

The study employs the scales developed by Riggio, Widaman, Tucker and Salinas (1991), which is divided into dynamic (interpersonal communication skills, body language, and reaction to events, social expertise, intelligence, and skills) and static (individual physical appearance, attire, facial attractiveness, and physical attractiveness) aspects.

B. Measurement of Employee's Professional Competency

In reference to Horng & Wang (2003), the professional competency of staff in international tourist hotel should include knowledge, attitude and skill as variable measurement dimensions. For the content validity of the questionnaire, it is confirmed and amended by five specialists and scholars.

C. Measurement of Service Attitude

This study incorporates Kuo's study (2007), which focused on verified results from exploratory factor analysis designed specifically for the service attitude of international tourist hotel service personnel. The service attitude is logically embodied in the service employees, and was divided into elements of friendliness, problem solving, empathy and proactive service.

D. Measurement of Self-Confidence

This study adopts the measurement scale developed by Teresa V. Crowe (2002), which is used generally by everyone when it comes to measurement of self-confidence. Appropriate wording changes were made in accordance with the features of international tourist hotels.

E. Reliability and Validity

Cronbach α values above 0.7 indicates high reliability (Guieford, 1965). After testing, the Cronbach α values of the physical attractiveness in this study were 0.89, 0.84 for professional competency, 0.81 for self-confidence and 0.91 for service attitude. With all research variable reliabilities above 0.8, this study's reliability is evidently sound. In terms of validity, this study incorporated suggestions from Kerlinger (1986) and performed criterion-related validity tests for the correlation coefficients between each item and total values to improve this study's related validity. After the factor analysis, every factor's load limit was above 0.5. The KMO value for physical attractiveness was 0.85, 0.85 for professional competency, 0.86 for self-confidence and 0.88 for service attitude.

2. Findings

A. Basic Data Analysis

For the supervisors, most interviewees were female, accounting for 57% of the total samples; most were 40.439 years old, accounting for 43% of the total; most were university graduates, accounting for 69% of the total; most were married, accounting for 66% of the total; most are supervisors or executives, accounting for 48%; in terms of income, most earned 1,250-1,531 USD per month, accounting for 38% of the total.

The evaluated service personnel had the following major characteristics, with the biggest groups indicated with the percentages provided here: 48% were between 30 and 39 years of age, 43% had a university education, and 57% majored in food and beverage. Of those surveyed, 84% of them were married, and regarding job type, 50% were front desk GSRs while 50% were other service personnel (this one-to-one split was a research design requirement). Finally, 30% have worked at the hotel for one to two years, and 29% had monthly salaries between 625 - 906 USD.

B. Relationship between Physical Attractiveness, Professional Competency and Service Attitude

This research categorized characteristics (dimensions) with four measurement variables used when surveying direct supervisors evaluating their service personnel: physical attraction, professional competency,

Table 1. Table of categorization for evaluation of characteristics

Variable	Characteristic/Dimensions
Physical Attraction.	●Passive Attraction. ●Active Attraction.
Professional Competency	●Knowledge ●Skills ●Attitude
Self-Confidence	Self-Confidence
Service Attitude	●Friendliness ●Problem Solving ●Empathy ●Enthusiasm

self-confidence, and service attitude. Then, by integrating these characteristics back into variables, this study established a main index and proceeded to analyze the structural equation model, as shown in Table 1.

I. Investigating the Structural Equation Model

This research used the aforementioned measurement variables, added measurement error and model error categories, and developed a pathway chart for the structure of this research, which was then analyzed using Amos Graphics 7.0. The structural equation model can be divided into two parts: the measurement model (which explains the relationship between observation variables and potential variables) and the structural equation model for the various potential variables (which explains the causal relationship between the potential variables). Because this research integrates its variable categories into respective overall variable indices, it investigates the causal relationships between observation variables only, which are represented with rectangles. The structural equation model was then expressed with a pathway chart, as shown in Figures 1 and 2: Pathway Coefficient Chart of How Direct Supervisors View Their Service Personnel (non-standardized and standardized).

The model suitability analysis results for the above charts are shown in Table 2.

As the Table 2 shows, the Degree of Freedom = 1, the chi-square value is 0.1, and P = 0.728. Clearly, since GFI=1, AGFI=0.993, and they are both greater than 0.9, this model should be considered suitable.

Figure 1. Pathway coefficient chart of how direct supervisors view their service personnel (non-standardized)

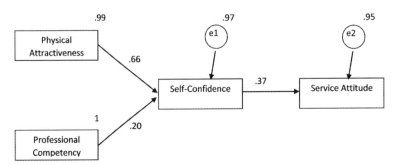

Figure 2. Pathway coefficient chart of how direct supervisors view their service personnel (standardized)

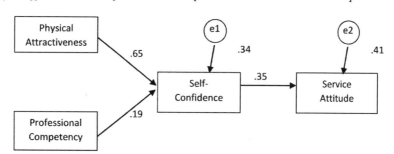

Table 2. Model suitability analysis table

Index	Standardized
Chi-square	0.1
Df	1
P	.728
GFI	1
AGFI	0.993
RMR	0.010
RMSEA	0.000

II. Model Internal Suitability Analysis Results

Analyzing the model's Internal Structure Fitness is an inherent quality of the analytical model. The assessment indicator for the model's inherent quality is the reliability of the various categories, which refers to the respective variables' R2 (Squared Multiple Correlation, SMC) values. The larger the R2 value, the better the results are, as it indicates a stronger causal relationship; an R2 value greater than 0.3 represents a strong causal factor (Shuen-Yu Chen, 2007). As shown in Figure 2, the Standardized Pathway Coefficient Chart, the R2 value for Physical Attraction, Professional Competence, and Self-Confidence is 0.41 towards Service Attitude, indicating that they explain Service Attitude well. Furthermore, the R2 value for Physical Attraction and Professional Competence is 0.34 for Self-Confidence, indicating that they explain Self-Confidence well. Therefore, this research model likely possesses a good Internal Structure Fitness level.

III. Overall Model Fitness Analysis Results

The Overall Model Fitness generally measures how well the overall model fits the observed data, as well as the overall model's External Structure Fitness. Hair et al. (1988) stated that Overall Model Fitness can be categorized into Absolute Fitness Statistics, Appreciation Fitness Statistics, and Simplified Fitness Statistics. This research follows the suggestion of Byrne (2001) and further inspects analysis results and modifies indices for analysis to obtain the final model. Fitness results for the overall theory model for this research are shown in Table 3.

Table 3. Overall model fitness analysis results

Statistics Verification Level	Fitness Standard	Verification Results	Suitability Judgement
Absolute Fitness Level Statistics			
X2	P<.05 (not significant)	0.1(p=.728>.05)	Yes
RMR value	<.05	0.010	Yes
RMSEA value	<.08	0.000	Yes
GFI value	>.09	1	Yes
AGFI value	>.09	0.993	Yes
Appreciation Fitness Statistics			
NFI value	>.90	0.996	Yes
RFI value	>.90	0.958	Yes
IFI value	>.90	1.031	Yes
Appreciation Fitness Statistics			
TLI value	>.90	1.458	Yes
CFI value	>.90	1	Yes
Simplified Fitness Statistics			
PGFI	>.50	0.607	Yes
PNFI	>.50	0.510	Yes
PCFI	>.50	0.541	Yes

This study's research pathway structure is shown in Figure 3 which is designed to explore the relationship between the physical attractiveness, professional competency, and service attitude, in order to test the hypotheses. The fitness values for the basic overall model all met the standards, thus achieving desired levels.

This result is focused on the study's hypotheses H1, H2 and H3a and b. According to Figure 3, results of the AMOS analysis on the causal relationship among physical attractiveness, professional competency and service attitude it shows that these three hypotheses H1, H2, and H3 a and b are supported. As for the path effect, results indicate that the direct effect of physical attractiveness on service attitude is 0.81, where there is no indirect effect. The direct effect of professional competency on service attitude is 0.75, where there is no indirect effect. The physical attractiveness, professional competency and self-confidence have reciprocal effects, which are 0.85 and 0.75 respectively.

Figure 3. The relationship model for physical attractiveness, professional competency, and service attitude

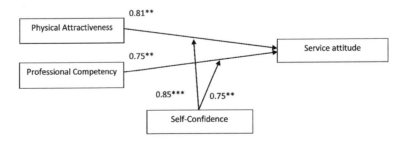

FUTURE RESEARCH DIRECTIONS

1. Direct supervisors of service personnel feel that a service person's physical attractiveness positively affects her service attitude when providing service to customers.

As this research shows, by the time a front line service person reaches the "moment of truth" of her service, her supervisor will have long been prejudiced into believing that customers expect certain qualities from service personnel. Therefore, as the research shows, a service person's physical attraction positively affects her supervisor's view of her service attitude. Previous supporting research is summarized below:

Megumi et al. (2003) suggest that physical attractiveness is important. In the studies of Dipboye, Arvey & Terpstra, (1977); Dipboye, Fromkin & Wiback, (1975); Cash, Gillen & Burns, (1977); Watkins & Johnston (2000), the investigation of physical attractiveness also suggest that the physical attractiveness of the job seeker may affect all other details. According to this study, before 'the moment of truth' service contact, the supervisors have already developed stereotypes and prejudices towards the first-line service staff: they believe that the service staff that meets the expectations of the consumers should concur to certain criteria. Therefore, the study shows that during service contact, the supervisors tend to have more positive feelings about the service attitudes of the personnel who are physically attractive. Previous studies are also supportive: Koering & Page (2002) found that dentists who are physically attractive deliver a better quality service; Spiess & Waring (2005) pointed out that if the industry people emphasize the physical attractiveness of the front-line service staff, it would improve the quality of service. Chuang Ming-chung (2006) found that the main factor affecting the hiring of first-line service personnel are their appearance and conduct of the person. This was also found to be true in previous research. For example, McArthur (1982) felt that in interpersonal relationships, it is easier for people to pay attention to each other's appearances and have their appearances reflect how they feel about people. Another study addressed how most people will first observe the appearance of others before they proceed to understand their inner qualities. Shou-Cheng Yang (2002) pointed out in her research that appearance not only affects what we assume about others' characteristics and what we expect of them in the future but also our evaluation of their abilities. Research results from Clifford and Walster (1974) showed that teachers' expectations of student performance are higher for students with greater external attractiveness. Furthermore, Romano, Schlia, Bordieri, and James (1989) found in their research that teachers with more attractive appearances have a greater likelihood of being rated as good teachers. One can easily understand from the aforementioned research that the more externally attractive a person is to others, the more others will expect from her in terms of performance and future. As a result, for an international tourist hotel industry that demands a high degree of service contact, great luxury and high service quality (Ruan Cheng-zong, 1994; Yao De-Xhsiong, 2001), this study explains why the industry people consider service staff who are physically attractive and have a commendable service attitude; thus, people with an attractive appearance have a better chance to be employed during an interview.

Service staff is in the front-line at international tourist hotels, they are the crucial point between personnel and public. Therefore, direct supervisors of the service personnel believe that as such, the service attitude of the service staff is important, and most job performances are evaluated by the service attitude in most service industries (Ren Jing-shyen, 2003). Tomplins (1993) suggests that the service attitude of the service staff is conveyed by body language and interaction, such as language, expressions and emotions, while the external image, including neat clothing and chic etiquette of the service personnel would influence the customers' satisfaction of service given by the service staff (Chen Meng-shiou,

1999). Hence, if the enterprise improves the quality of service attitude of the service staff, it would also increase positive evaluation of international tourist hotels.

2. Direct supervisors of service personnel feel that a service person's professional competency positively affects her service attitude when providing service to customers.

As this research has proven, the direct supervisors of service personnel feel that, in terms of servicing consumers, the greater the service person's professional competency (e.g. knowing the necessary language(s), communication skills, crisis management skills, when to use what cutlery, etc.), the better the attitude she displays when providing services. Professional competency, including knowledge, expertise and attitude, would influence the dependence of consumers on employees and improve the value of interaction (Bitner, 1994). Thus, the industrial sector want professional competency when providing service and consider it as important (Wang Li-lin, 2001). Siu (1998), Chung (2000), Formica & McCleary (2000) and other scholars also investigated the two hotel departments that have the most contact with customers, the "Food and Beverage Department" and the "Housekeeping Department" in Hong Kong, Italy and Korea and found that the training programs targeting employees' professional competency are important, because they affect service quality (attitude) of staff members. Maddux and Rogers (1980) found that professional employee competency positively affects consumer attitude; Crano (1970) found that consumers are more likely to agree with information provided by a highly professional staff member than with seemingly less professional staff; Woodside and Davenport (1994) also found that highly professional salesmen had more customers than less knowledgeable and less professional salesmen. In international tourist hotel industry, Chuang (2006) considers the most important factor that determines whether the basic service staff would be employed or not, their professional background; she suggests that direct supervisors of the service personnel believe that professional knowledge and competency affect the service process; therefore, it is important that the front-line employees possess wide-ranging professional competence (Mark J. Pescatore, 2005). According to this study, during the interaction process between the service personnel and the customers, supervisors believe that the professional conduct of the staff would positively affect the service attitude, supporting previous studies results, such as Formica & McCleary (2000), who suggest that training and developing professional competence in service staff is vital because such professional competence will influence their service attitudes.

3. Direct supervisors of service personnel believe that during the course of providing service, a service person's physical attractiveness and professional competence, through her self-confidence, will influence her service attitude. Between the two, self-confidence arising from being physically attractive is clearly more influential than self-confidence arising from professional competency.

By integrating the results from the empirical research herein, direct supervisors of service personnel were found to believe that if a service person is confident in her physical attractiveness and her display of professional competency, her service attitude will observably improve. Of those two characteristics, self-confidence inspired by physical attractiveness is clearly more influential than that inspired by professional competency. This research result agrees with research results from Li-Ling Wang (2001), which indicated that guest service personnel in international tourist hotels should possess such qualities as physical attractiveness, professionalism, motivation for improvement, self-confidence, and an amicable attitude. In previous literature, Kahle and Homer (1985) pointed out in their research that attraction from a superior physique and appearance plays a strongly suggestive role when people begin judging others, and attraction for a product or service can draw consumer attention (Ohanian, 1991). According to Eagly et al. (1991), people who are physically charismatic are often judged to possess many positive service qualities and are thus believed to have other positive qualities. Considerable research has demonstrated that physical attraction positively affects those who possess such a trait, and when the service person has a high self-esteem, his/her service attitude would have positive intents (Zhao, Seibert, and Hills 2005), it is supported by this study results. From the viewpoints of the international tourist hotel supervisors, during the service process, the self-confidence of the service staff would decide the quality of service. Hence, the self-confidence of the service staff is a vital factor during the service process. Usually, service personnel with sufficient self-confidence would reflect his/her and others' confidence with a smile and welcoming expression; therefore, supervisors consider the self-confidence of the service personnel affecting the quality of service attitude. In addition, supervisors believe that if the service personnel have an attractive good appearance and body language, he/she tend to have positive features during the service process; besides, people with high professional competency have a more positive influence on the consumers than people with a low professional competency. Confident service personnel would be more devoted to their service profession (Niu Han-jen, 2000).

Integrating the empirical results: direct supervisors of service staff believe - if the service employees have a high self-esteem, is physically attractive, and professional competent, he/she would have a better service attitude. While the physical attractiveness has a greater effect on the self-confidence than professional competency does, which supports the previous studies, results show that supervisors could inevitably judge a person by his/her appearances and select candidates with an outstanding appearance. For instance, Warhurst & Nickson (2007) found that enterprises would select service personnel with exceptional appearance and start to control the corporeality of the service personnel (Witz et al., 2003), through training courses to improve the appearance of the service staff, Solomon et al. (1985) discover that enterprises also put emphasis on the professional competency and expertise of the service personnel. These above empirical results show that the major reason is if enterprises select service personnel with outstanding looks, through professional training courses, it could enhance the self-confidence of service staff when providing service contact (Warhurst, Nickson, Witz & Cullen, 2000), and thus improve their service attitude.

4. The study recommends that those in the industry not just look at physical attraction and professional competence, but place greater emphasis on training in order to foster and maintain self-confidence for service personnel.

To increase service quality and effectiveness from service personnel in the field of customer service, human resources departments should design courses and activities that address any employee shortcomings, thus assisting service personnel to improve their work performance (Tania, 2007). The study discusses this idea in three parts:

a. In terms of physical attractiveness.

In pre-job training, consider the passive impression service employees give, such as whether they dress in a clean, coordinated manner and whether their appearance make customers feel comfortable.

Give them lessons in basic makeup techniques and make suitable individual adjustments so that they can make good first impressions when they interact with customers.

Regarding on-the-job training, focus on giving positive impressions and provide courses that train service personnel in overall mannerism, tones, and manners of speaking, smiling, attentiveness, gentleness, etc. during service. Doing so will raise the quality of service that the service personnel provides to the customers.

Finally, for training outside of work, hotels should host seminars and role-play sessions on subjects related to appearances and service processes, enabling seasoned employees to share and pass on their valuable customer service experience.

b.   In terms of professional competence.

In pre-job training, first understand whether the service person already possesses relevant credentials in F&B or hotel services; then, accounting for their existing skills, provide training in basic capabilities in terms of knowledge. One may also wish to consider whether the service person possesses good oral expression and communications abilities, knowledge of when to use what cutlery, common sense in fire safety, common sense in food safety, knowledge of restaurant operations, etc.

Regarding on-the-job training, mainly consider an employee's attitude and skills. Make the service personnel understand the level of professionalism required in customer service, and that this, in addition to whether or not they learn proactively, whether they are skilled in F&B services, etc., will affect their overall service performance. To do this, provide related training courses to accelerate the improvement of service for service personnel.

Regarding training outside of work, the most important thing is to enhance the service personnel's foreign language capabilities, since foreign guests check into international tourist hotels every day. Therefore, language, particularly English, training is quite important, and the study suggests that industry members hold training courses or activities that will help their service personnel attain relevant language training certifications.

c.   In terms of self-confidence.

In pre-job training, consider the adaptive ability and on-site reaction ability of service employees. Understand the service personnel's work performance throughout her service process, and have an experienced service person give her tutoring and emotional coaching.

Regarding on-the-job training, have the direct supervisor act favorably towards service employees and give them some decision making abilities, thus increasing their self-confidence.

Regarding training outside of work, provide service personnel with lessons related to their areas of service and increase their related confidence. The research recommends that after observing various service processes, direct supervisors hold discussions with the employee who performed the service afterwards to address what transpired, positively communicate with one another, and find a more suitable method for facing that situation. After coordinating such discussions, coach the service person on correct service methods and attitude and/or host courses on beauty, etiquette, makeup, etc. Through effective training of service personnel's positivity, establish the goal of having them strive towards attentive service, ultimately boosting service employees' self-confidence.

CONCLUSION

In the environment of market competition, service-focused hotels can build the brand image and enhance the competitive advantages through frontline staff who has constant interaction with consumers (Nickson et al., 2005) and are want growth in consumer value (Peppers & Rogers, 2004). Posthuma et al. (2002) point out that some factors of physical attractiveness can be improved by clothing, glasses/contact lenses, appropriate weight, courtesy, and adornment. Thus, enterprises can improve the customer's service experiences by aesthetic training, clothing, manners/etiquette and cosmetics (Warhurst, Nickson, Witz & Cullen, 2000; Witz, Warhurst & Nickson, 2003). In addition, results of the study show that the professional competency of an employee is a major factor that affects service attitude. Therefore, in addition to the given physical appearance, the training of professional competency and self-confidence could be enhanced by courses. Hence, enterprises do not have to select only candidates with an outstanding appearance in the interview process. Some aspects of physical attractiveness can be improved through a training program (e.g. courtesy and etiquette training, make-up program, dress sense, etc.) to better the external and internal beauty (static and dynamic attractiveness) and effectively enhance the service performance of employees', as well as increasing competitive advantages (Warhurst et al., 2000). Not many studies have analysed the consumer's subjective demand for service staff in international tourist hotels (the given and acquired conditions of staff); therefore, the study fills a blank in the psychology and human resource management; it is also valuable for recruiting, selecting and marketing management.

REFERENCES

Zamudio & Lichter. (2008). Bad attitudes and good soldiers: Soft skills as a code for tractability in the hiring of immigrant latina/os over native blacks in the hotel industry. *Social Problems, 11*, 573.

Bandura, A. (1986). *Social foundations of thought and action: A social cognitive theory*. Englewood Cliffs, NJ: Prentice Hall.

Bandura, A. (1997). *Self-efficacy: The exercise of control*. New York: Freeman.

Bandura, A. (1997). *Self-efficacy:The exercise of control*. New York: Freeman.

Benabou, R., & Tirole, J. (2003). Intrinsic and extrinsic motivation. *The Review of Economic Studies, 70*(3), 489–520. doi:10.1111/1467-937X.00253

Berger, J., Fisek, M. H., Norman, R. Z., & Zelditch, M. Jr. (1977). *Status characteristics and social interaction: An expectation states approach*. New York: Elsevier.

Bitner, M. J., Booms, B., & Tetreault, M. S. (1990). The service encounters:Diagnosing favorable and unfavorable incidents. *Journal of Marketing, 54*(1), 71–84. doi:10.2307/1252174

Bitner, M. J., Booms, B. H., & Mohr, L. A. (1994). Critical service encounter: The employee's viewpoint. *Journal of Marketing, 58*(4), 95–106. doi:10.2307/1251919

Burns, L. H. (1987). Infertility and the sexual health of the family. *Journal of Sex Education and Therapy, 13*, 30–34.

Buys, T. (2007). Professional competencies in occupational therapy work practice: What are they and how should these be developed? *Work (Reading, Mass.), 29*(1), 3. PMID:17627069

Cash, T. F., Gillen, B., & Burns, D. S. (1977). Sexism and beautyism in personnel consultant decision making. *The Journal of Applied Psychology, 62*(3), 301–310. doi:10.1037/0021-9010.62.3.301

Chang, C. H. (1989). *Psychology Dictionary*. Longman Group UK Limited.

Chang, M-C. (2006). *A Study on the Motivation of Purchasing Skin Care Products by the Female Consumers*. Takmang University Department of Business Administration.

Chen, M.-P. (2015). *Young people finding jobs difficult vs "Plastic Surgery" to enhance competitiveness,* Retrieved December 10, 2015, from http://www.laserone.com.tw/news_show_38.html

Chen, Y.-T. (2006). *The Effect of Personal Characteristics and Appearance Attraction of Salesperson on Business Performance-The Cases of Health care and Pharmaceutical Industries in Chinese Region*. (Unpublished Master's Thesis). Da-Yeh University, Changhua. Retrieved from http://handle.ncl.edu.tw/11296/ndltd/05486746407350309024

Chen, M-S. (1999). *Research on the influence of employees personality and QWL on work attitude and job performance in retail industry*. National Sun Yat-Sen University Department of Business Administration.

Chisholm, M. E., & Ely, D. P. (1976). *Media Presonnel in Education:A Competency Approach, Englewood Cliffs*. New York: Prentice-Hall.

Cho, Y.-C. (2007). *The relationships among core employability, professional abilities and future access choice of graduating students in the Universities of Technology*. (Unpublished master's thesis). National Changhua University of Education, Changhua. Retrieved from http://ir.ncue.edu.tw/ir/handle/987654321/3654

Chusmir, L. H., Koberg, C. S., & Stecher, M. D. (1992). Self-confidence of managers in work and social situations: A look at gender differences. *Sex Roles, 26*(11-12), 497–512. doi:10.1007/BF00289871

Clifford, M. M., & Walster, E. (1974). Research note: The effect of physical attractiveness on teacher expectations. *Sociology of Education, 46*(1), 248–258.

Crowe, T. V. (2002). *Translation of the Rosenberg self-esteem scale:From English to American sign language*. Baltimore, MD: University of Maryland.

Curry, D., Dobbins, G., & Ladd, R. (1994). Transfer of training and adult learning (TOTAL). *Journal of Continuing Social Work Education, 6*(1), 8–14.

Dion, K. K., Bersheid, E., & Walster, E. (1972). What is beautiful is good. *Journal of Personality and Social Psychology, 24*(3), 285–290. doi:10.1037/h0033731 PMID:4655540

Dipboye, R. L., Arvey, R. D., & Terpstra, D. E. (1977). Sex and physical attractiveness of raters and applicants as determinants of resume evaluations. *The Journal of Applied Psychology, 62*(3), 288–294. doi:10.1037/0021-9010.62.3.288

Dipboye, R. L., Fromkin, H. L., & Wiback, K. (1975). Relative importance of applicant sex, attractiveness, and scholastic standing in evaluation of job applicant resumes. *The Journal of Applied Psychology, 60*(1), 39–43. doi:10.1037/h0076352

Eagly, A. H., Ashmore, R. D., Makhijani, M. G., & Longo, L. C. (1991). What is beautiful is good, but …: A meta-analytic review of research on the physical attractiveness stereotype. *Psychological Bulletin, 110*(1), 109–128. doi:10.1037/0033-2909.110.1.109

Fischer, E., Gainer, B., & Bristor, J. (1997). The sex of the service provider: Does it influence perceptions of service quality? *Journal of Retailing, 73*(3), 361–382. doi:10.1016/S0022-4359(97)90023-3

Formica, S., & McCleary, K. (2000). Professional development needs in Italy. *The Cornell Hotel and Restaurant Administration Quarterly, 41*(2), 72–79. doi:10.1177/001088040004100219

Formkin, H. L. (1975). Relative importance of applicant sex, attractiveness, and scholastic standing in evaluation of job applicant resumes. *The Journal of Applied Psychology, 60*(1), 39–43. doi:10.1037/h0076352

Garner, D., & Kearney, C. A. (1997). The 1997 body image survey results. *Psychology Today, 1*(2), 30–84.

Han-jen. (2000). *The relationship of career commitment, self efficacy and job involvement MBA graduate student research conference.* Taipei, Taiwan.

Hatfeild, E., & Sprecher, S. (1986). *Mirror, mirror: The importance of looks in everyday life.* Albany, NY: State University of New York.

Hill, C. J. S. J. G., & Hanna, M. E. (1989). Selection Criteria for Professional Service Providers. *Journal of Services Marketing, 3*(4), 61–69. doi:10.1108/eb043366

Horng, J. S., & Wang, L. L. (2003). Competency analysis profile of F&B managers in international hotel managers in Taiwan. *Asia Pacific Journal of Tourism Research, 8*(1), 26–36. doi:10.1080/10941660308725453

Hosoda, , Stone-Romero, & Coats. (2003). The effects of physical attractiveness on job-related outcomes: A meta-analyses…. *Personnel Psychology, 56*, 431. doi:10.1111/j.1744-6570.2003.tb00157.x

Jarvis, P. (1990). *International dictionary of adult and continuing education.* London: Kogan Page.

Jing-Shyen. (2003). *The relationship between quality of working life and service attitude of international flight attendants.* National Taipei University of Nursing and Health Science Graduate Institute of Tourism & Health Science.

Johnson. (2001). *Self-esteem comes in all sizes: How to be happy and healthy at your natural weight.* Pub Group West.

Julie Baker. (1987). The role of the environment in marketing services:The consumer perspective. In J. A. Czepiel, C. A. Congram, & J. Shanahan (Eds.), *The Service Challenge:Integrating for Competitive Advantage* (p. 80). Chicago: American Marketing Association.

Keates, N. (1997). Hotels find hostility sells better than hospitality. *Wall Street Journal Europe, 12*, 7-8.

Kempen, G. I., Sanderman, R., Miedema, I., Meyboom-de Jong, B., & Ormel, J. (2000). Functional decline after congestive heart failure and acute myocardial infarction and the impact of psychological attributes: A prospective study. *Quality of Life Research: An International Journal of Quality of Life Aspects of Treatment, Care and Rehabilitation, 9*(4), 439–450. doi:10.1023/A:1008991522551 PMID:11131936

Kenichi. (2006). *The Professionalism.* Commonwealth Publishing Group.

Kerlinger, F. N. (1986). *Foundation of behavior research* (3rd ed.). New York: Holt, Rinehart & Winston. Comprehensive coverage of the scientific concepts and logical reasoning.

Koering, S. K., & Page, A. L. (2002). What if your dentist looked like tom cruise? Applying the match-up hypothesis to a service encounter. *Psychology and Marketing, 19*(1), 91–110. doi:10.1002/mar.1003

Koerning, S. K., & Page, A. L. (2002). What if your dentist looked like tom cruise? Applying the match-up hypothesis to a service encounter. *Psychology and Marketing, 19*(1), 91–110. doi:10.1002/mar.1003

Kohn, L. M., & Schooler, C. (1973). Occupational experience and psychological function: An assessment of reciprocal effects. *American Sociological Review, 38*(1), 97–118. doi:10.2307/2094334

Kuo, C. M. (2007). The importance of hotel employee service attitude and the satisfaction of international tourists. *Service Industries Journal, 27*(8), 1073–1085. doi:10.1080/02642060701673752

Li, T.-S. (1993). *translate.* The Core Competence of the Corporation. EMBA Magazine.

Lin, C.-C. (2007). *Business Times: Role of beauty in the employee's selection.* Retrieved December 13, 2013, from http://tw.myblog.yahoo.com/jw!G0Ap7lKABRXrE9O_lIvG.ITsGg--/article? mid=152

Lisa. (2003). *JiuJik: Job requirements.* Retrieved October 13, 2001, from http://www.jiujik.com/jsarticle. php?lcid=HK.B5&artid=3000006221&arttype =JINVT&artsection=JOB

Lockwood, A., & Jones, P. (1989). Creating positive service encounters. *The Cornell Hotel and Restaurant Administration Quarterly, 29*(4), 44–50. doi:10.1177/001088048902900411

Luoh, H. F., & Tsaur, S. H. (2009). Physical attractiveness stereotypes and service quality in customer-server encounters. *Service Industries Journal, 29*(8), 1093–1104. doi:10.1080/02642060902764517

Marshall, G. N. (1991). A multidimensional analysis of internal health locus of control beliefs: Separating the wheat from the chaff? *Journal of Personality and Social Psychology, 61*(3), 483–491. doi:10.1037/0022-3514.61.3.483 PMID:1941520

Maurer, T. (2001). Career-Relevant Learning and Development, Worker Age, and Beliefs About Self-Efficacy for Development. *Journal of Management, 27*(2), 123–140. doi:10.1177/014920630102700201

McCabe, M. P., & Ricciardelli, L. A. (2003). Body image and strategies to lose weight and increase muscle among boys and girls. *Health Psychology, 22*(1), 39–46. doi:10.1037/0278-6133.22.1.39 PMID:12558200

Mowday, R. (1978). The exercise of influence in organizations. *Administrative Science Quarterly, 23*(1), 137–156. doi:10.2307/2392437

Nickson, D., Warhurst, C., & Dutton, E. (2005). The Importance of Attitude and Appearance in the Service Encounter in Retail and Hospitality. *Managing Service Quality*, *15*(2), 195–208. doi:10.1108/09604520510585370

Ohanian, R. (1990). Construction and validation of a scale to measure celebrity endorsers' perceived expertise, trustworthiness, and attractiveness. *Journal of Advertising*, *19*(3), 39–52. doi:10.1080/0091 3367.1990.10673191

Overbaugh, R., & Lu, R. (2008). The Impact of a NCLB-EETT Funded Professional Development Program on Teacher Self-Efficacy and Resultant Implementation. *Journal of Research on Technology in Education*, *41*(1), 43–61. doi:10.1080/15391523.2008.10782522

Parasuraman, A., Zeithaml, V. A., & Berry, L. L. (1985). A conceptual model of service quality an its implications for future research. *Journal of Marketing*, *49*(4), 41–50. doi:10.2307/1251430

Parasuraman, A., Zeithaml, V. A., & Berry, L. L. (1988). Servqual: A multiple-item scale for measuring consumer perc. *Journal of Retailing*, *64*(1), 12–41.

Patzer, G. L. (1985). *The physical Attractiveness Phenomena*. New York: Plemun. doi:10.1007/978-1-4757-0202-6

Pescatore, M. J. (2005). *It's all about appearances*. New York: Government Video.

Pick, U. X., & Ruesga, C. (2007). Capacity building for decentralization in Mexico: A psychosocial approach. *International Journal of Public Sector Management*, *20*(2), 157–166. doi:10.1108/09513550710731517

Posthuma, R. A., Morgeson, F. P., & Campion, M. A. (2002). Beyond employment interview validity: A comprehensive narrative review of recent research and trends over time. *Personnel Psychology*, *55*(1), 1–81. doi:10.1111/j.1744-6570.2002.tb00103.x

Rapert, M. I., & Wren, B. M. (1998). Service quality as a competitive opportunity. *Journal of Services Marketing*, *12*(3), 223–235. doi:10.1108/08876049810219539

Rejeski & Miller. (2001). A marginal model for analyzing discrete outcomes from longitudinal surveys with outcomes subject to multiple-cause nonresponse. *Journal of the American Statistical Association*, *96*(455), 844.

Riggio, R. E., Widaman, K. F., Tucker, J. S., & Salinas, C. (1991). Beauty is more than skin deep: Component of attractiveness. *Basic and Applied Social Psychology*, *12*(4), 423–439. doi:10.1207/s15324834basp1204_4

Ruan. (1994). *A Study on the management type and performance of International Tourist Hotels - The Empirical study of Taiwan, U.S., Japan*. Chinese Culture University Graduate Institute of Tourism Industry.

Sasser, W. E., Olsen, R. P., & Wyckoff, D. D. (1987). *Management of service operations: Text and Case*. Boston: Alley and Bacon Inc.

Schunk, D. H., & Pajares, M. F. (2002). The development of academic self-efficacy. In A. Wigfield & J. S. Eccles (Eds.), *Development of achievement motivation* (pp. 16–32). San Diego, CA: Academic Press. doi:10.1016/B978-012750053-9/50003-6

Schwer, K., & Daneshvary, R. (2000). Keeping up one's appearance: Its importance and the choice of type of hair-grooming establishment. *Journal of Economic Psychology, 21*(2), 207–222. doi:10.1016/S0167-4870(99)00043-4

Sirgy, D. G., & Mangelburg, T. (2000). Retailing environment, self-congruity, and retail patronage:An integrative model and a research agenda. *Journal of Business Research, 49*, 127–138. doi:10.1016/S0148-2963(99)00009-0

Siu, Y-M. (1998). The Imbalance of Sexes in China: A Consequence of the 'One-Child' Policy?. In *China in the Post-Deng Era*. Hong Kong: The Chinese University Press.

Solmon, M. R., Surprenant, C. F., Czepiel, J. A., & Gutman, E. G. (1985). A role theory perspective on dyadic interactions:The service encounter. *Journal of Marketing, 51*, 86–96.

Speiss, L., & Waring, P. (2005). Aesthetic labour, cost minimisation and the labour Process in the Asia Pacific Airline Industry. *Employee Relations, 27*(2), 193–207. doi:10.1108/01425450510572702

Staats, A. W. (1981). Paradigmatic behaviorism, unified theory, unified theory construction methods, and the Zeitgeist of separatism. *The American Psychologist, 36*(3), 239–256. doi:10.1037/0003-066X.36.3.239

Tabachnick, B. G., & Fidell, L. S. (2007). Using multivariate statistics (5th ed.). Needham Heights, MA: Allyn and Bacon.

Timmerman, J. E., & Lytle, R. S. (2007). Exercises in tourism empowerment practice. *International Journal of Culture. Tourism and Hospitality Research, 1*(4), 273.

Tompkins, N. C. (1993). Employee satisfaction leads to customer service-employee relations. *Human Resource Magazines, 37*(3), 93–97.

Tsai, C.-W., & Lin, T. H. (2008). Would service employee's physical attractiveness affect service attitude consumer perceived and consumers' primary purchase intentions? -Empirical evidence from hotel industry.*14th Annual Asia Pacific Tourism Association Conference*, Bangkok.

Vithessonthi, C., & Schwaninger, M. (2008). Job motivation and self-confidence for learning and Development as predictors of support for change. *Journal of Organizational Transformation and Social Change, 5*(2), 141–157. doi:10.1386/jots.5.2.141_1

Von Berqen. (2006). College reaching out to firms: Community College of Phila. launches an effort to build partnerships with the business community, knight ridder tribune business news. Washington.

Wang, L-L. (2001). *Professional competencies required for food and beverage employees working front of the house in international tourist hotel*. National Taiwan Normal University Graduate Institute of Department of Human Development and Family Studies.

Warhurst, C., & Nickson, D. (2001). *Looking Good, Sounding Right: Style Counselling in the New Economy*. London: The Industrial Society.

Warhurst, C., & Nickson, D. (2007). Employee experience of aesthetic labour in retail and hospitality. *Work, Employment and Society, 21*(1), 103–120. doi:10.1177/0950017007073622

Warhurst, C., & Nickson, D. (2007). Employee experience of aethetic labour in retail and hospitality. *Work, Employment and Society, 21*(1), 103–120. doi:10.1177/0950017007073622

Warhurst, C., Nicoson, D., Witz, A., & Cullen, A. M. (2000). Aesthetic labour in interactive service work: Some case study evidence from the new glasgow. *Service Industries Journal, 20*(3), 1–18. doi:10.1080/02642060000000029

Watkins, L. M., & Johnston, L. (2000). Screening job applicants: The impact of physical attractiveness and application quality. *International Journal of Selection and Assessment, 8*(1), 76–84. doi:10.1111/1468-2389.00135

Watkins, L. M., & Johnston, L. (2000). Screening job applicants: The impact of physical attractiveness and application quality. *International Journal of Selection and Assessment, 8*(2), 76–84. doi:10.1111/1468-2389.00135

Wen-Jeng, L. (2001). Manufacturing human resources professional functions. *Sun Yat-Sen Management Review, 9*(4), 621–654.

Witz, A., Warhurst, C., & Nickson, D. (2003). The labour of aesthetics and the aesthetics of organization. *Organization, 10*(1), 33–54. doi:10.1177/1350508403010001375

Wood, W., & Stagner, B. (1994). Why are some people easier to influence than others? *Psychological insights and perspectives*, 149-174.

Woodside & Davenport. (1994). Linking Service Quality, Customer Satisfaction and Behavioral Intention. *Journal of Health Care Marketing, 9*(1), 5–17. PMID:10304174

Wu, M. L. (2007). *SPSS & the Application and Analysis of Statistics*. Taipei: Wu-Nan Book Inc.

Yang, S.-C. (2002). *The Effect of Physical Attractiveness on Self-Evaluation-Concerning with the Effect of Moderation of Similarity and Self-Aspects*. (Unpublished master's thesis). Chung Yuan Christian University, Taoyuan City.

Yao, D.-X. (2001). *Development and Planning for Hotel Industry 3ᵈ*. Taipei: Yang-chih Book.

Zhao, H., Seibert, S. E., & Hills, G. E. (2005). The Mediating Role of Self-Efficacy in the Development of Entrepreneurial Intentions. *The Journal of Applied Psychology, 90*(6), 1265–1272. doi:10.1037/0021-9010.90.6.1265 PMID:16316279

Chapter 15
Socially Responsible Practices in Hotels:
Factor Analysis and Descriptive Statistics

María Dolores Sánchez-Fernández
University of A Coruña, Spain

Rosa María Vaca-Acosta
University of Huelva, Spain

Alfonso Vargas-Sánchez
University of Huelva, Spain

ABSTRACT

The aim of this work is to study social responsible behavior in three, four and five star hotels found in Galicia and the Northern region of Portugal. To be able to carry out this investigation two types of analysis are carried out. First of all there is a descriptive statistical analysis about the group of variables contained in the used scale. Secondly a factor analysis is applied in which the factors that make up social responsibility in line with the triple dimension identified by Elkington (1997) are identified. The development of this methodology has made it possible to compare practices of social responsibility carried out by the hotels under study in two different countries, Spain and Portugal. From this investigation it can be concluded that the initial hypothesis is confirmed, corporations behave differently when it comes to social responsibility depending on the country they are in.

INTRODUCTION

Tourism is one of the main economic motors which Portugal and Spain rely on. But as well as in many other sectors, the crisis has had a strong impact on tourist activity in Spain and Portugal; however, despite the highs and lows in the first stage of the economic crisis, today, tourism has recuperated its importance in the economy. Based on official statistics from both countries it is possible to come to the conclusion that during the last four years, in both countries the tourism sector has recovered its importance in

DOI: 10.4018/978-1-5225-0201-2.ch015

the economy, recuperating the losses made in the first years of the economic crisis, a fact that is seen in the evolution of GNP. Employment is another of the representative factors of the economy, and in both countries the number of people working and the unemployment rate has grown much less than the national rate in this sector. The authors Alvarez, Vila, Fraiz and Rio (2013) and Lopes (2010) reinforce the importance that the tourism sector has for the economy of both countries.

Social corporate responsibility is nowadays in a prominent position due to the development over the years of different standards and regulations, pressures exerted by stakeholders, the implementation of CSR practices in organizations, and the interest from the scientific community, institutions as well as society in general. On the other hand it should be highlighted that in situations of economic crisis the adoption of socially responsible practices can be diminished by other interests (survival of the Organization, amongst others). The cultural factor also influences the degree of implementation CSR practices (Fanjul, 2010).

Due to this it is of interest to study social responsibility in the tourism sector in two bordering countries that have a similar culture and are going through a period of an economically diminished situation. The choice of the hotel subsector aims to add uniformity to the study to make a comparison in both countries.

The main objective of this research is to find out if the behavior of the hotels in this study in the field of social responsibility is different depending on the country where the activity of the organization takes place; Spain and Portugal. Therefore the following hypothesis is put forward in this investigation: corporations behave differently when it comes to social responsibility depending on the country they are in.

This research seeks to, on the one hand, in order to measure CSR, find the appropriate scale to implement in this research, adapt it to the object of study and validate it. Analysis of literature review and the application of the factor analysis technique are used to do this.

On the other hand it seeks to verify socially responsible behavior in hotels. In order to do so the descriptive statistical analysis technique is used making it possible to compare the set of items (practices) that make up each of the dimensions - social, environmental and economic (Elkington, 1997)-. Finally, the aim is to check if the practices implemented in hotels are in line with the proposals in the strategic plans of the representative institutions of the tourism sector in both countries.

As a result, to carry out this research work it is necessary to review the literature in the designated areas (socially responsible behavior, future prospects of tourism in both regions and the CSR measurement). An empirical study, using the techniques of descriptive statistical analysis and factor analysis is also necessary.

This paper explores how hotels in three, four and five star hotels located in Galicia (Northwest region of Spain) and in the Northern Region of Portugal apply social responsibility. These two regions border each other and have a similar culture although they belong to two different countries encompassed within the European Union.

This chapter is divided into seven sections. In the first section the main literature on socially responsible behavior in organizations, the future prospects of tourism in both countries and the monitoring of Corporate Social Responsibility (CSR) is reviewed. It is then followed by the main focus of the chapter with issues, controversies and problems. In the third section, the recommendations and solutions are put forward followed by future research directions. The conclusions are then presented followed by bibliographical references and the key terms and definitions.

BACKGROUND

1. Socially Responsible Behavior in Organizations

In this section the conceptualization of corporate social responsibility, the various factors that can influence the adoption of socially responsible behavior and the key figure which exerts influence on the implementation of socially responsible practices in organizations is analyzed.

The conceptualization of Corporate Social responsibility evolves with time, demands and situations facing organizations. Therefore, it is difficult to specify a permanent definition which is adapted to a type of organization. Based on this argument, this investigation is based on the definition of social responsibility proposed by Sanchez-Fernandez, Vargas-Sánchez and Remoaldo (2014) which derives from the conjunction of a series of features, based on the review of the academic literature (European Commission, 2011; Gessa, Ruiz & Jimenez, 2008; Martin, et al., 2008; Freeman, 1984; European Commission, 2001; Humble, 1975; Vela, 1977). Corporate social responsibilities are those practices implemented in organizations, which go beyond the legal obligations an Organization has, helping to meet the expectations of stakeholders. The company must adopt a proactive attitude in order to assure certain results. It is not identified as an isolated philanthropic activity but rather as a management phenomenon within the organization. Moreover, this concept is determined by a minimal limit; compliance with regulations and legislation pertaining to the organization and a maximum limit; endangering the survival of the company itself by carrying out socially responsible practices.

Different investigations (Galaskiewcz, 1991; Scott, 1995; Maigan & Ralston, 2002; Campbell, 2007; Lee, 2011; Brammer, Jackson & Matten, 2012) point out that one of the factors influencing the adoption of socially responsible behavior within companies is the location of the organization. The countries where they operate and the incentives offered by institutions also affect the limits and proactive factor of this behavior. The importance that CSR acquires in organizations has effects on the organization.

Galaskiewicz (1991) mentions that corporations tend to act with social responsibility if regulatory or cultural institutions offer a suitable set of incentives to act in a socially responsible way. Campbell (2007) argues that the institutions are a key element to limit or motivate companies in their commitment to socially responsible activities.

Various institutional studies have shown that the social behavior of organizations is determined by their interaction with the social actors who are responsible for channeling and focusing the institutional strengths of the companies (Lee, 2011). If companies were provided with a regulatory-normative framework and cognitive structures so that they adopt a socially responsible behavior, institutions would give importance and stability to this behavior (Scott, 1995). The responsibility of the company in the internal dimension must not be forgotten. Organizations have the responsibility of preventing the misconduct of employees by creating standards and codes within the Organization. This would not be a personal problem, but the fact that an employee does not have a socially responsible behavior affects the organization (Lee, 2011). In the same way, societies have the responsibility of preventing the misconduct of corporations by measuring the performance of institutions and establishing commitments for stakeholders (direct commitments).

Since the implementation of socially responsible practices in organizations lacks institutional support, the probability that stakeholders reward socially responsible behavior (CSR) or sanction socially irresponsible behavior is minimal Brammer, Jackson and Matten (2012). Organizations which are more likely to adopt CSR are those which have a relationship with unions, employees and other stakeholders (Campbell, 2007).

There are several key actors that have an influence in the companies when implementing corporate social responsibility (CSR) practices, amongst them are the managers who are identified as influential parts Campbell (2007). Drucker (1973) adds that the leading groups within organizations should consider which responsibilities they should adopt along with the objectives and in what areas. For Prieto (1979) the strategic Apex must assume an important role in the field of CSR. Godos and Fernández (2011) believe it is a key factor in the company's strategy.

The tourism sector is connected to the demand for greater quality of life and environmental protection (Gessa, Ruiz & Jimenez, 2008), so it is important for organizations to develop this activity in accordance with the customer's demand. In addition it is important to note that research in the tourism sector in the area of social responsibility creates great interest for academics (Manente, Minghetti & Mingotto, 2012; Boluk, 2013; Nyahuzvi, 2013; Martinez, Perez & Rodriguez, 2014; Zanfardini, Aguirre & Tamagni, 2015; among others).

2. Future Prospects of Tourism in Spain and Portugal

Future prospects of tourism in Spain and Portugal are oriented to achieving a sustainable balance in the efficient use of resources, the development of tourist activity and taking into account the impacts that they generate in the short, medium and long term. The main points of the strategic plans (Ministry of Economy and Employment, 2012; Ministry of Industry, Energy and Tourism, 2012; Northern Regional Coordination and Development Commission, 2014 and Tourism of Galicia, 2014) that state the future prospects intended to orient the tourism sector in both countries are then analyzed and presented.

Spain and Portugal aim to improve the promotion of their country brand through quality tourism taking advantage of all heritage resources being natural, gastronomic and cultural. They intend to focus on making the most of tourism resources (proper use of all its resources) dissociating themselves from pure consumption tourism and giving value to all their richness and finding an appropriate balance between care, protection and exploitation of different tourist activities.

In terms of infrastructure they intend to make improvements in environmental sustainability especially focusing on efficiency, energy and water saving and improving accessibility for all. One of the objectives specified in the strategic plans in both countries is to promote sustainable tourism. They also have entrepreneurship programs aimed at sustainability and social economy.

The lines of action in both countries have the same orientation as the triple dimension of social responsibility; social, economic and environmental field. They intend to establish a sustainable-oriented future. They aspire to be socially responsible tourism destinations.

In the mentioned strategic plans, hotels are one of the key pieces that help to achieve the objectives marked. They are companies that need to collaborate in the attainment of the strategic objectives in the tourism sector by creating plans for energy and water efficiency; incorporating environmental practices into their companies; adapting the accessibility and sustainability of its actions; valuing the orientation of new professions aimed at accessibility and sustainability, as well as the training of current employees and providing infrastructure for environmental sustainability.

They must also take into account the impact generated in the development of their activities as well as collaborating with the environment promoting their culture, landscape, heritage, among others; thus becoming the engine of their environment.

3. Monitoring CSR: Tools, Indexes and Scales

It is important to be able to measure the performance of CSR business-oriented. Brammer, Jackson and Matten (2012) and Claasen and Roloff (2012) characterized CSR as a multidimensional construct with a complex character, making it difficult to measure. They point out that many indicators of CSR are partial, since they contain explicit information while the implicit information is not easily detected or can be confused with a lack of responsibility. Aupperle, Carrol and Hatfield (1985); Singhapakdi et al. (1996);Quazi and O'Brien (2000); Martin et al. (2008); Perdomo and Escobar (2011) and Gallardo, Sanchez and Corchuelo (2013) have developed various instruments of CSR measurement using different approaches. Aupperle, Carrol and Hatfield (1985) developed a scale to measure individual values and attitudes by managers towards CSR based on the model of the four dimensions of Carroll (1979). Ruf, Muralidhar and Paul (1998) developed a scale to capture the multi-dimensional nature of CSR. Singhapakdi et al. (1996) designed a scale that allows to measure ethics and CSR; PRESOR (Perceived Role of Ethics and Social Responsibility), aimed at the measurement of single values of managers. Davis (1991) and Orpen (1987), Quazi and O'Brien (2000) developed a scale for measuring attitudes towards social responsibility based on previous studies.

Martin et al. (2008) have developed a scale composed of different sections based on the three dimensions of social responsibility for the measurement of CSR in the tourism sector. This scale is very laborious and extensive directed at managers of marinas. Gallardo, Sanchez and Corchuelo (2013) articulated a CSR scale that validated the perspective of the three dimensions (Elkington, 1997) in companies located in the province of Extremadura. This scale is enriched with aspects that extend the vision of the organization. These authors oriented questionnaires to the directors. It is a scale with an adequate and affordable extension that obtains information on the basis of a Likert scale of CSR practices developed by these organizations. This last scale is ideal for this investigation oriented at management which is based on triple dimension and is of a suitable size to incorporate it as a measuring scale.

The study carried out by Perdomo and Escobar (2011) pointed out that there is not a universal measurement for CSR, the reason why over time various measurements or approaches have arisen in different research projects. In addition to the scales proposed by various academics different surveys, reputation indexes, databases, analysis of various documents and indicators from the measuring instruments of the management of CSR such as those identified in Sanchez-Fernandez (2015) have appeared and evolved over the last years. The main focus of the chapter can be seen below.

MAIN FOCUS OF THE CHAPTER

Issues and Controversies

The unit under study are three, four and five-star hotels in Galicia and North of Portugal. This investigation is aimed at three, four and five star hotels given that these types of hotels are more likely to adopt socially responsible practices than one and two star hotels. These hotel categories establish socially responsible practices of sufficient size, entity, and foundations to collect information. On the other hand it is important to denote that the number of three, four and five-star hotels under study are a sufficient number to obtain an adequate sample and allow a vision of the hotels in the mentioned categories.

After the literature review a structured questionnaire is drawn up and adapted to the language of each country; Portuguese and Spanish, following the recommendations of Vitell, Ramos y Nishihara (2010). The paragraph that captures the features of categorization and classification of hotels, as well as the socio-demographic characteristics of respondents has been based on the variables contained in the reports prepared by recognized institutions of each country. These reports come from the National Statistical Institute of Portugal and Spain, the Statistical Institute of tourism and tourism satellite account. The section that contains information about the scale of corporate social responsibility is developed based on the studies of Gallardo, Sanchez and Corchuelo (2013). The scale adapted to the objects under study in this investigation derives from the scale proposed by the latter authors and is based on the three dimensions Elkington (1997) - social, economic and environmental. The set of items used in this study corresponds to the definitive set of items, those which remained in the scale after fulfilling the validity and reliability requisites they were subjected to and that came from the investigation by Gallardo, Sanchez and Corchuelo (2013). For their measurement a Likert type scale from 1 to 5 was used, corresponding to the lowest and highest respectively indicating if they were in disagreement or in accordance with the statements in the questionnaire. The proposed scale contains the following items (see Table 1).

The main objective of this research is to find out if the behavior of companies in the field of social responsibility is different depending on the country where the organization develops the activity. This is

Table 1. Items from the social responsibility scale

Dimension	Denomination	Reference
Environmental	Minimize environmental impact	DM1
	Use environmentally friendly product	DM2
	Energy saving	DM3
	Alternative energy sources	DM4
	Investment planning for reducing impact	DM5
	Reducing emissions	DM6
	Ecological articles	DM7
	Recyclable packaging	DM8
Economic	Quality products and services	DE1
	Products and services that fulfill a standard	DE2
	Better price levels	DE3
	Accurate information on products and services	DE4
	Consumer rights	DE5
Social	Employee quality	DS1
	Employee salary	DS2
	Creation of employment	DS3
	Employee training	DS4
	Conciliation policies	DS5
	Equal opportunities	DS6
	Employee dialogue mechanisms	DS7

(Source: Own elaboration based on Gallardo, Sanchez and Corchuelo, 2013)

the reason why three, four and five-star hotels were chosen in order to guide the investigation towards a new sector and add uniformity to the study thus making it possible to compare the two regions located in two different countries with similar culture. Consequently, on the one hand a descriptive statistical study is made to analyze the results of the items and on the other hand a factor analysis is made to analyze the set of factors and the aspects of social responsibility. All of this is to test the hypothesis put forward in the following paragraph. As can be seen in the literature, several studies (Galaskiewcz, 1991; Scott, 1995; Maigan& Ralston, 2002; Campbell, 2007; Lee, 2011; Brammer, Jackson &Matten, 2012) reflect that one of the factors influencing the adoption of socially responsible behavior by companies is the location of the premises of the Organization and the countries where they operate. Therefore the following hypothesis arises: corporations behave differently when it comes to social responsibility depending on the country they are in.

The questionnaire used to collect the necessary data was completed by each of the managers of the hotels under study. As can be seen in literature, company managers are considered to be of key importance when implementing CSR practices, (Campbell 2007) and therefore the hotel manager was considered an important informant to be able to analyze the object under study. It must be noted that both before and after the pre-test phase the questionnaire was revised by experts in the areas of tourism and social responsibility and management. Firstly the pre-test phase began in the month of April 2012. The data was collected via web forms, email and telephone. After the pre-test phase, the data was collected in the period between May and August of 2012 by email and regular mail, web forms, one on one visits, fax and telephone.

The response rate obtained was 30% (109 valid questionnaires); the most restrictive percentage level was accepted to validate the sample as it is in line with works such as those of Vargas-Sánchez and Riquel-Ligero (2015) with a response rate of 33.3%. Lower response rates were discarded in line with the works of Llamas-Sanchez, Garcia-Morales and Martin-Tapia (2013) with 21.33%; Šarotar, et al. (2013) with 13.3%; Gallardo, Sánchez and Corchuelo (2013) that obtained 11.07% response rate; others that were even lower such as Godos and Fernández (2011) with a percentage of 5%. The sample error obtained is 6%, where p=q=0. 5.

The data was submitted to descriptive statistical analysis and factor analysis, and the statistical package SPSS (version 18.0) was used in order to do so. The statistical methodology of the analysis follows.

STATISTICAL METHODOLOGY OF THE ANALYSIS

The descriptive statistics study was used in order to analyze the data to obtain the most precise idea possible of its features. This was achieved by paying attention to three basic aspects, central tendency, dispersion, and distribution manner. In this study when it came to central tendency, the mean, the mode and the median was analyzed. As for dispersion, standard deviation, the minimum and maximum was analyzed. Finally, distribution manner was analyzed using kurtosis and asymmetry.

A brief description of the steps followed for developing factor analysis was then performed. To know if the data was optimal the analysis factor was applied. This consisted in subjecting the data to different tests in order to analyze their behavior. Based on the criteria previously laid down in this paragraph, the results were interpreted and in order to obtain the most adequate set of variables and factors the most appropriate decisions were made.

In this work the application for factor analysis was the selection of variables. This type of analysis made it possible to select, from amongst a large group of variables, which were most involved in the description of the phenomenon under study. It also made it possible to only keep the initial variables that were closely correlated with the factors that were considered to be most important.

1. Test Analysis

The tests to which the variables were subjected in order to provide information by carrying out factor analysis are explained below. Prior to factor analysis the correlations matrix was studied in order to see if it was suitable to apply this technique. To do so the determinant of the correlations matrix was used. A visual inspection of the data was carried out in order to analyze it; in the correlations matrix, in which it should be noted that there is a substantial quantity of correlations greater than 0.3 (Aymerich & Meseguer, 2004) and the determinant of the correlations matrix whose value should be very low was checked. The next step was to carry out the Kaiser-Meyer-Olkin (KMO) test to verify if the partial correlations between the variables were sufficiently small. Verdú (2002) and Perez (2005) indicate that the level defined as the minimum for the KMO is 0.5. Then the data was subjected to Bartlett's sphericity test in order to test the null hypothesis, the correlations matrix was an identity matrix. The level of significance (sig) should be less than 0.05, the closest it is to zero (0) the better (Bartlett, 1951). Cronbach's alpha was used to study reliability, the minimum value defined by Nunnally (1978) is 0.7. Subsequently the communalities, the explained variance and the sedimentation graph were studied. Using the principal components method a communality close to 0 (zero) indicates that the factors did not explain the variability of a variable at all, whilst a value of 1 (one) would indicate that the variable was fully explained by the factors. The value of the explained variance must be within the range of 60-80%, since this was what was suitable for social research in the analysis of main components (APC), according to Wubneh (1987) and Wang (2005). Finally the matrix of major components was analyzed, and in the case of getting more than one factor after rotation, the matrix of rotated components using the Varimax rotation method and the components in rotated space graph was analyzed. Based on the components in the rotated space graph you could check the position of the different variables, this was how its grouping by factors was established.

2. Problems

Finally it must be pointed out that any empirical study is considered to be limited in some aspect, these limitations should be taken into consideration when interpreting the results and conclusions that emerge. They must also be taken into account for future research. First of all it must be stressed that this investigation has relied on measures based on the perceptions of hotel managers and therefore in all the cases the information comes from a single respondent. As a result, the possibility that the respondents' perceptions do not encompass the reality of the whole range of stakeholders that may be involved, both internal and external to the organization exists. On the other hand, it should be noted that the measures of some variables is based on respondents' subjective perceptions. The possibility of including character or objective nature measures in future studies that improve the measurement validity of the results obtained should be considered. Finally it must be pointed out that the factors contain a different set of variables in each of the cases analyzed, and this therefore implies a limitation in the research.

SOLUTIONS AND RECOMMENDATIONS

Firstly, the main features of the informant, in this case the hotel managers are presented. This is followed by the results of the descriptive statistical analysis and the analysis factor of the scale of corporate social responsibility under the three dimensions (social, economic and environmental).

In the analysis of gender note that more than half of the managers throughout the hotels in the two regions are men, only 30% are women. The percentage represented by women increases slightly in the North of Portugal being 34% compared to 28% in Galicia. Nine intervals that represent the age range of the hotel managers of hotels have been established, the minimum range being between 18 and 30 years old and the maximum range between 66 upwards. Generically, it is worth mentioning that senior men are younger than women in the same positions. In Galicia, those who occupy management positions are generally younger than in the North of Portugal. It must be emphasized that after a certain age, 60 years old in Spain and 55 years old in the North of Portugal, women have no representation in management positions. The latter analysis is then followed by the descriptive statistical analysis of the social responsibility scale.

1. Descriptive Statistical Analysis

The descriptive statistics study was used in order to analyze the data to obtain the most precise idea possible of its features. This is achieved by paying attention to three basic aspects, central tendency, dispersion, and distribution manner. In this study when it comes to central tendency, the mean, the mode and the median is analyzed. As for dispersion, standard deviation, the minimum and maximum is analyzed. Finally, distribution manner is analyzed using kurtosis and asymmetry. Table 2 shows the results obtained after submitting the data from both regions to descriptive statistics using SPSS (version 18).

The data presented in Table 2 is then analyzed taking into consideration that the number of items analyzed in Galicia are 65 and in the case of the North of Portugal are 44. In the environmental dimension, reducing emissions is the most valued item in the development of environmental practices in both regions. In Galicia energy saving appears second in order of importance in contrast to the Northern Region of Portugal where investment for reducing impact planning is valued more. All of them agree that the use of products with low environmental impact is the practice which is least applied in the hotels in the regions under study.

With reference to the economic dimension, all items are measured with the highest number (5), and exceed the 4.38 average. The less developed practice in Galicia is maintaining the best prices (DE3) in relation to the quality offered in contrast to the North of Portugal where this practice is of the most importance. The most applied practice in hotels in Galicia is that products and services have a high standard of quality (DE2). The least developed practice by the hotels located in the Northern Region of Portugal is to offer accurate information about

When it comes to the social aspect in the hotels located in the North of Portugal, the most important social practice *is* promoting the training and professional development of employees (DS4). The least important practice in the North of Portugal is the relationship between employees' wages (DS2) and the responsibilities and the benefits obtained. For the hotels located in Galicia, promoting equal opportunities (DS6) is the most important social practice. This phenomenon may be due to the dissemination and specific repercussion of the Equality Act which was applied in Galicia in the year 2007, as well as the

Table 2. Statistical-descriptive

D	Item	North Portugal								Galicia							
		x	M	X	σ	Mn	Mx	K	A	x	M	X	σ	Mn	Mx	K	A
ENVIRONMENTAL	DM1	4	4	4.11	0.66	3	5	-0.57	-0.11	4	4	3.86	0,66	2	5	0.14	-0.18
	DM2	4	4	3.66	0.89	1	5	0.86	-0.70	4	4	3.62	0,93	1	5	0.61	-0.70
	DM3	5	5	4.45	0.63	3	5	-0.41	-1.68	5	5	4.58	0,68	2	5	2.64	-1.68
	DM4	4	5	3.91	1.19	2	5	0.46	-0.70	4	5	4.28	0.80	2	5	-0.44	-0.70
	DM5	5	5	4.48	0.67	3	5	-0.24	-1.44	5	5	4.46	0.77	2	5	1.70	-1.44
	DM6	5	5	4.61	0.58	3	5	0.58	-3.28	5	5	4.80	0.54	2	5	1.25	-3.28
	DM7	4	4	4.11	0.78	3	5	-1.32	-1.07	4	4	4.05	0.83	2	5	2.01	-1.07
	DM8	5	5	4.34	0.78	3	5	-0.98	-1.69	5	5	4.52	0.73	2	5	2.90	-1.69
ECONOMIC	DE1	5	5	4.59	0.69	2	5	1.75	-1.88	5	5	4.62	0.63	2	5	1.83	-1.80
	DE2	5	5	4.66	0.61	3	5	1.64	-1.62	5	5	4.72	0.67	2	5	1.72	-2.77
	DE3	5	5	4.77	0.52	3	5	1.68	-2.30	5	5	4.38	0.76	1	5	1.65	-1.65
	DE4	5	5	4.57	0.63	3	5	0.36	-1.16	5	5	4.49	0.69	2	5	1.37	-1.61
	DE5	5	5	4.61	0.62	3	5	0.91	-1.38	5	5	4.60	0.66	2	5	1.20	-1.78
SOCIAL	DS1	5	5	4.50	0.73	2	5	2.08	-1.50	4	4	4.29	0.74	2	5	1.13	-1.01
	DS2	5	5	4.23	1.16	1	5	1.36	-1.50	4	5	4.05	0.96	2	5	0.40	-0.86
	DS3	5	5	4.39	0.75	2	5	0.98	-1.12	4	5	3.95	1.21	1	5	0.72	-1.23
	DS4	5	5	4.52	0.82	2	5	2.62	-1.79	4	5	4.26	0.96	1	5	2.02	-1.65
	DS5	5	5	4.27	1.02	2	5	1.49	-1.41	4	4	4.08	0.97	2	5	1.86	-1.35
	DS6	5	5	4.50	0.76	2	5	1.66	-1.48	5	5	4.63	0.80	3	5	2.33	-2.60
	DS7	5	5	4.43	0.87	2	5	1.66	-1.48	5	5	4.51	0.66	3	5	-0.09	-1.01

M: mode; X: average; σ: standard deviation; x: median; K: Kurtosis; Mn: minimum; Mx: maximum; A: asymmetry; D: dimensions

(Source: Own elaboration)

implementation of strong training measures and the dissemination of laws and regulations concerning this matter. The least important practice in Galicia, is the creation of employment (DS3) taking on trainees, creation of new jobs, etc. It is worth noting, due to its great difference, that this is the only practice that obtains a rating of under four.

In the mode analysis, the most frequent value in the data matrix in Portugal in all the variables is 5 except for environmental practices related to the minimization of the environmental impact, organic items and the use of products with a low environmental impact which is 4. Unlike the hotels located in Galicia, although many practices presented a rating of 5, there are practices in different areas with a rating equal to 4. In both regions there is no variable that has a value more frequent in the data matrixes lower than 4, and therefore the hotel managers state that they carry out CSR practices intensely. The hotels located in Portugal carry out practices in all areas in an intense manner, and in three of their practices the environmental aspect is not carried out so intensely, as opposed to the hotels located in Galicia, which carry out practices in a more or less intense way, in all CSR aspects.

The practices carried out in social, economic and environmental aspects in Galicia and the Northern Region of Portugal behave in an asymmetrically negative way, the values tend to gather more intensely on the right side of the mean.

From the descriptive statistical analysis, we can draw the conclusion that a different trend in the behavior of the hotels is revealed depending on their location when it comes to the three aspects of corporate social responsibility. Carrying out socially responsible practices in social and economic aspects in both regions is different, but there is a certain similarity in the case of practices related to the environmental aspect. The most highly rated aspect is the economic aspect with the social and environmental aspects coming in second and third place respectively in the hotels located in Galicia. The hotels in the Northern Region of Portugal carry out the economic aspect more and in second place practices related to the social and environmental aspect. The factor analysis can be seen below.

2. Factor Analysis

Corporate social responsibility dimension scales are studied under the factor analysis test. The data undergoes different tests using the statistical pack SPSS (version 18.0) and the spreadsheet program from the Microsoft Office pack (version 2003). The steps to apply and the criteria to be taken into consideration have been described in the previous section, main focus in the statistical methodology of the analysis section, and the results obtained can be seen below.

2.1. Environmental Dimension

Using the original variables that make up CSR practices in the environmental dimension, an analysis of the main components is carried out and the appropriate grouping of variables is decided, by obtaining a lower number of factors which make it possible to classify the variables of this aspect. Table 3 shows the summary of the environmental aspect scale tests in both regions (Galicia and North Portugal).

The environmental dimension scale, in both regions (Galicia and North Portugal), fulfils all the requirements previously established, after putting the data through a second phase of factor analysis testing. In the model of the Northern Region of Portugal, after the first phase of analysis, the DM3 (energy saving) and DM4 (energy sources) variables are eliminated; the communalities of these variables are not relevant, they have very low figures and a tendency towards zero. Clearly these variables do not add value to the factor in which they are located, and are therefore eliminated. Following the analysis in this second phase the established requirements are fulfilled and two factors are obtained as a result. Factor one, which has been referred to as Environmental practices of predisposition is composed of two items: minimizing environmental impact (DM1) and using products with low environmental impact (DM2), this factor is the same as the model of Galicia. And factor two, which has been referred to as Environmental practices of action consists of four items: investment in impact reduction planning (DM5), reduction of emissions (DM6), ecological articles (DM7) and recyclable containers and packaging (DM8), this last factor differs in one element to the model of Galicia.

The case of the model based on the data of Galicia, in the first phase of factor analysis the total explained variance is lower than the established criteria and three factors are identified. In this case this third factor is eliminated, consisting of the DM4 (energy sources) and (ecological articles) DM7 variables. These variables are removed as they do not pass the statistical tests to which they were subjected. After a second analysis, in the case of Galicia, the previously established requirements are also fulfilled

Table 3. Summary of the results of the Environmental Dimension scale tests

Test		North Portugal		Galicia	
Correlations matrix		>0.3	ok	>0.3	ok
Determinant value		0.044	ok	0.022	ok
KMO		0.747	ok	0.705	ok
Bartlett´s test of sphericity		0.000	ok	0.000	ok
Cronbach´s Alpha		0.825	ok	0.730	ok
Total explained variance		75.7%	ok	63.8%	ok
Tests	**Variables**	**Initial**	**Extraction**	**Initial**	**Extraction**
Communalities (principal components analysis extraction method)	Minimize environmental impact (DM1)	1	0.685	1	0.762
	Use environmentally friendly product (DM2)	1	0.788	1	0.742
	Energy saving (DM3)	--	--	1	0.518
	Alternative energy sources (DM4)	--	--	--	--
	Investment planning for reducing impact (DM5)	1	0.708	1	0.524
	Reducing emissions (DM6)	1	0.800	1	0.788
	Ecological articles (DM7)	1	0.693	--	--
	Recyclable packaging (DM8)	1	0.866	1	0.493
Tests	**Variables**	**Components**		**Components**	
		1	**2**	**1**	**2**
Rotated matrix components (Extraction method Analysis of main components. Rotation method: standardization Varimax with Kaiser. The rotation has coincided in 3 items).	Minimize environmental impact (DM1)	0.293	0.774	0.186	0.853
	Use environmentally friendly product (DM2)	0.063	0.885	0.075	0.858
	Energy saving (DM3)	--	--	0.719	0.026
	Alternative energy sources (DM4)	--	--	--	--
	Investment planning for reducing impact (DM5)	0.737	0.406	0.586	0.325
	Reducing emissions (DM6)	0.866	0.225	0.885	0.066
	Ecological articles (DM7)	0.823	0.122	--	--
	Recyclable packaging (DM8)	0.927	0.086	0.653	0.257
--: eliminated in the first phase					

(Source: Own elaboration)

obtaining two factors which are the same as the model of North Portugal, in which factor two differs slightly in the set of elements. Factor one, which has been referred to as Environmental practices of pre-disposition is composed of two items: minimizing environmental impact (DM1) and using products of low environmental impact (DM2). And factor two, which has been referred to as Environmental practices of action consists of four items: Energy saving (DM3), investment in impact reduction planning (DM5), reduction of emissions (DM6) and containers and recyclable packaging (DM8). It is worth taking note that in both models, Galicia and the Northern region of Portugal, the alternative energy sources item (DM4) is eliminated for failing to fulfill the established requirements.

2.2. Economic Dimension

The results after applying the different tests to the original variables that make up the development of CSR practices in the economic dimension are presented in Table 4.

In both regions, Galicia and North Portugal, the construct CSR practices in the economic dimension is composed of one single factor which includes all of the variables initially proposed, fulfilling, in this way, all the previously established criteria. In this case the models of both regions contain the same set of variables.

2.3. Social Dimension

Outlined in Table 5 is the summary of the results of the tests to which the data belonging to the CSR practices scale in the social dimension of both regions was subjected.

Table 4. Summary of the results of the Economic Dimension Scale

Tests		North Portugal		Galicia	
Correlations matrix		>0.3	ok	>0.3	ok
Determinant value		0.015	ok	0.027	ok
KMO		0.858	ok	0.775	ok
Bartlett´s test ofsphericity		0.000	ok	0.000	ok
Cronbach´s Alpha		0.925	ok	0. 867	ok
Total explained variance		77.5%	ok	60.9%	ok
Test	**Variables**	**Initial**	**Extraction**	**Initial**	**Extraction**
Communalities (principal components analysis extraction method)	Quality products and services (DE1)	1	0.860	1	0.718
	Products and services that fulfill a standard (DE2)	1	0.831	1	0.417
	Better price levels (DE3)	1	0.787	1	0.712
	Accurate information on products and services (DE4)	1	0.776	1	0.585
	Consumer rights (DE5)	1	0.622	1	0.617
Test	**Variables**	**Components**		**Components**	
		1		**1**	
Components matrix Extraction method: Principal components analysis. 1 Extracted component.	Quality products and services (DE1)	0.927		0.847	
	Products and services that fulfill a standard (DE2)	0.911		0.646	
	Better price levels (DE3)	0.887		0.844	
	Accurate information on products and services (DE4)	0.881		0.765	
	Consumer rights (DE5)	0.789		0.786	
--: eliminated in the first phase					

(Source: Own elaboration)

Table 5. Summary of the results of the Social Aspect scale tests

Tests		North Portugal		Galicia	
Correlations matrix		>0.3	ok	>0.3	ok
Determining value		0.001	ok	0.023	ok
KMO		0.825	ok	0.741	ok
Bartlett´s test of sphericity		0.000	ok	0.000	ok
Cronbach´s Alpha		0.938	ok	0. 801	ok
Total explained variance		74.2%	ok	64.2%	ok
Test	**Variables**	**Initial**	**Extraction**	**Initial**	**Extraction**
Communalities (principal components analysis extraction method)	Employee quality (DS1)	1	0.722	1	0.684
	Employee salary (DS2)	1	0.764	--	--
	Creation of employment (DS3)	1	0.615	--	--
	Employee training (DS4)	1	0.745	--	--
	Conciliation policies (DS5)	1	0.829	1	0.582
	Equal opportunities (DS6)	1	0.683	1	0.587
	Employee dialogue mechanisms (DS7)	1	0.838	1	0.715
Test	**Variables**	**Components**		**Components**	
		1		**1**	
Components matrix Extraction method: Principal components analysis. 1 Extracted component.	Employee quality (DS1)	0.850		0.817	
	Employee salary (DS2)	0.874		--	
	Creation of employment (DS3)	0.784		--	
	Employee training (DS4)	0.863		--	
	Conciliation policies (DS5)	0.911		0.763	
	Equal opportunities (DS6)	0.826		0.766	
	Employee dialogue mechanisms (DS7)	0.915		0.845	
--: eliminated in the first phase					

(Source: Own elaboration)

The models that apply the data from the Northern Region of Portugal fulfill all the established criteria. All the items proposed initially are included in one single factor. Unlike the Galician model, two factors are obtained in the first phase of the factor analysis. The minimum value established is not reached for the total variance explained, remaining well below 60%. In the second phase of the analysis three variables that make up the second factor (DS2, DS3 and DS4) are eliminated. These variables are eliminated as they did not pass the statistical tests to which they were subjected. Once this second phase has been carried out after the elimination of this set of variables, the fulfillment of the previously established requirements is confirmed. In the model of Galicia, the social aspect is made up of one single-factor, the same as the model of Portugal, but not because of the same set of items.

2.4. Discussion

After submitting the data from both regions, Galicia and North Portugal, the proposed hypothesis can be confirmed given the differences in the results obtained in both regions, corporations behave differently when it comes to social responsibility depending on the country they are in. This result is in line with those obtained by Campbel (2007).

One of the objectives of this study was to find a scale that makes it possible to measure CSR appropriately, adapt it to the object of study and validate it. The scale developed by Gallardo, Sanchez and Corchuelo (2013) fulfills the stipulated conditions. However the set of items proposed by the authors does not coincide with the results in this research. All the information is supplied by a smaller number of variables, in the case of social dimension and the environment. In the case of economic dimension they remain the same. The set of items is configured. The scale is valid for each of the regions studied, although the constructs contain a different set of variables in each of the cases, which represents a limitation for the research.

To verify socially responsible behavior performed a descriptive statistical analysis was carried out; comparing the importance given to CSR practices in both regions based on the study of the three dimensions identified by Elkington (1997).The conclusion reached was that, in general, socially responsible behavior in both countries was different, according to the findings of Campbell (2007). In a more detailed dimension analysis, environmental practices are fairly balanced in both regions. In both countries good practice has spread and proliferated quite well in this regard, and many are in line with economic savings; companies are expected to take advantage of the implementation of these practices. Those with greater variation are in the economic and social dimension. In the economic dimension, in Galicia, it should be noted that more importance is given to quality recognition, in line with what happens across the country (Spain), not being so in Portugal. The social factor in Galicia is framed by equal opportunities, whilst hotels are committed to practices that focus on training and developing staff. It is believed that due to the weakening of the economy, practices related to creating employment, hiring of new staff and interns takes on less importance for these companies.

On the other hand, after statistical analysis, it is verified that hotels give great importance to CSR, consistent with the sustainable development measures proposed by the institutions (Ministry of Economy and Employment, 2012; Ministry of Industry, Energy and Tourism, 2012; Northern Regional Coordination and Development Commission, 2014 and Tourism of Galicia, 2014). Especially in the implementation of environmental measures aimed at efficiency and saving (water, energy). Such is not the case for measures to reduce the environmental impact. In the social approach, the North of Portugal gives more importance to training measures. In the economic dimension more importance is given to quality recognition, especially in Galicia.

From this research work a series of implications that can help managers to define a strategy in the field of CSR arise. This type of organization has the need for social acceptance; therefore, all the efforts made to maintain good relations with the various pressure groups will be repaid to the organization in the form of resources of various kinds. This is why social responsibility policies in their broadest sense are especially necessary in this type of organization. A company that sides with institutional strategic plans implies taking advantage of all the potentiality and receiving institutional support. For the hotel managers it is important to promote their environment in a sustainable way, it allows for new partnerships and improving the use of resources, as well as an interesting economic return.

FUTURE RESEARCH DIRECTIONS

In this section there are future lines of research that are expected to provide continuity and amplitude to this investigation and help overcome the limitations encountered.

It is believed that a longitudinal study should be conducted over a period of time using the initial data obtained in this study as a starting point. It is proposed to conduct this study at a time when the economy of both countries is buoyant and compare the results with the results obtained in this study in a situation of economic crisis. With these results it would be possible to confirm if there is the same trend in a state of economic crisis and in a prosperous economic situation. This study would also allow verifying if the adoption of CSR practices is a fad with an expiry date, if they are maintained or if the implementation of such practices intensifies. It would be possible to see how social responsibility practices evolve at an organizational level.

On the other hand, the investigation will be aimed at hotel chains. This would allow a wider view of the strategy used in the larger units (chains) and compare it with the smaller units (hotels), allowing to check if the initial hypothesis is met equally by both the strategic vision of hotel chains and the vision of a hotel unit.

One way to complement this study would be to apply qualitative research methods. An investigation of specific hotel units through the application of the methodology of case studies could be conducted. The study would include hotels that implement socially responsibility practices and compare it to other hotels that do not implement these practices. By doing so, the investigation could show the motivations that lead to implement or not implement socially responsible practices.

It would be possible to propose another qualitative study using a different methodology. It would consist in conducting in depth interviews to gain insight into the reasons that lead companies to adopt CSR practices. Different points of view, opinions and reflections of different stakeholders (professionals, experts, associations, among others) from different areas (CSR, tourism, marketing, and organization of companies) would have to be considered in the interviews

Finally, a quantitative study that shows the possible limitations of this investigation would be conducted. In this case a survey would be carried out collecting information from various stakeholders instead of collecting information from a single interviewee, as in this investigation. This proposal is based on the studies of Kumar, Stern and Anderson (1993) who recommend the use of multiple interviewees to give more exactitude in the phase of data collection.

CONCLUSION

A conclusion can be drawn in this investigation from the descriptive statistical analysis that there is a different tendency in hotel behavior, from the analysis of the point of view of the three CSR aspects (Elkington, 1997). The participation of the hotels when it comes to carrying out social responsibility practices in social and economic aspects is different, but it is similar in the practices used in the environmental aspect. In this case, both Spain and Portugal have developed comprehensive environmental legislation under the umbrella of the European Union. In social aspects the legislation and regulations are different. In the case of Galicia social issues related to equal opportunities are promoted, and in Portugal less so. In Galicia issues relating to employment are left aside, as fewer work vacancies are created due to the economic crisis and the conditions depreciate. This also occurs in Portugal, but there is greater collaboration and awareness in this regard. In the economic field everything related to the interests of this aspect is a concern both in Galicia and in Portugal. Comparing these results with the future prospects that both countries want to achieve, it can be deduced that the institutions must continue strengthening the environmental behavior of these organizations, although it is possible to denote that they are working in the right direction. However, the lines of action in the social field are not obtaining good results, especially with regards to the issue of employment and workers. Due to the economic crisis in both countries, this aspect has suffered a major setback. The implementation of practices related to the economic aspect must also be insisted on in order to achieve the purposes framed within the sustainable strategic programs of both countries.

Considering all this it is possible to draw the conclusion that the hypothesis can be confirmed. The behavior of the hotels in both regions is different, there are small variations, despite being two adjoining regions and with a similar culture, although they belong to two different countries. Therefore, it could be possible to study the institutional paradigm in future research in order to implement appropriate actions to achieve the purposes framed within the strategic programs for sustainability.

The analysis of corporate social responsibility practices was carried out under the hypothesis of the statement extracted from Maigan and Ralston (2002), the tendency towards socially responsible behavior varies based on different countries. Based on the two types of analysis carried out in this study, the propensity of different behavior depending on the country in social and economic aspects in three, four and five star hotels, belonging to the northern region of Portugal and Galicia is confirmed. These hotels tend to have similar socially responsible behavior in the environmental aspect. The main motivations have been explained above.

It is also necessary to highlight that, based on the confirmatory factor analysis with Varimax rotation, the variables that are part of the CSR scale, based on the three aspects for three, four and five star hotels located in Galicia and North Portugal varies slightly from the set of items originally proposed in the scales. Comparing the results, the data from the model of the Northern Region of Portugal obtains better statistics compared with that of Galicia.

This study has made it possible to deduce that when it comes to strategic decision-making the leading figure is the hotel director, but as there are different interested parties involved that can influence making decisions in this area, the hotel director is not the only party from whom information may be collected. On the other hand, our study cannot be generalized to the entire country, Spain and Portugal, but it offers relevant data in research. The aim with these last two questions is to expand this study, and more details can be found in the section future lines of research.

REFERENCES

Alvarez García, J., Vila Alonso, M., Fraiz Brea, J. A., & Río Rama, M. C. (2013). Análisis de las relaciones de dependencia entre los factores críticos de la calidad y los resultados. Sector de alojamiento turístico en España. *Investigaciones Europeas de Dirección y Economía de la Empresa, 19*(2), 74–89. doi:10.1016/j.iedee.2012.08.001

Aupperle, K. E., Carroll, A. B., & Hatfield, J. D. (1985). An Empirical Examination of the Relationship between Corporate Social Responsibility and Profitability. *Academy of Management Journal, 28*(2), 446–463. doi:10.2307/256210

Aymerich Martínez, J., & Meseguer Artola, A. (2004). Investigación descriptiva: análisis de información. In A. Meseguer & J. Vilaseca (Eds.), *Coord), Estadística aplicada*. Catalunya: Fundació Universitat Oberta de Catalunya.

Bartlett, M. S. (1951). A further note on tests of significance in factor analysis. *British Journal of Psychology, 4*, 1–2.

Boluk, K. (2013). Using CSR as a tool for development: An investigation of the fair hotels scheme in Ireland. *Journal of Quality Assurance in Hospitality & Tourism, 14*(1), 49–65. doi:10.1080/152800 8X.2013.749382

Brammer, S., Jackson, G., & Matten, D. (2012). Corporate Social Responsibility and institutional theory: New perspectives on private governance. *Socio-economic Review, 10*(1), 3–28. doi:10.1093/ser/mwr030

Campbell, J. L. (2007). Why would corporations behave in socially responsible ways? An institutional theory of corporate social responsibility. *Academy of Management Review, 32*(3), 946–967. doi:10.5465/ AMR.2007.25275684

Carrol, A. B. (1979). A Three Dimensional Conceptual Model of Corporate Performance. *Academy of Management Review, 4*(4), 497–505.

Claasen, C., & Roloff, J. (2012). The Link between Responsibility and Legitimacy: The Case of De Beers in Namibia. *Journal of Business Ethics, 107*(3), 379–398. doi:10.1007/s10551-011-1045-0

Davis, C. F. (1991). Agents without principles? The spread of the poison pill through the intercorporate network. *Administrative Science Quarterly, 38*(4), 583–613. doi:10.2307/2393275

Drucker, P. (1973). *La Gerencia, tareas, responsabilidad y prácticas*. Buenos Aires: ElAteneo.

Elkington, J. (1997). *Cannibals with Forks: The Triple Bottom Line of 21st Century Business* (2nd ed.). Oxford: Capstone Publishing Ltd.

European Commission. (2001). *Libro verde. Fomentar un marco Europeo para la responsabilidad social de las empresas*. Retrieved January 22, 2015, from: http://eur-lex.europa.eu/LexUriServ/site/es/ com/2001/com2001_0366es01.pdf

European Commission. (2011). *Estrategia renovada de la UE para 2011-2014 sobre la responsabilidad social de las empresas*. Retrieved January 22, 2015, from: http://eur-lex.europa.eu/LexUriServ/ LexUriServ.do?uri=COM:2011:0681:FIN:ES:PDF

Fanjul, E. (2010, September-October). Factores culturales e internacionalización de la empresa. *ICE, 856*, 7–19.

Freeman, R. (1984). *Strategic management: A stakeholders approach*. Zürich: Pitman. Fremdenverkehrslehre.

Galaskiewicz, J. (1991). Making corporate actors accountable: Institution-building in Minneapolis-St. Paul. In W.W. Powell, & P.J. DiMaggio, P.J. (Eds.), The new institutionalism in organizational analysis (pp. 293-310). Chicago: University of Chicago Press.

Gallardo Vázquez, D., Sánchez Hernández, M. I., & Corchuelo Martínez-Azúa, M. B. (2013). Validación de un instrumento de medida para la relación entre la orientación a la Responsabilidad Social Corporativa y otras variables estratégicas de la empresa. *Revista de Contabilidad. Spanish Accounting Review, 6*(1), 11–23.

Gessa, A., Ruiz, A., & Jimenez, M. A. (2008). *La responsabilidad social corporativa como modelo de gestión hotelera. Implantación y desarrollo en la red de paradores. Estableciendo puentes en una economía global*. Madrid: ESIC Editorial.

Godos, J., & Fernández, R. (2011). ¿Cómo se percibe la dirección socialmente responsable por parte de los altos directivos de empresas en España? *Universia Business Review, 29*, 32–49.

Humble, J. (1975). *La responsabilidad social de la empresa*. Madrid: F. Universidad Empresa.

Kumar, N., Stern, L., & Anderson, J. (1993). Conducting interorganizational research using key informants. *Academy of Management Journal, 36*(6), 1633–1651. doi:10.2307/256824

Lee, M. D. P. (2011). Configuration of External Influences: The Combined Effects of Institutions and Stakeholders on Corporate Social Responsibility Strategies. *Journal of Business Ethics, 102*(2), 281–298. doi:10.1007/s10551-011-0814-0

Llamas-Sanchez, R., Garcia-Morales, V., & Martin-Tapia, I. (2013). Factors affecting institutional change: A study of the adoption of Local Agenda 21 in Spain. *Journal of Organizational Change Management, 26*(6), 1045–1070. doi:10.1108/JOCM-03-2012-0037

Lopes, E.R. (Ed.). (2010). *A constelação do turismo na economia portuguesa*. Mirandela: Edições Jornal Sol.

Maigan, I., & Ralston, D. A. (2002). Corporate social responsibility in Europe and the U.S: Insights from businesses' self-presentations. *Journal of International Business Studies, 33*(3), 497–514. doi:10.1057/palgrave.jibs.8491028

Manente, M., Minghetti, V., & Mingotto, E. (2012). Ranking assessment systems for responsible tourism products and corporate social responsibility practices. *Anatolia, 23*(1), 75–89. doi:10.1080/13032 917.2011.653633

Martín Rojo, I., Gaspar González, A. I., Caro González, F. J., Castellanos Verdugo, M., & Oviedo García, M. A. (2008). *La responsabilidad social corporativa en los puertos deportivos y clubes náuticos de Andalucía: Diagnóstico y propuestas de mejoras para la innovación turística*. Sevilla: C. y D. Consejería de Turismo.

Martínez, P., Pérez, A., & Rodríguez del Bosque, I. (2014). Exploring the role of CSR in the organizational identity of hospitality companies: A case from the Spanish tourism industry. *Journal of Business Ethics, 124*(1), 47–66. doi:10.1007/s10551-013-1857-1

Ministry of Economy and Employment. (2012). *Plano Estratégico Nacional do Turismo (PENT) Horizonte 2013-2015*. Retrieved January 15, 2015, from http://www.turismodeportugal.pt/Portugu%C3%AAs/turismodeportugal/publicacoes/Documents/PENT%202012.pdf

Ministry of Industry, Energy, and Tourism. (2012). *Plan Nacional e Integral de Turismo 2012-2015 (PNIT)*. Retrieved January 15, 2015, from http://www.tourspain.es/es-es/VDE/Documentos%20Vision%20Destino%20Espaa/Plan%20Nacional%20e%20Integral%20de%20Turismo%202012_2015_FINAL_RE-VISADO%20150313.pdf

Northern Regional Coordination and Development Commission. (2014). *Programa Operacional Regional do Norte 2014-2020*. Retrieved January 15, 2015, from http://www.norte2020.pt/sites/default/files/public/uploads/programa/po_norte2020.pdf

Nunnally, J. C. (1978). *Psychometric theory* (2nd ed.). New York: McGraw-Hill.

Nyahunzvi, D. K. (2013). CSR reporting among Zimbabwe's hotel groups: A content analysis. *International Journal of Contemporary Hospitality Management, 25*(4), 595–613. doi:10.1108/09596111311322943

Orpen, C. (1987). The attitudes of United States and South African Managers to Corporate Social Responsibility. *Journal of Business Ethics, 6*(2), 89–96. doi:10.1007/BF00382022

Perdomo, J., & Escobar, A. (2011). La investigación en RSE : Una revisión desde el management. *Cuadernos de Administración, 24*(43), 193–219.

Pérez López, C. (2005). *Métodos estadísticos avanzados con Spss*. Madrid: Thomson.

Prieto, G. (1979). Balance social de la empresa: Aspectos doctrinales. *Revue d'Economie Politique, 82*(Mayo-Agosto), 62.

Quazi, A. M., & O'Brien, D. (2000). An empirical test of a cross-national model of Corporate Social Responsibility. *Journal of Business Ethics, 25*(1), 33–51. doi:10.1023/A:1006305111122

Ruf, B. M., Muralidhar, K., & Paul, K. (1998). The development of a systematic, aggregate measure of Corporate Social Performance. *Journal of Management, 24*(1), 119–133. doi:10.1177/014920639802400101

Sánchez-Fernández, M. D. (2015). Ferramentas e instrumentos de gestão estratégica de responsabilidade social: Setor turismo. *Tourism and Hospitality International Journal, 4*(2), 71–88.

Sánchez-Fernández, M. D., Vargas-Sánchez, A., & Remoaldo, P. (2014). Institutional Context and Hotel Social Responsibility. *Kybernetes, 43*(3/4), 413–426. doi:10.1108/K-12-2013-0267

Šarotar Zizek, S., Mulej, M., Milfelner, B., & Potocnik, A. (2013). Social responsibility in Slovenia. *Systems: Connecting Matter, Life. Culture Technique, 1*(1), 95–109.

Scott, W. R. (1995). *Institutions and organizations*. Thousand Oaks: Sage.

Singhapakdi, A., Vitell, S. J., Rallapalli, K. C., & Kraft, K. L. (1996). The perceived role of Ethics and Social Responsibility: A scale development. *Journal of Business Ethics, 15*(11), 1131–1140. doi:10.1007/BF00412812

Tourism of Galicia. (2014). *Plan Integral de Turismo de Galicia 2014-2016*. Retrieved January 15, 2015, from http://issuu.com/turismodegalicia/docs/pitg_detallado_2014_03_05

Vargas-Sánchez, A., & Riquel-Ligero, F. (2015). Golf tourism, its institutional setting, and environmental management: A longitudinal analysis. *European Journal of Tourism Research, 9*, 41–56.

Vela Sastre, E. (1977). El balance social de la empresa. *Economía Industrial, 168*, 4–25.

Verdu Jover, A. J. (2002). *Relación entre flexibilidad y desempeño organizativo: una aproximación desde la perspectiva de la gestión de la calidad total*. Alicante: Universidad Miguel Hernández.

Vitell, S. J., Ramos, E., & Nishihara, C. M. (2010). The Role of Ethics and Social Responsibility in Organizational Success: A Spanish Perspective. *Journal of Business Ethics, 91*(4), 467–483. doi:10.1007/s10551-009-0134-9

Wang, C. H. (2005). Constructing multivariate process capability indices for short-run production. *International Journal of Advanced Manufacturing Technology, 26*(11-12), 1306–1311. doi:10.1007/s00170-004-2397-8

Wubneh, M. A. (1987). Multivariate analysis of socio-economic characteristics of urban areas in Ethiopia. *Afr. Urban Quaterly, 2*, 425–433.

Zanfardini, M., Aguirre, P., & Tamagni, L. (2015). *The evolution of CSR's research in tourism context: A review from 1992 to 2012*. Anatolia; doi:10.1080/13032917.2015.1083207

KEY TERMS AND DEFINITIONS

Bartlett's Test of Sphericity: Test that makes it possible to estimate the factorial scores' coefficients.

Communality: Communality is the proportion of variance with which each variable contributes to the final solution, namely the creation of factors.

Components in Rotated Space Graph: Graph that makes it possible to check the position of the different variables, that is, how the grouping by factors is established.

Correlations Matrix: Set of data that informs about the structure of correlations between the observed variables.

Cronbach's Alpha: A ratio used to measure the reliability of a measurement scale.

Kaiser-Meyer-Olkin: Index measuring the adequacy of sampling or sampling adequacy, also known by the acronym KMO.

Principal Components Analysis: Method which allows the reduction of an original set of variables to a smaller set of components/non-correlated factors that represent most of the information found in the original variables.

Chapter 16
Facilitating Hospitality and Tourism Management in Global Business

Kijpokin Kasemsap
Suan Sunandha Rajabhat University, Thailand

ABSTRACT

This chapter explains the overview of hospitality management; the overview of tourism management; product quality, service quality, price, customer satisfaction, and consumer trust in hospitality and tourism management; the significance of hospitality management in global business; the significance of tourism management in global business; and the managerial implications of hospitality and tourism management. Tourism and hospitality industry is one of the most important industries in the modern business world. It is essential to acquire a driving enthusiasm for customer service and a strong sense of professionalism to develop and maintain customer satisfaction in the hospitality and tourism industry. Effective hospitality and tourism management positively affects customer satisfaction, firm growth, and productivity in global business. The chapter argues that facilitating hospitality and tourism management in global business has the potential to enhance organizational performance and reach strategic goals in the digital age.

INTRODUCTION

From a practical business perspective, hospitality and tourism management sector is one of the most important sectors in the global economy (Israeli, 2014). From an academic perspective, the perspectives of hospitality and tourism management are the interdisciplinary fields that focus on many areas, such as management, strategic management, human behavior, organizational behavior, finance, yield management, planning, and marketing (Israeli, 2014). Tourism contributes to the growth of regional economies, thus providing a source of income for both resident households and local firms (Incera & Fernandez, 2015). Tourism is related to globalization and modernity (Wang, Niu, Lu, & Qian, 2015). Tourism is viewed as the development priority concerning government and international organizations (Tolkach & King, 2015).

DOI: 10.4018/978-1-5225-0201-2.ch016

Tourism has become one of the most growing service sectors in global business (Tang & Tan, 2015). Modeling tourism demand is important in countries where the income from tourism constitutes a considerable percentage of their gross domestic product (Akın, 2015). Tourism marketing can help facilitate the dynamic evolutions and the demands of tourism industry concerning the diversity of tourism marketing topics (Kasemsap, 2015a). The hospitality industry in many parts of the world is expected to realize the significant rates of growth in the next few years (Pirani & Arafat, 2014). Recognizing the importance of product and service quality, satisfaction, and trust every firm in the hospitality and tourism industry is becoming more concerned about managing and improving quality, satisfaction, and trust (Han & Hyun, 2015).

This chapter aims to bridge the gap in the literature on the thorough literature consolidation of hospitality and tourism management. The extensive literature of hospitality and tourism management provides a contribution to practitioners and researchers by describing the theory and applications of hospitality and tourism management in order to maximize the business impact of hospitality and tourism management in global business.

BACKGROUND

Research with the tourism and hospitality management realms has reached a certain degree of maturity, demonstrated by researchers via both qualitative and quantitative methods (Köseoglu, Sehitoglu, & Craft, 2015). An emergent contemporary hospitality literature is dedicated to the methodological appraisal and development (Robinson, Solnet, & Breakey, 2014). There are a number of scholarly works published by researchers that investigate the domains of tourism and hospitality management (Tsang & Hsu, 2011).

Many studies map the intellectual structure of tourism and hospitality management-related disciplines, such as organization studies (Ferreira, Pinto, & Serra, 2014), general management (Tahai & Meyer, 1999), strategic management (Nerur, Rasheed, & Natarajan, 2008), international management (Acedo & Casillas, 2005), knowledge management (Ponzi, 2002), human resource management (Fernandez-Alles & Ramos-Rodríguez, 2009), business ethics (Tseng, Duan, Tung, & Kung, 2010), information systems management (Culnan, 1987), and operations management (Pilkington & Liston-Heyes, 1999).

Contributions of economics to hospitality literature are largely empirical and microeconomics-related (Mohammed, Guillet, & Law, 2015). Many researchers recognize hospitality management as a field of study with a mission of preparing students for successful careers in this industry and helping the industry solve its problems (Lugosi, Lynch, & Morrison, 2009). The focus of hospitality management research should be on instrumental research that addresses the main challenges of hospitality industry, rather than topics that have little practical implications (Pizam, 2003). Tourism affects economic growth (Jalil, Mahmood, & Idrees, 2013). The tourism sector has become the main source of income for many countries contributing to their economies, generating markets for a wide variety of goods and services both directly and indirectly related to tourism (Eugenio-Martin & Campos-Soria, 2011).

PERSPECTIVES OF HOSPITALITY AND TOURISM MANAGEMENT

This section emphasizes the overview of hospitality management; the overview of tourism management; product quality, service quality, price, customer satisfaction, and consumer trust in hospitality and tourism management; the significance of hospitality management in global business; the significance of tourism management in global business; and the managerial implications of hospitality and tourism management.

Overview of Hospitality Management

The hospitality industry is a major industry that combines the components of product and service (Israeli, 2014). Given that performance in the hospitality sector is a multi-dimensional construct, there are various recognized measure approaches (e.g., the balanced scorecard) that combine quantitative and qualitative performance measures (Kaplan & Norton, 1996). However, hospitality leaders often adhere to one paradigm (e.g., production or service) which title their management and decision-making style as production-oriented or service-oriented perspective (Harris, 1999). Israeli et al. (2006) stated that hotel managers may lack a clear vision about managing hospitality performance under production and service paradigms.

Competency models have become a meaningful method for determining requisite skills in both hospitality and tourism education (Chung-Herrera, Enz, & Lankau, 2003) and operations (Tas, 1988). Competency models can serve a wide variety of organizational functions and can help develop managerial skills (Testa & Sipe, 2012). Many studies have described significant competencies in the hospitality field (Johanson, Ghiselli, Shea, & Roberts, 2011). Hospitality researchers have continued to indicate the fundamental competencies and curricular needs perceived to be important by practitioners in the hospitality areas (Fjelstul, 2007). Researchers have compared how students, educators, and practitioners effectively perceive such competencies in order to determine whether there is the broad stakeholder agreement on the skills needed for various roles in the hospitality industry (Raybould & Wilkins, 2005).

Managers should learn through work activities (Marsick, 2003). Pre-designed educational programs and training courses limit learning that reflects constantly changing work practices. In the hospitality industry, the pre-planned approach utilizing information and communication technology (ICT) (e.g., learning management system) drives management development provision (Li, Buhalis, Lockwood, & Benzine, 2007). Hospitality leaders should utilize the learning management system and ICT applications in their daily practices toward gaining potential to facilitate their learning in the hospitality industry (Li, Lee, & Law, 2012). Modern organizations that emphasize employees' learning requirements can achieve business objectives through building knowledge, transferring knowledge, and applying knowledge in the learning organizations (Kasemsap, 2016a).

Service quality and customer satisfaction is the fundamental goal of tourism organizations that takes a strategic approach (McCole, 2004). Customer value is positively correlated with customer satisfaction (Kasemsap, 2014a). The balance of business and people-related competencies is required for effective service leadership (Sandwith, 1993). The managerial success is related to the constant development in the hospitality industry (Testa & Sipe, 2012). Self-development is the most influential issue for the hospitality leaders (Kay & Russette, 2000). Hospitality leaders should professionally act, effectively organize the service standard, and provide organizational value (Yoon, Beatty, & Suh, 2001).

Overview of Tourism Management

Tourism is one of the most significant service industries in global business (Pérez & del Bosque, 2014). Tourism can be an impetus for the positive growth and economic success (Dodds & Kuehnel, 2010). However, if irresponsibly utilized, tourism can be a source for leakage, low fares and seasonal employment, instability and low job status, environmental degradation, displacement of local people, inflation, and the dilution of culture (Agarwal, 2002).

Sustainability has gained momentum in the tourism industry, where tourism organizations must play a role in the exercise of good governance practices (Martínez, Pérez, & del Bosque, 2013). Sustainability is considered as a multi-dimensional construct that equally emphasizes the economic, social, and environmental duties of companies (Panwar, Rinne, Hansen, & Juslin, 2006). Regarding sustainability, triple bottom line (TBL) include three dimensions (i.e., economic, social, and environmental perspectives) (Pérez & del Bosque, 2014).

The economic dimension is based on ensuring the feasible economic activities so that all stakeholders suitably receive the distributed socioeconomic benefits (Dyllick & Hockerts, 2002). The social dimension refers to the consideration for the cultural authenticity of host communities, the preservation of their architectural and living cultural assets and traditional values, and a contribution to intercultural understanding and tolerance (Dyllick & Hockerts, 2002). The environmental dimension refers to the optimal utilization of environmental resources, which is a crucial component of tourism development, protecting ecological processes, and conserving natural resources (Dyllick & Hockerts, 2002).

The academic literature contains the investigation of case studies of countries and tourist destinations that have sought to rebrand themselves by promoting cultural events, exhibitions, sports competitions and tourism (Lahav, Mansfeld, & Avraham, 2013). Kulendran and Dwyer (2009) indicated that investment in destination promotion and marketing has a positive effect on inbound tourism. The adoption of various public diplomacy means has limited effect when a destination is associated with risk due to war, violence, and instability (Taylor, 2006). The negative characteristics dominate the perception of the destination and harm its attempts to attract tourists (Avraham, 2015).

Tourism firms are required to adapt their strategies to fit the rapidly changing environment (Pechlaner & Sauerwein, 2002). A great deal of innovation is vital for tourism firms to increase their competitiveness through the establishment of new products, such as customization and ICT interaction (Sundbo, Orfila-Sintes, & Sorensen, 2007). Executive's human capital and social capital are important to provide a better quality of supervision of the strategic position of tourism firms to ensure that the firms are able to adapt to the changing environment (Ooi, Hooy, & Som, 2015). Regarding the increasing advances in technology, information technology (IT) and knowledge management applications effectively improve the strategic tools for providing the direct link between customers and tourism organizations, thus encouraging the communication channels in global tourism (Kasemsap, 2016b).

Although tourism development brings about a great deal of positive benefits, the residents of host communities can experience the negative socio-cultural changes in their daily lives (Jordan, Vogt, & DeShon, 2015). Theoretical frameworks (e.g., social exchange theory, power theory, and identity theory) are utilized to investigate the resident perceptions of, support for, and responses to tourism development (Nunkoo & Ramkissoon, 2012). Emotional and psychological well-being is an influential part of individuals' overall quality of life (Schalock, 1997). There is an increasing body of literature toward understanding how individuals' lives are affected beyond attitudes for tourism development (Kim, Uysal, & Sirgy, 2013).

Corporate social responsibility (CSR) is an innovative way to create value for society and tourism organizations (Starr, 2013). The aims of CSR in tourism management are to reinforce ties with community (Kasim, 2006), to engage with the social and environmental issues (Henderson, 2007), and to sustainably utilize tourism resources (Chhabra, 2009). Environmental protection and well-structured CSR strategies are the foundation of the environmental and socially responsible cultural tourism (Black,

2012), can help target the financial pressures experienced by heritage attractions which is expected to become more challenging (Garrod & Fyall, 2000).

Rural tourism, also called ecotourism, has been adopted by many countries in the world as one of the major rural policies to generate the rural vitality (Brandth & Haugen, 2011). Although there exists a fundamental debate about the driving agency of rural tourism, common understandings are converging to emphasize the importance of the public sector (Logar, 2010). Rural tourism is one of the major components representing the transition from an economy of production to an economy based on consumption in rural area (Woods, 2005).

Rural tourism is a composite of agricultural products, eco-products, cultural resources, and spatial amenities, involving diverse functions (e.g., economic, social, educational, environmental, recreational, and therapeutic activities) (Lee & Kim, 2010). Bel et al. (2015) stated that tourism has the potential to make a major contribution to the development of rural areas. Rural tourism facilitates rediscovering the values of rural resources that have been neglected in the modernization process of the world economy (Hwang & Lee, 2015). Rural tourism offers diverse implications for farm-based rural businesses and sustainable rural development plans (Lane, 1994).

Product Quality, Service Quality, Price, Customer Satisfaction, and Consumer Trust in Hospitality and Tourism Management

Product quality, service quality, satisfaction, and trust are recognized as the important concepts in explaining customer post-purchase behavior (Han & Hyun, 2015). Researchers explain that these variables contribute to creating positive intentions toward affecting customer retention and loyalty (Han, 2013). Conceptualizations of the perceived quality of products and services differ little in the extensive literature, but an essential aspect of this concept is the process of evaluating the products and services offered by a specific company for excellence against alternatives provided by competitors (Han & Ryu, 2006).

Product quality and service quality involve the two major facets (i.e., core-product and service-product performances) (Bitner, Booms, & Tetreault, 1990). Quality of core product indicates the performance of the basic product relative to its value (Clemmer, 1990) while service-product quality suggests the performances derived from interactions with service personnel (Price, Arnould, & Deibler, 1995). Product quality and service quality contribute to building customers' behavioral intentions (Cronin & Taylor, 1992). Keeping existing customers is about five times more profitable than attracting new customers (Chiu, Hsu, Lai, & Chang, 2012) as the increased customer retention is likely to improve business's profitability (Jiang & Rosenbloom, 2005).

Price is an increasingly vital topic in the hospitality and tourism industry (Han & Hyun, 2015). Customers tend to utilize price reasonableness when evaluating their experiences with a product and service (Ryu & Han, 2010). Customers utilize the reasonableness of price as a cue when estimating their product and service experiences and organizing their attitudes toward the provider (Varki & Colgate, 2001). Individuals' judgments about whether a firm's price is reasonable or unreasonable result in negative decisions concerning the firm (e.g., deciding to spread the negative word-of-mouth) and increase price sensitivity (Oliver & Swan, 1989). Customers tend to remember the perceived price rather than the actual price after evaluating price reasonableness compared to the reference prices offered by competitors (Oh, 2000).

A considerable body of literature has indicated the significance of price reasonableness in explaining consumer behavior (Crozier & Baylis, 2010). In a hospitality context, Han and Kim (2009) stated that reasonableness of price importantly affects individuals' intention formation. Price perception (e.g., expensive or cheap and reasonable or unreasonable perspectives) plays an important role in customers' decision-making processes (Ryu & Han, 2010). Customers' perceptions of a firm's price reasonableness in comparison to its competitors' prices is central in building the enthusiastic intentions and loyalty toward a firm (Han & Kim, 2009). Price reasonableness is a critical product and service cue affecting consumer decision making (Watchravesringkan, Yan, & Yurchisin, 2008).

While various conceptualizations of customer satisfaction have evolved over the past few decades, the general agreement among practitioners and researchers is that individual satisfaction is an evaluation of the overall experience of consumption (Oliver, 1997). If customers positively evaluate their overall consumption experiences, their satisfaction levels and readiness to repurchase will increase (Jani & Han, 2013). Many studies have offered the support for the essential role of quality and satisfaction in the intention formation (Lee, Lee, & Yoo, 2000; Ting, 2004). While the complicated character of the relationship between quality and customer satisfaction exists, quality acts as a significant predictor of customer satisfaction toward generating behavioral intentions (Han & Ryu, 2006). Quality is an important origin of customer satisfaction (Han & Ryu, 2006). The quality-satisfaction relationship is vital in establishing individual's intention (Ting, 2004).

Wang et al. (2014) indicated that consumer trust has attracted the increasing attentions from hospitality and tourism researchers since the 1990s. Consumer trust is largely investigated in hospitality sectors, especially in hotels (Lovell, 2009) and restaurants (Oh, 2002). Consumer trust is studied in the hospitality settings, such as tourism suppliers and travel (Macintosh, 2002), nature-based tourism provider (Zillifro & Morais, 2004), conference (Lee & Back, 2008), and airlines (Forgas, Moliner, Sánchez, & Palau, 2010).

For service businesses (e.g., tourism and hospitality industry), the unique natures (e.g., intangibility and inseparability of production and consumption) emphasize the consequential roles played by building and maintaining strong relationships with customers (McCole, 2002). Zillifro and Morais (2004) indicated that the inherent natures of tourism services (e.g., intangibility of service performance and lack of services transparency) lead to information asymmetry and opportunistic behavior. The existence of intense competition in the marketplace on the supply side makes business operations more challenging as switching costs for consumers are greatly lowered (Álvarez, Casielles, & Martín, 2009).

Consumer trust is viewed as a crucial aspect to sustain continuity in the consumer-provider relationship (Han & Hyun, 2013). Sirdeshmukh et al. (2002) defined consumer trust as the expectations held by the consumer that the service provider is reliable. Consumer trust serves as a powerful method for minimizing uncertainty and diminishing the sources of uncertainty (Pavlou, Liang, & Xue, 2007). Trust in a firm's practices refers to the organizational performance, policies, and practices (Santos & Basso, 2012). Consumer trust leads to the loyalty, irrespective of the magnitude of the level of the relationship between the company and its customers (Agustin & Singh, 2005). Consumer trust based on such satisfactory experiences acts as an influential determinant of the repeat purchase intention (Lankton, Wilson, & Mao, 2010).

Significance of Hospitality Management in Global Business

Ruetzler et al. (2014) stated that in hospitality management, strategic planning is critical in a competitive environment. Christou (2002) determined that managing guest problems and maintaining positive customer relations are the crucial skills indicated by hotel managers. Other dimensions of strategic planning include quality management, systems design, process improvement, teamwork, business policy, strategy analysis, and sustainability (Okumus, Wong, & Altinay, 2008). Although strategic planning remains a popular activity within organizations (Whittington & Cailluet, 2008), it is surprising that the subject has received relatively little attention in the tourism literature (Soteriou & Roberts, 1998).

Strategic planning is an important management tool for profit and non-profit making organizations in competitive and turbulent environments (Liu, Siguaw, & Enz, 2008). Slattery (2002) recognized the structure of hospitality as freestanding (e.g., hotels and cruise ships), operations within leisure venues (e.g., casinos and sports stadia), operations in travel venues (e.g., airports and train stations), and subsidized hospitality (e.g., workplaces and education). Earlier strategic planning research emphasized tourism enterprises (Phillips & Moutinho, 2000) with interest in not-for-profit tourism enterprises growing in more recent work (Soteriou & Coccossis, 2010). Contemporary developments in tourism highlight, the mixed nature of the industry involving private firms, public agencies, and not-for-profit associations (Andersson & Gertz, 2009).

Social networking sites involve blogs, photo sharing sites, message boards, and other online communities (Hanna, 2008). Social networking sites are the modern technological trends to reach the hospitality industry and hospitality managers should obtain the social media skills (Sieburgh & Berkus, 2007). Social media technology can enhance the organizational productivity by fostering the communication and collaboration of employees which aids knowledge transfer and makes organizations more profitable (Kasemsap, 2014b). Social media enables the development of knowledge value chain to customize information and delivery for a technological business growth (Kasemsap, 2014c). The capability of social media in building brand is essential in modern advertising (Kasemsap, 2015b). Social networking sites can be utilized to increase productivity and reduce employee turnover through developing team loyalty among employees (Ketter & Ellis, 2010).

Significance of Tourism Management in Global Business

Tourism remains a critical economic activity, which continues to grow (Phillips & Moutinho, 2014). Tourism incorporates both public and private sector organizations (Cooper, 2006). The current economic upturn suggests that tourism industry will not only experience another business cycle, but also a restructuring of the economic order (Phillips & Moutinho, 2014). Regarding cultural perspectives, the internationalization of tourism has brought attention not only to the cross-cultural peculiarities that arise from traveling internationally, but also to the inter-religious locus of modern tourism (Kirillova, Gilmetdinova, & Lehto, 2014). Modern business organizations must recognize the differences in cross-cultural values and develop strategies for reconciling these cross-cultural differences in the digital age (Kasemsap, 2015c). New hybrid cultures are emerging and blending elements of different culture origins (Kasemsap, 2015d).

Hospitality on the part of hosts leads to the feeling of welcome on the guest side and acts as a fundamental prerequisite for an enjoyable vacation (Mill & Morrison, 2009). Hosts who rely on tourism for economic benefits tend to perceive the presence of tourists in the area more favorably than other residents (Látková & Vogt, 2012). The success of tourism development should not be measured by the increased number of tourists or tourism revenues, instead it should be evaluated according to how it is integrated within the local economy, and to what extent the industry contributes to the well-being of local people (Buzinde, Kalavar, & Melubo, 2014). Both the positive and negative impacts of tourism influence residents' support (Sinclair-Maragh & Gursoy, 2015).

Ritchie (1999) drew the attention to the growing level of international competition in the tourism marketplace that makes strategic planning increasingly imperative. Competitiveness is defined as the capability a geographical area has to compete in international markets (Kogut, 1993). This vision is based on the theory of comparative advantage (Leamer, 1993). With this approach, the explanation of competitiveness in international tourism markets is limited to considering the cost advantages derived from the productive resources controlled by the tourism sector in each location and the endowments of factors in the space in which it is located (Camison & Fores, 2015). Pham et al. (2015) stated that the impacts on tourism are complicated due to the offsetting income and exchange rate effects.

Tourism development generates social harmony (Airey & Chong, 2010) and helps in the preservation of local cultures (Stronza & Gordillo, 2008) and the environment (Dwyer, Edwards, Mistilis, Roman, & Scott, 2009). Regardless of these economic, social, cultural, and environmental benefits, tourism activities are recognized as having negative effects (Gursoy, Jurowski, & Uysal, 2002). Tourism activities can likewise damage the natural and physical environment (Brida, Osti, & Barquet, 2010) on which tourism depends (Moeller, Dolnicar, & Leish, 2011). Sociological analysis of districts (Grandori, 1999) is relevant in the tourism sector which emphasizes the competition around human capital and knowledge-related resources (Galbreath & Galvin, 2008). The importance of the collective learning processes that occur around the firms located in a tourist district or destination (Camison & Fores, 2015).

The culture of host communities can be negatively influenced due to the erosion of traditional values (Besculides, Lee, & McCormic, 2002). Organizational culture is positively correlated with organizational climate (Kasemsap, 2014d). The strategic perspective of industrial districts emphasizes shared competence in the pattern of knowledge and information assets deposited in a territorial setting near the firm (Breukel & Go, 2009), such as the flows of knowledge, information, and experience circulation within the district with a certain degree of freedom (Hjalager, 2002); the existence of a common positioning and branding; and the culture, values, and vision established in the territory (Saxena, 2005).

Empirical studies show that income positively affects the decision to travel (Fleischer & Rivlin, 2009), and its effect is higher for individuals with the high levels of income (Nicolau & Mas, 2005). The income elasticity is below the unit value (Alegre & Pou, 2004), and has a value greater than one for the decision to travel abroad (Eugenio-Martin & Campos-Soria, 2011). Rapoport and Rapoport (1975) defined age as a major determinant of tourism expenditure behavior. Age conditions the different stages of the tourist participation pattern (Bernini & Cracolici, 2015).

Managerial Implications of Hospitality and Tourism Management

Executives and managers in the hospitality and tourism industry need to know what hospitality and tourism management is, the economic, environmental, social, and cultural impacts of hospital and tourism management in global business. In addition, executives and managers need to know the relationship between hospitality and tourism industry with other industries, the roles, and the responsibility of individual staff to plan and organize the hospitality and tourism businesses toward gaining sustainable competitive advantage in hospitality and tourism industry. In order to gain an advantageous edge in the competitive environment, hospitality and tourism practitioners should organize the relationship marketing and should recognize it as a strategic tool in the hospitality and tourism industry (Wang et al., 2014).

Hospitality industry encompass an extensive variety of service industries that include food service, tourism, and hotels. Hospitality industry can be empirically divided into two parts, namely entertainment areas (e.g., clubs and bars) and accommodation. Accommodation takes the form of public houses, resorts, inn, campgrounds, hotels, hostels, serviced apartments, and motels. The clubs and bars category include restaurants, fast foods, and nightclubs. The hospitality industry also includes tourism support commercial activities (e.g., airline cabin staff and travel agents). To encourage a tourist's preference for a specific destination, an effective tourism marketing strategy needs to gain a large share of first mentions among consumers who are choosing between competing travel destinations (Ruhanen, Whitford, & McLennan, 2015).

Hospitality and tourism consist of several nuances ranging from being both capital and labor intensive (Olsen, West, & Tse, 2008). The structure of the hospitality field includes the dispersed units, franchised, managed operations, and independent operators (Phillips & Moutinho, 2014). The intangible nature of the tourism experience renders complications. The generation of a valuable tourism experience depends on the provision of intangible services, which are derived from intangible resources, such as knowledge and innovative capability (Voelpel, Leibold, & Eckhoff, 2006). The adoption of tourism strategy ranges from destinations, trade associations to special events, and strategies for specific defined needs (Tribe, 2010).

While the attrition curve is a model that can be utilized to evaluate tourist awareness, preference, and intention to adopt a tourism experience, it is not a continuous phenomenon that can be employed to predict behavior (Ruhanen et al., 2015). Correlations between preference and arrival are a function of tourism product (Macfarlane & Jago, 2009). The development of accessible tourism product has to replicate tourist product offered to all tourists by concentrating on its competitive advantages in the perspectives of heritage resources (e.g., wealth, parks, and landscape) and creative resources (e.g., artistic, sports, nature, and adventure activities).

FUTURE RESEARCH DIRECTIONS

The classification of the extensive literature in the domains of hospitality and tourism management will provide the potential opportunities for future research. Sustainable tourism is tourism committed to generating a low impact on the surrounding environment and community by acting responsibly while generating income and employment for the local economy and aiding social cohesion. Customer relationship management (CRM) becomes one of the most important business strategies in the digital age, thus involving organizational capability of managing business interactions with customers in an effective manner (Kasemsap, 2015e). The relationship between sustainable tourism and CRM in the tourism and hospitality industry will be the beneficial issue for future research direction.

Social media platforms (e.g., Facebook and Twitter) and the Web 2.0 technologies are the technological tools to facilitate various marketing activities (e.g., advertising, personal selling, sales promotion, public relations, direct marketing, and brand building). Practitioners and researchers should explore the applications of social media platforms and the Web 2.0 technologies in promoting the tourism and hospitality services. Customer service is an array of significant activities designed to enhance the level of customer satisfaction. Understanding the importance of good customer service is essential for a healthy business in creating new customers, keeping loyal customers, and developing referrals for future customers. Good customer service is strongly related to how service quality is effectively managed and which holds a meaningful importance to customer satisfaction and customer loyalty. In the hospitality and tourism industry, customer service, customer satisfaction, and customer loyalty are certain to remain important topics for future research directions.

CONCLUSION

This chapter highlighted the overview of hospitality management; the overview of tourism management; product quality, service quality, price, customer satisfaction, and consumer trust in hospitality and tourism management; the significance of hospitality management in global business; the significance of tourism management in global business; and the managerial implications of hospitality and tourism management. Tourism and hospitality industry is one of the most important industries in the modern business world. Tourism occurs as a result of the different types of business that provide a range of products and services to tourists. It is essential to acquire a driving enthusiasm for customer service and a strong sense of professionalism to develop and maintain customer satisfaction in the hospitality and tourism industry.

Hospitality and tourism sector involves a wide variety of related sectors providing a range of services and facilities and a range of jobs in various departments. Career and job opportunities can be created due to the expansion of tourism and hospitality businesses toward business success and economic growth. Individual staff in the hospitality and tourism sector can work as chef, housekeeper, receptionist, concierge, marketing executive, travel agent, and tour operator. In the hospitality and tourism sector, the skills and abilities (e.g., automated ticketing and reservation systems, sales and marketing, information seeking, customer service, administration, accounting, and strategic planning) are required. Executives and managers in the hospitality and tourism industry must have the particular knowledge and skills (e.g., leadership skills, human resource management, facility management, and service management) to organize and control individual staff to effectively perform in the industry.

Effective hospitality and tourism management positively affects customer satisfaction, firm growth, and productivity in global business. The facilitation of hospitality and tourism management is vital for modern organizations that seek to serve suppliers and customers, increase business performance, strengthen competitiveness, and achieve continuous success in global business. Sustainable tourism, rural tourism, and responsible tourism are the emerging trends in the hospitality and tourism industry and should be studied for future research. Facilitating hospitality and tourism management has the potential to enhance organizational performance and reach strategic goals in global business.

REFERENCES

Acedo, J., & Casillas, C. (2005). Current paradigms in the international management field: An author co-citation analysis. *International Business Review*, *14*(5), 619–639. doi:10.1016/j.ibusrev.2005.05.003

Agarwal, S. (2002). Restructuring seaside tourism: The resort lifecycle. *Annals of Tourism Research*, *29*(1), 25–55. doi:10.1016/S0160-7383(01)00002-0

Agustin, C., & Singh, J. (2005). Curvilinear effects of consumer loyalty determinants in relational exchanges. *JMR, Journal of Marketing Research*, *42*(1), 96–108. doi:10.1509/jmkr.42.1.96.56961

Airey, D., & Chong, K. (2010). National policy-makers for tourism in China. *Annals of Tourism Research*, *37*(2), 295–314. doi:10.1016/j.annals.2009.09.004

Akın, M. (2015). A novel approach to model selection in tourism demand modeling. *Tourism Management*, *48*, 64–72. doi:10.1016/j.tourman.2014.11.004

Alegre, J., & Pou, L. (2004). Micro-economic determinants of the probability of tourism consumption. *Tourism Economics*, *10*(2), 125–144. doi:10.5367/000000004323142452

Álvarez, L. S., Casielles, R. V., & Martín, M. D. (2009). The role of commitment perceived by the consumer in service industries. *Management Review*, *7*(2), 141–175.

Andersson, T. D., & Gertz, D. (2009). Tourism as a mixed industry: Differences between private, public and not-for-profit festivals. *Tourism Management*, *30*(6), 847–856. doi:10.1016/j.tourman.2008.12.008

Avraham, E. (2015). Destination image repair during crisis: Attracting tourism during the Arab Spring uprisings. *Tourism Management*, *47*, 224–232. doi:10.1016/j.tourman.2014.10.003

Bel, F., Lacroix, A., Lyser, S., Rambonilaza, T., & Turpin, N. (2015). Domestic demand for tourism in rural areas: Insights from summer stays in three French regions. *Tourism Management*, *46*, 562–570. doi:10.1016/j.tourman.2014.07.020

Bernini, C., & Cracolici, M. F. (2015). Demographic change, tourism expenditure and life cycle behaviour. *Tourism Management*, *47*, 191–205. doi:10.1016/j.tourman.2014.09.016

Besculides, A., Lee, M. E., & McCormic, P. J. (2002). Residents' perceptions of the cultural benefits of tourism. *Annals of Tourism Research*, *29*(2), 303–319. doi:10.1016/S0160-7383(01)00066-4

Bitner, M. J., Booms, B. H., & Tetreault, M. S. (1990). The service encounter: Diagnosing favorable and unfavorable incidents. *Journal of Marketing*, *54*(1), 71–84. doi:10.2307/1252174

Black, G. (2012). *Transforming museums in the 21st century*. London, United Kingdom: Routledge.

Brandth, B., & Haugen, M. S. (2011). Farm diversification into tourism: Implications for social identity? *Journal of Rural Studies*, *27*(1), 35–44. doi:10.1016/j.jrurstud.2010.09.002

Breukel, A., & Go, F. M. (2009). Knowledge-based network participation in destination and event marketing: A hospitality scenario analysis perspective. *Tourism Management*, *30*(2), 184–193. doi:10.1016/j.tourman.2008.05.015

Brida, J. B., Osti, L., & Barquet, A. (2010). Segmenting resident perceptions toward tourism: A cluster analysis with multinomial a logit model of a mountain community. *International Journal of Tourism Research*, *12*(5), 591–602. doi: 10.1002/jtr.778

Buzinde, C. N., Kalavar, J., & Melubo, K. (2014). Community well-being amongst the Maasai in Tanzania. *Annals of Tourism Research*, *44*, 20–35. doi:10.1016/j.annals.2013.08.010

Camison, C., & Fores, B. (2015). Is tourism firm competitiveness driven by different internal or external specific factors?: New empirical evidence from Spain. *Tourism Management*, *48*, 477–499. doi:10.1016/j.tourman.2015.01.001

Chhabra, D. (2009). Proposing a sustainable marketing framework for heritage tourism. *Journal of Sustainable Tourism*, *17*(3), 303–320. doi:10.1080/09669580802495758

Chiu, C., Hsu, M., Lai, H., & Chang, C. (2012). Re-examining the influence of trust on online repeat purchase intention: The moderating role of habit and its antecedents. *Decision Support Systems*, *53*(4), 835–845. doi:10.1016/j.dss.2012.05.021

Christou, E. (2002). Revisiting competencies for hospitality management: Contemporary views of the stakeholders. *Journal of Hospitality & Tourism Education, 14*(1), 25–32. doi:10.1080/10963758.2002 .10696721

Chung-Herrera, B. G., Enz, C. A., & Lankau, M. J. (2003). Grooming future hospitality leaders: A competencies model. *The Cornell Hotel and Restaurant Administration Quarterly, 44*(3), 17–25. doi: 10.1177/001088040304400302

Clemmer, J. (1990). The three rings of perceived value. *The Canadian Manager, 15*(2), 12–15.

Cooper, C. (2006). Knowledge management and tourism. *Annals of Tourism Research, 33*(1), 47–64. doi:10.1016/j.annals.2005.04.005

Cronin, J. J., & Taylor, S. A. (1992). Measuring service quality: A reexamination and extension. *Journal of Marketing, 56*(3), 55–68. doi:10.2307/1252296

Crozier, G. K. D., & Baylis, F. (2010). The ethical physician encounters international medical travel. *Journal of Medical Ethics, 36*(5), 297–301. doi:10.1136/jme.2009.032789 PMID:20439336

Culnan, M. J. (1987). Mapping the intellectual structure of MIS, 1980–1985: A co-citation analysis. *Management Information Systems Quarterly, 11*(3), 341–353. doi:10.2307/248680

Dodds, R., & Kuehnel, J. (2010). CSR among Canadian mass tour operators: Good awareness but little action. *International Journal of Contemporary Hospitality Management, 22*(2), 221–244. doi:10.1108/09596111011018205

Dwyer, L., Edwards, D., Mistilis, N., Roman, C., & Scott, N. (2009). Destination and enterprise management for a tourism future. *Tourism Management, 30*(1), 63–74. doi:10.1016/j.tourman.2008.04.002

Dyllick, T., & Hockerts, K. (2002). Beyond the business case for corporate sustainability. *Business Strategy and the Environment, 11*(2), 130–141. doi:10.1002/bse.323

Eugenio-Martin, J. L., & Campos-Soria, J. A. (2011). Income and the substitution pattern between domestic and international tourism demand. *Applied Economics, 43*(20), 2519–2531. doi:10.1080/00036840903299698

Fernandez-Alles, M., & Ramos-Rodríguez, A. (2009). Intellectual structure of human resources management research: A bibliometric analysis of the Journal Human Resources Management 1985–2005. *Journal of the American Society for Information Science and Technology, 60*(1), 161–175. doi:10.1002/asi.20947

Ferreira, M. P., Pinto, C. P., & Serra, F. R. (2014). The transaction costs theory in international business research: A bibliometric study over three decades. *Scientometrics, 98*(3), 1899–1922. doi:10.1007/s11192-013-1172-8

Fjelstul, J. (2007). Competencies and opportunities for entry-level golf and club management careers: Perceptions from the industry. *Journal of Hospitality & Tourism Education, 19*(3), 32–38. doi:10.1080/10963758.2007.10696895

Fleischer, A., & Rivlin, J. (2009). Quality, quantity and duration decisions in household demand for vacations. *Tourism Economics, 15*(3), 513–530. doi:10.5367/000000009789036558

Forgas, S., Moliner, M. A., Sánchez, J., & Palau, R. (2010). Antecedents of airline passenger loyalty: Low-cost versus traditional airlines. *Journal of Air Transport Management, 16*(4), 229–233. doi:10.1016/j.jairtraman.2010.01.001

Frechtling, D. C., & Horvath, E. (1999). Estimating the multiplier effects of tourism expenditures on a local economy through a regional input-output model. *Journal of Travel Research, 37*(4), 324–332. doi:10.1177/004728759903700402

Galbreath, J., & Galvin, P. (2008). Firm factors, industry structure and performance variation: New empirical evidence to a classic debate. *Journal of Business Research, 61*(2), 109–117. doi:10.1016/j.jbusres.2007.06.009

Garrod, B., & Fyall, A. (2000). Managing heritage tourism. *Annals of Tourism Research, 27*(3), 682–708. doi:10.1016/S0160-7383(99)00094-8

Grandori, A. (1999). *Interfirm networks: Organization and industrial competitiveness.* London, United Kingdom: Routledge. doi:10.4324/9780203022481

Gursoy, D., Jurowski, C., & Uysal, M. (2002). Resident attitudes: A structural modeling approach. *Annals of Tourism Research, 29*(1), 79–105. doi:10.1016/S0160-7383(01)00028-7

Hall, C. M. (1998). *Introduction to tourism: Development, dimensions and issues.* Melbourne, Australia: Longman.

Han, H. (2013). The healthcare hotel: Distinctive attributes for international medical travelers. *Tourism Management, 36*(1), 257–268. doi:10.1016/j.tourman.2012.11.016

Han, H., & Hyun, S. S. (2013). Image congruence and relationship quality in predicting switching intention: Conspicuousness of product use as a moderator variable. *Journal of Hospitality & Tourism Research (Washington, D.C.), 37*(3), 303–329. doi:10.1177/1096348012436381

Han, H., & Hyun, S. S. (2015). Customer retention in the medical tourism industry: Impact of quality, satisfaction, trust, and price reasonableness. *Tourism Management, 46*, 20–29. doi:10.1016/j.tourman.2014.06.003

Han, H., & Kim, W. (2009). Outcomes of relational benefits: Restaurant customers' perspective. *Journal of Travel & Tourism Marketing, 26*(8), 820–835. doi:10.1080/10548400903356236

Han, H., & Ryu, K. (2006). Moderating role of personal characteristics in forming restaurant customers' behavioral intentions: An upscale restaurant setting. *Journal of Hospitality & Leisure Marketing, 15*(4), 25–53. doi:10.1300/J150v15n04_03

Hanna, E. (2008). Networking gets new meaning on the web. *Hotel & Motel Management, 223*(19), 30–58.

Harris, P. (1999). *Profit planning.* Oxford, United Kingdom: Butterworth–Heinemann.

Henderson, J. C. (2007). Corporate social responsibility and tourism: Hotel companies in Phuket, Thailand, after the Indian Ocean tsunami. *International Journal of Hospitality Management, 26*(1), 228–239. doi:10.1016/j.ijhm.2006.02.001

Hjalager, A. M. (2002). Repairing innovation defectiveness in tourism. *Tourism Management*, *23*(5), 465–474. doi:10.1016/S0261-5177(02)00013-4

Hosany, S., Ekinci, Y., & Uysal, M. (2006). Destination image and destination personality: An application of branding theories to tourism places. *Journal of Business Research*, *59*(5), 638–642. doi:10.1016/j.jbusres.2006.01.001

Hwang, J. H., & Lee, S. W. (2015). The effect of the rural tourism policy on non-farm income in South Korea. *Tourism Management*, *46*, 501–513. doi:10.1016/j.tourman.2014.07.018

Incera, A. C., & Fernandez, M. F. (2015). Tourism and income distribution: Evidence from a developed regional economy. *Tourism Management*, *48*, 11–20. doi:10.1016/j.tourman.2014.10.016

Israeli, A. A. (2014). An inter-paradigmatic agenda for research, education and practice in hospitality management. *International Journal of Hospitality Management*, *42*, 188–191. doi:10.1016/j.ijhm.2014.07.005

Israeli, A. A., Barkan, R., & Fleishman, M. (2006). An exploratory approach to evaluating performance measures: The managers' perspective. *Service Industries Journal*, *26*(8), 861–872. doi:10.1080/02642060601011665

Jalil, A., Mahmood, T., & Idrees, M. (2013). Tourism-growth nexus in Pakistan: Evidence from ARDL bounds tests. *Economic Modelling*, *35*, 185–191. doi:10.1016/j.econmod.2013.06.034

Jani, D., & Han, H. (2013). Personality, social comparison, consumption emotions, satisfaction, and behavioral intentions: How do these and other factors relate in a hotel setting? *International Journal of Contemporary Hospitality Management*, *25*(7), 970–993. doi:10.1108/IJCHM-10-2012-0183

Jiang, P., & Rosenbloom, B. (2005). Customer intention to return online: Price perception, attribute-level performance, and satisfaction unfolding over time. *European Journal of Marketing*, *39*(1/2), 150–174. doi:10.1108/03090560510572061

Johanson, M., Ghiselli, R., Shea, L. J., & Roberts, C. (2011). Changing competencies of hospitality leaders: A 25 year review. *Journal of Hospitality & Tourism Education*, *23*(3), 43–47. doi:10.1080/10963758.2011.10697012

Jordan, E. J., Vogt, C. A., & DeShon, R. P. (2015). A stress and coping framework for understanding resident responses to tourism development. *Tourism Management*, *48*, 500–512. doi:10.1016/j.tourman.2015.01.002

Kaplan, R. S., & Norton, D. P. (1996). *The balanced scorecard: Translating strategy into action*. Boston, MA: Harvard Business School Press.

Kasemsap, K. (2014a). The role of brand loyalty on CRM performance: An innovative framework for smart manufacturing. In Z. Luo (Ed.), *Smart manufacturing innovation and transformation: Interconnection and intelligence* (pp. 252–284). Hershey, PA: IGI Global. doi:10.4018/978-1-4666-5836-3.ch010

Kasemsap, K. (2014b). The role of social networking in global business environments. In P. Smith & T. Cockburn (Eds.), *Impact of emerging digital technologies on leadership in global business* (pp. 183–201). Hershey, PA: IGI Global. doi:10.4018/978-1-4666-6134-9.ch010

Kasemsap, K. (2014c). The role of social media in the knowledge-based organizations. In I. Lee (Ed.), *Integrating social media into business practice, applications, management, and models* (pp. 254–275). Hershey, PA: IGI Global. doi:10.4018/978-1-4666-6182-0.ch013

Kasemsap, K. (2014d). Unifying a framework of organizational culture, organizational climate, knowledge management, and job performance. In R. Perez-Castillo & M. Piattini (Eds.), *Uncovering essential software artifacts through business process archeology* (pp. 336–362). Hershey, PA: IGI Global. doi:10.4018/978-1-4666-4667-4.ch013

Kasemsap, K. (2015a). The role of marketing strategies in the tourism industry. In N. Ray (Ed.), *Emerging innovative marketing strategies in the tourism industry* (pp. 174–194). Hershey, PA: IGI Global. doi:10.4018/978-1-4666-8699-1.ch010

Kasemsap, K. (2015b). The role of social media in international advertising. In N. Taşkıran & R. Yılmaz (Eds.), *Handbook of research on effective advertising strategies in the social media age* (pp. 171–196). Hershey, PA: IGI Global. doi:10.4018/978-1-4666-8125-5.ch010

Kasemsap, K. (2015c). The roles of cross-cultural perspectives in global marketing. In J. Alcántara-Pilar, S. del Barrio-García, E. Crespo-Almendros, & L. Porcu (Eds.), *Analyzing the cultural diversity of consumers in the global marketplace* (pp. 37–59). Hershey, PA: IGI Global. doi:10.4018/978-1-4666-8262-7.ch003

Kasemsap, K. (2015d). The role of cultural dynamics in the digital age. In B. Christiansen & J. Koeman (Eds.), *Nationalism, cultural indoctrination, and economic prosperity in the digital age* (pp. 295–312). Hershey, PA: IGI Global. doi:10.4018/978-1-4666-7492-9.ch014

Kasemsap, K. (2015e). The role of customer relationship management in the global business environments. In T. Tsiakis (Ed.), *Trends and innovations in marketing information systems* (pp. 130–156). Hershey, PA: IGI Global. doi:10.4018/978-1-4666-8459-1.ch007

Kasemsap, K. (2016a). The roles of e-learning, organizational learning, and knowledge management in the learning organizations. In E. Railean, G. Walker, A. Elçi, & L. Jackson (Eds.), *Handbook of research on applied learning theory and design in modern education* (pp. 786–816). Hershey, PA: IGI Global. doi:10.4018/978-1-4666-9634-1.ch039

Kasemsap, K. (2016b). The roles of information technology and knowledge management in global tourism. In A. Nedelea, M. Korstanje, & B. George (Eds.), *Strategic tools and methods for promoting hospitality and tourism services* (pp. 109–138). Hershey, PA: IGI Global. doi:10.4018/978-1-4666-9761-4.ch006

Kasim, A. (2006). The need for business environmental and social responsibility in the tourism industry. *International Journal of Hospitality & Tourism Administration, 7*(1), 1–22. doi:10.1300/J149v07n01_01

Kay, C., & Russette, J. (2000). Hospitality-management competencies. *The Cornell Hotel and Restaurant Administration Quarterly, 41*(2), 52–63. doi:10.1177/0010880400004100217

Ketter, P., & Ellis, R. (2010). Six trends that will change workplace learning forever. *Training & Development, 64*(12), 34–40.

Kim, K., Uysal, M., & Sirgy, M. J. (2013). How does tourism in a community impact the quality of life of community residents? *Tourism Management, 36*(5), 527–540. doi:10.1016/j.tourman.2012.09.005

Kirillova, K., Gilmetdinova, A., & Lehto, X. (2014). Interpretation of hospitality across religions. *International Journal of Hospitality Management, 43,* 23–34. doi:10.1016/j.ijhm.2014.07.008

Kogut, B. (1993). *Country competitiveness: Technology and the organizing of work.* New York, NY: Oxford University Press.

Köseoglu, M. A., Sehitoglu, Y., & Craft, J. (2015). Academic foundations of hospitality management research with an emerging country focus: A citation and co-citation analysis. *International Journal of Hospitality Management, 45,* 130–144. doi:10.1016/j.ijhm.2014.12.004

Kulendran, N., & Dwyer, L. (2009). Measuring the return from Australian marketing expenditure. *Journal of Travel Research, 47*(3), 275–284. doi:10.1177/0047287508322786

Lahav, T., Mansfeld, Y., & Avraham, E. (2013). Public relations for rural areas. *Journal of Tourism & Travel Marketing, 30*(4), 291–307. doi:10.1080/10548408.2013.784148

Lane, B. (1994). What is rural tourism? *Journal of Sustainable Tourism, 2*(1/2), 7–21. doi:10.1080/09669589409510680

Lankton, N. K., Wilson, E. V., & Mao, E. (2010). Antecedents and determinants of information technology habit. *Information & Management, 47*(5/6), 300–307. doi:10.1016/j.im.2010.06.004

Látková, P., & Vogt, C. (2012). Residents' attitudes toward existing and future tourism development in rural communities. *Journal of Travel Research, 51*(1), 50–67. doi:10.1177/0047287510394193

Leamer, E. E. (1993). Factor-supply differences as a source of comparative advantage. *The American Economic Review, 83*(2), 436–439.

Lee, H., Lee, Y., & Yoo, D. (2000). The determinants of perceived service quality and its relationship with satisfaction. *Journal of Services Marketing, 14*(3), 217–231. doi:10.1108/08876040010327220

Lee, J. S., & Back, K. J. (2008). Attendee-based brand equity. *Tourism Management, 29*(2), 331–344. doi:10.1016/j.tourman.2007.03.002

Lee, S. W., & Kim, H. J. (2010). Agricultural transition and rural tourism in Korea: Experiences of the last forty years. In G. Thapa, P. Viswanathan, J. Routray, & M. Ahmad (Eds.), *Agricultural transition in Asia* (pp. 37–64). Bangkok, Thailand: Asian Institute of Technology.

Li, L., Buhalis, D., Lockwood, A., & Benzine, K. (2007). *The use of e-learning in training in the UK hospitality industry: An exploratory study.* Paper presented at the 6th European Conference on e-Learning (ECEL 2007), Copenhagen, Denmark.

Li, L., Lee, H., & Law, R. (2012). Technology-mediated management learning in hospitality organisations. *International Journal of Hospitality Management, 31*(1), 451–457. doi:10.1016/j.ijhm.2011.07.003

Liu, Z., Siguaw, J. A., & Enz, C. A. (2008). Using tourist travel habits and preferences to assess strategic destination positioning: The case of Costa Rica. *Cornell Hospitality Quarterly, 49*(3), 258–281. doi:10.1177/1938965508322007

Logar, I. (2010). Sustainable tourism management in Crikvenica, Croatia: An assessment of policy instruments. *Tourism Management, 31*(1), 125–135. doi:10.1016/j.tourman.2009.02.005

Lovell, G. (2009). Can I trust you? An exploration of the role of trust in hospitality service settings. *Tourism and Hospitality Planning & Development, 6*(2), 145–157. doi:10.1080/14790530902981548

Lugosi, P., Lynch, P., & Morrison, A. (2009). Critical hospitality management research. *Service Industries Journal, 29*(10), 1465–1478. doi:10.1080/02642060903038879

Macfarlane, I., & Jago, L. (2009). *The role of brand equity in helping to evaluate the contribution of major events.* Gold Coast, Australia: Sustainable Tourism Cooperative Research Centre.

Macintosh, G. (2002). Building trust and satisfaction in travel counselor/client relationships. *Journal of Travel & Tourism Marketing, 12*(4), 59–74. doi:10.1300/J073v12n04_04

Marsick, V. J. (2003). Invited reaction: Informal learning and the transfer of learning: How managers develop proficiency. *Human Resource Development Quarterly, 14*(4), 389–395. doi:10.1002/hrdq.1075

Martínez, R. P., Pérez, A., & del Bosque, I. R. (2013). Measuring corporate social responsibility in tourism: Development and validation of an efficient measurement scale in the hospitality industry. *Journal of Travel & Tourism Marketing, 30*(4), 365–385. doi:10.1080/10548408.2013.784154

McCole, P. (2002). The role of trust for electronic commerce in services. *International Journal of Contemporary Hospitality Management, 14*(2), 81–87. doi:10.1108/09596110210419264

McCole, P. (2004). Dealing with complaints in services. *International Journal of Contemporary Hospitality Management, 16*(6), 345–354. doi:10.1108/09596110410550789

Mill, R., & Morrison, A. (2009). *The tourism system.* Dubuque, IA: Kendall Hunt Publishing.

Moeller, T., Dolnicar, S., & Leish, F. (2011). The sustainability-profitability trade-off in tourism: Can it be overcome? *Journal of Sustainable Tourism, 19*(2), 155–169. doi:10.1080/09669582.2010.518762

Mohammed, I., Guillet, B. D., & Law, R. (2015). The contributions of economics to hospitality literature: A content analysis of hospitality and tourism journals. *International Journal of Hospitality Management, 44*, 99–110. doi:10.1016/j.ijhm.2014.10.010

Nerur, S., Rasheed, A., & Natarajan, V. (2008). The intellectual structure of the strategic management field: An author co-citation analysis. *Strategic Management Journal, 29*(3), 319–336. doi:10.1002/smj.659

Nicolau, J. L., & Mas, F. (2005). Stochastic modeling: A three-stage tourist choice process. *Annals of Tourism Research, 32*(1), 49–69. doi:10.1016/j.annals.2004.04.007

Nunkoo, R., & Ramkissoon, H. (2012). Power, trust, social exchange and community support. *Annals of Tourism Research, 39*(2), 997–1023. doi:10.1016/j.annals.2011.11.017

Oh, H. (2000). The effect of brand class, brand awareness, and price on customer value and behavioral intentions. *Journal of Hospitality & Tourism Research (Washington, D.C.), 24*(2), 136–162. doi:10.1177/109634800002400202

Oh, H. (2002). Transaction evaluations and relationship intentions. *Journal of Hospitality & Tourism Research (Washington, D.C.), 26*(3), 278–305. doi:10.1177/1096348002026003005

Okumus, F., Wong, K., & Altinay, L. (2008). Are we teaching strategic management right? *Journal of Teaching in Travel & Tourism, 8*(4), 329–350. doi:10.1080/15313220903047938

Oliver, R. L. (1997). *Satisfaction: A behavioral perspective on the consumer.* New York, NY: McGraw–Hill.

Oliver, R. L., & Swan, J. E. (1989). Consumer perceptions of interpersonal equity and satisfaction in transaction: A field survey approach. *Journal of Marketing, 53*(2), 21–35. doi:10.2307/1251411

Olsen, M. D., West, J., & Tse, E. C. Y. (2008). *Strategic management in the hospitality industry.* New York, NY: Prentice Hall.

Ooi, C. A., Hooy, C. W., & Som, A. P. M. (2015). Diversity in human and social capital: Empirical evidence from Asian tourism firms in corporate board composition. *Tourism Management, 48*, 139–153. doi: 10.1016/j.tourman.2014.11.002

Panwar, R., Rinne, T., Hansen, E., & Juslin, H. (2006). Corporate responsibility: Balancing economic environmental and social issues in the forest products industry. *Forest Products Journal, 56*(2), 4–12.

Pavlou, P. A., Liang, H., & Xue, Y. (2007). Understanding and mitigating uncertainty in online exchange relationships: A principal-agent perspective. *Management Information Systems Quarterly, 31*(1), 105–136.

Pechlaner, H., & Sauerwein, E. (2002). Strategy implementation in the Alpine tourism industry. *International Journal of Contemporary Hospitality Management, 11*(7), 359–365.

Pérez, A., & del Bosque, I. R. (2014). Sustainable development and stakeholder relations management: Exploring sustainability reporting in the hospitality industry from a SD-SRM approach. *International Journal of Hospitality Management, 42*, 174–187. doi:10.1016/j.ijhm.2014.07.003

Pham, T., Jago, L., Spurr, R., & Marshall, J. (2015). The Dutch disease effects on tourism: The case of Australia. *Tourism Management, 46*, 610–622. doi:10.1016/j.tourman.2014.08.014

Phillips, P. A., & Moutinho, L. (2000). The strategic planning index (SPI): A tool for measuring strategic planning effectiveness. *Journal of Travel Research, 38*(4), 369–379. doi:10.1177/004728750003800405

Phillips, P. A., & Moutinho, L. (2014). Critical review of strategic planning research in hospitality and tourism. *Annals of Tourism Research, 48*, 96–120. doi:10.1016/j.annals.2014.05.013

Pilkington, A., & Liston-Heyes, C. (1999). Is production and operations management a discipline? A citation/co-citation study. *International Journal of Operations & Production Management, 19*(1), 7–20. doi:10.1108/01443579910244188

Pirani, S. I., & Arafat, H. A. (2014). Solid waste management in the hospitality industry: A review. *Journal of Environmental Management, 146*, 320–336. doi:10.1016/j.jenvman.2014.07.038 PMID:25194519

Pizam, A. (2003). What should be our field of study? *International Journal of Hospitality Management, 22*(4), 339. doi:10.1016/j.ijhm.2003.09.001

Ponzi, L. J. (2002). The intellectual structure and interdisciplinary breadth of knowledge management: A bibliometric study of its early stage of development. *Scientometrics, 55*(2), 259–272. doi:10.1023/A:1019619824850

Price, L., Arnould, E., & Deibler, S. (1995). Consumers' emotional responses to service encounters. *International Journal of Service Industry Management, 6*(3), 34–63. doi:10.1108/09564239510091330

Rapoport, R., & Rapoport, R. N. (1975). *Leisure and the family life cycle*. London, United Kingdom: Routledge and Kegan Paul.

Raybould, M., & Wilkins, H. (2005). Over qualified and under experienced: Turning graduates into hospitality managers. *International Journal of Contemporary Hospitality Management, 17*(3), 203–216. doi:10.1108/09596110510591891

Ritchie, J. R. B. (1999). Crafting a value-driven vision for a national tourism treasure. *Tourism Management, 20*(3), 273–282. doi:10.1016/S0261-5177(98)00123-X

Robinson, R. N. S., Solnet, D. J., & Breakey, N. (2014). A phenomenological approach to hospitality management research: Chefs' occupational commitment. *International Journal of Hospitality Management, 43*, 65–75. doi:10.1016/j.ijhm.2014.08.004

Ruetzler, T., Baker, W., Reynolds, D., Taylor, J., & Allen, B. (2014). Perceptions of technical skills required for successful management in the hospitality industry: An exploratory study using conjoint analysis. *International Journal of Hospitality Management, 39*, 157–164. doi:10.1016/j.ijhm.2014.02.012

Ruhanen, L., Whitford, M., & McLennan, C. I. (2015). Indigenous tourism in Australia: Time for a reality check. *Tourism Management, 48*, 73–83. doi:10.1016/j.tourman.2014.10.017

Ryu, K., & Han, H. (2010). Influence of the quality of food, service, and physical environment on customer satisfaction and behavioral intention in quick-casual restaurants: Moderating role of perceived price. *Journal of Hospitality & Tourism Research (Washington, D.C.), 34*(3), 310–329. doi:10.1177/1096348009350624

Sandwith, P. (1993). A hierarchy of management training requirements: The competency domain model. *Public Personnel Management, 22*(1), 43–62. doi:10.1177/009102609302200104

Santos, C. P., & Basso, K. (2012). Do ongoing relationships buffer the effects of service recovery on customers' trust and loyalty? *International Journal of Bank Marketing, 30*(3), 168–192. doi:10.1108/02652321211222540

Saxena, G. (2005). Relationships, networks and the learning regions: Case evidence from the Peak District National Park. *Tourism Management, 26*(2), 277–289. doi:10.1016/j.tourman.2003.11.013

Schalock, R. L. (1997). *Quality of life: Application to persons with disabilities*. Washington, DC: AAMR.

Sieburgh, J., & Berkus, D. (2007). Social networking: Technology for a new generation. *Lodging Hospitality, 63*(5), 41.

Sinclair-Maragh, G., & Gursoy, D. (2015). Imperialism and tourism: The case of developing island countries. *Annals of Tourism Research, 50*, 143–158. doi:10.1016/j.annals.2014.12.001

Sirdeshmukh, D., Singh, J., & Sabol, B. (2002). Consumer trust, value and loyalty in relational exchanges. *Journal of Marketing, 66*(1), 15–37. doi:10.1509/jmkg.66.1.15.18449

Slattery, P. (2002). Finding the hospitality Industry. *Journal of Hospitality, Leisure, Sport and Tourism Education, 1*(1), 19–28. doi:10.3794/johlste.11.7

Soteriou, E. C., & Coccossis, H. (2010). Integrating sustainability into the strategic planning of national tourism organizations. *Journal of Travel Research, 49*(2), 191–205. doi:10.1177/0047287509336472

Soteriou, E. C., & Roberts, C. (1998). The strategic planning process in national tourism organizations. *Journal of Travel Research, 37*(1), 21–29. doi:10.1177/004728759803700103

Starr, F. (2013). *Corporate responsibility for cultural heritage: Conservation, sustainable development and corporate reputation*. Abingdon, United Kingdom: Routledge.

Stokburger-Sauer, N. E. (2011). The relevance of visitors' nation brand embeddedness and personality congruence for nation brand identification, visit intentions and advocacy. *Tourism Management, 32*(6), 1282–1289. doi:10.1016/j.tourman.2010.12.004

Stronza, A., & Gordillo, J. (2008). Community views of ecotourism. *Annals of Tourism Research, 35*(2), 448–468. doi:10.1016/j.annals.2008.01.002

Sundbo, J., Orfila-Sintes, F., & Sorensen, F. (2007). The innovative behaviour of tourism firms: Comparative studies of Denmark and Spain. *Research Policy, 36*(1), 88–106. doi:10.1016/j.respol.2006.08.004

Tahai, A., & Meyer, M. J. (1999). A revealed preference study of management journals' direct influences. *Strategic Management Journal, 20*(3), 279–296. doi:10.1002/(SICI)1097-0266(199903)20:3<279::AID-SMJ33>3.0.CO;2-2

Tang, C. F., & Tan, E. C. (2015). Does tourism effectively stimulate Malaysia's economic growth? *Tourism Management, 46*, 158–163. doi:10.1016/j.tourman.2014.06.020

Tas, R. E. (1988). Teaching future managers. *The Cornell Hotel and Restaurant Administration Quarterly, 29*(2), 41–43. doi:10.1177/001088048802900215

Taylor, P. A. (2006). Getting them to forgive and forget: Cognitive based marketing responses to terrorist acts. *International Journal of Tourism Research, 8*(3), 171–183. doi:10.1002/jtr.570

Testa, M. R., & Sipe, L. (2012). Service-leadership competencies for hospitality and tourism management. *International Journal of Hospitality Management, 31*(3), 648–658. doi:10.1016/j.ijhm.2011.08.009

Ting, D. H. (2004). Service quality and satisfaction perceptions: Curvilinear and interaction effect. *International Journal of Bank Marketing, 22*(6), 407–420. doi:10.1108/02652320410559330

Tolkach, D., & King, B. (2015). Strengthening community-based tourism in a new resource-based island nation: Why and how? *Tourism Management, 48*, 386–398. doi:10.1016/j.tourman.2014.12.013

Tribe, J. (2010). *Strategy for tourism*. Oxford, United Kingdom: Goodfellow Publishers.

Tsang, N. K. F., & Hsu, C. H. C. (2011). Thirty years of research on tourism and hospitality management in China: A review and analysis of journal publications. *International Journal of Hospitality Management, 30*(4), 886–896. doi:10.1016/j.ijhm.2011.01.009

Tseng, H., Duan, C., Tung, H., & Kung, H. (2010). Modern business ethics research: Concepts, theories, and relationships. *Journal of Business Ethics, 91*(4), 587–597. doi:10.1007/s10551-009-0133-x

Varki, S., & Colgate, M. (2001). The role of price perceptions in an integrated model of behavioral intentions. *Journal of Service Research, 3*(3), 232–240. doi:10.1177/109467050133004

Voelpel, S. C., Leibold, M., & Eckhoff, R. A. (2006). The tyranny of the balanced scorecard in the innovation economy. *Journal of Intellectual Capital, 7*(1), 43–60. doi:10.1108/14691930610639769

Wang, D., Niu, Y., Lu, L., & Qian, J. (2015). Tourism spatial organization of historical streets: A post-modern perspective: The examples of Pingjiang Road and Shantang Street, Suzhou, China. *Tourism Management, 48*, 370–385. doi:10.1016/j.tourman.2014.12.007

Wang, L., Law, R., Hung, K., & Guillet, B. D. (2014). Consumer trust in tourism and hospitality: A review of the literature. *Journal of Hospitality and Tourism Management, 21*, 1–9. doi:10.1016/j.jhtm.2014.01.001

Wang, S., & Xu, H. (2015). Influence of place-based senses of distinctiveness, continuity, self-esteem and self-efficacy on residents' attitudes toward tourism. *Tourism Management, 47*, 241–250. doi:10.1016/j.tourman.2014.10.007

Watchravesringkan, K., Yan, R., & Yurchisin, J. (2008). Cross-cultural invariance of consumers' price perception measures: Eastern Asian perspective. *International Journal of Retail & Distribution Management, 36*(10), 759–779. doi:10.1108/09590550810900982

Whittington, R., & Cailluet, L. (2008). The craft of strategy. *Long Range Planning, 41*(3), 241–247. doi:10.1016/j.lrp.2008.03.003

Woods, M. (2005). *Rural geography*. New York, NY: Sage Publications.

Yoon, M. H., Beatty, S. E., & Suh, J. (2001). The effect of work climate on critical employee and customer outcomes: An employee-level analysis. *International Journal of Service Industry Management, 12*(5), 500–521. doi:10.1108/EUM0000000006095

Zillifro, T., & Morais, D. B. (2004). Building customer trust and relationship commitment to a nature-based tourism provider: The role of information investments. *Journal of Hospitality & Leisure Marketing, 11*(2/3), 159–172. doi:10.1300/J150v11n02_11

ADDITIONAL READING

Abrate, G., Fraquelli, G., & Viglia, G. (2012). Dynamic pricing strategies: Evidence from European hotels. *International Journal of Hospitality Management, 31*(1), 160–168. doi:10.1016/j.ijhm.2011.06.003

Benavides-Chicón, C. G., & Ortega, B. (2014). The impact of quality management on productivity in the hospitality sector. *International Journal of Hospitality Management, 42*, 165–173. doi:10.1016/j.ijhm.2014.07.004

Brown, E. A., Arendt, S. W., & Bosselman, R. H. (2014). Hospitality management graduates' perceptions of career factor importance and career factor experience. *International Journal of Hospitality Management, 37*, 58–67. doi:10.1016/j.ijhm.2013.10.003

Buultjens, J., & Gale, D. (2013). Facilitating the development of Australian indigenous tourism enterprises: The business ready program for indigenous tourism. *Tourism Management Perspectives, 5,* 41–50. doi:10.1016/j.tmp.2012.09.007

Buzinde, C. N., & Manuel-Navarrete, D. (2013). The social production of space in tourism enclaves: Mayan children's perceptions of tourism boundaries. *Annals of Tourism Research, 43,* 482–505. doi:10.1016/j.annals.2013.06.003

Ford, R. (2012). Tourist destination governance: Practice, theory, and issues. *International Journal of Contemporary Hospitality Management, 24*(5), 810–812. doi:10.1108/ijchm.2012.24.5.810.1

Gardner, B. (2012). Tourism and the politics of the global land grab in Tanzania: Markets, appropriation and recognition. *The Journal of Peasant Studies, 39*(2), 377–402. doi:10.1080/03066150.2012.666973

Gunter, U., & Onder, I. (2015). Forecasting international city tourism demand for Paris: Accuracy of uni- and multivariate models employing monthly data. *Tourism Management, 46,* 123–135. doi:10.1016/j.tourman.2014.06.017

Han, H., & Hwang, J. (2013). Multi-dimensions of the perceived benefits in a medical hotel and their roles in international travelers' decision-making process. *International Journal of Hospitality Management, 35*(1), 100–108. doi:10.1016/j.ijhm.2013.05.011

Honma, S., & Hu, J. L. (2012). Analyzing Japanese hotel efficiency. *Tourism and Hospitality Research, 12*(3), 155–167. doi:10.1177/1467358412470558

Hwang, S. N., & Chang, T. Y. (2003). Using data envelopment analysis to measure hotel managerial efficiency change in Taiwan. *Tourism Management, 24*(4), 357–369. doi:10.1016/S0261-5177(02)00112-7

Jordan, E. J., Vogt, C. A., Kruger, L. E., & Grewe, N. (2013). The interplay of governance, power and citizen participation in community tourism planning. *Journal of Policy Research in Tourism, Leisure and Events, 5*(3), 270–288. doi:10.1080/19407963.2013.789354

Ketter, E., & Avraham, E. (2012). The social revolution of tourism marketing: The growing power of users in social media tourism campaigns. *Place Branding and Public Diplomacy, 8*(4), 285–294. doi:10.1057/pb.2012.20

Kim, W., Jun, H. M., Walker, M., & Drane, D. (2015). Evaluating the perceived social impacts of hosting large-scale sport tourism events: Scale development and validation. *Tourism Management, 48,* 21–32. doi:10.1016/j.tourman.2014.10.015

Lai, I. K. W., & Hitchcock, M. (2015). Importance–performance analysis in tourism: A framework for researchers. *Tourism Management, 48,* 242–267. doi:10.1016/j.tourman.2014.11.008

Lemelin, R. H., Koster, R., & Youroukos, N. (2015). Tangible and intangible indicators of successful aboriginal tourism initiatives: A case study of two successful aboriginal tourism lodges in Northern Canada. *Tourism Management, 47,* 318–328. doi:10.1016/j.tourman.2014.10.011

Loda, M. D., & Amos, C. (2014). Temporal orientation and destination selection. *Journal of Hospitality Marketing & Management, 23*(8), 907–919. doi:10.1080/19368623.2014.891963

Meneses, O. A. M., & Teixeira, A. A. C. (2011). The innovative behaviour of tourism firms. *Economics and Management Research Project: An International Journal*, *1*(1), 25–35.

Nunkoo, R., Gursoy, D., & Ramkissoon, H. (2013). Developments in hospitality marketing and management: Social network analysis and research themes. *Journal of Hospitality Marketing & Management*, *22*(3), 269–288. doi:10.1080/19368623.2013.753814

Nyaupane, G. P., & Poudel, S. (2011). Linkages among biodiversity, livelihood, and tourism. *Annals of Tourism Research*, *38*(4), 1344–1366. doi:10.1016/j.annals.2011.03.006

Singal, M. (2014). The business case for diversity management in the hospitality industry. *International Journal of Hospitality Management*, *40*(1), 10–19. doi:10.1016/j.ijhm.2014.02.009

Tang, L., & Jang, S. (2014). Information value and destination image: Investigating the moderating role of processing fluency. *Journal of Hospitality Marketing & Management*, *23*(7), 790–814. doi:10.1080/19368623.2014.883585

Vila, T. D., Darcy, S., & Gonzalez, E. A. (2015). Competing for the disability tourism market: A comparative exploration of the factors of accessible tourism competitiveness in Spain and Australia. *Tourism Management*, *47*, 261–272. doi: 10.1016/j.tourman.2014.10.008

Wells, V. K., Manika, D., Gregory-Smith, D., Taheri, B., & McCowlen, C. (2015). Heritage tourism, CSR and the role of employee environmental behaviour. *Tourism Management*, *48*, 399–413. doi:10.1016/j.tourman.2014.12.015

Wong, T., & Wickham, M. (2015). An examination of Marriott's entry into the Chinese hospitality industry: A brand equity perspective. *Tourism Management*, *48*, 439–454. doi:10.1016/j.tourman.2014.12.014

Xue, L., Kerstetter, D., & Buzinde, C. N. (2015). Residents' experiences with tourism development and resettlement in Luoyang, China. *Tourism Management*, *46*, 444–453. doi:10.1016/j.tourman.2014.08.005

KEY TERMS AND DEFINITIONS

Corporate Social Responsibility: A company's sense of responsibility toward the community and environment in which it operates.

Customer Satisfaction: The degree of satisfaction provided by the products or services of a company as measured by the number of repeat customers.

Hospitality Industry: The industry related to hotel, motels, inns, or such businesses providing transitional lodging, with or without food.

Product Quality: The group of features and characteristics of a saleable good which determine its desirability and which can be controlled by a manufacturer to meet certain basic requirements.

Service: A valuable action or effort performed to satisfy a need or to fulfill a demand.

Service Quality: An evaluation of how well a delivered service conforms to the client's expectations.

Strategic Planning: A systematic process of envisioning a desired future, and translating this vision into broadly defined goals and a sequence of steps to achieve them.

Tourism: The marketing of the enjoyable features of a travel destination, and the provision of facilities and services for the pleasurable tourists.

Compilation of References

Aaker, D., & Day, G. (1990). Marketing Research. (4th ed.). Wiley.

Abernathy, W., & Clark, K. B. (2007). Innovation: Mapping the winds of creative destruction. *Research Policy, 14*(1), 3–22. doi:10.1016/0048-7333(85)90021-6

Aburdene, P. (2007). *Megatrends 2010: The rise of conscious capitalism.* Hampton Roads Publishing.

Acedo, J., & Casillas, C. (2005). Current paradigms in the international management field: An author co-citation analysis. *International Business Review, 14*(5), 619–639. doi:10.1016/j.ibusrev.2005.05.003

Ackers, L. (2013). Internet mobility, co-presence and purpose: contextualising internationalisation in research careers. *Sociología Y tecnociencia/Sociology & Technoscience/Sociologia E Tecnociência, 3*(3), 117–141.

Adger, W. N., Hughes, T. P., Folke, C., Carpenter, S. R., & Rockstrom, J. (2005). Social-Ecological Resilience to Coastal Disasters. *Science, 309*(5737), 1036–1039. doi:10.1126/science.1112122 PMID:16099974

Agarwal, S. (2002). Restructuring seaside tourism: The resort lifecycle. *Annals of Tourism Research, 29*(1), 25–55. doi:10.1016/S0160-7383(01)00002-0

Aggelopoulos, S., Kamenidou, I., & Pavloudi, A. (2008). Women's business activities in Greece: The case of agro-tourism. *Tourism, 56*, 371–384.

Agier, M. (2011). *Antropologia da cidade: Lugares, situações e movimentos.* São Paulo: Editora Terceiro Nome.

Agustin, C., & Singh, J. (2005). Curvilinear effects of consumer loyalty determinants in relational exchanges. *JMR, Journal of Marketing Research, 42*(1), 96–108. doi:10.1509/jmkr.42.1.96.56961

Ahl, H. (2006). Why Research on Women Entrepreneurs Needs New Directions. *Entrepreneurship: Theory & Practice, 30*(5), 595–621. doi:10.1111/j.1540-6520.2006.00138.x

Ahl, H., & Nelson, T. (2010). Moving forward: Institutional perspectives on gender and entrepreneurship. *International Journal of Gender and Entrepreneurship, 2*(1), 5–9. doi:10.1108/17566261011044259

Air Transport Action Group. (2014). *Aviation Benefits beyond Borders.* Geneva: ATAG.

Airey, D., & Chong, K. (2010). National policy-makers for tourism in China. *Annals of Tourism Research, 37*(2), 295–314. doi:10.1016/j.annals.2009.09.004

Airports Council International Europe. (2015). *Economics Report 2014.* Brussels: ACI Europe.

Airports Council International. (2015). *Airport Connectivity Report.* Montreal: ACI.

Akın, M. (2015). A novel approach to model selection in tourism demand modeling. *Tourism Management, 48,* 64–72. doi:10.1016/j.tourman.2014.11.004

Aksoy, S., Atilgan, E., & Akinci, S. (2003). Airline Services Marketing by Domestic and Foreign Firms: Differences from the Customers' Viewpoint. *Journal of Air Transport Management, 9*(6), 343–351. doi:10.1016/S0969-6997(03)00034-6

Alegre, J., & Pou, L. (2004). Micro-economic determinants of the probability of tourism consumption. *Tourism Economics, 10*(2), 125–144. doi:10.5367/000000004323142452

Altman, M. (2005). *Treading Water.* Thai Day.

Alvarez García, J., Vila Alonso, M., Fraiz Brea, J. A., & Río Rama, M. C. (2013). Análisis de las relaciones de dependencia entre los factores críticos de la calidad y los resultados. Sector de alojamiento turístico en España. *Investigaciones Europeas de Dirección y Economía de la Empresa, 19*(2), 74–89. doi:10.1016/j.iedee.2012.08.001

Álvarez, L. S., Casielles, R. V., & Martín, M. D. (2009). The role of commitment perceived by the consumer in service industries. *Management Review, 7*(2), 141–175.

Álvarez, L. S., Martín, A. M. D., & Casielles, R. V. (2007). Relationship marketing and information and communication technologies: Analysis of retail travel agencies. *Journal of Travel Research, 45*(4), 453–463. doi:10.1177/0047287507299593

Alvarez, M., & Asugman, G. (2006). Explorers versus planners: A study of Turkish tourists. *Annals of Tourism Research, 33*(2), 319–338. doi:10.1016/j.annals.2005.12.001

Anderson, R. I., Fish, M., Xia, Y., & Michello, F. (1999). Measuring efficiency in the hotel industry: A stochastic frontier approach. *Hospital Management, 18*(1), 45–57. doi:10.1016/S0278-4319(98)00046-2

Anderson, R., Lewis, D., & Parker, M. (2000). Hotel industry efficiency: An advanced linear programming examination. *American Business Review, 18*(1), 40–48.

Andersson, S., Berglund, K., Gunnarsson, E., & Sundin, E. (2012). *Promoting Innovation - Policies, practices and procedures* (Vinnova Re). VINNO VA –Verket för Innovationssystem /Swedish Governmental Agency for Innovation System.

Andersson, T. (1996). *Traditional key ratio analysis versus data envelopment analysis: a comparison of various measurements of productivity and efficiency in restaurants.* London: Cassell.

Andersson, T. D., & Gertz, D. (2009). Tourism as a mixed industry: Differences between private, public and not-for-profit festivals. *Tourism Management, 30*(6), 847–856. doi:10.1016/j.tourman.2008.12.008

Ansoms, A. (2005). Resurrection after civil war and genocide: Growth, poverty and inequality in post-conflict Rwanda. *European Journal of Development Research, 17*(3), 495–508. doi:10.1080/09578810500209577

Anson, C. (1999). Planning for peace: The role of tourism in the aftermath of violence. *Journal of Travel Research, 38*(1), 1–5. doi:10.1177/004728759903800112

Aoyama, Y., Olds, K., Dicken, P., Kelly, P., Kong, L., & Yeung, H. (2001). Globalisation and the Asia-Pacific: Contested Territories. *Economic Geography, 77*(2), 201. doi:10.2307/3594066

AR-Media. (2015). *Augmented reality and the future of printing and publishing opportunities and perspectives.* Retrieved from: http://www.inglobetechnologies.com/docs/whitepapers/AR_printing_whitepaper_en.pdf

Ashcraft, K. L. (2009). Gender and diversity: other ways of making a difference. In M. Alvesson, T. Bridgman, & H. Willmott (Eds.), *The Oxford Handbook of Critical Management Studies* (pp. 304–327). Oxford, UK: Oxford University Press. doi:10.1093/oxfordhb/9780199237715.003.0015

Ashford, N., Mumayiz, S., & Wright, P. (2011). *Airport Engineering: Planning, Design and Development of 21st Century Airports* (4th ed.). New York, NY: John Wiley and Sons. doi:10.1002/9780470950074

Ashley, C., Roe, D., & Goodwin, H. (2001). *Pro-Poor Tourism Strategies: Making Tourism Work For The Poor. A review of experience.* Available at: http://www.propoortourism.info/documents/AshleyetalPPTStrats.pdf

Assaf, A. G., & Barros, C. P. (2013). A global benchmarking of the hotel industry. *Tourism Economics, 19*(4), 811–821. doi:10.5367/te.2013.0230

Assaf, A. G., & Josiassen, A. (2015). Frontier Analysis: A State-of-the-Art Review and Meta-Analysis. *Journal of Travel Research.* doi:10.1177/0047287515569776

Assaf, A., Barros, C. P., & Josiassen, A. (2010). Hotel efficiency: A bootstrapped metafrontier approach. *International Journal of Hospitality Management, 29*(3), 468–475. doi:10.1016/j.ijhm.2009.10.020

Association of European Airlines. (2014). *Flightpath 2019: A Blueprint for the Future.* Brussels: AEA.

Augé, M. (1998). *El viaje imposible: el turismo y sus imágenes.* Barcelona: Editorial Gedisa.

Augmented Reality Blog. (2015). *How augmented reality can revolutionize the hospitality industry.* Retrieved from: http://www.augmentedrealitytrends.com/augmented-reality/hospitality-industry.html

Aupperle, K. E., Carroll, A. B., & Hatfield, J. D. (1985). An Empirical Examination of the Relationship between Corporate Social Responsibility and Profitability. *Academy of Management Journal, 28*(2), 446–463. doi:10.2307/256210

Australian Agency for International Development (AusAID). (2012). *Australia Development Partner Handover Report 2012* (Unpublished). Díli, East Timor.

Avraham, E. (2015). Destination image repair during crisis: Attracting tourism during the Arab Spring uprisings. *Tourism Management, 47*, 224–232. doi:10.1016/j.tourman.2014.10.003

Aymerich Martínez, J., & Meseguer Artola, A. (2004). Investigación descriptiva: análisis de información. In A. Meseguer & J. Vilaseca (Eds.), *Coord), Estadística aplicada.* Catalunya: Fundació Universitat Oberta de Catalunya.

Azim, R., & Hassan, A. (2013a). *Understanding Recent Wireless and Mobile Technological Changes for Business Management Practises.* The 6th International Conference on Business Market Management (BMM). The University of Bamberg. Available at: http://bit.ly/Ns5u1C

Azim, R., & Hassan, A. (2013b). *Analysing the impact of mobile and wireless technology on Business Management Strategies.* The 6th International Conference on Business Market Management (BMM). The University of Bamberg. Available at: http://bit.ly/Ns5u1C

Azim, R., & Hassan, A. (2013). Impact analysis of wireless and mobile technology on business management strategies. *Journal of Information and Knowledge Management, 2*(2), 141–150.

Azuma, R. (1997). A survey of augmented reality. *Presence (Cambridge, Mass.), 6*(4), 355–385. doi:10.1162/pres.1997.6.4.355

Bai, B., Law, R., & Wen, I. (2008). The impact of website quality on customer satisfaction and purchase intentiond: Evidence from Chinese online visitors. *International Journal of Hospitality Management, 27*(3), 391–402. doi:10.1016/j.ijhm.2007.10.008

Bakas, F. E. (2014). *Tourism, female entrepreneurs and gender: Crafting economic realities in rural Greece.* (PhD Thesis). University of Otago, Dunedin, New Zealand.

Baker, M., & Riley, M. (1994). New perspectives on productivity in hotels: Some advances and new directions. *International Journal of Hospitality Management, 13*(4), 297–311. doi:10.1016/0278-4319(94)90068-X

Baldini, G., Oliveri, F., Braun, M., Seuschek, H., & Hess, E. (2012). Securing disaster supply chains with cryptography enhanced RFID. *Disaster Prevention and Management, 21*(1), 51–70. doi:10.1108/09653561211202700

Baloglu, S., & McCleary, K. W. (1999). US International Pleasure Travellers' Images of Four Mediterranean Destinations: A Comparison of Visitors and Nonvisitors. *Journal of Travel Research, 38*(2), 114–129. doi:10.1177/004728759903800207

Baltzell, D. E. (1991). *The Protestant Establishment revisited*. New Brunswick, NJ: Transaction Publishers.

Bandura, A. (1986). *Social foundations of thought and action: A social cognitive theory*. Englewood Cliffs, NJ: Prentice Hall.

Bandura, A. (1997). *Self-efficacy: The exercise of control*. New York: Freeman.

Bandura, A. (1997). *Self-efficacy:The exercise of control*. New York: Freeman.

Banks, M. (2001). *Visual methods in social research*. London: Sage.

Barata, M. J. (2010). O Que e Quem é um Povo? O conceito de autodeterminação e o debate sobre a ontologia do actor internacional. In *Proceedings of Congress da APCP* (pp. 1-10). Retrieved July 4, 2015, from http://repositorio.ismt.pt/handle/123456789/254

Barker, D. K. (2005). Beyond Women and Economics: Rereading "Women's Work.". *Signs (Chicago, Ill.), 30*(4), 2189–2209. doi:10.1086/429261

Baron, S., & Harris, K. (2008). Consumers as resource integrators. *Journal of Marketing Management, 24*(1-2), 113–130. doi:10.1362/026725708X273948

Barros, C. P. (2005). Measuring efficiency in the hotel sector. *Annals of Tourism Research, 32*(2), 456–477. doi:10.1016/j.annals.2004.07.011

Bartlett, M. S. (1951). A further note on tests of significance in factor analysis. *British Journal of Psychology, 4*, 1–2.

Baum, T. (2013). *International Perspectives on Women and Work in Hotels*. Geneva: Catering and Tourism.

BCTL. (2011). *Evolução Economia Nacional. In: Annual Report –Financial Year 2010-2011*. Retrieved November, 13, 2015, from https://www.bancocentral.tl/Download/Publications/Annual_Rep/Full_Report.pdf

BCTL. (2012). *Um ano de evolução da economia nacional 2011-12*. Retrieved November, 13, 2015, from https://www.bancocentral.tl/Download/Publications/Eco_Outlook_2012.pdf

BCTL. (2014). *Evolução Recente da Economia Nacional. In: Annual Report–Financial Year 2014*. Retrieved November, 13, 2015, from https://www.bancocentral.tl/Download/Publications/Annual_Rep/2014/Pt/BCTL_AR_2014_portuguese_Total.pdf

BCTL. (2015). Petroleum Fund of East Timor. *Quarterly Report, 11*(28). Retrieved July 4, 2015, from: http://www.bancocentral.tl/Download/Publications/Quarter-Report39_en.pdf

Bel, F., Lacroix, A., Lyser, S., Rambonilaza, T., & Turpin, N. (2015). Domestic demand for tourism in rural areas: Insights from summer stays in three French regions. *Tourism Management, 46*, 562–570. doi:10.1016/j.tourman.2014.07.020

Bel, G., & Fageda, X. (2005). Is a Mixed Funding Model for the Highway Network Sustainable Over Time? The Spanish Case. *Research in Transportation Economics, 15*, 187–203. doi:10.1016/S0739-8859(05)15015-X

Benabou, R., & Tirole, J. (2003). Intrinsic and extrinsic motivation. *The Review of Economic Studies, 70*(3), 489–520. doi:10.1111/1467-937X.00253

Benavides-Chicón, C. G., & Ortega, B. (2014). The impact of quality management on productivity in the hospitality sector. *International Journal of Hospitality Management, 42*(0), 165–173. doi:10.1016/j.ijhm.2014.07.004

Berendien, L., Douglas, A., & Zambellis, J. (2011). An Application of the Airport Service Quality Model in South Africa. *Journal of Air Transport Management, 17*(4), 224–227. doi:10.1016/j.jairtraman.2010.08.001

Berendien, L., & Liebe, L. (2010). The Perceived Value of Devices to Passengers Across the Airline Activity Chain. *Journal of Air Transport Management, 16*(1), 12–15. doi:10.1016/j.jairtraman.2009.02.002

Berger, J., Fisek, M. H., Norman, R. Z., & Zelditch, M. Jr. (1977). *Status characteristics and social interaction: An expectation states approach.* New York: Elsevier.

Berkeley.edu. (2005). *UC Berkeley team visits Thailand to open dialogue on impacts of tourism.* Author.

Bernardino, L., & Jones, M. (2008). *Internationalization and performance: an empirical study of high-tech SMEs in Portugal.* Bookonomics Lda.

Bernini, C., & Cracolici, M. F. (2015). Demographic change, tourism expenditure and life cycle behaviour. *Tourism Management, 47*, 191–205. doi:10.1016/j.tourman.2014.09.016

Bertaux, D., & Kohli, M. (1984). The life story approach: A continental view. *Annual Review of Sociology, 10*(1), 215–237. doi:10.1146/annurev.so.10.080184.001243

Besculides, A., Lee, M. E., & McCormic, P. J. (2002). Residents' perceptions of the cultural benefits of tourism. *Annals of Tourism Research, 29*(2), 303–319. doi:10.1016/S0160-7383(01)00066-4

Beyer, K. W. (2009). *Grace Hopper and the invention of the information age.* Cambridge, MA.: MIT Press.

Bieger, T., & Laesser, C. (2004). Information Sources for Travel Decisions: Toward a Source Process Model. *Journal of Travel Research, 42*(4), 357–371. doi:10.1177/0047287504263030

Bieger, T., & Wittmer, A. (2006). Air transport and tourism: Perspectives and challenges for destinations, airlines and governments. *Journal of Air Transport Management, 12*(1), 40–46. doi:10.1016/j.jairtraman.2005.09.007

Bitner, M. J., Booms, B. H., & Mohr, L. A. (1994). Critical service encounter: The employee's viewpoint. *Journal of Marketing, 58*(4), 95–106. doi:10.2307/1251919

Bitner, M. J., Booms, B., & Tetreault, M. S. (1990). The service encounters:Diagnosing favorable and unfavorable incidents. *Journal of Marketing, 54*(1), 71–84. doi:10.2307/1252174

Black, G. (2012). *Transforming museums in the 21st century.* London, United Kingdom: Routledge.

Blake, M. K., & Hanson, S. (2005). Rethinking innovation: Context and gender. *Environment & Planning, 37*(4), 681–701. doi:10.1068/a3710

Boeing. (2015). *Boeing's working on augmented reality, which could change space training, ops.* Retrieved from: http://bit.ly/1SquO89

Boisjoly, R., & Argenti, J. (1978). Corporate Collapse: The Causes and Symptoms. *Southern Economic Journal, 45*(2), 638. doi:10.2307/1057698

Bolton, K., & Graddol, D. (2012). English in China today. *English Today, 28*(3), 3–9. doi:10.1017/S0266078412000223

Boluk, K. (2013). Using CSR as a tool for development: An investigation of the fair hotels scheme in Ireland. *Journal of Quality Assurance in Hospitality & Tourism, 14*(1), 49–65. doi:10.1080/1528008X.2013.749382

Bonham, C., Edmonds, C., & Mak, J. (2006). The Impact of 9/11 and Other Terrible Global Events on Tourism in the United States and Hawaii. *Journal of Travel Research, 45*(1), 99–110. doi:10.1177/0047287506288812

Bonn, I., & Rundle-Thiele, S. (2007). Do or die—Strategic decision-making following a shock event. *Tourism Management, 28*(2), 615–620. doi:10.1016/j.tourman.2006.04.021

Botterill, D. (2001). The epistemology of a set of tourism studies. *Leisure Studies, 20*(3), 199–214. doi:10.1080/02614360127084

Bradshaw, S. (2002). Exploring the gender dimensions of reconstruction processes post-hurricane Mitch. *Journal of International Development, 14*(6), 871–879. doi:10.1002/jid.932

Brammer, H. (1990). Floods in Bangladesh: Geographical Background to the 1987 and 1988 Floods. *The Geographical Journal, 156*(1), 12. doi:10.2307/635431

Brammer, S., Jackson, G., & Matten, D. (2012). Corporate Social Responsibility and institutional theory: New perspectives on private governance. *Socio-economic Review, 10*(1), 3–28. doi:10.1093/ser/mwr030

Bramwell, B., & Lane, B. (2003). Tourism and sustainable development in an economic downturn. *Journal of Sustainable Tourism, 11*(1), 1–2. doi:10.1080/09669580308667188

Bramwell, B., & Lane, B. (2014). The "critical turn" and its implications for sustainable tourism research. *Journal of Sustainable Tourism, 22*(1), 1–8. doi:10.1080/09669582.2013.855223

Brandth, B., & Haugen, M. S. (2011). Farm diversification into tourism: Implications for social identity? *Journal of Rural Studies, 27*(1), 35–44. doi:10.1016/j.jrurstud.2010.09.002

BrazilianCooperationAgency (ABC). (2012). *Cooperação Brasileira – Parceiros para o Desenvolvimento: Relatório para a Transição 2012* (Unpublished). Díli, East Timor.

Breda, Z., & Ferreira, A. (2013, July). *Turismo em Timor-Leste: passaporte para o desenvolvimento?* Paper presented at Timor Conference 2013, Díli, East Timor.

Breda, Z. (2010). *Redes relacionais e a internacionalização da economia do turismo. Departamento de Economia, Gestão e Engenharia Industrial.* Aveiro: University of Aveiro.

Breeze, M. (2014). *How augmented reality will change the way we live.* Retrieved from: http://tnw.co/1nEDN6O

Breukel, A., & Go, F. M. (2009). Knowledge-based network participation in destination and event marketing: A hospitality scenario analysis perspective. *Tourism Management, 30*(2), 184–193. doi:10.1016/j.tourman.2008.05.015

Brida, J. B., Osti, L., & Barquet, A. (2010). Segmenting resident perceptions toward tourism: A cluster analysis with multinomial a logit model of a mountain community. *International Journal of Tourism Research, 12*(5), 591–602. doi:10.1002/jtr.778

Brida, J. G., Driha, O. M., Ramón-Rodríguez, A. B., & Scuderi, R. (2015). Dynamics of internationalisation of the hotel industry: The case of Spainnull. *International Journal of Contemporary Hospitality Management, 27*(5), 1024–1047. doi:10.1108/IJCHM-11-2013-0527

Briedenhann, J., & Wickens, E. (2004). Tourism routes as a tool for the economic development of rural areas—vibrant hope or impossible dream? *Tourism Management, 25*(1), 71–79. doi:10.1016/S0261-5177(03)00063-3

Britton, S. (1991). Tourism, capital, and place: Towards a critical geography of tourism. *Environment and Planning. D, Society & Space, 9*(4), 451–478. doi:10.1068/d090451

Brix, H., Koottatep, T., & Laugesen, C. (2007). Wastewater treatment in tsunami affected areas of Thailand by constructed wetlands. *Water Science and Technology, 56*(3), 69. doi:10.2166/wst.2007.528 PMID:17802840

Brocato, E. D., Voorhees, C. M., & Baker, J. (2012). Understanding the Influence of Cues from Other Customers in the Service Experience: A Scale Development and Validation. *Journal of Retailing, 88*(3), 384–398. doi:10.1016/j.jretai.2012.01.006

Brooner, F., & de Hoog, R. (2012). Economizing strategies during an economic crisis. *Annals of Tourism Research, 39*(2), 1048–1069. doi:10.1016/j.annals.2011.11.019

Bruni, A., Poggio, B., & Gherardi, S. (2005). *Gender and entrepreneurship: an ethnographic approach.* New York: Routledge. doi:10.4324/9780203698891

Buchholz, R. (2014). *Augmented reality: New opportunities for marketing and sales.* Retrieved from: http://bit.ly/1nMCLYO

Buell, F. (1994). *National culture and the new global system.* Baltimore, MD: JHU Press.

Buhalis, D. (2003). *eTourism: Information technology for strategic tourism management.* London: Pearson.

Buhalis, D., Leung, D., & Law, R. (2011). E-Tourism: Critical Information and Communication Technologies for Tourism Destinations. In Destination Marketing and Management. CAB International.

Buhalis, D., Costa, C., & Ford, F. (Eds.). (2006). *Tourism business frontiers.* London: Routledge.

Buhalis, D., & Law, R. (2008). Progress in information technology and tourism management: 20 years on and 10 years after the Internet—The state of eTourism research. *Tourism Management, 29*(4), 609–623. doi:10.1016/j.tourman.2008.01.005

Buhalis, D., & Michopoulou, E. (2011). Information Enabled Tourism Destination Marketing: Addressing the Accessibility Market. *Current Issues in Tourism, 14*(2), 145–168. doi:10.1080/13683501003653361

Buhalis, D., & O'Connor, P. (2005). Information communication technology – revolutionising tourism. *Tourism Recreation Research, 30*(3), 7–16. doi:10.1080/02508281.2005.11081482

Burgess, L., & Cooper, J. (2000). A model of internet Commerce Adoption (MICA). In S. M. Rahman & M. S. Raisinghani (Eds.), *Electronic Commerce: Opportunity and Challenges* (pp. 189–201). IGI Global.

Burke, K. C. (2012). Women's Agency in Gender-Traditional Religions: A Review of Four Approaches. *Social Compass, 6*(2), 122–133. doi:10.1111/j.1751-9020.2011.00439.x

Burnett, J. (1998). A strategic approach to managing crises. *Public Relations Review, 24*(4), 475–488. doi:10.1016/S0363-8111(99)80112-X

Burns, L. H. (1987). Infertility and the sexual health of the family. *Journal of Sex Education and Therapy, 13*, 30–34.

Bushell, R., & Sheldon, P. J. (Eds.). (2009). *Wellness and tourism: Mind, body, spirit, place.* New York: Cognizant Communication.

Butcher, J. (2003). *The Moralisation of Tourism.* London: Routledge.

Button, K., & Taylor, S. (2000). International air transportation and economic development. *Journal of Air Transport Management, 6*(4), 209–222. doi:10.1016/S0969-6997(00)00015-6

Buys, T. (2007). Professional competencies in occupational therapy work practice: What are they and how should these be developed? *Work (Reading, Mass.), 29*(1), 3. PMID:17627069

Buzinde, C. N., Kalavar, J., & Melubo, K. (2014). Community well-being amongst the Maasai in Tanzania. *Annals of Tourism Research, 44*, 20–35. doi:10.1016/j.annals.2013.08.010

Calahan, D. (2011). Consuming and erasing Portugal in the Lonely Planet guide to East Timor. *Postcolonial Studies, 14*(1), 95–109. doi:10.1080/13688790.2011.542117

Caldieron, J. M. (2013). Safety Perception and Tourism Potential in the Informal Neighborhood of "La Perla", San Juan, Puerto Rico. *International Journal of Safety and Security in Tourism, 4*, 1–23.

Calgaro, E., & Lloyd, K. (2008). Sun, sea, sand and tsunami: Examining disaster vulnerability in the tourism community of Khao Lak, Thailand. *Singapore Journal of Tropical Geography, 29*(3), 288–306. doi:10.1111/j.1467-9493.2008.00335.x

Calof, J. L., & Beamish, P. W. (1995). Adapting to foreign markets: Explaining internationalization. *International Business Review, 4*(2), 115–131. doi:10.1016/0969-5931(95)00001-G

Camison, C., & Fores, B. (2015). Is tourism firm competitiveness driven by different internal or external specific factors?: New empirical evidence from Spain. *Tourism Management, 48*, 477–499. doi:10.1016/j.tourman.2015.01.001

Campbell, J. L. (2007). Why would corporations behave in socially responsible ways? An institutional theory of corporate social responsibility. *Academy of Management Review, 32*(3), 946–967. doi:10.5465/AMR.2007.25275684

Canclini, N. G. (2013). *Culturas híbridas*. São Paulo: EDUSP.

Candela, G., & Figini, P. (2012). *The economics of tourism destinations*. Berlin: Springer. doi:10.1007/978-3-642-20874-4

Cantallops, A. S., & Cardona, J. R. (2015). Holiday destinations: The myth of the lost paradise? *Annals of Tourism Research, 55*(4), 171–173. doi:10.1016/j.annals.2015.10.002

Capterra. (n.d.). *Best Hospitality Property Management*. Retrieved March 25, 2015, from http://www.capterra.com/hospitality-property-management-software/

Carrion, R. S. M., & Santos, C. G. (2011). Sobre a governança da cooperação internacional para o desenvolvimento: Atores, propósitos e perspectivas. *Revista de Administração Pública, 45*(6), 1847–1868.

Carrol, A. B. (1979). A Three Dimensional Conceptual Model of Corporate Performance. *Academy of Management Review, 4*(4), 497–505.

Carvalho, I., Costa, C., Lykke, N., & Torres, A. (2014). An Analysis of Gendered Employment in the Portuguese Tourism Sector. *Journal of Human Resources in Hospitality & Tourism, 13*(4), 405–429. doi:10.1080/15332845.2014.888509

Cash, T. F., Gillen, B., & Burns, D. S. (1977). Sexism and beautyism in personnel consultant decision making. *The Journal of Applied Psychology, 62*(3), 301–310. doi:10.1037/0021-9010.62.3.301

Castillo-Canalejo, A. M., & Sánchez Cañizares, S. M. (2014). Community-based island tourism: The case of Boa Vista in Cape Verde. *International Journal of Culture. Tourism and Hospitality Research, 8*(2), 219–233.

Catalyst. (2015). *2014 Catalyst Census: Women Board Directors*. New York: Author.

Causevic, S., & Lynch, P. (2011). Phoenix tourism: Post-conflict tourism role. *Annals of Tourism Research, 38*(3), 780–800. doi:10.1016/j.annals.2010.12.004

CAVR. (2005). Chega! Relatório da CAVR. Díli, East Timor: CAVR.

CAVR. (2010). Timor-Oriental, Autodeterminação e a Comunidade Internacional – Audiência pública Nacional, 15-17 março 2004. Díli, East Timor: CAVR.

Cazals, C., Florens, J.-P., & Simar, L. (2002). Nonparametric frontier estimation: A robust approach. *Journal of Econometrics, 106*(1), 1–25. doi:10.1016/S0304-4076(01)00080-X

Chalmers, W. D. (2013). *America's Vacation Deficit Disorder: Who Stole Your Vacation?* Bloomington, IL: Universe.

Chambers, E. (2009). *Native tours: the anthropology of travel and tourism.* Waveland Press.

Chand, M. (2010). The impact of HRM practices on service quality, customer satisfaction and performance in the Indian hotel industry. *International Journal of Human Resource Management, 21*(4), 551–566. doi:10.1080/09585191003612059

Chang, M-C. (2006). *A Study on the Motivation of Purchasing Skin Care Products by the Female Consumers.* Takmang University Department of Business Administration.

Chang, C. H. (1989). *Psychology Dictionary.* Longman Group UK Limited.

Chang, M. K., & Cheung, W. (2001). Determinants of the intention to use Internet/ WWW at work: A confirmatory study. *Information & Management, 39*(1), 1–14. doi:10.1016/S0378-7206(01)00075-1

Chang, T.-Y., & Horng, S.-C. (2010). Conceptualizing and Measuring Experience Quality: The Customer's Perspective. *Service Industries Journal, 30*(14), 2401–2419. doi:10.1080/02642060802629919

Charness, G., & Gneezy, U. (2012). Strong Evidence for Gender Differences in Risk Taking. *Journal of Economic Behavior & Organization, 83*(1), 50–58. doi:10.1016/j.jebo.2011.06.007

Chen, M.-P. (2015). *Young people finding jobs difficult vs "Plastic Surgery" to enhance competitiveness,* Retrieved December 10, 2015, from http://www.laserone.com.tw/news_show_38.html

Chen, M-S. (1999). *Research on the influence of employees personality and QWL on work attitude and job performance in retail industry.* National Sun Yat-Sen University Department of Business Administration.

Chen, Y.-T. (2006). *The Effect of Personal Characteristics and Appearance Attraction of Salesperson on Business Performance-The Cases of Health care and Pharmaceutical Industries in Chinese Region.* (Unpublished Master's Thesis). Da-Yeh University, Changhua. Retrieved from http://handle.ncl.edu.tw/11296/ndltd/05486746407350309024

Chen, C.-F. (2007). Applying the stochastic frontier approach to measure hotel managerial efficiency in Taiwan. *Tourism Management, 28*(3), 696–702. doi:10.1016/j.tourman.2006.04.023

Chen, J. S., & Gursoy, D. (2001). An investigation of tourists' destination loyalty and preferences. *The International Journal of Contemporary Hospitality Management, 13*(2), 79–85. doi:10.1108/09596110110381870

Chen, J., Johnson, C., & Gherissi-Labben, T. (2013). Cross-cultural examination of decision elements: Youth tourism in Switzerland. *Anatolia, 24*(2), 162–172. doi:10.1080/13032917.2012.741529

Chen, J., Koh, Y., & Lee, S. (2011). Does the Market Care About RevPAR? A Case Study of Five Large U.S. Lodging Chains. *Journal of Hospitality & Tourism Research (Washington, D.C.), 35*(2), 258–273. doi:10.1177/1096348010384875

Chester, D. (1995). Blaikie, Piers, Cannon, Terry, Davis, Ian and Wisner, Ben, "At Risk: Natural Hazards, People's Vulnerability and Disasters" (Book Review). *Third World Planning Review, 17*(3), 357.

Chhabra, D. (2009). Proposing a sustainable marketing framework for heritage tourism. *Journal of Sustainable Tourism, 17*(3), 303–320. doi:10.1080/09669580802495758

Chiang, W., Tsai, H., & Wang, L. (2004). A DEA evaluation of Taipei hotels. *Annals of Tourism Research, 31*(3), 712–715. doi:10.1016/j.annals.2003.11.001

China Council for International Cooperation (CECID). (2012). *China Development Partner Handover Report 2012* (Unpublished). Díli, East Timor.

China Internet Network Information Center (CNNIC). (2014). *Statistical Report on Internet Development in China.* Retrieved March 5, 2015, from http://www1.cnnic.cn/IDR/ReportDownloads/201411/P020141102574314897888.pdf

China Internet Watch (CIW). (2015). *China, the Largest Outbound Tourism Market in 3 Consecutive years.* Retrieved May 25, 2015, from http://www.chinainternetwatch.com/13152/the-largest-outbound-tourism-market-3-consecutive-years

Chisholm, M. E., & Ely, D. P. (1976). *Media Presonnel in Education:A Competency Approach, Englewood Cliffs.* New York: Prentice-Hall.

Chitturi, R., Raghunathan, R., & Mahajan, V. (2008). Delight by Design: The Role of Hedonic Versus Utilitarian Benefits. *Journal of Marketing, 72*(3), 48–63. doi:10.1509/jmkg.72.3.48

Chiu, C., Hsu, M., Lai, H., & Chang, C. (2012). Re-examining the influence of trust on online repeat purchase intention: The moderating role of habit and its antecedents. *Decision Support Systems, 53*(4), 835–845. doi:10.1016/j.dss.2012.05.021

Cho, Y.-C. (2007). *The relationships among core employability, professional abilities and future access choice of graduating students in the Universities of Technology.* (Unpublished master's thesis). National Changhua University of Education, Changhua. Retrieved from http://ir.ncue.edu.tw/ir/handle/987654321/3654

Cho, S., Woods, R. H., Jang, S., & Erdem, M. (2006). Measuring the impact of human resource management practices on hospitality firms' performances. *International Journal of Hospitality Management, 25*(2), 262–277. doi:10.1016/j.ijhm.2005.04.001

Christou, E. (2002). Revisiting competencies for hospitality management: Contemporary views of the stakeholders. *Journal of Hospitality & Tourism Education, 14*(1), 25–32. doi:10.1080/10963758.2002.10696721

Chung-Herrera, B. G., Enz, C. A., & Lankau, M. J. (2003). Grooming future hospitality leaders: A competencies model. *The Cornell Hotel and Restaurant Administration Quarterly, 44*(3), 17–25. doi: 10.1177/0010880403044400302

Chusmir, L. H., Koberg, C. S., & Stecher, M. D. (1992). Self-confidence of managers in work and social situations: A look at gender differences. *Sex Roles, 26*(11-12), 497–512. doi:10.1007/BF00289871

Cisco (2014). *Cisco Connected World Technology Report.* Retrieved February 15, 2015, from http://www.cisco.com/c/en/us/solutions/enterprise/connected-world-technology-report/index.html

Claasen, C., & Roloff, J. (2012). The Link between Responsibility and Legitimacy: The Case of De Beers in Namibia. *Journal of Business Ethics, 107*(3), 379–398. doi:10.1007/s10551-011-1045-0

Claros, E., & Di Tella, A. (2014). *Tourism in the EU economy.* European Parliament.

Clemmer, J. (1990). The three rings of perceived value. *The Canadian Manager, 15*(2), 12–15.

Clifford, M. M., & Walster, E. (1974). Research note: The effect of physical attractiveness on teacher expectations. *Sociology of Education, 46*(1), 248–258.

CNN News. (2005). Land Wars in Post-Tsunami World. *CNN News.*

Cohen, E. (1972). Towards a Sociology of International Tourism. *Social Research, 39*, 64–82.

Cohen, E. (1979). Rethinking the sociology of tourism. *Annals of Tourism Research, 6*(1), 18–35. doi:10.1016/0160-7383(79)90092-6

Cohen, E. (1982). "The Pacific Islands, from utopian myth to consumer Product". *The Disenchantment Paradise. Cathiers du Turisme, Serie B., 27,* 1–17.

Cohen, E. (1983). Insiders and Outsiders: The Dynamics of Development of Bungalow Tourism on the Islands of Southern Thailand. *Human Organization, 42*(2), 158–162. doi:10.17730/humo.42.2.45767335470438t0

Cohen, E. (1984). The sociology of tourism: Approaches, issues, and findings. *Annual Review of Sociology, 10*(1), 373–392. doi:10.1146/annurev.so.10.080184.002105

Cohen, E. (1985). Tourism as play. *Religion, 15*(3), 291–304. doi:10.1016/0048-721X(85)90016-8

Cohen, E. (2007). Authenticity and Commoditisation in Tourism. *Annals of Tourism Research, 1*(15), 371–386.

Coles, T., Hall, C. M., & Duval, D. T. (2006). Tourism and post-disciplinary enquiry. *Current Issues in Tourism, 9*(4-5), 293–319. doi:10.2167/cit327.0

Collins, D., & Tisdell, C. (2002). Age-Related Lifecycles: Purpose Variations. *Annals of Tourism Research, 29*(3), 801–818. doi:10.1016/S0160-7383(01)00081-0

Connell, J. (2006). Medical Tourism: Sea, Sun, Sand and Surgery. *Tourism Management, 27*(6), 1093–1100. doi:10.1016/j.tourman.2005.11.005

Conrady, R., & Buck, M. (2011). *Trends and issues in global tourism 2011*. London: Springer. doi:10.1007/978-3-642-17767-5

Cooper, C. (2006). Knowledge management and tourism. *Annals of Tourism Research, 33*(1), 47–64. doi:10.1016/j.annals.2005.04.005

Coppola, D. (2015). *Introduction to international disaster management* (3rd ed.). Oxford, UK: Butterworth-Heinemann.

Costa, C., Caçador, S., Carvalho, I., Breda, Z., & Costa, R. (2014). The Influence of Gender and Education-related Variables on Career Development: The Case of Portuguese and Brazilian Tourism Graduates. In The Tourism Education Futures Initiative: Activating Change in Tourism Education. Routledge.

Costa, C., Carvalho, I., & Breda, Z. (2011). Gender inequalities in tourism employment: The Portuguese case. *Revista Turismo & Desenvolvimento, 15,* 37–52.

Council Regulation (EC) No 550/2004 of the European Parliament and of the Council of 10 March 2004 on the provision of air navigation services in the single European sky (the service provision Regulation) OJ96/10

Council Regulation (EEC) No 2407/92. The introduction of harmonised requirements for an operating licence for EU airlines

Coviello, N. E. (2006). The network dynamics of international new ventures. *Journal of International Business Studies, 37*(5), 713–731.

Cox, D., & Rigby, J. (2013). *Innovation policy challenges for the 21st century*. New York: Routledge.

Creswell, J. W. (2003). *Research Design Qualitative, Quantitative and Mixed Methods Approaches* (2nd ed.). Thousand Oaks, CA: Sage.

Creswell, J. W. (2007). *Qualitative inquiry & research design. Choosing among five approaches*. Thousand Oaks, CA: SAGE.

Cronin, J. J., & Taylor, S. A. (1992). Measuring service quality: A reexamination and extension. *Journal of Marketing, 56*(3), 55–68. doi:10.2307/1252296

Crotts, J. C., & Mazanec, J. A. (2013). Diagnosing the impact of an event on hotel demand: The case of the BP oil spill. *Tourism Management Perspectives, 8*, 60–67. doi:10.1016/j.tmp.2013.07.002

Crouch, D., & Desforges, L. (2003). The sensuous in the tourist encounter. *Tourist Studies, 3*(1), 5–22. doi:10.1177/1468797603040528

Crowe, T. V. (2002). *Translation of the Rosenberg self-esteem scale:From English to American sign language.* Baltimore, MD: University of Maryland.

Crozier, G. K. D., & Baylis, F. (2010). The ethical physician encounters international medical travel. *Journal of Medical Ethics, 36*(5), 297–301. doi:10.1136/jme.2009.032789 PMID:20439336

Cuban Embassy in Díli. (2012). *Republic of Cuba Development Partner Handover Report 2012* (Unpublished). Díli, East Timor.

Cuhls, K., & Johnston, R. (2008). Corporate foresight. In C. Cagnin, M. Keenan, R. Johnston, F. Scapolo, & R. Barré (Eds.), *Future-Oriented Technology Analysis* (pp. 102–114). Springer Berlin Heidelberg. doi:10.1007/978-3-540-68811-2_8

Cullen, K., & Helsel, C. (2010). *The Evolving Dynamics of Revenue Management. In Advanced Robust and Nonparametric Methods in Efficiency Analysis: Methodology and Applications* (Vol. 4). Springer Science & Business Media.

Culnan, M. J. (1987). Mapping the intellectual structure of MIS, 1980–1985: A co-citation analysis. *Management Information Systems Quarterly, 11*(3), 341–353. doi:10.2307/248680

Cummings, J. (2005). *Andaman Coast Post-Tsunami Landscape: Island Recover.* TAT Governor Corner.

Curry, D., Dobbins, G., & Ladd, R. (1994). Transfer of training and adult learning (TOTAL). *Journal of Continuing Social Work Education, 6*(1), 8–14.

Cyr, D., Head, M., Larios, H., & Pan, B. (2009). Exploring human images in website design: A multi-method approach. *Management Information Systems Quarterly, 33*(3), 539–566.

D'Alessandro-Scarpari, C. (2011). Local territories, their power and their actions: Development as a weapon for peace. World Journal of Science, *Technology and Sustainable Development, 8*(2-3), 263–275.

Dadwal, S., & Hassan, A. (2015). The Augmented Reality Marketing: A Merger of Marketing and Technology in Tourism. In N. Ray (Ed.), *Emerging Innovative Marketing Strategies in the Tourism Industry* (pp. 78–96). Hershey, PA: IGI Global. doi:10.4018/978-1-4666-8699-1.ch005

Dale, C., & Robinson, N. (2001). The theming of tourism education: A three-domain approach. *International Journal of Contemporary Hospitality Management, 13*(1), 30–35. doi:10.1108/09596110110365616

Danilda, I., & Thorslund, J. G. (2011). *Innovation & Gender.* Västerås: Edita Västra Aros AB.

Dann, G. M. (2011). Anglophone hegemony in tourism studies today. *Enlightening Tourism: A Pathmaking Journal, 1*(1), 1-30.

Dann, G. (2009). How international is the International Academy for the Study of Tourism? *Tourism Analysis, 14*(1), 3–13. doi:10.3727/108354209788970180

Davis, C. F. (1991). Agents without principles? The spread of the poison pill through the intercorporate network. *Administrative Science Quarterly, 38*(4), 583–613. doi:10.2307/2393275

Day, A. (1997). A Model for Monitoring Web Site Effectiveness. *Internet Research*, *7*(2), 109–115. doi:10.1108/10662249710165244

De Neufville, R., & Odoni, A. (2013). *Airport Systems: Planning, Design and Management*. New York, NY: McGraw-Hill.

Debord, G. (1998). *Comments on the Society of the Spectacle* (Vol. 18). London: Verso.

Decrop, A. (1999). Triangulation in qualitative tourism research. *Tourism Management*, *20*(1), 157–161. doi:10.1016/S0261-5177(98)00102-2

Deem, R. (1996). No time for a rest? An exploration of women's work, engendered leisure and holidays. *Time & Society*, 5.1, 5-25.

Delic, J. M. (2011). *Trends in Slum Tourism*. Available at: https://dspace.lib.uoguelph.ca/xmlui/handle/10214/2473

Denscombe, M. (2010). *The good research guide* (4th ed.). Maidenhead, UK: Open University Press.

Denzin, N. K., & Lincoln, Y. (2011). *The SAGE Handbook of Qualitative Research*. SAGE Publications.

Diekmann, A., & Hannan, K. (2012). Touristic mobilities in India's slum spaces. *Annals of Tourism Research*, *39*(3), 1315–1336. doi:10.1016/j.annals.2012.02.005

Dion, K. K., Bersheid, E., & Walster, E. (1972). What is beautiful is good. *Journal of Personality and Social Psychology*, *24*(3), 285–290. doi:10.1037/h0033731 PMID:4655540

Dipboye, R. L., Arvey, R. D., & Terpstra, D. E. (1977). Sex and physical attractiveness of raters and applicants as determinants of resume evaluations. *The Journal of Applied Psychology*, *62*(3), 288–294. doi:10.1037/0021-9010.62.3.288

Dipboye, R. L., Fromkin, H. L., & Wiback, K. (1975). Relative importance of applicant sex, attractiveness, and scholastic standing in evaluation of job applicant resumes. *The Journal of Applied Psychology*, *60*(1), 39–43. doi:10.1037/h0076352

Dobruszkes, F. (2009a). Does liberalisation of air transport imply increasing competition? Lessons from the European case. *Transport Policy*, *16*(1), 29–39. doi:10.1016/j.tranpol.2009.02.007

Dobruszkes, F. (2009b). New Europe, new low-cost air services. *Journal of Transport Geography*, *17*(6), 423–432. doi:10.1016/j.jtrangeo.2009.05.005

Dodds, R. (2011). Koh Phi Phi: Moving Towards or Away from Sustainability? *Asia Pacific Journal of Tourism Research*, *15*(3), 251–265. doi:10.1080/10941665.2010.503615

Dodds, R., Graci, S., & Holmes, M. (2010). Does the tourist care? A comparison of tourists in Koh Phi Phi, Thailand and Gili Trawangan, Indonesia. *Journal of Sustainable Tourism*, *18*(2), 207–222. doi:10.1080/09669580903215162

Dodds, R., & Kuehnel, J. (2010). CSR among Canadian mass tour operators: Good awareness but little action. *International Journal of Contemporary Hospitality Management*, *22*(2), 221–244. doi:10.1108/09596111011018205

Dodgson, M., & Gan, D. (2010). *Innovation: a very short introduction*. Oxford, UK: Oxford University Press. doi:10.1093/actrade/9780199568901.001.0001

Doolin, B., Burgess, L., & Cooper, J. (2002). Evaluating the use of the web for tourism marketing: A case study from New Zeland. *Tourism Management*, *23*(5), 557–561. doi:10.1016/S0261-5177(02)00014-6

Doong, H., Law, R., & Wang, H. (2009). An initial investigation of integrating innovation diffusion models for drawing first-time visitors. *Journal of Travel & Tourism Marketing*, *26*(1), 19–29. doi:10.1080/10548400802656702

Dos Santos, J. R. (2005). Antropología, comunicación y turismo: la mediación cultural en la construcción del espacio turístico de una comunidad de pescadores en Laguna, Sc. Brasil. *Estudios y Perspectivas en Turismo, 14*(4), 293-313.

Drucker, P. (1973). *La Gerencia, tareas, responsabilidad y prácticas*. Buenos Aires: ElAteneo.

Duarte, R. (2010). *Exploring the Social Impacts of Favela Tourism*. Wageningen University. Retrieved from www.slumtourism.net/download/Duarte2010.pdf

Dubisch, J. (1993). "foreign chickens" and other outsiders: Gender and community in Greece. *American Ethnologist, 20*(2), 272–287. doi:10.1525/ae.1993.20.2.02a00040

Durbin, S. (2011). Creating Knowledge through Networks: A Gender Perspective. *Gender, Work and Organization, 18*(1), 90–112. doi:10.1111/j.1468-0432.2010.00536.x

Durkheim, E. (1997). *The division of labor in society*. New York, NY: Simon and Schuster.

Dürr, E. (2012a). Encounters Over Garbage: Tourists And Lifestyle Migrants In Mexico. *Tourism Geographies, 3*(2), 339–355. doi:10.1080/14616688.2012.633217

Dürr, E. (2012b). Urban Poverty, Spatial Representation and Mobility: Touring a Slum in Mexico. *International Journal of Urban and Regional Research, 36*(4), 706–724. doi:10.1111/j.1468-2427.2012.01123.x

Dürr, E., & Jaffe, R. (2012). Theorising Slum Tourism in Latin America and the Caribbean: Performing, Negotiating and Transforming Inequality. *European Review of Latin American and Caribbean Studies, 93*, 113–123.

Dwyer, L., Edwards, D., Mistilis, N., Roman, C., & Scott, N. (2009). Destination and enterprise management for a tourism future. *Tourism Management, 30*(1), 63–74. doi:10.1016/j.tourman.2008.04.002

Dwyer, L., Gill, A., & Seetaram, N. (2012). *Handbook of Research Methods in Tourism: quantitative and qualitative approaches*. Cheltenham, UK: Edward Elgar Publishing Ltd. doi:10.4337/9781781001295

Dyllick, T., & Hockerts, K. (2002). Beyond the business case for corporate sustainability. *Business Strategy and the Environment, 11*(2), 130–141. doi:10.1002/bse.323

Eagly, A. H., Ashmore, R. D., Makhijani, M. G., & Longo, L. C. (1991). What is beautiful is good, but …: A meta-analytic review of research on the physical attractiveness stereotype. *Psychological Bulletin, 110*(1), 109–128. doi:10.1037/0033-2909.110.1.109

Easterby-Smith, M., Thorpe, R., & Lowe, A. (2012). *Management Research* (4th ed.). London: Sage.

Edensor, T. (2001). Performing tourism, staging tourism (Re) producing tourist space and practice. *Tourist Studies, 1*(1), 59–81. doi:10.1177/146879760100100104

Edwards, E. (1992). Anthropology and photography, 1860-1920. New Haven, CT: Yale University Press in association with the Royal Anthropological Institute, London.

Edwards, D., Mistilis, N., Roman, C., Scott, N., & Cooper, C. (2008). *Megatrends underpinning tourism to 2020: Analysis of key drivers for change*. CRC for Sustainable Tourism.

Ekachai, S. (1998). What it all boils down to is greed. *The Bangkok Post*.

Elkington, J. (1997). *Cannibals with Forks: The Triple Bottom Line of 21st Century Business* (2nd ed.). Oxford: Capstone Publishing Ltd.

Elsaid, E., & Ursel, N. D. (2011). CEO succession, gender and risk taking. *Gender in Management: An International Journal, 26*(7), 499–512. doi:10.1108/17542411111175478

Engel, J., Blackwell, R., & Miniard, P. (1995). *Consumer Behaviour* (8th ed.). Fort Worth, TX: Dryden.

Erfurt-Cooper, P., & Cooper, M. (2009). *Health and Wellness Tourism. Spas and Hot Springs*. Bristol: Channel View Publications.

Erin, A. (2014). *7 Alternatives to Google AdWords for Small Businesses*. Retrieved April 26, 2015, from http://www.sitepronews.com/2014/10/08/7-alternatives-google-adwords-small-businesses

Ernst, A. T., Jiang, H., Krishnamoorthy, M., & Sier, D. (2004). Staff scheduling and rostering: A review of applications, methods and models. *European Journal of Operational Research*, *153*(1), 3–27. doi:10.1016/S0377-2217(03)00095-X

Escalona, F. M. O. D., & Thirkettle, A. (2011). General theory of tourism? the case of war and terrorism. *International Journal of Tourism Anthropology*, *1*(3), 208–225. doi:10.1504/IJTA.2011.043706

Eugenio-Martin, J. L., & Campos-Soria, J. A. (2011). Income and the substitution pattern between domestic and international tourism demand. *Applied Economics*, *43*(20), 2519–2531. doi:10.1080/00036840903299698

Eugenio-Martin, J. L., & Campos-Soria, J. A. (2014). Economic crisis and tourism expenditure cutback decision. *Annals of Tourism Research*, *44*, 53–73. doi:10.1016/j.annals.2013.08.013

EUROCONTROL. (2015). *NM Annual Network Operations Report 2014*. Brussels: EUROCONTROL.

EUROCONTROL-FAA. (2013). *Comparison of ATM-related performance: USA – Europe*. Brussels: EUROCONTROL.

European Commission. (2001). *Libro verde. Fomentar un marco Europeo para la responsabilidad social de las empresas*. Retrieved January 22, 2015, from: http://eur-lex.europa.eu/LexUriServ/site/es/com/2001/com2001_0366es01.pdf

European Commission. (2010). Europe 2020 – A European strategy for smart, sustainable and inclusive growth. Brussels: Author.

European Commission. (2011). *Estrategia renovada de la UE para 2011-2014 sobre la responsabilidad social de las empresas*. Retrieved January 22, 2015, from: http://eur-lex.europa.eu/LexUriServ/LexUriServ.do?uri=COM:2011:0681:FIN:ES:PDF

European Commission. (2014). *State aid: Commission adopts new guidelines for state aid to airports and airlines*. Brussels: European Commission.

European Commission. (2015a). *Public consultation on the EU Aviation Package: Background information*. Available at: http://ec.europa.eu/transport/modes/air/consultations/doc/2015-aviation-package/background.pdf

European Commission. (2015b). *Air: Single European Sky*. Available at: http://ec.europa.eu/transport/modes/air/single_european_sky/index_en.htm

European Commission. (2015c). *Commission Regulation (EU) 2015/340 of 20 February 2015 laying down technical requirements and administrative procedures relating to air traffic controllers' licences and certificates pursuant to Regulation (EC) No 216/2008 of the European Parliament and of the Council, amending Commission Implementing Regulation (EU) No 923/2012 and repealing Commission Regulation (EU) No 805/2011*. Brussels: European Commission.

Fahrer, N. (2012). *Innovation and other useless things: a jump-start for discussions*. New York: Norman Fahrer.

Fairburn-Dunlop, P. (1994). Gender, Culture and Tourism Development in Western Samoa. In V. Kinnaird & D. Hall (Eds.), *Tourism: A Gender Analysis* (pp. 121–141). Chichester, New York: Wiley.

Falk, M., & Hagsten, E. (2015). Modelling growth and revenue for Swedish hotel establishments. *International Journal of Hospitality Management*, *45*, 59–68. doi:10.1016/j.ijhm.2014.11.009

Fanjul, E. (2010, September-October). Factores culturales e internacionalización de la empresa. *ICE*, *856*, 7–19.

Faria, V. S. (2011). *O desempenho da administração transitória das Nações Unidas em Timor-Leste: um estudo e análise do mandato do Conselho de Segurança das Nações Unidas segundo resolução n. 1272, de 1999.* LembahManah.

Faulkner, B. (2001). Towards a framework for tourism disaster management. *Tourism Management, 22*(2), 135–147. doi:10.1016/S0261-5177(00)00048-0

Fenstermaker, S., & West, C. (2013). *Doing gender doing difference.* Hoboken, NJ: Francis Taylor.

Ferguson, L., & Alarcón, D. M. (2014). Gender and sustainable tourism: Reflections on theory and practice. *Journal of Sustainable Tourism,* 1–16. doi:10.1080/09669582.2014.957208

Fernandez-Alles, M., & Ramos-Rodríguez, A. (2009). Intellectual structure of human resources management research: A bibliometric analysis of the Journal Human Resources Management 1985–2005. *Journal of the American Society for Information Science and Technology, 60*(1), 161–175. doi:10.1002/asi.20947

Fernández-Morales, A., & Mayorga-Toledano, M. C. (2008). Seasonal concentration of the hotel demand in Costa del Sol: A decomposition by nationalities. *Tourism Management, 29*(5), 940–949. doi:10.1016/j.tourman.2007.11.003

Ferreira, M. P., Pinto, C. P., & Serra, F. R. (2014). The transaction costs theory in international business research: A bibliometric study over three decades. *Scientometrics, 98*(3), 1899–1922. doi:10.1007/s11192-013-1172-8

Fesenmaier, D. R., Cook, S., Sheatsley, D., & Patkose, M. (2009). *Travellers' Use of the Internet: 2009 Edition.* Washington, DC: Travel Industry Association.

Fesenmaier, D. R., & O'Leary, J. T. (2006). The transformation of consumer behavior. In D. Buhalis & C. Costa (Eds.), *Tourism business frontiers: Consumers, products and industry* (pp. 9–18). Oxford, UK: Elsevier.

Figueroa-Domecq, C., Pritchard, A., Segovia-Pérez, M., Morgan, N., & Villacé-Molinero, T. (2015). Tourism gender research: A critical accounting. *Annals of Tourism Research, 52*(0), 87–103. doi:10.1016/j.annals.2015.02.001

Finger, M. (2015, Spring). Liberalisation of air traffic management services: what role for EUROCONTROL? *Skyway,* 40-41.

Fink, S. (2000). *Crisis management.* New York, NY: American Management Association.

Finnish Tourist Board. (2005). Hyvinvointi- ja wellness-matkailun peruskartoitus. Helsinki: Finnish Tourist Board A:144. Suunnittelukeskus Oy.

Fischer, E., Gainer, B., & Bristor, J. (1997). The sex of the service provider: Does it influence perceptions of service quality? *Journal of Retailing, 73*(3), 361–382. doi:10.1016/S0022-4359(97)90023-3

Fjelstul, J. (2007). Competencies and opportunities for entry-level golf and club management careers: Perceptions from the industry. *Journal of Hospitality & Tourism Education, 19*(3), 32–38. doi:10.1080/10963758.2007.10696895

Fleischer, A., Peleg, G., & Rivlin, J. (2011). The Impact of Changes in Household Vacation Expenditures on the Travel and Hospitality Industries. *Tourism Management, 32*(4), 815–821. doi:10.1016/j.tourman.2010.07.003

Fleischer, A., & Rivlin, J. (2009). Quality, quantity and duration decisions in household demand for vacations. *Tourism Economics, 15*(3), 513–530. doi:10.5367/000000009789036558

Fodness, D., & Murray, B. (1998). A typology of tourist information search strategies. *Journal of Travel Research, 37*(2), 108–119. doi:10.1177/004728759803700202

Forgas, S., Moliner, M. A., Sánchez, J., & Palau, R. (2010). Antecedents of airline passenger loyalty: Low-cost versus traditional airlines. *Journal of Air Transport Management, 16*(4), 229–233. doi:10.1016/j.jairtraman.2010.01.001

Formica, S., & McCleary, K. (2000). Professional development needs in Italy. *The Cornell Hotel and Restaurant Administration Quarterly, 41*(2), 72–79. doi:10.1177/001088040004100219

Forret, M. L., & Dougherty, T. W. (2004). Networking behaviors and career outcomes: Differences for men and women? *Journal of Organizational Behavior, 25*(3), 419–437. doi:10.1002/job.253

Fox, B. (2006). Motherhood as a class act: the many ways in which "Intensive mothering" is entangled with social class. In K. Bezanson & M. Luxton (Eds.), *Social reproduction: feminist political economy challenges neo-liberalism.* Montreal: McGill-Queen's University Press.

Francescon, S. (2012). *Generic integrity and innovation in tourism texts in English.* Academic Press.

Frechtling, D. C., & Horvath, E. (1999). Estimating the multiplier effects of tourism expenditures on a local economy through a regional input-output model. *Journal of Travel Research, 37*(4), 324–332. doi:10.1177/004728759903700402

Freeman, R. (1984). *Strategic management: A stakeholders approach.* Zürich: Pitman. Fremdenverkehrslehre.

Freire-Medeiros, B. (2007). Selling the favela: Thoughts and polemics about a tourist destination. *Revista Brasileira de Ciencias Sociais, 22*(65), 61–72.

Freire-Medeiros, B. (2009). The favela and its touristic transits. *Geoforum, 40*(2), 580–588. doi:10.1016/j.geoforum.2008.10.007

Freire-Medeiros, B. (2012). *Touring Poverty.* Oxon, UK: Routledge.

French Development Agency (AFD). (2012). *France Development Partner Handover Report 2012* (Unpublished). Díli, East Timor.

Frenzel, F. (2014). Slum Tourism and Urban Generation: Touring Inner Johannesburg. *Urban Forum, 25*, 431-447. doi:10.1007/s12132-014-9236-2

Frenzel, F., & Koens, K. (2012). Slum Tourism: Developments in a Young Field of Interdisciplinary Tourism Research. *Tourism Geographies, 14*(2), 195–212. doi:10.1080/14616688.2012.633222

Frenzel, F., Koens, K., & Steinbrink, M. (Eds.). (2012). *Slum-Tourism: Power Poverty Ethics.* Oxon, UK: Routledge.

Frenzel, F., Koens, K., Steinbrink, M., & Rogerson, C. M. (2015). Slum Tourism: State of the art. *Tourism Review International, 18*(4), 237–252. doi:10.3727/154427215X14230549904017

Fried, H. O., Lovell, C. K., & Schmidt, S. S. (2008). *The measurement of productive efficiency and productivity growth.* Oxford University Press. doi:10.1093/acprof:oso/9780195183528.001.0001

Frontier Economics. (2014). *Setting airport regulated charges: the choice between single till and dual till.* London: Frontier Economics.

Fuengprichavai, R. (1998). At the movies or at the beach, where were you. *Nation (New York, N.Y.).*

Galaskiewicz, J. (1991). Making corporate actors accountable: Institution-building in Minneapolis-St. Paul. In W.W. Powell, & P.J. DiMaggio, P.J. (Eds.), The new institutionalism in organizational analysis (pp. 293-310). Chicago: University of Chicago Press.

Galbreath, J., & Galvin, P. (2008). Firm factors, industry structure and performance variation: New empirical evidence to a classic debate. *Journal of Business Research, 61*(2), 109–117. doi:10.1016/j.jbusres.2007.06.009

Gallardo Vázquez, D., Sánchez Hernández, M. I., & Corchuelo Martínez-Azúa, M. B. (2013). Validación de un instrumento de medida para la relación entre la orientación a la Responsabilidad Social Corporativa y otras variables estratégicas de la empresa. *Revista de Contabilidad. Spanish Accounting Review, 6*(1), 11–23.

García-Altés, A. (2005). The development of health tourism services. *Annals of Tourism Research, 32*(1), 262–266. doi:10.1016/j.annals.2004.05.007

Garland, A. (1997). *The beach.* New York: Riverhead Books.

Garner, D., & Kearney, C. A. (1997). The 1997 body image survey results. *Psychology Today, 1*(2), 30–84.

Garrod, B., & Fyall, A. (2000). Managing heritage tourism. *Annals of Tourism Research, 27*(3), 682–708. doi:10.1016/S0160-7383(99)00094-8

Gartner Incorporated. (2014). *Gartner technology research.* Retrieved from: http://gtnr.it/1nvU5Bb

Geertz, C. (1994). Thick description: Toward an interpretive theory of culture. *Readings in the Philosophy of Social Science,* 213-231.

Geertz, C. (1973). *The interpretation of cultures: Selected essays* (Vol. 5019). New York: Basic books.

Gefen, D., & Heart, T. (2006). On the need to include national culture as a central issue in e-commerce trust beliefs. *Journal of Global Information Management, 14*(4), 1–30. doi:10.4018/jgim.2006100101

Gentile, C., Spiller, N., & Noci, G. (2007). How to sustain the customer experience: An overview of experience components that co-create value with the customer. *European Management Journal, 25*(5), 395–410. doi:10.1016/j.emj.2007.08.005

George, B. P., Inbakaran, R., & Poyyamoli, G. (2010). To Travel or Not to travel: towards understanding the theory of nativistic motivation. *Turizam: znanstveno-stručni časopis, 58*(4), 395-407.

George, R., & Booyens, I. (2014). Township tourism demand: tourists' perceptions of safety and security. *Urban Forum, 25,* 449-467. doi:10.1007/s12132-014-9228-2

German International Cooperation Agency (GIZ). (2012). *Germany Development Partner Handover Report 2012* (Unpublished). Díli, East Timor.

Germann Molz, J. (2014). *Travel Connection: Tourism, technology and togetherness in a mobile world.* Abingdon, UK: Routledge.

Gessa, A., Ruiz, A., & Jimenez, M. A. (2008). *La responsabilidad social corporativa como modelo de gestión hotelera. Implantación y desarrollo en la red de paradores. Estableciendo puentes en una economía global.* Madrid: ESIC Editorial.

Gherardi, S., & Murgia, A. (2014). What makes a "good manager"? Positioning gender and management in students' narratives. *Equality, Diversity and Inclusion:International Journal (Toronto, Ont.), 33*(8), 690–707. doi:10.1108/EDI-05-2013-0040

Ghobarah, A., Saatcioglu, M., & Nistor, I. (2006). The impact of the 26 December 2004 earthquake and tsunami on structures and infrastructure. *Engineering Structures, 28*(2), 312–326. doi:10.1016/j.engstruct.2005.09.028

Gibson-Graham, J. K. (2006). *The end of capitalism (as we knew it): a feminist critique of political economy.* Minneapolis, MN: University of Minnesota Press.

Giddens, A. (1971). *Capitalism and modern social theory: An analysis of the writings of Marx, Durkheim and Max Weber.* Cambridge, UK: Cambridge University Press. doi:10.1017/CBO9780511803109

Giddens, A. (1992). *The transformations of intimacy.* Cambridge, MA: Polity.

Gitelson, R. J., & Crompton, J. (1983). The planning horizons and sources of information used by pleasure vacationers. *Journal of Travel Research, 21*(3), 2–7. doi:10.1177/004728758302100301

Gitelson, R. J., & Perdue, R. R. (1987). Evaluating the role of state welcome centers in disseminating travel related information in North Carolina. *Journal of Travel Research, 25*(1), 15–19. doi:10.1177/004728758702500403

Glover, P., & Prideaux, B. (2009). Implications of Population Ageing for the Development of Tourism Products and Destinations. *Journal of Vacation Marketing, 15*(1), 25–37. doi:10.1177/1356766708098169

Godos, J., & Fernández, R. (2011). ¿Cómo se percibe la dirección socialmente responsable por parte de los altos directivos de empresas en España? *Universia Business Review, 29*, 32–49.

Goffman, E. (1959). *The presentation of self in everyday life*. Garden City, NY: Anchor.

Goodwin, H. (2009). Reflections on 10 years of Pro-Poor Tourism. *Journal of Policy Research in Tourism. Leisure and Events, 1*(1), 90–94. doi:10.1080/19407960802703565

Gössling, S., Hall, C. M., Peeters, P., & Scott, D. (2010). The future of tourism: Can tourism growth and climate policy be reconciled? A mitigation perspective. *Tourism Recreation Research, 35*(2), 119–130. doi:10.1080/02508281.2010. 11081628

Goswami S. (2013). The Slums: A Note On Facts And Solution. *Indian Streams Research Journal,* (3), 1-10.

Graburn, N. H. (1983). The anthropology of tourism. *Annals of Tourism Research, 10*(1), 9–33. doi:10.1016/0160-7383(83)90113-5

Graburn, N. H. (1983). the Anthropology of Tourism. *Annals of Tourism Research, 10*(1), 1–9. doi:10.1016/0160-7383(83)90110-X

Graham, A. (2014). *Managing Airports: An International Perspective* (4th ed.). Oxford: Routledge.

Graham, A., Forsyth, P., & Papatheodorou, A. (2008). *Aviation and Tourism*. Aldershot: Ashgate.

Grandori, A. (1999). *Interfirm networks: Organization and industrial competitiveness*. London, United Kingdom: Routledge. doi:10.4324/9780203022481

Gražulevičiūtė-Vileniškė, I., & Zaleskienė, E. (2014). Landscape Research Trends and Some Insights from Rurban Landscape. *Environmental Research. Engineering and Management, 67*(1), 43–53.

Greene, W. H. (1997). Frontier production functions. Handbook of applied econometrics, 2, 81-166.

Gretzel, U., & Yoo, K. (2008). Use and impact of online travel reviews. In P. O'Connor, W. Hopken, & U. Gretzel (Eds.), *Information and Communication Technologies in Tourism 2008* (pp. 35–46). Vienna, Austria: Springer-Verlag Wien. doi:10.1007/978-3-211-77280-5_4

Grönroos, C. (2008). Service Logic Revisited: Who Creates Value? And who Co-creates? *European Business Review, 20*(4), 298–314. doi:10.1108/09555340810886585

Grönroos, C. (2011). Value Co-creation in Service Logic: A Critical Analysis. *Marketing Theory, 11*(3), 279–301. doi:10.1177/1470593111408177

Groot, E., & Simons, I. (2015). Power and empowerment in community-based tourism: Opening Pandora's box? *Tourism Review, 70*(1), 72–94. doi:10.1108/TR-06-2014-0035

Grougiou, V., & Pettigrew, S. (2011). Senior Customers' Service Encounter Preferences. *Journal of Service Research, 14*(4), 475–488. doi:10.1177/1094670511423785

GSMA. (2015). *The mobile economy 2015*. Retrieved June 2, 2015 from: http://gsmamobileeconomy.covaibalem

Guimaraes, T. (2012). Industry clockspeed's impact on business innovation success factors. *European Journal of Innovation Management, 14*(3), 322–344. doi:10.1108/14601061111148825

Guizzardi, A., & Mazzocchi, M. (2010). Tourism demand for Italy and the business cycle. *Tourism Management, 31*(3), 367–377. doi:10.1016/j.tourman.2009.03.017

Gursoy, D. (2001). *Development of travellers' information search behaviour model*. (Unpublished doctoral dissertation). Polytechnic Institute and State University, Blacksburg, VA.

Gursoy, D. (2003). Prior product knowledge and its influence on the traveller's information search behaviour. *Journal of Hospitality & Leisure Marketing, 10*(3/4), 113–131. doi:10.1300/J150v10n03_07

Gursoy, D., & Chi, C. G. (2008). Travellers' information search behavior. In H. Oh (Ed.), *Handbook of Hospitality Marketing Management* (pp. 266–295). Oxford, UK: Elsevier.

Gursoy, D., Jurowski, C., & Uysal, M. (2002). Resident attitudes: A structural modeling approach. *Annals of Tourism Research, 29*(1), 79–105. doi:10.1016/S0160-7383(01)00028-7

Gursoy, D., & McCleary, K. W. (2004). An integrative model of tourist's information search behaviour. *Annals of Tourism Research, 31*(2), 353–373. doi:10.1016/j.annals.2003.12.004

Gursoy, D., & Umbreit, W. T. (2004). Tourist information search behaviour: Cross-cultural comparison of European Union Member States. *International Journal of Hospitality Management, 23*(1), 55–70. doi:10.1016/j.ijhm.2003.07.004

Gustafson, P. (2006). Work-related travel, gender and family obligations. *Work, Employment and Society, 20*(3), 513–530. doi:10.1177/0950017006066999

Guthrie, J. P. (2001). High-involvement work practices, turnover, and productivity: Evidence from New Zealand. *Academy of Management Journal, 44*(1), 180–190. doi:10.2307/3069345

Hall, C. M., Williams, A. M., & Lew, A. A. (2004). Tourism: Conceptualizations, institutions, and issues. *A Companion to Tourism*, 3-21.

Hall, C. (1999). *Sustainable tourism: a geographical perspective*. Harlow: Pearson Education.

Hall, C. M. (1998). *Introduction to tourism: Development, dimensions and issues*. Melbourne, Australia: Longman.

Hall, D. (2002). Brand development, tourism and national identity: The re-imaging of former Yugoslavia. *Brand Management, 9*(4-5), 323–334. doi:10.1057/palgrave.bm.2540081

Hall, M. C., & Allan, W. (2008). *Tourism and innovation*. Oxon, UK: Routledge.

Hall, M. C., & Page, S. J. (2014). *The geography of tourism and recreation: Environment, space and place*. London: Routledge.

Hall, R. M. (1976). *Beyond Culture*. New York, NY: Doubleday.

Hall, R. M. (1990). *Understanding Cultural Difference*. Boston, MA: Intercultural Press Inc.

Halpern, N., & Graham, A. (2013). *Airport Marketing*. Oxford: Routledge.

Han, H. (2013). The healthcare hotel: Distinctive attributes for international medical travelers. *Tourism Management, 36*(1), 257–268. doi:10.1016/j.tourman.2012.11.016

Han, H., & Hyun, S. S. (2013). Image congruence and relationship quality in predicting switching intention: Conspicuousness of product use as a moderator variable. *Journal of Hospitality & Tourism Research (Washington, D.C.)*, *37*(3), 303–329. doi:10.1177/1096348012436381

Han, H., & Hyun, S. S. (2015). Customer retention in the medical tourism industry: Impact of quality, satisfaction, trust, and price reasonableness. *Tourism Management*, *46*, 20–29. doi:10.1016/j.tourman.2014.06.003

Han, H., & Kim, W. (2009). Outcomes of relational benefits: Restaurant customers' perspective. *Journal of Travel & Tourism Marketing*, *26*(8), 820–835. doi:10.1080/10548400903356236

Han, H., & Ryu, K. (2006). Moderating role of personal characteristics in forming restaurant customers' behavioral intentions: An upscale restaurant setting. *Journal of Hospitality & Leisure Marketing*, *15*(4), 25–53. doi:10.1300/J150v15n04_03

Han-jen. (2000). *The relationship of career commitment, self efficacy and job involvement MBA graduate student research conference*. Taipei, Taiwan.

Hanna, E. (2008). Networking gets new meaning on the web. *Hotel & Motel Management*, *223*(19), 30–58.

Hannam, K., Sheller, M., & Urry, J. (2006). Editorial: Mobilities, immobilities and moorings. *Mobilities*, *1*(1), 1–22. doi:10.1080/17450100500489189

Hardiman, N., & Burgin, S. (2010). Adventure recreation in Australia: A case study that investigated the profile of recreational canyoners, their impact attitudes, and response to potential management options. *Journal Of Ecotourism*, *9*(1), 36–44. doi:10.1080/14724040902863333

Harnisch, O. (2008). Productivity Management in the Hospitality Industry. *Hospitalitynet.org*. Retrieved from http://www.hospitalitynet.org/news/4035884.html

Harris, P. (1999). *Profit planning*. Oxford, United Kingdom: Butterworth–Heinemann.

Harvey, D. (2006). *Spaces of global capitalism*. London: Verso.

Harvey, D. (2007). Neoliberalism as Creative Destruction. *The Annals of the American Academy of Political and Social Science*, *610*(1), 21–44. doi:10.1177/0002716206296780

Hashim, N., Murphy, J., & Law, R. (2007). A review of hospitality website design frame-works. In M. Sigala, L. Mich, & J. Murphy (Eds.), *Information and communication technologies in tourism*. Wien: Springer.

Hassan, A. (2013). Perspective Analysis and Implications of Visitor Management - Experiences from the Whitechapel Gallery, London. *Anatolia: An International Journal of Tourism and Hospitality Research*. DOI: 10.1080/13032917.2013.797916

Hassan, A., & Shabani, N. (2015). *eMarketing Adoption in Tourism and Hospitality Industry in London: Industry Analysis and Some Narratives*. The 4th International Interdisciplinary Business-Economics Advancement Conference (IIBA). Available at: http://bit.ly/1BQqGnI

Hassan, A. (2012a). Key Components for an Effective Marketing Planning: A Conceptual Analysis. *International Journal of Management & Development Studies*, *2*(1), 68–70.

Hassan, A. (2012b). Rationalization of Business Planning Through the Current Dynamics of Tourism. *International Journal of Management & Development Studies*, *2*(1), 61–63.

Hassan, A. (2015). The Customization of Electronic Word of Mouth: An Industry Tailored Application for Tourism Promotion. In S. Rathore & A. Panwar (Eds.), *Capturing, Analyzing and Managing Word-of-Mouth in the Digital Marketplace* (pp. 61–75). Hershey, PA: IGI Global.

Hassan, A. (in press). Destination Image Formation: The Function Analysis of Augmented Reality Application. In M. Khosrow-Pour (Ed.), *The Encyclopaedia of Information Science and Technology* (4th ed.). Hershey, PA: IGI Global.

Hassan, A., & Dadwal, S. (in press). Search Engine Marketing – An Outlining of Conceptualization and Strategic Application. In W. Ozuem & G. Bowen (Eds.), *Competitive Social Media Marketing Strategies*. Hershey, PA: IGI Global.

Hassan, A., & Donatella, P. S. (in press). Google AdSense as a Mobile Technology in Education. In J. L. Holland (Ed.), *Handbook of Research on Wearable and Mobile Technologies in Education*. Hershey, PA: IGI Global. doi:10.4018/978-1-5225-0069-8.ch011

Hassan, A., & Iankova, K. (2012). Strategies and Challenges of Tourist Facilities Management in the World Heritage Site: Case of the Maritime Greenwich, London. *Tourism Analysis, 17*(6), 791–803. doi:10.3727/108354212X13531051127348

Hassan, A., & Jung, T. (in press). Augmented Reality as an Emerging Application in Tourism Education. In D. H. Choi, A. Dailey-Hebert, & J. S. Estes (Eds.), *Emerging Tools and Applications of Virtual Reality in Education*. Hershey, PA: IGI Global.

Hassan, A., & Rahman, M. (2015). Macromarketing Perspective in Promoting Tourism: The Case of the Buddhist Vihara at Paharpur. *Tourism Spectrum, 1*(2), 13–19.

Hassan, A., & Rahman, M. (in press). World Heritage Site as a Label in Branding a Place. *Journal of Cultural Heritage Management and Sustainable Development*.

Hassan, A., & Ramkissoon, H. (in press). Augmented Reality for Visitor Experiences. In J. N. Albrecht (Ed.), *Visitor Management*. Oxfordshire, UK: CABI.

Hassan, A., & Sharma, A. (in press). Wildlife Tourism: Technology Adoption for Marketing and Conservation. In M. A. Khan & J. K. Fatima (Eds.), *Wilderness of Wildlife Tourism*. Waretown: Apple Academic Press, Inc.

Hatfeild, E., & Sprecher, S. (1986). *Mirror, mirror: The importance of looks in everyday life*. Albany, NY: State University of New York.

Hax, A. C. (2010). *Reinventing your business strategy*. New York: Springer.

Hays, S., Page, S. J., & Buhalis, D. (2013). Social media as a destination marketing tool: Its use by national tourism organisations. *Current Issues in Tourism, 16*(3), 211–239. doi:10.1080/13683500.2012.662215

Hedman, E-L. (2005). The Politics of the Tsunami Response. *Forced Migration Review*.

Henderson, J. (1999). Managing the Asian Financial Crisis: Tourist Attractions in Singapore. *Journal of Travel Research, 38*(2), 177–181. doi:10.1177/004728759903800212

Henderson, J. (2005). Influence: The Impact of language, credibility and gender. *The Conservator, 29*(1), 63–72. doi:10.1080/01410096.2005.9995213

Henderson, J. C. (2007). Corporate social responsibility and tourism: Hotel companies in Phuket, Thailand, after the Indian Ocean tsunami. *International Journal of Hospitality Management, 26*(1), 228–239. doi:10.1016/j.ijhm.2006.02.001

Hernandez-Garcia, J. (2013). Slum tourism, city branding and social urbanism: The case of Medellin, Colombia. *Journal of Place Management and Development, 6*(1), 43–51. doi:10.1108/17538331311306122

Hiernaux, N. (2000). La fuerza de lo efímero. In *En Alicia Lindon Villoria (comp). La vida cotidiana y su espacio-temporalidad*. Editorial Anthropos.

Hill, C. J. S. J. G., & Hanna, M. E. (1989). Selection Criteria for Professional Service Providers. *Journal of Services Marketing*, *3*(4), 61–69. doi:10.1108/eb043366

Hiltunen, P., Jokelainen, J., Ebeling, H., Szajnberg, N., & Moilanen, I. (2004). Seasonal variation in postnatal depression. *Journal of Affective Disorders*, *78*(2), 111–118. doi:10.1016/S0165-0327(02)00239-2 PMID:14706721

Himitian, E. (2012). Hubo más de medio millón de divorcios en la última década. *La Nación*. Available http://www.lanacion.com.ar/1453694-hubo-mas-de-medio-millon-de-divorcios-en-la-ultima-decada

Hindley, B. (2004). *Trade Liberalization in Aviation Services: Can the Doha round free flight?* Washington, DC: American Enterprise Institute Press.

Hjalager, A. M., Konu, H., Huijbens, E. H., Björk, P., Nordin, S., & Tuohino, A. (2011). Innovating and re-branding Nordic wellbeing tourism. Oslo: NICe.

Hjalager, A.-M. (2014). Disruptive and sustaining innovations: the case of rural tourism. In Handbook of Research on Innovation in Tourism Industries (pp. 56-83). Edward Elgar. doi:10.4337/9781782548416.00009

Hjalager, A. M. (2002). Repairing innovation defectiveness in tourism. *Tourism Management*, *23*(5), 465–474. doi:10.1016/S0261-5177(02)00013-4

Hjalager, A.-M. (2010). A review of innovation research in tourism. *Tourism Management*, *31*(1), 1–12. doi:10.1016/j.tourman.2009.08.012

Hockings, P. (2003). *Principles of visual anthropology*. Berlin: Mouton de Gruyter.

Hofstede, G. (1991). *Cultures and Organizations*. New York: McGraw Hill.

Hofstede, G. (2001). *Culture's Consequences: Comparing Values, Behaviours, Institutions, and Organizations Across Nations*. Sage Publications.

Hofstede, G. (2011). Dimensionalizing cultures: The Hofstede model in context. *Online Readings in Psychology and Culture*, *2*(1). doi:10.9707/2307-0919.1014

Hofstede, G., & Hofstede, G. J. (2005). *Cultures and Organizations: Software of the Mind* (2nd ed.). McGraw-Hill.

Hofstede, G., Hofstede, G. J., & Minkov, M. (2010). *Cultures and organizations: software of the mind: intercultural cooperation and its importance for survival* (3rd ed.). New York: McGraw Hil.

Hoggart, K., Black, R., & Buller, H. (2014). *Rural Europe*. Routledge.

Holbrook, M. B., & Hirschmann, E. C. (1982). The Experiential Aspects of Consumption: Consumer Fantasies, Feelings, and Fun. *The Journal of Consumer Research*, *9*(2), 132–140. doi:10.1086/208906

Hollinshead, K. (2009). Review - tradition and the declarative reach of tourism: Recognizing transnationality - the articulation of dynamic aboriginal being. *Tourism Analysis*, *14*, 537–555. doi:10.3727/108354209X12596287114417

Holloway, J. C. (2004). *Marketing for tourism*. Essex, UK: Pearson Education Limited.

Horng, J. S., & Wang, L. L. (2003). Competency analysis profile of F&B managers in international hotel managers in Taiwan. *Asia Pacific Journal of Tourism Research*, *8*(1), 26–36. doi:10.1080/10941660308725453

Hosany, S., Ekinci, Y., & Uysal, M. (2006). Destination image and destination personality: An application of branding theories to tourism places. *Journal of Business Research*, *59*(5), 638–642. doi:10.1016/j.jbusres.2006.01.001

Hosany, S., & Witham, M. (2010). Dimensions of cruisers' experiences, satisfaction, and intention to recommend. *Journal of Travel Research*, *49*(3), 351–364. doi:10.1177/0047287509346859

Hosoda, , Stone-Romero, & Coats. (2003). The effects of physical attractiveness on job-related outcomes: A meta-analyses.... *Personnel Psychology*, *56*, 431. doi:10.1111/j.1744-6570.2003.tb00157.x

Hossain, S. (2005). Poverty, Household Strategies and Coping with Urban Life: Examining 'Livelihood Framework' in Dhaka City, Bangladesh. *Bangladesh e-. Journal of Sociology (Melbourne, Vic.)*, *2*(1), 1–12.

Howard, D. R., & Gitelson, R. J. (1989). An analysis of the differences between state welcome center users and nonusers: A profile of Oregon vacationers. *Journal of Travel Research*, *27*(1), 38–40. doi:10.1177/004728758902700406

Howey, R. M., Savage, K. S., Verbeeten, M. J., & Van Hoof, H. B. (1999). Tourism and hospitality research journals: Cross-citations among research communities. *Tourism Management*, *20*(1), 133–139. doi:10.1016/S0261-5177(98)00099-5

Hsu, J., & Aristil, J. C. (2014). *Haiti: Tourism Development on Île-à-Vache Island – Reconstruction or Another Disaster?* Retrieved 4 July, 2015, from http://www.globalresearch.ca/haiti-tourism-development-on-ile-a-vache-island-reconstruction-or-another-disaster/5393046

Huan, T., Beaman, J., & Shelby, L. (2004). No-escape natural disaster. *Annals of Tourism Research*, *31*(2), 255–273. doi:10.1016/j.annals.2003.10.003

Hu, B. A., & Cai, L. A. (2004). Hotel labor productivity assessment: A data envelopment analysis. *Journal of Travel & Tourism Marketing*, *16*(2-3), 27–38. doi:10.1300/J073v16n02_03

Hu, J.-L., Chiu, C.-N., Shieh, H.-S., & Huang, C.-H. (2010). A stochastic cost efficiency analysis of international tourist hotels in Taiwan. *International Journal of Hospitality Management*, *29*(1), 99–107. doi:10.1016/j.ijhm.2009.06.005

Humble, J. (1975). *La responsabilidad social de la empresa*. Madrid: F. Universidad Empresa.

Hwang, J. H., & Lee, S. W. (2015). The effect of the rural tourism policy on non-farm income in South Korea. *Tourism Management*, *46*, 501–513. doi:10.1016/j.tourman.2014.07.018

Hwang, S., & Chang, T. (2003). Using data envelopment analysis to measure hotel managerial efficiency change in Taiwan. *Tourism Management*, *24*(4), 357–369. doi:10.1016/S0261-5177(02)00112-7

Hystad, P., & Keller, P. (2008). Towards a destination tourism disaster management framework: Long-term lessons from a forest fire disaster. *Tourism Management*, *29*(1), 151–162. doi:10.1016/j.tourman.2007.02.017

IKEA. (2015). *2014 IKEA Catalogue Comes To Life with Augmented Reality*. Retrieved from: http://bit.ly/1uQHR86

Inácio, R. O., Kern, J., Xavier, T. R., & Wittmann, M. L. (2013). Desenvolvimento regional: uma análise sobre a estrutura de um consórcio intermunicipal. *Revista de Administração Pública*, *47*(4), 1041-1065.

inc. (2015). *3 smart ways augmented reality is changing the customer experience*. Retrieved from: http://www.inc.com/eric-holtzclaw/using-augmented-reality-to-enhance-the-customer-experience.html

Incera, A. C., & Fernandez, M. F. (2015). Tourism and income distribution: Evidence from a developed regional economy. *Tourism Management*, *48*, 11–20. doi:10.1016/j.tourman.2014.10.016

Inglehart, R. (1997). *Modernization and Postmodernization. Cultural, economic, and political change in 43 societies*. Princeton, NJ: Princeton University Press.

Ingram, J., Franco, G., Rio, C., & Khazai, B. (2006). Post-disaster recovery dilemmas: Challenges in balancing short-term and long-term needs for vulnerability reduction. *Environmental Science & Policy, 9*(7-8), 607–613. doi:10.1016/j.envsci.2006.07.006

International Air Transport Association. (2013). *IATA Economic Briefing – Infrastructure Costs.* Geneva: IATA.

International Civil Aviation Organization. (2003). *Commercialization and Liberalization* (working paper). Available at: www.icao.int/meetings/atconf6/.../workingpapers/atconf6-wp006_en.pdf

International Civil Aviation Organization. (2006). *Economic Contribution of Civil Aviation. International Civil Aviation Organization, 2006 Edition CD-ROM.* Aviatech Publications.

International Civil Aviation Organization. (2008). Ownership, Organisation and Regulatory Practices of Airports and Air Navigation Services Providers (report). Montreal: ICAO.

International Civil Aviation Organization. (2012a). Doc 9082 ICAO's Policies on Charges for Airports and Air Navigation Services. Montreal: ICAO.

International Civil Aviation Organization. (2012b). Doc 9980: Manual on Privatization in the Provision of Airports and Air Navigation Services. Montreal: ICAO.

International Civil Aviation Organization. (2013a). *Air Navigation Services Providers (ANSPs) Governance and Performance.* working paper. Available at: http://www.icao.int/Meetings/atconf6/Documents/WorkingPapers/ATConf.6.WP.073.2.en.pdf

International Civil Aviation Organization. (2013b). Doc 9161: Manual on Air Navigation Services Economics. Montreal: ICAO.

International Relations and Security Network (ISN). (2012). *China, Corporations and Internet Censorship.* Retrieved March 11, 2015, from http://www.isn.ethz.ch/Digital-Library/Articles/Special-Feature/Detail/?lng=en&id=138039&contextid774=138039&contextid775=138031&tabid=138031

Internet World Stats. (2015). *Internet users in the world.* Retrieved March 3, 2015, from http://www.internetworldstats.com/stats.htm

Ionnides, D., & Apostolopoulos, Y. (1999). Political instability, war, and tourism in Cyprus: Effects, management, and prospects for recovery. *Journal of Travel Research, 38*(1), 51–56. doi:10.1177/004728759903800111

Iresearch. (2012). *A research report on the Chinese online travellers' behaviours in 2012.* Retrieved January 17, 2015, from http:// www.iresearch.com.cn

Irish Aid. (2012). *Irish Aid Development Partner Handover Report 2012* (Unpublished). Díli, East Timor.

Israeli, A. A. (2014). An inter-paradigmatic agenda for research, education and practice in hospitality management. *International Journal of Hospitality Management, 42,* 188–191. doi:10.1016/j.ijhm.2014.07.005

Israeli, A. A., Barkan, R., & Fleishman, M. (2006). An exploratory approach to evaluating performance measures: The managers' perspective. *Service Industries Journal, 26*(8), 861–872. doi:10.1080/02642060601011665

Itim International. (2015). *National Culture.* Retrieved March 15, 2015, from http://geert-hofstede.com/national-culture.html

Itim International. (2015). *What about China?* Retrieved April 20, 2015, from http://geert-hofstede.com/china.html

Itim International. (2015). *What about the UK?* Retrieved April 20, 2015, from http://geert-hofstede.com/united-kingdom.html

Jafari, J. (1990). Research and scholarship: the basis of tourism education. *Journal of Tourism Studies, 1*(1), 33-41.

Jafari, J. (2001). The scientification of tourism. In V. L. Smith & M. Brent (Eds.), *Hosts and guests revisited: Tourism issues of the 21st century* (pp. 28–41). New York: Cognizant Communications.

Jafari, J. (2005). Bridging out, nesting afield: Powering a new platform. *Journal of Tourism Studies, 16*(2), 1–5.

Jafari, J., & Aaser, D. (1988). Tourism as the subject of doctoral dissertations. *Annals of Tourism Research, 15*(3), 407–429. doi:10.1016/0160-7383(88)90030-8

Jalil, A., Mahmood, T., & Idrees, M. (2013). Tourism-growth nexus in Pakistan: Evidence from ARDL bounds tests. *Economic Modelling, 35*, 185–191. doi:10.1016/j.econmod.2013.06.034

Jallat, F., & Schultz, C. J. (2011). Lebanon: from cataclysm to opportunity: crisis management lessons for MNCs in the tourism sector of the Middle East. *Journal of World Business, 46*(4), 476–486. doi:10.1016/j.jwb.2010.10.008

Jang, S., Bai, B., Hong, G., & O'Leary, J. T. (2004). Understanding Travel Expenditure Patterns: A Study of Japanese pleasure Travelers to the United States by Income Level. *Tourism Management, 25*(3), 331–341. doi:10.1016/S0261-5177(03)00141-9

Jani, D., & Han, H. (2013). Personality, social comparison, consumption emotions, satisfaction, and behavioral intentions: How do these and other factors relate in a hotel setting? *International Journal of Contemporary Hospitality Management, 25*(7), 970–993. doi:10.1108/IJCHM-10-2012-0183

Japan International Cooperation Agency (JICA). (2012). *Embassy of Japan & JICA Development Partner Handover Report 2012* (Unpublished). Díli, East Timor.

Jarvenpaa, S. L., Tractinsky, N., & Saarinen, L. (1999). Consumer trust in an Internet store: A cross-cultural validation. *Journal of Computer-Mediated Communication, 5*(2), 1–37.

Jarvis, P. (1990). *International dictionary of adult and continuing education.* London: Kogan Page.

Jiang, P., & Rosenbloom, B. (2005). Customer intention to return online: Price perception, attribute-level performance, and satisfaction unfolding over time. *European Journal of Marketing, 39*(1/2), 150–174. doi:10.1108/03090560510572061

Jing-Shyen. (2003). *The relationship between quality of working life and service attitude of international flight attendants.* National Taipei University of Nursing and Health Science Graduate Institute of Tourism & Health Science.

Johanson, M., Ghiselli, R., Shea, L. J., & Roberts, C. (2011). Changing competencies of hospitality leaders: A 25 year review. *Journal of Hospitality & Tourism Education, 23*(3), 43–47. doi:10.1080/10963758.2011.10697012

Johns, N., Howcroft, B., & Drake, L. (1997). The use of data envelopment analysis to monitor hotel productivity. *Progress in Tourism and Hospitality Research, 3*(2), 119–127. doi:10.1002/(SICI)1099-1603(199706)3:2<119::AID-PTH74>3.0.CO;2-2

Johnson. (2001). *Self-esteem comes in all sizes: How to be happy and healthy at your natural weight.* Pub Group West.

Johnson, G. (1988). Rethinking incrementalism. *Strategic Management Journal, 9*(1), 75–91. doi:10.1002/smj.4250090107

Johnson, K. (2009). Corporate sperm count and boiled frogs. *Int J Contemp Hospitality Mngt, 21*(2), 179–190. doi:10.1108/09596110910935679

Johnson, M. P. (2011). Gender and types of intimate partner violence: A response to an anti-feminist literature review. *Aggression and Violent Behavior, 16*(4), 289–296. doi:10.1016/j.avb.2011.04.006

Jones, P., & Siag, A. (2009). A re-examination of the factors that influence productivity in hotels: A study of the housekeeping function. *Tourism and Hospitality Research, 9*(3), 224–234. doi:10.1057/thr.2009.11

Jordan, E. J., Norman, W. C., & Vogt, C. A. (2012). A cross-cultural comparison for online travel information search behaviours. *Tourism Management Perspectives, 6*(1), 15–22.

Jordan, E. J., Vogt, C. A., & DeShon, R. P. (2015). A stress and coping framework for understanding resident responses to tourism development. *Tourism Management, 48*, 500–512. doi:10.1016/j.tourman.2015.01.002

Jordan, F. (1997). An occupational hazard? Sex segregation in tourism employment. *Tourism Management, 18*(8), 525–534. doi:10.1016/S0261-5177(97)00074-5

Jornal Diário Nacional. (2015, August 28). *Dragon Star Shipping Fasilita Barco Rapido – Dili-Oecusse Oras Tolu Deit*. Retrieved from: http://www.jndiario.com/2015/08/31/dragon-star-shipping-fasilita-barco-rapido-dili-oecusse-oras-tolu-deit/

Julie Baker. (1987). The role of the environment in marketing services:The consumer perspective. In J. A. Czepiel, C. A. Congram, & J. Shanahan (Eds.), *The Service Challenge:Integrating for Competitive Advantage* (p. 80). Chicago: American Marketing Association.

Jung, T., Chung, N., & Leue, M. (2015). The determinants of recommendations to use augmented reality technologies: The case of a Korean theme park. *Tourism Management, 49*, 75–86. doi:10.1016/j.tourman.2015.02.013

Juniper Research. (2015). *Mobile augmented reality IFx1 2013-2018*. Retrieved from: http://www.juniperresearch.com/researchstore

Jüttner, U., Schaffner, D., Windler, K., & Maklan, S. (2013). Customer Service Experiences: Developing and Applying a Sequential Incident Laddering Technique. *European Journal of Marketing, 47*(5/6), 738–769. doi:10.1108/03090561311306769

Kaewkuntee, D. (2006). Land Tenure, Land Conflicts and Post-Tsunami Relocation in Thailand. *Mekong Update and Dialogue, 9*(2).

Kandampully, J. (2013). Service Management a New Paradigm in Health and Wellness Services. In J. Kandampully (Ed.), *Service Management in Health & Wellness Services* (pp. 1–6). Dubuque, IA: Kendall Hunt.

Kaplan, R. S., & Norton, D. P. (1996). *The balanced scorecard: Translating strategy into action*. Boston, MA: Harvard Business School Press.

Karake Shalhoub, Z. (2007). Internet Commerce Adoption in the GCC Countries. *IRMA International Conference, Managing Worldwide Operations & Communications with Information Technology*.

Kasemsap, K. (2014a). The role of brand loyalty on CRM performance: An innovative framework for smart manufacturing. In Z. Luo (Ed.), *Smart manufacturing innovation and transformation: Interconnection and intelligence* (pp. 252–284). Hershey, PA: IGI Global. doi:10.4018/978-1-4666-5836-3.ch010

Kasemsap, K. (2014b). The role of social networking in global business environments. In P. Smith & T. Cockburn (Eds.), *Impact of emerging digital technologies on leadership in global business* (pp. 183–201). Hershey, PA: IGI Global. doi:10.4018/978-1-4666-6134-9.ch010

Kasemsap, K. (2014c). The role of social media in the knowledge-based organizations. In I. Lee (Ed.), *Integrating social media into business practice, applications, management, and models* (pp. 254–275). Hershey, PA: IGI Global. doi:10.4018/978-1-4666-6182-0.ch013

Kasemsap, K. (2014d). Unifying a framework of organizational culture, organizational climate, knowledge management, and job performance. In R. Perez-Castillo & M. Piattini (Eds.), *Uncovering essential software artifacts through business process archeology* (pp. 336–362). Hershey, PA: IGI Global. doi:10.4018/978-1-4666-4667-4.ch013

Kasemsap, K. (2015a). The role of marketing strategies in the tourism industry. In N. Ray (Ed.), *Emerging innovative marketing strategies in the tourism industry* (pp. 174–194). Hershey, PA: IGI Global. doi:10.4018/978-1-4666-8699-1.ch010

Kasemsap, K. (2015b). The role of social media in international advertising. In N. Taşkıran & R. Yılmaz (Eds.), *Handbook of research on effective advertising strategies in the social media age* (pp. 171–196). Hershey, PA: IGI Global. doi:10.4018/978-1-4666-8125-5.ch010

Kasemsap, K. (2015c). The roles of cross-cultural perspectives in global marketing. In J. Alcántara-Pilar, S. del Barrio-García, E. Crespo-Almendros, & L. Porcu (Eds.), *Analyzing the cultural diversity of consumers in the global marketplace* (pp. 37–59). Hershey, PA: IGI Global. doi:10.4018/978-1-4666-8262-7.ch003

Kasemsap, K. (2015d). The role of cultural dynamics in the digital age. In B. Christiansen & J. Koeman (Eds.), *Nationalism, cultural indoctrination, and economic prosperity in the digital age* (pp. 295–312). Hershey, PA: IGI Global. doi:10.4018/978-1-4666-7492-9.ch014

Kasemsap, K. (2015e). The role of customer relationship management in the global business environments. In T. Tsiakis (Ed.), *Trends and innovations in marketing information systems* (pp. 130–156). Hershey, PA: IGI Global. doi:10.4018/978-1-4666-8459-1.ch007

Kasemsap, K. (2016a). The roles of e-learning, organizational learning, and knowledge management in the learning organizations. In E. Railean, G. Walker, A. Elçi, & L. Jackson (Eds.), *Handbook of research on applied learning theory and design in modern education* (pp. 786–816). Hershey, PA: IGI Global. doi:10.4018/978-1-4666-9634-1.ch039

Kasemsap, K. (2016b). The roles of information technology and knowledge management in global tourism. In A. Nedelea, M. Korstanje, & B. George (Eds.), *Strategic tools and methods for promoting hospitality and tourism services* (pp. 109–138). Hershey, PA: IGI Global. doi:10.4018/978-1-4666-9761-4.ch006

Kasim, A. (2006). The need for business environmental and social responsibility in the tourism industry. *International Journal of Hospitality & Tourism Administration, 7*(1), 1–22. doi:10.1300/J149v07n01_01

Kay, C., & Russette, J. (2000). Hospitality-management competencies. *The Cornell Hotel and Restaurant Administration Quarterly, 41*(2), 52–63. doi:10.1177/001088040004100217

Kaytaz, M., & Gul, M. C. (2014). Consumer response to economic crisis and lessons for marketers: The Turkish experience. *Journal of Business Research, 67*(1), 2701–2706. doi:10.1016/j.jbusres.2013.03.019

Keates, N. (1997). Hotels find hostility sells better than hospitality. *Wall Street Journal Europe, J2,* 7-8.

Keegan, W., & Schlegelmilch, B. (2001). *Global marketing management* (6th ed.). Harlow, UK: Pearson Education Limited.

Kempen, G. I., Sanderman, R., Miedema, I., Meyboom-de Jong, B., & Ormel, J. (2000). Functional decline after congestive heart failure and acute myocardial infarction and the impact of psychological attributes: A prospective study. *Quality of Life Research: An International Journal of Quality of Life Aspects of Treatment, Care and Rehabilitation, 9*(4), 439–450. doi:10.1023/A:1008991522551 PMID:11131936

Kenichi. (2006). *The Professionalism.* Commonwealth Publishing Group.

Kerlinger, F. N. (1986). *Foundation of behavior research* (3rd ed.). New York: Holt, Rinehart & Winston. Comprehensive coverage of the scientific concepts and logical reasoning.

Ketter, P., & Ellis, R. (2010). Six trends that will change workplace learning forever. *Training & Development, 64*(12), 34–40.

Kevan, S. M. (1993). Quests for cures: A history of tourism for climate and health. *International Journal of Biometeorology, 37*(3), 113–124. doi:10.1007/BF01212620 PMID:7691761

Kilic, H., & Okumus, F. (2005). Factors influencing productivity in small island hotels: Evidence from Northern Cyprus. *International Journal of Contemporary Hospitality Management, 17*(4), 315–331. doi:10.1108/09596110510597589

Kim, S. (2013, July). *Iraq seeks threefold tourism rise despite unrest.* Retrieved 20 December, 2014, from http://www.telegraph.co.uk/travel/travelnews/10214243/Iraq-seeks-threefold-tourism-rise-despite-unrest.html

Kim, D. Y., Lehto, X. Y., & Morrison, A. M. (2007). Gender differences in online travel information search: Implications for marketing communications on the internet. *Tourism Management, 28*(2), 423–433. doi:10.1016/j.tourman.2006.04.001

Kim, E., Mattila, A. S., & Baloglu, S. (2011). Effects of gender and expertise on consumers' motivation to read online hotel reviews. *Cornell Hospitality Quarterly, 52*(4), 399–406. doi:10.1177/1938965510394357

Kimes, S. E. (2011). The future of hotel revenue management. *Journal of Revenue and Pricing Management, 10*(1), 6272. doi:10.1057/rpm.2010.47

Kim, J.-H., Ritchie, J. R. B., & McCormick, B. (2012). Development of a Scale to Measure Memorable Tourism Experiences. *Journal of Travel Research, 51*(1), 12–25. doi:10.1177/0047287510385467

Kim, K., Uysal, M., & Sirgy, M. J. (2013). How does tourism in a community impact the quality of life of community residents? *Tourism Management, 36*(5), 527–540. doi:10.1016/j.tourman.2012.09.005

Kim, S. S., Prideaux, B., & Prideaux, J. (2007). Using tourism to promote peace on the Korean Peninsula. *Annals of Tourism Research, 34*(2), 291–309. doi:10.1016/j.annals.2006.09.002

Kinnaird, V., & Hall, D. (1996). Understanding Tourism Processes: A Gender Aware Framework. *Tourism Management, 17*(2), 95–102. doi:10.1016/0261-5177(95)00112-3

Kirillova, K., Gilmetdinova, A., & Lehto, X. (2014). Interpretation of hospitality across religions. *International Journal of Hospitality Management, 43*, 23–34. doi:10.1016/j.ijhm.2014.07.008

Klaus, P., & Maklan, S. (2011). Bridging the Gap for Destination Extreme Sports: A Model of Sports Tourism Customer Experience. *Journal of Marketing Management, 27*(13/14), 1341–1365. doi:10.1080/0267257X.2011.624534

Klaus, P., & Maklan, S. (2012). EXQ: A Multiple-item Scale for Assessing Service Experience. *Journal of Service Management, 23*(1), 5–33. doi:10.1108/09564231211208952

Klein, N. (2007). *The shock doctrine.* New York: Metropolitan Books/Henry Holt.

Knowles, C., & Sweetman, P. (2004). *Picturing the social landscape.* New York, NY: Routledge.

Koering, S. K., & Page, A. L. (2002). What if your dentist looked like tom cruise? Applying the match-up hypothesis to a service encounter. *Psychology and Marketing, 19*(1), 91–110. doi:10.1002/mar.1003

Kogut, B. (1993). *Country competitiveness: Technology and the organizing of work.* New York, NY: Oxford University Press.

Kohn, L. M., & Schooler, C. (1973). Occupational experience and psychological function: An assessment of reciprocal effects. *American Sociological Review, 38*(1), 97–118. doi:10.2307/2094334

Koh, S., Yoo, J. J.-E., & Boeger, C. A. (2010). Importance performance analysis with benefit segmentation of spa goers. *International Journal of Contemporary Hospitality Management*, 22(5), 1–20.

Konisranukul, W., & Tuaycharoen, N. (2010). *Public Participation In Sustainable Island And Tourism Planning*. Faculty Of Science And Technology.

Konu, H. (2010). Identifying potential wellbeing tourism segments in Finland. *Tourism Review*, 65(2), 41–51. doi:10.1108/16605371011061615

Konu, H., & Laukkanen, T. (2010). Predictors of tourists' wellbeing holiday intentions in Finland. *Journal of Hospitality and Tourism Management*, 17(1), 144–149. doi:10.1375/jhtm.17.1.144

Korea International Cooperation Agency (KOICA). (2012). *Korea International Cooperation Agency (KOICA) Development Partner Handover Report 2012* (Unpublished). Díli, East Timor.

Korstanje, M. E. (2010). The power of projective drawings: A new method for researching tourist experiences. *e-Review of Tourism Research*, 8(5), 85-101.

Korstanje, M. E., & Skoll, G. (2015). Exploring the Fear of Travel: study revealing into tourist´s mind. *Revista Turismo: estudos e práticas*, 4(1), 56-63.

Korstanje, M., & Skoll, G. (2014). The inception of the rational platform. *Turismo y Desarrollo Local*, (17), 1-9.

Korstanje, M. (2007). The Origin and meaning of Tourism: An ethimologycal study. *E-Review of Tourism Resarch*, 5(5), 100–108.

Korstanje, M. (2009). "Interpretando el Génesis del Descanso: Una aproximación a los mitos y rituales del turismo". *Pasos. Revista de Turismo y Patrimonio Cultural*, 7(1), 99–113.

Korstanje, M. (2015). Entry: Paradise Tourism. In *Encyclopedia of tourism. Jafar Jafari & Xiao Honggen. Print to head*. Wien: Springer.

Korstanje, M., & Busby, G. (2010). Understanding the Bible as the roots of physical displacement: The origin of tourism. *E-Review of Tourism Research*, 8(3), 95–111.

Köseoglu, M. A., Sehitoglu, Y., & Craft, J. (2015). Academic foundations of hospitality management research with an emerging country focus: A citation and co-citation analysis. *International Journal of Hospitality Management*, 45, 130–144. doi:10.1016/j.ijhm.2014.12.004

Ko, T. (2005). Development of a tourism sustainability assessment procedure: A conceptual approach. *Tourism Management*, 26(3), 431–445. doi:10.1016/j.tourman.2003.12.003

Kotiranta, A., Kovalainen, A., & Rouvinen, P. (2007a). *Female Leadership and Firm Profitability*. Finnish Business and Policy Forum.

Kotiranta, A., Kovalainen, A., & Rouvinen, P. (2007b). *Female Leadership and Firm Profitability*. EVA. Retrieved from http://www.europeanpwn.net/files/eva_analysis_english.pdf

Kounavis, C. D., Kasimati, A. E., & Zamani, E. D. (2012). Enhancing the tourism experience through mobile augmented reality: Challenges and prospects. *International Journal of Engineering Business Management*, 4, 1–6.

Kozak, M. W. (2014). Innovation, Tourism and Destination Development: Dolnośląskie Case Study. *European Planning Studies*, 22(8), 1604–1624. doi:10.1080/09654313.2013.784597

Krakover, S. (2000). Partitioning seasonal employment in the hospitality industry. *Tourism Management, 21*(5), 461–471. doi:10.1016/S0261-5177(99)00101-6

Kralisch, A., Eisend, M., & Berendt, B. (2005). Impact of culture of Website navigation behaviour. In *Proceedings of the 11th International Conference on Human-Computer Interaction.*

Krauss, E. (2005). *Wave of destruction.* London: Vision.

Krawczyk, K. (2015). *Google is easily the most popular search engine, but have you heard who's in second?* Retrieved April 22, 2015, from http://www.digitaltrends.com/web/google-baidu-are-the-worlds-most-popular-search-engines

Krippendorf, J. (1984). *Holiday makers.* Oxford, UK: Heinemann-Butterworth.

Krippendorf, J. (1975). *Die Landschaftsfresser: Tourismus u. Erholungslandschaft.* Bern: Hallwag.

Krippendorf, J. (1982). Towards new tourism policies: The importance of environmental and sociocultural factors. *Tourism Management, 3*(3), 135–148. doi:10.1016/0261-5177(82)90063-2

Krippendorf, J. (1986). The new tourist—turning point for leisure and travel. *Tourism Management, 7*(2), 131–135. doi:10.1016/0261-5177(86)90025-7

Krippendorf, J. (1987). Ecological approach to tourism marketing. *Tourism Management, 8*(2), 174–176. doi:10.1016/0261-5177(87)90029-X

Krippendorf, J. (1987). *The Holiday-makers: Understanding the Impact of Travel and Tourism.* Oxford, UK: Butterworth-Heinemann.

Krippendorf, J. (1989). *Fur einen Anderen Tourimus: Probleme-Perspektiven.* Frankfurt Am Main: Fischer-Taschenbuch Verl.

Krippendorf, J. (1995). *Freizeit & Tourismus: eine Einfuhrung in Theorie und Politiks.* Bern: FIF.

Krippendorf, J. (2010). *Holiday makers.* Oxford, UK: Taylor & Francis.

Krongkaew, M. (2004). The development of the Greater Mekong Subregion (GMS): Real promise or false hope? *Journal of Asian Economics, 15*(5), 977–998. doi:10.1016/j.asieco.2004.09.006

Krutwaysho, O., & Bramwell, B. (2010). Tourism policy implementation and society. *Annals of Tourism Research, 37*(3), 670–691. doi:10.1016/j.annals.2009.12.004

Kulendran, N., & Dwyer, L. (2009). Measuring the return from Australian marketing expenditure. *Journal of Travel Research, 47*(3), 275–284. doi:10.1177/0047287508322786

Kulik, C. T., & Olekalns, M. (2012). Negotiating the Gender Divide: Lessons From the Negotiation and Organizational Behavior Literatures. *Journal of Management, 38*(4), 1387–1415. doi:10.1177/0149206311431307

Kumar, N., Stern, L., & Anderson, J. (1993). Conducting interorganizational research using key informants. *Academy of Management Journal, 36*(6), 1633–1651. doi:10.2307/256824

Kumar, V., Venkatesan, R., & Reinartz, W. J. (2006). Knowing what to sell when to whom. *Harvard Business Review*, (May), 131–145. PMID:16515161

Kuo, C. M. (2007). The importance of hotel employee service attitude and the satisfaction of international tourists. *Service Industries Journal, 27*(8), 1073–1085. doi:10.1080/02642060701673752

Kuo, H., Chen, C., Tseng, W., Ju, L.-F., & Huang, B.-W. (2008). Assessing Impacts of SARS and Avian Flu on International Tourism Demand to Asia. *Tourism Management, 29*(5), 917–928. doi:10.1016/j.tourman.2007.10.006

Kyläheiko, K., Jantunen, A., Puumalainen, K., Saarenketo, S., & Tuppura, A. (2011). Innovation and internationalization as growth strategies: The role of technological capabilities and appropriability. *International Business Review, 20*(5), 508–520. doi:10.1016/j.ibusrev.2010.09.004

Lacanau, G. (2003). *El rito sagrado de las vacaciones: alimentos y género en la Argentina de 1930-1950. In Gastronomía y Turismo: cultura al plato* (pp. 203–216). Buenos Aires: CIET.

Laesser, C. (2011). Health travel motivation and activities: Insights from a mature market – Switzerland. *Tourism Review, 66*(1/2), 83–89. doi:10.1108/16605371111127251

Lahav, T., Mansfeld, Y., & Avraham, E. (2013). Public relations for rural areas. *Journal of Tourism & Travel Marketing, 30*(4), 291–307. doi:10.1080/10548408.2013.784148

Laing, J., & Weiler, B. (2008). Mind, Body and Spirit: Health and Wellness Tourism in Asia. In J. Cochrane (Ed.), *Asian Tourism: Growth and Change* (pp. 379–389). Amsterdam: Elsevier. doi:10.1016/B978-0-08-045356-9.50037-0

Lane, B. (1994). What is rural tourism? *Journal of Sustainable Tourism, 2*(1/2), 7–21. doi:10.1080/09669589409510680

Lankton, N. K., Wilson, E. V., & Mao, E. (2010). Antecedents and determinants of information technology habit. *Information & Management, 47*(5/6), 300–307. doi:10.1016/j.im.2010.06.004

Lao Hamutuk. (2013). *South Coast petroleum infrastructure project*. Retrieved July 4, 2015, from http://www.laohamutuk.org/Oil/TasiMane/11TasiMane.htm

Látková, P., & Vogt, C. (2012). Residents' attitudes toward existing and future tourism development in rural communities. *Journal of Travel Research, 51*(1), 50–67. doi:10.1177/0047287510394193

Leamer, E. E. (1993). Factor-supply differences as a source of comparative advantage. *The American Economic Review, 83*(2), 436–439.

Leavy, P. (2014). *The Oxford Handbook of Qualitative Research*. Oxford, UK: Oxford University Press. doi:10.1093/oxfordhb/9780199811755.001.0001

Lee, H. A., Denizci Guillet, B., & Law, R. (2013). An Examination of the Relationship between Online Travel Agents and Hotels: A Case Study of Choice Hotels International and Expedia.com. *Cornell Hospitality Quarterly, 54*(1), 95–107. doi:10.1177/1938965512454218

Lee, H., Lee, Y., & Yoo, D. (2000). The determinants of perceived service quality and its relationship with satisfaction. *Journal of Services Marketing, 14*(3), 217–231. doi:10.1108/08876040010327220

Lee, J. S., & Back, K. J. (2008). Attendee-based brand equity. *Tourism Management, 29*(2), 331–344. doi:10.1016/j.tourman.2007.03.002

Lee, K. (2006). Fahn, James David. 2003. A Land on Fire. The Environmental Consequences of the Southeast Asian Boom. Boulder, CO: Westview Press. *Global Environmental Politics, 6*(4), 135–136. doi:10.1162/glep.2006.6.4.135

Lee, M. D. P. (2011). Configuration of External Influences: The Combined Effects of Institutions and Stakeholders on Corporate Social Responsibility Strategies. *Journal of Business Ethics, 102*(2), 281–298. doi:10.1007/s10551-011-0814-0

Lee, S. W., & Kim, H. J. (2010). Agricultural transition and rural tourism in Korea: Experiences of the last forty years. In G. Thapa, P. Viswanathan, J. Routray, & M. Ahmad (Eds.), *Agricultural transition in Asia* (pp. 37–64). Bangkok, Thailand: Asian Institute of Technology.

Lee, Y., & Harrald, J. (1999). Critical issue for business area impact analysis in business crisis management: Analytical capability. *Disaster Prevention and Management*, 8(3), 184–189. doi:10.1108/09653569910275382

Lehto, X. Y., Brown, S., Chen, Y., & Morrison, A. M. (2006). Yoga tourism as a niche within the wellness tourism market. *Tourism Recreation Research*, 31(1), 5–14. doi:10.1080/02508281.2006.11081244

Leigh, J., Webster, C., & Ivanov, S. (Eds.). (2013). *Future Tourism: Political, Social and Economic Challenges*. Abingdon, UK: Routledge.

Leiper, N. (1981). Towards a cohesive curriculum tourism: The case for a distinct discipline. *Annals of Tourism Research*, 8(1), 69–84. doi:10.1016/0160-7383(81)90068-2

Lemke, F., Clark, M., & Wilson, H. (2011). Customer Experience Quality: An Exploration in Business and Consumer Contexts Using Repertory Grid Technique. *Journal of the Academy of Marketing Science*, 39(6), 846–869. doi:10.1007/s11747-010-0219-0

Lewis, B. R., & McCann, P. (2004). Service failure and recovery: Evidence from the hotel industry. *International Journal of Contemporary Hospitality Management*, 16(1), 6–17. doi:10.1108/09596110410516516

Li, L., Buhalis, D., Lockwood, A., & Benzine, K. (2007). *The use of e-learning in training in the UK hospitality industry: An exploratory study*. Paper presented at the 6th European Conference on e-Learning (ECEL 2007), Copenhagen, Denmark.

Liff, S., & Ward, K. (2001). Distorted Views Through the Glass Ceiling: The Construction of Women's Understandings of Promotion and Senior Management Positions. *Gender, Work and Organization*, 8(1), 19–36. doi:10.1111/1468-0432.00120

Li, L., & Buhalis, D. (2006). eCommerce in China: The case of travel. *International Journal of Information Management*, 26(2), 153–166. doi:10.1016/j.ijinfomgt.2005.11.007

Li, L., Lee, H., & Law, R. (2012). Technology-mediated management learning in hospitality organisations. *International Journal of Hospitality Management*, 31(1), 451–457. doi:10.1016/j.ijhm.2011.07.003

Lin, C.-C. (2007). *Business Times: Role of beauty in the employee's selection*. Retrieved December 13, 2013, from http://tw.myblog.yahoo.com/jw!G0Ap7lKABRXrE9O_lIvG.ITsGg--/article? mid=152

Li, N., & Kirkup, G. (2007). Gender and cultural differences in Internet use: A study of China and the UK. *Computers & Education*, 48(2), 301–317. doi:10.1016/j.compedu.2005.01.007

Lindberg, M. (2012). A Striking Pattern. Co-construction of Innovation, Men and Masculinity in Sweden's Innovation policy. In S. Andersson, K. Berglund, E. Gunnarsson, & E. Sundin (Eds.), *Promoting Innovation. Policies, Practices and Procedures*. Stockholm: VINNOVA.

Lisa. (2003). *JiuJik: Job requirements*. Retrieved October 13, 2001, from http://www.jiujik.com/jsarticle.php?lcid=HK.B5&artid=3000006221&arttype =JINVT&artsection=JOB

Li, T.-S. (1993). *translate*. The Core Competence of the Corporation. EMBA Magazine.

Litvin, S. W., Goldsmith, R. E., & Pan, B. (2008). Electronic word-of-mouth in hospitality and tourism management. *Tourism Management*, 29(2), 458–468. doi:10.1016/j.tourman.2007.05.011

Liu, Z., Siguaw, J. A., & Enz, C. A. (2008). Using tourist travel habits and preferences to assess strategic destination positioning: The case of Costa Rica. *Cornell Hospitality Quarterly*, 49(3), 258–281. doi:10.1177/1938965508322007

Li, X. (2014). An analysis of labour productivity growth in the Canadian tourism/hospitality industry. *Anatolia*, 25(3), 374–386. doi:10.1080/13032917.2014.882850

Li, X., & Petrick, J. F. (2008). Tourism marketing in an era of paradigm shift. *Journal of Travel Research, 46*(3), 235–244. doi:10.1177/0047287507303976

Llamas-Sanchez, R., Garcia-Morales, V., & Martin-Tapia, I. (2013). Factors affecting institutional change: A study of the adoption of Local Agenda 21 in Spain. *Journal of Organizational Change Management, 26*(6), 1045–1070. doi:10.1108/JOCM-03-2012-0037

Lockwood, A., & Jones, P. (1989). Creating positive service encounters. *The Cornell Hotel and Restaurant Administration Quarterly, 29*(4), 44–50. doi:10.1177/001088048902900411

Logar, I. (2010). Sustainable tourism management in Crikvenica, Croatia: An assessment of policy instruments. *Tourism Management, 31*(1), 125–135. doi:10.1016/j.tourman.2009.02.005

Lopes, E.R. (Ed.). (2010). *A constelação do turismo na economia portuguesa*. Mirandela: Edições Jornal Sol.

Lovell, G. (2009). Can I trust you? An exploration of the role of trust in hospitality service settings. *Tourism and Hospitality Planning & Development, 6*(2), 145–157. doi:10.1080/14790530902981548

Lugosi, P., Lynch, P., & Morrison, A. (2009). Critical hospitality management research. *Service Industries Journal, 29*(10), 1465–1478. doi:10.1080/02642060903038879

Luoh, H. F., & Tsaur, S. H. (2009). Physical attractiveness stereotypes and service quality in customer-server encounters. *Service Industries Journal, 29*(8), 1093–1104. doi:10.1080/02642060902764517

Lusa. (2015a, June 25). *Construtora sul-coreana ganha contrato de 720MD para projeto em Timor-Leste*. Retrieved from: http://noticias.sapo.tl/portugues/info/artigo/1445592.html

Lusa. (2015b, Jun 13). *Timor-Leste recebe com êxito enchente de turistas de cruzeiro australiano*. Retrieved June, 23, 2015, from http://www.sapo.pt/noticias/timor-leste-recebe-com-exito-enchente-de_557bfaea60753b3619188ed6

Lusch, R. F., Vargo, S. L., & O'Brien, M. (2007). Competing through service: Insights from service-dominant logic. *Journal of Retailing, 83*(1), 5–18. doi:10.1016/j.jretai.2006.10.002

Lusch, R. F., & Webster, F. E. Jr. (2011). A stakeholder-unifying, cocreation philophy for marketing. *Journal of Macromarketing, 31*(2), 129–134. doi:10.1177/0276146710397369

Ma, B. (2010). *A Trip into the Controversy: A Study of Slum Tourism Travel Motivations*. 2009-2010 Penn Humanities Forum on Connections. Available at: http://repository.upenn.edu/uhf_2010/12

Maccannell, D. (1988). Turismo e Identidad [Tourism & Identity]. Madrid: Juncar Edition.

MacCannell, D. (1988). Turismo e Identidad [Tourism & identity]. Madrid: Juncar.

MacCannell, D. (2009). Dmitri Shalin Interview with Dean MacCannell about Erving Goffman entitled "Some of Goffman's Guardedness and Verbal Toughness Was Simply a Way of Giving Himself the Space and Time That He Needed to Do the Work That He Really Loved". *Bios Sociologicus: The Erving Goffman Archives,* 1-37.

MacCannell, D. (1973). Staged authenticity: Arrangements of social space in tourist settings. *American Journal of Sociology, 79*(3), 589–603. doi:10.1086/225585

MacCannell, D. (1976). *The tourist: A new theory of the leisure class*. Berkeley, CA: University of California Press.

MacCannell, D. (1976). *The Tourist: A New Theory of the Leisure Class*. New York: Schocken Books Inc.

MacCannell, D. (1984). Reconstructed ethnicity tourism and cultural identity in third world communities. *Annals of Tourism Research, 11*(3), 375–391. doi:10.1016/0160-7383(84)90028-8

MacCannell, D. (1992). *Empty meeting grounds: The tourist papers*. London: Routledge. doi:10.4324/9780203412145

MacCannell, D. (2001). Tourist agency. *Tourist Studies*, *1*(1), 23–37. doi:10.1177/146879760100100102

MacCannell, D. (2011). *The ethics of sightseeing*. Berkeley, CA: University of California Press. doi:10.1525/california/9780520257825.001.0001

MacCannell, D. (2012). On the ethical stake in tourism research. *Tourism Geographies*, *14*(1), 183–194. doi:10.1080/14616688.2012.639387

Macfarlane, I., & Jago, L. (2009). *The role of brand equity in helping to evaluate the contribution of major events*. Gold Coast, Australia: Sustainable Tourism Cooperative Research Centre.

Macintosh, G. (2002). Building trust and satisfaction in travel counselor/client relationships. *Journal of Travel & Tourism Marketing*, *12*(4), 59–74. doi:10.1300/J073v12n04_04

Mack, N., Woodsong, C., MacQueen, K. M., Guest, G., & Namey, E. (2005). *Qualitative research methods: A data collector's field guide*. Family Health International.

Maigan, I., & Ralston, D. A. (2002). Corporate social responsibility in Europe and the U.S: Insights from businesses' self-presentations. *Journal of International Business Studies*, *33*(3), 497–514. doi:10.1057/palgrave.jibs.8491028

Mair, H. (2005). Tourism, health and the pharmacy: Towards a critical understanding of health and welness tourism. *Tourism*, *53*(4), 335–346.

Mak, A., Wong, K. K., & Chang, R. C. (2009). Health or self-indulgence? The motivations and characteristics of spagoers. *International Journal of Tourism Research*, *11*(2), 185–199. doi:10.1002/jtr.703

Malo, M. C., Beundia-Martinez, I., & Vezina, M. (2012). A conceptualization of women's collective entrepreneurship: From strategic perspectives to public policies. In M. A. Galindo & D. Ribeiro (Eds.), *Women's entrepreneurship and economics*. New York: Springer. doi:10.1007/978-1-4614-1293-9_14

Manasakis, C., Apostolakis, A., & Datseris, G. (2013). Using data envelopment analysis to measure hotel efficiency in Crete. *International Journal of Contemporary Hospitality Management*, *25*(4), 510–535. doi:10.1108/09596111311322907

Manente, M., Minghetti, V., & Mingotto, E. (2012). Ranking assessment systems for responsible tourism products and corporate social responsibility practices. *Anatolia*, *23*(1), 75–89. doi:10.1080/13032917.2011.653633

Mansfield, C. (2005). *Traversing Paris: French Travel Writing Practices in the Late Twentieth Century: An Analysis of the Work of Annie Ernaux, François Maspero and Jean Rolin. VDM* Verlag.

Marcello, M., Baggio, M. R., Buhalis, D., & Longhi, C. (2014). Tourism management, marketing, and development: volume I: the importance of networks and ICTs. New York: Palgrave McMillan.

Marchante, A. J., & Ortega, B. (2012). Human Capital and Labor Productivity: A Study for the Hotel Industry. *Cornell Hospitality Quarterly*, *53*(1), 20–30. doi:10.1177/1938965511427698

Marcos, M. C., Garcia-Gavilanes, R., Bataineh, E., & Pasarin, L. (2013). *Cultural Differences on Seeking Information: An Eye Tracking Study*. Retrieved April 28, 2015, from http://repositori.upf.edu/bitstream/handle/10230/20943/CHI_mcmarcos.pdf?sequence=1

Marshall, C., & Rossman, G. (2006). *Designing Qualitative Research (4th ed.)*. Thousand Oaks, CA: Sage Publications.

Marshall, G. N. (1991). A multidimensional analysis of internal health locus of control beliefs:Separating the wheat from the chaff? *Journal of Personality and Social Psychology*, *61*(3), 483–491. doi:10.1037/0022-3514.61.3.483 PMID:1941520

Marshall, P. (1997). *Research Methods: How to Design and Conduct a Successful Project*. Oxford, UK: How To Books, Ltd.

Marsick, V. J. (2003). Invited reaction: Informal learning and the transfer of learning: How managers develop proficiency. *Human Resource Development Quarterly, 14*(4), 389–395. doi:10.1002/hrdq.1075

Martín Rojo, I., Gaspar González, A. I., Caro González, F. J., Castellanos Verdugo, M., & Oviedo García, M. A. (2008). *La responsabilidad social corporativa en los puertos deportivos y clubes náuticos de Andalucía: Diagnóstico y propuestas de mejoras para la innovación turística*. Sevilla: C. y D. Consejería de Turismo.

Martínez, P., Pérez, A., & Rodríguez del Bosque, I. (2014). Exploring the role of CSR in the organizational identity of hospitality companies: A case from the Spanish tourism industry. *Journal of Business Ethics, 124*(1), 47–66. doi:10.1007/s10551-013-1857-1

Martínez, R. P., Pérez, A., & del Bosque, I. R. (2013). Measuring corporate social responsibility in tourism: Development and validation of an efficient measurement scale in the hospitality industry. *Journal of Travel & Tourism Marketing, 30*(4), 365–385. doi:10.1080/10548408.2013.784154

Mason, P., & Cheyne, J. (2000). Residents' Attitudes to Proposed Tourism Development. *Annals of Tourism Research, 27*(2), 391–411. doi:10.1016/S0160-7383(99)00084-5

Maurer, T. (2001). Career-Relevant Learning and Development, Worker Age, and Beliefs About Self-Efficacy for Development. *Journal of Management, 27*(2), 123–140. doi:10.1177/014920630102700201

McCabe, M. (2013). *The Routledge handbook of tourism marketing*. New York: Routledge.

McCabe, M. P., & Ricciardelli, L. A. (2003). Body image and strategies to lose weight and increase muscle among boys and girls. *Health Psychology, 22*(1), 39–46. doi:10.1037/0278-6133.22.1.39 PMID:12558200

McCole, P. (2002). The role of trust for electronic commerce in services. *International Journal of Contemporary Hospitality Management, 14*(2), 81–87. doi:10.1108/09596110210419264

McCole, P. (2004). Dealing with complaints in services. *International Journal of Contemporary Hospitality Management, 16*(6), 345–354. doi:10.1108/09596110410550789

McDonald, S. (2011). What's in the "old boys" network? Accessing social capital in gendered and racialized networks. *Social Networks, 33*(4), 317–330. doi:10.1016/j.socnet.2011.10.002

Mcmeekin, A., Tomlinson, M., Green, K., & Walsh, V. (2009). *Innovation by demand: an interdisciplinary approach to the study of demand and its role in innovation (new dynamics of innovation and competition MUP)*. Manchester, UK: Manchester University Press.

Meethan, K. (2006). Introduction: narratives of place and self. In Tourism Consumption and Representation. CABI.

Meethan, K. (2003). Mobile Cultures? hybridity, tourism and cultural change. *Journal of Tourism and Cultural Change, 1*(1), 11–28. doi:10.1080/14766820308668157

Meethan, K. (2004). To stand in the shores of my ancestors. In T. Coles & D. Timothy (Eds.), *Tourism, Disaporas and Space* (pp. 139–150). London: Routledge.

Meethan, K. (2005). Tourism in global society. Place, culture, consumption. *Relaciones Estudios de Historia Social (Madrid, Spain), 26*(103), 270–277.

Meethan, K. (2014). Mobilities, Ethnicities and Tourism. In A. Lew, M. C. Hall, & A. Williams (Eds.), *Tourism*. New York, NY: Willey Blackwell. doi:10.1002/9781118474648.ch19

Mei, X. Y., Arcodia, C., & Ruhanen, L. (2012). Towards tourism innovation: A critical review of public polices at the national level. *Tourism Management Perspectives, 4*, 92–105. doi:10.1016/j.tmp.2012.05.002

Mekawy, M. A. (2012). Responsible slum tourism: Egyptian experience. *Annals of Tourism Research, 39*(4), 2092–2113. doi:10.1016/j.annals.2012.07.006

Merklen, D. (2013). Las Dinámicas contemporáneas de la individuación. In *Individuación, precariedad, inseguridad.* Buenos Aires: Paidos.

Merriam, S. B. (2014). *Qualitative Research: A Guide to Design and Implementation.* San Francisco: John Wiley & Sons.

Meschkank, J. (2011). Investigations into slum tourism in Mumbai: Poverty tourism and the tension between different constructions of reality. *GeoJournal, 76*(1), 47–62. doi:10.1007/s10708-010-9401-7

MFTL (Ministry of Finance of East Timor). (2015). *Aprovação unânime do Orçamento Geral do Estado para 2015.* Retrieved July 4, 2015, from https://www.mof.gov.tl/wp-content/uploads/2015/01/MoF_Press_Release_Budget_2015-_pt.pdf

Mich, L., Franch, M., & Gaio, L. (2003). Evaluating and Designing the Quality of Web Sites. *IEEE MultiMedia, 10*(1), 34–43. doi:10.1109/MMUL.2003.1167920

Michopoulou, E., & Buhalis, D. (2013). Information Provision for Challenging Markets: The Case of the Accessibility Requiring Market in the Context of Tourism. *Information & Management, 50*(5), 229–239. doi:10.1016/j.im.2013.04.001

Middleton, V. T. C., Fyall, A., Morgan, M., & Ranchhod, A. (2009). *Marketing in travel and tourism.* Oxford, UK: Butterworth Heinemann.

Mihart, C. (2012). Impact of Integrated Marketing Communication on Consumer Behaviour: Effects on Consumer Decision – Making Process. *International Journal of Marketing Studies, 4*(2), 121–129. doi:10.5539/ijms.v4n2p121

Miles, W. S. (2010). Dueling border tours: Jerusalem. *Annals of Tourism Research, 37*(2), 555–559. doi:10.1016/j.annals.2009.11.003

Miller, A. L., Lambert, A. D., & Speirs Neumeister, K. L. (2012). Parenting Style, Perfectionism, and Creativity in High-Ability and High-Achieving Young Adults. *Journal for the Education of the Gifted, 35*(4), 344–365. doi:10.1177/0162353212459257

Miller, H., Engemann, K., & Yager, R. (2006). Disaster planning and management. *Communications Of The International Information Management Association, 6*(2), 25–36.

Mill, R., & Morrison, A. (2009). *The tourism system.* Dubuque, IA: Kendall Hunt Publishing.

Ministry of Economy and Employment. (2012). *Plano Estratégico Nacional do Turismo (PENT) Horizonte 2013-2015.* Retrieved January 15, 2015, from http://www.turismodeportugal.pt/Portugu%C3%AAs/turismodeportugal/publicacoes/Documents/PENT%202012.pdf

Ministry of Industry, Energy, and Tourism. (2012). *Plan Nacional e Integral de Turismo 2012-2015 (PNIT).* Retrieved January 15, 2015, from http://www.tourspain.es/es-es/VDE/Documentos%20Vision%20Destino%20Espaa/Plan%20Nacional%20e%20Integral%20de%20Turismo%202012_2015_FINAL_REVISADO%20150313.pdf

Mitchell, L. S., & Murphy, P. E. (1991). Geography and tourism. *Annals of Tourism Research, 18*(1), 57–70. doi:10.1016/0160-7383(91)90039-E

Mitropoulos, P., & Tatum, C. B. (2008). Forces driving adoption of new information technologies. *Journal of Construction Engineering and Management,* (September-October), 340–348.

Moeller, T., Dolnicar, S., & Leish, F. (2011). The sustainability-profitability trade-off in tourism: Can it be overcome? *Journal of Sustainable Tourism, 19*(2), 155–169. doi:10.1080/09669582.2010.518762

Mohammed, I., Guillet, B. D., & Law, R. (2015). The contributions of economics to hospitality literature: A content analysis of hospitality and tourism journals. *International Journal of Hospitality Management, 44*, 99–110. doi:10.1016/j.ijhm.2014.10.010

Morey, D., & Dittman, D. (1995). Evaluating a hotel's GM performance: A case study in benchmarking. *The Cornell Hotel and Restaurant Administration Quarterly, 36*(5), 30–35.

Morgan, O., Sribanditmongkol, P., Perera, C., Sulasmi, Y., Van Alphen, D., & Sondorp, E. (2006). Mass Fatality Management following the South Asian Tsunami Disaster: Case Studies in Thailand, Indonesia, and Sri Lanka. *PLoS Medicine, 3*(6), e195. doi:10.1371/journal.pmed.0030195 PMID:16737348

Morrison, A. M. (2013). *Marketing and managing tourism destinations.* Oxon, UK: Routledge.

Moutinho, L., Rate, S., & Ballantyne, R. (2013). Futurecast: an exploration of key emerging megatrends in the tourism arena. In C. Costa, E. Pnayik, & D. Buhalis (Eds.), *Trends in European Tourism Planning and Organisation* (pp. 313–325). Bristol, UK: Channel View Publications.

Mowday, R. (1978). The exercise of influence in organizations. *Administrative Science Quarterly, 23*(1), 137–156. doi:10.2307/2392437

Mulder, N. (2000). *Inside Thai society.* Chiang Mai, Thailand: Silkworm Books.

Müller, H., & Lanz Kauffman, E. (2001). Wellness Tourism: Market analysis of a special health tourism segment and implications for the hotel industry. *Journal of Vacation Marketing, 7*(1), 5–17. doi:10.1177/135676670100700101

Muñoz De Escalona, F. (2014). La Epistemología Y El Turismo (Epistemology and Tourism). *Anuario de Turismo y Sociedad, 15*(1), 187–203.

Murphy, P., Pritchard, M. P., & Smith, B. (2007). The destination product and its impact on traveller perceptions. *Tourism Management, 21*(1), 43–52. doi:10.1016/S0261-5177(99)00080-1

Musteen, M., Francis, J., & Datta, D. K. (2010). The influence of international networks on internationalization speed and performance: A study of Czech SMEs. *Journal of World Business, 45*(3), 197–205. doi:10.1016/j.jwb.2009.12.003

Mutinelli, M., & Piscitello, L. (1998). The entry mode choice of MNEs: An evolutionary approach. *Research Policy, 27*(5), 491–506. doi:10.1016/S0048-7333(98)00063-8

Naisbitt, J., & Aburdene, P. (1990). *Megatrends 2000.* New York: William Morrow.

Narayan, M., Pritchett, T., & Kapoor, M. (2009). *Moving Out of Poverty. Success from the Bottom Up.* The World Bank and Palgrave Macmillan. doi:10.1596/978-0-8213-7215-9

NATS. (2015). *Seamless Exceeding expectations on the ground and in the air.* Available at: http://www.nats.aero/wp-content/uploads/2013/01/NATS-Corporate-Brochure.pdf

Nelson, J. A. (2014). Are women really more risk-averse than men? A re-analysis of the literature using expanded methods. *Journal of Economic Surveys*, 1–20. doi:10.1111/joes.12069

Nerur, S., Rasheed, A., & Natarajan, V. (2008). The intellectual structure of the strategic management field: An author co-citation analysis. *Strategic Management Journal, 29*(3), 319–336. doi:10.1002/smj.659

Neves, G. N. S. (2007). O paradoxo da cooperação em Timor-Leste. In K. Silva & D. S. Simião (Eds.), *Timor-Leste por trás do palco: cooperação internacional e a dialética da formação do Estado* (pp. 97–121). Belo Horizonte: UFMG.

Nickson, D., Warhurst, C., & Dutton, E. (2005). The Importance of Attitude and Appearance in the Service Encounter in Retail and Hospitality. *Managing Service Quality, 15*(2), 195–208. doi:10.1108/09604520510585370

Nicolau, J. L., & Mas, F. (2005). Stochastic modeling: A three-stage tourist choice process. *Annals of Tourism Research, 32*(1), 49–69. doi:10.1016/j.annals.2004.04.007

Nielsen, H., & Spenceley, A. (2010). *The success of tourism in Rwanda: gorillas and more.* Retrieved September, 20, 2012, from http://anna.spenceley.co.uk/files/publications/nature%20based%20tourism/Tourism_Rwanda%20gorillas.pdf

Nielsen, J. (2014). *Millennials: much deeper than their facebook pages.* Retrieved February 15, 2015, from http://www.nielsen.com/us/en/insights/news/2014/millennials-much-deeper-than-their-facebook-pages.html

Nisbet, R. A. (1993). *The sociological tradition.* New Brunswick, NJ: Transaction publishers.

Noikorn, U. (1998). Green protest at film slammed. *The Bangkok Post.*

Northern Regional Coordination and Development Commission. (2014). *Programa Operacional Regional do Norte 2014-2020.* Retrieved January 15, 2015, from http://www.norte2020.pt/sites/default/files/public/uploads/programa/po_norte2020.pdf

Norwegian Agency for Development Cooperation (NORAD). (2012). *Norway Development Partner Handover Report 2012* (Unpublished). Díli, East Timor.

Novelli, M., Morgan, N., & Nibigira, C. (2012). Tourism in a post-conflict situation of fragility. *Annals of Tourism Research, 39*(3), 1446–1469. doi:10.1016/j.annals.2012.03.003

Noy, C., & Cohen, E. (Eds.). (2012). *Israeli backpackers: From tourism to rite of passage.* New York: SUNY Press.

Nunkoo, R., & Ramkissoon, H. (2012). Power, trust, social exchange and community support. *Annals of Tourism Research, 39*(2), 997–1023. doi:10.1016/j.annals.2011.11.017

Nunnally, J. C. (1978). *Psychometric theory* (2nd ed.). New York: McGraw-Hill.

Nyahunzvi, D. K. (2013). CSR reporting among Zimbabwe's hotel groups: A content analysis. *International Journal of Contemporary Hospitality Management, 25*(4), 595–613. doi:10.1108/09596111311322943

Nyberg, A.-C. (2009). *Making Ideas Matter: Gender, Technology and Women's Invention.* Luleå University.

O'neill, J. W., & Mattila, A. S. (2006). Strategic Hotel Development and Positioning The Effects of Revenue Drivers on Profitability. *The Cornell Hotel and Restaurant Administration Quarterly, 47*(2), 146–154. doi:10.1177/0010880405281519

OBrien, P. W. (2011). Business, Management and Poverty Reduction: A Role for Slum Tourism? *Journal of Business Diversity, 11*(1), 33–46.

Office for National Statistics (ONS). (2014). *Internet Access – Households and Individuals 2014.* Retrieved March 5, 2015, from http://www.ons.gov.uk/ons/dcp171778_373584.pdf

Ohanian, R. (1990). Construction and validation of a scale to measure celebrity endorsers' perceived expertise, trustworthiness, and attractiveness. *Journal of Advertising, 19*(3), 39–52. doi:10.1080/00913367.1990.10673191

Oh, H. (2000). The effect of brand class, brand awareness, and price on customer value and behavioral intentions. *Journal of Hospitality & Tourism Research (Washington, D.C.), 24*(2), 136–162. doi:10.1177/109634800002400202

Oh, H. (2002). Transaction evaluations and relationship intentions. *Journal of Hospitality & Tourism Research (Washington, D.C.), 26*(3), 278–305. doi:10.1177/1096348002026003005

Okazaki, S. (2005). Mobile advertising adoption by multinationals: Senior executives' initial responses. *Internet Research, 15*(2), 160–180. doi:10.1108/10662240510590342

Okazaki, S., & Hirose, M. (2009). Does gender affect media choice in travel information search? On the use of mobile Internet. *Tourism Management, 30*(6), 794–804. doi:10.1016/j.tourman.2008.12.012

Okumus, F., & Karamustafa, K. (2005). Impact of an Economic Crisis; Evidence from Turkey. *Annals of Tourism Research, 32*(4), 942–961. doi:10.1016/j.annals.2005.04.001

Okumus, F., Wong, K., & Altinay, L. (2008). Are we teaching strategic management right? *Journal of Teaching in Travel & Tourism, 8*(4), 329–350. doi:10.1080/15313220903047938

Oliver, R. L. (1997). *Satisfaction: A behavioral perspective on the consumer.* New York, NY: McGraw–Hill.

Oliver, R. L., & Swan, J. E. (1989). Consumer perceptions of interpersonal equity and satisfaction in transaction: A field survey approach. *Journal of Marketing, 53*(2), 21–35. doi:10.2307/1251411

Olsen, M. D., West, J., & Tse, E. C. Y. (2008). *Strategic management in the hospitality industry.* New York, NY: Prentice Hall.

Olsen, R. (2000). Toward a politics of disaster: Losses, Values, Agenda and Blame. *International Journal of Mass Emergencies and Disasters, 18*(2), 265–287.

Olsson, T., & Väänänen-Vainio-Mattila, K. (2013). Expected User Experience of Mobile Augmented Reality Services. *Personal and Ubiquitous Computing, 17*(2), 287–304. doi:10.1007/s00779-011-0494-x

Ooi, C. A., Hooy, C. W., & Som, A. P. M. (2015). Diversity in human and social capital: Empirical evidence from Asian tourism firms in corporate board composition. *Tourism Management, 48,* 139–153. doi: 10.1016/j.tourman.2014.11.002

Orpen, C. (1987). The attitudes of United States and South African Managers to Corporate Social Responsibility. *Journal of Business Ethics, 6*(2), 89–96. doi:10.1007/BF00382022

Overbaugh, R., & Lu, R. (2008). The Impact of a NCLB-EETT Funded Professional Development Program on Teacher Self-Efficacy and Resultant Implementation. *Journal of Research on Technology in Education, 41*(1), 43–61. doi:10.1080/15391523.2008.10782522

Panwar, R., Rinne, T., Hansen, E., & Juslin, H. (2006). Corporate responsibility: Balancing economic environmental and social issues in the forest products industry. *Forest Products Journal, 56*(2), 4–12.

Papatheodorou, A. (2002). Civil Aviation Regimes and Leisure Tourism in Europe. *Journal of Air Transport Management, 8*(6), 381–388. doi:10.1016/S0969-6997(02)00019-4

Papatheodorou, A., Rossello, J., & Xiao, H. (2010). Global economic crisis and tourism: Consequences and perspectives. *Journal of Travel Research, 49*(1), 39–45. doi:10.1177/0047287509355327

Pappas, N. (2010). Terrorism and Tourism: The Way Travelers Select Airlines and Destinations. *Journal of Air Transport Studies, 1*(2), 76–96.

Parasuraman, A., Zeithaml, V. A., & Berry, L. L. (1985). A conceptual model of service quality an its implications for future research. *Journal of Marketing, 49*(4), 41–50. doi:10.2307/1251430

Parasuraman, A., Zeithaml, V. A., & Berry, L. L. (1988). Servqual: A multiple-item scale for measuring consumer perc. *Journal of Retailing, 64*(1), 12–41.

Parise, S., Guinan, P., & Weinberg, B. (2008). *The secrets of marketing in a web 2.0 world.* Retrieved April 4, 2015, from http://online.wsj.com/article/SB122884677205091919.html

Park, C., & Jun, J.-K. (2003). A cross-cultural comparison of Internet buying behaviour: Effects of Internet usage, perceived risks, and innovativeness. *International Marketing Review, 20*(5), 534–553. doi:10.1108/02651330310498771

Parsons, W. (1996). Crisis management. *Career Development International, 1*(5), 26–28. doi:10.1108/13620439610130614

Patzer, G. L. (1985). *The physical Attractiveness Phenomena.* New York: Plemun. doi:10.1007/978-1-4757-0202-6

Paustian-Underdahl, S. C., Walker, L. S., & Woehr, D. J. (2014). Gender and perceptions of leadership effectiveness: A meta-analysis of contextual moderators. *The Journal of Applied Psychology, 99*(6), 1129–1145. doi:10.1037/a0036751 PMID:24773399

Pavlou, P. A., Liang, H., & Xue, Y. (2007). Understanding and mitigating uncertainty in online exchange relationships: A principal-agent perspective. *Management Information Systems Quarterly, 31*(1), 105–136.

Payne, A. F., Storbacka, K., & Frow, P. (2008). Managing the co-creation of value. *Journal of the Academy of Marketing Science, 36*(1), 83–96. doi:10.1007/s11747-007-0070-0

Pearce, P. L. (1982). *The social psychology of tourist behaviour.* New York: Pergamon Press.

Pechlaner, H., & Sauerwein, E. (2002). Strategy implementation in the Alpine tourism industry. *International Journal of Contemporary Hospitality Management, 11*(7), 359–365.

Peng, H., Xu, X., & Chen, W. (2013). Tourist Behaviours in Online Booking: A New Research Agenda. *Communications in Information Science and Management Engineering, 3*(6), 280–285.

Penn State. (2013). *Factors identified that influence willingness to use new information technology.* Retrieved from: http://news.psu.edu/story/267639/2013/03/07/science-and-technology/factors-identified-influence-willingness-use-new

Perdomo, J., & Escobar, A. (2011). La investigación en RSE : Una revisión desde el management. *Cuadernos de Administración, 24*(43), 193–219.

Pérez López, C. (2005). *Métodos estadísticos avanzados con Spss.* Madrid: Thomson.

Pérez, A., & del Bosque, I. R. (2014). Sustainable development and stakeholder relations management: Exploring sustainability reporting in the hospitality industry from a SD-SRM approach. *International Journal of Hospitality Management, 42*, 174–187. doi:10.1016/j.ijhm.2014.07.003

Performance Review Unit. (2004). *ATM Cost-Effectiveness (ACE) 2002 Benchmarking Report.* Brussels: EUROCONTROL.

Performance Review Unit. (2014). *ATM Cost-Effectiveness (ACE) 2012 Benchmarking Report with 2013-2017 Outlook.* Brussels: EUROCONTROL.

Pescatore, M. J. (2005). *It's all about appearances.* New York: Government Video.

Pesonen, J., & Palooja, O. M. (2010). Comparing Internet Commerce Adoption Between the Finnish and the European Independent Accommodation Companies. In *Information and Communication Technologies in Tourism 2010,Proceedings of the International Conference.* doi:10.1007/978-3-211-99407-8_5

Pesonen, J., & Komppula, R. (2010). Rural Wellbeing Tourism: Motivations and Expectations. *Journal of Hospitality and Tourism Management, 17*(1), 150–157. doi:10.1375/jhtm.17.1.150

Pettersson, K. (2007). *Men as male as the norm? A gender perspective on innovation policies in Denmark, Finland and Sverige*. Stockholm: Nordregio.

Pham, T., Jago, L., Spurr, R., & Marshall, J. (2015). The Dutch disease effects on tourism: The case of Australia. *Tourism Management, 46*, 610–622. doi:10.1016/j.tourman.2014.08.014

Phillips, P. A., & Moutinho, L. (2000). The strategic planning index (SPI): A tool for measuring strategic planning effectiveness. *Journal of Travel Research, 38*(4), 369–379. doi:10.1177/004728750003800405

Phillips, P. A., & Moutinho, L. (2014). Critical review of strategic planning research in hospitality and tourism. *Annals of Tourism Research, 48*, 96–120. doi:10.1016/j.annals.2014.05.013

Pick, U. X., & Ruesga, C. (2007). Capacity building for decentralization in Mexico: A psychosocial approach. *International Journal of Public Sector Management, 20*(2), 157–166. doi:10.1108/09513550710731517

Piermartini, R., & Rousova, L. (2008). *Liberalization of Air Transport Services and Passenger Traffic*. Available at: http://www.wto.org/english/res_e/reser_e/ersd200806_e.pdf

Pilkington, A., & Liston-Heyes, C. (1999). Is production and operations management a discipline? A citation/co-citation study. *International Journal of Operations & Production Management, 19*(1), 7–20. doi:10.1108/01443579910244188

Pine, J. B. II, & Gilmore, J. H. (1999). *The experience Economy: work is theatre and every business a stage*. Boston: Harvard Business School Press.

Pirani, S. I., & Arafat, H. A. (2014). Solid waste management in the hospitality industry: A review. *Journal of Environmental Management, 146*, 320–336. doi:10.1016/j.jenvman.2014.07.038 PMID:25194519

Pizam, A. (2003). What should be our field of study? *International Journal of Hospitality Management, 22*(4), 339. doi:10.1016/j.ijhm.2003.09.001

Pleumarom, A. (2004). *Tourism and the Tsunami disaster with a focus upon Thailand*. Third World Network.

Plog, S. (2001). Why Destination Areas Rise and Fall in Popularity. *The Cornell Hotel and Restaurant Administration Quarterly, 32*, 14–24.

Ponzi, L. J. (2002). The intellectual structure and interdisciplinary breadth of knowledge management: A bibliometric study of its early stage of development. *Scientometrics, 55*(2), 259–272. doi:10.1023/A:1019619824850

Poon, A. (1993). *Tourism, technology, and competitive strategies*. Wallingford: CAB International.

Porter, M. (2001). Strategy and the Internet. *Harvard Business Review, 79*(3), 63–78. PMID:11246925

Portuguese Development Agency (IPAD). (2012). *Portugal Development Partner Handover Report 2012* (Unpublished). Díli, East Timor. Retrieved 20 June, 2014, from http://timor-leste.gov.tl/?cat=39&lang=pt&bl=16

Posthuma, R. A., Morgeson, F. P., & Campion, M. A. (2002). Beyond employment interview validity:A comprehensive narrative review of recent research and trends over time. *Personnel Psychology, 55*(1), 1–81. doi:10.1111/j.1744-6570.2002.tb00103.x

Prahalad, C. K., & Ramaswamy, V. (2004). *The future of competition. Co-creating unique value with customers*. Delhi: Harvard Business School Press.

Prebensen, N. K., & Foss, L. (2011). Coping and co-creating in tourist experiences. *International Journal of Tourism Research, 13*(1), 54–67. doi:10.1002/jtr.799

Price, L., Arnould, E., & Deibler, S. (1995). Consumers' emotional responses to service encounters. *International Journal of Service Industry Management, 6*(3), 34–63. doi:10.1108/09564239510091330

Prieto, G. (1979). Balance social de la empresa: Aspectos doctrinales. *Revue d'Economie Politique, 82*(Mayo-Agosto), 62.

Privitera, D. (2015). Tourist Valorisation of Urban Poverty: An Empirical Study on the Web. *Urban Forum, 6*(4), 373-390. doi:10.1007/s12132-015-9259-3

Prote. (2015). *iBeacon*. Retrieved from: http://bit.ly/1embSQh

Putnam, R. D. (1995). Bowling alone: America's declining social capital. *Journal of Democracy, 6*(1), 65–78. doi:10.1353/jod.1995.0002

Quan, S., & Wang, N. (2004). Towards a structural model of the tourist experience: An illustration from food experiences in tourism. *Tourism Management, 25*(3), 297–305. doi:10.1016/S0261-5177(03)00130-4

Quazi, A. M., & O'Brien, D. (2000). An empirical test of a cross-national model of Corporate Social Responsibility. *Journal of Business Ethics, 25*(1), 33–51. doi:10.1023/A:1006305111122

Quinlan Cutler, S., & Carmichael, B. A. (2010). The dimensions of the tourist experience. In M. Morgan, P. Lugosi, & J. R. Ritchie (Eds.), *The tourism and leisure experience. Consumer and managerial perspectives* (pp. 3–26). Bristol, UK: Channel View Publications.

Ramchander, P. (2004). *Towards the responsible management of the socio-cultural impact of township tourism*. University of Pretoria, Department of Tourism Management. Available at: http://upetd.up.ac.za/thesis/available/etd-08262004-130507/

Ranson, G. (2012). Men, Paid Employment and Family Responsibilities: Conceptualizing the "Working Father.". *Gender, Work and Organization, 19*(6), 741–761. doi:10.1111/j.1468-0432.2011.00549.x

Rapert, M. I., & Wren, B. M. (1998). Service quality as a competitive opportunity. *Journal of Services Marketing, 12*(3), 223–235. doi:10.1108/08876049810219539

Rapoport, R., & Rapoport, R. N. (1975). *Leisure and the family life cycle*. London, United Kingdom: Routledge and Kegan Paul.

Raybould, M., & Wilkins, H. (2005). Over qualified and under experienced: Turning graduates into hospitality managers. *International Journal of Contemporary Hospitality Management, 17*(3), 203–216. doi:10.1108/09596110510591891

Rayport, J. F., & Bernard, J. J. (2004). Best face forward. *Harvard Business Review, 82*(12), 47–52. PMID:15605565

Regulation (EEC) No 2408/92. The access for Community air carriers to intra-Community air routes.

Regulation (EEC) No 2409/92. The full freedom with regard to fares and rates.

Rejeski & Miller. (2001). A marginal model for analyzing discrete outcomes from longitudinal surveys with outcomes subject to multiple-cause nonresponse. *Journal of the American Statistical Association, 96*(455), 844.

República Democrática de Timor-Leste. (n.d.a). *Programa do V Governo Constitucional*. Retrieved 20 June, 2014, from http://timor-leste.gov.tl/?cat=39&lang=pt&bl=7569

República Democrática de Timor-Leste. (n.d.b). *Programa do VI Governo Constitucional*. Retrieved 20 June, 2014, fromhttp://timor-leste.gov.tl/?cat=39&lang=pt&bl=11688

Rice, A., & Haynes, K. (2005). *Post-tsunami reconstruction and tourism: a second disaster?* London: Tourism Concern.

Richardson, B. (1994). Crisis Management and Management Strategy-Time to "Loop the Loop"? *Disaster Prevention and Management, 3*(3), 59–80. doi:10.1108/09653569410795632

Richardson, B., Nwankwo, S., & Richardson, S. (1994). Understanding the Causes of Business Failure Crises. *Management Decision, 32*(4), 9–22. doi:10.1108/00251749410058635

Richter, L. K. (1983). Tourism politics and political science: A case of not so benign neglect. *Annals of Tourism Research, 10*(3), 313–335. doi:10.1016/0160-7383(83)90060-9

Richter, L. K. (1989). *The politics of tourism in Asia*. Honolulu, HI: University of Hawaii Press.

Richter, L. K. (1999). After political turmoil: The lessons of rebuilding tourism in three Asian countries. *Journal of Travel Research, 38*(1), 41–45. doi:10.1177/004728759903800109

Ridgeway, C. L. (2009). Framed before we know it how gender shapes social relations. *Gender & Society, 23*(2), 145–160. doi:10.1177/0891243208330313

Riggio, R. E., Widaman, K. F., Tucker, J. S., & Salinas, C. (1991). Beauty is more than skin deep:Component of attractiveness. *Basic and Applied Social Psychology, 12*(4), 423–439. doi:10.1207/s15324834basp1204_4

Rigg, J., Law, L., Tan-Mullins, M., & Grundy-Warr, C. (2005). The Indian Ocean tsunami: Socio-economic impacts in Thailand. *The Geographical Journal, 171*(4), 374–379. doi:10.1111/j.1475-4959.2005.00175_3.x

Riley, M. (1990). The labour retention strategies of UK hotel managers. *Service Industries Journal, 10*(3), 614–618. doi:10.1080/02642069000000063

Ritchie, B. (2004). Chaos, crises and disasters: A strategic approach to crisis management in the tourism industry. *Tourism Management, 25*(6), 669–683. doi:10.1016/j.tourman.2003.09.004

Ritchie, B. W., Burns, P., & Palmer, C. (2005a). Preface. In *Tourism Research Methods, integrating theory with Practice* (pp. ix–x). Wallingford: CABI Publishing. doi:10.1079/9780851999968.0000

Ritchie, B. W., Burns, P., & Palmer, C. (2005b). Introduction: reflection on the Practice Research. In *Tourism Research Methods, integrating theory with Practice* (pp. 1–8). Wallingford: CABI Publishing. doi:10.1079/9780851999968.0001

Ritchie, J. R. B. (1999). Crafting a value-driven vision for a national tourism treasure. *Tourism Management, 20*(3), 273–282. doi:10.1016/S0261-5177(98)00123-X

Ritchie, J. R., & Hudson, S. (2009). Understanding and meeting the challenges of consumer/tourist experience research. *International Journal of Tourism Research, 11*(2), 111–126. doi:10.1002/jtr.721

Rittichainuwat, B. (2006). Tsunami recovery: A case study of Thailand's Tourism. *The Cornell Hotel and Restaurant Administration Quarterly, 47*(4), 390–404. doi:10.1177/0010880406289994

Rittichainuwat, B. (2011). Ghosts: A Travel Barrier to Tourism Recovery. *Annals of Tourism Research, 38*(2), 437–459. doi:10.1016/j.annals.2010.10.001

Roberts, L., & Hall, D. (2001). *Rural tourism and recreation: principles to practice*. Wallingford: Cabi Publishing. doi:10.1079/9780851995403.0000

Robertson, L. (2007). Taming space: Drug use, HIV, and homemaking in downtown eastside Vancouver. *Gender, Place and Culture, 14*(5), 527–549. doi:10.1080/09663690701562198

Robinson, R. N. S., Solnet, D. J., & Breakey, N. (2014). A phenomenological approach to hospitality management research: Chefs' occupational commitment. *International Journal of Hospitality Management, 43*, 65–75. doi:10.1016/j.ijhm.2014.08.004

Rogers, M. E. (1962). *Diffusion of Innovations*. New York: Free Press.

Rogerson, C. M. (2008). Shared Growth in Urban Tourism: Evidence from Soweto, South Africa. *Urban Forum, 19*(4), 395–411.

Rogerson, C. M. (2004). Urban tourism and small tourism enterprise development in Johannesburg: The case of township tourism. *GeoJournal, 60*(3), 249–257. doi:10.1023/B:GEJO.0000034732.58327.b6

Rogerson, C. M. (2013). Urban tourism, economic regeneration and inclusion: Evidence from South Africa. *Local Economy, 28*(2), 188–202. doi:10.1177/0269094212463789

Rolfes, M. (2010). Poverty tourism: Theoretical reflections and empirical findings regarding an extraordinary form of tourism. *GeoJournal, 75*(5), 421–442.

Rosenbaum, G. (2013). Toward an understanding of how entrepreneurs access and use networks/social capital to internationalize: A gender perspective. In H. Etemad, T. K. Madsen, E. S. Rasmussen, & P. Servais (Eds.), *Current Issues in International Entrepreneurship* (pp. 296–316). Cheltenham, UK: Edward Elgar Publishing. doi:10.4337/9781781953426.00018

Ruan. (1994). *A Study on the management type and performance of International Tourist Hotels - The Empirical study of Taiwan, U.S., Japan*. Chinese Culture University Graduate Institute of Tourism Industry.

Ruetzler, T., Baker, W., Reynolds, D., Taylor, J., & Allen, B. (2014). Perceptions of technical skills required for successful management in the hospitality industry: An exploratory study using conjoint analysis. *International Journal of Hospitality Management, 39*, 157–164. doi:10.1016/j.ijhm.2014.02.012

Ruf, B. M., Muralidhar, K., & Paul, K. (1998). The development of a systematic, aggregate measure of Corporate Social Performance. *Journal of Management, 24*(1), 119–133. doi:10.1177/014920639802400101

Ruhanen, L., Whitford, M., & McLennan, C. I. (2015). Indigenous tourism in Australia: Time for a reality check. *Tourism Management, 48*, 73–83. doi:10.1016/j.tourman.2014.10.017

Ryan, C. (1991). *Recreational tourism: A social science perspective*. London: Routledge.

Ryan, C. (2002). *The Tourist Experience*. New York: Continuum Books.

Ryan, C. (2005). Ethics in Tourism Research: objectivies and Personal Perspectives. In *Tourism Research Methods, integrating theory with Practice* (pp. 9–20). Wallingford: CABI Publishing. doi:10.1079/9780851999968.0009

Ryu, K., & Han, H. (2010). Influence of the quality of food, service, and physical environment on customer satisfaction and behavioral intention in quick-casual restaurants: Moderating role of perceived price. *Journal of Hospitality & Tourism Research (Washington, D.C.), 34*(3), 310–329. doi:10.1177/1096348009350624

Sakata, K., & MacKenzie, C. (2004). The Accumulation of Human Capital and the Sectoral Shifts Hypothesis for Different Age Groups. *Mathematics and Computers in Simulation, 64*(3-4), 459–465. doi:10.1016/S0378-4754(03)00111-3

Salazar, N. B. (2010). Towards an anthropology of cultural mobilities. *Crossings: Journal of Migration & Culture, 1*(1), 53–68.

Salazar, N. B. (2013). *Envisioning Eden: Mobilizing imaginaries in tourism and beyond* (Vol. 31). Oxford, UK: Berghahn Books.

Saltman, K. (2007). *Schooling in Disaster Capitalism: How the Political Right is using Disaster to Privatise Public Schooling*. Teacher Education Quarterly Spring.

Salvadori, N., & Balducci, R. (2005). *Innovation, unemployment, and policy in the theories of growth and distribution.* Cheltenham, UK: Edward Elgar Publishing. doi:10.4337/9781845428167

Sánchez-Fernández, M. D. (2015). Ferramentas e instrumentos de gestão estratégica de responsabilidade social: Setor turismo. *Tourism and Hospitality International Journal, 4*(2), 71–88.

Sánchez-Fernández, M. D., Vargas-Sánchez, A., & Remoaldo, P. (2014). Institutional Context and Hotel Social Responsibility. *Kybernetes, 43*(3/4), 413–426. doi:10.1108/K-12-2013-0267

Sanchez-Ollero, J. L., García Pozo, A., Marchante-Lara, M., Okumus, F., & Okumus, F. (2015). Measuring the effects of quality certification on labour productivity: An analysis of the hospitality sector. *International Journal of Contemporary Hospitality Management, 27*(6), 1100–1116. doi:10.1108/IJCHM-02-2014-0057

Sandwith, P. (1993). A hierarchy of management training requirements: The competency domain model. *Public Personnel Management, 22*(1), 43–62. doi:10.1177/009102609302200104

Santos, C. P., & Basso, K. (2012). Do ongoing relationships buffer the effects of service recovery on customers' trust and loyalty? *International Journal of Bank Marketing, 30*(3), 168–192. doi:10.1108/02652321211222540

Sariisik, M., Sari, D., Sari, S., & Halis, M. (2011). Tourism sector in order to recovering from the recession: Comparison analyses from Turkey. *Procedia: Social and Behavioral Sciences, 24*, 181–187. doi:10.1016/j.sbspro.2011.09.070

Sarker, S. (2007). *Innovation, market archetypes and outcome: An integrated framework*. New York: Physica-Verlag.

Šarotar Zizek, S., Mulej, M., Milfelner, B., & Potocnik, A. (2013). Social responsibility in Slovenia. *Systems: Connecting Matter, Life. Culture Technique, 1*(1), 95–109.

SAS Institute Inc. (2015). *Digital marketing-what is it and why it matters*. Retrieved from: http://bit.ly/1cRj6SG

Sasser, W. E., Olsen, R. P., & Wyckoff, D. D. (1987). *Management of service operations: Text and Case*. Boston: Alley and Bacon Inc.

Saunders, M., Lewis, P., & Thornhill, A. (2003). *Research methods for business students*. Harlow, UK: Prentice Hall.

Saunders, M., Lewis, P., & Thornhill, A. (2007). *Research Methods for Business Students* (4th ed.). Harlow, UK: Pearson Education Limited.

Saxena, G. (2005). Relationships, networks and the learning regions: Case evidence from the Peak District National Park. *Tourism Management, 26*(2), 277–289. doi:10.1016/j.tourman.2003.11.013

Schalock, R. L. (1997). *Quality of life: Application to persons with disabilities*. Washington, DC: AAMR.

Scheyvens, R. (2002). *Tourism for Development: Empowering Communities*. Harlow: Pearson Education.

Schlumberger, C., & Weisskopf, N. (2014). *Ready for Takeoff? The Potential for Low-Cost Carriers in Developing Countries*. Washington, DC: World Bank Group. doi:10.1596/978-1-4648-0282-9

Schmitt, B. H. (1999). *Experiential Marketing*. New York: The Free Press.

Schul, P., & Crompton, J. L. (1983). Search behaviour of international vacationers: Travel-specific lifestyle and sociodemographic variables. *Journal of Travel Research, 22*(3), 25–31. doi:10.1177/004728758302200206

Schunk, D. H., & Pajares, M. F. (2002). The development of academic self-efficacy. In A. Wigfield & J. S. Eccles (Eds.), *Development of achievement motivation* (pp. 16–32). San Diego, CA: Academic Press. doi:10.1016/B978-012750053-9/50003-6

Schwer, K., & Daneshvary, R. (2000). Keeping up one's appearance: Its importance and the choice of type of hair-grooming establishment. *Journal of Economic Psychology, 21*(2), 207–222. doi:10.1016/S0167-4870(99)00043-4

Scott, W. R. (1995). *Institutions and organizations*. Thousand Oaks: Sage.

SE1 Media Ltd. (2015). *Key trends in online customer behaviour: Experience driven content strategies*. Retrieved January 25, 2015, from http://thinkdigital.travel/opinion/key-trends-in-online-customer-behaviour-experience-driven-content-strategies

Seaton, A. V. (1998). The history of tourism in Scotland: Approaches, sources and issues. *Tourism in Scotland, 1*(2), 35–41.

Sekaran, U. (2000). *Research Methods for Business: A Skill – Building Approach* (3rd ed.). New York: John Wiley & Sons Inc.

Shabani, N., & Hassan, A. (2015). *Innovative Technology Diffusion in Hospitality: Concept and Industry Perspective*. The 5th International Interdisciplinary Business-Economics Advancement Conference (IIBA). Available at: http://bit.ly/1BQqGnI

Shavinina, L. V. (2003). *The international handbook on innovation*. Oxford, UK: Elsevier Science Limited.

Shaw, G., Bailey, A., & Williams, A. (2011). Aspects of service-dominant logic and its implications for tourism management: Examples from the hotel industry. *Tourism Management, 32*(2), 207–214. doi:10.1016/j.tourman.2010.05.020

Shaw, G., & Williams, A. M. (2004). *Tourism and tourism spaces*. London, UK: SAGE.

Shelby-Biggs, B. (2000). *The Two faces of Leo*. The Envirolink Network.

Sheldon, P. J. (1991). An authorship analysis of tourism research. *Annals of Tourism Research, 18*(3), 473–484. doi:10.1016/0160-7383(91)90053-E

Sheldon, P., & Bushell, R. (2009). Introduction to wellness and tourism. In R. Bushell & P. J. Sheldon (Eds.), *Wellness and Tourism. Mind, Body, Spirit, Place* (pp. 3–18). New York: Cognizant Communication.

Sheldon, P., & Dwyer, L. (2010). The Global Financial Crisis and Tourism: Perspectives of the Academy. *Journal of Travel Research, 49*(3), 3–4. doi:10.1177/0047287509353191

Shen, Y., Ong, S. K., & Nee, A. Y. C. (2011). Vision-based hand interaction in augmented reality environment. *International Journal of Human-Computer Interaction, 27*(6), 523–544. doi:10.1080/10447318.2011.555297

Sieburgh, J., & Berkus, D. (2007). Social networking: Technology for a new generation. *Lodging Hospitality, 63*(5), 41.

Sigala, M. (2003). The information and communication technologies productivity impact on the UK hotel sector. *International Journal of Operations & Production Management, 23*(10), 1224–1245. doi:10.1108/01443570310496643

Sigala, M. (2004). Using data envelopment analysis for measuring and benchmarking productivity in the hotel sector. *Journal of Travel & Tourism Marketing, 16*(2-3), 39–60. doi:10.1300/J073v16n02_04

Sigala, M., Christou, E., & Gretzel, U. (2012). *Social media in travel, tourism and hospitality: Theory, practice and cases*. Ashgate Publishing, Ltd.

Sigala, M., Jones, P., Lockwood, A., & Airey, D. (2005). Productivity in hotels: A stepwise data envelopment analysis of hotels' rooms division processes. *Service Industries Journal, 25*(1), 61–81. doi:10.1080/0264206042000302414

Simon, S. J. (2001). The impact of culture and gender on web sites: An empirical study. *The Data Base for Advances in Information Systems, 32*(1), 18–37. doi:10.1145/506740.506744

Sinclair-Maragh, G., & Gursoy, D. (2015). Imperialism and tourism: The case of developing island countries. *Annals of Tourism Research, 50*, 143–158. doi:10.1016/j.annals.2014.12.001

Singh, A., & Schmidgall, R. S. (2002). Analysis of financial ratios commonly used by US lodging financial executives. *Journal of Retail & Leisure Property, 2*(3), 201–213. doi:10.1057/palgrave.rlp.5090210

Singhapakdi, A., Vitell, S. J., Rallapalli, K. C., & Kraft, K. L. (1996). The perceived role of Ethics and Social Responsibility: A scale development. *Journal of Business Ethics, 15*(11), 1131–1140. doi:10.1007/BF00412812

Sirdeshmukh, D., Singh, J., & Sabol, B. (2002). Consumer trust, value and loyalty in relational exchanges. *Journal of Marketing, 66*(1), 15–37. doi:10.1509/jmkg.66.1.15.18449

Sirgy, D. G., & Mangelburg, T. (2000). Retailing environment, self-congruity, and retail patronage:An integrative model and a research agenda. *Journal of Business Research, 49*, 127–138. doi:10.1016/S0148-2963(99)00009-0

Siu, Y-M. (1998). The Imbalance of Sexes in China: A Consequence of the 'One-Child' Policy?. In *China in the Post-Deng Era*. Hong Kong: The Chinese University Press.

Skalpe, O., & Sandvik, K. (2002). The economics of quality in the hotel business. *Tourism Economics, 8*(4), 361–376. doi:10.5367/000000002101298188

Slattery, P. (2002). Finding the hospitality Industry. *Journal of Hospitality, Leisure, Sport and Tourism Education, 1*(1), 19–28. doi:10.3794/johlste.11.7

Slaughter, R. (1995). *Future tools and techniques*. Melbourne: DDM.

Smeral, E. (2009). The Impact of the Financial and Economic Crisis on European Tourism. *Journal of Travel Research, 48*(1), 3–13. doi:10.1177/0047287509336332

Smeth, J. N., Allvine, F. C., Uslay, C., & Dixit, A. (2007). *Deregulation and Competition, Lessons from the Airline Industry*. Singapore: Sage Publications.

Smith, M., & Puczkó, L. (2013). Regional trends and predictions for global health tourism. In Wellness Tourism: A Destination Perspective. Abingdon, UK: Routledge.

Smith, M., & Puczkó, L. (2014). *Health Tourism and Hospitality: Spas, Wellness and Medical Travel*. Routledge.

Smith, M., & Puzckó, L. (2009). *Health and Wellness Tourism*. Oxford, UK: Butterworth-Heinemann.

Snepenger, D., Meged, K., Snelling, M., & Worrall, K. (1990). Information search strategies by destination-naive tourists. *Journal of Travel Research, 29*(1), 13–16. doi:10.1177/004728759002900104

Soares, R., Barkiewicz, M. J., Mulligan-Ferry, L., Fendler, E., & Wai Chun Jun, E. (2013). *2013 Catalyst Census: Fortune 2013 Women Executive Officers and Top Earners*. Retrieved September 18, 2015, from http://www.catalyst.org/knowledge/statistical-overview-women-workplace

Solmon, M. R., Surprenant, C. F., Czepiel, J. A., & Gutman, E. G. (1985). A role theory perspective on dyadic interactions:The service encounter. *Journal of Marketing, 51*, 86–96.

Sondergaard, M. (1990). Hofstede's consequences: A study of reviews, citations and replications. *Organization Studies, 15*(3), 447–456. doi:10.1177/017084069401500307

Song, H., Lin, S., Witt, S., & Zhang, X. (2010). Impact of Financial/Economic Crisis on Demand for Hotel Rooms in Hong Kong. *Tourism Management, 32*(1), 172–186. doi:10.1016/j.tourman.2010.05.006

Song, H., Wong, K., & Chon, K. (2003). Modeling and Forecasting the Demand for Hong Kong Tourism. *International Journal of Hospitality Management, 22*(4), 435–451. doi:10.1016/S0278-4319(03)00047-1

Sonmez, S., Apostolopoulos, Y., & Tarlow, P. (1999). Tourism in Crisis: Managing the Effects of Terrorism. *Journal of Travel Research, 38*(1), 13–18. doi:10.1177/004728759903800104

Soteriou, E. C., & Coccossis, H. (2010). Integrating sustainability into the strategic planning of national tourism organizations. *Journal of Travel Research, 49*(2), 191–205. doi:10.1177/0047287509336472

Soteriou, E. C., & Roberts, C. (1998). The strategic planning process in national tourism organizations. *Journal of Travel Research, 37*(1), 21–29. doi:10.1177/004728759803700103

Spanish Agency of International Cooperation for Development (AECID). (2012). *AECID (Spanish Agency of International Cooperation for Development) Development Partner Handover Report 2012* (Unpublished). Díli, East Timor.

Speiss, L., & Waring, P. (2005). Aesthetic labour, cost minimisation and the labour Process in the Asia Pacific Airline Industry. *Employee Relations, 27*(2), 193–207. doi:10.1108/01425450510572702

Srite, M., Thatcher, J. B., & Galy, E. (2008). Does within-culture variation matter? An empirical study of computer usage. *Journal of Global Information Management, 16*(1), 1–25. doi:10.4018/jgim.2008010101

Staats, A. W. (1981). Paradigmatic behaviorism, unified theory, unified theory construction methods, and the Zeitgeist of separatism. *The American Psychologist, 36*(3), 239–256. doi:10.1037/0003-066X.36.3.239

Stamboulis, Y., & Skayannis, P. (2003). Innovation strategies and technology for experience-based tourism. *Tourism Management, 24*(1), 35–43. doi:10.1016/S0261-5177(02)00047-X

Starr, F. (2013). *Corporate responsibility for cultural heritage: Conservation, sustainable development and corporate reputation*. Abingdon, United Kingdom: Routledge.

Steinbauer, A., & Werthner, H. (2007). Consumer Behaviour in e-Tourism. In M. Sigala, L. Mich, & J. Murphy (Eds.), *Information and Communication Technologies in Tourism 2007* (pp. 65–76). Vienna: Springer Vienna. doi:10.1007/978-3-211-69566-1_7

Steinbrink, M. (2012). We did the Slum! – Urban Poverty Tourism in Historical Perspective. *Tourism Geographies, 14*(2), 1–22. doi:10.1080/14616688.2012.633216

Stokburger-Sauer, N. E. (2011). The relevance of visitors' nation brand embeddedness and personality congruence for nation brand identification, visit intentions and advocacy. *Tourism Management, 32*(6), 1282–1289. doi:10.1016/j.tourman.2010.12.004

Stoltzfus, G., Nibbelink, B. L., Vredenburg, D., & Hyrum, E. (2011). Gender, Gender Role, and Creativity. *Social Behavior and Personality: An International Journal, 39*(3), 425–432. doi:10.2224/sbp.2011.39.3.425

Stone, P., & Sharpley, R. (2008). Consuming dark tourism: A thanatological perspective. *Annals of Tourism Research, 35*(2), 574–595. doi:10.1016/j.annals.2008.02.003

Straub, D. W. (1994). The effect of culture on IT diffusion: E-mail and fax in Japan and the US. *Information Systems Research, 5*(1), 23–47. doi:10.1287/isre.5.1.23

Stronza, A., & Gordillo, J. (2008). Community views of ecotourism. *Annals of Tourism Research, 35*(2), 448–468. doi:10.1016/j.annals.2008.01.002

Sugarman, D. B., & Frankel, S. L. (1996). Patriarchal ideology and wife-assault: A meta-analytic review. *Journal of Family Violence, 11*(1), 13–40. doi:10.1007/BF02333338

Sundbo, J., Orfila-Sintes, F., & Sorensen, F. (2007). The innovative behaviour of tourism firms: Comparative studies of Denmark and Spain. *Research Policy, 36*(1), 88–106. doi:10.1016/j.respol.2006.08.004

Suontausta, H., & Tyni, M. (2005). *Wellness-matkailu – hyvinvointi matkailun tuotekehityksessä.* Helsinki: Edita Prima Oy.

Svetasreni, S. (2009). *Tourism Management in a Critical Period. JATA World Tourism Congress.*

Swan, G. M. P. (2009). *The economics of innovation: an introduction.* Cheltenham, UK: Edward Elgar Publishing.

Swarbrooke, J. (1999). *Sustainable tourism management.* Wallingford, UK: CABI Pub.

Tabachnick, B. G., & Fidell, L. S. (2007). Using multivariate statistics (5th ed.). Needham Heights, MA: Allyn and Bacon.

Tahai, A., & Meyer, M. J. (1999). A revealed preference study of management journals' direct influences. *Strategic Management Journal, 20*(3), 279–296. doi:10.1002/(SICI)1097-0266(199903)20:3<279::AID-SMJ33>3.0.CO;2-2

Tang, C. F., & Tan, E. C. (2015). Does tourism effectively stimulate Malaysia's economic growth? *Tourism Management, 46*, 158–163. doi:10.1016/j.tourman.2014.06.020

Tangwisutijit, N., & Warunpitikul, Y. (2005). *Post-Tsunami Development – The lessons not learned.* Third World Network.

Tan, T. F., & Netessine, S. (2014). When Does the Devil Make Work? An Empirical Study of the Impact of Workload on Worker Productivity. *Management Science, 60*(6), 1574–1593. doi:10.1287/mnsc.2014.1950

Tas, R. E. (1988). Teaching future managers. *The Cornell Hotel and Restaurant Administration Quarterly, 29*(2), 41–43. doi:10.1177/001088048802900215

Taylor, P. A. (2006). Getting them to forgive and forget: Cognitive based marketing responses to terrorist acts. *International Journal of Tourism Research, 8*(3), 171–183. doi:10.1002/jtr.570

Testa, M. R., & Sipe, L. (2012). Service-leadership competencies for hospitality and tourism management. *International Journal of Hospitality Management, 31*(3), 648–658. doi:10.1016/j.ijhm.2011.08.009

Tews, J., & Merritt, S. (2007). *Independent travel website satisfaction study.* Retrieved March 15, 2015, from http://businesscenter.jdpower.com/news/pressrelease.aspx?ID=2007277

Teye, V., Sonmez, S., & Sirakaya, E. (2002). Residents' Attitudes toward Tourism Development. *Annals of Tourism Research, 29*(3), 668–688. doi:10.1016/S0160-7383(01)00074-3

Thakran, K., & Verma, R. (2013). The Emergence of Hybrid Online Distribution Channels in Travel, Tourism and Hospitality. *Cornell Hospitality Quarterly, 54*(3), 240–247. doi:10.1177/1938965513492107

The Nation. (2004). Tsunami Warning rejected to protect Tourism. *The Nation.*

The New Zealand Aid Programme. (2012). *New Zealand Aid Programme Development Partner Handover Report 2012* (Unpublished). Díli, East Timor.

The Phuket Gazette. (2006). Big Phi Phi Meeting makes small progress. *The Phuket Gazette.*

Thirkettle, A., & Korstanje, M. E. (2013). Creating a new epistemiology for tourism and hospitality disciplines. *International Journal of Qualitative Research in Services, 1*(1), 13–34. doi:10.1504/IJQRS.2013.054342

Thomaz, L. F. (2008). *Achegas para a compreensão de Timor-Leste.* Instituto Português do Oriente, Fundação Oriente.

Thompson, G. M. (1998a). Labor scheduling, part 1: Forecasting demand. *The Cornell Hotel and Restaurant Administration Quarterly, 39*(5), 22–31. doi:10.1177/001088049803900507

Thompson, G. M. (1998b). Labor scheduling, Part 2: Knowing how many on-duty employees to schedule. *The Cornell Hotel and Restaurant Administration Quarterly, 39*(6), 26–37. Retrieved from http://cqx.sagepub.com/content/39/6/26

Thompson, G. M. (1999a). Labor Scheduling, Part 3: Developing a workforce schedule. *The Cornell Hotel and Restaurant Administration Quarterly, 40*(1), 86–94. doi:10.1016/S0010-8804(99)80019-6

Thompson, G. M. (1999b). Labor Scheduling, Part 4: Controlling workforce schedules in real time. *The Cornell Hotel and Restaurant Administration Quarterly, 40*(3), 85–96.

Thompson, G. M., & Goodale, J. C. (2006). Variable employee productivity in workforce scheduling. *European Journal of Operational Research, 170*(2), 376–390. doi:10.1016/j.ejor.2004.03.048

Timmerman, J. E., & Lytle, R. S. (2007). Exercises in tourism empowerment practice. *International Journal of Culture. Tourism and Hospitality Research, 1*(4), 273.

Ting, D. H. (2004). Service quality and satisfaction perceptions: Curvilinear and interaction effect. *International Journal of Bank Marketing, 22*(6), 407–420. doi:10.1108/02652320410559330

Ting, P., Wang, S., Bau, D., & Chiang, M. (2013). Website Evaluation of the Top 100 Hotels Using Advanced Content Analysis and eMICA Model. *Cornell Hospitality Quarterly, 54*(3), 284–293. doi:10.1177/1938965512471892

Tolkach, D., & King, B. (2015). Strengthening community-based tourism in a new resource-based island nation: Why and how? *Tourism Management, 48*, 386–398. doi:10.1016/j.tourman.2014.12.013

Tolkach, D., King, B., & Pearlman, M. (2007). Prospects for the establishment of a community-based tourism network in Timor-Leste. In M. Lech, N. C. Mendes, A. B. Silva, B. Bougthon, & A. C. Ximenes (Eds.), *Peskiza foun konaba Timor-Leste* (pp. 302–307). Hawthorn: Swinburne Press.

Tompkins, N. C. (1993). Employee satisfaction leads to customer service-employee relations. *Human Resource Magazines, 37*(3), 93–97.

Topi, H., & Tucker, A. (Eds.). (2014). *Computing Handbook: Information Systems and Information Technology* (3rd ed.). Boca Raton, FL: Taylor & Francis Group.

Tourism of Galicia. (2014). *Plan Integral de Turismo de Galicia 2014-2016*. Retrieved January 15, 2015, from http://issuu.com/turismodegalicia/docs/pitg_detallado_2014_03_05

Towner, J. (1985). The Grand Tour: A key phase in the history of tourism. *Annals of Tourism Research, 12*(3), 297–333. doi:10.1016/0160-7383(85)90002-7

Towner, J., & Wall, G. (1991). History and tourism. *Annals of Tourism Research, 18*(1), 71–84. doi:10.1016/0160-7383(91)90040-I

Tracey, J. B., & Hinkin, T. R. (2008). Contextual factors and cost profiles associated with employee turnover. *Cornell Hospitality Quarterly, 49*(1), 12–27. doi:10.1177/0010880407310191

Trakolis, D. (2001). Local Peoples' Perceptions of Planning and Management Issues in Prespes Lakes National Park, Greece. *Journal of Environmental Management, 61*(3), 227–241. doi:10.1006/jema.2000.0410 PMID:11381950

Tretheway, M., & Mak, D. (2006). Emerging Tourism Markets: Ageing and Developing Economies. *Journal of Air Transport Management, 12*(1), 21–27. doi:10.1016/j.jairtraman.2005.09.008

Tribe, J. (1997a). The indiscipline of tourism. *Annals of Tourism Research, 24*(3), 638–657. doi:10.1016/S0160-7383(97)00020-0

Tribe, J. (2005). New tourism research. *Tourism Recreation Research, 30*(2), 5–8. doi:10.1080/02508281.2005.11081468

Tribe, J. (2006). The truth about tourism. *Annals of Tourism Research, 33*(2), 360–381. doi:10.1016/j.annals.2005.11.001

Tribe, J. (2007). Critical tourism: Rules and resistance. In I. Altejevic, A. Pritchard, & N. Morgan (Eds.), *The critical turn in tourism studies: Innovative research methodologies* (pp. 29–40). Oxford, UK: Elsevier. doi:10.1016/B978-0-08-045098-8.50007-6

Tribe, J. (2009). *Philosophical Issues in tourism.* Bristol: Channelview.

Tribe, J. (2010). *Strategy for tourism.* Oxford, United Kingdom: Goodfellow Publishers.

Tribe, J. (2010). Tribes, territories and networks in the tourism academy. *Annals of Tourism Research, 37*(1), 7–33. doi:10.1016/j.annals.2009.05.001

Tsai, C., & Chen, C. (2010). An earthquake disaster management mechanism based on risk assessment information for the tourism industry-a case study from the island of Taiwan. *Tourism Management, 31*(4), 470–481. doi:10.1016/j.tourman.2009.05.008

Tsai, C.-W., & Lin, T. H. (2008). Would service employee's physical attractiveness affect service attitude consumer perceived and consumers' primary purchase intentions? -Empirical evidence from hotel industry.*14th Annual Asia Pacific Tourism Association Conference*, Bangkok.

Tsang, N. K. F., & Hsu, C. H. C. (2011). Thirty years of research on tourism and hospitality management in China: A review and analysis of journal publications. *International Journal of Hospitality Management, 30*(4), 886–896. doi:10.1016/j.ijhm.2011.01.009

Tseng, H., Duan, C., Tung, H., & Kung, H. (2010). Modern business ethics research: Concepts, theories, and relationships. *Journal of Business Ethics, 91*(4), 587–597. doi:10.1007/s10551-009-0133-x

Tucker, H. (2007). Undoing Shame: Tourism and Women's Work in Turkey. *Journal of Tourism and Cultural Change, 5*(2), 87–105. doi:10.2167/jtcc089.0

Turban, E., McLean, E. R., & Wetherbe, J. C. (2008). *Information technology for management.* John Wiley and sons, Inc.

Turner, B. L., Kasperson, R. E., Matson, P. A., Mccarthy, J. J., Corell, R. W., Christensen, L., & Schiller, A. et al. (2003). A framework for vulnerability analysis in sustainability science. *Proceedings of the National Academy of Sciences of the United States of America, 100*(14), 8074–8079. doi:10.1073/pnas.1231335100 PMID:12792023

Tveteraas, S., Roll, K. H., Jørgensen, H., & Tveterås, R. (2015). *Workload Management and Staff Performance in the Hospitality Sector.* Paper presented at the Nordic Symposium of Tourism and Hospitality, Reykjavik, Iceland.

Tveteraas, S., Asche, F., & Lien, K. (2014). European tour operators' market power when renting hotel rooms in Northern Norway. *Tourism Economics, 20*(3), 579–594. doi:10.5367/te.2013.0291

Tynan, C., & McKechnie, S. (2009). Experience marketing: A review and reassessment. *Journal of Marketing Management, 25*(5-6), 501–517. doi:10.1362/026725709X461821

Tzanelli, R. (2007). *The cinematic tourist: Explorations in globalization, culture and resistance.* Abingdon, UK: Routledge.

UNDP, World Bank, & FAO. (2005). *Joint Tsunami Disaster Assessment Mission.* Ft. Belvoir: Livelihood Recovery and Environmental Rehabilitation.

Un-Habitat. (2013). *Streets as Public Spaces and Drivers of Urban Prosperity*. Available at: http://mirror.unhabitat.org

United Nations World Food Programme (WFP). (2012). *United Nations World Food Program Development Partner Handover Report 2012* (Unpublished). Díli, East Timor.

United Nations World Tourism Organization. (2012). *Global Report on Aviation: Responding to the needs of new tourism markets and destinations*. Madrid: UNWTO.

United Nations World Tourism Organization. (2015). *UNWTO Tourism Highlights 2015 Edition*. Madrid: UNWTO.

United States Agency for International Development (USAID). (2012). *The US Mission Development Partner Handover Report 2012* (Unpublished). Díli, East Timor.

Uriely, N. (2005). The tourist experience. Conceptual developments. *Annals of Tourism Research, 32*(1), 199–216. doi:10.1016/j.annals.2004.07.008

Urry, J. (1988). Cultural change and contemporary holiday-making. *Theory, Culture & Society, 5*(1), 35–55. doi:10.1177/026327688005001003

Urry, J. (2002). *The Tourist Gaze*. London: Sage Publications.

Urry, J. (2007). *Mobilities*. Cambridge, MA: Polity Press.

Van Esterik, P. (2000). *Materialising. Thailand*. Oxford, UK: Berg.

Varey, R. J. (2013). Marketing in the flourishing society megatrend. *Journal of Macromarketing, 33*(4), 354–368. doi:10.1177/0276146713489150

Vargas-Sánchez, A., & Riquel-Ligero, F. (2015). Golf tourism, its institutional setting, and environmental management: A longitudinal analysis. *European Journal of Tourism Research, 9*, 41–56.

Vargo, S. L., & Lusch, R. F. (2004). Evolving to a new dominant logic for marketing. *Journal of Marketing, 68*(1), 1–17. doi:10.1509/jmkg.68.1.1.24036

Vargo, S. L., & Lusch, R. F. (2008). Service-dominant logic: Continuing the evolution. *Journal of the Academy of Marketing Science, 36*(1), 1–10. doi:10.1007/s11747-007-0069-6

Varki, S., & Colgate, M. (2001). The role of price perceptions in an integrated model of behavioral intentions. *Journal of Service Research, 3*(3), 232–240. doi:10.1177/109467050133004

Vela Sastre, E. (1977). El balance social de la empresa. *Economía Industrial, 168*, 4–25.

Verdu Jover, A. J. (2002). *Relación entre flexibilidad y desempeño organizativo: una aproximación desde la perspectiva de la gestión de la calidad total*. Alicante: Universidad Miguel Hernández.

Verge, T., & de la Fuente, M. (2014). Playing with different cards: Party politics, gender quotas and women's empowerment. *International Political Science Review, 35*(1), 67–79. doi:10.1177/0192512113508295

Verma, R., Stock, D., & McCarthy, L. (2012). Customer preferences for online, social media, and mobile innovations in the hospitality Industry. *Cornell Hospitality Quarterly, 53*(2), 183–186. doi:10.1177/1938965512445161

Vickers, A. (2012). *Bali: a paradise created*. Singapore: Tuttle.

Villarreal, E. (2009). Capitalizing on Disaster: Taking and Breaking Public Schools - By Kenneth J. Saltman. *Anthropology & Education Quarterly, 40*(4), 438–439. doi:10.1111/j.1548-1492.2009.01059.x

Villiers, C. (1989). Boiled Frog Syndrome. *Management Today*, 121-124.

Virilio, P. (2006). Velocidad y política: Ensayo sobre dromología [Speed and politics: An essay on dromology]. Los Angeles, CA: Semiotext (e).

Vitell, S. J., Ramos, E., & Nishihara, C. M. (2010). The Role of Ethics and Social Responsibility in Organizational Success: A Spanish Perspective. *Journal of Business Ethics*, *91*(4), 467–483. doi:10.1007/s10551-009-0134-9

Vithessonthi, C., & Schwaninger, M. (2008). Job motivation and self-confidence for learning and Development as predictors of support for change. *Journal of Organizational Transformation and Social Change*, *5*(2), 141–157. doi:10.1386/jots.5.2.141_1

Voelpel, S. C., Leibold, M., & Eckhoff, R. A. (2006). The tyranny of the balanced scorecard in the innovation economy. *Journal of Intellectual Capital*, *7*(1), 43–60. doi:10.1108/14691930610639769

Vogt, C. A., & Fesenmaier, D. R. (1998). Expanding the functional information search model. *Annals of Tourism Research*, *25*(3), 551–578. doi:10.1016/S0160-7383(98)00010-3

Voigt, C., & Pforr, C. (Eds.). (2013). *Wellness tourism. A destination perspective*. Abingdon, UK: Routledge.

Von Berqen. (2006). College reaching out to firms: Community College of Phila. launches an effort to build partnerships with the business community, knight ridder tribune business news. Washington.

von Groddeck, V., & Schwarz, J. O. (2013). Perceiving megatrends as empty signifiers: A discourse-theoretical interpretation of trend management. *Futures*, *47*, 28–37. doi:10.1016/j.futures.2013.01.004

Vuylsteke, A., Wen, Z., Baesens, B., & Poelmans, J. (2009). *Consumers' Online Information Search: A Cross-Cultural Study between China and Western Europe*. Retrieved April 28, 2015, from http://www.aabri.com/OC09manuscripts/OC09043.pdf

Vyncke, F., & Brengman, M. (2010). Are culturally congruent websites more effective? An overview of a decade of empirical evidence. *Journal of Electronic Commerce Research*, *11*, 14–29.

Walle, A. H. (1997). Quantitative versus qualitative tourism research. *Annals of Tourism Research*, *24*(3), 524–536. doi:10.1016/S0160-7383(96)00055-2

Wan, C. S. (2002). The web sites of international tourist hotels and tour wholesalers in Taiwan. *Tourism Management*, *23*(2), 155–160. doi:10.1016/S0261-5177(01)00048-6

Wang, L-L. (2001). *Professional competencies required for food and beverage employees working front of the house in international tourist hotel*. National Taiwan Normal University Graduate Institute of Department of Human Development and Family Studies.

Wang, C. H. (2005). Constructing multivariate process capability indices for short-run production. *International Journal of Advanced Manufacturing Technology*, *26*(11-12), 1306–1311. doi:10.1007/s00170-004-2397-8

Wang, D., Niu, Y., Lu, L., & Qian, J. (2015). Tourism spatial organization of historical streets: A postmodern perspective: The examples of Pingjiang Road and Shantang Street, Suzhou, China. *Tourism Management*, *48*, 370–385. doi:10.1016/j.tourman.2014.12.007

Wang, J., & Ritchie, B. W. (2012). Understanding accommodation managers' crisis planning intention: An application of the theory of planned behaviour. *Tourism Management*, *33*(5), 1057–1067. doi:10.1016/j.tourman.2011.12.006

Wang, L., Law, R., Hung, K., & Guillet, B. D. (2014). Consumer trust in tourism and hospitality: A review of the literature. *Journal of Hospitality and Tourism Management*, *21*, 1–9. doi:10.1016/j.jhtm.2014.01.001

Wang, S., & Xu, H. (2015). Influence of place-based senses of distinctiveness, continuity, self-esteem and self-efficacy on residents' attitudes toward tourism. *Tourism Management, 47*, 241–250. doi:10.1016/j.tourman.2014.10.007

Wang, Y. (2009). The Impact of Crisis Events and Macroeconomic Activity on Taiwan's International Inbound Tourism Demand. *Tourism Management, 30*(1), 75–82. doi:10.1016/j.tourman.2008.04.010

Wang, Y. C., & Fesenmaier, D. R. (2006). Identifying the success factors of Web-based marketing strategy: An investigation of convention and visitors bureaus in the United States. *Journal of Travel Research, 44*(3), 239–249. doi:10.1177/0047287505279007

Warhurst, C., & Nickson, D. (2001). *Looking Good, Sounding Right: Style Counselling in the New Economy*. London: The Industrial Society.

Warhurst, C., & Nickson, D. (2007). Employee experience of aesthetic labour in retail and hospitality. *Work, Employment and Society, 21*(1), 103–120. doi:10.1177/0950017007073622

Warhurst, C., Nicoson, D., Witz, A., & Cullen, A. M. (2000). Aesthetic labour in interactive service work: Some case study evidence from the new glasgow. *Service Industries Journal, 20*(3), 1–18. doi:10.1080/02642060000000029

Watchravesringkan, K., Yan, R., & Yurchisin, J. (2008). Cross-cultural invariance of consumers' price perception measures: Eastern Asian perspective. *International Journal of Retail & Distribution Management, 36*(10), 759–779. doi:10.1108/09590550810900982

Watkins, L. M., & Johnston, L. (2000). Screening job applicants: The impact of physical attractiveness and application quality. *International Journal of Selection and Assessment, 8*(1), 76–84. doi:10.1111/1468-2389.00135

Weaver, D., & Lawton, L. (2014). *Tourism Management* (5th ed.). Queensland: Wiley.

Wei, R., & Su, J. (2012). The statistics of English in China: An analysis of the best available data from government sources. *English Today, 28*(3), 10–14. doi:10.1017/S0266078412000235

Wen-Jeng, L. (2001). Manufacturing human resources professional functions. *Sun Yat-Sen Management Review, 9*(4), 621–654.

Werthner, H., & Klein, S. (1999). *Information technology and tourism - a challenging relationship*. Vienna: Springer-Verlag. doi:10.1007/978-3-7091-6363-4

Whittington, R., & Cailluet, L. (2008). The craft of strategy. *Long Range Planning, 41*(3), 241–247. doi:10.1016/j.lrp.2008.03.003

Whyte, K. P., Selinger, E., & Outterson, K. (2011). Poverty tourism and the problem of consent. *Journal of Global Ethics, 7*(3), 337–348. doi:10.1080/17449626.2011.635689

Wickens, E. (2002). The sacred and profane: A tourist typology. *Annals of Tourism Research, 29*(4), 834–851. doi:10.1016/S0160-7383(01)00088-3

Williams, S. (2015). *China Inbound: how to prepare for Chinese guests*. Retrieved April 16, 2015, from http://www.hoteliermiddleeast.com/23481-china-inbound-how-to-prepare-for-chinese-guests/1/print

Williams, A. M., & Shaw, G. (2011). Internationalization and innovation in tourism. *Annals of Tourism Research, 38*(1), 27–51. doi:10.1016/j.annals.2010.09.006

Williams, C. (2008). Ghettourism and Voyeurism, or challenging stereotypes and raising consciousness? Literary and non-literary forays into the favelas of Rio de Janeiro. *Bulletin of Latin American Research, 27*(4), 483–500. doi:10.1111/j.1470-9856.2008.00280.x

Williams, S., & Lew, A. A. (2014). *Tourism Geography: Critical Understandings of Place, Space and Experience.* Abingdon, UK: Routledge.

Willis, K., & Dawson, B. (2011). *Theories and practices of development.* London: Routledge.

Witz, A., Warhurst, C., & Nickson, D. (2003). The labour of aesthetics and the aesthetics of organization. *Organization, 10*(1), 33–54. doi:10.1177/1350508403010001375

Wong, Y. (2012). Influences on Chinese online buying behaviour and decision making: The case of online booking for tourism products. *The International Hospitality and Tourism Student Journal, 4*(2), 135–145.

Wood, W., & Stagner, B. (1994). Why are some people easier to influence than others? *Psychological insights and perspectives*, 149-174.

Woodside & Davenport. (1994). Linking Service Quality, Customer Satisfaction and Behavioral Intention. *Journal of Health Care Marketing, 9*(1), 5–17. PMID:10304174

Woods, M. (2005). *Rural geography.* New York, NY: Sage Publications.

Wood, W., & Eagly, A. H. (2010). Gender. In *Handbook of Social Psychology* (5th ed.; pp. 629–667). New York, NY: Oxford University Press. doi:10.1002/9780470561119.socpsy001017

World Economic Forum. (2013). *The Travel and Tourism Competitiveness Report 2013.* Geneva: World Economic Forum.

Wubneh, M. A. (1987). Multivariate analysis of socio-economic characteristics of urban areas in Ethiopia. *Afr. Urban Quaterly, 2*, 425–433.

Wu, M. L. (2007). *SPSS & the Application and Analysis of Statistics.* Taipei: Wu-Nan Book Inc.

Wynne, C., Berthon, P., Pitt, L., Ewing, M., & Napoli, J. (2001). The impact of the Internet on the distribution value chain- the case of the South African tourism industry. *International Marketing Review, 18*(4), 420–431. doi:10.1108/EUM0000000005934

Xiang, Z., & Gretzel, U. (2010). Role of social media in online travel information search. *Tourism Management, 31*(2), 179–188. doi:10.1016/j.tourman.2009.02.016

Yang, S.-C. (2002). *The Effect of Physical Attractiveness on Self-Evaluation-Concerning with the Effect of Moderation of Similarity and Self-Aspects.* (Unpublished master's thesis). Chung Yuan Christian University, Taoyuan City.

Yang, C. C. (2004). Exploring factors affecting the adoption of mobile commerce in Singapore. *Telematics and Informatics, 22*(3), 257–277. doi:10.1016/j.tele.2004.11.003

Yao, D.-X. (2001). *Development and Planning for Hotel Industry 3*^{d}. Taipei: Yang-chih Book.

Yasarata, M., Altinay, L., Burns, P., & Okumus, F. (2010). Politics and sustainable tourism development: Can they co-exist? Voices from North Cyprus. *Tourism Management, 31*(3), 345–356. doi:10.1016/j.tourman.2009.03.016

Ye, Q., Law, R., Gu, B., & Chen, W. (2011). The influence of user-generated content on traveller behaviour: An empirical investigation on the effects of e-word-of-mouth to hotel online bookings. *Computers in Human Behavior, 27*(2), 634–639. doi:10.1016/j.chb.2010.04.014

Yin, R. K. (2012). *Applications of Case Study Research.* Thousand Oaks, CA: SAGE Publication.

Yin, R. K. (2009). *Case study research. Design and methods.* Thousand Oaks, CA: SAGE.

Yoon, M. H., Beatty, S. E., & Suh, J. (2001). The effect of work climate on critical employee and customer outcomes: An employee-level analysis. *International Journal of Service Industry Management, 12*(5), 500–521. doi:10.1108/EUM0000000006095

Yovcheva, Z., Buhalis, D., & Gatzidis, C. (2012). Smartphone augmented reality applications for tourism. *e-Review of Tourism Research, 10*(2), 63-66.

Yu, C.-S., & Tao, Y. H. (2009). Understanding business-level innovation technology adoption. *Technovation, 29*(2), 92–109. doi:10.1016/j.technovation.2008.07.007

Zamudio & Lichter. (2008). Bad attitudes and good soldiers: Soft skills as a code for tractability in the hiring of immigrant latina/os over native blacks in the hotel industry. *Social Problems, 11*, 573.

Zanfardini, M., Aguirre, P., & Tamagni, L. (2015). *The evolution of CSR's research in tourism context: A review from 1992 to 2012.* Anatolia; doi:10.1080/13032917.2015.1083207

Zhang, W. (2009). *The Motivations, Constraints and Decision Making of Beijing Outbound Tourism.* Hamilton, New Zealand: University of Waikato.

Zhao, H., Seibert, S. E., & Hills, G. E. (2005). The Mediating Role of Self-Efficacy in the Development of Entrepreneurial Intentions. *The Journal of Applied Psychology, 90*(6), 1265–1272. doi:10.1037/0021-9010.90.6.1265 PMID:16316279

Zhong, Y. G., & Couch, S. (2007). Hospitality Students' Perceptions of Facilitators and Constraints Affecting Women's Career Advancement in the Hospitality Industry. *Family and Consumer Sciences Research Journal, 35*(4), 357–373. doi:10.1177/1077727X07299993

Zhou, M. (2014). Gender difference in web search perceptions and behaviour: Does it vary by task performance? *Computers & Education, 78*(1), 174–185. doi:10.1016/j.compedu.2014.06.005

Zillifro, T., & Morais, D. B. (2004). Building customer trust and relationship commitment to a nature-based tourism provider: The role of information investments. *Journal of Hospitality & Leisure Marketing, 11*(2/3), 159–172. doi:10.1300/J150v11n02_11

Zizek, S. (2004). *L'epidemia dell'immaginario.* Roma: Meltemi.

About the Contributors

Nikolaos Pappas is currently an associate professor in aviation and tourism at the University of West London. He holds a doctorate (PhD) in tourism development and planning, and a post-doctorate (PDoc) in risk and crisis management, both from the University of Aegean, Greece. His professional engagement with tourism and hospitality industry has started in 1990. Since 2001 he works as an academic in Greece and United Kingdom. From 1998 and on he has been involved in a series of internationally funded research projects, and he has more than 40 publications in internationally recognised scientific journals and conferences. He is also a reviewer in several esteemed journals of the field such as Annals of Tourism Research, Tourism Management, Journal of Sustainable Tourism, International Journal of Contemporary Hospitality Management, and Current Issues in Tourism. His research interests and publication activity mainly include tourism development and planning, crisis management, hospitality management, and destination marketing.

Ilenia Bregoli is a Senior Lecturer in Marketing at the Lincoln Business School (UK). She was awarded her PhD at the Catholic University of Milan (Italy). Her research is focused on destination branding; destination governance; experiential marketing in multi-stakeholder environments; and wine tourism. She has published in the Journal of Travel Research, Tourism Analysis and the International Journal of Tourism Research.

* * *

Thiago Allis is a Full Lecturer at University of São Paulo (USP), full lecturer at São Carlos Federal University (UFSCar), Brazil (2008-2015), and visiting lecturer at Timor Lorosa'e National University. PhD in Regional and Urban Planning (2012), University of São Paulo (USP), Brazil, Master in Latin American Integration (2006), University of São Paulo (USP), Brazil. Research interests: Tourism (territorial and cultural issues), urban tourism, post-conflict tourism, urban mobility and transportation.

Alexandros Apostolakis is an assistant professor in Tourism Marketing at the Department of Business Administration, School of Management and Economics, Technological Educational Institute of Crete. He is also a visiting research fellow at the University of Portsmouth, UK, and an affiliate lecturer at the Greek Open University. Alexandros graduated with a bachelor's degree (BSc) in Economics with Politics from the University of Plymouth, UK in 1999. He carried on with a postgraduate degree (MSc) in Local and Regional Economic Analysis from the University of Portsmouth, UK in 2000 and a PhD degree from the same University in 2005. His thesis examined individual tourists' preferences for two cultural resources in the island of Crete, Greece. Alexandros's research interests and publication activity mainly focuses on the tourism industry (the examination of individual preferences through stated preferences discrete choice modelling) and comprises of over 30 contributions to textbooks and peer – reviewed academic journals. In particular, Dr Apostolakis has been conducting research on the evaluation of individual preferences for future policy initiatives in hospitality, tourism and the cultural sector. Alexandros acts as associate editor in the Anatolia Journal, and the Regional Science Enquiry Journal. At the same time, he acts as guest editor and reviewer for all mainstream high impact peer review journals in the tourism field (Annals of Tourism Research, Tourism Management, Tourism Economics, Journal of Travel Research and others).

Pavlos Arvanitis is Senior Lecturer in Tourism and Air Travel at Southampton Solent University, UK. His research interests focus on tourism and air transport, regional tourism development and airport development as a means of tourism development. His work has been published at international peer reviewed journals and presented at numerous conferences.

Fiona Eva Bakas is an emerging tourism researcher, with a PhD Tourism and Gender from Otago University, NZ and an MSc Ecotourism from Portsmouth University, UK. She is currently a Postdoctoral Research Fellow at Aveiro University, Portugal, and a member of the Research Unit in Governance, Competitiveness and Pubic Policies (GOVCOPP), investigating the role of gender equality in boosting innovative forms of economic growth in tourism. Taking an interest in tourism also outside academic settings she has become an associate of NGO Equality in Tourism. Fiona´s research interests are gender, work, tourism, sustainability, handicrafts, entrepreneurship and feminist economics.

Maria Helena Mattos Barbosa dos Santos is a Full Lecturer at São Carlos Federal University (UFSCar), Brazil since 2007, and visiting lecturer at Timor Lorosa'e National University (2012), East Timor. PhD in History and Fundamentals of Architecture and Urbanism (2015), São Paulo University (USP), Brazil, Master in Hospitality and Tourism (2006), Vale do Itajaí University (UNIVALI). Research interests: Tourism (leisure and cultural issues), urban and cultural tourism, politics and policies of tourism and heritage preservation, post-conflict tourism, urban anthropology.

Zélia Breda holds a PhD in Tourism, a MA in Chinese Studies (Business and International Relations) and a BSc in Tourism Management and Planning from the University of Aveiro, where she is Assistant Professor and Director of the MA in Tourism Management and Planning. She is an integrated member of the Research Unit 'Governance, Competitiveness and Public Policies', and a founding member and vice-president of the Observatory of China and the Portuguese Institute of Sinology. She is also member of the editorial and scientific boards of a few academic national and international journals, as well member of the organizing and scientific committees of international tourism conferences. She has authored and co-authored several national and international papers and communications on tourism development, networks, tourism in China and Goa (India), gender and tourism, and internationalisation of the tourism economy. She has also been taking part of several research projects in the tourism field, both as member of the team and as consultant.

Carlos Costa is a Full Professor and Head of the Department of Economics, Management, Industrial Engineering and Tourism at the University of Aveiro (Portugal). He holds a PhD and MSc in Tourism

Management (University of Surrey, UK), and a BSc in Urban and Regional Planning (University of Aveiro, Portugal) and is an integrated member of Research Unit GOVCOPP. He is editor of the Journal of Tourism & Development (Revista de Turismo e Desenvolvimento). Carlos is the leader of the Tourism Research Unit and of the PhD Tourism Programme at the University of Aveiro. He is Scientific Coordinator of "idtour-unique solutions" (a tourism spin-off company of the University of Aveiro) and is involved in a number of national and international tourism projects.

Marília Durão is a Research Fellow at the University of Aveiro, Portugal, and has been granted a Doctoral scholarship by the Portuguese Foundation for Science and Technology (FCT). She holds a Masters degree in Tourism Planning and Management from the University of Aveiro where she is currently a PhD candidate in the Tourism Doctoral Program. Her PhD thesis is devoted to employee turnover, well-being at work and job burnout in the tourism industry. Over the past few years she has been actively involved in several research projects whose topics are closely related to her research interests and publications, namely development and management of tourism destinations, socio-economic impact assessment, human resources management, employment and gender equality in the tourism sector. She is also member of the Research Unit in Governance, Competitiveness and Pubic Policies (GOVCOPP) within the Tourism and Development Group.

Marina Efthymiou is Lecturer in Aviation and Tourism at University of West London. Previously she was working at the European Organisation for the Safety of Air Navigation, EUROCONTROL. Her research interests focus on Performance Indicators in Air Traffic Management, Airport Planning and Development, as. well as Transport and Tourism Policy

Azizul Hassan is a PhD candidate at the Cardiff Metropolitan University, UK and a member of the Tourism Consultants Network of the Tourism Society, UK. His main areas of research interest are technology supported marketing in tourism, innovative marketing dynamics, destination branding in tourism, cultural heritage tourism, heritage interpretation and sustainable management/marketing alternatives for cultural heritage industries.

Anne-Mette Hjalager is Professor at University of Southern Denmark. She works with innovation issues, and she is interested in rural and regional development issues in particular. She edits the Journal of Gastronomy and Tourism.

Christian Kahl received his PhD at FSU Jena in Germany where he concentrates his study as well his research on international teaching and learning methods, cultural education and education history. Over the last ten years he lived in China and Malaysia where he widespread his research interest on cultural differences in teaching and learning. Currently he is working as a senior lecturer at the Graduate School of Hospitality and Tourism Management at Taylor's University in Malaysia and teaches Intercultural Management as well provides teaching training in and outside of the university. In 2013 he gave training to the Westin Hotel Management on how to work with Generation Y graduates, to support the hotel philosophy of harmonious working culture. In 2014 he received several best paper awards for his research on cultural understanding and cultural management of Generation Y youth in today's society.

Kijpokin Kasemsap received his BEng degree in Mechanical Engineering from King Mongkut's University of Technology Thonburi, his MBA degree from Ramkhamhaeng University, and his DBA degree in Human Resource Management from Suan Sunandha Rajabhat University. He is a Special Lecturer at Faculty of Management Sciences, Suan Sunandha Rajabhat University based in Bangkok, Thailand. He is a Member of International Association of Engineers (IAENG), International Association of Engineers and Scientists (IAEST), International Economics Development and Research Center (IEDRC), International Association of Computer Science and Information Technology (IACSIT), International Foundation for Research and Development (IFRD), and International Innovative Scientific and Research Organization (IISRO). He also serves on the International Advisory Committee (IAC) for International Association of Academicians and Researchers (INAAR). He has numerous original research articles in top international journals, conference proceedings, and book chapters on business management, human resource management, and knowledge management published internationally.

Henna Konu, Lic.Sc. (Econ. and B.A.) is Project manager/Researcher at the University of Eastern Finland, Centre for Tourism Studies and she has worked in various national and international tourism research and development projects. Her research interests are in service development, customer involvement, consumer/tourist experiences, experiential services, and wellbeing and nature tourism. She is currently writing her doctoral dissertation on the customer involvement in experiential tourism service development. She is also a substitute member of Management Committee of COST action IS1204 Tourism, Wellbeing and Ecosystem Services. Her publications include articles in several scientific journals and she has also co-authored several book chapters in international edited books in tourism field.

Maximiliano Emanuel Korstanje is an associate professor at University of Palermo, Argentina. Editor in Chief of the International Journal of Safety and Security in Tourism. With more than 650 published papers in peer review journals, Korstanje is concerned in the study of risk, capitalism and mobility. He co-edits 10 journals, and takes part of editorial board list of other 25 specialized journals. From 2010 his biography is a point of entry in Marquis Who´s Who in the World. He was awarded as Outstading reviewer 2012/2013 for Emerald Group Publishing, UK. Because his contribution to the sociology of tourism, Korstanje has been nominated to three honorary doctorates.

Elina (Eleni) Michopoulou is a Senior Lecturer in Business Management at University of Derby. She teaches on subjects relating to the management and marketing of Tourism, Hospitality, Events and Spa industries. She holds a PhD in Accessible Tourism Information Systems from University of Surrey, UK. Her research interests include technological applications and information systems in tourism, online consumer behaviour and technology acceptance.

Delia G. Moisa is a former student from the University of Derby, where she obtained a degree in Travel and Tourism Management. Her working experience in the Chinese tourism and hospitality industry, alongside her passion for cultures and technology are the factors which motivated her to research the travellers' behaviour in the online environment.

Lourdes Cisneros Mustelier is Dean of the National University of La Habana, Cuba. She has gained great traction in cultural studies of tourism and hospitality worldwide. Now, with countless publications, Lourdes serves as a Dean of Tourism Department in the National University of la Habana, Cuba.

Andreas Papatheodorou is the Dean of the London College of Hospitality and Tourism at the University of West London. Previously he was an Associate Professor at the University of the Aegean and the Director of the Laboratory for Tourism Research and Studies at the same university. An Oxford MPhil and DPhil graduate, Professor Papatheodorou has published extensively in the areas of air transport and tourism; he has been involved in a large number of research and consulting projects.

Isabel Pinho has a PhD in Management from University of Aveiro, Portugal and a Post-doctorate in Higher Education from Federal University of Rio Grande do Sul, Brazil. Expert in Knowledge Management, Data Management and Research Evaluation. Has a MSc in Information Management and a MSc in Public Management from University of Aveiro, Portugal. Reviewer: Studies in Higher Education (Dorchester-on-Thames)-Web of Science Member of Latin American Studies Association, University of Pittsburgh Member of GOVCOPP - Governance, Competitiveness and Public Policies.

Donatella Privitera is an Associate Professor of economic geography at University of Catania, Italy, with a M.S. Degree in Agri-Business from the Catholic University of Milan. Prior to becoming a full-time academic, she has had experience working in a multinational company (Kraft General Food, Italy) in marketing. She has taught the economy of landscape and marketing of agricultural products for the Faculty of Agriculture at University Mediterranea, Reggio Calabria. She is currently teaching economic geography with a speciality in tourism and regional development. She is a member of Italian Geographic Society (SGI), Society Italian of Agricultural Economists (SIDEA). She is a member of Lab ReTMES Research for Mediteranean entrepreneurship and startups and of International Advisory Board of International Journal of Sustainable Economies Management. She has presented paper at several conferences, published in international books and mainly associated with her research in the following areas: economic and tourism geography; sustainable cities; information and communication technologies with rural development; green economy; regional planning and its implications for tourism. She has participated in EU project HERODOT- INTERREG IIIB and she is participating in cooperative national research projects. She is a nominated expert for the Calabria and Sicily to manage projects involving university-industry knowledge transfer.

Roya Rahimi completed her PhD in Tourism and Hospitality Management at 2013 and joined University of Wolverhampton, Business School as lecturer in September 2014 where she teaches across tourism, hospitality, leisure and events subject areas. While undertaking her PhD studies, she was a Research Assistant at Management Department of Izmir University (2009-2010) and, in broadening her knowledge and academic experience; she became a PhD visiting Scholar at University of Wolverhampton (2010-2011). From February 2013 to August 2014, Roya worked as a Visiting Lecturer in Hospitality Management at University of Sunderland. Her research interests are Customer Relationship Management (CRM), Organisational Culture and Human Resource Management in Hospitality Industry. She has expertise in Quantitative Research Methods and her work has been presented at various international conferences and has been published in a variety of journals and books. Her industry experience includes seven years of experience working in the hotel industry in number of international hotels in various countries. She is acting as the director of Visiting Scholar Scheme at University of Wolverhampton.

María Dolores Sánchez-Fernández is a PhD "Competitiveness, Innovation and Development" and a Lecturer at the University of A Coruña (Spain), Faculty of Economics and Business, Department of

Analysis and Business Management, Business Organization area. She is also part of the GREFIN (University of A Coruña) and GEIDETUR (University of Huelva) research groups and associate researcher at the Centre of CICS research at the University of Minho. Member of the Development of Business and Social Responsibility Association (ADRES). She has been the author or co-author of several articles published in indexed journals. She has participated in over 100 communications in national and international conferences and is a member of the scientific committee. She reviews international scientific magazines in Spain, United States and Brazil. Her main research topics are: Corporate Social Responsibility, quality, tourism, the hotel industry and human resources.

Faye Taylor is a Lecturer in Marketing within the Nottingham Business School of Nottingham Trent University, UK. Her PhD concerned the influence of political economy and interpretations of sustainability upon the post disaster tourism redevelopment of Koh Phi Phi Island, Thailand. Her current research interests lie in the political economy and ethics of tourism development.

Kaarina Tervo-Kankare is a tourism geographer working in Finland. Her previous research has dealt with rural and peripheral tourism, nature-based tourism, climate change and adaptation, and sustainable tourism.

Chien-Wen Tsai is an associate professor at Chinese Culture University in Taiwan. Her research interests are human resource management, marketing management, organization behavior and issues about ethics.

Anja Tuohino has worked in various research and development projects as a researcher and project manager at the University of Eastern Finland (until 12.2009 University of Joensuu). Currently she is development manager at the Center for Tourism Studies at the University of Eastern Finland. She has over 10 years experience in national and international project activities. Before her academic career she worked for more than 15 years in business sector in various administrative positions. She holds PhD degree in Geography, with majors in human geography and tourism and minor studies in EU studies, sociology and business studies. Her research interests are in lake tourism development, wellness and well-being tourism and in innovation policy. She is a member of Management Committee of COST IS1204 Tourism, Well-being and Ecosystem Services. She has also published various academic research papers nationally and internationally.

Rosa María Vaca-Acosta is a PhD "Competitiveness, Innovation and Development" and a Lecturer at the University of Huelva (Spain), Faculty of Economics and Business, Department of Business Organization area. She is also part of GEIDETUR (University of Huelva) research groups and associate researcher at the Centre of CICS research at the University of Minho. She has been the author or co-author of several articles published in indexed journals. She has participated in 70 communications in national and international conferences and is a member of the scientific committee. She reviews international scientific magazines in Spain. Her main research topics are: Corporate Social Responsibility, quality, tourism, the hotel industry and human resources.

Alfonso Vargas-Sánchez, PhD, is a full professor of strategic management at the Spanish University of Huelva. He heads its research group on "Innovation and Development Strategies in Tourist Firms"

(GEIDETUR). He is also the author of a number of papers published in journals such as Tourism & Management Studies; Journal of Tourism and Development; Journal of Travel Research; Annals of Tourism Research; Journal of Sustainable Tourism; Journal of Heritage Tourism; Tourism Management; International Journal of Contemporary Hospitality Management; Journal of Hospitality Marketing & Management, among others.

Shengnan Zhang works as a Senior Guest Relations Officer at one of the 5-star luxury resort in Maldives. She has around 3 years of experience in the Guest Service field including China, Malaysia and Maldives. She developed an interest in hotel industry after experiencing working in several hotels in China in early 2010. Later on, Shengnan went to overseas to strengthen her knowledge of hospitality industry in 2011. She holds a Master Degree in International Hospitality Management from the University of Taylor's, Malaysia and University of Toulouse, France.

Index

A

ACI 45, 53, 57
Addiopizzo-Travel 69
Addiopizzo Travel 58-59, 62-66
agencies 10, 15, 49, 88, 90-92, 96, 104, 106, 140, 170, 289
airlines 41-45, 47-49, 51-53, 114, 288
airports 41-45, 47-49, 51-53, 57, 105, 211, 289
air transport liberalisation 45
ANS 48-49, 51-54, 57
ANSP 49, 57
ANSPs 42, 49, 51-53
anti-Mafia movement 62, 64, 69
Asian tsunami 163-164, 170
Augmented Reality 130-131, 133, 136, 139-140, 147

B

Bartlett's Test of Sphericity 282
boiled frog syndrome 164, 166, 183, 189

C

capitalism 72, 163-164, 170-171, 176-177, 182-184, 189, 211
case study 25, 30, 32, 34-35, 39, 62, 66, 176, 199
CDO 53, 57
clean slate 163-164, 170, 174-176, 178, 182
co-creation 58-61, 66-67, 69
co-creation of experiences 61, 66, 69
Colonialism 93, 110
Communality 269, 282
communities 4, 13, 26-27, 32-34, 54, 60, 75, 101, 105, 150, 154, 159, 167, 169-171, 174, 184, 210, 286, 289-290
competency 239, 242, 244-247, 250, 252-253, 255, 285

competitive advantage 25, 29, 39, 60, 114, 239, 290
Components in Rotated Space Graph 269, 282
consumer behaviour 2-4, 15, 59, 207
consumption 24, 54, 60-62, 71-72, 74-75, 129-133, 139, 141, 152, 156, 190-191, 199-203, 207, 210-211, 216, 226, 265, 287-288
corporate social responsibility 263-265, 267, 270, 272, 278, 286, 305
correlations matrix 269, 282
crisis 74, 79, 90, 163, 165-167, 169, 171, 174, 181-182, 189-194, 197, 199-203, 207, 216, 252, 262-263, 277-278
Cronbach's Alpha 269, 282
CSR scale 266, 278
culture 1-3, 6-10, 13-16, 26-27, 62, 72, 96-98, 100, 105, 213, 263, 265, 268, 278, 286, 289-290
customer satisfaction 202, 283-285, 287-288, 291-292, 305

D

decolonization 89-90, 110
descriptive statistical analysis 262-263, 268, 270, 272, 276-277
digital marketing 131, 138
Digital Tourism Marketing 130, 136, 139, 147
disaster 2, 163-171, 174, 176-177, 179, 181-184, 189, 213
disaster capitalism 163-164, 170-171, 176-177, 183-184
disaster vulnerability 164, 181, 189
discourse 74, 101, 112, 114-117, 120, 123, 171, 183, 189
divorce 70-71, 73-79, 84

E

EC 45, 51, 57
economics 4, 47, 112, 123, 129, 213, 284

Become an IRMA Member

Members of the **Information Resources Management Association (IRMA)** understand the importance of community within their field of study. The Information Resources Management Association is an ideal venue through which professionals, students, and academicians can convene and share the latest industry innovations and scholarly research that is changing the field of information science and technology. Become a member today and enjoy the benefits of membership as well as the opportunity to collaborate and network with fellow experts in the field.

IRMA Membership Benefits:

- **One FREE Journal Subscription**

- **30% Off Additional Journal Subscriptions**

- **20% Off Book Purchases**

- Updates on the latest events and research on Information Resources Management through the IRMA-L listserv.

- Updates on new open access and downloadable content added to Research IRM.

- A copy of the Information Technology Management Newsletter twice a year.

- A certificate of membership.

IRMA Membership $195

Scan code to visit irma-international.org and begin by selecting your free journal subscription.

Membership is good for one full year.

Printed in the United States
By Bookmasters